CAMBRIDGE STUDIES IN

INTERNATIONAL AND COMPARATIVE LAW: NEW SERIES

General Editor:

SIR ROBERT Y. JENNINGS

Judge of the International Court of Justice
Formerly Whewell Professor of International Law,
University of Cambridge

THE LEGAL REGIME OF FOREIGN PRIVATE INVESTMENT IN THE SUDAN AND SAUDI ARABIA

BOOKS IN THIS SERIES

F. H. Lawson and B. S. Markesinis: *Tortious liability for unintentional harm in the Common law and the Civil law*

A. A. Cançado Trindade: *The application of the rule of exhaustion of local remedies in international law: its rationale in the international protection of individual rights*

THE LEGAL REGIME OF FOREIGN PRIVATE INVESTMENT IN THE SUDAN AND SAUDI ARABIA

A Case Study of Developing Countries

FATH EL RAHMAN ABDALLA EL SHEIKH

LL.M. (*University of Khartoum*), PH.D. (*Cantab.*)

CAMBRIDGE UNIVERSITY PRESS

Cambridge

London New York New Rochelle Melbourne Sydney

in association with

KHARTOUM UNIVERSITY PRESS

Published by the Press Syndicate of the University of Cambridge
The Pitt Building, Trumpington Street, Cambridge CB2 1RP
32 East 57th Street, New York, NY 10022, USA
296 Beaconsfield Parade, Middle Park, Melbourne 3206, Australia

First published 1984

Printed in Great Britain by the University Press, Cambridge

Library of Congress catalogue card number: 83–7611

British Library Cataloguing in Publication Data

El Sheikh, Fath el Rahman Abdalla
The legal regime of foreign private investment in the Sudan and Saudi Arabia. – (Cambridge studies in international and comparative law. New series)
1. Investments, Foreign – Law and legislation – Sudan 2. Investments, Foreign – Law and legislation – Saudi Arabia
I. Title
346.2406′92

ISBN 0 521 25286 5

CONTENTS

PART THREE
REMEDIES

PREFACE

This book deals with the legal regime of foreign private investment in the Sudan and Saudi Arabia, countries which have similar ethnical, religious and social backgrounds, albeit many diverse political and economic characteristics. Yet both countries fall within the category of the 'developing countries', which have been for decades victims of an existing international economic order which heavily tilts the scale against these countries.

The Sudan is the largest country in Africa. Economically, it enjoys a strategic location, lying in close proximity to the lucrative and rapidly growing Middle Eastern markets. Despite its numerous constraints, its untapped potential has attracted the attention of the Arabs, and the international business community, as a highly promising place for investment.

Because of lack of adequate capital and technical know-how, foreign private investment is of paramount importance for the economic development of the Sudan. Public investment hitherto has hobbled the progress of the national economy by burdening the country with the accumulation of massive debts, now at astronomical proportions. Hence the obvious and urgent need of the country for foreign capital makes the legal study of foreign private investment a timely necessity. Saudi Arabia, on the other hand, being one of the richest countries in terms of financial resources, and though it has emerged as an influential international economic power, yet needs foreign investment to import the appropriate technology, expertise and know-how for the realization of its huge developmental goals.

This book is primarily concerned with the exposition of the legal regime pertaining to foreign private investment in the two countries within the framework of international law. The crucial question is that of the control and standard of treatment and protection furnished to foreign investment. This is examined in the context of the current international investment climate, reflected in the conflict between the developed and developing countries over the international law rules governing foreign investment; a conflict which appears especially in the North–South dialogue.

The study falls into three parts. Part One, consisting of three chapters, deals with certain preliminary issues.

Chapter 1 provides an economic and political perspective on the needs of the Sudan and Saudi Arabia, since the legal issues can hardly be properly understood except in this perspective.

Chapter 2 deals with the initial question of the definition of the term 'foreign investment', both under the investment laws and treaties; which necessarily also delimits the scope of the issues that properly fall within the purview of this study. This chapter, furthermore, sets out the formal and substantive rules governing the admission of foreign investment and the formation of business organizations which run the investment activities.

Chapter 3 addresses itself to the impediments that actually face foreign investors, with special consideration of those impediments which could be eliminated by legal reform. The purpose of this chapter is to shed light on the basic nature of the problem, and to show why it is necessary to have a legal regime for the encouragement and protection of foreign private investment.

Part Two is the core of the book. It deals specifically with the form and content of encouragement and protection. It is composed of Chapters Four to Nine, inclusive.

Chapter 4 outlines the legal incentives which are fiscal in nature. A critical analysis of the efficacy of the administrative mechanism endowed with the power of granting investment licences and incentives constitutes the cardinal approach in this chapter. The main purpose is to explore how far the incentives effectively combat the impediments.

Chapter 5 deals with the unilateral guarantees of constitutional clauses, legislation and policy statements which are designed for the protection of foreign private investment. The chief purpose of this inquiry is to elucidate their legal effects both under municipal law and international law.

Chapter 6 is confined to investment treaties. It examines, in particular, the standard of treatment to be accorded to foreign investments and the relation between the investment laws and treaties, as well as their legal effect both under municipal law and international law. The desirability of concluding a multilateral investment convention and a survey of the suggested drafts therefor is embarked upon. Special attention is directed towards the legal effect of the Charter of Economic Rights and Duties of States and its impact on the international investment climate.

Chapter 7 is confined to the divisive issue of compensation in cases of nationalization of foreign investment. The Sudanese practice in this respect is examined at length, and comparatively evaluated.

Chapter 8 investigates the insurance of foreign investments by some capital-exporting countries, notably by the United States and West Germany. On the international level, the Guarantee Programme of the Arab Corporation for

Investment Guarantee sponsored by the Arab States, and the proposal of the World Bank for establishing an International Investment Insurance Agency are also discussed in this chapter.

Chapter 9 is the principal theme. It focuses on all legal aspects of economic development agreements between foreign investors and the State.

Part Three is designed for remedies. It consists of Chapters 10 and 11.

Chapter 10 explores the courses which an aggrieved foreign investor can pursue to obtain relief if his investment is destroyed or adversely affected.

Chapter 11 investigates the unilateral sanctions which may be taken by the home States of the investors against the investee State to secure redress for economic injuries of these investors, if other devices prove ineffective.

This book is the outcome of a study completed in 1979 for the Ph.D. degree in the University of Cambridge on 'The Legal Aspects of Foreign Private Investment in the Democratic Republic of the Sudan'. The notion of expanding the study to include Saudi Arabia as well has been precipitated by the genuine desire to explore the regime regulating foreign investment in that country, in an attempt to proffer a vivid account of how far the prevailing Islamic practices have contributed in the development of international rules on the subject. The reader will find more material on Sudanese law than on Saudi law. The reason is obvious. Being a Sudanese lawyer, I am well acquainted with the Sudanese legal system, a facility which was not available to me in the secretive system of Saudi Arabia.

In undertaking the study on which this book is based and in preparing it for publication, I have become indebted to many people. I owe an immense debt of gratitude to my supervisor, Professor R. Y. Jennings, Jesus College, Cambridge University, who both supervised the work when it was in dissertation form and read the manuscript. His sustained encouragement, suggestions and guidance were invaluable, without which this work would have been really difficult. I would like also to thank my colleague Mr Mohammed Nour El Din El Tahir who kindly agreed to read the manuscript and who gave me the benefit of his advice. I would like also to thank Sayed Hussein El Sayed and Saud El Shwaf, Attorneys at Law, Riyadh, for their support and help in providing me with material on Saudi law.

As the original manuscript of this book was prepared for publication in 1980, there have since been some changes in the law which warrant writing a short addendum, to update the work to some extent.

I wish to express my profound thanks to the Sudan Government and the Ford Foundation for granting me scholarships and grants which made the preparation and publication of this book possible.

I am also indebted to my colleagues, the people whom I interviewed and the staff of the Squire Law Library, Cambridge, for providing and assisting me in finding the required material. I am so grateful to Mrs S. Barry of Cambridge, for typing the manuscript. My grateful thanks also go to Miss Amanda Chapman for her work in checking it.

My deep thanks go to my wife, Widad, for her patience and continuing support. I must, however, add that I alone bear the responsibility for anything mentioned in this book.

Finally, I wish to record my gratitude to the publishers for their co-operation in the production of this book.

Fath El Rahman Abdalla El Sheikh

ABBREVIATIONS

A.A.A.I.D.	Arab Authority for Agricultural Investment and Development
A.A.L.C.C.	African and Asian Legal Consultative Committee
A.B.A.J.	*American Bar Association Journal*
A.B.S.I.D.	Arab Board for Settlement of Investment Disputes
A.C.	Appeal Cases (English Law Reports: Decisions of the House of Lords and the Privy Council from 1891)
A.C.P.	African-Caribbean-Pacific countries
A.D.	Annual Digest of Public International Law Cases (now International Law Reports
A.E.C.U.	African Economic and Customs Union
All E.R.	All England Law Reports
Am.Econ.Rev.	*American Economic Review*
Att.Gen.	Attorney-General
A.I.D.	Agency for International Development
A.J.C.L.	*American Journal of Comparative Law*
A.J.I.L.	*American Journal of International Law*
A.P.I.C.	The Arab Petroleum Investment Corporation
Am.Soc.Int.Law Proceed.	*American Society of International Law Proceedings*
Bus.Lawyer	*Business Lawyer*
B.Y.B.I.L.	*British Yearbook of International Law*
C.B.I.	Confederation of British Industry
C.B.R.	*Canadian Bar Review*
C.E.R.D.S.	Charter of Economic Rights and Duties of States
Columb.J.Trans.L.	*Columbia Journal of Transnational Law*
Camb.L.J.	*Cambridge Law Journal*
C.L.P.	*Current Legal Problems*
Calif.L.Rev.	*California Law Review*
Columb.L.R.	*Columbia Law Review*
C.M.	Council of Ministers
Cmd and Cmnd	Command Papers (British)
C.Rev.	*Criminal Review*

C.R.O.	Central Records Office
C.S.	Civil Suit
D.A.C.	Development Association Committee
D.R.S.G.	*Democratic Republic of the Sudan Gazette*
Econ.J.	*Economic Journal*
E.C.O.S.O.C.	Economic and Social Council (United Nations)
E.E.C.	European Economic Community
E.R.	English Reports
F.A.O.	Food and Agriculture Organization
F.B.J.	*Federal Bar Journal*
F.C.N.	American Friendship, Commerce and Navigation Treaties
F.C.S.C.	United States Foreign Claims Settlement Commission
Ford.L.Rev.	*Fordham Law Review*
G.A.	General Assembly of the United Nations
G.A.T.T.	General Agreement on Tariffs and Trade
Grotius Society	*Grotius Society Transactions*
Harv.Int.L.J.	*Harvard International Law Journal*
Harv.L.R.	*Harvard Law Review*
I.B.R.D.	International Bank for Reconstruction and Development (World Bank)
I.C.C.	International Chamber of Commerce
I.C.J.Rep.	*International Court of Justice Reports*
I.C.L.Q.	*International and Comparative Law Quarterly*
I.C.S.I.D.	International Centre for Settlement of Investment Disputes
I.D.A.	International Development Association
I.F.C.	International Finance Corporation
I.I.I.A.	International Investment Insurance Agency
Indian J.I.L.	*Indian Journal of International Law*
I.L.C.	International Law Commission
Int.L.L.	*International Lawyer*
I.L.M.	*International Legal Materials*
I.L.O.	International Labour Organization
I.L.R.	International Law Reports
I.M.F.	International Monetary Fund
I.T.O.	International Trade Organization
J.A.L.	*Journal of African Law*
J. of B.L.	*Journal of Business Law*
J.M.A.S.	*Journal of Modern African Studies*

J.P.L.	*Journal of Public Law*
J.Transn.L.	*Journal of Transnational Law*
J.W.T.L.	*Journal of World Trade Law*
K.B.	King's Bench (English Law Reports: 1901–52)
KH.HC.	Khartoum High Court
L. of N.	League of Nations
L.N.T.S.	League of Nations Treaty Series
L.Q.R.	*Law Quarterly Review*
L.S.D.R.S.G.	*Legislative Supplement to the Democratic Republic of the Sudan Gazette*
M.J.	Ministry of Justice
Neth.Int.L.R.	*Netherlands International Law Review*
N.I.O.C.	National Iranian Oil Company
N.Y.U.L.R.	*New York University Law Review*
O.A.P.E.C.	Organization of Arab Petroleum Exporting Countries
O.A.S.	Organization of American States
O.A.U.	Organization of African Unity
O.E.C.D.	Organization for Economic Co-operation and Development
O.P.E.C.	Organization of Petroleum Exporting Countries
O.P.I.C.	Overseas Private Investment Corporation
P.C.I.J.	Permanent Court of International Justice
Petromin	General Petroleum and Minerals Organization
Q.B.	Queen's Bench (English Law Reports: 1891–1900: 1952–?)
Rev. Belge D.I.	*Revue Belge de Droit International*
R.S.G.	*Republic of the Sudan Gazette*
S.A.B.I.C.	Saudi Arabia Basic Industries Corporation
S.A.M.A.	Saudi Arabia Monetary Agency
S.D.R.	Special Drawing Rights (I.M.F.)
S.L.J.R.	*Sudan Law Journal and Reports*
S.L.R.	*Sudan Law Reports*
S.L.S.D.R.S.G.	*Special Legislative Supplement to the Democratic Republic of the Sudan Gazette*
T.I.A.S.	Treaties and other International Acts Series
Tex.Int.L.J.	*Texas Journal of International Law*
U.N.	United Nations
U.N.A.A.R.	*United Nations Arbitral Award Reports*
U.N.C.I.T.R.A.L.	United Nations Commission on International Trade Law

U.N.C.T.A.D.	United Nations Conference on Trade and Development
U.N.D.P.	United Nations Development Programme
U.N.I.D.O.	United Nations Industrial Development Organization
U.N.R.I.A.A.	*United Nations Reports of International Arbitral Awards*
U.N.T.S.	United Nations Treaty Series
U.N.Y.B.I.L.C.	*United Nations Yearbook of the International Law Commission*
U.S.T.I.A.	United States Treaties and International Agreements
W.L.R.	Weekly Law Reports (English Law Reports)
Y.B.I.L.	*Yearbook of International Law*
Y.L.J.	*Yale Law Journal*

GLOSSARY OF ARABIC WORDS USED

Figh	Writings of Muslim jurists
Geziva	Island
Jizyah	Capitation tax
Omodias	Districts
Sunna	Teachings of the Prophet Mohammed
Zakat	Alms tax

TABLE OF CASES

(1) Permanent Court of International Justice

(2) International Court of Justice

(3) Sudanese Cases

(4) Decisions of Foreign Municipal Courts and Arbitral Awards

TABLE OF STATUTES

(1) Sudan

(2) Saudi Arabia

(3) Statutes of other countries

TABLE OF TREATIES

PART ONE

CERTAIN PRELIMINARY ISSUES

1

FOREIGN INVESTMENT IN POLITICO-ECONOMIC PERSPECTIVE

The legal regime of foreign investment in the Sudan and Saudi Arabia, as in other countries, cannot operate in isolation from politico-economic factors general to the international arena; nevertheless, such a legal regime also reflects national policy, and it is, accordingly, necessary at the outset to describe not only the general factors, but also the Sudanese and Saudi national policies towards foreign investment.

1. Economic nationalism and the new international economic order

The international investment climate is today greatly affected by the economic nationalism which has recently dominated the Third World. Many developing countries were at one time colonies, mostly of the industrialized western powers from where foreign investment traditionally comes.[1] Accordingly, developing countries tend to cling to their independence, and are suspicious of any foreign relationships which might seem to endanger the newly-obtained sovereignty. The popular objective is to achieve 'economic independence'.[2] In the words of Professor Arthur Lewis:

> At present, most of the less developed countries are in a state of reaction against nineteenth-century imperialism. They have acquired a distaste for foreign capital and foreign administration, and they are more anxious to protect themselves from future exploitations than to take advantage of current opportunities.[3]

The emphasis of developing countries on their economic nationalism has been articulated in several statements of principle in United Nations resolutions over the last twenty-five years. Thus in 1952, the General Assembly of the United

Nations passed a resolution on the exploitation of natural resources, which among other things recommended: 'All member states to refrain from acts, direct or indirect, designed to impede the exercise of the sovereignty of any State over its natural resources.'[4] In 1955, the developing countries succeeded in convincing the Third Committee of the General Assembly to adopt article 1 of the Draft Human Rights Covenant which reads:

> The peoples may for their own ends freely dispose of their natural wealth and resources without prejudice to any obligations arising out of international economic co-operation, based upon the principle of mutual benefit and international law. In no case may a people be deprived of its own means of subsistence.[5]

Again in 1962, the General Assembly of the United Nations passed the Resolution on the Permanent Sovereignty over Natural Resources. Its operative principle 1 reads:

> The right of peoples and nations to permanent sovereignty over their natural resources must be exercised in the interest of their national development and the well-being of the people of the State concerned.[6]

The climax of this economic nationalism pursued by the developing nations has been their claim to a new international economic order, formulated in the United Nations Declaration on the Establishment of a New International Economic Order,[7] and the Charter of Economic Rights and Duties of States, 1974.[8] The essence of this is the claim that every State has the right to full and permanent sovereignty over its natural resources and all economic activities within its territory; and that every State has the right to exploit these natural resources and to control all economic activities within its territory. This comprehends the right of every State to exploit these natural resources by nationalization of enterprises in accordance with its own legislation; and that foreign investment disputes should be settled in the national courts according to local law. These documents have also emphasized that transnational corporations should not interfere in the internal affairs of investee States.

The spirit of these declaratory principles has been respected in the United Nations Report of Eminent Persons.[9] This report addressed itself to a number of problems relating to the activities of multinational corporations and foreign private investment. It stressed the need for a code to regulate the activities of multinational corporations through which foreign private investment is channelled to developing countries. In accordance with the Group of Eminent Persons' recommendation,[10] the Economic and Social Council of the United Nations established the Commission on Transnational Corporations to deal with issues concerning multinational enterprises, and in particular to formulate a code of conduct for transnationals.[11] This topic and other similar issues are also under extensive discussion in the United Nations Conference on Trade and Development (U.N.C.T.A.D.) and in the north–south dialogue, in which fora the developing countries are seeking to restructure the whole world economy and the international financial institutions. This move has tended to encounter resistance from the industrialized countries which have often favoured rather the *status quo*.[12]

But, as the capital and technological needs of the developing countries are so great, and cannot at present be met from domestic funds, these countries also realize the importance of foreign private capital to exploit their natural resources so as to achieve their economic development goals through quick industrialization.[13] Accordingly, they invite and welcome foreign capital, provided that it is under control and does not dominate their economies and impinge on their sovereignty. This was unequivocally stated by Kwame Nkrumah, the ex-President of Ghana, in the following terms:

> The struggle against neo-Colonialism is not aimed at excluding the capital of the developed world from operating in less developed countries. It is aimed at preventing the financial power of the developed countries being used in such a way as to impoverish the less developed. Non-alignment, as practised by Ghana and many other countries, is based on co-operation with all States, whether they be capitalist, socialist or have a mixed economy. Such a policy, therefore, involves foreign investment from capitalist countries, but *it must be invested in accordance with a national plan drawn up by the government of the non-aligned State with its own interests in mind*. The issue is not what return the foreign investor receives on his investments. He may, in fact, do better for himself if he invests in a non-aligned country than if he invests in a neo-colonial one.[14] (My italics.)

On the other hand, some of the developing countries, instead of extending inducements to foreign investment, create impediments which discourage it. These impediments are reflected in restrictions on transfer of profits and capital, discriminatory taxation, exclusion from certain sectors of the economy, in addition to some rules imposing employment of a certain number of indigenous workers, immigration and import licence restrictions.[15] More serious impediments are the risks of confiscation, nationalization without compensation and discriminatory treatment.[16]

2. Investment patterns in the international investment climate

(a) Joint ventures, production-sharing agreements and similar arrangements

Resulting from widespread adherence to the concepts of the welfare state and economic nationalism, there has been a rapid increase of direct state participation in investment in many countries. The most recent pattern of this sort of participation has been the emergence of different forms of joint ventures between foreign investors and recipient countries; striking examples of this new trend are found in Egypt and Chile, where many of the development projects take this shape.[17] Even in the oil sector, however, the traditional concession agreements are gradually giving way to production-sharing agreements such as the agreement concluded by the Sudan with the Chevron Company, which is modelled on the Indonesian agreements, the pioneer in this field.[18] The advantage of this type of arrangement is that it enables the co-operation of foreign capital in countries not willing to accept direct foreign capital in the traditional form. Similarly, foreign investment nowadays takes the pattern of licensing arrangements; co-operative agreements; investment contracts which are either self-liquidating or restricted to certain functions to be performed by the multinational company; profit-sharing agreements, especially in the mining sector, and disinvestment patterns.[19]

(b) Triangular arrangements

This is the most recent feature of foreign investment patterns in developing countries. As in the Sudan, it combines western technology and expertise with O.P.E.C. capital for the development of the non-oil developing countries.[20]

Indeed, O.P.E.C. can participate with the western firms in investment in non-oil developing countries in various ways. They may purchase shares in parent companies or even in their subsidiaries. By so doing, they can influence the types and amounts of investments undertaken by the parent companies in non-oil developing countries as well as in their own economies. The recent acquisition by Kuwait and Iran, respectively, of shares in a British and a German firm, apparently assumed this form.[21]

O.P.E.C. may also acquire a dominant interest in developing countries jointly with western firms whose contribution in the investment project will be in the form of supplying management, technology, and trade names in return for equity shares.[22] At present, there are several investment projects of this nature. Egypt, for instance, planned to erect a vehicle assembly plant, to be installed in a duty-free zone. The annual production capacity of the project was expected to be 10,000 Landrovers for Arab markets. This project will combine O.P.E.C. capital of about $50 million provided by Saudi Arabia with British technical know-how and Egyptian manpower.[23] A similar project for the construction of a 'float process glass' manufacturing plant, to supply the Egyptian and other Arab markets, was recently being negotiated between the Kuwait Investment Company, Egypt and the United Kingdom company, Pilkington.[24]

(c) Four-cornered arrangements

Again, more than three parties may be involved in an investment project; one of these parties may be an international institution such as the International Finance Corporation (I.F.C.), which adds to the attractiveness of a project for potential Arab investors. The financing schedule envisaged for a proposed $62 million chemical fertilizer plant in Jordan is of this type. The American firm constructing it will take a 25% share of the capital; Jordan will be a 50% majority shareholder. The I.F.C. will take a 5% holding. The remaining 20% will be allotted to the public and the rest of the Arab world.[25]

3. The role of international organizations in improving the investment climate

Global and regional[26] organizations, governmental or non-governmental,[27] have directly or indirectly contributed to a great extent in improving the investment climate in developing countries, at least in the following respects.

(a) Drafting of investment conventions and codes

International organizations have made extensive studies of the drafting of conventions, and codes, for the encouragement and protection of foreign private investment. With the exception of the World Bank Convention on the Settlement of Investment Disputes between States and Nationals of other States,[28] and the investment conventions sponsored by the Arab League,[29] none of the proposed conventions or codes has yet been agreed upon. None the less, these draft conventions and codes must have a persuasive effect in the drafting of national investment laws, as well as bringing to light discrepancies amongst legal instruments, thus spurring perhaps a movement towards a general consensus in the future.

(b) Rendering of technical advice and research

International organizations have played a direct role also in ameliorating the investment climate by rendering technical advice, studies and researches to developing countries, thus helping these countries to pursue properly-thought-out economic policies. This task is usually performed by the United Nations specialized agencies.[30] These studies furnish sufficient data for feasibility studies to potential foreign investors. Furthermore, the very rendering of the study, the evaluating of the economic potentialities of a developing country by an international organization, must add to the credibility of that country in the eyes of foreign entrepreneurs.

(c) Sharing in investment with private investors

Certain international organizations, such as the World Bank and its affiliates, either participate directly with local or foreign private investors in, or themselves finance, investment projects.[31] The establishment of development banks and funds, especially the O.P.E.C. Special Fund and the development funds of the Arab oil-rich countries such as the Kuwait, Abu Dhabi and Saudi Arabia has helped to finance heavy investment projects, particularly in the infrastructural sector. Also, the accumulation of surpluses of oil money in the hands of the Arabs has led to the formation of many Arab financing institutions which provide credit facilities and syndicated loans to potential investors on a commercial basis.[32] These financing institutions are designed to recycle Arab money to poorer countries, a strategy which should work favourably for the Sudan. This direct involvement in the investment process by these international organizations and financing institutions has a positive psychological effect on the participation of foreign investors and persuades others to follow suit. It also strengthens the investors' belief in the profitability of the investment.

How far these international politico-economic factors have their impact on the investment climate and the legal regime of foreign investment in the Sudan and Saudi Arabia will be seen below.

4. Sudanese and Saudi foreign investment policies

(a) Sudan[33]

(i) *Foreign capital and socialism in the Sudan*

The flow of foreign private capital to the Sudan was to a great extent adversely affected by the 21 October Revolution, 1964, which ended the Abboud military regime. Indeed, this Revolution marked a turning-point in the Sudan's economic and social development. Socialist slogans calling for state economy and nationalization of foreign trade and property were publicly raised by the communists and in other socialist quarters. Though this did not ripen into any hard state policy at that time, yet it had its effect on foreigners, who began to liquidate their enterprises in the Sudan. Accordingly, the flow of foreign private capital was at that time much discouraged.

In 1970 these socialist principles were positively implemented by the dissolved

Revolutionary Command Council of the '25 May Revolution, 1969', which nationalized all commercial banks and more than seventy major companies.[34]

(ii) *Openness policy*

After the failure of the left-wing *coup* in July 1971, it became necessary to create political stability. This could only be achieved by the active participation of large numbers of people in the Government's administration and policy. These measures are vital for the success of the great development programme upon which the Government has embarked. The experience of the abortive left-wing *coup* produced far-reaching changes. Theoretical, socialist-inspired plans of nationalization and socialization and close partnership with the Soviet bloc gave way to a new reappraisal of the economic scene. After two years' consideration, the measures of confiscation and nationalization were reversed. Eventually, this new policy resulted in a partial return to the private sector.[35] This brought prospects of a renewal of foreign investment. Private enterprise became respectable, while foreign investors were welcomed.[36] The Sudan economy has changed into public, co-operative, private and mixed sectors, with the State as regulator in some sectors and entrepreneur in others.[37] This policy has now been reflected in constitutional provisions.[38]

The public sector was to be a pioneer sector and to lead progress in all fields of development and to be based on public ownership and subject to people's control.[39] The co-operative sector was to be based on the collective ownership by all members participating in co-operative societies. The State was to care for the co-operative societies and the law was to regulate their formation and management.[40]

On the other hand, the private sector was to be based on non-exploiting private ownership. The State was to protect and encourage it and organize its functions so as to enable it to play a positive and active role in the national economy.[41] The mixed sector is based on joint ownership between the State and the private sector.[42] It is within this constitutional framework that foreign investment legislation and policy in the Sudan are now to be considered.

To restore confidence and attract foreign investors, investment legislation has been improved in 1974, 1975, 1976 and more recently in 1980.[43] These new laws provide for general tax holidays, protection of sales as well as complete freedom of transfer of profits and capital. A number of financial institutions[44] sprang up to help investors and to channel funds to profitable and nationally-desirable ventures. The Government adopted an investment policy of 'openness' to the whole world,[45] with the exception of South Africa and Israel.

(iii) *Arab–Sudanese joint ventures and western technology*

Luckily enough, these developments coincided with the accumulation of financial resources in the hands of traditional Arab oil-exporting nations, which are very conservative, anti-communist, anti-Socialist and favour private enterprise. The scene was thus now set for the Sudan to become a major target for private and Government investment on the part of the oil-rich Arab world, notably that of the Gulf States, Saudi Arabia and Kuwait.[46] Numerous schemes have been embarked upon to develop the country economically and socially. A high point of this movement was reached in August 1976 when a formal agreement was announced between the Sudan Government and the Arab Fund for Social and Economic Development which consists of twenty Arab countries. The agreement was for an investment of about £4,000 million, mainly in agricultural projects and allied industries, over the next decades. The overall plan covered a 25-year period, until the year 2000, by which time Sudan was expected to be producing the greater part of the Arab world's food.[47]

By the start of 1980s, however, these plans had become a thing of the past, victims of the Sudan's infrastructural bottlenecks and severe economic problems. By 1980 A.A.A.I.D. had only succeeded in launching four small projects.[48]

In 1976 President Nimeiri visited the United States and one of the objectives of that visit was to invite American investors to the Sudan.[49] And a Sudan–American Business Council was formed to encourage American investments in the Sudan. This in turn led to a massive influx of different types of businessmen and financiers, mostly from Europe and the United States.[50] If the Arabs provide the money, and the Sudan labour and natural resources, it will be Europe and the United States that will be expected to supply the tools, technology and expertise.[51] Consequently, foreign investment in the Sudan, as in many countries, has assumed new patterns of business institutions, in the form of multinational companies and joint ventures among the Government or its agencies,[52] foreign and local investors in manufacturing and agro-industry[53] and exploitation of mineral resources. There is no predetermined systematic formula as regards the percentage of the shareholding of the Government. However, Government majority shareholding is usually preferred, a practice which is, indeed, favoured even by some industrialized countries themselves,[54] because of the control of the investment that it affords.

(iv) *Effect of political stability and national unity on foreign investment*

The investment climate in the Sudan has been enhanced to a great extent by the ratification of the Peace Settlement Agreement[55] on 27 March 1972, which solved

Table 1. *The six-year plan for social and economic development 1977–78 to 1982–83*★

Investment allocations (£S m)

Sector	Total allocation: Value	Total allocation: % of total sector	Public sector: Value	Public sector: % of total sector	Private sector: Value	Private sector: % of total sector	Mixed sector: Value	Mixed sector: % of total sector
Agricultural & irrigation	715	26.8	425	27.1	40	5.9	250	59.5
Industry, mining, power and tourism	535	20.0	335	21.3	80	11.8	120	28.5
Transport and communications	500	18.7	320	20.4	130	19.1	50	12.0
Social services	695	26.0	265	16.9	430	63.2	—	—
Reserves	225	8.5	225	14.3	—	—	—	—
Total	2,670	100	1,570	100	680	100	420	100

Sources of finance (£S m)

Source	Public sector: Amount	Public sector: % of total allocations	Private and mixed sectors: Amount	Private and mixed sectors: % of total allocations	Total: Amount	Total: % of total allocations
Domestic resources	735	27.5	550	20.5	1,285	48.1
Public sector	450	16.8	—	—	450	16.8
Private savings	—	—	550	20.5	550	20.5
Deficit financing	285	10.7	—	—	285	10.7
External resources	835	31.4	550	20.5	1,385	51.9
Total	1,570	59.0	1,100	41.0	2,670	100.0

★ *Source*: Ministry of Planning (Khartoum).

Table 2. *Projected private sector investment six-year plan**

Sector	Amounts in Sudanese pounds			% per sector
	Mixed	Private	Total	
Agriculture	250	40	290	26.4
Industry	120	80	200	18.2
Transport	50	130	180	16.4
Services (mainly housing)	—	430	430	39.0
Total	420	680	1,100	100

* *Source*: *Economic Survey* 1976/77, Research and Studies of Economic Policy Administration, Ministry of Finance and National Economy, Khartoum.

the Southern Question and ended the guerrilla war which had lasted for seventeen years in the southern Sudan. This Settlement Agreement gave the southern Sudan a regional autonomy. The Agreement also brought a new attitude of sympathy for the Sudan from many countries. Nowadays, huge development projects are under execution by many foreign investors, friendly countries and international institutions. The most influential and attractive development project, which it is hoped may change the life of many southerners, is the Junglei Canal Project which has been undertaken by a joint venture between the Sudan Government and Egypt, utilizing the western technology of a French firm in digging the canal and preparing the land for cultivation.

More recently, President Nimeiri wisely issued a general amnesty to all his conservative political opponents of the dissolved National Front in July 1977. As a result, a relative national reconciliation has been obtained, as some members of the National Front returned to the Sudan and stopped fighting the regime.[56]

Undoubtedly, this positive step towards overall national unity is constructive. It will achieve political stability, which is the foremost requirement for the alleviation of the fears of foreign investors about the reversal of investment policy and laws, which might otherwise follow from changes of the political system; a turn of events not unlikely in a country like the Sudan. Accordingly, foreign investment should be attracted and encouraged. It is to be expected that the rhetoric of the Sudan's socialist policies will not be allowed to get in the way of foreign enterprise or investment. In fact, businessmen, as will be shown later, now have more freedom to invest and transfer profits in the Sudan than anywhere else in the Third World.

(b) Saudi Arabia

(i) *Industrialization*

Unlike the Sudan, Saudi Arabia, having a relatively stable political system, and being one of the richest countries in the world, is a lucrative place in which to invest. In the aftermath of the 1973–74 rise in oil prices, Saudi Arabia has accumulated enormous financial surpluses; and being the strongest of the O.P.E.C. group, it possesses increasing international economic power. This financial ability characterizes Saudi Arabia as a major capital-exporting country, especially to the Sudan. But, to achieve industrialization, it also needs foreign capital, in terms of technology and expertise, and this compels the Kingdom to be also a capital-importing country to which heavy investment is flowing.

The overall objective of Saudi Arabia is to transform its economy from overwhelming dependence on the export of crude oil into a diversified industrial economy; for the oil may deplete in the future. Since 1974, Saudi Arabia has launched successive Five-Year Plans in which it has allocated billions of dollars for infrastructural development to prepare its free economy for the desired industrialization. The ultimate target is to set up a hydrocarbon-based petrochemical industry. And this strategy should be easy to achieve, the resources of the Kingdom being abundant. The key project is to build giant gas-gathering and treatment systems, planned to cost $4.7 billion. The resultant 1.6 million cubic feet of gas per day would be made available both for export and for use by a number of industrial projects located primarily in the traditional oil-producing area, the Eastern Province – but including some to be located in the Western Province as well.[57] These industrial schemes have enticed the attention of foreign firms, on whose technology and expertise the implementation basically depends. The Saudi determination to change its economy into a giant industrial and export-oriented petrochemical economy is evident in the approval of the Third Five-Year Plan, 1980–85, which allocates billions of Saudi riyals to expand industrial investments in the oil and mineral sectors. Investment in productive industries will rise to 37.3% of the total, compared with 25.1% under the previous plan.[58]

(ii) *Institutions for industrial promotion*

To secure the establishment of the best industrial base, it has become obvious that there is a need to create new institutions to administer the new Saudi petrochemical and mineral process projects. The General Petroleum and Minerals Organization (Petromin) was established to administer the oil and gas sectors and is to be the Saudi partner of any foreign company becoming involved in refinery projects.[59] In 1975 there was a general reorganization of the Saudi central administration. The Central Planning Organization was granted the status of a Ministry, and a new Ministry of Industry and Electricity was created, of which the Foreign Capital Investment Committee[60] is the adjunct. In December of the same year a Royal Commission for Jubail and Yanbu was formed, whose task was to eliminate bureaucracy holding back the building of the gigantic port, road and other infrastructural development necessary for the two industrial zones at Jubail and Yanbu. Finally, in August 1976, the Saudi Arabia Basic Industries Corporation (S.A.B.I.C.) was created, under the auspices of the Ministry of Industry and Electricity, with a capital of 10 billion Saudi riyals ($2.8 billion). This State company was charged with undertaking the new industrial projects assigned to the Ministry of Industry and Electricity – these were the ventures in the petrochemical, iron, steel and aluminium sectors.

The positive role played by Aramco in the development of the oil industry in Saudi Arabia should not be ignored. Though complete take-over of the company by the Saudi Government is being finalized, Aramco will be resurrected as a service company which would concentrate decreasingly on the international marketing of oil, and increasingly on project management within the Kingdom.[61]

(iii) *Investment pattern*

The recent investment pattern in Saudi Arabia concentrates on the joint venture approach. The new export-oriented projects are characterized by the formation of joint ventures between foreign private investors and State agencies or Saudi nationals up to a fifty-fifty basis.[62] The Saudi insistence on the joint-venture formula seems to have stemmed from their fear of failure. By having foreign partners, they will ensure the buying of reliable plant, operating it efficiently and finding world markets for the products. It is said that, by insisting that foreign partners have a financial and managerial share in the plant, the Saudis are attempting to write their own insurance policy.

5. Conclusions

No doubt foreign investors would be more attracted to Saudi Arabia than to the Sudan. This is because the foreign investor's main concern is to generate profits, and these are likely to be more easily obtained in Saudi Arabia, an oil-rich country. Another inducement is that foreign investors would find a better infrastructure in Saudi Arabia, which has huge financial resources enabling it to build that infrastructure to the best international standards. Hence, foreign investors will not be requested to make any significant contribution to the overall initial costs of ports, roads, power stations, telecommunication systems, airport, housing and educational facilities. The reverse is true with regard to the Sudan, whose financial inability cripples it from shouldering any responsibility for infrastructural development. And, consequentially, foreign investors are required in the Sudan constructively to undertake this expensive task. But, despite this negative factor, and other numerous constraints, the Sudan's untapped potential has attracted the attention of the Arabs and the international business community as a highly promising place for investment.

It remains to be seen in the coming chapters how far these discrepancies in the financial situations, and the foregoing politico-economic factors, influence the legal regimes regulating foreign investment in the Sudan and Saudi Arabia.

2

PREREQUISITES FOR THE ADMISSION OF INVESTMENTS

For foreign investment to be admitted into the Sudan and Saudi Arabia under the present laws, there are certain substantive and procedural requirements which have to be satisfied initially. Once these requirements have been duly met, a foreign investor in either country will be entitled to claim those protection measures which will be discussed in later chapters, and may also enjoy certain incentives. In the following pages, it is proposed to examine these initial requirements, and to see how far the Sudan and Saudi Arabia agree or disagree in this respect.

1. What investments are eligible?

The first basic requirement is that an investment must be a 'foreign investment' of the kind that falls within the scope of the investment policy embodied in the investment laws and treaties. What, then, is the meaning of the term 'foreign investment' in Sudanese and Saudi investment laws and treaties?

Foreign investment ultimately involves three parties: the capital-exporting countries – of which the foreign investors are usually nationals, the foreign investors themselves, and the capital-importing country.[1]

'Foreign private investment' means simply an investment made by a foreigner; thus there are two components, namely, the 'foreign investor' and the 'investment'. Each of these components needs to be dealt with separately, first in respect of natural persons, and then in respect of juridical persons.

(a) The meaning of 'foreign investor'

A foreign investor may either be a natural or a juridical person.

(i) *Natural persons*

Generally, a foreign national, under both the Sudanese and Saudi laws, is a person who has not acquired Sudanese or Saudi nationality in accordance with the nationality laws of those countries,[2] and who, at the time of the investment and throughout the period of investment, does not voluntarily acquire such nationality.

The general rule under international law is that it is for each State to decide who has its nationality. The means and methods by which a State confers its nationality are, in principle, a matter for the domestic law. This rule was restated by the Permanent Court of International Justice in its *Advisory Opinion in the Nationality Decrees in Tunis and Morocco* Case,[3] and is confirmed by many writers.[4]

The Sudan has followed this practice in the treaties it has concluded with other States. Thus the Treaty between the Republic of the Sudan and the Federal Republic of Germany concerning the Encouragement and Protection of Investments, 1963[5] (cited hereinafter as the Sudan–German Investment Protection Treaty), provides:

For the purpose of this treaty, the term 'national' shall mean:

(a) in respect to the Federal Republic of Germany, Germans within the meaning of the Basic Law for the Federal Republic of Germany;
(b) in respect to the Republic of the Sudan, a person who is a Sudanese within the meaning of the Nationality Act.

This same definition had been adopted in the German–Pakistan Treaty,[6] as well as in other German investment protection treaties with other countries.

More recently, Article 1 of the Agreement between the Democratic Republic of the Sudan and the Swiss Confederation Concerning the Encouragement and Reciprocal Protection of Investment, 1974[7] (cited hereinafter as the Sudan–Swiss Investment Protection Agreement), defined the term 'nationals' as:

physical persons who, according to the respective legislation of each contracting party, are considered citizens of that country.

It is interesting to note that as yet Saudi Arabia has not concluded investment bilateral treaties with other capital-exporting countries, as the latter consider the investment regime in Saudi Arabia relatively stable; a belief which may be shaken by the spectacle of the general unrest in the Gulf area after the Iranian Revolution.

The Convention on the Settlement of Investment Disputes between States and Nationals of Other States 1966,[8] does not define the term 'foreign investment', though it debars an investor with dual nationality and prevents him from making use of the jurisdiction of the Centre established by the convention if he holds the nationality of the State which is also a party to an investment dispute.[9]

(ii) *Juridical persons*

There are four possible tests of the nationality of a company or corporation. The first test is the rule of the 'siège sociale'. Thus the Investment Code of Zaire defines a resident juridical person as:

any corporate body whose registered office or main establishment is in the Democratic Republic of the Congo.[10]

The Indonesian Foreign Investment Law of 1967 provides:

1. An enterprise as defined in Article 1, which is operated wholly or for the most part in Indonesia as an independent business unit, must be a legal entity according to Indonesian law and have its domicile in Indonesia.
2. The government will determine whether an enterprise is operated entirely or for the most part in Indonesia as an independent business unit.[11]

From this provision, it seems that foreign investors in Indonesia mainly assume Indonesian nationality if their activities are directly conducted in that country. On the other hand, it is not clear whether the requirement that a foreign company must have a head office in a certain country means that it acquires the nationality of that country. In civil law systems, the law of the location of the seat of control of a company, the '*siège sociale*', determines its nationality. This test was acknowledged by the Permanent Court of International Justice in the *Wimbledon* Case,[12] where the only feature of the company that France was protecting was the location of its seat of control which, being in Paris, established the company's nationality as French according to French law.

During the two World Wars another test – the factor of effective control – was adopted to determine the nationality of a corporation.[13] Occasionally, the notion of control has also been resorted to, by analogy, for the purpose of justifying protection of the alien shareholders of a company which is incorpoated in the respondent State and has its '*siège control*' or its domicile there.[14]

The Commonwealth countries, generally, adopt the incorporation test, according to which the nationality of a juridical person is determined by the law of the country in which it is incorporated. The incorporation test was also applied by the International Court of Justice in the *Anglo-Iranian Oil* Case (Preliminary Objection) 1955,[15] where the Court expressly noted that the company was incorporated under the laws of the United Kingdom and then referred to it immediately thereafter as 'this British company'.[16] More recently the same test was applied by the court in the *Barcelona Traction, Light and Power Co.* Case.[17]

The Sudan is not a Commonwealth country,but as might be expected, it does apply the incorporation test. There is no express provision to this effect in the

Sudanese Nationality Act, 1957, nor in the investment laws or the Companies Ordinance, 1925.[18]

The Saudi law is explicit on this point. Thus, under Article 14 of the Companies Law, 1965[19] apart from joint venture, every company incorporated under that law shall have its head office in the Kingdom, and it shall be deemed of the Saudi nationality, though not vested with the same rights as those vested in Saudi nationals. This provision is modified, to some extent, by Article 2 of the Foreign Capital Investment Law, 1979[20] which adopts as the criterion of nationality a total Saudi Arabian shareholding in the corporation. Accordingly, the nationality of the corporation under Saudi law is determined by three requirements, all of which must be satisfied, namely: head office, place of incorporation and that all shareholders must be Saudis.

Another possible test to determine the nationality of a juridical person is, of course, the 'substantial interest' test. This test was adopted by the United States during the Second World War period. For a company to have the protection of the United States, 50% or more of the economic interest should be owned by United States nationals.[21] However, under the present commercial treaties, the United States favours the incorporation test, though sometimes the 'substantial interest' test is used.[22] This test of 'substantial interest' has been adopted by the Sudan, as will be seen in a moment, for the purposes of investment treaties.

The Sudan–Swiss Investment Protection Agreement,[23] for its own purposes, defines the term 'companies' as including 'companies, institutions or foundations with legal personality, as well as partnerships, firms or limited partnerships and other associations without legal personality in which nationals of either contracting party have a substantial interest, either directly or indirectly'. Different treaties of the Sudan reflect requirements of the law of the other contracting State. Thus, in order to conform with Swiss notions of the nationality test for juridical persons, the Sudan–Swiss Agreement adopts the 'substantial interest' test, according to which a person can have an interest without control. This may contradict the basic Sudanese nationality law if it adopts the incorporation test.[24] However, the 'substantial interest' test is not the same as the 'control' test, though normally it coincides with it in its actual operation. In short, this is a rather wide definition of a juridical person, because it includes partnerships as well as associations without legal personality.

Article 8(4) of the Sudan–German Investment Protection Treaty provides that:

the term 'companies' shall mean:

(a) in respect of the Federal Republic of Germany any juridical person as well as any commercial or other company or association with or without legal personality, having its seat in the territory of the Federal Republic of Germany and lawfully existing consistent with legal provisions, irrespective of whether the liability of its partners, associates or members is limited or unlimited and whether or not its activities are directed at profit,

(b) in respect of the Republic of the Sudan any company with a limited liability incorporated in the territory of the Republic of the Sudan, or any juridical person or any association of persons lawfully constituted in accordance with its legislation.

Thus, the parties to a treaty may well use identical tests for determining the nationality of a juridical person; yet this still does not disturb the rule that nationality is determined by the municipal law of each country. In deciding which company acquires its nationality, it may use one of the tests of '*siège sociale*', 'incorporation' or 'substantial interest'. It may also select two of them together or all three of them, as the case may be. While the nationality of a company under the German law is determined by the '*siège sociale*' test, the Sudanese counterpart adopts the incorporation test. This disagreement is due to the origin and background of the two legal systems. Thus, the German definition reflects the civil law system view, while the Sudanese reflects the common law view, which generally adheres to the incorporation test. The German definition of 'company' has been incorporated in German treaties with other countries.[25]

There are some regional conventions on the protection of foreign investment which employ the test of '*siège control*' or that of 'substantial interest' to determine the nationality of a juridical person. Thus, the Andean Common Regime of Protection of Foreign Capital and of Trademarks, Patents, Licences and Royalties, 1971[26] adopts the latter by defining a foreign enterprise as:

An enterprise whose capital in the hands of national investors amounts to less than 51% or, if that percentage is higher, it is not reflected in the opinion of the proper national authority, in the technical, financial, administrative and commercial management of the enterprise.[27]

Conversely, Article 63 of the Lomé Convention of 1975,[28] concluded among the European community and the African-Caribbean-Pacific countries (A.C.P.) and which is primarily concerned with trade co-operation, stabilization of export receipts, financial and technical co-operation, defines for its own purposes 'companies or firms of a Member State or of an A.C.P. State' broadly as meaning:

companies or firms formed in accordance with the law of a Member State or A.C.P. State and whose registered office, central administration or principal place of business is in a Member State or A.C.P. State; however a company or firm having only its registered office in a Member State or A.C.P. State must be engaged in an activity which has an effective and continuous link with the economy of that Member State or A.C.P. State.

Clearly, according to this article, the nationality of a company or a firm is determined by blending together the tests of '*siège sociale*', place of registration (incorporation) and that it is not enough for the company or firm to acquire the nationality of a member or A.C.P. State by only having its registered office there, but it must contribute to the development of the State concerned. This is a novel provision.

The Abs–Shawcross Draft Convention of 1959 seems to adopt the incorporation and the control tests concurrently. Thus in paragraph (a) of Article IX, nationals are defined as including in relation to a party to the convention '(i) companies which under the municipal law of that party are considered national companies of that party, and (ii) companies in which nationals of that party have directly or indirectly a controlling interest. Companies includes both juridical persons recognised as such by the law of a party and associations even if they do not possess legal personality'.[29]

From the foregoing, it is clear that the nationality of a company under the investment protection treaties and conventions is determined by the criteria of incorporation and '*siège sociale*'.

(b) The meaning of investment[30]

(i) *Legislation*

Having attempted to define 'foreign investor', it is necessary to define 'investment', first in the Sudan law and then in Saudi Arabian law.

(1) *Sudan law*

The Approved Enterprises 'Concessions' Act, 1956[31] (repealed), which was the first investment legislation in the Sudan, had referred only to the term 'approved enterprise'. It meant simply an 'industrial or similar undertaking in the Sudan which in the opinion of the Minister of Commerce, Industry and Supply, was an approved enterprise'. This was not a definition at all, but simply an authority to the Minister to decide in each case.

Though the Organization and Promotion of Industrial Investment Act, 1967[32] (repealed), had repealed the previous legislation, yet again it failed to provide any positive definition of foreign investment. It only defined 'capital employed' as:

> the total fixed assets of an enterprise including the fixed assets of the enterprise resulting from profits ploughed back before deducting the depreciation.[33]

A more elaborate definition of the term 'capital' has been furnished by the Industrial Investment Act, 1974[34] which provides in section 4:

> Capital means the capital employed in the 'establishment'[35] at the beginning of investment which consists of fixed and circulating assets plus any subsequent additions whether in the form of fixed assets (machinery, equipment and constructions) or cash or by way of employing the profits gained by the establishment if added to original capital provided that the additions shall

be made with the approval of the Minister of Industry and Mining after consultation with the Minister of Finance, National Economy and Planning.[36]

A definition of the term 'investment' was introduced in section 2 of the Organization and Encouragement of Investment in Economic Services Act, 1973[37] (cited hereinafter as the Investment in Economic Services Act), which defines the term 'invested capital' as:

the fixed and circulating capital and the shares owned by the enterprise, including assets owned in consequence of re-investment of its profits without including depreciation.

The same definition has been incorporated in the most recent legislation on investment in the agricultural sector in the Sudan, namely, the Promotion and Encouragement of Agricultural Investment Act, 1976[38] (cited hereinafter as the Agricultural Investment Act) (repealed).

Foreign Currency

The omission of 'foreign currency' from the definition of capital in the previous Sudanese investment laws raised the question whether or not it was obligatory on a foreign investor to finance his investment project by foreign currency only, or whether it was permissible to use local currency instead. In practice, the Bank of Sudan usually rejects applications to repatriate capital and remit profits owned by foreigners who decide to leave the Sudan for good, if they did not originally bring into the Sudan foreign currency which had been duly registered in the Bank of Sudan. Their money was required to be put in a 'blocked account'.[39] They were allowed to transfer abroad only a reasonable amount of money[40] according to the discretion of the Governor of the Bank of Sudan.[41]

Capital goods and raw materials

A foreign investor may import capital goods as capital to be invested in the Sudan provided that the foreign currency used in buying such goods came from a source outside the Sudan. It must come from the investor's overseas funds.[42] Capital goods include machinery, equipment, spare parts and accessories as well as raw materials, semi-processed materials or products.[43]

Re-invested profits

Re-investment of profits generated from investments which have already been made is also considered as capital in the Sudan if the particular Minister approves their addition to the original capital as the case may be.[44]

New definitions

To remedy the shortcomings of the three Sudanese investment laws and to unify them in one law to be applied to all investments, a Law Reform Commission was set up (hereinafter referred to as the Investment Law Commission).[45] The Draft Bill on the National, Arab and Foreign Investment (see *post*, pp. 77–81) prepared by this Commission, culminated in the Encouragement of Investment Act, 1980[46] which has repealed and replaced the three investment laws. This Act defines in section 3 'foreign capital' to be invested in the Sudan as to include:

(a) the foreign exchange transferred to the Sudan at the exchange price current at the time of transfer through a bank working in the Sudan for the utilization thereof in execution of a project;
(b) machinery, equipment and means of transport financed from abroad and necessary for the execution of a project, provided that they are in accordance with up-to-date technical development suitable for the Sudan as prescribed by the Minister of Finance and National Economy;
(c) the foreign hard currency to be utilized on the preliminary and feasibility studies and the establishment fees to be incurred by the foreign investors within the limits approved by the Minister;
(d) profits and returns from projects if added to the original capital or to be re-invested separately in another project with the consent of the Minister;
(e) intangible assets, like patents, trade marks, technical know-how, securities, rights *in rem*, investment contracts, etc. (Presumably this definition includes goodwill as well.)

Surprisingly enough, the word 'investment' is not defined at all by the new Act. It only refers to the word 'project', which is then defined generally to include any establishment or economic activity that might fall within the particular sectors in which investment is permitted in accordance with the Act.

It is worth noting the definition employed by the Egyptian Law No. 43 of 1974,[47] which partly inspired the Sudan new investment law. Under the Egyptian law, 'invested capital' means: 'free foreign exchange, machinery, equipment, primary material and commodity requirements imported from abroad, provided that such are compatible with modern technological developments and have not been previously used'. It also means 'intangible assets such as patents and duly registered trade marks, free foreign exchange spent on preliminary studies, research and incorporation; profits realised by the investment project in increasing its capital or if invested in another project'.[48]

(2) *Saudi law*

Under Article 1 of the Foreign Capital Investment Law, 1979,[49] foreign *capital* is defined as any coins, currency notes, securities, machinery, equipment, spare parts, raw materials, products, transportation facilities and intangible rights, such as patents, trade marks and similar assets.

Though capital is defined in such a wide pattern by the Saudi law, it does not explicitly mention expertise. Notwithstanding this omission, according to one practitioner,[50] the law, as applied, really means expertise too. This wide interpretation is supported by the fact that the purpose behind the invitation of foreign capital to Saudi Arabia is not for the capital in *stricto senso* but for the expertise and technology which that country needs in order to achieve the goal of industrialization, by exploiting its accumulating oil and mineral wealth, and to help its population to acquire the technical knowledge for a better standard in managing the developmental projects already embarked upon.

(ii) *Treaties*

Article 8(1) of the Sudan–German Investment Protection Treaty, 1963,[51] gives an elaborate definition of the term 'investment' in the following terms:

> the term 'investment' shall comprise every kind of asset and more particularly, though not exclusively:
>
> (a) movable and immovable property as well as any other rights *in rem*, such as mortgages, liens, pledges, usufructs and similar rights;
> (b) shares or other kinds of interest in companies;
> (c) titles to money or to any performance having an economic value;
> (d) copyrights, industrial property rights, technical processes, trade-names and goodwill [*sic*];
> (e) business concessions under public law, including concessions regarding the prospecting for, or the extraction or winning of natural resources, as give to their holder a legal position of some duration.
>
> Any alteration of the form in which assets are invested shall not affect their classification as investment, provided that such alteration is not contrary to the admission, if any, granted in respect of the assets originally invested.

This is the widest definition of 'investment' one can get anywhere. Not only does it include all types of property, whether real or personal, but also includes any interest or rights therein, tangible or intangible, in addition to technology, patents and copyrights.[52] This categorization accommodates all types of investments, direct or equity (portfolio).

Article 1 of the Sudan–Swiss Investment Protection Agreement, 1974, defines the term 'investment' so as to include every kind of asset belonging to nationals or companies of either contracting party and established in accordance with its legislation. In particular, though not exclusively, it includes movable and immovable property as well as any other rights *in rem*, such as mortgages, liens, pledges, usufructs and similar rights. It also includes shares or other kinds of interests in companies, claims to money or to any performance having an economic value. The Agreement, like the Sudan–Swiss Investment Protection Treaty, 1963, also includes in its definition of 'investment',[53] copyrights, industrial property rights, technical processes, know-how, trade marks, business concessions including concessions to search for, extract or exploit natural resources. It also includes in the definition of 'investment', business names. But its novelty lies in the fact that it excludes 'goodwill' altogether from the concept of 'investment'. This is narrower than the Sudan–German Agreement, which seems to include goodwill in the definition of investment.

The investment guaranty treaties concluded by the United States with developing countries reveal a practice of using the term 'investment' to include 'currency, credits, assets or investments on account of which such payment is made',[54] but not goodwill.

(iii) *Draft conventions*

Several draft conventions on the protection of foreign investment use the word 'property' and not 'investment'. The Abs–Shawcross Draft Convention[55] is a typical example of this. In paragraph (h) of Article IX, property is defined as including 'all property rights and interests, whether held directly or indirectly. A member of a company is deemed to have an interest in the property of the company'. Strangely enough, although this Draft Convention is headed 'Draft Convention on Investment Abroad', investment is not defined. Schwarzenberger[56] praised this wide formulation of property as being in conformity with international law. But he seems to have gone too far in saying that the terms 'investment' and 'property' are treated as synonyms and cover all types of interests and rights in property.[57] He went further in saying that, 'unless otherwise stated, foreign investments are intended to include proprietary and portfolio investments abroad as well as medium and long-term credits or loans for the import of equipment or services into another country'.[58] But under international law, property and investment are not always the same. International law always speaks of alien property, which does not always mean investment. Property may often not be invested. Furthermore, it has long been established that, although international law does not possess its own definition of property, the concept is well recognized by that system in different forms as being mainly regulated by municipal law.[59]

So, investment seems to be the correct term, and it includes all forms of invested property, which embraces also know-how.

2. Where to invest in the Sudan and Saudi Arabia

(a) The right of a State to regulate investment within its territory

The practice of developing countries reveals a uniform adherence in exercising their right under international law to regulate foreign investment in their territories.[60]

(b) Conformity with the economic and social plans

(i) *The Sudan*

In the Sudan the following conditions are to be satisfied before foreign investment can be admitted in various economic sectors:

(1) Industry

Under section 5 of the Industrial Investment Act, 1974, which lays down the policy governing foreign investment, foreign investment is encouraged in the 'establishment' that satisfies any one of the following conditions:

(i) that it shall be of defence or strategic importance;
(ii) that its produce or manufacturing shall depend upon local raw materials or the setting up thereof will encourage the production of such materials;
(iii) that its produce or manufacturing will have the effect of dispensing wholly or partially with importation or make a contribution in exportation;
(iv) that it shall directly or indirectly provide potential employment for Sudanese people;
(v) that its work shall contribute in achieving the aims of economic co-operation and integration with Arab and African states.

This provision thus enshrines the investment policy in the industrial sector in legal terms. Furthermore, foreign investment is encouraged, if it fulfils the above-mentioned conditions, in the industrial sector,[61] in agricultural products, animal products or mineral extracts, mining,[62] prospecting for petroleum[63] or any other industrial activity as may be determined by the Minister of Power and Mining.

(2) *Economic services*

Under sections 4 and 6 of the Investment in Economic Services Act, 1973, foreign investment is encouraged in economic services if it contributes to the realization of the State's economic plans and the acceleration of economic growth in the Sudan. Special consideration shall be given to an investment enterprise when its owner agrees to its being placed in the area in which the Minister of Finance, National Economy and Planning considers its placing would more effectively contribute to implementing the State's economic development plan and the policy of rural development, with a view to achieving the integration of the economy.[64] It is worth noting that the Investment in Economic Services Act did not define in clear terms the economic services. However, it mentioned some of them, which include the following:

(a) tourism
(b) transport
(c) warehousing
(d) equipment of pesticides and agricultural production
(e) any other economic activities that may help to serve and develop the national economy as decided by the Minister of Finance, National Economy and Planning.[65]

Banking is not expressly included in these economic services, though the Bank of Sudan Act, 1959[66] has been recently amended in such a way as to allow the formation of new foreign banks in the Sudan despite the fact that the then existing foreign banks were nationalized in 1970. Till now, however, at least seven foreign banks have been formed, including three American banks.[67] According to this new amendment, the only requirement for forming a foreign bank in the Sudan is to obtain a licence from the Bank of Sudan and the approval of the Minister of Finance, National Economy and Planning. It seems that the admission of foreign banks falls solely within the discretionary power conferred on the Ministry of Finance, National Economy and Planning by paragraph (e) of section 5 of the Investment in Economic Services Act, 1973. Sometimes the issue is subject to the approval of the Council of Ministers and the assent of the President before the Minister can exercise his discretionary power.

(3) *Agriculture*

According to the Agricultural Investment Act, 1976 investment in the agricultural sector is encouraged in all projects working in agricultural or animal production and husbandry for local production, export or both, or any other project on which the Minister of Agriculture, Food and Natural Resources may decide, within the policy of the agricultural development plan which aims at achieving the following objectives:

(a) achieving self-sufficiency in agricultural products and commodities;
(b) production of the maximum amount of agricultural products and commodities that increase the Sudan's export and hard currency reserves.
(c) introducing varieties of cash crops that insure the Sudan economy against the risk of depending on only one cash crop;
(d) achieving a just distribution of agricultural development opportunities in different parts of the Sudan, with a view to raising the standard of living and the rate of national income;
(e) integration in kind in agricultural production, both in its botanic and animal sections, and also achieving functional integration between agriculture and industry.[68]

All these statutory conditions and objectives stipulated by the Sudanese investment laws mentioned above have been resurrected in section 6 of the Encouragement of Investment Act, 1980 which repealed the previous investment laws. Section 5 of this Act gives the Ministerial Committee for Investment established by the Act, the right to determine for investment any other economic activity, in addition to what is stipulated by the Act.

(ii) *Saudi Arabia*

In contrast to the Sudan, Saudi Arabia has launched huge development plans for diversifying its economy. These call for industrialization which can make use of the derivatives of petroleum and the wasted natural gas.[69] And obviously, unlike the Sudan, fertile land for agriculture is very scanty, as most of the Arabian peninsula is desert. Industrialization in Saudi Arabia is carried out by both the public and private sectors. The Kingdom adheres to the concept of a free economy. The Government intervenes only when it is essential for the welfare of the people. It encourages private investors to take part in both the process of development and its benefits. For economic diversification, the Government has been continuously encouraging the private sector to undertake industrial and other investments.[70]

Under the present law, foreign capital is encouraged in the Kingdom if it satisfies two basic conditions, namely:

(a) it shall be invested in development projects, which do not include petroleum and mineral extraction projects;[71]
(b) the investment shall be accompanied by foreign technical know-how and expertise.[72]

The development projects eligible for investment are to be determined by the Ministry of Industry and Electricity on the recommendations of the Foreign Investment Committee[73] within the guidelines of the Development Plan[74] from time to time.

As regards banking, the Saudi policy has shifted towards 'Saudization'. Thus, as of May 1977, all banks operating in the Kingdom were required to have a minimum participation of 60% by Saudi nationals within a period of one year, and this has now largely been accomplished, with the exception of only three foreign banks, Bank Melli Iran, the United Bank Limited of Pakistan and the Banque del Liban et d'Outre Mer.[75]

By the same token, trading and commercial activities are confined to Saudi nationals. If a foreign entity, which does not have a Saudi partner, enters into a contract with a Government agency, it must appoint a Saudi service agent.[76]

3. Entry visa, residence and work permits

Having decided where to invest, a foreign investor needs to obtain an entry visa to the country of his choice so as to carry out feasibility studies on the potentialities of investment in the sectors he has chosen. If he is then satisfied with the 'investment climate' and decides to start his investment, again he needs a residence permit. Equally, he must obtain work permits from the competent labour authorities for his foreign employees and workers, which is a long process in Saudi Arabia.[77] The procedure for obtaining visas and permits is well regulated by the immigration laws,[78] and hence does not require special consideration here. Suffice it to state that issuing of entry visas is entrusted to the Passports Departments and consulates or diplomatic missions abroad.

The validity of the immigration provisions under international law is well established. It is generally recognized that a State is under no duty, in the absence of treaty provisions, to admit or not to admit aliens into its territory. Even if it does allow entry to an alien, it may do so on such conditions as it may deem fit for its national security and economic policy in this regard. This fundamental principle of international law has been confirmed by many jurists[79] as well as international conferences, conventions[80] and the practice of States.[81]

(a) Modification of immigration laws in favour of foreign investors

These immigration rules being so stringent, attempts have been made in the Sudan to mitigate their rigour by special legislation and treaties to encourage foreign investors.

In the first place, section 16 of the Organization and Promotion of Industrial Investment Act, 1967 (repealed) provided that the Ministry of Industry and Mining might submit recommendations to the concerned Government or semi-government bodies, by which the investment enterprise was to be sponsored, regarding application of the investment enterprise relating to residence permits for its managers and skilled foreign workers necessary for working in the Sudan. These recommendations were to be given special consideration. In case of refusal by the sponsoring body of these recommendations, it was to state in writing the justifying reasons.

This provision has not been reproduced in the current investment laws though there are scattered provisions which allow of wide discretionary powers to grant any facilities or concessions to foreign enterprises.[82]

The Exchange of Notes between the Sudanese and the West German delegations annexed to the Sudan–German Investment Protection Treaty, 1963 emphasized the necessity of simplifying the immigration laws in order to encourage and promote investment by nationals of either party. Thus the Sudanese delegation stated that:

To facilitate and promote investments made by German nationals or companies in the territory of the Republic of the Sudan in accordance with Article 1 of the treaty[83] ...the Republic of the Sudan undertakes to grant the necessary permits to German nationals who in connection with such investments desire to enter into and stay in the Republic of the Sudan and to carry on activity there as employees, unless reasons of public order or security or public health or morality warrant otherwise.[84]

Equally, Article 4 of the Sudan–Swiss Investment Protection Agreement, 1974, provides that:

Either contracting party shall facilitate in its territory such investment and shall grant to that effect necessary permits including permits for the implementation of manufacturing agreements, for technical, commercial or administrative assistance as well as for the employment of consultants and other qualified personnel of the other contracting party or a *Third State*.

However, either contracting party may refuse entry of employments *for security reasons*. (My italics.)

The novelty in this provision is that it introduces a provision in favour of nationals of a third party, not a party to the agreement. Moreover, it is very elaborate and detailed.[85]

Furthermore, article 8 of the Convention on Investment of the Arab Capital and its Transfer among the Arab States, 1971, expressly provided that an Arab investor shall have the right to reside in the territory of the host country so as to conduct his investment activities.

However, if an investor is not covered by the German or any other treaty, the situation would be that the general rules of international law will apply, which entrench the sovereign right of a State to decide whether or not to admit aliens into its territory.

4. How to invest

If a foreign investor decides to embark upon any investment project in the Sudan or Saudi Arabia, and if he has satisfied the requirements of the immigration laws, there are still some other procedural formalities which he must satisfy. He has to elect in what manner and shape he is going to conduct his business activity, and the following formalities, *inter alia*, must be satisfied at the outset.

(a) Duty to obtain a licence

(i) *Sudan*

Before taking any step in setting his investment in motion, a foreign investor must obtain a licence from a competent authority. Under the previous legislation, if he intends to invest in the industrial sector, he has to obtain a licence to that effect from the Minister of Industry, who may grant such a licence after considering the recommendation of the Advisory Committee for Industrial Development formed under section 6 of the Industrial Investment Act, 1974. The Advisory Committee is normally constituted of high officials from the Ministries of Industry, of Finance, National Economy and Planning, of Local Government, and from the Bank of Sudan, as well as other officials from other departments like the Council of National Planning, Central Electricity and Water Corporation and other members to be appointed by the Minister of Industry.[86] This Advisory Committee usually advises the Ministry of Industry on all matters, and in particular on:

(a) Considering all applications submitted by investors for the grant of licences or renewal thereof, or by crafts' owners for the grant of concessions, facilities or guarantees and submitting recommendations thereabout to the Minister of Industry.
(b) Submitting reports to the Minister of Industry about the indications of industrial development and the difficulties facing industrial development and recommending appropriate solutions therefor.
(c) Considering the reports submitted by the competent officials of the Ministry of Industry and submitting recommendations thereto to the Minister.
(d) Giving opinion on any matter referred to it by the Minister of Industry.

Similarly, a foreign investor who intends to invest in petroleum extraction and mining must obtain an exploration licence to that effect from the Minister of Energy with the approval of the President on the recommendation of the Board of Petroleum Affairs and the Mines and Quarries Board set up under the Petroleum Resources Act, and the Mines and Quarries Act, and regulations thereunder, respectively. As regards investment in the agricultural sector, the licence used to be obtained from the Minister of Agriculture, Food and Natural Resources on the recommendations of the Advisory Committee for Development and Promoting Agricultural Investment.[87] Apart from the petroleum and mining sectors all licence issuing has now been consolidated under one authority by sections 17 and 18 of the Encouragement of Investment Act, 1980 whereby the investment licence will be obtained from the Minister of Finance and National Economy subject to the conditions stipulated by that Act and the regulations passed thereunder. The Minister will be guided by the advice of the Consultative Committee, which is more or less a consolidation of the previous Advisory Committees established under the previous three laws.

(ii) *Saudi Arabia*

The general principle is that no foreign investor may do business in Saudi Arabia without Government approval to do so. This approval can be obtained either from the Ministry of Commerce or through the Ministry of Industry and

Electricity. The exception to this general principle is the oil companies and, to some degree, the service organizations.[88]

As regards commercial activities, a foreign company doing work for a Government agency must obtain a temporary licence for that particular work. The licence must specify the scope of the work and the duration of the contract. Once this temporary licence is given and a new work is obtained, which is not encompassed by the licence, that work and the relevant duration of time would be added to the licence.[89] At one time this temporary licence was issued in the form of a commercial registration which in practice has ceased to exist.

Another form of authorization for starting investment in Saudi Arabia is through a licence from the Foreign Capital Investment Committee in the Ministry of Industry constituted under the Foreign Capital Investment Law, 1979.[90] Similar to the Sudanese counterpart, this committee is usually formed of high officials from Government departments or agencies related to investment and sponsoring or regulating the economic development plans.[91] The Committee, like the Sudanese Investment Advisory Committees, acts as an advisory organ for the Minister of Industry, and in particular:

(a) to propose the projects that will be classified as development projects;
(b) to consider Foreign Investment applications.[92]

Additionally, the Committee is empowered to examine any complaints or claims submitted by foreign investors or other parties concerned arising out of questions governed by the investment legislation, and to submit its recommendations on these matters to the competent authorities. Wider than this, the Saudi Investment Committee, unlike the Sudanese Advisory Committees, has jurisdiction to recommend penalties to be imposed on any project violating the investment legislation. The Saudi Committee is also the competent body for drafting rules of procedure for the implementation of the investment legislation. It must also consider all matters referred to it by the Minister.

After filling in all the relevant forms and presenting the relevant documents,[93] and if the Committee recommends to the Minister of Industry that the temporary licence be issued, the Minister may then issue that licence by a ministerial decision, a copy of which goes to the Ministry of Commerce, where another procedure thereupon starts.

The activities, however, that are licensed by the Foreign Capital Investment Committee are limited, and do not encompass such activities as marketing, management, advertising, research and the whole field of the consulting activities. In theory, it may be possible to persuade the Committee to recommend a licence to a branch office of a company without any Saudi participation. Actually, there are very few such licences. The Committee is reluctant to issue any licence, if there is no Saudi participation.

Again theoretically, if a foreign company undertakes activities that are not of the type that are licensed by the Foreign Capital Investment Law, it is possible that the Minister of Commerce would issue a licence to such a company. This issue is under review by the Council of Ministers at the time of writing.

There is a minority view that there are some exceptional cases where no licence is required. Examples are said to be the activities of consulting companies and the offices of technical and scientific services.[94] This is not correct. It is true that the situation of consulting firms is not as yet clear under Saudi law, as is the case of commercial firms. But in practice the requirement of temporary licence does actually apply, at least for a Government agency. Furthermore, there is a requirement of the employment of a Saudi agent in the same type of speciality, for Government contracts.

(b) Registration of foreign investment

On the other hand, there are several companies doing business in the Kingdom without licences from any authority. From a technical point of view, these companies are perhaps doing business illegally. To remedy this awkward situation, a method of filing for registration has been developed by practitioners on behalf of these companies. This serves as a constructive type of notice which would give them some sort of status.

Foreign companies working in Saudi Arabia under special agreements were formerly not bound to obtain licences from the Foreign Capital Committee. Recently, however, the minister of Commerce has issued Decision no. 680 dated 10 October 1978, requiring foreign companies contracting with Government departments or foreign companies sub-contracting with such companies to apply to the Ministry of Commerce within thirty days from the signing of the contract for a licence to establish an office in the Kingdom for the performance of the works contracted by them. This new policy would seem not to be applicable to a foreign company which is a partner in a Saudi limited liability partnership, and at the same time has a technical and management services agreement with such a partnership. But the question is how to distinguish 'management' from 'assigning' and 'sub-contracting' the project or any part thereof from the Saudi limited liability partnership to the foreign partner. Would that project or a part of it be outside the scope of the technical and management agreement? According to one practitioner,[95] if the project amounts to assigning of sub-contracting and/or is outside the scope of the technical and management agreement, then the foreign partner has to comply with the licensing and registration formalities.

Apart from the complexities of commercial registration, which we shall deal with below, foreign capital is usually deposited in any commercial bank, and not in the Saudi Arabia Monetary Agency (S.A.M.A.), which is equivalent to the

Bank of Sudan. Obviously, this is due to the absence of strict exchange control such as applies rigorously in the Sudan.

(c) Procedure for forming business institutions

(i) *Sudan*

A foreign investor in the Sudan can either elect to form a company or partnership with other foreign or local investors, or enter into a joint venture with the Government or any of its agencies or corporations, together with other private investors.

(1) *Companies*

The substantive and procedural rules that govern the formation of a company whether private or public are contained in the Companies Ordinance 1925[96] as amended from time to time. Under part VIII of this ordinance, no company incorporated outside the Sudan, which on 15 March 1939 had not established a place of business in the Sudan and had not registered the documents required to be registered, shall establish a place of business in the Sudan, unless registered with the Registrar of Companies.[97] In the case of a company incorporated outside the Sudan, which has entered into a contract with the Government for the execution of any work in the Sudan, and which has to establish a place of business in the Sudan solely for that purpose, the registration shall be deemed to be limited to such work and for such time as is necessary for the execution of such work in accordance with the conditions of the contract.[98]

Applications for registration are to be made to the Registrar of Companies before commencing business and the application is to be accompanied by all the necessary documents, namely:

(a) a certified copy of the charter, statute or memorandum and articles of association of the company or other instrument constituting or defining the constitution of the company;[99]
(b) a list of the directors of the company containing all particulars;[100]
(c) the names and addresses of some one or more persons resident in the Sudan authorized to accept on behalf of the company service of process and any notices required to be served on the company;[101]
(d) a certified copy of a power of attorney enabling some person ordinarily resident in the Sudan to act for the company in the Sudan.[102]

After a foreign investor has satisfied all these conditions, the Registrar of Companies must submit the application to the Attorney-General who may authorize or refuse registration.[103]

Upon receiving the authorization of the Minister for the registration of the company, the Registrar of Companies retains and registers the charter, statutes or memorandum and articles. He also publishes the same, at the cost of the company, in the Gazette.[104]

These procedural requirements are mandatory and cannot be dispensed with at all. Any company failing to comply with them is liable to a fine.[105]

If any alterations take place in the original documents and particulars, a return is to be delivered to the Registrar within two months of such alterations.[106] It is also obligatory on every foreign company carrying on business in the Sudan, to make and deliver a copy of its balance sheet in every calendar year.[107] Not only this, but it must also state in every prospectus the country where it is incorporated and whether it is limited.

Under section 94(9), no shares in any company can be allotted to a non-Sudanese without the previous consent of the Attorney-General and any allotment of shares made without obtaining such consent shall be void.[108]

In practice foreign companies may either be registered in the Sudan as subsidiaries of foreign companies or registered or incorporated in the Sudan 'with foreign capital' in several sectors of the economy other than public utilities such as railways, electricity and broadcasting. Insurance is reserved only to the State and Sudanese nationals.[109] On the other hand, concession companies like the Arabic Gum Company and Oil Seeds Company, which are public companies working in imports and exports, are also confined to Sudanese nationals and the Government only.[110]

In the case of investment in petroleum extraction, according to section 8(a) of the Petroleum Resources Act, 1972,[111] no licence shall be granted to a company incorporated outside the Sudan unless such company is duly registered in the Sudan under the Companies Ordinance, as mentioned above. In the case of leases, a more stringent condition is required by sub-section (b) of the same section, which makes it obligatory on a foreign company not only to be registered, but also to be 'formed' in the Sudan.[112] It is unclear whether the word 'formed' used in this sub-section means 'incorporated'. Despite the reference to companies 'incorporated' outside the Sudan in the preceding sub-section which might weaken the inference that the word 'formed' means 'incorporated', yet it is the opinion of the writer that the legislature must have intended 'incorporated' rather than 'formed'. This issue presents certain problems as regards the diplomatic protection of companies incorporated in the Sudan if they are injured by spoliatory measures by the Sudanese Government (see *post*, pp. 293–9).

(2) *Partnership or business name*

The substantive rules governing the formation of partnerships in the Sudan are derived from English law, namely the Partnership Act, 1893,[113] and the body of case law built around it.[114] But when a partnership is duly formed, it has to be registered with the Registrar of Partnerships in accordance with the Partnerships Registration Ordinance, 1933.[115] In the case of business names, registration thereof must take place under the Registration of Business Names Ordinance, 1933,[116] as amended by the Registration of Business Names Act, 1970.[117]

It is not clear whether or not it is permissible for a foreign investor to carry out his investment activities without utilizing any of these forms of business institution. The Sudanese investment laws deal with the terms 'establishment', 'project', 'craft' and 'enterprise', without explaining their legal nature. They never refer to any particular form of business institution such as companies or partnerships. In view of this uncertainty, it seems that it is necessary for a foreign investor at least to have a 'business name', and this coincides with the current policy of the Government.

(ii) *Saudi Arabi*

As far as the forms of doing business in Saudi Arabia are concerned, the relevant legislative instrument governing this is the Companies Regulations of 1965.[118] This envisages eight different forms of business entities and describes the procedure for their formation, dissolution, as well as their relationship with third parties and all other pertinent matters. It has been observed by one scholar[119] that some of these eight entities created by the law enjoy all the corporate qualities known to western systems of jurisprudence, while others enjoy only some of these qualities. About 90%of foreign investors prefer to do business in Saudi Arabia by forming mixed enterprises and joint ventures with Saudi nationals.[120] Unlike the Sudan, the pattern of joint ventures between foreign investors and the Government is rare in Saudi Arabia.

The relevant business entity for a foreign investor is the limited liability company, or partnership in the American conception. Despite the substantial legal differences between a company and a partnership in the common law system, it should be pointed out that the two terms in the Arabic language are the same, and it is very difficult, even for the most able Arab lawyers, to differentiate between the two concepts in Saudi law.

The limited liability company is that which is formed of at least two or more partners who are responsible for the debts of the company to the extent of their private shares in the capital. The number of partners must not exceed fifty.[121] The capital of a limited liability company shall not be less than 50,000 Saudi riyals, and must be divided into shares of equal value, which must not be represented by negotiable instruments.[122]

A limited liability company is not allowed to resort to public subscription for raising its capital or for obtaining loans.[123] It cannot carry on insurance activities, savings or banking.[124] A limited liability company must be incorporated pursuant to articles of association signed by all the partners, giving the particulars prescribed by the Minister of Commerce and the basic information[125] listed in Article 161 of the Companies Regulations, 1965.

Within thirty days of the formation of the company, the managers or partners must apply for the notorization of the articles of association with a Notary Public.[126] The practice is that the Ministry of Commerce after approving the articles of association usually writes to the Notary Public of the town where the headquarters of the company is situate and asks him to notarize the articles. The foreign partner and the Saudi partner have to appear in person, or by proper representation before the Notary Public. Then, the articles must, thereafter, be published in the Official Gazette which is in Mecca. After this, the partners must go back to the Ministry of Commerce, which will ask for evidence that the partners have deposited with a commercial bank the capital of the company. Though the law stipulates that the minimum capital should be 50,000 Saudi riyals, in practice this amount is not enough. The Minister usually requires the foreign partner to be serious, and this could only be proved if the foreign partner raises the capital of the joint venture from the statutory amount to 2,000,000 riyals. The justification seems to be that the Minister expects the foreign partner to come with expertise, know-how and management; so his contribution to the capital must be realistic.

The foreign partner must also file with the Ministry of Commerce a registration from his home country, which should also be notarized, certified and it should have the final Saudi Embassy stamp in the country of origin. After all these lengthy procedures the company will be registered in the Commercial Register and the Companies Register at the Ministry of Commerce. These formalities would formalize the legal presence of the foreign investor in the Kingdom, which actually starts the moment he gets the licence from the Ministry of Industry.

These provisions apply equally to branches of foreign companies which have their head office abroad.[127] Thus, under Article 228 of the Companies Regulations no foreign company shall establish branches, agents[128] or representative offices, nor shall it carry on any business in the Kingdom without obtaining a licence from the Ministry of Commerce.

As regards trade marks, the governing law is the Registration of Trade Marks Law, 1939 which describes the method of registration,[129] the types of trade marks eligible for registration[130] and the duration of the protection.[131]

5. Conclusions

There is a discrepancy between the definition of 'investment' in Sudanese investment laws and in Sudanese bilateral treaties so far concluded with some capital-exporting countries. While the investment treaties categorize 'investment' into certain specified types of property, interest and securities therein, yet the investment law envisages only general descriptions of 'capital', which fall short of the precise definition of 'investment'. The formulation would seem to be wider than the treaty provision, as the term 'capital' could accommodate any form of property.

This flexibility in the legislation explains the fact that, under an investment law, the investee State will often try to assert its policy and sovereign right in formulating its own concept of property under its municipal legal system. In the treaty process, we find two sovereign States negotiating the terms of a treaty on an equal basis. Each side tries to assert its own will, and disagreement on major issues develops in the course of the negotiation. To come to an agreement, each negotiating party has to give something in the end. The outcome may be that certain terms agreed upon in the treaty will depart from the municipal law of either party. How then can the problem be solved?

This raises the further question: what is the place or status of treaties in the Sudanese and Saudi municipal laws? Are they to prevail over statutes or be inferior to them? Can a treaty be repealed by a later statute or law if it is discovered that it actually contradicts an earlier statute? This also raises the question whether a treaty, which is known to be better than the law, is worthwhile to a foreign investor. These and several other questions will be answered in chapter 6.

3

IMPEDIMENTS TO FOREIGN INVESTMENT

1. Introduction

It is obviously not possible to furnish a complete list of the factors impeding the investment of foreign capital in the developing countries generally.[1] These countries are widely different from each other in culture, economic potentialities, development, and in many other respects; and the factors tending to limit the flow of foreign capital to the developing regions are likewise of varying character and origin. The complete or partial elimination of some of these limiting factors may or may not in fact improve the rate of flow of foreign capital, for remaining obstacles may still keep the flow at a low level. But most of the countries need to eliminate one or more of the more effective impediments if they are to increase the flow of foreign capital.

The present study deals only with those impediments which could be removed through legal reform or state guarantees and incentives. The Sudan and Saudi Arabia have attracted a considerable amount of foreign capital; yet it remains true that investment of foreign capital meets with impediments. The removal of these impediments is more important than the creation of new incentives; because the former tend to stifle the effect of the latter.

This chapter will now describe the obstacles that might still be encountered by the foreign investor in the Sudan and Saudi Arabia. Not all impediments are pertinent to each of these two countries. Though both of them share a common cultural heritage, and to some extent, ethnic characteristics, they differ in other respects, notably in economic capacity and political structure. These variations, as will be seen, make the impediments less likely to discourage the flow of foreign capital to Saudi Arabia than to the Sudan. For this reason, this chapter will mainly concentrate on the Sudan.

2. Socio-economic impediments

There are several non-legal factors which generally discourage investment initiatives. It is beyond the purview of this study to deal in detail with these socio-economic factors; but, a brief description may help the understanding of their adverse effect on the legal rules regulating foreign investment.

Normally, a foreign investor will have certain factors in his mind before taking the risk of investing in a particular country; the most obvious is the economic condition of the country. He is also anxious to know as far as may be the future government policy towards foreign investment in the host country. In the majority of cases, the economic background of many developing countries does not favour foreign investment, because of the general economic conditions of these countries. The following are, *inter alia*, some obstacles which help to impede foreign investment in the Sudan, and in Saudi Arabia, to a lesser degree.

(a) Competing opportunities

One of the disincentives for a foreign investor in a developing country is the existence of competing opportunities for highly profitable investments in the already developed countries. This has been considered in some quarters as the principal factor in the shortage of private international investment in developing areas.[2] This factor is predominant in the Sudan where it is extremely difficult to compete with opportunities for investment in areas like Australia, Canada or even India. Prospective foreign investors are always looking for high rates of profit, especially in risky enterprises such as petroleum extraction and mining, which are still in the exploration stages in the Sudan. Obviously, this factor is not so important in Saudi Arabia; at present, the Kingdom is booming, and there is a wide range of highly profitable investments, especially in the industrial and petro-chemical sectors.

(b) Absence of sizeable market

This not only limits the amount but also determines the particular form of the investment. It is said that foreign investors will not invest in any industry designed for the local market, if the latter is too small to allow for a reasonably sized industry as well as the possibility of future expansion.[3] The majority of foreign investors are attracted towards industries producing for the export market. This is not so in the Sudan, the reason being that there is a sizeable local market, especially in textiles and food stuffs, notably in the sugar industry. Having a population of nearly twenty-two million, the Sudan until now has imported sugar and textiles in large quantities from different countries. For this reason the investment policy, as envisaged by the Six-Year Plan, 1977–1983,[4] concentrates on agro-industry so as to achieve self-sufficiency, and hence save foreign currency.

Obviously, there will be very little room for exports in case of surplus; and even if this is obtained, it will not be attractive for foreign investors to indulge in export trade of this nature.

It is also unlikely that Sudanese manufactured goods can compete internationally with their counterparts originating in the industrialized countries. This is partly because of their low quality, but primarily because of the unjust situation afflicting the developing countries in general in the existing international economic order. Under the present system these countries are actually barred from free access to international markets and technology. Though the G.A.T.T.[5] has tried to secure a code for regulating international trade, yet its system proved unsatisfactory to the developing countries, despite the introduction in their favour of the generalized non-discriminatory preferential tariff treatment for products originating in their territories. As mentioned before, the resulting discontent of the developing countries has been articulated in the resolutions of the General Assembly of the United Nations on the New International Economic Order and has occupied the continuing north–south dialogue in the U.N.C.T.A.D. (see *ante*, pp. 2–3 and *post* pp. 27–140).

(c) The big gap in the infrastructure and the basic facilities

There are other serious impediments to foreign investment in the Sudan. The country suffers from very poor communications and transport systems.[6] The failure of successive governments to improve these systems has thrown the task, when it has been tackled at all, on to the shoulders of reluctant entrepreneurs.[7] At present, the Sudan finds it difficult to obtain the minimum amount of foreign exchange for procuring necessary spare parts and fuel. In fact, the huge development projects embarked upon are beyond the present capacity of the Sudanese economy to absorb. This has led to the failure of the majority of the new projects in most of the economic sectors. Consequently, the Government has been compelled to abide by the advice of the I.M.F.[8] to slacken the rapid development so as to stabilize the economy, which has suffered from lavish and uncontrolled public expenditure since independence in 1956.[9]

It has been alleged[10] that banking and credit facilities are often inadequate and related business institutions are not always adequately equipped with qualified personnel in the developing areas. This is not wholly true for the Sudan. The Sudanese banking system has been re-organized in such a manner as to help in supplying investment projects. In addition, the previous investment laws[11] stipulated that the competent banking institutions should give priority to financing investment enterprises. Prudently, this intention has been seriously frustrated by the Bank of Sudan imposing restrictions and ceilings on the commercial banks' lending capacities to cope with scarcity of capital and lack of money liquidity.

In Saudi Arabia the banking system is established well up to the standard recognized by the western world; this despite the invalidity of interest in Islamic jurisprudence. Interest has in fact been catered for by considering it as banking charges or fees. More importantly, the Saudi Arabian Monetary Agency rarely interferes with banking transactions, and hence there is no stringent exchange control, as is the case in the Sudan.

Another chronic problem which would face a foreign investor in the Sudan and Saudi Arabia is that of accommodation and of establishing offices, which even if obtained, would be at high cost. In the Sudan, this emanates from the absence of housing planning and the loopholes in the Rent Restriction Acts[12] which fail to control the soaring rents, which have reached astronomical figures. Equally, in Saudi Arabia finding accommodation is an acute problem despite the huge constructions embarked upon. The situation is aggravated by the inapplicability of the Rent Act in many cases.

(d) Political and financial instability

The most serious impediment to foreign investment is political instability. Most of the developing countries have been colonies at one time, and their attitude towards foreign investment is governed by a reaction to their previous conditions. Some of these countries are ruled by totalitarian factions, often subservient to foreign interests. Their emergence as political units coincided with the deep division of the world into two opposed main 'blocs', i.e. the west and the east. Each of these 'blocs' tried hard to dominate the evolution of the newly-emerging developing country, to make it either capitalist or socialist. As a consequence, the political climate in most developing countries is today stormy and unpredictable. Not only governments and parties but political regimes as well, change rapidly. Undoubtedly, this has consequences for the legal regulations of the economic affairs of these countries. Thus a change in government may result in excessive central control, important constitutional or legislative changes, or a violation by a subsequent government of the commitments of its predecessor.[13]

Sudan offers a typical example of the effect of political instability on foreign investment. The first investment legislation[14] was introduced during the first parliamentary experience at the dawn of independence in 1956. The provisions of this legislation were reproduced more elaborately in the Promotion and Encouragement of Industrial Investments Act of 1967 (repealed). Despite the assurances and guarantees set out in these Acts, foreign enterprises did not escape the sweeping confiscation and nationalization measures taken by the present regime in its early period in 1970. The lesson learned from these hasty and haphazard measures has been reflected in the current investment laws and treaties which contain generous concessions and guarantees to foreign investment, which will be discussed later.

So, before a foreign investor takes the decision to invest in a particular country, he has to consider whether there is a favourable political climate, and this is highly unpredictable. It is left to the assessment of a foreign inestor alone, as a businessman, whether or not to venture to invest in a particular country, keeping in mind the consequences and risks that might result from political instability.

It is worth mentioning that the stability of the present regime in the Sudan may be maintained by the recent reconciliation settlement accomplished by President Nimeiri with some of his Conservative political opponents who have strongly pledged full support to the regime, and recognized the Socialist union as the only party in the country in accordance with the present constitution. This achievement, together with the previous settlement in the Southern Sudan, if genuinely observed, means that political instability will no longer be so serious an impediment to foreign investment in the Sudan. Yet even if the stability of the present regime is maintained, the system itself is discouraging to foreign investment. The frequent reshuffling of Governments and sacking of ministers disrupts the decision-making process and results in changes in policies. The succeeding Minister, in order to prove his capability and talents, often reverses the policy of his predecessors and accordingly pending investment licences are rejected on the pretext of non-compliance with the new policy, though they might have satisfied the previous policy. In such a disturbed system it is hard to imagine a sufficiently positive response of foreign investors to the invitation to invest in the Sudan.

Closely related to political instability is financial instability.[15] Its importance as an impediment to foreign investment is evident. Financial instability in the developing countries which import foreign capital is the main reason for the predominance of direct foreign investment. It is difficult at this point to elaborate on the devastated financial conditions of the Sudan. Like any other developing country, it is suffering from shortage of foreign exchange and currency reserves. Suffice it to say that Sudan, at the time of writing, is the only country listed by the I.M.F. as having negative foreign exchange reserves. Moreover, its rapidly growing foreign debts soared in July 1978 to $1.5 billion;[16] and the repeated devaluation of the Sudanese pound by an effective 20% has escalated the economic crisis of the Sudan.[17] Thus, there has been a dramatic rise in the prices of imports and essential commodities and a reduction of export earnings in Sudanese pound terms, and the rate of inflation is running at high double figures.[18]

On the other hand, political and financial instability do not constitute any obstacle to foreign investment in Saudi Arabia, as the system is relatively stable, both politically and financially. But the outbreak of war between Iran and Iraq at the time of writing will inevitably have an adverse effect on financial and political stability not only in Saudi Arabia but throughout the Arabian Gulf, as the Saudi Arabian Government fully supports Iraq. However, at present the Saudi riyal is well covered by gold, though in recent years the devaluation of the dollar, the trading currency of oil, has created some embarrassment in the international currency markets. In order to maintain a stable value of the riyal, it is linked with the Special Drawing Rights (S.D.R.) of the I.M.F. which consists of sixteen major world currencies. A band of 7.25% around the S.D.R./riyal parity is being utilized to insulate the value of the riyal from destablizing movements in one or more of the major currencies.

3. State measures affecting the investment climate

Nowadays the State increasingly interferes with the economy in varying degrees. This may itself create obstacles to the flow of foreign capital to a developing country which needs it most. However, the following are the main State measures that have their negative effect on foreign investment in the Sudan and Saudi Arabia.

(a) The 'screening' of foreign investment

One of the things usually cited as constituting an obstacle to foreign investment in developing countries is the imposition of restrictions or conditions on the entry of foreign capital. A typical example of such restrictions is 'screening'.[19] In order to import his capital, the foreign investor needs the prior approval of the competent Government authority to which he should submit his application in the first place. To reach a decision, the competent authority must take into consideration the general economic policy adopted by the government in the national plan.

In principle, 'screening' is inevitable. It finds justification in many considerations of economic policy, the most important being the concern over the conditions of the capital-importing country's balance-of-payments, a factor which is of particular relevance to the Sudan. Equally important is the avoidance of excessive concentration of foreign investment in a few fields. Furthermore, control over the entry and direction of capital is an indispensable condition for the operation of national economic planning. Finally, 'screening' is an effective way of excluding foreign investors from certain sectors of the economy, which are reserved to the State itself or its nationals for reasons of security and avoiding foreign domination (see *ante*, pp. 24–32).

Nevertheless, 'screening' has been condemned by foreign investors as a serious stumbling-block to the flow of foreign capital. Its removal has been advocated as a necessary pre-condition for the increase of foreign investments.[20] It seems that the removal of 'screening' could only be welcomed where it has resulted in the establishment of a governmental bureaucracy which may be, to some extent, antagonistic to foreign investment.

As described in the preceding chapter, in the Sudan the previous legislation on investment consisted essentially of sectoral investment laws,[21] administered by separate ministries.[22] Each of these investment laws provided for a separate 'screening board' in the form of an advisory committee to consider the different applications for investment in the prescribed sector (see *post*, p. 73). Thus, the application of these investment laws by separate organs presented duplication and multiplication as well as conflict of jurisdiction among ministries – particularly where a single project integrated several stages of production. Which law, for example, would apply to a project whose purpose was to grow, mill, store and transport rice? Any attempt to apply a separate law to different stages of production would, of course, result in confusion, a multiplication of bureaucratic red tape, and, in the end, a formidable obstacle to foreign investment. Generally speaking, such fragmentation of investment legislation and authority is not conducive to large, integrated agro-industrial projects – precisely the kind of projects upon which Sudanese economic development depends. For these reasons the three sectoral investment laws were repealed and a single investment law was passed, the Encouragement of Investment Act, in 1980, which is applicable to all investments. This Act creates only one administering investment authority, the Bureau of Investment, which we shall discuss later.

Unlike the Sudan, as mentioned before, Saudi Arabia has, from the beginning, only one investment law, the Foreign Capital Investment Law, which is administered by Ministry of Industry and Electricity under the guidance of 'the Foreign Capital Investment Committee'. And in most other countries, a single law governs all types of investments. In Egypt, for example, the legal framework of the new policy of *al-infitah* (openness) is to be found in one act – Law No. 43 of 1974[23] (as amended by Law No. 32 of 1977).

Experience shows that the Sudanese and Saudi as well as other Arab screening boards are generally rigid in their approach. They are sometimes arbitrary in their application of the investment laws and regulations. In most cases, the classification and inquiries into the projected enterprise's plans and prospects result in unnecessary delays. Even after their proposed projects are approved by the highest authorities, foreign investors often still have to tackle more than a dozen government offices to see their projects through.

Nevertheless, the lawfulness of the practice of 'screening' cannot be challenged under international law.[24] In fact there is nothing to complain about, provided the operational principles are well formulated and judiciously applied.

(b) Restrictions on the entry of foreign capital

As indicated in the preceding chapter, the business activities open to foreign investors must conform with the economic and social development plan whereby certain sectors are reserved only to the Government and Sudanese or Saudi nationals, as the case may be.[25]

In most developing countries, however, there are today certain additional restrictions which are directed especially against foreign investment. Such restrictions are usually aimed at achieving not the total exclusion of aliens but the increased participation of local capital in foreign-financed enterprises. The operation of domestic participation usually takes place when the investment legislation requires domestic partnerships with foreign investors. Thus investment laws in some developing countries make domestic partnership a pre-condition for the establishment of any commercial enterprise by foreign investors. Often the law fixes the percentage of the requisite domestic-capital participation. For example, no company is allowed to engage in the exploitation of natural resources in Brazil unless 51% of its capital is locally owned.[26] On the other hand, some developing countries adopt a liberal view by admitting foreign investors to invest in all sectors of their economy. In addition, they do not necessarily insist on national participation either in the capital or in the management of the enterprise. Typical examples are found in countries like Venezuela[27] or Kenya.[28]

Insistence on national participation in foreign enterprises has become very common amongst the developing countries. This has led the General Assembly of the United Nations to recognize the importance of this practice and encourage it. Thus, in its resolution no. 2158 of 28 November 1966, it emphasized the importance of foreign capital to the exploitation of natural resources of the developing countries on condition that there should be Government supervision of the activities of the foreign enterprises. It also recognized the right of every developing country to increase its shares in the management of foreign enterprises so that it receives the maximum share in the profits and dividends on equitable grounds.[29]

As mentioned before (pp. 24–6), though the Sudanese investment laws do not contain any provision on national participation, yet it is the current policy of the present regime to enter into joint ventures with multinational companies and foreign businessmen. Similarly, but with a firm policy which is indirectly legalized, according to the Saudi investment law, foreign investment cannot enjoy tax exemption and other incentives unless at least 25% of the invested capital is provided by Saudi nationals.[30] This is an indirect statutory imposition of national participation.

Whatever might be the merits and demerits of local participation in the foreign investment enterprises, it is resented by some foreign investors as hampering foreign investment, while others have found it profitable. This is because the latter rely either on the pressing need for services they furnish or on the legal arrangements, such as managing contracts, which permit them to have effective control over the operation of the investment enterprises.

Majority national participation, though it is desirable from a nationalistic point of view, is yet prone to fetter, to a greater or lesser extent, the activities of the foreign enterprise. On the other hand, if it is required, minority participation is possible, and that is hardly to be regarded as an impediment to foreign investment. Still it may be disadvantageous to foreign investors because of sharing the profits, and the possibility of friction between the parties. Nevertheless, one scholar[31] advocates that local participation is sometimes advantageous to foreign investors as it assures a knowledge of local conditions, economic as well as political or cultural. It is also said that local participation provides some sort of security against hostile measures by the government.[32] Eventually, it may even assist in increasing goodwill in countries which are antagonistic to foreign capital.

(c) Labour legislation

Some developing countries are anxious to obtain the utmost benefit of industrialization for their nationals by insisting that a certain percentage of the labour force of all foreign-owned enterprises must be formed of their nationals. They aim at raising the general level of employment and reducing the prevailing shortage of native skilled labour.

In the case of unskilled labour, a foreign investor finds no problem since usually there is a large unskilled labour force; certainly this is so in the Sudan. For this reason it seems that there is a convincing justification for insisting on employing local labour. The real problem is raised by limitations on the employment of skilled labour or managerial and administrative staff. Here, foreign investors often emphasize the complications and inefficiency likely to occur because of the absence of experienced and qualified personnel. They stress their urgent need for foreign technical and managerial personnel in order to ensure the efficient operation of their enterprises.[33] It is observed that:

the corporation cannot be expected to invest in the developing of new technologies appropriate to the typical situation in developing countries of scarcity of capital and abundance of *unskilled, uneducated, illiterate labour and in the mass training of blue-collar, white-collar,* and especially *executive native personnel.*[34] (My italics.)

To remove any obstacle in this respect, labour legislation should be flexible enough to permit the employment of foreign personnel and technicians whenever it is considered necessary. Indeed, the practice of countries varies. Some of them insist that certain proportions of nationals must be employed in the investment project. Thus, in Burma 25% of skilled personnel must be Burmese nationals,[35] while in Pakistan the required percentage is 50. According to Article 45 of the Saudi Labour and Workers' Regulation the percentage of the Saudi workers engaged by the employer shall not be less than 75% of his total workforce, nor their wages constitute less than 51% of this workers' total wages. Where Saudi workers with the necessary technical proficiency or academic qualifications are not available, the Minister of Labour may provisionally reduce the Saudi percentage. But, as labourers are scarce in Saudi Arabia, this exception is not strictly adhered to, and hence the foreign investor is usually compelled to hire, not only foreign labourers, but also administrative personnel. This is obtainable at high wages and salaries, which adds to the cost of the investment. By the same token, the Egyptian Company Law, 1954[36] stipulates that a minimum of 75% of the administrative, technical, clerical and accounting personnel of branches of foreign companies operating in Egypt must be Egyptians receiving not less than 65% of the total emoluments paid by the branch. In addition, Egyptian nationals must constitute at least 90% of the unskilled labour force and be entitled to 80% of the total wages paid by the company.

Not only may limitations be imposed on the employment of nationals, but also limitations are frequently imposed on the members of the boards of directors or equivalent bodies of domestic corporations. Thus in Egypt, for instance, the majority of the members of any company's board of directors must be Egyptian nationals.[37] In some other countries, provisions require only that the majority of board of directors be residents, and not necessarily citizens of the investee State.[38]

In the Sudan, under the previous legislation, there was no express provision insisting on employment of Sudanese nationals in the foreign investment projects. But, the new legislation, the Encouragement of Investment Act, 1980[39] provides that the investment will be encouraged if it secures jobs for the Sudanese nationals. Moreover, it is the policy now that Sudanese nationals must be employed whenever they are qualified for the jobs. This policy is sometimes incorporated in development agreements.[40] According to the immigration laws and policy directives, the employment of aliens in the Sudan is confined only to the preparation of specialized and highly technical matters. Ironically enough, the work force is now problematic in the Sudan. There is an alarming shortage of skilled Sudanese technicians and administrative personnel. This is because of the increasing brain drain, as the highly qualified Sudanese have been attracted by generous salaries in the Arab oil-producing countries, especially Saudi Arabia

Owing to discontent among the Sudanese trade unions, as a result of the soaring inflation which has dramatically raised the cost of living, there has been a rapid increase in strikes over pay claims and the improvement of conditions of service. This has been so, despite the banning of the right to strike. Undoubtedly, strikes are not uncommon today everywhere, but it should be emphasized that their proliferation inevitably causes disruption to existing investments and discourages others. Furthermore, businessmen disapprove of the existing Sudanese machinery for solving industrial disputes and termination of service.[41] They claim that the requirement for the approval of the Labour Office for unilateral dismissals restricts their freedom to dismiss, and therefore deprives them of an important management prerogative. And more discouraging in this respect is the frequent imposition of the minimum statutory wages by the government on private enterprises which certainly adds to the cost of the investment.

(d) Nationalization and expropriation

The most dangerous risk to a foreign investor is the taking of his property without compensation or with inadequate compensation. In this respect, fear of expropriation and nationalization constitutes a serious impediment to foreign investment. The taking by a State of property owned by aliens within its territory has been a familiar feature of eighteenth and nineteenth-century international law. The Russian nationalization in this century gave impulse to nationalization, and since the Second World War many States have adopted expropriatory or nationalization measures.[42] The era of European nationalization seems now to be over and the present trend is more closely associated with the policy of the developing countries. Since 1951, nationalization of foreign-owned property has taken place *inter alia* in Iran,[43] Egypt,[44] Indonesia,[45] Cuba,[46] Ghana,[47] Tanzania,[48] Sudan, and recently in Libya.[49] This repeated experience confirms foreign private investors in their fear that investments abroad are open to the danger of nationalization and expropriation by the State of the *situs*.

Whatever might be the status and the 'social function' of private property in the present stage of development of international law, the most generally accepted view is that, under customary international law, a State can expropriate and nationalize foreign property situate in its territory, provided that proper or appropriate compensation be paid.[50] Despite the obligation of the expropriating State to pay compensation, the fear of expropriation and nationalization is still one of the major impediments to foreign private investment. This is because the existence of an obligation to compensate on the part of the expropriating state may not be always sufficient assurance to foreign investors; especially so, when they fear that such compensation may be inadequate or may be granted only after a long time.[51] The uncertainty is exacerbated by the Charter of Economic Rights and Duties of States[52] which purports to confine the whole issue of compensation within the municipal law of the nationalizing State, thus eroding international law rules on the subject.

The effect of expropriation and nationalization as impediments to foreign private investment is best illustrated by the Sudanese practice, when the dissolved Revolutionary Command Council nationalized and confiscated some foreign property in 1970 (see *post*, pp. 209–25). The effect of these hasty measures caused a very serious setback to the Sudanese economy to the extent that it was near to utter collapse. No more foreign capital ventured to flow to the Sudan till the nationalization and confiscation measures were reversed in 1972.[53]

(e) Exchange control

One of the continuing difficulties in the economic growth of the developing countries is that they suffer constantly from balance-of-payments and foreign exchange problems. To protect their balance-of-payments position they put limitations and restrictions on capitals outflow and international transactions as well as exports and imports.

The operations of foreign private enterprises are affected by any exchange control laws which are made to safeguard the interests of the investee State. In some cases, such laws not only restrict the remittance of earned profits or the repatriation of capital, but also create multiple exchange rates. The Afghanistan Law of 18 November 1958[54] permitted the remittance of only 15% per annum of profits at the official exchange rate and the excess through the 'free' or 'black market' rate.[55]

Exchange control also affects foreign enterprises by making it difficult for foreign technicians and managerial personnel, because of limitations imposed on the transfer of their salaries abroad. Not only this, but also the operation of the foreign enterprise itself may turn out to be difficult or impossible, because of the restrictions on importing equipment, machinery and spare parts. This is in addition to restrictions that might be placed on exports and securities.

In the Sudan, exchange control was governed by the Finance (Exchange Control) Regulations, 1976.[56] Under these regulations, dealing in foreign currencies in the Sudan is completely prohibited except by authorized dealers (commercial banks).[57] These regulations also place restrictions on export,[58] imports,[59] securities,[60] transfer of insurance policies[61] and collection of debts.[62] These restrictive provisions have been temporarily modified by the Organization of Dealings in Foreign Currency Regulations, 1979, as amended up to 1980 which has revoked the 1976 regulations. Under section 16 of these new regulations investors travelling abroad are entitled to carry foreign currency notes or any other means of payment in foreign currency provided that they declare them at the point of entry and departure.[63] If this relaxation is perpetuated, exchange control will no longer be an impediment to foreign investment in the Sudan. But, the policy is still in its experimental phase, and it is unknown for how long this phase will last.

In the oil-rich countries there are no strict exchange restrictions as such. In Saudi Arabia, the Saudi Arabia Monetary Agency, which is equivalent to the Bank of Sudan, is only concerned with the functions of regulating banking activities,[64] the issue of currency, and the regulation of deposits held and loans and investments made by commercial banks.[65]

Customary international law recognizes the right of control by a State over its currency as an attribute of sovereignty.[66] This was confirmed by the Permanent Court of International Justice in the case of *Serbian and Brazilian Loans.*[67] Consequently, a general devaluation of currency or the imposition of restrictions on its transfer by a State for what it deems to be the public interest will not normally constitute an international delinquency. Accordingly, the devaluation of the Sudanese pound so as to clear the way to agreement with the I.M.F. on balance-of-payments support is valid under international law. In *Tabar Claim (No. 3)*, it was held by the United States International Claims Commission that 'international law and the usual commercial treaties are no bar to exchange restrictions. So long as the control measures are not discriminatory, no principle of international law is violated.'[68] In practical terms, this rule is qualified by the concept of abuse of rights and the existence of obligation under conventional international law.[69]

. It is normal that a State will protest against a spoliatory or discriminatory foreign exchange control law which adversely affects the interest of its nationals. Nwogugu[70] contended that a discriminatory exchange regulation may violate the most-favoured-nation treatment (see *post*, pp. 112–14) stipulated in the G.A.T.T.[71] with respect to charges imposed on the international transfer of payments. He cited with approval the case of *re Helbert Wagg & Co.*[72] In that case it was held that English courts will not recognize a foreign exchange law which is not *bona fide*, but was passed 'in reality with some object not in accordance with the usage of nations'.[73] It seems that *bona fide* currency exchanges made for the public interest cannot be challenged internationally even when they cause loss to foreigners.[74] If exchange control regulations are arbitrary and confiscatory in effect, no valid justification can be found for them in international law. But their imposition, regardless of their legality, discourages foreign investors who prefer to have unfettered hands to remit their profits and repatriate capital. The existing deteriorating standing of the Sudan negative foreign reserves invites the application of the exchange control regulations vigorously.

To some extent the Articles of Agreement of the International Monetary Fund are an attempt to regulate some of the problems of world currency convertibility and exchange control. The purposes of the Fund, *inter alia*, are:

(i) To promote exchange stability, to maintain orderly exchange arrangements among members and to avoid competitive exchange depreciation.[75]

(ii) To assist in the establishment of a multilateral system of payments in respect of current transactions between members and in the elimination of foreign exchange restrictions which hamper the growth of the world trade.[76]

The Articles of Agreement impose certain legal obligations on member States. Under the original Article IV,[77] the par value of the currency of each member shall be expressed in terms of gold or in United States dollars. This has been modified by adopting the Special Drawing Rights system, which abolished the previous arrangement of linking the par value with the dollar. A member can alter the par value of its currency to 'correct' a fundamental disequilibrium only after consultation with the Fund. Members have full discretion to exercise such controls as are necessary to regulate international capital transfers. But Article VIII(2)(a) forbids the imposition of restrictions on the making of payments and transfers for current international transactions without the approval of the Fund. Furthermore, no member of the Fund shall engage in, or permit any of its fiscal agencies to engage in, any discriminatory currency arrangements or multiple currency practices except as authorized under the Agreement or approved by the Fund.[78]

The drafting of the Fund Agreement has been much criticized by many scholars[79] for the uncertainty it has produced. There is little evidence that the I.M.F. has had the expected results. The member States are slow or even reluctant in fulfilling their obligations under the Agreement. For this reason, so far at least, the I.M.F. Agreement has not produced a standard code of behaviour for currency regulations.

Indisputably, exchange control regulations are of paramount importance to the Sudan for the conservation of foreign exchange to purchase essential goods and equipment for industrialization. Nevertheless, reasonable and permanent relaxation should be maintained in favour of foreign investors to transfer abroad their profits and capital; otherwise further investment may not be forthcoming from the same source. How far this relaxation of exchange control is obtained will be investigated later.

(f) Taxation

(i) *International double taxation*

One of the most important factors that persuades a foreign investor to run the risk of investing capital in a particular country is the potentiality for profits in that country. As taxation involves a considerable cut of income or profit, it is in fact counted as an impediment to foreign investment. Taxation may operate in two ways. In the first place, it may be an impediment to foreign investment, though as a normal business risk. Secondly, it can be used as an effective incentive, by taking certain measures. In this respect, taxation is the sole element of the investment climate which directly affects a basic economic factor, namely the investment's rate of return. This chapter will examine the negative effect of taxation as an impeding element to foreign investment. Its positive effect as an incentive will be reserved for the next chapter.

Taxation may operate as an impediment to foreign investment in either of two ways. In the first place, a foreign investor may be subject to international double taxation. On the other hand, he may be discriminated against or excessively taxed. International double taxation 'arises where various sovereign States exercise their sovereign power to subject the same person to taxes of a substantially similar character on the same subject'.[80] This usually happens when a person is subject to taxation both in the host and his home country. It may also arise when the tax system of each country adopts different criteria like nationality, residence, domicile or the place where property is situate, whereby a foreign investor finds himself subject to more than one tax system at the same time.[81] This results from the absence of any customary international law limitation on the tax jurisdiction of a State.[82]

States are free to formulate their tax legislation on any principle. They invariably claim extra-territorial tax jurisdiction. Thus, in Britain, according to Schedule D, income tax is charged in respect of the annual profits or gains arising or accruing:

(a) to any person (including companies) resident in the U.K. for any trade, profession or vocation whether it is carried on in the U.K. or elsewhere, or from any employment which is outside the U.K.;
(b) to any person residing in the U.K. from any trade, profession or vocation whether it is carried on in the U.K. or elsewhere, or from any employment which is outside the U.K.;
(c) to any person, whether a British subject or not, although not resident in the U.K., from

any property whatever in the U.K., or from any trade, profession or vocation exercised within the United Kingdom.[83]

Accordingly, every person resident in the United Kingdom is liable to income tax on his world-wide income, unless special arrangements to avoid double taxation are made by treaties. In the United States income tax jurisdiction is based on nationality and the source of income. Subject to treaties on double taxation, all United States nationals, no matter where they reside, and all United States corporations, are liable to United States income tax.[84] And as there are no double taxation treaties, tax credits, or provisions deeming foreign subsidiary income to be that of the parent[85] in Saudi Arabia, double taxation is an impediment to foreign investment in that country. But, despite its negative effect on the profit-gaining of foreign companies, this element does not seriously discourage foreign investors from taking the risk of investing in the Kingdom. This is because there are other factors which ameliorate this impediment, particularly the high probability, if not the certainty, of the economic gain of the investment.

Double taxation is unreservedly condemned by businessmen as it hinders the development of international trade and investment. Some national courts refuse to enforce claims to taxes when made within their jurisdictions by a foreign State.[86]

(ii) *Discriminatory and excessive taxation*

Taxation also adversely affects foreign investment where there is discrimination againt aliens, excessive taxation and the imperfect functioning of the capital-importing country's tax system. To attract foreign investment, discrimination and excessive taxation should be avoided. They cannot be challenged as unlawful in international law, except in so far as they become virtually confiscatory in character.[87] Unfortunately, the present Sudanese taxation system is not accurate enough to secure just and equitable tax assessments. Taxes are frequently assessed haphazardly which results sometimes in exacting more than due from some taxpayers while others are left to evade taxes through loopholes in the operative tax legislation. Additionally, the department of taxation lacks an adequate qualified cadre.

4. Commercial law

The investment of foreign capital in a particular developing country may be obstructed by the existence of out-of-date commercial law. The situation may be devastating when there is a great uncertainty or there are serious gaps in the commercial law. The fields most commonly found inadequate for modern commercial transactions include company law, bankruptcy, patents, trade marks, insurance, banking and capital markets. The Sudanese commercial law is a typical example. Apart from the areas of contracts, sale of goods and agency,[88] the other branches of commercial law suffer from uncertainty and ambiguity. They were enacted a long time ago during the colonial period, and for this reason they are not well adapted to the complexities of the modern business institutions.[89] The majority of them derive their origin from English law. In some cases the courts have to apply English law to fill in the gaps.[90] The situation has been realized and now legal reform is entrusted to the Law Reform Commission to revise and re-draft all the Sudanese laws. It is hoped that the Law Reform Commission takes into consideration the need to simplify the Sudanese commercial law to such an extent as to attract more foreign investment. Provisions such as those requiring the incorporation of foreign companies in the Sudan to be mandatory should not be included in the new law (see *ante*, p. 33). In fact this stipulation does not serve to control the activities of foreign companies, as it is thought. On the contrary, it helps transnational companies investing in the Sudan to acquire Sudanese nationality by incorporation, which facilitates the competition of these companies in investment opportunities with the indigenous investors. More effectively, this also spreads the risks facing transnational companies in many countries in cases of nationalization or similar measures. The incorporation of a branch of a foreign company in the Sudan will economically benefit that company in down-stream operations and inter-affiliate transactions and transfer-pricing which can be accomplished by other branches of the same company incorporated elsewhere.[91] For these reasons it is wise to leave the door open for negotiation. The criteria should be the adjustment of interests, as well as the benefit accruing to the national economy from the mobility of the foreign company. Because a free mobility will definitely tighten the grip of that company on the natural resources, it may arouse the nationalistic feeling; which might eventually lead the government to take spoliatory measures against the investing company, so that in the end further investments from other sources will be discouraged.

Particular attention should also be directed towards the need for a modern and streamlined company law under which foreign investors can be able to operate freely without encountering restrictions on the distribution of profits.[92] The new law should also contain provisions on protection of minority shareholders and corporate capital structure. How far these suggestions are going to be implemented is difficult to predict. These issues are to be considered by the newly constituted Law Reform Commission which is mainly composed of orthodox Islamic-oriented groups who claim the application of strict Islamic law. If this is accomplished, Islamic law should be liberally and flexibly implemented, otherwise this would discourage rather than encourage the flow of foreign private capital to the Sudan, as foreign investors are always worried about certain basic concepts which are usually pertinent to foreign investment, namely, insurance and interest on loans.

It is well known that Saudi Arabia is generally governed by Islamic law. This law does not prevail in the fashion that prevailed 1,400 years ago. The Saudi Arabian Government regulates for the day-to-day needs of the people. This is reflected in the application of a body of regulations in all aspects of commercial activities. The Commercial Code, which was issued in 1931, came into being before the recent explosion of commercial activity in the country. It seems that the bulk of Saudi legislation is patterned indirectly on civil law models. It has been contended by one practitioner[93] that the Saudi commercial code, which, in turn, was based on the Ottoman Code, was believed to originate in the French system.[94] Also the Regulation of Companies provides for the formation of many types of corporate institutions, some of which do not exist in the Anglo-American jurisprudence, but are perfectly familiar on the continental system. In this respect, commercial law in Saudi Arabia can be considered as a partial impediment to foreign investment. The English lawyer and the American attorney will find it difficult to render advice to their clients in such a system, without the collaboration of Saudi or Arab lawyers.

Another hurdle in this area in Saudi Arabia is that not all law is in the form of legislation. The greater part of the law is to be found in the mass of scholarly writing produced by Islamic legal scholars over the centuries. In most cases, these books and treatises are not available to foreign legal advisers, as they have not yet been translated.

In the case of construction and procurement contracts, a foreign investor will be faced in Saudi Arabia with the requirement of furnishing bank contract performance guarantees. Saudi Arabia's tendering law[95] requires the posting of bid bonds of 1% at the time the bid is submitted and a performance guarantee of 5% when the contract is signed.[96] The raising of these causes considerable difficulties when the contract levels begin reaching the hundred million or billion dollar level. To ease these requirements, performance guarantees need no longer only be issued by a commercial bank as a letter of credit. They can take the form of an insurance certificate covering at least 25% of the total value of the contract, payable on the first call without recourse to the courts or to arbitration.[97]

5. Translation

A serious impediment usually encountered by foreign investors in the Arab countries generally, and Saudi Arabia in particular, is the problem of translation from foreign languages into Arabic. In Saudi Arabia, all instruments and documents, applications, tender documents, correspondence etc. should be presented to the authorities in Arabic. This makes translation in the Kingdom a very lucrative industry, which is usually run by big firms with no legal personnel. Such a phenomenon leads to legal disputes over the Arabic prevailing text. Experience suggests that the Saudi courts adhere only to the Arabic authentic text. In one case a dispute arose between a Saudi landlord and an American company, the tenant, over a mistaken translation of a stipulation in a lease. The English version stipulated that the last instalment of the rent should be paid after three years and a half from taking possession of the premises, while the Arabic version stipulated that the instalment should be paid at the end of the third year. The Civil Rights Commission, which was the competent court to decide the case, rendered its judgment according to the Arabic version, despite an argument that the court should have investigated the actual intentions of the parties from the previous correspondence and the circumstances of the case.[98]

To avoid such a situation, it is prudent to have the translation revised by an Arab *lawyer* to ascertain that both the foreign and the Arabic versions are consistent in all respects.

6. Conclusions and reform

Impediments to foreign investment are not of a purely legal nature. There are some psychological, socio-economic and political considerations which have their influence on a foreign investor's decision whether to take the risk to invest in a particular country. Thus, two eminent writers[99] observed that 'the desire to preserve a certain market in spite of heavy import duties or sudden outside competition, the faith in the long-term prospects of a poorly developed country with rich possibilities, or quite frequently, the personal connections or inclinations of the top executive in charge will be the key factors far more often than the question of legal security'. Undoubtedly, these are subjective factors which are left to the sole judgment of the foreign investor as a businessman, and hence they fall outside the scope of this study.

Though it is incontestable that there is now a general international economic recession, yet the existing international economic order is unfair to the developing countries. It has engendered certain economic crises in these countries which hamper their economic development. This could best be combated by the international community as a whole revising the existing monetary system and adopting new multilateral measures in the light of the United Nations General Assembly resolutions and the recommendations of the U.N.C.T.A.D.[100]

On the other hand, there are some impediments which are not of a purely economic nature and, therefore, can be ameliorated by national legal reform. Professor Salacuse[101] proposed that the existing Sudanese bureaucratic screening could be eradicated by enacting a single law to be applicable to all investments, domestic and foreign as well. The administration of this law should be entrusted to a top-level investment commission or board functioning under the close auspices of the Ministry of Planning. He proposed further that the investment commission should be chaired by a minister of a prestigious status to be accountable directly to the President.[102] The Commission should be endowed with wide powers to decide on every investment issue, in co-ordination with other departments.

These suggestions served as a momentum in stimulating reform. Thus, in an attempt at reforming the existing system, a special Technical Reform Commission was formed.[103] The terms of reference of this Commission were, first, to make a technical study for unifying the existing investment laws in one single integrated law prescribing the ways and means towards encouraging foreign investment in various economic sectors. Secondly, in the light of the above study, to consider the desirability of establishing an executive bureau for supervising and implementing the new law which must interact with the specialized State departments to co-ordinate all efforts in allocating foreign investments in development schemes and programmes.

After intensive deliberations and hearing the opinions and evidence of the officials to whom the administration of the existing investment laws had been entrusted, the Commission was able to evaluate the sectoral administration of the investment laws. This unique approach placed the Commission in an ideal situation to identify the inefficiency of the existing paraphernalia. In its final report, the Commission suggested a Draft Bill[104] which would have the effect of repealing all of the five investment laws in force.[105] Part Two of the Draft Bill deals with the constitution, function and powers of the Central Bureau for Investment which would be the only administering authority of the new single investment law, to be applicable to all kinds of investments, classified as the national, Arab and foreign investments.[106] The Central Bureau would have a separate legal entity and a perpetual personality. It would consist of a Central Committee, a permanent Secretariat and several specialized departments to be formed subsequently by such special regulations as may be deemed to be feasible. The whole system would be placed under the auspices of the Ministry of National Planning.[107]

The function of the Central Bureau is to encourage investment in the private, mixed and co-operative sectors according to certain priorities.[108] To achieve such objective, the Bureau must be very effective in making *ad hoc* feasibility studies for eligible and suitable investment projects. It must also make the necessary publicity which will attract capital from inside and outside the Sudan as well as supervising all investment activities and furnishing all facilities to investors. As is proposed by the Draft Bill, the Bureau will issue the necessary regulations and grant investment licences.[109] By another provision the power of granting the incentives is bestowed upon the Minister of Planning.[110]

The Central Committee, which is the most active organ of the Bureau, will be composed of representatives from those ministries and departments which are related to investment, particularly those in the economic, agricultural and industrial sectors, in the same manner as is the case in the formation of the Advisory Committees under the previous system, with the addition of the Attorney-General.[111]

A single administering authority is surely desirable to avoid the inter-sectoral disunities and to help to co-ordinate more easily the activities of the different sectors of the economy. But the writer seriously doubts whether the proposed Central Bureau would achieve this goal. In the first place, the proposed machinery is both confusing and paradoxical. Instead of modifying and simplifying the existing system, it introduces its own anomalies which would result from the overlapping and duplication of the powers of the Minister of Planning with those of the Bureau. For example, it is unclear which authority would have the power to grant investment licences and incentives – is it the Minister or the Bureau individually, or both of them jointly, or the Council of Ministers? It is worth noting that such a power should be bestowed upon the Bureau and not the Minister, in order to avoid preferential treatment which might be tainted by political motivation. This suggestion applies equally to Saudi Arabia.

Furthermore, anything under the Draft Bill is left to be determined by special regulations; which eventually leads to a situation where there are several regulations contradicting each other. By so doing, the Bill is providing, through the back door, the same anomalies as the existing system. Ironically, it does not delimit categorically the powers and jurisdiction of the Minister of Planning and the Central Committee: an issue which lies at the heart of any reform.

In 1979 a ministerial committee was set up to reconsider the Draft Bill, and the effort culminated in the promulgation of the Encouragement of Investment Act[112] in 1980, which has, somewhat, eradicated the shortcomings of the Draft Bill. The Act creates an Investment Bureau, which consists of a General Secretariat and a Ministerial Committee for Investment. These two organs will jointly be the administering authority of the new single investment law, which will be applicable to both national and foreign investments, as well. The third category, Arab investment, has been deleted, and it is apparently classified as foreign.[113] The General Secretariat consists of a Secretary-General, a Technical Committee and a Consultative Committee. The whole system will be placed under the auspices of the Ministry of Finance and National Economy.[114]

The function of the General Secretariat for Investment is to encourage investment in the public, co-operative, mixed and private sectors according to certain priorities.[115] To achieve such objectives, the Technical Committee must be very effective in making *ad hoc* feasibility studies for eligible and suitable investment projects. It must also make the necessary publicity which will attract capital from inside and outside the Sudan as well as supervising all investment activities and furnishing all facilities to investors.[116]

The Consultative Committee, which is the most active organ of the Bureau, will be chaired by the Secretary-General and consists of representatives from those ministries and departments which are directly related to investment, provided that it includes four representatives from the private sector, each to be appointed for three renewable years. Unlike the Advisory Committees formed under the previous legislation, the Consultative Committee will not be a permanent statutory organ composed of certain identifiable officials, but will be established by Presidential Order, which means that the membership of the Committee is subject to the reorganization of ministries and departments from time to time.[117] This is a flexible provision as it offsets the danger of static provision which requires amendment of the law in every case, a process which takes time, creates uncertainty and causes disruption in the investment decision-making process. The Committee should liaise with the prospective investor to save him the trouble of getting approval from a large number of government agencies and departments. In addition the Committee will undertake promotional activities to encourage investment in the Sudan[118]

As with the Consultative Committee, the formation of the Ministerial Committee is left by the new law to the President, who may reconstitute it from time to time so as to allow for amalgamation or disintegration of ministries as the case may be.[119] The Ministerial Committee is empowered to frame the general policy for encouragement of investment in the light of the objects set out in the Act. It also determines the priorities in granting the licences, privileges and facilities. Furthermore, it must issue all the necessary directions, regulations and orders for the proper implementation of the Act.[120] In this sense, it performs a supervisory function, a task which in the past was unwisely entrusted to the minister in each case.

The issuing of investment licences is entrusted to the Minister of Finance and National Economy who must act on the recommendations of the Consultative Committee and any other competent minister.[121]

Whether this reform will succeed in achieving the desired objectives depends on the interpretation to be put on the provisions of the new law, and only time and the future can tell whether the lesson will be learned from past experience. One merit of the new act lies in its generality, which leaves room for flexibility and discretion, but the problem is how to regulate the exercise of that discretion.

It is hoped that the regulations to be issued under the law will fill in any loopholes that might be discovered by the new administering machinery. Another merit of the new law is its attempt to lay down some demarcation to the jurisdiction and power of each organ of the Investment Bureau. It, for example, elevates the role of the Consultative Committee in considering investment applications and plays down the part played by the Ministerial Committee, formerly the deciding body under the Draft Bill. The new law also gives the Secretary-General, who is the Chairman of the Consultative Committee, considerable powers of recommendation and discretion in his own right.

In the previous Draft Bill, approval was not only required for the original investment but also for all subsequent financial transactions. Under the new law only major changes have to be approved.

Despite these changes, which may offset certain impediments, doubts continue as to whether legislation alone can really improve the investment climate in the Sudan. As for foreign investors, they say that, even with the statutory changes, investment opportunities in other Middle East States are more favourable. With bottlenecks continuing in Port Sudan, a widespread lack of basic commodities and power cuts, sizeable foreign investment is still a long way off.

As regards the impediments emanating from taxation, exchange control and fear of expropriation, nationalization and similar measures, they can be moderated by the State establishing specific incentives and guarantees to investors, unilaterally or in collaboration with other States. This is usually obtained by national laws, treaties and development agreements between the State and foreign investors. These are the major topics which form the crux of this book. To these issues, the ensuing chapters are devoted.

PART TWO

ENCOURAGEMENT AND PROTECTION: FORM AND CONTENT

4

LEGAL INCENTIVES

1. Introduction

As mentioned in the preceding chapter, there are certain impediments which hamper the flow of foreign investment to the Sudan, and in a lesser degree also to Saudi Arabia, and so tend to create an unfavourable investment climate. Consequently these two developing countries have been impelled to try to attract foreign capital by removing these impediments, as well as by providing additional incentives, thus producing a more satisfactory investment climate. The United Nations has acknowledged the need for such measures on many occasions.[1] One of its reports states: 'any measure impairing the assets of any investor in a given country is likely to affect negatively the decision of potential investors in other fields of activity and even in other countries.'[2]

This report was welcomed by many capital-importing countries, which accordingly have taken measures to minimize the impediments and increase the incentives with a view to attracting more foreign capital. These incentives are presented in national legislations, treaties, development agreements and detailed governmental statements. Most of them are in the form of fiscal concessions which make the early years of an investment project more attractive. The justification of this policy is to enable business enterprises financed with foreign capital to settle down and make a good start in the host country.

The Sudanese and Saudi investment laws[3] in particular provide the following incentives.

2. Tax holidays

Income and business profits tax relief

(i) *Sudan*

At present, investors in the Sudan may enjoy certain tax concessions, such as exemption from payment of business profits tax for a period of five years, calculated from the date of commencement of production. This exemption may be extended for another period of five years, if the total annual profits do not exceed 10% of the capital of the establishment. Any increase of profits above this limit will be taxed according to the prescribed rates.[4]

The above statutory exemption may also be extended for an extra period of five years, for establishments that have increased their capital in the first ten years, provided that the exemption in this case is at the same percentage as that by which the capital has been increased. If the percentage of profits in such a case is below 10% of the total capital after the increase, there must be a complete exemption.[5]

Investment in oil extraction and mining is regulated by the Petroleum Resources and Mineral Resources Acts, which empower the Minister of Mining to conclude agreements with companies, and these agreements furnish to these companies more concessions than those accorded by the investment laws. Thus, under Article IX of the Petroleum Production-Sharing Agreement between the Sudan and Chevron Co. (Sudan), 1975 (see p. 412, n. 12 to ch. 9) the contractors are exempted during the entire life of the agreement (thirty years) from all taxes and duties, including those respecting extracting, producing and transporting of petrol. However, when the oil flows, the contractor has to pay all Sudanese taxes on his share of the oil.

Perhaps the most extensive tax exemption ever accorded is that furnished to Faisal's Islamic Bank, recently established in the Sudan. Under section 7 of its constituent Act, all capital of the bank, the funds deposited therein for the purpose of investment, and all the salaries and wages of its employees are exempted from all taxes for an indefinite period. In addition to this exaggerated concession, the bank is entitled to any other exemption or incentives under any other law in force.[6]

Under the Investment in the Economic Services Act, 1975 a tourist enterprise may be exempted wholly or in part from payment of business profits tax for five years, provided that it has a capital of at least fifty thousand Sudanese pounds. In the case of a non-tourist enterprise, the capital of which amounts to at least fifty thousand Sudanese pounds, the exemption applies only for three years.[7] Apparently, there is no reason for this differentiation between tourist enterprises and other categories of economic service enterprises other than, presumably, a

Government policy aimed at encouraging investment in tourism more than in any other economic sector. Furthermore, if the capital of an investment enterprise of this category, i.e. providing economic services amounts to one hundred and fifty thousand Sudanese pounds, the exemption from business profits tax may be granted for six years.[8]

These exemptions do not stand alone. The Minister of Finance, Planning and National Economy may recommend the Council of Ministers to grant an investment enterprise any sort of facilities not provided for by the investment laws.[9]

Under the previous investment legislation of 1956,[10] which was applicable to all investments, for assessing business profits tax up to 5% of the profits of approved enterprise is exempted from tax, and profits in excess of this figure are to be taxed at half the normal rate. The length of this relief varies according to the amount of capital invested.[11]

The above statutory provisions on tax exemption stipulated by the previous Sudanese investment laws are consolidated in sections 8 and 9 of the Encouragement of Investment Act, 1980. The exemption from business profits tax will be for five years, which may be extended subject to certain conditions to other five years. And the exemption may be total or partial.

These tax exemptions and the other concessions to be accorded to investors do not apply as of right. They depend rather on the discretion of the Minister of Finance and National Economy. The Minister's discretion in according these tax exemptions and other concessions to investors is not absolute. In exercising this discretion the Minister must take into consideration the type, extent, period of the concessions and the extent of the achievement of the investment project for the economy in the light of the policies and priorities determined by the Ministerial Committee, and the recommendation of the Consultative Committee.[12]

(ii) *Saudi Arabia*

In the case of industrial and agricultural projects under article 7 of the Saudi Foreign Capital Investment Law, 1979 foreign capital which has fulfilled the conditions provided for in that law shall be exempted from income tax and company tax for a period of ten years.[13] In other projects the exemption from such taxes shall be for a period of five years only. This provision underlies the basic Saudi policy towards foreign investment, which, as mentioned before (see *ante*, pp. 11–12), aims at the diversification of the economy and seeks alternative sources for State revenue, which depends mainly on oil.

An important feature of this Saudi provision is that, once the foreign capital has satisfied the prerequisites stipulated by the law, the tax exemption applies as of right. It does not depend on any discretion, as is the case in the Sudanese investment laws (see *ante*, pp. 58–9). This attitude is indeed encouraging and demonstrates how far the Kingdom is anxious to invite foreign investment. But, in the Sudan, after all, economic necessity justifies its reluctance to recognize such a right, because the national revenue depends heavily on taxation, an element which is not so important to the oil-rich Kingdom.

A pre-requisite, however, for any tax exemption in Saudi Arabia is that Saudi capital shall not be less than *twenty-five per cent* of the total capital of the project, and that such percentage shall be maintained throughout the period of exemption. By this device joint ventures between foreign and Saudi investors are made mandatory, if the tax exemption is to be enjoyed. But the practice has revealed that the Saudis are only sleeping partners and do not acquire any equity shares in the investment enterprises. They would be content only to receive annual remunerations from the foreign partners, the real owners of the enterprises. This practice tends to stifle the policy of the law, of controlling the investment and helping the Saudis to have access to technology, expertise and international markets by being active partners in the investment enterprises.

3. Depreciation allowance

(a) Sudan

Sometimes investment incentives include initial allowances in the form of accelerated depreciation of the cost of buildings, plant and machinery for tax purposes.[14] In the Sudan, depreciation is calculated during the years of complete tax exemption at the prescribed rates in every working shift (eight hours). The investment enterprise may appropriate a reserve within the expenditure to meet any increases in the prices of fixed assets when there is a need for their replacement, provided that the reserve does not exceed 75% of the value of the instalments of depreciation.[15] Any loss incurred during the period of complete or partial exemption is to be considered as if incurred during the last year of such a period. The expenses incurred before production begins, and depreciation deductions arising within the period of exemption, are deemed to be a loss liable to be deducted from the profits.[16]

The Sudanese investment laws do not fix a rate for depreciation. It seems that depreciation rates are worked out on a case-by-case basis by the Taxation Department.

(b) Saudi Arabia

A detailed list of the allowable rates of depreciation has been drawn up by the Tax Department. Higher rates may be negotiated where there are abnormal working conditions. Depreciation is normally made on the basis of a certain specified percentage in relation to each item which does not in all cases exceed 25%.[17] Since profits or losses on disposal of fixed assets, whether ranking for depreciation or not, are regarded as normal business items, there are no recapture provisions on the sale of ranking assets. An adjustment would be made if the 'book' and 'tax-written' values differ, but the normal practice is to use an acceptable tax basis for accounting purposes.

4. Relief from customs duties

(a) Sudan

Investment enterprises may be exempted from payment of customs duties, surcharges and other similar duties relating to imported machinery, equipment or apparatus necessary for production. Virtually the exemption applies to all imported goods used by the industry. Apparently, the policy behind this relief is that to impose custom dues will discourage the importation of plant and equipment, which is precisely what a developing country wants to be imported. The exemption is also applicable to spare parts, raw materials, semi-manufactured or intermediary materials imported into the Sudan by the investment enterprise. The exemption, in the latter case, is granted only on the condition that nothing similar can be found in the Sudan, and also subject to determination by the Ministry of Finance and National Economy of the amount of the raw materials exempted, in respect of each case.[18]

Not only that, but exemption may also be given in the Sudan to an investment enterprise from payment of any excise duties imposed upon any local raw materials introduced by the enterprise into its products. Alternatively, under the previous legislation, the investment enterprise may be reimbursed for excise duties and other taxes or duties of whatsoever nature, whether direct or indirect, which it has paid. This incentive applies only in respect of production to be exported, or packing materials used in exporting or for everything connected with exports, after deducting 10% of the total duties reimbursed.[19]

To restrict the repudiation of this customs duties' relief, section 12 of the Encouragement of Investment Act 1980 emphasizes that no duties or local rates may be imposed or increased upon investment enterprises during the exemption period without the approval of the Minister of Finance and National Economy.[20] Under the Industrial Investment Act, 1974 this restriction was intended to be applicable only to industrial enterprises. Nevertheless, in practice its operation was extended to investment in other sectors, especially in economic services. Such a wide interpretation finds support in the wording of section 10(4) of the Investment in Economic Services Act, which incorporates in general terms the provisions of the Industrial Investment Act by way of reference.

This exemption from customs and excise duties has been left untouched by section 10 of the Encouragement of Investment Act, 1980, which also accords exemption from *export* duties on manufactured or semi-manufactured goods produced by the investment enterprise. The justification is obvious – to encourage industry and increase Sudanese exports so as to enhance the capacity of the industrial sector to earn foreign exchange for the ailing economy.

Relief from customs duties may also be conferred by a contract. This is usually the case in the development agreements[21] for the exploitation of natural resources like petroleum and minerals. For instance, article XII of the Petroleum Production-Sharing Agreement between the Democratic Republic of the Sudan and the Chevron Company (Sudan), 1975, provides that contractors and sub-contractors engaged in carrying on operations under the Agreement will be exempted from customs duties and all related fees with respect to the importation of machinery, equipment, vehicles, spare parts, tyres, aircraft, boats, chemical materials, food stuffs, movable property and any other items connected with petroleum operations. The exemption is applicable only if a certificate from the Minister of Energy and Mining or his representative confirms that the items to be exempted from customs duties are to be used solely in carrying out the operations envisaged by the agreement. Furthermore, the same article extends the exemption to expatriate employees and technicians of the contractors and their sub-contractors. Each expatriate employee is permitted to import, free of customs duties, reasonable household and personal effects. Such properties must be imported for the sole use of the employee and his family, and provided that they are not allowed to be resold in the Sudan except in accordance with the regulations to be prescribed by the Government.

The exemption provided by the above petroleum agreement is not applicable to any imported items if it is the opinion of the Minister of Energy and Mining that reasonably formulated items of the same kind and quality can be manufactured locally. In this respect, however, special consideration must be given to their availability and timely delivery at a price comparable to the cost of imported items before paying custom duties. Any of the items imported in the Sudan either exempted or non-exempted from customs duties, excise duties, taxes of whatsoever kind under the agreement may be exported by the importing party at any time without paying any export duties or other taxes.[22]

To establish more effective incentives to investors in the petroleum industry, this Petroleum Agreement exempts the contractor from the requirements of obtaining import and export licences, and other financial burdens in respect of exporting petroleum.[23]

Identical agreements were concluded with three other American companies engaged in petroleum exploration.[24] Also provisions to the same effect were contained in agreements with other foreign companies digging for minerals throughout the Sudan.[25]

A more emphatic provision on exemption from customs duties can be found in the Contract for the Formation of the Arab Investment Company of 1974.[26] Under Articles 10 and 11 the company is exempted in the participant States from all duties and royalties during the whole period of its operation. Article 11 specifically confers on the company the right to enjoy all the privileges and incentives provided for by the investment laws of the countries party to the contract.

(b) Saudi Arabia

Machinery, tools, equipment, spare parts, primary and semi-processed raw materials, bags, cylinders, and containers imported for existing or new industrial establishments will be exempted from customs duties. Additionally, preferential tariff treatment is provided to protect locally-produced goods, where necessary.[27]

5. Other Incentives

(a) Sudan

Under sections 5, 6 and 11 of the Encouragement of Investment Act, 1980 all investments, whatever their origin, and indeed also national investments, are eligible to enjoy additional incentives. There may be an allocation of land at a reduced price necessary for the setting up of the investment enterprise. The reduced price may be payable by instalments, in which case the first instalment will not be more than the cost of the essential services such as the supply of water and electricity. Special consideration will be given for the future expansion of the enterprise.[28]

Moreover, under section 13 of the Encouragement of Investment Act, 1980 an investment enterprise may be granted facilities in the form of reduction of the prices of the electricity, of freight applied on machinery, equipments and raw materials. Reduction in local rates may also be granted.[29] More generously, the previous legislation provided for necessary measures to be taken to ensure the provision of raw materials, intermediary commodities and spare parts required to be imported from abroad for the purposes of the investment enterprise.[30]

Perhaps more important than any other incentive is that which was furnished by section 11(2) of the Sudanese Industrial Investment Act, which is unscathed by section 14 of the Encouragement of Investment Act, 1980. Under this section the investor can enjoy a monopolistic position, through the imposition of high tariffs and import restrictions or prohibition on competing foreign products. This provides some protection to the domestic industry from outside competition.

(b) Saudi Arabia

In Saudi Arabia, foreign capital enjoys, under Article 7 (a) of the Foreign Capital Investment Law, 1979, privileges enjoyed by national capital under the Law of the Protection and Promotion of National Industries[31] in respect to industrial projects only. This incorporation by reference of additional incentives concerns mainly the allocation of land at nominal price, and the supply of electric power, gas and fuel at subsidized cost. In addition, the Saudi Industrial Development Fund makes loans of up to 50% of the total project cost for a term of five to ten years, with a grace period of about one to five years, and at a low 'administrative fee'. Also, the Saudi Investment Bank Corporation provides medium and long-term financing for national and foreign investment enterprises, provided that the latter have 100% collateral guarantees from another bank.[32]

6. Double taxation treaties

As Saudi Arabia has not entered into any double taxation treaties with developed countries, and is considered unlikely to do so, the discussion in this section is concerned only with the Sudan.

(a) Historic survey

As mentioned in the preceding chapter, international double taxation is one of the more serious impediments to foreign investment and world trade.

The elimination of international double taxation has been a subject of extensive studies since the period of the League of Nations. A number of expert studies were carried out between 1921 and 1946.[33] These studies reached the conclusion that double taxation could best be eliminated through the conclusion of tax conventions. The League of Nations prepared two model tax conventions to be studied by interested States.[34]

The view adhered to by many authorities is that business income should be taxed only at source. In 1953, the United Nations Economic and Social Council recognized that the taxation by capital-exporting countries of foreign-earned income had a nullifying effect on the tax incentives granted by developing countries to foreign investments. It recommended that: 'The highly developed countries, acting unilaterally or when concluding tax agreements, should give special consideration to the feasibility of taking action to ensure that such income [from foreign investment] is taxable only or primarily in the country in which the income was produced.'[35] The International Chamber of Commerce also supported this view.[36]

The problem of double taxation has recently been a topic for comment by the Group of Eminent Persons studying the impact of multinational corporations in the development process.[37] In their report, they condemned the existing practice of taxing multinational corporations in the host as well as home countries. Ideally, they believed that there should be an international standardization of tax arrangements which must be neutral in their impact on foreign investment. To achieve this result, concerted international action was urgently called for to explore alternative approaches and reach a consensus on broad general principles. This would eventually develop guidelines to facilitate the establishment of a network of bilateral treaties between the developed and developing countries for the avoidance of double taxation.

(b) Elimination of double taxation by bilateral treaties

Usually the accepted device for eliminating double taxation is the conclusion of bilateral treaties between capital-exporting and capital-importing countries. This device helps to a great extent in encouraging foreign investment in the developing countries generally.[38] During the last two decades there has been an increasing number of double taxation treaties,[39] with the distinctive characteristic of the creation of incentives for investment in developing countries. As the developed countries have extensive investments in the developing countries, they practically bear the entire financial burden resulting from double taxation treaties.

The Sudanese practice in this respect has not yet proceeded very far. The Agreement between the Democratic Republic of the Sudan and the Republic of Italy, 1969[40] offers, however, an example. Under Article 2, each contracting party undertakes to exempt the public or private enterprises of the other party from all taxes on income arising from the exercise of maritime and air navigation in its territory. A criticism that may be levelled against this agreement is that it operates only in cases of investments in maritime and air navigation. To be entitled to an exemption under this agreement, it is essential that the ship or aircraft which performed the activities in the territory of either of the two countries must be sailing or flying under the flag of the other country.[41] The exemption contemplated by the agreement will apply also in favour of Sudanese and Italian maritime and air enterprises participating in a common pool, management or in an international organization.[42]

Double taxation treaties operate as incentives to foreign investment in either of two ways. First, they may result in exemption of foreign income from taxation in the capital-exporting country. Under this arrangement, dividends, interests and royalties earned by foreign enterprises are taxed at source, while the investor's home country grants him relief by complete exemption from its taxes. This has recently been extensively accorded to the British investors in the Sudan under the Convention between the Government of the United Kingdom and Northern Ireland and the Government of the Democratic Republic of the Sudan for the Avoidance of Double Taxation and the Prevention of Fiscal Evasion with Respect to Taxes on Income and Capital, 1977.[43] Thus the Convention, endorsing the principle that income should only be taxed at source, provides, in Articles 10–13, that dividends, interest, royalties, capital gains may be taxed in the State in which they arise. As regards income from immovable property, Article 6 provides that it may be taxed in the contracting State in which such property is situated.[44]

Secondly, a tax credit system may be utilized, whereby some industrialized countries like Japan, the United States and the United Kingdom usually grant relief to income from the developing countries by the 'tax sparing' or 'tax credit' method. Under this system, the investor is allowed to credit against his home State taxes any foreign taxes paid at the source. Article 23 of the Sudan-United Kingdom Convention, thus endorsing this practice of allowing credit against United Kingdom tax of tax payable abroad, eliminates double taxation for British investments in the Sudan as follows:

(a) Sudan tax payable under the laws of the Sudan and in accordance with this convention, whether directly or by deduction, on profits, income or chargeable gains from sources within the Sudan (excluding in the case of a dividend, tax payable in respect of the profits out of which the dividend is paid) shall be allowed as a credit against any United Kingdom tax computed by reference to the same profits, income or chargeable gains to which the Sudan tax is computed;

(b) in the case of a dividend paid by a company which is a resident of the Sudan to a company which is a resident of the United Kingdom and which controls directly or indirectly at least 10% of the voting power in the company paying the dividend, the credit shall take into account (in addition to any Sudan tax creditable as indicated in the above paragraph) the Sudan tax payable by the company in respect of the profits out of which such dividend is paid.

Paragraph (2) of the same article goes further, to elucidate and define widely the scope of Sudan tax so as to include any amount which would have been payable as Sudan tax, but for an exemption or reduction which is certified by the Director of Taxation as having been given with a view to encouraging industrial, commercial, agricultural, scientific or educational development under the operative Sudanese investment laws or any subsequent provisions dealing with the same.

Similarly, Article XV(1) of the U.S.–Pakistan Treaty of 1957,[45] allowed Pakistan tax paid on income emanating from Pakistan to be credited against

United States tax. A more explicit provision of this kind is manifested in the Japan–India Treaty of 1960.[46] After providing for credit against Japanese tax for tax already paid in India, it went on to provide that:

There shall be deemed to have been paid by the taxpayer the amount by which Indian tax has been reduced by the special incentive measures designed to promote economic development in India, . . . provided that the scope of the benefit accorded to the taxpayer by the said measures effective on the date of signature of the present agreement is not increased.[47]

This pattern has also been followed in the same standard terms in the Agreement between the United Kingdom and Pakistan, 1961.[48] Under Article XIV(2)(b), the Pakistan tax which could be credited against United Kingdom tax includes:

Any amount which would have been payable as Pakistan tax for any year but for an exemption granted for that year of any part thereof (under certain tax legislations providing tax holiday for foreign investments), so far as they were in force on, and have not been modified since, the date of the signature of this Agreement, or have been modified only in minor respects so as not to affect their general character.

This treaty also allows, as 'Pakistan tax':

Any other provision or statutory rule which subsequently be made granting an exemption which is agreed by the taxation authorities of the contracting Governments to be of a substantially similar character, if it has not been modified thereafter or has been modified only in minor respects so as not to affect its general character.[49]

More than this, under the same treaty, credit will be given for agricultural income tax levied by the government of any province in Pakistan, and any tax of a substantially similar character imposed after the signature of the agreement.[50] These are generous and far-reaching provisions. If they are fully exercised, foreign enterprises would be enabled to enjoy the utmost benefit of the tax holiday granted in countries where they carry on business.

There are two other features of double taxation treaties. One is that the industrial and commercial profits of an enterprise belonging to one party in the territory of the other are not to be taxed in the latter, unless the business or trade is carried out through a permanent establishment.[51] Even then, the country of its *situs* is, by treaty, empowered to tax only those profits arising from the establishment within its territory and not its world-wide income.[52]

Another feature of double taxation treaties is of recent origin. This is the protection furnished by these treaties to foreign investors against discriminatory taxation. Article 25 of the United Kingdom–Sudan Double Taxation Convention, provides that:

(1) The nationals of a contracting State shall not be subjected in the other contracting State to any taxation or any requirement connected therewith which is other or more

burdensome than the taxation and connected requirements to which nationals of that other State in the same circumstances are or may be subjected.

(2) The taxation on a permanent establishment which an enterprise of a contracting State has in the other contracting State shall not be less favourably levied in that other State than the taxation levied on enterprises of that other State carrying on the same activities.

(3) Enterprises of a contracting State, the capital of which is wholly or partly owned or controlled, directly or indirectly, by one or more residents of the other contracting State, shall not be subjected in the first-mentioned contracting State to any taxation or any requirement connected therewith which is other or more burdensome than the taxation and connected requirements to which other similar enterprises or that first-mentioned State are or may be subjected.

This latter provision seems to be intended to accommodate the increasing emergence of joint ventures between Sudanese businessmen and British investors.

The Convention between Sweden and Ceylon, 1957[53] had a similar clause, but with less precision. By Article XVI (2):

The enterprises of one of the territories shall not be subjected in the other territory, in respect of profits attributable to their permanent establishment in that other territory, to any taxation which is other, higher or more burdensome than the taxation to which the enterprises of that other territory, and, in the case of companies, to which enterprises of that other territory incorporated in that other territory, are or may be subjected in respect of the like profits.

This type of provision casts on a developing country an obligation of a kind that provides an effective guarantee against discriminatory, or arbitrary, taxation on foreign investment. What is important to a foreign investor in this case is the standard of treatment. He needs to know whether it is 'national treatment', or a 'most-favoured-nation treatment standard' because, of course, the former may change? In relation to discriminatory or arbitrary taxation, Nwogugu[54] advocated that it was sufficient that foreign investment should receive national treatment. This finds place in section 7 of the Sudan Encouragement of Investment Act, 1980 which prohibits discrimination between foreign and national investments.

Perhaps more important than the question of national treatment, is double taxation; and it would be advisable for the Sudan to eliminate the deterring effect of double taxation by concluding bilateral treaties with other capital-exporting countries. This depends largely on the readiness of richer countries to help the developing world generally. Undoubtedly, the best method of eradicating double taxation and also indeed of guarding against the occurrence of discriminatory taxation, is the conclusion of a multilateral treaty to be adhered to by all States, developed and developing. This task is for the United Nations, and previous studies should be taken into consideration. But, in reality, it is not easy to achieve a multilateral treaty relating to foreign investment, as will be shown in chapter 6.

7. Critical evaluation

(a) Procedure for acquisition of incentives

While the nature and extent of investment incentives are of vital importance to foreign investors, no less important is the procedure that must be followed to ensure the enjoyment of these incentives. A foreign investor must apply to the appropriate authority for a licence to invest in a certain business activity (see *ante*, pp. 28–30). His application will be referred to the competent advisory (consultative) committee or board which will determine whether or not the application satisfies the basic statutory requirements. If the advisory (consultative) committee reaches a decision in his favour, the appropriate Minister may give him a licence which indicates the quality and extent of the incentives. Thus, apart from the right to transfer abroad profits and capital, in cases of liquidation see *post*, pp. 102–3), the granting of other incentives, under the Sudanese investment laws, lies exclusively within the discretion of the Minister, the exercise of which is unpredictable. There are, indeed, general guidelines,[55] which may be followed by the Minister and the advisory committee. But these are expressed in general terms which widen rather than limit the discretion.[56] This opens the door for political influence and leads to preferential treatment and discrimination even among investors of the same nationality. This remark applies with equal force to the cancellation and revocation of licences, which are also entrusted to the Minister under special conditions.[57]

The investment licence is called an 'approving instrument'. The question is: will this 'approving instrument' be characterized as a contract between the foreign investor and the Government? The answer to this question is very difficult. The formation of a contract requires mutuality of the contracting parties which is lacking in the case of an 'approving instrument'. Incentives conferred by contracts and treaties are more specific, and are determined beforehand, as these are effective legal instruments obtained by mutual consent through lengthy negotiations. Their unreasonable revocation may give rise to an international obligation, and thus should exclude ministerial discretion (see *post*, chs. 6 and 9).

As shown in the preceding chapter (see *ante*, pp. 42–3), there is a rigidity in the application of the screening system, resulting from the application procedure for licences. All application forms have been framed in such a way that they are to be applicable to all cases alike, irrespective of the nature and size of a particular investment. Neither the Industrial Investment Act nor the Agricultural Investment Act required a minimum investment, and in theory all incentives were available to any investment regardless of size. This is also the case under the Saudi law. Conversely, the Investment in Economic Services Act required a minimum of £50,000 to be eligible for a tax concession.[58]

The investment laws of some countries are designed in such a way that the nature and extent of the incentives have a direct relationship to the size and importance of the investment to be attracted. The more important the investment, the greater will be the incentives. To achieve this objective, investment laws often provide for two or more investment categories or regimes: for instance, 'approved investments' and 'pioneer investment' to which different incentives are attached on the basis of the importance of the category to the country's economic development.[59] Notwithstanding the absence of an explicit statutory provision to this effect in the previous Sudanese Industrial Investment Act, the officials at the Ministry of Industry have indicated that in practice they follow certain guidelines to determine the types of investment eligible to receive specified incentives. Their practice was neither uniform nor certain. However, the situation has been, to some extent, improved by section 8(2) of the Encouragement of Investment Act, 1980 which provides that the type, extent, and period of incentives must be specified in accordance with the extent of the achievement of the investment project for the national economy.

It is suggested that the licence application forms should be diversified so as to furnish material for *ad hoc* feasibility studies for the various investment projects. The automatic filling-in of the present standard forms does not help much in pursuing the necessary supervision and analysis. In fact, some investors present fictitious projects without feasibility studies. They are only interested in the financing facilities or participation in business administration without risking capital. Sometimes successful applicants sell their investment licences to investors who, for one reason or another, failed to obtain licences. There are, up to now, more than twenty-nine approved licences for establishing textile factories but very few of them have actually come into existence. To deal with these anomalies, the Technical Commission for reforming the investment laws rightly recommended that there must be some criteria for ensuring the capability of the investor actually to provide the necessary capital for implementing the investment project, before any licence be issued. Reliance might, for example, be made on letters of credit opened in a bank for the importation of machinery and equipment necessary for constructing the investment project or establishment.

(b) Misuse of incentives

In the Sudan there has been frequent abuse of incentives and facilities such as exemption from taxation and excise duties.[60] Thus, after obtaining the exemption, the investor often sells the exempted goods or utilizes them for other purposes than that envisaged by the investment laws; especially building materials, which are very rare. The Commission recommended that it was desirable to control the misuse of incentives, but made no specific suggestions. Indeed, supervision in this field is very difficult and it needs both strenuous efforts and trained personnel.

(c) Problems relating to land

As regards the acquisition of land necessary for constructing the investment enterprises, practice has shown that most of the investors insist that their investments be in Khartoum Province where the prices of land are very high. There is no overall national plan for a functional exploitation of land for various investment projects. Additionally, there are many practical and legal problems relating to settlement of land disputes, and to the removal of encumbrances and charges on land for investors: a process which takes a long time.[61] There is also the problem of fixing the basic sale price of land. Ironically, the Commission[62] suggested that there should be no fixed basic sale price. It seems that the right solution is to make the investor pay a reasonable price, taking into account the continuous rise in land prices, the kind and size of the investment and the site of the land to be utilized for the investment project. In the case of joint ventures between the public sector and foreign investors, the Commission is of the opinion that the latter must pay part of the compensation to be paid to the dispossessed owner, or that the price of the land must be included in the cost of the investment project.[63] From an economic point of view this proposal may be sound, but, unfortunately, it would tend to discourage rather than encourage foreign investment; especially since compensation to be paid to the dispossessed owner may be high owing to the rapid increase in land prices. A better solution would be to apportion the expenses by fixing the basic sale price in such a way that it provides some revenue to the State.

(d) Registration of foreign capital

It has been observed that there is a lack of enthusiasm on the part of foreign investors to register their capital as investment in the Sudan.[64] It is curious that there has been no systematic collection of data of foreign or national investments, so the statistics for determining the balance-of-payments are lacking.

(e) Inconsistency with economic plans

The application of the Sudan Industrial Investment Act has revealed that the overwhelming majority of the present industries established under the Act are small-size industries, such as plastic or perfumes, owned by individuals, and depending on imported raw materials. This is entirely inconsistent with the proclaimed economic policy pursued by the present Government which aims at encouraging the formation of public companies for the heavy industries that depend on local raw materials, and which are believed to assist in the transfer of technology and expertise to the country.

(f) Taxation

In this regard, the Commission observed that the non-existence of a qualified cadre for assessing the tax exemption has allowed loopholes for tax avoidance.[65] This observation is of particular importance in relation to depreciation allowances which involve many accounting complexities.

Two criticisms can be levelled against the present Sudanese tax incentives in relation to long-term investments. In the first place, it is said that tax exemptions apply only during the early years of an investment enterprise, and so will be of limited attraction to long-term investments.[66] Also, this limited concession will not protect an investment enterprise against high and arbitrary taxation at a later period. Concerning the first point, one author[67] has contended that tax incentives in their present form are designed primarily to help out an industry during the initial years of operation, when there may be strong competition from other enterprises. He conceded that once on its feet the new enterprise should be able to fend for itself. But this is not always the case. The new enterprise might not earn enough profit to meet its current expenses, let alone payment of taxation. It is to be admitted that long-term investments are less attracted by temporary preferential treatment than by a low normal rate of taxation, fair means of assessment, and impartial and competent administration.[68]

As regards the second criticism, this can be guarded against by creating binding obligations on States not to discriminate against foreign investments. Such obligations can be embodied in contracts or treaties. In principle, it would be difficult to impose any standard of treatment on host States because of the prevailing economic nationalism in the wake of the Charter of Economic Rights and Duties of States.[69]

Understanding the anxieties of foreign investors, some developing countries have expressed their willingness to take more positive steps to assure them of reasonable taxation measures. For instance, the Chilean Law of 1960 authorizes the President to give the following guarantees to new industrial establishments for periods between fifteen and twenty years:

1. that there will be no increases in the rates of income tax on movable capital or dividends or profits obtained from the new investment;

2. there will be no new legislation that might entail discriminatory treatment in calculating income obtained from the new capital as distinct from that in force at the time of the approval of the investment;
3. that there would be no new taxes which might be considered discriminatory to the new business, or to its produce in their sale and transport.[70]

In Saudi Arabia the tax exemption is very effective in attracting foreign investment, despite the fact that it is linked with the requirement of national participation. One important tax, namely *Zakat*, a form of religious alms tax, applies in any event and, by its nature, only to Saudi nationals. The taxation system is well organized and it has checks on the activities of foreign enterprises in the Kingdom.

(g) Customs duties

There is still capricious categorization of items to be exempted from customs duties in the Sudan. There is no settled policy on identifying and determining the duration and scope of the exemption. This has led to a substantial loss of revenue. There should be a rationality between the customs exemption and the economic return from the investment project, taking into consideration the purpose and function of the incentive for encouraging foreign investment.

(h) Mining

The Investment Law Reform Commission suggested that it would be unwise for the Government to indulge individually in the mining industry at this stage, because of the high expenses involved and the lack of technical know-how. The Commission supported the creation of joint ventures between the Government and foreign investors in the ratio of 51% for the Government and 49% for the investor. To encourage foreign investors to invest in the mining sector, the Commission recommended that it would be advantageous not to impose too onerous terms on screening formalities in this field, especially at the exploration stage (see *ante*, pp. 42–4).

Having examined the practical problems that arose through the very short period of applying the previous Sudanese investment laws, it remains to be seen how far the suggested reform will succeed in dealing with the shortcomings.

8. The Encouragement of the National, Arab and Foreign Investment Draft Bill, 1978

The Draft Bill[71] prepared by the Sudan Investment Laws Reform Commission, after being revised, has culminated in the Encouragement of Investment Act of

1980. But before dealing with this Act, it is important first to examine the Draft Bill so as to give the reader a vivid account of the development of the reform.

The Draft Bill invites comments on the following points.

(a) Title

From its title, the Bill is designed to be applied to national, Arab and foreign investments. The earmarking of Arab investment as a distinct category implies that it is not foreign *stricto sensu*. The reason behind this is the heavy investment projects sponsored by the Arab Funds for the implementation of the master plan aiming at making the Sudan the food-basket of the Arab World (see *ante*, pp. 7–8). Moreover, the reference to the Arab investment in the title of the Bill seems to imply that a privileged and preferential treatment may be accorded.

A flaw in the title of the Draft Bill is that it omits to include the word 'Protection' altogether. The use of such a word would have a persuasive effect from the start.

(b) Quality and quantity of incentives

Under Part One of the Draft Bill and the *Incentive Regulations* (to be enacted; my italics), an investment project may be granted reduction in the following:

(1) business profits tax;
(2) customs duties;
(3) rents of governmental land necessary for the project;
(4) fees for issuing the necessary investment licences.[72]

The tax reduction will not be granted unless the investor proves to the conferring authority that the project will benefit from the incentives and to that extent no benefit will accrue to another State.[73] The purpose of such a provision is to take cognizance of treaties on double taxation (see *ante*, pp. 51–2).

To ascertain the genuineness of investors, it is made obligatory not to grant any of the incentives unless feasibility studies are presented and approved by the Central Committee on the recommendations of the competent authorities.[74]

On policy grounds, the quality and quantity of investment incentives to be granted depend on all or some of the following factors, namely:

(1) that the investment project must achieve the objectives of the investment law as specified under section 5 of the Draft Bill:[75]
(2) the amount of the net return that will be secured by the investment project to the national economy;
(3) the investor must undertake initially to provide the necessary capital and technical, administrative and market knowledge for establishing the project. Additionally, he must

train the indigenous Sudanese personnel at all levels so as to take over the administration within a scheduled time with the approval of the Central Committee;[76]

(4) the investor must undertake to provide the basic infrastructure or establish his investment in an area which has the basic infrastructure;

(5) the investment project must depend on the local raw materials;

(6) any other requirements that might be imposed by the Incentives Regulations.

From the foregoing, it is apparent that the policy of the Government is to cut down the incentives, as they cause great losses in revenue to the national budget.[77] Incentives such as a reduction in the rates for electricity and water supplies are deleted altogether from the Draft Bill; the other incentives are to be in the form of reduction, and not complete exemption, which is the case under the previous investment laws as examined above. This change of attitude is to be welcomed as it secures to the State a direct revenue in terms of tax levies, though it might discourage potential investors. It is admitted that the existing investment incentives are to be counted as the most generous among the Third World, and indeed in some cases exaggerated.[78] However, if they are to be modified, this has to be accomplished gradually, taking into consideration the size and type of each investment. Oddly, the Faisal Islamic Bank has been accorded total exemption from all taxes and duties for unlimited period by special Law-decree (see p. 378, n. 6 to ch. 4). This is a striking example of the inconsistency in the general policy of the Government towards foreign investment generally, and the lack of co-ordination and uniformity in the legislation in particular.

(c) Power of granting incentives

Under section 7 of the Draft Bill the Central Committee is the competent authority for determining the quantity and quality of incentives on the recommendations of other competent authorities. The decision of the Committee will be submitted to the Minister of Planning for approval within thirty days, and his approval will be inferred if he does not expressly disapprove the decision of the Committee. In case of disapproval, the matter may be taken to the Council of Ministers for reconsideration. This is a most confusing provision. It is inconceivable that the matter will in fact be taken to the Council of Ministers if the Minister of Planning disagrees with the decision of the Central Committee. And usually matters would be submitted to the Council of Ministers with supporting recommendations of the Minister concerned.[79] A better procedure would have been to allow the aggrieved investor to appeal personally against the decision of the Minister. To whom should the appeal be addressed?

Under the present Sudanese constitutional system, it is constitutionally doubtful to vest the appellate authority in the Council of Ministers which strictly has no constitutional existence. Under the Permanent Constitution of the Sudan, 1973,[80] embodying a presidental system, executive powers are vested in the President alone. He is empowered to appoint a Prime Minister to assist him in carrying out his duties.[81] The President also is empowered to appoint ministers to run the ministries assigned to them. The ministers are to be executive authorities in their ministries.[82] This does not mean that there is a Council of Ministers as a constitutional institution which has its separate legal entity and constitutional powers. In practice, it is true that the Prime Minister presides over the ministers sitting jointly. But to avoid the constitutional dilemma that might arise in relation to the legal status of the decisions then taken, these were expressed and issued in the name of the Prime Minister at one time. The Prime Minister has been for a considerable time the President himself, and when appointing a Prime Minister the latter should exercise his power by special delegation from the President.

The appeal of an aggrieved investor against the decision of the Minister of Planning must be addressed to the Prime Minister or the President himself and thereafter to the courts. It should not be addressed to the 'Council of Ministers' as this does not exist at all under the present constitution of the Sudan.

It would have been wise to entrust the task of granting the incentives and the investment licences to the Central Committee and not to the Minister. This would avert the danger of political influence. Perhaps the best solution is to make the Minister the chairman of the Central Committee as is the case in the Egyptian investment law,[83] which lies at the background of the Draft Bill. Such a suggestion would actually cut short all technicalities and formalities, in addition to creating an effective machinery for a decision-making process.

(d) Joint ventures and co-operative projects

These issues receive attention for the first time in the Draft Bill.[84] They have top priority among incentives and facilities. In fact, the provision on joint ventures is consistent with the existing structure of the Sudanese mixed economy. The Draft Bill tried to give statutory recognition to the various joint ventures which had already been embarked upon, especially in the industrial sector (see *ante*, p. 10). The Bill was pragmatic in not fixing the percentage of State participation in joint ventures so as not to disturb previous agreements and the existing practice which varies from one agreement to another.

(e) Cancellation of licences and incentives

Under section 14 of the Draft Bill the power to cancel investment licences and incentives is vested in the Central Committee though the granting of these, as noted earlier, is for the Minister. Here also, the same problem arises. The appeal against the decision of the Committee will be addressed to the Minister and the Council of Ministers.

9. The Encouragement of Investment Act, 1980

The Draft Bill gave birth to the Encouragement of Investment Act, 1980 which has adopted some of the reforms proposed by the Draft Bill. In many respects it removes the anomalies of the Draft Bill and the disunity of the previous legislation. Under section 8 of the Encouragement of Investment Act the Minister of Finance and National Economy is the competent authority to issue the investment licences and grant incentives and facilities with the consultation of the competent Ministers and on the advice of the Consultative Committee. The granting of any incentive and the kind and duration thereof depend on how far the investment project will achieve the objectives set out by section 6 of the Act and the policies and priorities prescribed by the Ministerial Committee.

Under section 18 of the Act investment licences, facilities and privileges are granted subject to the following conditions.

(a) No alteration or amendment in the size of the investment project or the purpose for which the licence is granted and no transfer of the project from its licensed place should be made save with the written consent of the Minister.

(b) No transfer of the ownership or leasehold of the whole or any part of the project should be made save with the written consent of the Minister.

(c) The machines, equipment, materials or spare parts with respect to which privileges or facilities have been granted under the Act should not be used for any purpose other than for which the licence was granted save with the written consent of the Minister.

(d) The land allotted for the project under the Act should not be used for any other purpose or mortgaged save with the written consent of the Minister.

(e) The owner of the investment project must present every year to the Secretary General for Investment a copy of the annual accounts of the project signed by a certified accountant.

(f) The owner of the project must provide the Secretary General every year with reports about the progress of the operation or execution of the project and the productivity of the project after commencement of production.

These conditions, if strictly observed, would give the Government a leverage to control investment and prevent the misuse of incentives for other purposes which were not intended by the legislature, the essential elements which were utterly neglected by the previous Sudanese investment legislation. The new law does not only contain such precautionary provisions for controlling investment, but also furnishes additional reasons which lead to the cancellation and revocation of investment licences. Thus, under section 23(1) the Minister of Finance and National Economy may cancel any licence, privilege or facilities granted under the Act in the following cases:

(a) If the investor has not established the project within the period specified in the licence or any extension thereof.
(b) If the investor has broken any of the terms according to which any privileges, facilities or licences have been granted under the Act.
(c) If the investor has provided any false information or used unlawful means by which he obtained a benefit under the Act.
(d) If the investment project, without reasonable cause, stopped.
(e) If the investor interfered in the politics and internal affairs of the State.
(f) If the continuation of the project threatens the safety and security of the Sudan or if the foreign investor has been deported for security reasons, unless he has sold his investment to a Sudanese national or the State before the order cancelling his licence.

In all these cases the investor must repay to the Government the financial benefits which he has gained from the facilities or privileges if the benefits accrued to him as a result of the occurrence of the event or contingency which gave rise to the cancellation of the investment licence or facilities. This penalty clause aims at offsetting the negative sides of foreign investment – foreign domination of the national economy and using multinationals as instruments of foreign policy by the industrialized countries. These issues have for years dominated the north–south dialogue, as we shall see in chapter 6.

The aggrieved investor against whom an order of cancellation is passed by the Minister under section 23(1) has the right to appeal against the decision of the Minister to the Ministerial Committee, and its decision is final. This has not carried the reform reached by the Draft Bill any further.

10. Conclusions

Theoretically, foreign investment in the Sudan and Saudi Arabia enjoys the most generous incentives ever found in any developing country. How far these incentives eliminate the impediments surveyed in the preceding chapter is a question of degree.

It is indisputable that the investment incentives result in substantial losses of revenue to the national budget in terms of tax and customs exemptions, which are the main direct sources of revenue to the Sudanese government to cover its current public expenditure and provide the basic services to the society. But on the other hand, drastically to reduce these incentives would have an adverse psychological effect on foreign investors. They would eventually be sceptical about the attitude of the Government towards foreign investment. It is true that tax exemptions and customs relief, though, are useful temporary incentives, yet they are not generally the only weighty factors in the investment decision-making process. They essentially serve as a signal from the Government of a capital-importing country to foreign investors that they are welcomed. To secure effective tax concessions, there must be a fair, steady and permanent means of assessment entrusted to an impartial and competent administration. No doubt this would attract long-term investments rather than the temporary preferential treatment.

In order to avoid political influence in granting investment licences and incentives, it is strongly recommended that such a task should be conferred on a statutory board or commission instead of leaving the whole issue to the discretion of a minister. It is also recommended that all investments must be formalized in contracts to be negotiated and agreed upon between the investors and the board. This instrumentality would firmly establish effective devices for protecting the interests of investors as the present 'approving instruments', moulded in investment licences, can hardly be characterized as contracts[85].

A multilateral effort is required for the elimination of double taxation. This depends on co-operation between the developed and developing countries. As will be explained later, experience has shown that it is not easy, at present, to agree on any multilateral convention related to foreign investment in view of the prevailing international investment climate (see ch. 6). However, to encourage foreign investment, it is advisable for the Sudan to conclude bilateral treaties with capital-exporting countries with as wide a scope as the United Kingdom–Sudan Convention on double taxation, which is the most comprehensive and constructive instrument in this respect. Such an arrangement will furnish a more persuasive tax incentive to foreign investors than the legislative measures which might not be easily invoked in the international sphere (see *post*, pp. 104–7).

The Sudanese Encouragement of Investment Act of 1980 introduces major reforms to the previous investment legal regime in the Sudan. In principle the idea of having a single investment law, as in Saudi Arabia, spelling out the general rules and leaving the details to be specified by subordinate instruments, is quite sound.

The Sudan's problems may be particularly difficult to solve because they stem essentially from inefficiency, maladministration and obstructive bureaucracy. In fact, it is not very difficult to enact an Utopian investment law in the Sudan, but the real difficulty has always been how to apply the law to achieve the desired objectives. How far this is predictable is beyond speculation. Much will depend on the political ideology prevailing at the particular time, which will have its impact on the content and function of the law.

What is significant for foreign investors is not the quantum and qualities of incentives, but their effective enjoyment and guarantee of their permanence. There should be an effective legal machinery for the protection of the acquired rights of foreign investors to enjoy these incentives without any disturbance. In the domestic sphere, foreign investors might claim to be accorded a full guarantee to have access to the local courts. Furthermore, they might demand that provisions like section 23 of the Encouragement of Investment Act, 1980 which purports to oust the jurisdiction of the Sudanese courts in cases of cancellation and revocation of investment licences, must be repealed. The decisions of the Minister cancelling or revoking the investment licences must be subject to judicial review in all cases (see *post*, pp. 284–90). But, this may sometimes cause delay as the Sudanese litigation system is very slow and time-consuming and the judiciary at present lacks enough judges to tackle the sophisticated problems of foreign investment.

From an international law point of view, several questions may be posed. In the first place, what is the legal status of the unilateral measures of a capital-importing country granting foreign investors certain incentives in relation to particular investments? Secondly, how can foreign investors be protected, under international law, against the repudiation of these incentives by the same government which granted them, or by a subsequent government? Thirdly, what will be the cause of action in the latter case? Is it possible for a foreign investor or his home State to plead an investment statute before an international tribunal or to invoke the doctrine of estoppel to substantiate the claim? These and similar issues will be considered in the ensuing chapters.

5
UNILATERAL GUARANTEES

1. Introduction

A serious impediment to foreign private investment in a developing country is the fear of loss through expropriation, nationalization and similar measures.[1] Any developing country that seeks to encourage the flow of foreign private capital to be invested in its territory is anxious to moderate these fears by establishing assurances and guarantees to foreign investors of the security of their investments. Indeed, the International Chamber of Commerce concedes that 'the fear of expropriation has probably been considered one of the main impediments to the international flow of private capital'.[2]

Apart from the early period of President Nimeiri's regime,[3] the Sudan, has, since independence in 1956, repeatedly assured foreign investors that their investments would not be nationalized or expropriated except for public purposes and on payment of just compensation. Equally, foreign investors have been assured that they would be allowed to transfer abroad their profits and capital.

In this chapter it is proposed to examine the form and content of these guarantees, to see to what extent they really provide protection to foreign investment both under municipal and international law.

It should be emphasized that the term 'guarantee' is not used here in its strict legal sense, but only to denote the various promises and undertakings given unilaterally by the State to foreign investors in relation to their investments.

2. Guarantee against expropriation, nationalization and similar measures

Usually, the assurances and guarantees against expropriation, nationalization and similar measures promised unilaterally by the State to foreign investors are found in constitutional clauses, items of legislation and official policy statements. The purpose of these devices is to confirm the desire of the government to protect foreign investment against arbitrary measures.

(a) Constitutional clauses

(i) *Sudan*

(1) *The right of private ownership*

This constitutes the corner-stone of the guarantee against any spoliatory action which may be inflicted on a foreign investment. Article 33 of the Permanent Constitution of the Sudan, 1973[4] provides that:

> the right of private ownership shall be guaranteed for all citizens, unless it is against public interest, and its inheritance and donation in accordance with the law are guaranteed. The State recognizes the useful social role played by private ownership in the field of production and in appreciation of its responsibility. [sic]

It is evident that this constitutional clause, though expressed in vague and general terms, emphasizes the useful social function played by private property in production within the framework of the national economic policy. As it appears, this clause, in addition to the awkward translation, is defective in other respects. As regards the guarantees to foreign investment, it is rather vague and ambiguous. This results partly from the word 'citizens'. Though the word 'citizens' is qualified by the word 'all', still there is a possibility of different interpretations which might curtail the operation or at least restrict the scope of the guarantee envisaged by the clause as a whole, and consequently exclude foreign investment altogether. Thus, it could be interpreted as being restricted only to Sudanese nationals, to the exclusion of foreigners; and in that case, foreign investors would find themselves without constitutional protection of their investments in the Sudan. This interpretation, if it be correct, implies that the framers of the constitution, to all intents and purposes, aimed at confining protection and guarantees to domestic private ownership only, and to the exclusion to foreign property.

To solve this problem, however, it is necessary to find out the intention of the framers by referring to other provisions in the constitution itself as well as subordinate legislation. In the first place, Article 40 of the Constitution provides that 'no Sudanese shall be deported from Sudanese lands or prevented from entering them'. By using the word 'Sudanese' and not 'citizen' as is the case in Article 33, it is possible to infer that the framers of the Constitution intend that Article 33 includes Sudanese citizens and aliens as well. The reason is that, as mentioned before, under international law a State cannot be put under a duty to admit aliens into its territory or deport them therefrom. But the problem is more complicated because of Article 45, which provides that 'every citizen shall have the right to participate in elections and referendums [sic]'. Furthermore, Article 122 provides that a person shall be eligible for the membership of the

People's Assembly if he is a Sudanese. This has been reproduced in section 17 of the People's Assembly Act 1973[5] and section 16 of the Regulations of the People's Assembly Election, 1974.[6] Such provisions only give legislative recognition to the general rule common to the majority of States that aliens have no political rights. Thus, in the United Kingdom, the resident alien is distinguishable from the national. He may not vote nor be a candidate in any election, nor hold any public office, nor own, command nor be a pilot of a British ship.[7]

The concept of citizenship is used when a national or a naturalized person owes allegiance to a State and is entitled to its protection. In addition, this status confers on him certain rights and privileges regardless of his residence.[8] Consequently, it is hardly conceivable that the concept of citizenship be extended to include aliens.

In view of the above, it might be argued that Article 33 of the Permanent Constitution of the Sudan provides no guarantee whatever of the right of private ownership to foreign investors in the Sudan. Had the word 'person' been used instead of 'citizen', the problem could have been solved. On the other hand, it is possible to interpret Article 33 so widely as to include aliens in the light of the policy of the present regime, which aims at attracting foreign capital to be invested in the Sudan. This is suggested by the applicability of the investment laws to aliens and Sudanese nationals alike.

(2) *Content of guarantee against illegal expropriation or nationalization*

Article 34 of the Permanent Constitution of the Sudan provides that:

> No private property shall be *confiscated* except *for a public interest, in accordance with the law* and on *payment of a fair compensation* [*sic*]. (My italics.)

This constitutional clause entrenches in a bill of right respect for private property. It provides some constitutional protection against confiscation by abusive executive or administrative measures by providing that confiscation should be in accordance with the law and for a public interest.

Unfortunately, this clause is not free from defects; in particular in the use of the word 'confiscation'. It is to be noted also that the clause poses two important questions in relation to foreign private investment. Firstly, how can the limitation of public interest be tested? Secondly, by what standard will compensation be fixed? The public interest issue will be examined below in relation to legislation, while compensation is the subject of chapter 8. But first it will be useful to look at that word 'confiscation'.

Terminology

Does the word 'confiscation' used in Article 34 mean expropriation, 'taking' or 'nationalization'? To understand the meaning of the term 'confiscation' it is necessary to consider also the legal meaning of expropriation and nationalization, both of which are very controversial. Neither the investment laws nor the treaties define these terms. They just refer to them in general terms. In some cases the word 'nationalization' is used instead of 'expropriation' and vice versa.[9] In most cases they are mentioned separately, as referring to different connotations. The problem is further mystified by the use of the neutral word 'taking'[10] in preference to either of the other two terms. Indeed, what constitutes expropriation is difficult to determine in the abstract: Professor Wortley[11] used the term 'expropriation' as including nationalization and confiscation. Professor Christie[12] tried to analyse all States' interference with private property since the Nazi regime, in an attempt to formulate a specific definition of the term 'expropriation'. In his view, what is important is not the wording of the description of the State's interference, but the effect of the interference on the proprietor's right to enjoy his property. In this respect the duration of the interference is important. Thus, interference with an alien's property may amount to expropriation even when no explicit attempt is made to affect the legal title of the property, and even though the respondent State may specifically disclaim any such intention.[13] After discussing the decision of the Permanent Court of International Justice in the much discussed case of *German Interests in Polish Upper Silesia*,[14] and international arbitral awards like the *Norwegian Claims* case,[15] as well as the literature of the American Foreign Claims Settlement Commission, Professor Christie came to no conclusion other than that each case needs separate consideration. In addition, he mentioned valuable general guidelines which might be of great help in specific areas of expropriation, namely, State monopoly, forced sales in apprehension of expropriation or persecution and refusal to permit alienation of real property.

There have been attempts, nevertheless, to define 'expropriation' in terms of 'taking'. Thus under the Harvard Draft Convention on the International Responsibility of States for Injuries to Aliens,[16] 'taking of property' is defined as follows:

> A taking of property includes not only taking of property as outright taking of property, but also any such unreasonable interference with the use, enjoyment, or disposal of property as to justify an inference that the owner thereof will not be able to use, enjoy, or dispose of the property within a reasonable period of time after the inception of such interference.

It seems, then, that a crucial consideration in determining what constitutes a taking will be the duration of the interference.[17]

The editors of the *Netherlands International Law Review*,[18] while commenting on the Indonesian seizure of the property of Dutch nationals, were of the opinion that the assumption of managerial control is a determining factor in constituting a sufficient taking which gives rise to a claim for full compensation.[19] This is a somewhat far-fetched interpretation of the State's action, as the assumption of control may not be for very long duration. However, this is a factor which is totally different from the above criterion, viz, the duration of the interference. Furthermore, the editors contended that the refusal to grant permission in advance for the transfer of operating profits to the owners may be a relevant factor in deciding what constitutes expropriation.[20] This is a remarkable contention; for, according to that view, if the Sudanese Government were to repudiate its promise to allow foreign investors to transfer abroad the profits generated from their investments, it might be argued that this act by itself was sufficient to imply that an expropriation had taken place. This may be termed 'partial expropriation' in relation to investment profits.

On the other hand, Friedmann,[21] who considered expropriation as a legal procedure by which private property might be taken away by the State, proposed the following definition:

> Expropriation means the procedure by which a State in time of peace and for reasons of public utility appropriates a private property right, with or without compensation so as to place it at the disposal of its public services, or of the public generally.

According to this view, it seems that the two elements of expropriation are nationalization and confiscation. The more normal use of confiscation is as a penalty for a breach of public law such as a criminal code. This is permissible under international law which permits the sanction of breaches of a State's public law by means of confiscation and similar measures, as a matter of territorial sovereignty.[22] Thus, international tribunals have recognized the validity of the confiscation of a ship in pursuance of a local law prohibiting the particular trade in which the ship was engaged.[23] Similarly, penal measures properly so called are on the same footing as confiscations carried out for non-observance of sanitary regulations, or as police measures.[24] Under such measures, no compensation is usually awarded, and for this reason confiscation is considered as expropriation without compensation, unlike nationalization which is an expropriation with compensation.[25]

On the other hand, Professor White[26] speaks of nationalization as the term used 'to describe the process whereby property, and rights and interests in property are transferred from private to public ownership by agents of the State acting on the authority of a legislative or executive measure'. She rightly distinguishes nationalization from expropriation, at least in the duration of the processes of transfer which they respectively authorize. In her view an expropriation law is one which will operate for individual cases at any time in the future and for so long as the law remains in force. 'In contrast, a nationalisation law usually provides for transfer to the State or to a State-controlled body to be carried out upon the enactment of the law, and does not contemplate future transfers to be carried out after an indefinite period of time.'[27]

But this distinction does not alter the fact that both expropriation and nationalization are related concepts and share common attributes. And though these terms are used interchangeably,[28] it would, nevertheless, seem sensible that each term should be used to signify different processes.[29] As a matter of strict legal terminology, the term 'nationalization' should be used as a general 'taking' which has the effect of economic reform of a certain sector of the economy whereby private property in that sector be transferred to the State. Expropriation is appropriately used for individual cases and not on a large scale. But, for more practical purposes the two terms may be, and commonly are, used interchangeably.

Proposed clause

The use of the word 'confiscation' in Article 34 of the Constitution of the Sudan is unfortunate. Confiscation is a punishment for breach of a public law, and in the usual situation compensation should not be awarded at all. But there is no alternative, as long as the clause remains, except to interpret the word 'confiscation' as meaning 'expropriation' or 'taking', which is true of the Arabic version. The confusion has resulted from the mistaken translation of the corresponding Arabic word نزع which actually means 'expropriation', and not 'confiscation'. For Article 34 of the Constitution to make legal sense in relation to existing legislative provisions, to be discussed below, it has to read:

> No private property shall be expropriated except for a public interest, in accordance with the law, and on payment of a fair compensation.

This would also, of course, then extend to nationalization.

It might be added that Article 34 of the Constitution of the Sudan has been misplaced. It should have been under the chapter dealing with the fundamental rights, rather than with the fundamental principles. This difference is important for investors, as the fundamental rights are enforceable by the Sudanese courts, as will be seen in chapter 10, while the fundamental principles are not. They are only declaratory and indicative of the Government's economic policies.

(ii) *Saudi Arabia*

Saudi Arabia is a monarchy, and the power is in the King in Council. This means the constitutional authority is the King and the Council of Ministers. There are two regulations which govern the functions and the powers of the Council of

Ministers. The first was promulgated in 1954 and the second was promulgated in 1958.[30] The Saudi Arabian Constitution is based on Moslem law, which says that those who rule should be good shepherds, and should look after the interests of the people.

Accordingly, to search for a constitutional guarantee for foreign investment in Saudi Arabia one must investigate Islamic jurisprudence, which in theory has established the first written constitution, the Koran, as supplemented by the Sunna and the Figh. But one may say without hesitation that, in principle, the status of private property in Islamic law is well recognized and established, provided that it is not utilized for purposes violating the teachings of Islam. This is a basic principle which does not require any further investigation. And as Saudi Arabia has for years maintained a capitalist economy within the context of the doctrine of the welfare state, it is apparent that the status of private ownership is uncontestable in the economic sectors, where it is permitted according to the national plans.

Does the element of foreignness of the private property modify this conclusion? The answer is in the negative. It is generally recognized that Islamic law, as a principle, protects the life and property of the non-Moslems, be they subjects of the Moslem State or resident aliens and tourists. Under orthodox Islamic law aliens who are non-Moslems are required to pay annually the capitation tax (*jizyah*), subject to certain exceptions.[31] It is noteworthy that this aspect of taxation is not adhered to at present in Saudi Arabia, for Islamic law does not prevail in the fashion that prevailed 1,400 years ago. The Saudi Arabian Government regulates the day-to-day needs. It has been conceded by one jurist[32] that classical Islamic theory has now undergone a process of far-reaching modification as a result of the participation of the old and new Islamic States in the community of nations. In the modern context, Islamic cultural values do not conflict with the existence of an international order and the notion of a law governing the relations between States, in particular in the domain of State responsibility for injuries to aliens.

One can safely say that, even though there are no written constitutional clauses guaranteeing foreign investment against illegal expropriation, as there are in the Sudan, such a guarantee is accommodated within Islamic law, the legal system prevailing in Saudi Arabia. Its existence is actually guaranteed by the nature of the Saudi economy which is based on private ownership. Islam encourages the investment of property, as the Moslem may pay *Zakat* out of his capital resources, excluding fixed assets. If the original capital is not invested, however, but kept in gold or silver, *Zakat* must then be paid out of this capital, which would thus gradually be diminished. So, foreign private investment in Saudi Arabia enjoys full protection against expropriation and nationalization, subject to the limitations imposed by the law. Even in the rare case of the nationalization of Aramco, the nationalization measure was implemented gradually within the time limit envisaged by the text governing the transaction and the long-run relationship.

(iii) *Constitutions of other developing countries*

Property protection clauses in the constitutions of other developing countries have no standard formulation. Some of them contain quite detailed provisions on the protection of private property generally. Thus, Article 34 of the Egyptian Constitution of 1971,[33] unlike the Sudan Constitution, provides that:

> Private property is inviolable and should not be put under sequestration except in cases based on law and a court verdict. Property may not be expropriated except for public welfare, and its owners are to be compensated according to the law.

Furthermore, Article 35 provides:

> (a) Nationalisation of property is not allowed except for consideration of public welfare and in accordance with the law, and its owners are to be compensated.
> (b) General confiscation of money is not allowed, and private confiscation is only possible by a court verdict.[34]

Constitutional clauses like this are useful formal devices for protecting foreign investment. They ensure some judicial protection against administrative measures, as confiscation is made possible only subject to a court verdict. Another merit of the Egyptian constitution is that it is specific about different types of State measures, namely sequestration, expropriation, nationalization and confiscation.

There have been effective property protection clauses in the recent constitutions of some African States. A striking example is the Sierra Leone Constitution of 1961.[35] Under Article 17 (1):

> No property of any description shall be compulsorily taken possession of, and no interest in or right over property of any description shall be compulsorily acquired, except where the following conditions are satisfied, that is to say:
>
> (a) the taking of possession is necessary in the interests of defence, public safety, public order, public morality, public health, town and country planning or the development and utilization of any property in such a manner as to promote the public benefit; and
> (b) the necessity therefor is such as to afford reasonable justification for the causing of any hardship that may result to any person having an interest in or right over the property; and
> (c) provision is made by a law applicable to that taking of possession or acquisition:
> (i) for the prompt payment of adequate compensation; and
> (ii) securing any person having an interest in or right over the property, a right of access to a court or other authority for the determination of the taking of possession of acquisition of the property, interest or right, and the amount of any compensation to which he is entitled, and for the purpose of obtaining prompt payment of that compensation.

A similar provision, but with much elaboration on the question when private property can be compulsorily taken, is found in Article 18 of the Jamaican Constitution, 1962.[36]

It is noteworthy that the constitution of Sierra Leone may be considered among the most effective and powerful unilateral devices for protecting foreign investment in the developing world. It follows the prevailing and accepted view that private property may be taken in exercise of the power of eminent domain. More importantly, it provides for the payment of prompt and adequate compensation, thus digesting the classical rules of international law. In domestic spheres, it assures foreign investors access to the courts for settlement of disputes[37] pertaining to all aspects of expropriation. In cases where determination of property claims does not fall within the jurisdiction of the courts, reference is made to 'other authority', which probably refers to administrative organs or special committees.

(b) Legislation

(i) *Sudan*

Section 16 of the Sudan Industrial Investment Act, 1974[38] provides that:

The capital invested in the Democratic Republic of the Sudan shall enjoy the following guarantees:

(a) It shall not be placed under sequestration or confiscation except by a decision of a competent court in accordance with the existing laws.

(b) It shall not be nationalized except when the high interest of the country so requires and, in such case, the following basis shall be taken into consideration:

  (i) the investor shall be given a just compensation after evaluating his property according to such price as may be current at the time of nationalization;

  (ii) evaluation shall be made within six months from the date of making the nationalization order and the value of compensation shall be paid by annual payments not exceeding five years in the same currency or currencies, brought for the purpose of investment.

  (iii) In case a dispute arises as to assessment of the value of compensation, the investor shall be entitled to request the submission of the dispute to a committee of arbitration to be constituted of one member representing the investor, another representing the Government and a third to be chairman of the committee of arbitration agreed upon by the two members referred to.

Identical provisions are contained in the Agricultural Investment Act, 1976.[39] Section 10(4), on the other hand, of the Investment in Economic Services Act, 1973, incorporates the investment guarantees set out in section 16 of the Industrial Investment Act, 1974, but only by reference.

These provisions were repealed and replaced in section 19 of the Encouragement of Investment Act, 1980 as follows:

Notwithstanding the provisions of any other law, any capital invested in the Sudan shall enjoy the following guarantees:

(a) it shall not be nationalized except for the public good and by virtue of a law; and in such case the following rules shall be followed:
   (i) the investor shall be granted after evaluation of his property, just compensation at the price current at the time of nationalization;
   (ii) the evaluation shall be completed within a maximum period of six months commencing from the date of order of nationalization; payment and transfer of compensation shall be in yearly instalments within a period not exceeding five years in the same currency of capital or any other currency agreed to;

(b) it shall not be subject to sequestration or confiscation save with the order of a competent court issued in accordance with the laws in force.

These provisions pose several questions. First, under what circumstances will private investment be placed under sequestration or be confiscated under the existing Sudanese laws? Secondly, what are the limitations in international law on the right of States to nationalize or expropriate foreign private property within its territory? Thirdly, how can compensation be assessed in case of nationalization so as to assure foreign investors a just compensation? Fourthly, how will this compensation actually be paid? And finally, how will disputes on compensation be settled?

The last three questions will be answered in chapters 8 and 10, respectively. It is the first and second questions which are relevant here.

(1) *When private investment is placed under sequestration or is confiscated*

It is very important that foreign investors should be acquainted with all the Sudanese laws and regulations which might expose their investments to dangers and risks, especially from interference by the State. Obviously, this can be avoided by observing the operative laws and refraining from illegal acts that entail legal penalties. Under the existing Sudanese law, private investment can be exposed to jeopardy in many situations. Thus, under section 194 of the Customs Ordinance, 1939[40] the court, upon a conviction, must declare forfeit any means of conveyance used in smuggling; and, under section 195 of the same ordinance, the court must declare forfeit the smuggled, prohibited or restricted goods. The forfeiture under this ordinance is mandatory in addition to other penalties.[41] The forfeiture envisaged by the Customs Ordinance is limited only to the subject-matter of the charge. In no case will it be extended to the rest of the property of the accused.

Private investment may also be confiscated under the Sudan Penal Code, 1974[42] (revised and re-enacted) and the State Security Act, 1973.[43] Under the latter, the property of a convicted person shall be confiscated if it is proved to the satisfaction of the court that he has been involved in any offence relating to offensive action against a foreign country with the intention of engaging the Sudan to declare war against that country; or exporting goods to an enemy country in state of war with the Sudan.[44] This provision prohibits all commercial and business transactions with countries like Israel and South Africa.[45]

Unlike the Customs Ordinance, the Penal Code and the State Security Act extend confiscation to all property of the convicted person whether it be movable or immovable. Private property may also be confiscated under the State Security Act in offences against the constitution. In this case, confiscation lies within the discretion of the court and is not mandatory. Its effect is limited only to the property or benefit acquired from the commission of the offence.[46] It is, of course, elementary international law that a State possesses the sovereign right to try and punish aliens for all infractions of its penal laws committed inside its territory.[47] This has been extended to cover even political crimes. In *Eisler* v. *United States*,[48] the United States Court of Appeal held that an alien is under a duty to testify before a Congressional Committee in the same way as a citizen. In the words of A. J. Clark,

> An alien resident owes a temporary allegiance to the Government of the U.S., and he assumes duties and obligations which do not differ materially from those of native-born or naturalised citizens; he is bound to obey all the laws of the country, not immediately relating to citizenship, and is equally amenable with citizens for any infractions of these laws.

In *Sudan Government* v. *Steiner*,[49] a German mercenary was tried and convicted by a Sudanese court martial for offences related to assisting guerrilla troops (*Anyanya*) to wage war in Southern Sudan against the central Government.

Section 4 of the Sudan Penal Code, 1974 provides that:

> (1) Every person shall be liable to punishment in the Sudan:
>
> (a) who by any act done outside the Sudan is a party whether as principal or abettor to any offence committed either wholly or in part in the Sudan; or
>
> (b) who by any act done in the Sudan abets the doing of a thing outside the Sudan which is an offence in the Sudan and is also an offence under any law in force in the place where the thing is done or intended to be done.

Foreign private investment may also be put under sequestration. Under section 267 of the Criminal Procedure Act, 1974[50] (revised and re-enacted), the court by way of execution of judgments and orders, can put the property of the convicted person under sequestration or order its acquisition and sale for the satisfaction of fines.

Foreign as well as Sudanese private property was subjected to sweeping confiscation and sequestration measures in 1970. Being inspired by extreme socialist policy for social and economic reforms, the now-dissolved Revolutionary Command Council passed three laws of this kind. These were the Central Bureau for Public Control Act,[51] 1970, the Acquisition Act,[52] 1970 and the Custody Act,[53] 1970. With the exception of the Acquisition Act, these laws have now been repealed.

Though the statutory powers and functions of the Central Bureau were set out in detail in its constituent Act, they were exceeded to the extent that the Bureau encroached on the jurisdiction of the courts and the police. The Bureau was supposed to exercise the functions of the Ombudsman in order to achieve administrative reform but, instead, it stretched its arms everywhere. Not only were recommendations for confiscation made to the dissolved Revolutionary Command Council, but also confiscation measures were carried out by the unilateral measures of the Public Commissioner who was the head of the Bureau. The outcome of this chaotic legal situation was that many foreign investments were confiscated and their owners were ordered to leave the country without compensation except for travelling expenses. At that time there was virtually no protection of foreign investment and no foreign capital was forthcoming as the investment climate was so unpropitious.

Similar measures were taken under the Acquisition Act and the Sequestration Act, 1970[54] whereby foreign investors were deprived of their investments in various degrees. The legality of all these measures was not questioned either in the Sudanese courts or in the international sphere. As regards the first, foreign investors had no right of access to Sudanese courts, this having been made impossible for two reasons. First, at the time when the laws under which these measures were taken, there was no constitutional right for anyone to challenge the laws or the decisions taken thereunder. This was because the Transitional Constitution of the Sudan, 1964[55] had been suspended before these laws were enacted. Second, the jurisdiction of the courts was expressly ousted by the Republican Order no. 1.[56] The operative provision of the Republican Order (repealed) provided that Sudanese courts had no jurisdiction to challenge any decisions of the Council of Ministers and the Revolutionary Command Council. Also under the Exercise of the Judicial Power Act, 1972 (repealed),[57] the Sudanese courts had no jurisdiction to challenge 'acts of State'. What constitutes an 'act of State' under the Sudanese law is difficult to ascertain in abstract.[58] Consequently, foreign investors whose property had been taken, in the early days of this decade, were left without remedies because they had been denied access to Sudanese courts. What was left to them was to attempt to invoke the diplomatic intervention of their home States, which might initiate international action on their behalf on the ground of denial of justice (see *post*, pp. 293–9). In fact, very few countries filed diplomatic protests on behalf of their nationals before the confiscation measures were reversed.[59]

To remove the doubts and fears of foreign investors from future coercive measures, the Sudanese government has passed three investment laws.[60] The genuineness of this policy is clearly reflected in the proviso that sequestration and confiscation of capital to be invested in the Sudan must be 'within the existing laws'.[61] The effectiveness of such a clause in providing a guarantee against future repudiation of the existing promises by a different future regime is dubious.[62]

(2) *Limitations on the right of a State to nationalize or expropriate foreign private property within its territory*

Expropriation and nationalization must be for public interest

As stated above, article 34 of the Constitution and section 16 of the Sudan Industrial Investment Act[63] provide that capital invested in the Sudan shall not be nationalized except when the high interest of the country so requires. This provision incorporates the limitation put by international law on the right of a State to nationalize or expropriate foreign private property within its territory. It is generally accepted that, under international law, if nationalization were not for a public purpose, but, for example, were meant to benefit a private person, then the State of the alien whose property has been nationalized has good reason for asserting that the nationalization measure is contrary to international law.[64]

The principle of public purpose in relation to nationalization is usually embodied in the nationalization laws.[65] Though the Sudanese nationalization laws of 1970[66] did not expressly mention this principle as a justification for nationalizing some banks and companies, the principle was expressly referred to in the resolution of the dissolved Revolutionary Command Council implementing the nationalization laws. This resolution stated that the nationalization measures were aimed at achieving economic reform and towards establishing a State economy according to the socialist policy then embarked upon.[67] The principle of public purpose can also be inferred from the Banks Nationalization Act, 1970[68] which provided that all the nationalized banks must be transformed into sharing companies to be owned by the State through the Bank of Sudan.

The limitation of the State's right to nationalize or expropriate private foreign property only to public purposes has been confirmed by the United Nations General Assembly resolutions on several occasions. Resolution 1803 (XVII) of December 1962 stated that:

> Nationalization, expropriation, or requisition shall be based on grounds or reasons of public utility, security, or the national interests which are recognized as overriding purely individual or private interests, both domestic and foreign.[69]

In the *German Interests in Polish Upper Silesia* case, the Permanent Court of International Justice observed that international law permits the expropriation of property for reasons of public utility.[70]

Yet, although most of the authorities support the view that a public purpose is necessary, the principle can hardly be said to have been established beyond doubt. Some scholars[71] deny the existence of the public utility limitation on the ground that the motives for nationalization or expropriation are irrelevant in international law. In any event there is the difficulty that the nationalising State is the sole judge of a critical situation. Thus, it is said that 'if the legislature has the sole power to determine what is for the public benefit...questions of motive or inducement become immaterial for all practical purposes'.[72] Nevertheless the abuse of the notion of public purpose cannot be excluded; as, for example, when assets are transferred out of public ownership into private hands, as in *Barcelona Traction*.[73] But, of course, this is not expropriation, at least in form.

Time-limitation on expropriation and nationalization: a self-imposed limitation

In addition to the limitation of 'public interest', some developing countries introduce in their investment laws an additional limitation, whereby foreign investment is not to be expropriated or nationalized for a limited period, for example, ten or twenty years after the operation of business has begun. For example, the Indonesian Act No. 78[74] guaranteed that foreign enterprises ought not to be expropriated for certain limited periods. A maximum guarantee period of twenty years was assured to industrial enterprises, while agricultural estates enjoyed such a privilege for thirty years. Similarly, under Article 6(1) of the Burmese Investment Act, 1959,[75] 'no enterprise shall be nationalized for a period of ten years from the date on which commercial operation commences; provided that the President may, after taking into consideration public interest and the magnitude of investment, extend the aforesaid period up to twenty years'.

Such a time-limit qualification is not preferred by the majority of States, because it unduly fetters the right of a State to regulate private property within its territory for achieving economic growth in accordance with its economic policy. Consequently, like the Sudan, they retain their sovereign right to expropriate foreign investment in accordance with their internal laws.[76]

Non-discrimination

Under international law, expropriation or nationalization must not be discriminatory against aliens or any group of aliens.[77] It must apply to all properties in a similar situation. Under the new Sudanese investment law,[78] apart from treaty obligations,[79] no distinction is to be made between national and foreign establishments in relation to concessions and guarantees. The nationalization measures of 1970 did not discriminate between Sudanese nationals and foreigners.

Where nationalization tends to affect a single undertaking in the field where there are no national interests capable of being affected, it seems that the nationalization of foreign investment will not be illegal.[80]

An example of discrimination is exemplified by the Cuban Nationalisation Law No. 851 of 6 July 1960, which was specifically directed against American companies.[81] This was invoked by Cir. J. Waterman, in the *Sabbatino case*.[82]

(ii) *Saudi Arabia*

The Foreign Capital Investment Law of 1979 does not contain any provision on the protection of foreign investment in Saudi Arabia against expropriation, nationalization and similar measures. The reason for the omission of such a provision is obvious: the status of the private enterprise is well established in the Saudi capitalist economy. It is interesting to note that when one counsel asked: 'What protection does a foreign investor have against expropriation in Saudi Arabia?', the answer was: 'All the protection that any investor needs. Trust in God, and believe what the government of Saudi Arabia says. We never think of it because it is just inconceivable.'[83] But the Saudi Arabian Government does not specify this view in its laws. Nevertheless, it may be conceded that the protection of foreign investment against expropriation under the Saudi law is implied by its conduct, as well as its statements of policy. Furthermore, in Islamic law no one shall be arbitrarily deprived of his property. This has been laid down in complete and perfect form.[84]

This does not mean that foreign private investment is inviolable in Saudi Arabia. It is a basic principle of Islamic law that the State has the sovereign right to regulate all economic activities within its territory and direct and utilize them for the interest of the whole community.[85] This is also reflected in rules of modern international law as voiced in recent resolutions of the United Nations. Islam has its own concept of socialism which accommodates private ownership, provided that it serves its social function. Accordingly, one may say, without more ado, that foreign investment may be confiscated if it is directed to illegal purposes according to Islamic law. Thus, it is inconceivable to concede protection to a factory engaging in liquor or alcoholic beverage production.

Foreign investment may also be expropriated or nationalized for public purposes, provided that adequate and effective compensation be paid. The important point is that Islam is against the outright and absolute right of the State to nationalize private property. But it is a general principle of Islamic jurisprudence that if private ownership comes into conflict with the public interest, the latter prevails.[86] And the recent nationalization measures in Iran and Libya are clear demonstrations of the existence of the concept of nationalization in the Islamic economic ideology; this is without the divisions and factions of certain Islamic groupings and the political motivation behind those measures. In the wake of the tension in the Arabian Gulf at the time of writing, foreign investors in Saudi Arabia may feel, to some extent, that their investments are, in terms of legal provisions, less well protected against expropriation and nationalization and similar measures, despite the present stable monarchy regime.

(c) Policy statements

Government guarantees against illegal expropriation, nationalization or similar measures may be expressed in the form of official statements from time to time. Apart from the early era of President Nimeiri's regime, successive Sudanese Governments had issued policy statements assuring foreign investors of the security of their investments in the Sudan. Thus, the Minister of Foreign Affairs of Abboud's military regime (1958–64) stated:

> one of the main points of our foreign policy is to promote and encourage foreign investment in the Sudan. The declared objective of the new industrialised policy of the government of the Sudan is to give a maximum scope to the private enterprise in the development of the resources of our country. That is why all enterprises are given the most careful consideration by all the relevant Ministries and Departments which are always ready to provide the required information regarding investment opportunities and problems in the Sudan and offer advice and guidance to the prospective investors. *Every possible help is given to foreign and local Investors in obtaining facilities given under the Approved Enterprises Act.*[87] (My italics.)

The economic policy of Abboud's military government in favour of foreign investment was spelt out in the same statement in the following words:

> We welcome foreign capital and its investments in our country whether it comes from government or private enterprise. We also welcome loans by international institutions like the International Bank for Reconstruction and Development and the other specialised agencies of the United Nations.
>
> Further, we welcome foreign aid from any country *provided it does not impinge on our national sovereignty or influence our stated national foreign policy*. The Sudan, in spite of its limited resources, has contributed and will continue to contribute towards the strengthening of the international organisations which seek to promote economic progress and stability in the world.
>
> We are in need of foreign loans and aid; we therefore shall do our best to create a favourable atmosphere to attract them. Our motive in encouraging foreign investment is derived from our very deep desire to develop our country in both the economic and social fields. The Sudan is fully conscious of its financial obligations and will continue as before to discharge its commitments fully in this respect.[88] (My italics.)

The main objective of this policy was to encourage industrial and similar enterprises by means of tax relief and concessions. This was to assure potential foreign investors that their interests would be safeguarded. This policy was, to some extent, successful. The total amount of approved foreign investment by the end of 1960 was approximately £S 15 million.[89]

Since 1972, when the confiscation measures were reversed, policy statements have been frequently issued inside[90] and outside the Sudan re-inviting foreign capital to be invested in the Sudan.[91] During his State visit to the United Kingdom in 1973, President Nimeiri assured the British businessmen of the security of their investments in the Sudan according to the new investment policy then embarked upon.[92]

Similarly, the Saudi Arabian government has issued policy statements inviting foreign capital. This has recently been affirmed in the industrial objectives policies as follows:

> The Government welcomes foreign capital as well as foreign expertise and their participation in the industrial development projects in cooperation with Saudi businessmen. The Government, recognizing the benefits to the industrial development of the Kingdom of the entry of foreign capital accompanied by administrative and technical capability and ability for international marketing, assures investors that it will always avoid imposing any restrictions on the entry and exit of money to and from the Kingdom and that *it shall continue its policy based on the respect of private ownership in the Islamic Law* (*Sharia*).[93] (My italics.)

The technique of policy statements has been followed by governments of other developing countries in concrete terms. Thus the parliamentary statement of the Prime Minister of India in 1949 declared that:

> If any foreign concern is compulsorily acquired, Government will pay compensation on a fair and equitable basis.[94]

Government statements such as these obviously have some weight as indicating good faith towards foreign investment, at least in countries with stable governments. Much depends on the political system of each country; but the political atmosphere in the Sudan, as in very many developing countries, is disturbed and change in a political regime cannot be ruled out; and a policy statement by one government may be reversed by its successor. And such policy statements can hardly be characterized in legal form. They are public statements of policy intentions, but are not legally binding. They are, accordingly, not legal devices for protecting foreign investment; unless, indeed, they are embodied in legal form in contracts or municipal legislation, in which case even successive governments should consider themselves bound by such instruments; and municipal courts would be more ready to enforce them.

3. Guarantee of permission to transfer profits and capital abroad[95]

(a) The guarantee in theory

The most important guarantee to foreign investors is the assurance of freedom to remit their profits. The present Sudanese practice in this respect may be considered as the most generous in the Third World. All profits earned from investing any foreign capital in the investment enterprises are able to be transferred outside the Sudan, after paying all the prescribed taxes, duties and obligations to the Government.[96] In the case of liquidation of any investment, it is obligatory on the Government to approve the re-transfer of the net capital originally imported, in the same currency in which it was imported or in any currency agreed upon. The transfer must be at the rate of exchange applicable at the time of transfer.[97] This may, of course, operate unfavourably to foreign investors, as the rate of exchange is subject to fluctuation; and in the absence of a treaty to the contrary, the devaluation of the State's currency is permissible under customary international law,[98] provided that the devaluation is in the interest of economic and monetary stabilization and solvency.[99] Accordingly, the Sudan would not be liable in international law for any loss incurred by foreign investors who intend to repatriate their capital, which could be worth less than the original capital as a result of the devaluation of the Sudanese pound. The only way of adequately protecting foreign investors against this kind of loss would be to give them the right to transfer their original capital at the rate of exchange which is applicable at the time of the repatriation or at the rate applicable at the time when the capital was imported, whichever is more favourable to them.

(b) Reality and side-effects of application of the guarantee

Foreign investors enjoy in law extensive concessions and guarantees in the Sudan over transfer of profits and capital in case of liquidation. In practice, these guarantees may encounter several obstacles. Sudan is among the poorest countries in the world and suffers from serious deficits in hard currency, and such a shortage is a deeply-rooted problem of the Sudanese economy. Some of the problems which can be expected to arise from this situation have not yet been met in practice simply because foreign investment has been so limited that actual profits, and indeed liquidation, have not occurred on any scale. In the opinion of the writer, transfer of profits should be allowed only after a certain period from starting production, say two or three years. This would help in allocating sufficient hard currency to meet the claims of foreign investors as well as enhancing the country's balance-of-payments. It would also be easier and more expedient if any transfer were made by instalments. An alternative would be to allow only a specified portion of the profits, leaving the rest to be re-invested.

As regards transfer of capital in case of liquidation, it is noteworthy that Sudanese investment laws leave loopholes. A foreign investor can enjoy all the tax concessions and other incentives during the initial years, and then after the expiration of the grace period he may decide to liquidate his business in the Sudan. He will then claim the right to repatriate his capital abroad without having made any positive contribution to the economic growth of the country. By so doing, he enjoys the best of both worlds. To cater for this defect, it would be wise to allow repatriation of capital in cases of liquidation only after two or three years from the expiration of the tax exemption period.

(c) Investment laws of other developing countries

The attitude of other developing countries towards the right of foreign investors to transfer their profits and capital in cases of liquidation is not uniform. Some countries adopt a liberal view, like the Sudan, in allowing foreign investors to transfer all their invested capital, profits, and the salaries of foreign employees to their home States: for example, Kenya, Liberia,[100] Ethiopia[101] and Venezuela.[102] Others leave the door open for negotiations between foreign investors and the capital-importing country to agree on the amount of capital and profits to be transferred in each case. Mauritania[103] is an example.

Very few developing countries adopt a wholly restrictive view over this problem of transfers. But the principle of allowing foreign investors to repatriate the invested capital and remit profits, and also salaries of foreign employees, to the home State, is usually subjected to restrictions on the amount to be transferred. Transfer is often permitted only after a certain period from starting operations. For instance, Egypt allows a foreign investor to repatriate his capital imported in foreign currency only after five years from its importation.[104] Furthermore, the Egyptian investment law permits foreign employees and technicians to transfer only 50% of their salaries.[105] The same pattern has been adopted in Somalia.[106] Indonesia permits foreign investors to transfer abroad profits up to 60% after payment of taxes. As regards dividends, only 30% is allowed to be transferred abroad. Foreign employees, under the Indonesian law, are permitted to remit only 20% of their salaries.[107] This practice finds parallels in other countries, like Syria[108] and Brazil.[109]

But there does appear to be an increasing tendency among the development countries to waive exchange control restrictions in favour of foreign investors wishing to transfer abroad their profits and capital.[110]

4. The effectiveness of constitutional and legislative promises

The effectiveness of the constitutional and legislative guarantees discussed above must depend, to a great extent, on their prospects of permanence and of enforceability. Without this they are bound to fall short of that security which foreign investors are anxious to receive.

Guarantees contained in municipal legislation but which are not also incorporated in specific terms in a contract between an investor and the host country are not of great value. They represent only a unilateral measure which poses many difficulties. For instance, there is a question whether an investment statute creates a cause of action on an international level. Nwogugu[111] stated that, when he was writing, there was no investment statute in any developing country which provided a remedy if the government failed to live up to its promises. It is different where concessions are also embodied in a contract containing an arbitration clause such as in countries like Argentina[112] and Chile where investments are formalized through investment contracts with the government.

The permanence of an investment statute is uncertain, and the investment guarantees thereunder may totally cease to exist if the statute is repealed by a successor government. According to the doctrine of parliamentary sovereignty, one parliament cannot bind its successor. Also a change of government or an alteration of the existing political ideology may easily result in the repealing of the investment statute which contains investment guarantees. Nevertheless, an investment statute may be of some value in providing an expression of good faith of a State which intends to admit foreign investment into its territory. In a country which enjoys a considerable degree of political stability, the investment statute also represents a moral reassurance guaranteeing private investment, but this may last only for the life of a particular government or a party in power.

In substance, the existing constitutional and legislative provisions offer some kind of legal protection to foreign investment before the Sudanese courts. This will be investigated in detail in chapter 10, when dealing with settlement of disputes.

If a Sudanese Government were to nationalise or confiscate a foreign investment contrary to the guarantees contained in the investment laws, would it be possible, apart from the theory of 'vested rights',[113] to plead these laws before an international tribunal? According to Nwogugu,[114] a municipal law which furnishes incentives and guarantees to foreign investments constitutes a representation and hence creates an estoppel against the investee State. This view was put forward by Freidmann in the following words:[115]

> Where...a State invites, by prospectus or general advertisement, foreign capital to invest in the development of certain utilities or industries, and foreign entrepreneurs have responded

to this invitation, an expropriation without compensation clearly justifies the application of the principles of estoppel or *venire contra factum proprium*. The government must be held estopped from acting contrary to reasonable expectations that it has itself created. (My italics.)

This view finds support in an *obiter dictum* of the International Court of Justice in the *Barcelona Traction* case[116] in the following words:

When a State admits into its territory foreign investments or foreign nationals, whether natural or juristic persons, *it is bound to extend to them the protection of the law and assumes obligation concerning the treatment to be afforded to them*. (My italics.)

More recently, the World Court observed in the *Nuclear Tests*[117] case that:

It is well recognised that declarations made by way of unilateral acts, concerning legal or factual situations, may have the effect of creating legal obligations... When it is the intention of the State making the declaration that it should become bound according to its terms, that intention confers on the declaration the character of a legal undertaking, the State being thenceforth legally required to follow a course of conduct consistent with the declaration.[118]

The principle of estoppel is well established in municipal and international law.[119] There is no reason in principle why it should not be applied to a representation made to foreign investors by the investee State. But the burden would lie on the investor or his home State to show that the investment was embarked upon while the investment law was in force and in good faith. The plea of estoppel would be stronger if, after the enactment of the investment law, the establishment by an investor of a certain business activity had been approved by the investee State under that law.

As regards the effect of property protection clauses contained in constitutions, it is submitted that the security assured to the foreign investors cannot be very strong. Many constitutions confer on all individuals resident in the State's territory the right to contest the legality of an act of expropriation coupled with guarantee to have access to the municipal courts. In the Sudan, a foreign investor whose investment has been expropriated can only challenge the reasons for expropriation if they are not in accordance with the law. He cannot challenge the quantum of compensation before the Sudanese courts as this is expressly entrusted by law[120] to arbitral committees.

Constitutional provisions which incorporate principles of international law are not without value in respect of the municipal law itself;[121] they act as guidelines for municipal judges or administrative officials to whom the function of settling investment disputes is entrusted; especially in relation to the assessment of compensation. Moreover, they do provide some protection because they are usually difficult to change. Sudan adheres to the accepted view that the constitution could only be amended by observing the rules prescribed in the constitution itself. This was followed in 1967, when the constituent Assembly amended the Transitional Constitution of the Sudan (Amended), 1964,[122] by securing the two-thirds majority vote required by the constitution. The same procedure has been prescribed for the amendment of the existing constitution. The amendment must also be assented to by the President.[123] Needless to say, however, it is not difficult to secure the required majority in a one-party system. In fact, a change was implemented in a single night-session in 1974 in order to incorporate deterrent provisions in the present Constitution. The purpose of the amendment was to constitutionalize all the detention measures taken by the Minister of Interior under section 93(h) of the Criminal Procedure Act, 1974. This section was challenged before the Supreme Court as being unconstitutional. But before the Court gave judgment, the constitution had been amended restrospectively, whereby all the detention measures were constitutionalized.

This incident shows that the present constitutional provisions on protection of private investment are of limited value to foreign investors. The possibility of their repeal cannot be considered out of the question under the existing regime. If a decision were taken to repeal or amend these provisions, it would be very easy to secure the two-thirds majority, as a considerable number of the members of the People's Assembly is appointed and not elected. However, it may be conceded that the amendment of the Constitution would be frustrated if the President refused to assent to the proposed amendment. But again this is inconceivable, because the initiative to amend the Constitution is an issue of high policy which cannot be initiated without the prior decision of the Executive Committee of the Socialist Union, the supreme political organ of the State, of which the President himself is the chairman.[124]

5. Conclusions

The Permanent Constitution of the Sudan, 1973, in a formal sense furnishes considerable protection to foreign private investment from expropriation and nationalization; for this must be according to law, and for the public interest, and fair compensation should be paid. These and similar constitutional protective clauses are theoretically valuable domestically to challenge, before the Sudanese courts, any measures purporting to encroach on the guarantees assured to foreign investment. But they cannot create future obligations in relation to other States, unless they are contained in treaties. They are more useful than the investment statutes as regards permanence and duration of continuity, because they can only be altered or repealed by a special constitutional procedure. Even so, they are of limited effect. The government in power can secure the required majority to amend the constitution.

The Sudanese investment laws theoretically guarantee to foreign investors the right to transfer abroad their profits and repatriate capital in cases of liquidation. This is certainly a basic requirement. Without it the incentives and other guarantees are of relatively little value. Nevertheless, the way it works in practice does not conform to the realities of a developing country like the Sudan. Putting severe restrictions on the right to repatriate capital and transfer abroad profits, will undobutedly deprive foreign investors from reaping the fruits of their investments. On the other hand, giving them an unfettered freedom over how much to repatriate, and when, is difficult to maintain in view of the critical situation of the Sudan's balance-of-payments. It is prudent to take a position somewhere between the two extremes. Accordingly, repatriation of capital should be allowed, but only after a certain period, and profits should be remitted by instalments.

As regards guarantees against illegal expropriation and nationalization, the Sudanese investment laws incorporate the general rule of international law that foreign investment can be nationalized for public interest on the payment of just compensation.

If a foreign investor is denied before the Sudanese courts any of the guarantees assured by the Constitution and investment laws, his home state may invoke the doctrine of 'estoppel' to plead the Constitution or the law before an international tribunal.

Despite the absence of an express statutory provision guaranteeing foreign investment in Saudi Arabia against expropriation or nationalization, yet in Islamic jurisprudence foreign investment will find all the protection it needs. The invitation of foreign capital by the Saudi Government is a unilateral tacit undertaking which should be respected according to Islamic law. In the international arena this tacit undertaking would be sufficient basis for invoking the doctrine of estoppel to substantiate an international claim.

6

INVESTMENT TREATIES: BILATERAL AND MULTILATERAL

1. Introduction

The preceding chapter has shown that purely unilateral guarantees and other measures by a capital-importing country, including even constitutional guarantees, are not usually sufficient protection for foreign private investment, because the guarantee that is still lacking is that Governments will continue to adhere to the policy manifested in the investment laws. This situation is common amongst developing countries, which are loathe to attenuate their repeated assertions of sovereignty over their natural resources. They resent being committted too far, and this makes the achievement of any stable legal regime for the protection of investment by unilateral devices very hard to establish or maintain. The Sudan is no exception; whereas Saudi Arabia is a different case, given the stability of the Government and the legal regime.

It is important, therefore, to examine the investment treaties to explore how far they provide an alternative method of protection; and this also requires examination of the relation between treaties and the national law of an investee State; and of the question, which prevails over the other in case of conflict.

In this chapter it will also be useful to consider a multilateral investment convention, and the various proposals that have been made for such a convention. But, it is difficult to draft an acceptable convention on the protection of foreign investment because of the opposed attitudes of the developed and developing countries. Also, for the Sudan and Saudi Arabia, it is necessary to take into account their peculiar situation, as members of two different regional organizations. Both of them are members of the Arab League; the Sudan is also a member of the Organization of African Unity (O.A.U.). This is in addition to their membership of the United Nations. This tripartite capacity has caused the Sudan to adopt incompatible stances on several issues in international economic relations. The Arab League is always preoccupied with the idea of creating a regional legal regime for the encouragement and protection of Arab capital accumulating in the hands of the rich Arab oil conservative countries. The African organization is less enthusiastic about this and tends to be dominated by nationalistic and revolutionary regimes which are instinctively antagonistic to foreign investment. Thus, the First Economic Summit of the O.A.U., which took place in April 1980 at Lagos (Nigeria), has entrenched the concept of self-reliance in accordance with a Plan of Action which was unanimously adopted by the African Heads of State and government attending the Summit conference.[1]

Accordingly, this chapter addresses itself to five particular issues. First, it examines the standards of treatment that have been accorded to investors and their property by investee States, both in their treaties and national laws, in order to see how far these same standards have inspired the content of the rules on protection in the bilateral investment treaties discussed below. Secondly, it investigates the kinds of protection actually accorded under these treaties. Thirdly, it surveys the previous draft multilateral conventions, and elucidates how far it may be possible to secure a multilateral convention for the protection of foreign investment. Fourthly, it analyses the legal effect of the Charter of Economic Rights and Duties of States and the other related resolutions of the General Assembly of the United Nations on the New International Economic Order, with particular reference to the formulating of a code of conduct for transnational corporations. Finally, it explores the legal effect of the investment treaties in municipal law of the two countries.

2. Standard of treatment of foreign investment in State practice and in international law

Before dealing with the kinds of protection furnished to foreign investments by treaties, it is important to establish as a reference standards by which the lawfulness of any particular State measure can be judged in general international law. Though the legal status of aliens is determined by the municipal law of each State, yet international law and the practice of States have imposed certain restrictions upon the discretion of the host State. Aliens are generally treated according to one or more of the following standards.

(a) The standard of identical treatment

Under this standard, States promise to grant each other's nationals identical treatment in certain matters.[2] In other words, States apply the doctrine of reciprocity. A State, in order to obtain similar treatment for its nationals in certain matters like diplomatic immunity, extradition, and commerce, finds itself compelled to accord other States a corresponding treatment. For example, Article

11 of the French Civil Code provides that 'aliens should enjoy in France the same civil rights which are or shall be accorded to Frenchmen by the treaties of the nation to which that alien belongs'.[3]

This standard, though often tacitly accorded in relations between States, is not usually resorted to by the Sudan. Nevertheless, the official translation of Article 11 of the Agreement on Economic Integration among the Democratic Republic of the Sudan, Egypt and Libya, 1970,[4] stipulates that 'the contracting Parties have to enact laws and conclude treaties with a view to secure[5] [sic] to their nationals identical treatment in economic and business activities'.

(b) The standard of national treatment

This standard provides for equality of treatment between aliens including foreign investors and the nationals of the host country. A general definition of this standard is given by the United States Friendship, Commerce and Navigation Treaties (F.C.N.) with other countries. Thus, one F.C.N. treaty defines the national treatment in the following terms:

> treatment accorded within the territories of a party upon terms no less favourable than the treatment accorded therein, in like situations, to nationals, companies, products, vessels or other objects, as the case may be.[6]

The English authentic text of Article 2(1) of the Sudan–German Investment Protection Treaty recognized the standard of national treatment in the following words:

> Investment owned by, or under the effective control of, nationals or companies of either Contracting Parties [sic] shall in the territory of the other Contracting Party not be treated less favourable [sic] by that party than it treats investments of its own nationals or companies or investments of nationals or companies of any third State.

The same provision was incorporated in other treaties which West Germany had concluded with other developing countries like Pakistan,[7] Indonesia,[8] and Ceylon (Sri Lanka).[9]

The Sudan–German Treaty is here explicit, in indicating in Article 2(2), the areas where national treatment is accorded to German investments as including occupational, business matters, management, use or enjoyment of investment incentives.[10]

Article 3 of the Sudan–Swiss Investment Protection Agreement,[11] in blending together national and most-favoured-nation treatments in one clause, provides that either Contracting Party must give fair and equitable treatment to foreign investments; and that this treatment must be at least equal to that granted to nationals or companies of either party, or equal to the treatment granted to nationals or companies of the most-favoured-nation (see *post*, pp. 112–14), if the latter is more favourable. But the article contains a proviso to the effect that the treatment so granted does not apply to privileges which either party accords to nationals and companies of a third State because of its membership in an international organization or association, a customs union, a common market or a free trade area. As far as the Sudan is concerned, it is possible that the proviso might apply to the Agreement on Economic Integration between Egypt and the Sudan, 1970, and the Convention on the Transfer of Arab Capital among the Arab States, 1970 (see p. 367, n. 47 to ch. 1).

The best approach is to introduce detailed provisions governing the scope and function of the 'standard of national treatment' to be accorded to foreign investments instead of mentioning it in general terms, which tends to confuse rather than clarify the situation. Thus on matters like conditions of establishment and access to courts, Friendship, Commerce and Navigation treaties give national treatment to nationals and companies of one contracting party in the territory of the other.[12] This is very useful to foreign investors sometimes, because the stipulation of equal treatment between nationals and aliens alike may ameliorate the investment climate, and obviate complaints about the privileged position of aliens. Nevertheless, a difficulty may arise if the national treatment should fall below the minimum standard required by international law. In this case, it seems that more than national treatment might be required.[13] One author[14] pointed out that 'if a State has a low standard of justice towards its own nationals, an alien's position is in a sense a privileged one, for the standard of treatment to which international law entitles him is an objective one, and he need not, even though nationals must, submit to unjust treatment'. Schwarzenberger[15] has asserted that when there is a conflict between national treatment and the minimum standard of international law, equality of treatment is not enough. The situation is perplexing, and aggravated because the exact nature and extent of this minimum standard of international law has not been fully defined. Beckett[16] thought that 'the standard is not an exacting one, and full allowances are made under it for the conditions of the country concerned. The minimum standard would be higher in a highly developed European country than in a sparsely inhabited and only partially developed territory like Africa or Asia'. On the other hand, Nwogugu[17] thought that, in each case, the prevalent national standard of treatment will be evaluated in the light of civilized treatment of aliens and of the principles of natural justice. As an example of this, he said that in the case of expropriation the correct standard is restitution or equivalent compensation. However, to secure a high standard of treatment to foreign investment, it is prudent to replace the national standard of treatment by such a contingent standard which would ensure an equitable and fair treatment to foreign investment.[18]

The standard of national treatment seems to be adopted by the Sudanese investment laws which are designed to apply to national and foreign investments alike. In spite of the absence of any express provision on the type of treatment to be accorded, section 15 of the Industrial Investment Act provides that no distinction is to be made between national and foreign establishments, public or private, in granting investment licences, concessions and facilities. This is taken to imply that foreign investment in the Sudan is accorded national treatment, at least in the industrial sector. More generously, the Agricultural Investment Act[19] confers on the Minister of Agriculture the discretion to give certain establishments or crafts preferential treatment if they are set up in particular areas. The justification for this special treatment is to encourage agricultural investment in rural areas instead of concentrating it in urban districts. Eventually, this privileged status is applicable to both foreign and national investment without any discrimination. But still, the possibility of conferring further special and preferential treatment to foreign establishments by treaties cannot be excluded.

The Saudi investment law is silent on this point, and one has to refer to Islamic law, which as a general principle, offers aliens a special standard of treatment, not less than equality with Moslems.[20]

Latin-American countries[21] generally adopt the standard of national treatment, the reason being that these countries also have been sensitive about their sovereignty and independence. They naturally resented the idea of committing themselves to according foreigners treatment more favourable than that accorded to their own nationals. The logical solution would be the coalescence of national and international standards resulting from human rights law, which is, of course, a much newer phenomenon than the *Calvo* doctrine.

(c) Most-favoured-nation treatment

This standard of treatment has been used for a long time in the United States' Friendship, Commerce and Navigation treaties. It is defined in one treaty as:

> Treatment accorded within the territories of a party upon terms no less favourable than the treatment accorded therein, in like situations, to nationals, companies, products, vessels or other objects, as the case may be, of any third party.[22]

The International Court of Justice has described this standard as 'the maintenance at all times of fundamental equality without discrimination among the countries concerned',[23] but did not extend its use between the treaties at issue.

This standard of treatment is expressly recognized by the Sudan–German Investment Protection treaty in relation to restitution, indemnification, compensation, returns from investment or other valuable considerations, for loss resulting from war or revolution in the territory of either party.[24] In fact, this is a most important protective clause for German investors in the Sudan, because if they were to be accorded *national* treatment in the matters envisaged by this treaty, they would get no protection, as it is always the case that Sudanese nationals who suffer any losses to their property as the result of armed conflict or revolution or civil riots receive no compensation.

The Sudan–Swiss Investment Protection Agreement, 1974 and the Investment Treaty between the Sudan and France of 1979, refer to the most-favoured-nation treatment in general terms without indicating its actual operation and scope. Thus Article 2 of the former treaty provides that:

> Either contracting party shall protect within its territory the investments by nationals or companies of the other contracting party and shall ensure fair and equitable treatment to such investments.
>
> This treatment shall be at least equal to that granted by each contracting party to its own nationals or companies, or equal to the treatment granted to nationals or companies of the most-favoured-nation, if the latter is more favourable.[25]

The novelty of this clause is that it blends the national and most-favoured-nation treatments into one formula, thus giving the Swiss investors the choice between the two standards, whichever is more favourable to them in the particular situation.[26] Such a clause, in effect, would widen the standard of treatment by reference to which the lawfulness or unlawfulness of State's measures affecting foreign investment can be ascertained. Furthermore, applying the two standards concurrently is advantageous, as the benefits of both standards can be enjoyed cumulatively.[27]

Under Article 11 of the Provisional Agreement between the United States of America and the Kingdom of Saudi Arabia in Regard to Diplomatic and Consular Representation, Juridical Protection, Commerce and Navigation, 1933,[28] the two contracting parties promised to accord to each other unconditional most-favoured-nation treatment in respect of import, export and other duties and changes affecting commerce and navigation as well as in respect of transit, warehousing and other facilities. Under the same Article, every concession with respect to any duty, change or regulation affecting commerce or navigation accorded or to be accorded by either party to any foreign country will become immediately applicable without request and without compensation to the commerce and navigation of the other party.

Despite the fact that the above Article explicitly offered unconditional most-favoured-nation treatment, yet Article IV of the same agreement has restricted the scope of the most-favoured-nation treatment change, by providing that the clause should not extend to the treatment which was accorded (at the time when the agreement was signed) by the United States to the commerce of Cuba and the Panama Canal Zone or any of the dependencies of the United States.

The most-favoured-nation treatment standard has received the attention of the International Law Commission. Thus the Commission, when dealing with the issue under a generalized system of preferences proposed the following:

The exercise of rights arising under a most-favoured-nation clause for the beneficiary State and for persons or things in a determined relationship with that State is subject to compliance with the relevant laws of the granting State. These laws, however, shall not be applied in such a manner that the treatment of the beneficiary State and persons or things in a determined relationship with that State becomes less favourable than that of the third State or of persons or things in the same relationship with that third State.[29]

Obviously, the purpose of this draft article is to put some restriction on the right of the granting State to enact laws that diminish the scope and effect of the standard of treatment given in the particular case.

Whatever might be the merits and demerits of either standards of national or most-favoured-nation treatments, the choice between them lies solely with the granting State. Here, economic and social realities will no doubt have their impact. Many States are hostile to any limitations put on their sovereignty in this respect.

(d) International law standard

International law provides a minimum standard of treatment for aliens which a State cannot violate without incurring international responsibility. International law demands that the treatment of aliens should not fall below the standard of international civilization as an objective goal.[30] This entails restricting the State's liberty of action by the right of other States to be assured that a certain minimum in this respect will not be overstepped. This had been plainly demonstrated in the *Neer* case in the following words;

The treatment of an alien, in order to constitute an international delinquency, should amount to an outrage, to bad faith, to wilful neglect of duty, or to an insufficiency of governmental action so far short of international standards that every reasonable and impartial man would readily recognize its insufficiency. Whether the insufficiency proceeds from deficient execution of an intelligent law or from the fact that the laws of the country do not empower the authorities to measure up to international standards is immaterial.[31]

The standard is not expressly stated in the old bilateral treaties concluded by the Sudan; yet an inference to that effect can be deduced from the Sudan–German Investment Protection Treaty, which states that 'investments by nationals or companies of either contracting party shall enjoy full protection and security in the territory of the other contracting party'.[32]

The international law standard finds treaty expression in the United States' Friendship, Commerce and Navigation treaties. Article V of the U.S.–Italian Treaty, 1948[33] provides that 'the nationals of each High Contracting party shall receive within the territory of the other the full protection and security required by international law'. A similar provision is recently expressed in Article 3 of the Investment Treaty between the Sudan and France, 1979. This treaty provision stipulates that the treatment required by international law shall not be less than the most-favoured-nation treatment.

Nwogugu[34] rightly explained the international standard as meaning, in concrete terms, 'fair treatment, free access to the courts, respect for human rights. In relation to foreign investment, this standard stipulates the payment of fair, adequate and effective compensation in cases of expropriation or nationalization.'[35]

It is not settled whether or not nowadays international law does actually establish an obligation on the host State to grant aliens more than equal treatment with its nationals, when the national standard falls below the international standard. A restrictive view denies any international obligation on the host State to accord aliens more than equality of treatment with its nationals. This view rests on the doctrine of State sovereignty. It has been consistently followed by the Latin-American States,[36] and at present the other developing countries seem to follow the same path. Their collective and unanimous view has been formulated in the Charter of Economic Rights and Duties of States, 1974 (see *post*, pp. 128–41).

3. Bilateral treaties

(a) Kinds of protection

The protective measures provided by bilateral investment treaties assume the following patterns, namely:

(i) *Promises facilitating establishment of investment activities*[37]

Under Article 1 of the Sudan–German Investment Protection Treaty,[38] each contracting party promises to promote as far as possible in its territory investments by nationals or companies of the other party, in accordance with its legislation, policies, and administrative practices.

The Sudan–Swiss Agreement[39] is more specific on this point. Under Article 4 either contracting party is not to impair by unreasonable or discriminating measures the management, maintenance, use, enjoyment, extension and, should it so happen, liquidation of such investments. In particular, under this article, the parties promise to facilitate such investments in their territories.

The practice is usually adopted in the vast majority of commercial treaties, especially those which the United States concludes with developing countries. In British treaty practice, most-favoured-nation treatment is promised for participation in business activities,[40] while the American Friendship, Commerce and Navigation treaties (F.C.N.) usually promise national treatment in this area.[41]

(ii) *Exchange control*

Transfer of capital and profits forms an essential background to the existence and operation of a foreign-owned business enterprise. As demonstrated before (see *ante*, pp. 000–00) there are two opposing aspects of the problem of exchange control. On the one hand, a developing country like the Sudan would claim that exchange control is one of the effective devices for combating its balance-of-payments problems. On the other hand, foreign investors are anxious to be assured of the right to transfer freely their capital and profits, otherwise foreign investment will not be forthcoming to the investee State. The previous chapter has shown empirically how far the Sudanese investment laws dealt with the problem in favour of foreign investors.

Under the Sudan–German Treaty, German investors have the right to transfer their profits, and capital in cases of liquidation. If no other arrangement is admitted by the appropriate agencies, transfers must be made without undue delay and at the rate of exchange effective for current transactions on the day the transfer is made. The treaty goes on to elaborate on the rate of exchange applicable to current transactions as to be based on the par value agreed with the International Monetary Fund. This rate of exchange must be within such a spread regarded by the Fund as commensurate with the obligations of members under section 3 of Article IV of the Fund's Articles of Agreement.[42] If at the time of transfer no rate of exchange exists in respect of a particular contracting party, the official rate fixed by a contracting party for its currency in relation to the United States dollar or to another freely convertible currency or to gold must be paid. If no such rate of exchange has been fixed, the appropriate agencies of either of the two countries in which territory the investment is situate must admit an equitable and fair rate of exchange.[43] This is taken to mean in this latter case that the rate of exchange for transferring profits and capital of German investors will be determined by the Bank of Sudan, which is the normal procedure.

The Sudan–Swiss Agreement is much more specific on the point of exchange control. Under Article V, Swiss investors have the right to transfer from the Sudan profits, instalments in payments of loans, expenses spent for the management of investment abroad, additional funds necessary for maintenance and development of investments, payments for technical, commercial or administrative assistance, and the proceeds of liquidation. However, unlike the German treaty, this agreement provides that, in the case of expropriation, the compensation must be settled in the currency of the country of origin.[44] Consequently, this can be extended by analogy to cover cases of transfer of profits and capital under the same agreement.

Undoubtedly, the German treaty and the Swiss agreement virtually provide firm guarantees on the right to repatriate capital and remit profits abroad. They are not free from criticism, however, as not conforming to the realities of the Sudanese economy. There could well be a time when their complete implementation would be utterly impossible owing to the deteriorating situation of the Sudan's foreign reserves and especially of hard currency.

(iii) *Guarantees against expropriation*

The security of private investment in an investee State is one of the vital considerations which influence foreign investors in deciding whether or not to invest their capital in that State. Bilateral treaties are useful instruments for providing effective protection in this respect. Article 3 of the Sudan–German Treaty provides that investments by nationals or companies of either contracting party must be protected to the fullest extent and be secured in the territory of the other contracting party. More emphatically, the same article provides that the investments envisaged by the treaty are not to be expropriated except for the public benefit and against compensation.[45] Article 5 of the Investment Treaty between the Sudan and France covers full guarantee aginst all types of interference with investments.

Ironically, the English authentic translation of Article V of the Sudan–Kuwaiti Economic Agreement,[46] provides:

> The two contracting parties shall not *confiscate* the capital investments belonging to either party or to their respective subjects, in either country only if a *fair* and *immediate* compensation is paid in the same currency of the original capital investment. (My italics.)

It seems that the word 'confiscate' was employed as meaning the same as expropriation, although confiscation, as pointed out earlier, is strictly a penalty and hence entails no obligation to pay compensation at all.

Conversely, the Egypt–Sudan Investment Agreement[47] provides for complete protection without any specific mention of any particular contingency. This can be interpreted so widely as to provide security against all risks including expropriation itself.

Similarly, but with more precision, Article 6 of the Sudan–Swiss Agreement provides that either party is under a duty not to take any measure of expropriation, nationalization or dispossession, either direct or indirect, against investments by nationals or companies of the other party, except under due process of law and provided that provisions be made for *effective* and *adequate* compensation. The amount of compensation must be fixed at the time of expropriation, nationalization or dispossession. It must be settled in the currency of the country of origin of the investment and must be paid to the investor without undue delay (see ch. 8). This agreement, however, displays a typical example of the traditional treaty approach in providing legal protection to foreign investment, which has been followed in many commercial treaties. Thus, the American F.C.N. treaties prescribe the obligation to grant equitable treatment to foreign property. Property belonging to foreign nationals and companies is accorded most constant protection and security. Under the U.S.–China F.C.N. Treaty,[48] each party undertook to grant property owned by nationals of the other protection and security in accordance with the requirements of international law. In addition to such a general protective clause, the F.C.N. treaties contain detailed provisions on expropriation, nationalization and similar measures. A striking example can be found in the U.K.–Iran F.C.N. Treaty of 1959. Article 15 of this treaty provides that:

> The nationals and companies of one High Contracting Party shall receive equitable treatment in any territory of the other in respect of any measure of requisition, civil or military, or of disposal, limitation, restriction or expropriation affecting their property, rights and interests of any company of the other High Contracting Party in which they own interests, and shall receive *prompt*, *adequate* and *effective* compensation for any such measure.[49]

This clause contains two important issues. First, it covers all possible forms of taking of private property, and particularly indirect or 'creeping' expropriation. Secondly, the security promised applies to the rights and interests of British nationals and companies in an Iranian company.

(iv) *Settlement of disputes*

The German and Swiss treaties discussed above, like many other investment treaties, contain detailed provisions on the methods and procedure to be adopted in solving investment disputes. This will be discussed in chapter 10.

(v) *Shortcomings*

The German and Swiss treaties do not contain elaborate provisions like the U.K.–Iran F.C.N. Treaty. Their provisions are too general to provide specific guarantees, except against expropriation and protecting the right to remit profits, and repatriate capital abroad. They fail altogether to provide for protection of foreign investment against discriminatory taxation, a matter which is usually taken care of in commercial treaties. For example, under the United States treaties each contracting party must accord national and most-favoured-nation treatment to foreign investment enterprises in respect of payment of and collection of fees, taxes and all other charges on property.[50] The combination of these two standards of treatment in matters of taxation operates, in the opinion of Albrecht,[51] 'to provide fiscal treatment to aliens which is at least as favourable as that accorded to nationals, and even more favourable than that accorded to nationals if such more favourable treatment has been accorded to any other State'.

The German and Swiss treaties under discussion, unlike the Investment Treaty between the Sudan and France, also omitted to provide any guarantee on two important issues, namely the right to acquire and dispose of property, and access to courts. The capacity to acquire and dispose of property freely is considered as an important corollary of the right of the investor to organize and operate his business enterprise in a foreign country. In the Sudan it has been the policy of the Government to ban the acquisition of real property of foreigners; but, it is believed that this policy will be relaxed in order to implement the investment laws. To leave the matter exclusively to administrative discretion may risk unreasonable exercise of the discretion. It is expedient to regulate all aspects of the acquisition and disposal of real property by treaties or special laws. Additionally, an investment treaty should also state unequivocally the standard of treatment to be accorded in this respect. F.C.N. treaties grant national treatment for the acquisition of such leaseholds as may be necessary for the execution of treaty-approved purposes, e.g. resident, or construction of a factory and offices. In other aspects of real property acquisition, a *de facto* reciprocity arrangement is usually adopted in United States' treaties in which national treatment is granted.[52]

Without giving the foreign investor the right of access to local courts, any promise of protection would be devoid of legal effectiveness. As will be shown later, in chapter 10, under the existing Sudanese laws any person has the right to pursue his claim in the Sudanese courts, but the permanence of this right is far from being assured. For this reason, treaty provisions are more effective than the municipal laws. Under the F.C.N. treaties national treatment is also granted with regard to access to local courts and employment in legal proceedings of advocates, attorneys or agents. These treaties also assure foreign nationals the right to employ interpreters of their own choice in judicial proceedings. Such guarantees are essential for the implementation of the general principle of natural justice that all parties before courts must be capable of presenting their case to the tribunal and be able to understand and follow the proceedings.[53]

4. Multilateral conventions

(a) Regional conventions

Owing to its geographical situation, and historical and cultural backgrounds, the Sudan has acquired the dual membership of two important regional organizations, the Arab League and the Organization of African Unity. This dual capacity qualifies it to be a party to several agreements and conventions sponsored by these two organizations. This comment is partially applicable to Saudi Arabia, which is an important member of the Arab League. Thus, the Arab States, with a view of strengthening economic relations among themselves, and in accordance with Article 11 of the Arab League Pact and Article 1 of the Agreement for Economic Unity among the Arab League Countries, 1969,[54] concluded the Convention on the Investment of Arab Capital and its Transfer among the Arab States, 1971.[55] Article 6 of this convention provides, *inter alia*, that the host State has the right to nationalize, confiscate or acquire private capital for the public interest. Should this take place, Arabe investors are entitled to adequate and effective compensation to be paid within a reasonable time. They are also given the right in the member States to transfer their invested capital, profits and compensation.[56] The convention also contains provisions on the right of establishment and residence, and incorporates by reference all the concessions and facilities furnished by the investment laws of the member States.[57]

The basic characteristic of this convention is that it is expressed in general terms, leaving the details to be set out in the municipal legislation of each member State.[58] Obviously, the advantage of this generalization is that it leaves room for flexibility. However, this could ideally be achieved if the details were contained in contracts between Arab investors and the host State rather than leaving the whole issue to the domestic legislation of the member States.

An unique legal instrument is the Contract for the Formation of the Arab Investment Company, 1974.[59] The novelty of this is that it contains an absolute guarantee against nationalization, confiscation, sequestration[60] or acquisition of the assets of the company by any State party to the contract.[61] Since these measures are ruled out initially, the issue of compensation is not mentioned at all. Accordingly, if any State party to the contract nationalizes or confiscates the assests of the company, this action by itself will constitute a breach of the contract. Like the previous Convention on Transfer of Arab Capital, the contract of the Arab company incorporates by reference all the facilities and concessions under the investment laws of the member States.[62]

(b) A multilateral convention or investment code

As treaties are binding only on States party to them, it has become important since the Second World War to adopt a code of State practice relating to foreign investment. This could be in the form of a multilateral treaty binding on several States, or on all concerned States. Indeed, if foreign investment is to be encouraged and protected it is essential to extend the conventional protection to cover many countries. The increased consciousness of international economic problems together with the rise of international organizations have led to the formation of an enthusiastic movement for the adoption of an international code or a multilateral convention. The United Nations Secretary General in his Progress Report on the International Flow of Private Capital, 1960, after surveying the protective provisions in bilateral investment treaties, concluded that:[63]

> It is not likely that this technique could offer a comprehensive solution to the problem; the expansion of such a bilateral network is not only a necessarily slow process, but is bound to remain highly selective in its geographical scope, especially since some capital-supplying countries are likely to be in a better position for securing such treaty protection for their investors than others.

As mentioned before, the notion of concluding a multilateral convention on foreign investments has been supported by some international organizations, governmental and non-governmental, but no final draft has been agreed upon. It is important to examine briefly some of the proposals, in an attempt to explore the reasons obstructing the conclusion of such a convention, and then how the problem might be solved.

(i) *The Havana Charter for an International Trade Organization*

This was the first main general multilateral effort to introduce a code on protection of foreign investment. It was suggested by the International Trade Organization (I.T.O.),[64] at Havana, 1948. The charter laid down certain General Rules[65] regarding treatment and protection of foreign investment in the territories of the contracting parties. The protection and regulation of foreign investment was set out in Article 12. It recognized the need to create good opportunities and adequate security for all foreign investment as a leading factor in the continuous flow of private capital to poor countries.[66] Specifically, this article gave each contracting party the right:

- (i) to make any appropriate safeguards necessary to ensure that foreign investment was not used as a basis for interference in its internal affairs or national policies;
- (ii) to determine whether and to what extent and upon what terms it would allow future foreign investment;

(iii) to prescribe and give effect on just terms to requirements as to the ownership of existing and future investments;

(iv) to prescribe and give effect to other reasonable requirements with respect to existing and future investment.[67]

In fact these provisions emphasize the sovereign rights of capital-importing countries rather than adjusting the balance of interests of all parties concerned. Because of this bias the charter did not attract support from capital-exporting countries.

With regard to protection of foreign investment, the charter did not contain adequate and concrete provisions. The relevant provisions maintained only that foreign investment should be protected, but opened the door for several qualifications and exceptions. Thus, Article 12(2) provided that capital-importing States were merely required:

(i) to provide reasonable opportunties for investment acceptable to them and adequate security, for existing and future investment, and

(ii) to give due regard to the desirability of avoiding discrimination as between foreign investments.[68]

Further, Article 11(1)(h) provided that: 'No member shall take unreasonable and unjustifiable action within its territory injurious to the rights or interests of nationals of other members in the enterprise, skills, capital, arts or technology which they have supplied.'

Making the protection of foreign investment subject to such vague terms as 'just', 'appropriate' and ' reasonable' is to add a new uncertainty and really does not provide any protection at all. It is, indeed, very difficult to ascertain the degrees of unreasonableness and what is ' appropriate' or 'just' in every case, without specific standards and criteria to clothe these general terms. In the last analysis, the matter would fall completely within the unilateral judgment of a capital-importing country. Moreover, the Havana Charter was strongly criticized as giving too much attention to the avoidance of discrimination, which is not by any means the only impediment to foreign investment.[69] One writer observed that the charter did more to affirm the right of the developing countries to interfere with investments than the rights of the investors themselves.[70]

(ii) *The Economic Agreement of Bogota, 1948*[71]

This agreement was a regional effort by some American States to increase the flow of foreign capital for developing purposes. Chapter IV of the Agreement dealt exclusively with private investment. The relevant provisions on fair treatment and non-discrimination are similar to the Havana Charter, though with more elaboration and clarity. Under the agreement, a general guarantee of 'equitable treatment' and especially of non-discrimination was granted. Obligations were cast on contracting States to reduce excessive taxes and 'impose no unjustifiable restrictions' on the transfer of earnings and capital. Expropriation must be accompanied by payment of fair compensation in a prompt, adequate and effective manner.[72] Article 24 of the Agreement stipulated that foreign capital should be subject to national law. This has been considered by the capital-exporting countries as unsatisfactory, because there may be situations where local laws fall below the international law standards of treatment of aliens and their property. The Agreement was also condemned by foreign investors, as it was rendered meaningless by many reservations attached to it by several signatories which made their national laws superior to the provisions of the Agreement. However, like the Havana Charter the Bogota Agreement never became a legally binding instrument. Only three Governments – Costa Rica, Honduras and Panama – ratified it.[73]

(iii) *The I.C.C. Code of Fair Treatment for Foreign Investments*

A remarkable proposal for an international investment convention is that of the world business organization, the International Chamber of Commerce (I.C.C.), in 1949. It drew up a draft international code of Fair Treatment for Foreign Investments.[74] The code would prohibit the imposition of 'discriminatory, political, or administrative measures intended to hamper investments'.[75] In the event of expropriation, the code provided for 'fair compensation' to be paid according to international law.[76] Similarly, the code assured investors of the right to transfer their interests, dividends, capital and other funds outside the investee State.[77] Although the issue of interference by investors in the internal sphere of the investee State received some attention in the introduction report, no provision was made for it, nor were corresponding obligations of investors made in the proposed code. This exposed the code to criticism from some scholars.[78]

The International Businessmen's Conference convened under the auspices of the I.C.C. at Karachi in December 1960, recommended a review by the I.C.C. of its draft code in the light of new developments. The conclusions of the conference centred on, *inter alia*, the payment of adequate, effective and prompt compensation, fair treatment for investments and the importance of joint ventures.[79]

(iv) *The Abs–Shawcross Draft Convention on Investment Abroad*[80]

This Draft Convention was an outcome of two separate drafts[81] suggested by two different groups, which were blended in one draft. Under the unified draft convention, fair and equitable treatment and constant protection are granted to foreign-owned property. Unlike the previous proposals, this draft convention tried to restate the traditional rules of international law. Thus, no discriminatory measures against foreign investment were allowed. Expropriation should be allowed only under due process of law, and where adequate and effective compensation was paid.[82]

The convention has also not escaped criticism as not paying due regard to the interests of recipient States.[83] It failed to effect a balance between the rights of investors and developing States.[84]

(v) *The O.E.C.D. Draft Convention on the Protection of Foreign Property, 1963*[85]

This represents recent western interests. It was prepared by the Committee of the Organization for Economic Co-operation and Development. The draft consists of fourteen articles, mainly emphasizing the obligations arising from the nationalizing of foreign property, the general standard of treatment and performance of undertaking. It did not produce anything new, but only declared the old customary international law rules on the protection of private property abroad. Apart from being very short, it commanded approval, in preference to other proposals, for its pragmatism.[86] As the majority of foreign capital invested in the Sudan primarily comes from the member countries of the O.E.C.D., this draft convention has special importance for the Sudan. What matters in this respect is the standard for assessing compensation in cases of expropriation and nationalization. The standard adopted by this Draft Convention is similar to that envisaged by the Sudanese investment laws.[87]

The effort of the O.E.C.D. to achieve a multilateral convention on the protection of foreign investment did not stop at this level. In 1969, a Code of Liberalization of Capital Movements[88] was established under a decision of the Council of the O.E.C.D. According to this code, members of the O.E.C.D. undertake general and specific obligations to eliminate restrictions on the movements of capital to the fullest extent for effective economic co-operation. All members agreed to treat all non-resident-owned assets on an equal footing regardless of the date of their formation, and to permit the liquidation and transfer of such assets. Beyond this, the members are to grant any authorization that may be required for the conclusion and execution of the transactions and for transfers specified in the code.

(vi) *The Harvard Draft*

In 1961 the Harvard Law School produced a draft convention on the Responsibility of States for Injuries to the Economic Interests of Aliens.[89] Though this draft convention is not directly related to foreign investment yet its relevant provisions provide that the deliberate destruction by a State of alien-owned property is wrongful unless such action is authorized by a competent tribunal or State authority on grounds of *ordre public*, health and morality. Even in these exceptional cases, the destruction of property should neither be discriminatory nor constitute an abuse of the power of eminent domain.[90] When alien-owned property is taken for public purpose, it must be accompanied by the payment of prompt compensation under certain specified criteria.[91]

(vii) *Other efforts*

The idea of concluding a multilateral convention for the protection of foreign private property or investment has gained the support of a number of international private groups,[92] jurists[93] and the International Law Commission.[94]

(c) Failure of proposals for an investment convention

Although most of the proposals surveyed above contain similar provisions, none of them has led to an acceptable multilateral convention. There are several reasons, mainly of a political and economic nature. Some proposals have been condemned primarily for being concerned only with the interests of investors, and consequently failing to balance the interests and obligations of all parties.[95] An effective investment code or convention should not be a one-sided instrument. It should regulate comprehensively the whole relationship between a host State and foreign investors.[96] As the protection sought for foreign investment must finally be offered by capital-importing countries, it is unrealistic to design any convention without their co-operation and consultation. Only a few of the above proposals did, in fact, give enough attention to this sensitive point.

Another reason is that most of the capital-importing countries have been at one time colonies of the capital-exporting countries. To them the newly gained independence and sovereignty are previous achievements which must be preserved. They fear political and economic domination possibly resulting from a convention with those countries from which they have won political independence. Nor are they keen to be committed in such a way as possibly to fetter future decisions about following the way of a political ideology leading to an ideal of a progressive society. In this way, political and psychological aspects of the problem have distorted international relations in the last decade. One writer[97] observed that:

'There is no place here for the exponent of "pure law", untrammelled by political considerations, economic, and cultural differences'.

Moreover, even if the capital-importing countries were willing to participate in efforts towards the conclusion of an international investment convention, nevertheless the capital-exporting countries could not guarantee that substantial amounts of new foreign capital would in fact be invested in the capital-importing countries. For those governments have only a limited control over the disposition of the funds of the private citizens, and over the giant transnational companies which manipulate the economies of the capital-exporting countries themselves, let alone the capital-importing countries. Furthermore, even if the legal obstacles were removed, economic factors might well have their impact in discouraging foreign investments in some, or in the majority of capital-importing countries. Consequently, a capital-importing country would have to accept certain definite obligations without any corresponding undertakings on the part of the capital-exporting countries.

In fact it is not only the capital-importing countries that are to be blamed for the failure of the previous proposals for a multilateral investment convention. If a multilateral convention is to accord some protection to foreign investment, the sovereignty of all States participating in it would have to be limited to some extent. To many capital-exporting countries, this is not acceptable. They are not prepared to undertake far-reaching commitments in this connection. They are reluctant to commit themselves in the sphere of domestic economic policy; and sometimes a federal system of government also makes more difficult the acceptance of such commitments.[98]

The failure in the last two decades to agree on an acceptable investment convention might be thought to suggest that there is a basic disagreement among States about the recent rules of international law. This suggestion is strengthened by the undoubtedly wide divergences of opinion of writers on the legal rules applicable to foreign investment. Nevertheless, the present attitude of the developing countries in so frequently providing guarantees and security to foreign investment does not justify this pessimistic conclusion about the basic law. But, as long as there exists a divergence between the interests of the capital-exporting and capital-importing countries, a multilateral agreement must be difficult to achieve. None the less, it does not follow at all that the relevant law is not in the process of development and consolidation. Indeed, it is arguable that to try just now to embody it in a single rigid code would be counter-productive.

(d) The Charter of Economic Rights and Duties of States[99]

The adoption of this Charter by the General Assembly of the United Nations in 1974 marked a new phase of development in international relations and economic co-operation. Taken together with the other two important documents, the Declaration on the Establishment of a New Economic Order,[100] and the Programme of Action on the Establishment of a New Economic Order,[101] the three documents disclose the new militancy at the United Nations of the developing countries, which have so profoundly increased their political power over the last decade.

However, what is relevant to the present study is Article 2 of the Charter which is the most contentious article. It expresses in concrete and clear terms that:

(1) Every State has and shall freely exercise full permanent sovereignty, including possession, use and disposal, over all its wealth natural resources and economic activities.
(2) Each State has the right:
  (a) To regulate and exercise authority over foreign investment within its national jurisdiction in accordance with its law and regulations and in conformity with its national objectives and priorities. No State shall be compelled to grant preferential treatment to foreign investment;
  (b) to regulate and supervise the activities of transnational corporations within its national jurisdiction and take measures to ensure that such activities comply with its laws, rules and regulations and conform with its economic and social policies. Transnational corporations shall not intervene in the internal affairs of a host State. Every State should, with full regard for its sovereign rights, co-operate with other States in the exercise of the right set forth in this paragraph;
  (c) to nationalize, expropriate or transfer ownership of foreign property in which case appropriate compensation should be paid by the State adopting such measures, taking into account its relevant laws and regulations and all circumstances that the State considers pertinent. In any case where the question of compensation gives rise to a controversy, it shall be settled under the domestic law of the nationalizing State and by its tribunals unless it is freely and mutually agreed by all States concerned that other peaceful means be sought on the basis of the sovereign equality of States and in accordance with the principle of free choice of means.

The above-mentioned provisions were intended to generate new norms in many areas relating to foreign investment, namely:

(1) the principle of permanent sovereignty over natural resources;
(2) the treatment of foreign investment;
(3) the diplomatic protection of aliens abroad;
(4) regulation and supervision of activities of transnational corporations;
(5) nationalization and terms of compensation.

This chapter examines the effect of the Charter of Economic Rights and Duties and States on the traditional rules of international law on the first four issues i.e.

the principle of permanent sovereignty, treatment of foreign investment, diplomatic protection and supervision of activities of transnational corporations.[102]

Before embarking upon these issues, it is important initially to determine the legal nature of the Charter of Economic Rights and Duties of States in an attempt to see to what extent it is binding on all States.

(i) *The legal force of the Charter*

Peter D. Maynard[103] has observed that:

> Generally speaking, resolutions or declarations of the General Assembly are not legally binding. The Charter is no exception. However, the reasons for characterisation of the Charter as non-binding may vary, owing to the controversy regarding the nature of U.N. resolutions.

Actually, there is no widespread consensus on the nature of the United Nations General Assembly resolutions. Thus, in the extreme view, Brierly[104] advocates that resolutions of the General Assembly are almost only recommendatory or hortatory. He writes:

> apart from its control over the budget, all that the General Assembly can do is to discuss and recommend and initiate studies and consider reports from other bodies...its decisions are not directions telling the member States what they are or are not to do.

This argument is in line with Article 10 of the Charter of the United Nations which provides that the General Assembly may make recommendations to the members of the United Nations on any questions or matters; and that Article does not specify that the resolutions of the General Assembly are binding.

This view has received the support of a considerable number of commentators.[105] More recently, Brown and Tepe characterized the Charter of Economic Rights and Duties of States (C.E.R.D.S.) as having a 'weakening effect on international law', and remarked:

> The most fundamental weakness of the Charter is its overall failure to state clearly that the economic rights and duties of States are subject to international law or at least that international law is pertinent.
>
> The failure of the Charter fundamentally to accord to international law its proper governing role in international relations is compounded by the substantial efforts made in substantive provisions of the Charter to undermine existing rules of international law believed by less developed countries to be insufficiently biased in their directions.[106]

Similarly, Haight observed that:

> Whatever the initial objectives of this exercise may have been, the six negative votes cast against the Charter as a whole and the many separate provisions clearly establish that it cannot have legal pretensions.

General Assembly Resolutions do not in any way have the force of law. Under the United Nations Charter, the General Assembly may discuss and make recommendations, but it is not a law-making body and its Resolutions, no matter how solemnly expressed or characterized, nor how often repeated do not make or have binding force.[107]

The same view has been recently advocated by Professor René-Jean Dupuy as sole Arbitrator in an *ex parte* arbitral Award in the Arbitration between the Government of Libya Arab Republic and California Asiatic Oil Company and Texaco Overseas Petroleum Company, 1977.[108] He stated, however, in part: 'The principles stated in this resolution were therefore assented to by a great many States representing not only all geographical areas but also all economic systems.'[109]

Indeed, the affirmative vote of several developed countries with a market economy was made possible in particular by the inclusion in Resolution 1803 (XVII) of two references to international law, and one passage relating to the importance of international co-operation for economic development. According to the representative of Tunisia:

the result of the debate on this question was that the balance of the original draft resolution was improved – a balance between on the one hand, the unequivocal affirmation of the inalienable right of States to exercise sovereignty over natural resources and, on the other hand, the reconciliation or adaptation of this sovereignty to international law, equity and the principles of international cooperation.[110]

The reference to international law, in particular in the field of nationalization, was therefore an essential factor in the support given by several western countries to Resolution 1803 (XVII), unlike the C.E.R.D.S. which does not expressly refer at all to international law.

On the contrary, the voting procedure under which the Resolution 3281 (XXIX) by which the C.E.R.D.S. was adopted, was notably different. The C.E.R.D.S. was adopted with a roll-call vote by the General Assembly, and the statements made by the delegates showed clearly and explicitly what was the position of each main group of countries. The most developed western countries were opposed to abandoning the compromise solution in Resolution 1803 (XVII). The analysis of votes on specific sections of the Charter is most significant in so far as paragraph 2(c) of Article 2 is concerned, which limits consideration of characteristics of compensation to the municipal law and tribunals of the nationalizing State with exclusion of international law. This was voted for by 104 to 16, with 6 abstentions. All of the industrialized countries with market economies abstained or voted against it.[111]

Dupuy succinctly observed:

The absence of any connection between the procedure of compensation and international law and the subjection of this procedure solely to municipal law cannot be regarded by this Tribunal except as a *de lege ferenda* formulation which even appears *contra legem* in the eyes of many developed countries.

This attitude is further reinforced by the general practice of and relations between States with respect to foreign investments which is consonant, not with the provisions of Article 2(c) of the C.E.R.D.S. conferring exclusive jurisdiction on domestic legislation and courts, but with the exception stated at the end of this paragraph. Thus, a great many investment agreements (see ch. 9) entered into between industrialized countries or their nationals, on the one hand, and developing countries on the other, state objectively the standards of compensation. Furthermore, they provide that, in case of dispute regarding the level of such compensation, resort is frequently made to international tribunals. The ratification of more than sixty-five States, by 1974, of the Convention on the Settlement of Investment Disputes between States and Nationals of Other States, 1965[112] is strikingly indicative of this practice.

Additionally, even though Article 2 of the C.E.R.D.S. does not explicitly refer to international law, it does not escape all norms of international law.[113] Paragraph 2 of Article 33 states that: 'in interpretation and application, the provisions of the present Charter are interrelated and each provision should be construed in the context of other provisions'. Among the fundamental elements of international economic relations in the Charter, principle (j) in Chapter 1 is headed as follows:

Fulfilment in good faith of international obligations.

Analysing the scope of these various provisions, Ambassador Castaneda, who chaired the Working Group charged with drawing up the Charter, formally stated that the principle of performance in good faith of international obligations laid down in chapter 1(j) of the C.E.R.D.S. applies to all matters governed by it, including, in particular, matters referred to in Article 2. He concludes as follows:

The Charter accepts that international law may operate as a factor limiting the freedom of the State should foreign interests be affected, even though Article 2 does not state this explicitly. This stems legally from the provisions included in other Articles of the Charter which should be interpreted and applied jointly with those of Article 2.[114]

Can the C.E.R.D.S. be considered as a codification and progressive development of international law in the essence of Article 13(a) of the United Nations Charter? The answer seems to be in the negative. There is no direct reference to codification and progressive development of international law. At a late stage in the negotiations in the Second Committee, the sponsors introduced revisions of the fourth and thirteenth preambular paragraphs of the C.E.R.D.S. The former revision dedicated the Charter 'to promote' instead of 'to codify and develop rules for', the establishment of the new international economic order. The latter revision deleted the characterization of the Charter 'as a first step in the codification and progressive development of this subject'.[115] This view is supported by Brown and Tepe.[116]

Conversely, Professor White concedes that the C.E.R.D.S. is regarded by a large majority of members of the United Nations as a codification and progressive development of legal norms for the development of international relations on a just and equitable basis.[117]

At the other pole, one might place the views of Judge Alvarez, who took the position that United Nations resolutions practically have the force of law. In his dissenting statement in 1951 in the Advisory Opinion on Reservations to the Convention on the Prevention and Punishment of the Crime of Genocide,[118] he said that resolutions 'have not yet acquired a binding character, but they may acquire it if they receive the support of public opinion'. He added that public opinion had on a number of occasions condemned violations of United Nations resolutions 'with more force than if it had been a mere breach of a convention of minor importance'. His conclusion is that 'the Assembly of the United Nations is tending to become an actual legislative power'.[119]

Between the two extremes of Brierly and Alvarez there are several writers who take a middle position, suggesting that resolutions of the United Nations General Assembly may be legislative or quasi-legislative.[120]

It seems that the C.E.R.D.S. has no binding force, unlike a treaty. This conclusion finds support in Article 38 of the Statute of the International Court of Justice which does not enlist resolutions of the General Assembly as sources of International Law to be applied. The Charter itself has not referred to international law. Despite its wordings and heading it cannot be characterized as a convention as it was not adopted unanimously. The developed countries voted against or abstained on the Charter as a whole and a number of its provisions, especially Article 2. As a matter of fact, during the early stages of negotiations, the developing countries were in favour of a treaty. Morocco and Zaire suggested the form of a 'convention' or a 'convenant'.[121] While the developed countries opposed the idea of treaty,[122] they suggested that the C.E.R.D.S. should be a declaration. Peter D. Maynard thought that the apparent rejection of the treaty option put the question of the legal nature of the final document in greater uncertainty.[123]

There are probably some publicists who would concede that the Charter, as adopted, is legally binding upon States. Thus, the delegate from Argentina said during the plenary session of the United Nations General Assembly that the C.E.R.D.S. is 'an instrument of economic international law'.[124] But this would probably be a minority point of view. Whatever may be the legal nature of the

C.E.R.D.S. at present, it would be unrealistic to ignore the current move towards a new international economic order which necessitates the revision of many of the traditional international law rules on foreign investment. And the Charter can be considered as one of the main pointers towards that objective. To say that the Charter has no legal force does not mean that it is devoid of legal significance. As it is adopted by an overwhelming majority of States it could be evidence of potential customary international law of the near future. The fact that the six developed countries have entered reservations to some provisions of the Charter underlies their fear that it might engender customary norms through the practice of States and repeated reference by international organizations, especially the General Assembly of the United Nations, which has referred to the Charter in its recent resolutions on the New International Economic Order since 1975. Furthermore, incorporating the provisions of the C.E.R.D.S. in the national laws of many countries, especially confining the settlement of disputes to domestic tribunals, may indirectly place the C.E.R.D.S. as a source of international law under the guise of general principles recognized by civilized nations, as accommodated in Article 38 of the Charter of the United Nations. This issue of settling investment disputes under the local jurisdiction has its relevance in the Sudanese and Saudi laws, which will be discussed in chapter 10.

(ii) *The principle of permanent sovereignty over natural resources*

This principle is an excellent example of conflict of interests between the capital-exporting and capital-importing countries.[125] On the one hand, the capital-exporting countries seek guarantees against arbitrary conduct on the part of host countries with respect to foreign investors and foreign investments; on the other hand, the capital-importing countries seek to conduct independent economic policies in accordance with their national objectives.

One result has been the preparation of ample studies,[126] and the elaboration of various formulations of the principle of permanent sovereignty over the natural resources over the last two decades. Since 1952, when the Chilean delegate first introduced the notion of 'permanent sovereignty over natural resources' into the debate on the Human Rights Covenant,[127] economic dependence has become a major theme of the principle of permanent sovereignty. Article 25 of the Covenants on Economic, Social and Cultural Rights, 1966, states that there is 'an inherent right of all peoples to enjoy and utilize fully and freely their natural wealth and resources'.[128]

The principle of permanent sovereignty over natural resources has been recognized in many resolutions of the United Nations which set out the criteria for its exercise. These resolutions have at times received the support of both developed and developing countries.

The basic themes of the principle of permanent sovereignty over natural resources are self-determination and political independence. These have become remarkably prominent as the result of the emergence of a great number of developing countries from colonialism.

While a balanced formulation of the principle of permanent sovereignty was approved unanimously in resolution 1803 (XVII), 1962,[129] Article 2 of the Charter of Economic Rights and Duties of States has perhaps carried the situation too far.[130] Article 2, on permanent sovereignty over natural resources and its various aspects, is probably the most controversial article. Its wording suggests a multiplicity of potential economic and legal dimensions, varying from codes of conduct for transnational corporations to the applicability of the 'Calvo Clause',[131] from the precise enunciation of the principle of permanent sovereignty, to the effect of political risk upon flows of private investment to developing countries.

Two issues must in particular be discussed in connection with Article 2. First, the text asserts that a State has the right of permanent sovereignty not only over its 'natural resources' but also over its 'wealth' and 'economic activities'. The term 'economic activities' is of relatively recent origin in the context of permanent sovereignty resolutions. Neither of these terms, 'wealth' or 'economic activities', has been defined by a pertinent international legal instrument. This uncertainty opens the door for wide interpretations, such as to include economic activities which are outside the territorial jurisdiction of a State, and this is possibly incompatible with the traditional rules of international law. In so far as this line of interpretation is feasible it can be argued that the C.E.R.D.S. does in fact create a novelty and one that lies awkwardly in the C.E.R.D.S. itself. For, as Peter D. Maynard[132] observed:

> if, for example, these terms indicate that the jurisdiction of a State over its 'wealth' and 'economic activities' may be exercised extra-territorially there is an apparent self-contradiction in relation to the concept of exclusive jurisdiction within a State's own territory as enunciated in paragraph 2(a).

Another issue concerning Article 2 of the C.E.R.D.S. is that paragraph 2(c) includes the words 'transfer of ownership'. The wording permits a transfer of ownership to be carried out by the State in such a way that the property in question passes from one private individual to another, and not from the private sector to the public sector, as might happen in the case of a nationalization. This raises a question, *inter alia*, whether a transfer of ownership is for a public purpose (see *ante*, pp. 97–8), or whether it is a case of unjust enrichment.

(iii) *Treatment of foreign investment and diplomatic protection*

The second sentence of paragraph 2(a) of Article 2 of the charter asserts:

No State shall be compelled to grant preferential treatment to foreign investment.

The view of developing countries is that the principle of sovereign equality is incompatible with the requirement of preferential treatment for aliens. Thus, according to this formulation, States may grant preferential treatment at their discretion, but are not compelled to do so.

Undoubtedly, this view is ultimately incompatible with the international rule that requires the application of a minimum standard of treatment of aliens and their property. Accordingly, the formulation of Article 2(2)(a) of the Charter appears to deprive a foreign investor of an important part of that diplomatic protection by the State of his nationality, which traditional international law permitted.

(iv) *Regulation and supervision of activities of transnational corporations: International Code of Conduct*

(1) *Origin*

The Declaration on the Establishment of a New International Economic Order and its accompanying Programme of Action both reasserted the right of every State to control and supervise the activities of transnational corporations within its territory.[133] However, neither the Declaration nor the Programme of Action treated this issue in specific terms. The latter stated that all efforts should be made to formulate, adopt and implement international regulations. Five of the elements within which the Code would deal were listed as follows:

(a) to prevent interference in the internal affairs of the countries where they operate and their collaboration with racist regimes and colonial administrations;
(b) to regulate their activities in host countries, to eliminate restrictive business practices and to conform to the national development plans and objectives of developing countries, and in this context facilitate, as necessary, the review and revision of previously concluded arrangements;
(c) to bring about assistance, transfer of technology and management skills to developing countries on equitable and favourable terms;
(d) to regulate the repatriation of profits accruing from their operations, taking into account the legitimate interest of all parties concerned;
(e) to promote reinvestment of their profits in developing countries.

Similarly, Article 2(2)(b) of the Charter of Economic Rights and Duties of States has reasserted in general terms the right of each State to regulate and supervise the activities of transnational corporations within its national jurisdiction and to take measures to ensure that such activities comply with its laws, rules and regulations and conform with its economic and social policies. Furthermore, 'transnational corporations shall not intervene in the internal affairs of a host State'. As depicted above, the developed countries opposed this Article because the absence of direct reference to 'international obligations' could admit the possibility of transnational corporations being discriminated against.[134]

It is believed that the above instruments sufficiently established the parameters within which the codes of conduct regulating the activities of transnational corporations could be achieved by the United Nations Commission[135] on Transnational Corporations and other organizations[136] embarking on the same task.

(2) *Need for the Code*

Discussions on the nature, role, operations and strategies of transnational corporations have revolved around two main themes. On the one hand, it has been stressed that transnational corporations have the requisite economic power and resources to act as effective instruments of development, particularly in developing countries. On the other hand, the pervasive role attributed to transnational corporations in the world and the disclosure of certain instances of corporate misconduct have engendered a grave concern about the impact of these corporations on economic development and political and social affairs, both at the national and international level. The various international and regional efforts towards the promulgation of a multilateral code for the regulation of the activities of the transnational corporations stem from this concern about the negative aspects of the operations of these corporations, as well as the recognition that national regulation and control is evidently inadequate to deal effectively with the vast global strategies of transnational corporations. Thus under the Sudanese Companies Act, only public companies are required to file balance sheets, and profit and loss accounts. And even this is hardly ever complied with. The Registrar of Companies does not penetrate the accounts. So there is lack of supervision by anyone. Also there is no restriction on a non-Sudanese being a director of a company. Such a director may be non-resident, and this entails cash remuneration, flight tickets, hotel and other similar expenses.

Another area of absence of control over transnational corporations under the Sudanese company law is the use of capital. Some companies bring a small amount of capital to the Sudan, then borrow from the local banks sums beyond the paid-up capital; and sometimes they mortgage the uncalled capital instead of calling it up.[137]

As to tax evasion, companies in the Sudan pay tax-free salaries to employees and directors, and then pay tax on these salaries and charge it to deductable expenditure of the company before tax. This results in loss of revenue to the State.

Though the Sudanese Government is trying to control transnational corporations by structuring the investment pattern in joint ventures, in which the State acquires majority shareholding, this is not an effective device, and it is a fallacy to assume that this majority shareholding in the private sector confers control of the enterprise upon the Sudanese. According to Professor K. Vasdev, transnationals usually succeed in controlling the investment enterprise through the mechanism of:

(a) entrenchment of the office of the directors;
(b) management agreements;
(c) restriction on transferability of shares.

Transnationals usually operate abroad through affiliates and subsidiaries. It appears from the writer's experience in the Technical Committee for Revising the Confiscation Measures, that such corporate arrangements involve over-invoicing of raw materials, tools, machinery and spare parts. This observation is also relevant to the appropriateness of technology to be furnished by transnationals to developing countries. Sometimes a second-hand painted machine is presented as new. The case of the Port Sudan–Khartoum pipeline is a clear example, which had been of public concern. In fact this case can be considered as a glaring example of how far the developing countries are at the mercy of transnational corporations in the search for technology, because these countries lack the expertise to test the appropriateness of the furnished technology. This negative aspect of transnationals was brought into the limelight in the deliberations of the U.N. training course on Regulating and Negotiating with Transnational Corporations, which was mentioned before. In this course, the issue of regulating the transfer of technology was concentrated upon, and the U.N.I.D.O. Draft International Code of Conduct on the Transfer of Technology of 1979 was critically evaluated.[138]

However, there are a very few provisions in Sudanese Company law which offer some control over companies, though inadequate. Under section 97 of the Companies Ordinance 1925, the failure of the company to file with the Registrar verified copies of contracts for allotment of shares for consideration otherwise than in cash, in exchange for services or property, will expose the company to a penalty of £S50 per day. But this is a dead provision which, due to no reason other than mere apathy, has never been invoked. Companies have been running for years with non-compliance of this provision. Another indirect control is found in section 19 which provides that, subject to the approval of the President of the Republic, the Minister of Finance and National Economy may, if he is of the opinion that it is not in the public interest that any company shall continue to carry on business in the Sudan, direct the Registrar to cancel the registration of such a company. This jurisdiction has been transferred recently to the Attorney-

General. Upon receiving such direction the Registrar shall forthwith make a cancellation order which shall operate and have effect as if it were a winding-up order made by the court in accordance with the provisions of the same legislation.

Under parts XII and XIII of the Saudi Companies Regulation there are some elements of control over foreign companies in terms of subjecting their activities to the Saudi laws and there are vigorous punishments for violation of the regulation.[139]

Generally, developing countries fear that transnational corporations may have become too dominating and too diffuse to be governed effectively by any single nation. They see themselves as relatively powerless against transnational corporations both in negotiating with them and in enforcing their national laws and regulations. Obtaining information about the practice of these corporations, for example, appears difficult for the developing countries when the headquarters and major officers of the company are elsewhere.[140]

(3) *Practical problems*

Transnational corporations strongly attack the Charter of Economic Rights and Duties of States as it emphasizes the sovereign right of the host countries to fetter these corporations' activities and denies them the right of diplomatic protection by their home States.[141] They also resent any idea of formulating codes of conduct which restrict their practices. For this reason, it was alleged that they have become less enthusiastic to invest in countries which have tightened control on their corporate practices and relocate in other countries that take a more benign view of their practices.[142] Nevertheless, this contention was partly refuted by the Mexican Ambassador, Alfonso Garcia Robles, in the following words:

> As you may know, Mexico is the only Latin American country which has never accepted the so-called guarantee agreement and it maintains in its Constitution the so-called *Calvo* clause. Why, then, are so many transnational corporations and private investors interested in investing in Mexico? Perhaps because those profits can be freely taken out of the country; perhaps it is because the country has political stability.[143]

(4) *Legal nature and contents of the Code*

The Inter-governmental Working Group established by the United Nations Commission on Transnational Corporations to draft a code of conduct relating to transnational corporations has now reached an advanced stage. Its discussions centred around a working paper[144] prepared by the United Nations Centre on Transnational Corporations, embodying, for purposes of discussion only, broad, tentative 'common elements' of the position which the Group might adopt on the substantive provisions of the Code. The working paper marked a new phase towards consensus on major issues between the developed and developing countries. But still, some controversial issues remain to be resolved, especially on nationalization; compensation; jurisdiction; diplomatic protection; reference to international law as regards the standard of treatment to be accorded to multinational corporations; the issue of definition of multinational enterprise of Eastern Europe; and finally the issue of implementation at the international level. But in the last analysis, the first part of the fourth session of the Commission on Transnational Corporations which started in March, 1978 showed that the stalemate presented by Article 2 of the Charter of Economic Rights and Duties of States and the first session[145] of the Commission might be overcome in the near future. Some of the major issues which have emerged during the deliberations of the Group are summarized below.

Conduct to be affected by the Code

A basic issue that emerged during the early stages of the Working Group's deliberations was whether the code of conduct should be addressed exclusively to transnational corporations or whether it should encompass the treatment of transnational corporations by Governments. The developing countries at first insisted that the only issue before the Working Group was the regulation of the conduct of the transnational corporations and that the conduct of Governments was outside the purview of the code.[146] This position was strongly resisted by the developed countries, which ultimately succeeded in including the treatment of transnational corporations by Governments within the orbit of the proposed code. Thus, as at present structured, the Code consists of two parts: part A, which deals with the regulation of transnational corporations and part B which prescribes standards to be observed by governments in relation to transnational corporations.[147]

Legal nature and form of the Code

Preliminary discussions on the nature and form of the Code have focused on several alternatives, viz. whether the code be binding, voluntary, or binding in part and voluntary in part, or an international agreement or convention which is binding on states party to it, but contains a voluntary code of conduct for transnational corporations. The Working Group has prudently deferred consideration of these issues as well as the modalities for the implementation of the code till agreement is reached on the substantive provisions of the Code.[148] However, the general assumption is that the Code will be voluntary. The adoption of even a voluntary code will have a substantial impact on the parties concerned. For host Governments it may serve as a model for national legislation,[149] which may require transnational corporations operating in their territory to state that they will adhere to the principles and specific provisions included in the Code. Furthermore, specific provisions of the Code, regarding disclosure of information to the public or trade unions, may prove difficult for transnationals to ignore. For the corporations, a voluntary code will have the practical effect of moral persuasion. Thus, reporting of restrictive trade practices or illicit payments by accountants may be embarrassing for multinational corporations.[150]

Substantive provisions of the Code

Apart from the standards regarding nationalization and compensation, there has almost been agreement on 'common elements', which more or less reflected what has been initially asserted in the developing countries' 'areas of concern' submitted in the first session of the Commission, and hence this marks a tremendous victory for these countries. Thus, the formulations tentatively agreed upon covered all aspects of activities of transnational corporations: non-political interference in the affairs of the countries in which they operate; economic, social and cultural contribution to development of these countries; submission to local laws and jurisdiction; respect of sovereignty; ownership and control; balance-of-payments; taxation; disclosure of information, etc.[151] In return, the proposed code prescribes that transnational corporations should be treated by their host countries in a fair and equitable manner consistent with the interests of all concerned and in accordance with national regulations and administrative practices, as well as *international* norms and contractual obligations which have freely been assumed. Non-discriminatory treatment is to be assured by the prescription that, subject to the requirements of public order and national security, transnational corporations should be accorded national treatment, in situations where their operations are comparable to those of domestic enterprises. This formulation, however, allows for according transnational corporations special treatment if there are no comparable domestic enterprises. Taken as a whole, the latter proposed prescription is a deviation from what Article 2(2)(b) of the Charter of Economic Rights and Duties of States envisages: confining the standard of treatment to the national law only. This is a step forward which might persuade the developed countries to support the code in some way.

If these tentative formulations are agreed upon in an international agreement or convention, then a new era will emerge which would eliminate many uncertainties and create modern international norms which would indirectly give legal impetus to the Charter of Economic Rights and Duties of States and other resolutions of the General Assembly of the United Nations on the New International Economic Order; as mentioned before, these resolutions have been given 'due respect' by the Commission as the broad skeleton for the Code.

(v) *The aftermath of the Charter of Economics Rights and Duties of States*

It is questionable whether Article 2 of the Charter of Economic Rights and Duties of States can be considered a contemporary authoritative expression of the international law regarding the status of foreign investment. The value of Article 2 is diminished by the fact that a reconciliation between the positions of developing and developed countries was not achieved, particularly on paragraphs 2(a) and 2 (c).

Though the Charter is not considered as having any binding force by the developed countries, especially the United States,[152] yet it has a considerable political and moral importance. The Charter, together with the Declaration and Programme of Action of the Sixth Special Session of the General Assembly of the United Nations, has been called 'the new foundations of the new international economic order'.[153]

The moral impetus of the Charter calls for a wide variety of measures in favour of the developing countries. Thus, it should, perhaps, be seen in the context of a long-term process of consensus -- creation. In the end, the Charter can be described as a new movement of the developing countries to take on their active role in the evolution of new international norms, just as they have demonstrated their discontent with the traditional rules of international law in this matter. This new move has met resistance in the developed countries. From a practical point of view, they repeatedly and publicly refused to consider the Charter as having any legal force. Accordingly, they tend to lessen its potential effects by bilateral treaties with the developing countries in which they produce the traditional rules.

But one may ask why the developing countries, though firmly asserting the binding force of the Charter, do actually follow such a paradoxical approach in entering into these bilateral treaties? The reasons for this pragmatic approach are obvious. Obviously, the chief motive for developing countries to enter into these treaties is to enhance their international reputation and credit-worthiness and, thus, to attract foreign capital. In many cases, however, more specific reasons have a bearing. Leaving aside the economic considerations peculiar to the relationship between the two contracting states, which might have been a contributory factor in some treaties, there are often considerations of a political nature. The application of a national investment guarantee programme, as will be shown in the next chapter, or the granting of special aid or technical assistance to a developing country might, for instance, be dependent upon the existence of a bilateral treaty containing suitable provisions on the treatment of property of nationals of the other contracting party. Developing countries which expect to make investments in the territory of the contracting partner may see practical advantages in the condition of reciprocity. This may in particular apply to investments of oil-exporting countries in industrial countries; they may also regard bilateral treaties as providing a useful pattern for similar countries in a regional context or otherwise.[154] This finds support in treaties concluded by the Sudan with some Arab countries.[155]

Conversely, the principal reason for the developed countries to see the conclusion of these treaties seems to be the desire to obtain greater security for the investments of their nationals made in the territory of the other contracting party. The respect that these treaties are receiving is apparent from a fairly recent large-scale measure of expropriation from which foreign enterprises protected by relevant treaties appear to have been deliberately excluded.[156]

One may hope that by a pragmatic approach and repeated reference, the gap between the developed and developing countries can be bridged. This would give the Charter a potential influence for the evolution of new norms consistent with the issues raised by the developing countries towards a New International Economic Order which would accommodate the interests of all.

In view of the above, it is hardly possible to imagine the conclusion of a convention on foreign investment. Any draft would not receive the unanimous support of all countries as long as the contention between the developing and developed world is basically unresolved.

5. Nature and effect of treaty obligation

(a) Under international law

Treaties are instruments of public international law which are binding on States party to them. The general rule of customary international law is that a State is bound to carry out in good faith the obligations which it has assumed by a treaty (*pacta sunt servanda*).[157] This rule is firmly established and recognized by all authorities. There is no case in which any tribunal ever repudiated this rule or questioned its validity. And it has been authoritatively stated in Article 26 of the Vienna Convention on the Law of Treaties, 1969.

The legal impact of the norm *pacta sunt servanda* in relation to protection of foreign investment is that, if a State undertakes in a treaty to respect and protect foreign investment within its territory, the obligation must be respected and performed. As treaties form an essential source of international law, any breach of a treaty obligation will eventually amount to an international delinquency. The international responsibility emanating from breach of treaty obligations to respect and protect foreign private property is well established by decided cases and a great body of legal literature.[158] Treaty promises concerning matters of investment are not exceptional.

As regards expropriation in violation of treaty promises, the well-settled general rule is that the act itself is unlawful and entails an international tortious liability. This rule is applicable regardless of the validity of the act of expropriation in municipal law, the existence or absence of public purpose and even the payment or non-payment of adequate compensation.[159] The rule in this area has been plainly stated by the Permanent Court of International Justice in the much discussed case of the *Chorzow Factory* (Indemnity).[160] After the First World War, there were some changes in the boundary between Germany and Poland. The two countries concluded the Geneva Convention of 1922 to regulate private property in Upper Silesia. Under the Convention each party undertook to respect private property in their respective portions. Article 6 of the Convention prohibited the liquidation in Polish Upper Silesia of the property rights and interests of German nationals and companies. Poland introduced a law which deprived some German nationals of their property in Polish Upper Silesia. In its previous judgment on the same case the Permanent Court held that the Polish law was incompatible with the Convention.[161] The Court observed that:

> It is a principle of international law that the breach of an engagement involves an obligation to make reparation in an adequate form. Reparation therefore is the indispensable complement of a failure to apply a convention and there is no necessity for this to be stated in the convention itself.[162]

The difficulties over treaties do not usually lie, however, in the determination of their legal effect in the abstract, but in determining whether a particular violation has or has not occurred. Much depends on the language used and the conduct and intention of the parties to the treaty in each particular case. Characterization of the instrument may also give rise to the dispute, raising the question whether or not a treaty obligation has actually been created.[163]

Some writers regard treaties as unnecessary for the protection of foreign investments.[164] This view rests on the thesis that the rights and obligations created in treaties are subject to international customary law which contains elaborate rules for the protection of private property situated abroad. It is true that treaty provisions dealt with so far in the present study did not create new rules in international law, particularly on expropriation, nor established a special rule constituting an exception to the existing general rules. They just gave conventional validity to the customary rules whose validity has continuously been questioned. Nevertheless, treaties are useful devices in providing international standards for judging the lawfulness or unlawfulness of an expropriation. The implication of this advantage makes it legitimate for the State whose national's property has been expropriated to intervene diplomatically even before formal exhaustion of local remedies. This usually happens when the municipal law to be applied by the local tribunals falls short of the standards established by the treaty. If the treatment accorded to foreign investors is more favourable than the minimum standards stipulated in the treaties, then the expropriating State ought to extend such treatment to foreign investors as well, by virtue of its promise to grant national treatment. On the other hand, if the national treatment falls short of the treatment prescribed in the treaty, then the treaty treatment applies. The effect of a treaty in this respect is that a State will be under a conventional obligation towards foreign investors which is completely distinct from its obligation under customary international law not to discriminate against them.

The legal effect and importance of treaty promises in protecting foreign investment is best recognized in the case of exchange control and other restrictions. This is because in these areas no customary legal rule pre-exists, and, in its absence, exchange control measures are inevitably permitted. Treaty promises lift exchange restrictions, though in various degrees and extent. Additionally, exchange restrictions and other fiscal measures, if they are to be imposed, ought to conform to certain standards in order to be permitted under the treaties.[165]

Furthermore, treaties usually contain valuable provisions on the intricate problem of the settlement of investment disputes, if diplomatic intervention proves to be unsatisfactory in any particular instance. It will be seen in chapter 10 how far bilateral treaties, such as the German and Swiss treaties concluded by the Sudan, will effectively contribute in solving investment disputes.

(b) Under municipal law

Foreign investors may invoke treaty provisions before municipal courts or administrative organs against any administrative act which contravenes the treaty. But the value of this course depends on the status of the particular treaty in the municipal law of the Sudan. This eventually is associated with the constitutional system, the administration of justice, as well as the relation between municipal and international law in the investee State.

To start with, the prevailing view in the Anglo-American jurisprudence is that customary international law is part of the 'law of the land'.[166] As regards treaties, the generally accepted view in English law is that treaties affecting private rights which are required to be enforced by English courts must require Parliament to enact the necessary legislation, or to vote the funds. This is usually implemented by an enabling Act of Parliament which gives the treaty the status of a statute.[167] To that extent, binding treaties which are instruments of international law do not form part of 'the law of the land' unless expressly made so by the legislature.

The regulation of the relation between international and Sudanese municipal law is omitted altogether from the constitution. Notwithstanding this omission, the Sudanese courts, having accepted the inheritance of English common law, seem to have applied the English common law doctrine that international law is part of the law of the land, in the absence of a repugnant legislative provision. Thus, recently, the Supreme Court applied the international law rules on diplomatic immunity in the case of *S.G.* v. *Gamaat Ilool-el-Aswad.*[168] In this case, some Palestinians forcibly occupied the Saudi Arabian Embassy at Khartoum and murdered three diplomats, including the American ambassador to the Democratic Republic of the Sudan. The issue was whether the Sudanese courts had jurisdiction to try the surrendering offenders for the crimes they committed in a foreign embassy situated in the territory of the Sudan. The district court's decision, which was rightly upheld by the Supreme Court, was that it had jurisdiction on the particular facts of the case.

A case more direct in point is *Juba-Omdurman Bank* v. *Bessi International And Another.*[169] In this case the Khartoum Province Court applied the international law rule that a nationalization law should not apply extraterritorially.

As regards the status of treaties in the municipal law of the Sudan, if they contradict a later statute, the situation is very obscure. The question has never arisen before the Sudanese courts. In the opinion of one scholar,[170] 'local courts would afford a little protection to foreign investments in the case of legislative action in violation of the treaty promises. The prevailing view in the courts of most States is that a later treaty prevails over an earlier statute.'[171] This rule is actually applied with caution. The practical view supported by classical international lawyers is that the courts generally recognize a presumption in favour of the continuing validity of the treaty and may require direct and clear statutory language in order to admit the treaty's invalidation.[172]

Article 103 of the Permanent Constitution of the Sudan provides as follows:

> The President of the Republic concludes and ratifies treaties; he communicates them to the People's Assembly, together with any relevant information. Upon ratification by the President the treaties shall come into force. *Peace treaties, alliance treaties,* and *all treaties concerning change of boundaries* or *pertaining to sovereignty or affecting the Regime or imposing new obligations on the State or requiring an expenditure not provided for in the budget or requiring legislative amendment* or affecting the *civil rights of individuals,* shall not come into force until ratified by the People's Assembly. (My italics.)

Of direct relevance to this Article is the decision by the Italian Court of Cassation in *De Marco* v. *Warenhandelsgesellschaft*[173] which reads in part as follows:

> Once an international treaty has been approved in the ways laid down by the fundamental law of the State, it *has the force of law* and may be invoked by private persons independently of any provision of the government, with the exception only of those parts which by their nature or by the express provisions of the Treaty need some such provision in order to be enforceable. (My italics.)

Accordingly, Article 103 can be interpreted as meaning the following:

There are certain treaties which can be enforced without the ratification of the People's Assembly. But the question is: are these treaties to be considered as laws? The answer must be in the negative for two reasons. In the first place, according to Article 102 of the Constitution, the legislative function is exercised by the People's Assembly and the President jointly. The Procedure for enacting the ordinary law, is that a bill passed by the People's Assembly is to become law from the date of the signature of the President.[174] In the case of treaties that require the approval of the Assembly, the procedure is reversed. Secondly, if at any time the Assembly is not at session or in cases of urgency, the President may issue Provisional Republican Orders having the force of Law. But they must be submitted to the Assembly within fifteen days from the date of issue if the Assembly is at session, or at first meeting in case of dissolution, or propagation or end of session. If such provisional orders are not submitted as prescribed or are submitted but not passed by the Assembly, they must be invalidated without retrospective effect.[175]

In the light of the above interpretation, it may be concluded that treaties which are to be concluded by Republican orders without the ratification of the Assembly, theoretically have no legal force as laws before the Sudanese courts. They need enabling legislation for their enforcement. But, in practice, though the issue has not been entertained by the courts, it is inconceivable that the Sudanese Courts would refuse to apply a treaty ratified by a Republican order only, if there is no express legislative provision to the contrary. Republican orders, though not laws, have in effect the force of law. This may be a convenient way to interpret the phrase 'come into force'. Undoubtedly, those treaties which are to be ratified only by the President will produce international obligations regardless of their status as laws in the municipal law of the Sudan. But the difficulty is how to delimit the application of this categorization. In the end, the matter will depend on the nature of the treaty in each case.

It can safely be asserted that investment protection treaties, like the German and Swiss treaties discussed above, fall within the categories enlisted by Article 103 of the Constitution which require for their enforcement the ratification of the People's Assembly. This interpretation is justifiable because the investment treaties impose new obligations on the State to conform to certain standards of treatment and protection against non-commercial risks. They also affect the budget by granting tax exemptions and according guarantees to remit profits and repatriate capital abroad. By so doing, they indirectly require an expenditure not provided for in the budget, especially the foreign exchange budget. They may also require legislative amendments in specific laws such as the customs, immigration and land laws. Consequently, it is right to conclude that investment treaties should be ratified by both the President and the People's Assembly, which virtually is the current practice. Such treaties will eventually have legal force like any other statutes. In fact, it had been the practice since independence in 1956, apart from the existing practice, that all treaties had to be approved by the legislature through an enabling Act of Parliament.

As noted before, investment treaties differ in varying degrees from the investment laws, especially in scope of protection and guarantees to foreign investment. What then will be the situation if a treaty provision contradicts an earlier statute or vice versa? Which is to prevail, the treaty or the law? As investment treaties are considered as part of the municipal law of the Sudan, the answer to this question is very simple. The issue will be only of interpretation and construction. The interpretation of Laws and General Clauses Act, (revised and re-enacted), 1974,[176] introduced general principles of construction. Under section 6:

(1) The provisions of any law shall be construed in such manner as to achieve the purpose for which it has been enacted and in all cases the construction which achieves such purpose shall be preferred to any other construction.
(2) If any provision in any law is inconsistent with any provision of the Constitution such provision of the Constitution shall prevail to the extent of such inconsistency.
(3) The provisions of a subsequent law shall prevail over the provisions of a preceding law to the extent of any inconsistency.
(4) Any special law or any special provision in any law in respect of any matter shall be deemed to be an exception to any general law or general provision in any law governing such matter.

From the above, it is theoretically right to say that the status of treaties in the municipal law of the Sudan is the same as that of the American view: where a treaty and an act of Congress are wholly inconsistent with each other, and the two cannot be reconciled, the one later in point of time must prevail.[177]

In Saudi Arabia, the conclusion of investment treaties, as mentioned before, is not frequent, except on rare occasions on a multilateral basis, such as the Convention on the Settlement of Investment Disputes between States and Nationals of Other States which was ratified by a royal decree. There is also the Investment Guarantee Agreement with U.S.A. These treaties will be discussed later in chapter 10 and the next chapter. But what is important here is the status of these and similar treaties which might be concluded or ratified by the Government of Saudi Arabia. From a general point of view, it is well recognized in Islamic law that a treaty concluded by the Moslem ruler must be respected. This rule was established by the Prophet in the early days of Islam[178] The question is: what will be the attitude of the Saudi courts and the Grievances Board if a treaty contravenes a later statute? As the legislation in Saudi Arabia is promulgated by means of royal decrees, and also ratification of treaties, it seems likely that the Saudi courts would follow the American and the Sudanese practice: the latest decree must prevail, despite the absence of an express provision on the point.

As the bilateral investment treaties concluded by the Sudan with Germany and the Swiss Confederation were ratified before the three investment laws, the latter are to prevail over the former, as there is some contradiction between the two in basic issues relating to foreign investment. So far, there is no case where the issue has been raised, and for this reason the present discussion is hypothetical.

It is to be conceded that the intention of the legislature in promulgating the Sudanese investment laws is to improve the investment climate by furnishing incentives and guarantees to foreign investors. To give this policy an effective legal sanctity, it is necessary to promise foreign investors that rights acquired under separate previous treaties are to be respected and protected, otherwise, foreign investors will have a shaky confidence in the application and continuity of the investment laws themselves. Accordingly, the better view is to regard the legislative and treaty provisions on foreign investment as complementing each other. Thus, German and Swiss investors who decided to invest their capital in the Sudan have to comply with the investment legislative provisions on screening, establishment and all the required provisions, administrative or legal, for setting up their investment enterprises. On the other hand, they are to enjoy the standard of treatment and the other guarantees accorded by the treaties, as long as they have not been expressly declared to be inoperative by the investment laws. Such an interpretation will inevitably give effect to the intention of the legislature to encourage and protect foreign investment in the Sudan.

If a later treaty is inconsistent with any of the investment laws, this will present no difficulty at all, as the general rules of construction will apply to uphold the treaty in preference to the law. The intention of the legislature in this latter case is taken to supersede or modify the investment laws so as to accord certain foreign investors a special legal regime by the treaty.

Functionally, treaties have little effect in furnishing protection to foreign investment before local courts, unless they have the force of law.[179] Their effectiveness would depend on the nature of the question involved. Thus, they may be effective in the cases of tax measures and exchange control. In the first situation, usually the tasks of tax assessment and imposition are often entrusted to junior officials who are subject to judicial or hierarchical control. It is believed that local courts would examine the formal validity of the acts involved, but not their necessity or advisability.

(c) Effect of municipal law on treaty obligations under international law

The general rule of customary international law is that a treaty subsists as an international obligation although it may not be enforceable by the municipal courts or administrative authorities. A State cannot plead the provisions of its constitution or legislation as a ground for non-observance of its international obligations. Judicial decisions, State practice and the opinion of jurists leave not the slightest doubt on this rule. The Permanent Court of International Justice confirmed it as of the corner-stones of jurisprudence in its judgment in the case of *Wimbledon*,[180] where the Court observed that:

> neutrality orders, issued by an individual State could not prevail over the provisions of the Treaty of Peace.[181]

This principle was subsequently reaffirmed by the Court on several occasions. The most explicit formulation includes the following:

> It is a generally accepted principle of international law that in the relations between powers who are contracting parties to a treaty, the provisions of municipal law cannot prevail over those of the treaty.[182]

The same view has been recognized in the jurisprudence of the International Court of Justice in many decisions.[183]

The principle was also acknowledged in arbitral awards[184] as well as the practice of States,[185] and by distinguished writers.[186] More recently, at the thirteenth plenary session of the United Nations Conference on the Law of Treaties, 1968 the following clause was agreed, which became Article 27 of the Vienna Convention on the Law of Treaties, 1969:

> A party may not invoke the provisions of its internal law as justification for its failure to perform a treaty.[187]

Accordingly, the Sudan and Saudi Arabia, cannot plead their municipal laws before an international tribunal to justify the breach of a treaty provision. In order to avoid such a contingency, it seems that the better solution would be, before introducing any legislation, to take into account the existing international obligations emanating from treaties.[188]

6. Conclusions

Being instruments of international law, bilateral treaties provide the most effective devices for the protection of foreign private investment. Unlike resolutions of the United Nations General Assembly, they are binding in international law on States party to them. More importantly, 'the spreading network of these agreements concluded in similar terms assists in strengthening international law, in improving the standard of international morality, and in reducing potential friction'.[189] It is true that the protection under bilateral treaties is not directly addressed to foreign investors like the investment laws and development agreements. This is because of the nature of treaties which are international instruments between States only. This very unique nature of treaties adds to their legal force and sanctity. States must observe treaty obligations in good faith (*pacta sunt servanda*).

The effect of treaties in assuring legal protection to foreign investment before municipal courts cannot be determined in the abstract. The issue depends on the constitutional law of each particular country. There is a great divergence of States' practice in this respect. Though there is no express provision as to the exact status of treaty in the Sudanese municipal law, yet it would seem that the Anglo-American doctrine of considering customary international law as part of the law of the land is recognized by the Sudanese courts. The practice and the law conceded that treaties are usually ratified by special ratification acts, and by virtue of this, they are statutes. The status of each particular treaty in relation to any law depends on its date of ratification. If it contradicts a certain statute, the later in point of time prevails. This rule may also be applicable in Saudi Arabia. As regards the bilateral investment protection treaties so far concluded by the Sudan, it is clear that some of them were concluded and ratified before the Sudanese investment laws, and, eventually, the latter prevail over the former in case of conflict. Till now, there is no case where a conflict is reported to have arisen. This is due to the willingness of President Nimeiri's Government to extend to foreign investment the application of the present legislative provisions in order to encourage foreign investment, as long as this does not cause a breach of international obligation arising from treaties. But this is not always guaranteed, as it depends on the policy of the government in power.

In order to create an effective international regime on the protection of foreign investment, it is advantageous to conclude a multilateral convention or an investment code. This investment code or convention must be declaratory of general principles and not containing detailed provisions. The details should be formalized in contracts between foreign investors and investee States. The convention must contain specific sanctions for its breach and regulate the whole issue on which States hold divergent views at present, i.e. standard of treatment, compensation etc. Sufficient room must be left for the increasing feature of joint ventures between the investee States or local nationals and investors of different nationalities, as well as transnational corporations. Under the proposed convention, foreign investors must be prepared to accept the obligation of contributing to the economic growth of developing countries which, in return, have to accord some protection to foreign investments in their territories. Though the developing countries may confine the whole arrangement pertaining to foreign investment within their municipal spheres, as is advocated in the Charter of Economic Rights and Duties of States, the compensation must be reasonable, and effectively paid within a reasonable time, taking into consideration the balance-of-payments of the investee State.

On the other hand, the investee State has to be assured of its sovereign right to control the activities of transnational corporations in its territories. These transnational corporations should refrain from all interference in the internal affairs of the investee state, and they should not be used as instruments of foreign policy of foreign countries.

Though the adoption of a multilateral convention on the protection of foreign private investment may be highly desirable in order to improve the investment climate and for that reason should attract the support of the Sudan and Saudi Arabia, yet the present situation of international relations hardly encourages further efforts towards that end. The issue needs a pragmatic approach and high diplomacy. Both the developed and developing countries hold extreme views on the basic issues relating to foreign investment. The Charter of Economic Rights and Duties of States presents the highest point of disagreement. However, this is a theoretical demonstration which does not conform to realities. Thus while the developing countries stuck firm to their position all through the negotiations which finally led to the adoption of the Charter, yet their subsequent practice is not consistent with its provisions, particularly on treatment of foreign investment and compensation. They do produce in their investment laws the traditional international law rules as developed and supported by the developed countries which reject the new norms propounded by the Charter. At the other end of the spectrum, the developed countries tend to emasculate or negate the effect of the Charter by bilateral arrangements with the developing countries which find themselves compelled to enter into such arrangements. An obvious explanation of this paradoxical approach is that the developing countries are in need of foreign capital to accelerate their economic growth. One may argue that this course might be rendered unnecessary in view of the accumulation of petrodollars in the hands of oil-producing countries (O.P.E.C.), especially the Arab countries. Such an argument assumes a particular concern for the Sudan. However, this argument cannot be sustained, because, as noted before, foreign capital is not enough for economic development. Of equal importance are expertise and technical know-how. These can only be supplied by the western developed countries.

Perhaps through the process of pragmatism, the Charter would give birth to new legal norms that would receive the support of both the developed and developing countries. Now that more than five years have elapsed since the Charter was adopted, some countries of the Group of 77,[190] notably Brazil and India, have been industrialized and accordingly their views on the Charter may have altered considerably. As the dialogue between the north and south is still continuing, a compromise might be reached, thus gearing the momentum towards agreement on certain rules which may provide a skeleton for an investment convention or code. Till that stage is reached, the protection of foreign investment has to be secured through the case-by-case method by bilateral treaties. The bilateral treaties concluded by the Sudan with other countries and such as that with West Germany and the Swiss Confederation present the most constructive and conducive demonstration.

The position of Saudi Arabia is awkward. On the one hand, it is one of the richest countries in the world in terms of wealth, and hence it is a capital-exporting country. Accordingly, from this standpoint the Charter does not appeal to it, as it leaves the security of Saudi investments abroad at stake due to the absence of the traditional formula on compensation in the Charter. On the other hand, Saudi Arabia is embarking on a huge development plan which calls for the diversification of the economy and industrialization. This necessitates the invitation of foreign technology and expertise to implement the plan. And actually the Saudi Government has succeeded in achieving this goal by booming its resources, a process which attracted foreign firms from different parts of the world. But the most important observation to make is that all these investing firms are obligated to adapt themselves to the local laws, a technique which is a clear application of Article 2 of the Charter of Economic Rights and Duties of States.

7
INVESTMENT INSURANCE PROGRAMMES

1. Purpose and scope

The concept of insuring foreign private investment against the political risks of expropriation, inconvertibility and war, revolution and insurrection has emerged as an answer to many relatively new problems. In the wake of the Charter of Economic Rights and Duties of States, there has been, to a large extent, an increasing departure from the traditional standards of international law. The Charter demonstrated a militant economic nationalism by the developing countries in asserting their sovereign right to confine the whole issue of foreign investment exclusively within their national laws. This reflected the sense of insecurity over foreign investment, and a lack of confidence in existing protection, whether economic or legal.[1] On the other hand there is an urgent need for flow of foreign capital across international boundaries to the developing countries.

For these reasons, the insurance of private investment abroad has become one of the principal contemporary instruments and techniques devised in response to the new challenge, i.e. how to provide adequate protection for investments in foreign countries. Furthermore, insurance offered some sort of protection to investors against what is often their principal worry, i.e. the political stability of the investee country.

The concept of investment insurance is still in its inception. In international law, it has not been extensively treated in recent legal literature; albeit several proposals have been put forward. This chapter is designed to consider some major aspects of this recent phenomenon of insuring investment abroad against non-commercial risks, particularly from the international-law point of view. Insurance of commercial risks, such as inflation and devaluation, falls outside the purview of this chapter.

Some developed countries have adopted national investment insurance schemes. The earliest of these schemes were those adopted by the United States, West Germany, Japan and recently the United Kingdom. The question is: do these national investment insurance schemes have any positive effect on the international investment climate so as to encourage and protect foreign investments in those areas which need much foreign capital?

This chapter will cover only those national and international investment insurance programmes applicable to the Sudan and Saudi Arabia, or which are likely to be so applicable; this includes particularly the investment insurance programmes sponsored by the United States and Germany. On the international plane, this study will consider only the Arab Guarantee scheme sponsored by the Inter-Arab Investment Corporation, and the Investment Insurance Programme proposed by the World Bank. To the extent that is relevant and permissible, reference will also be made to some proposals put forward by individuals and other international institutions.

The issues will be discussed in the following order: first, the discussion of certain issues raised by investment insurance under international law (section 2). Secondly, the national insurance programmes, and this covers only the American and the German programmes (section 3). Thirdly, the international programmes of the Arab Guarantee and the proposed Investment Insurance Agency of the World Bank (section 4).

2. Certain issues raised by investment insurance under international law

(a) The role of insurance in international claims

(i) *Subrogation*

Insurance of foreign investment involves the application of the mechanism of subrogation which lies at the heart of insurance law. Under this doctrine, the insurer steps into the shoes of the insured in typical cases of valid insurance transactions. His rights derive from the rights of the insured.[2] The accepted view is that the insurer does not acquire an 'original right'; his right arises later when the insured risk occurs, and the insured is paid the insurance benefits. Basically, the doctrine of subrogation cannot confer on the insurer rights which did not belong to the insured.[3] Neither can it, operating as it does in the domain of private law, confer on the claim of the insurer the national character of the original claim. This is because nationality is regulated *jure imperii* by the State of which the victim of the internationally wrongful act is a national.

In the light of these general observations it is vital to examine the relationship of insurance to the traditional rules of diplomatic protection and nationality of claims. Mainly, this entails the examination of several related issues, discussed below.

(ii) *The locus standi of insurers in international claims*

(1) *New approach*

Meron defines the term '*locus standi*' as 'the standing of a State to present claim of an insurer to an international tribunal, or to espouse it through diplomatic channels'.[4] He conceded that the wrongdoing State should not be allowed to escape liability because the injured party and his insurer do not have the same nationality. He asserts that 'while *de lega lata* the State of the insured has a clear standing to press the claim in the international plane, the State of the insurer should, *de lege ferenda*, be given standing with respect to the interests of the insurer in cases where the State of the insured would not present a claim'. In his thesis, there should be neither legal default by the wrongdoing State, nor double claims by the State of the insured and by the State of the insurer.

(2) *The traditional rules on diplomatic protection and nationality of claims*

These innovative ideas are difficult to reconcile with the international traditional rules of diplomatic protection and nationality of claims, so recently reaffirmed by the International Court of Justice in the *Barcelona Traction* case, 1976.[5] The Court reaffirmed unequivocally that diplomatic protection is based on the breach by the defendant State of an international obligation towards the plaintiff State in respect of its nationals, and underlined the exclusivity of the right of that State to bring a claim in respect of the breach.

Furthermore, the traditional rules of nationality of claims require that the claimant individual should have the nationality of the claimant State from the time when the injury was suffered, and until the time of the adjudication of the claim, or, at least its presentation.[6] These rules still prevail under customary international law. The question is: how can these traditional rules be reconciled with the modern concept of insurance of foreign investments whereby a claim can be espoused internationally by the insurer's home State when the insured and insurer possess different nationalities?

(3) *When insurer and insured have the same nationality*

Here there will be no difficulty. The practice of national commissions[7] as well as the international arbitral tribunals[8] have allowed claims by insurers as subrogees, against the State responsible for the internationally wrongful act. In case of claims submitted by both the insured and the insurer, usually international arbitral tribunals apportion the award and reduce the claim of the insured by the amount actually paid to him by the insurer.[9] However, it is suggested that such a measure is not justified, because the mobility of claims between the nationals of the same State, whether by subrogation or otherwise, is within the domestic competence of the State, and is governed by its municipal law, and hence should not be the concern of other States.[10]

As long as the nationality of the claim is not affected, the changes in the ownership of the claim, in accordance with the domestic law of the claimant State, the defendant State should not, in principle, go beyond the legal arrangements made between the insurer and the insured, provided they were not obviously *mala fide* and resulted in payments in excess of the insured value.[11]

(4) *When insurer and insured have different nationalities*

In this case a problem would really arise. Nevertheless, in a number of older cases of marine insurance, *locus standi* of insurers possessing nationality different from that of the insured was recognized.[12] Meron distinguished these cases as being irrelevant to investment insurance, because they were marine insurance and the decisions may have been affected by the belief that, under the peculiar institution of the maritime law, where total loss involves abandonment by the owner, the insurer acquires title directly rather than through the operation of the doctrine of subrogation.[13]

This, in his view, does not dispose of the difficulty posed by the nationality of claims rules. He concedes that the national character of the ship at the time of the injury could not be affected by abandonment, and since the national character differed from that of the insurers, this must be fatal for their *locus standi*. Rightly he observes that national character is usually determined by the State concerned *jure imperii* while the doctrines of abandonment and subrogation operate in private law only.[14] Though Meron cites several opinions[15] and decisions[16] of national and international claim commissions in favour of rejecting claims by insurers who possess different nationalities from that of the insured, strangely enough he comes to establish the reverse. Relying on an *obiter dictum* expressed by the International Court of Justice in the *Barcelona Traction* case,[17] he has tried by analogy to establish the *locus standi* of the Government of the insurer to present a claim against the respondent State. He expressed his view in the following words:

> The Court, in considering the right of Belgium to exercise diplomatic protection of Belgian shareholders in a Canadian Company with respect to measures taken in relation to the Company, rather than the shareholders, insisted on a clear – though perhaps unduly formalistic and economically artificial – distinction between a direct injury to a legal right of the Company, and indirect injury to simple, economic interests of the shareholders, regarding only the former, and not the latter, as involving the international responsibility of a State.[18]
> By analogy, the Court would have recognized the standing of the State of the insurer with respect to an internationally illegal act directly prejudicing the rights of an insurance company (i.e. expropriation without compensation) but not *qua* insurer – by contract – of others who suffered from an internationally wrongful act.

Finally, the Court was of the opinion that considerations of equity, required no more than the possibility for one protector State to intervene, primarily the national State of the company, and secondarily, the national State of the shareholders.[19]
However, the Court regarded the secondary right (by analogy, the right of the insurers) as coming into existence only when the original right (by analogy, of the State of the insured) ceases to exist, and not merely when it is not exercised.[20]

Though the analogy might seem attractive between the capacity of the national States of the aggrieved shareholders and that of insurers to espouse their claims internationally or diplomatically, it is very difficult to maintain such an argument in the absence of an investment treaty. The customary rules on diplomatic protection and nationality of claims are too firmly established to allow of such an analogy. The right of shareholders to have their injuries redressed by their home States can be claimed from the time of the acquisition of the shares, but in the case of insurers their rights in the insurance policies arise only when the risks insured against take place and the insured has received his claim. Only at that moment the doctrine of subrogation arises.

Meron himself is aware of the weaknesses of the position he prefers, and proposes the alternative of presenting the 'claim in the name of the insured, the victim of an internationally wrongful act, and that the State should not be permitted to demand the disclosure of insurance contracts, nor to benefit from them'.[21] Furthermore, the same writer suggests another alternative solution. Thus, the insurer could pay the insured an amount equal to the promised insurance benefits, but the transaction would be presented as a loan repayable out of the prospective recovery from the tortfeasor – the respondent State. He added that 'in order to avoid difficulties resulting from the nationality of claims rules, such techniques are actually used, jointly with contractual obligations of the insured towards the insurer to press the insured's national Government to proceed with the claim against the Government responsible for the internationally wrongful act'.[22] Under this arrangement the claim continues to be 'owned' by the insured, subrogation does not come into play, and hence the rules of nationality of claims are observed. Again, this alternative technique would be contrary to the exercise of diplomatic protection. A national cannot press his home State to espouse a diplomatic claim on his behalf. The right to exercise diplomatic protection is discretionary.[23] A State may sometimes be reluctant to espouse a claim of its nationals for many political reasons.[24]

The best approach is to regulate the issue of insuring foreign investments by treaty. It is well known that, in practice, nationality of claims and diplomatic protection may be tempered by treaties.[25] The device of national insurance programmes does not in fact raise such complicated issues. As will be discussed below, in the vast majority of these insurance programmes, both the insurer and the insured are of the same nationality. With regard to international insurance programmes, the concept is still discussed on theoretical levels, except on regional basis.

(iii) *The effect of insurance contract on the liability of the respondent State towards the insured*

Suppose that an insurer has paid the insured the benefits of the insurance, can the respondent State which committed the international wrong invoke the performance of the insurance contract to deny its international responsibility towards the home State of the insured?

The answer seems to be partially in the negative. Insurance contracts are based on the principle of indemnity, i.e. their objective is to confer a benefit not greater than the loss suffered. The rule of subrogation is related to this principle of indemnity and provides for the right of the insurer to be reimbursed out of the recovery from the third party.[26] Of course, the possibility of an unjust enrichment by the injured party cannot be excluded at all. If in such circumstances only the claim of the insured would be internationally protected, the danger of double claims would be minimized.[27]

It is generally assumed that a contract of insurance is personal in nature in the sense that it runs to the insured and its existence does not affect the third party's liability to the insured.[28] The mobility of claims among the nationals of the same State should be of no international concern. It is governed by the domestic law within the reserved domain.[29] The responsibility of the respondent State arises under international law as the result of causing the wrongful act which caused directly the injury to the national of the claimant State. The insurance contract is too remote in this case. Only if the respondent State is a party in one way or another to the contract can it invoke it to deny its international responsibility, which arises exclusively under a separate norm of international law. Of course, the respondent State can deny its international responsibility if the claim is espoused by the home State of the insurer who possesses a different nationality from the insured. Its defence in this case, as stated above, will be based on the nationality of claim principle and not on the ground that the insured has been paid by the insurer in accordance with the insurance contract.[30]

From the foregoing it is obvious that under the existing rules of nationality of claims,[31] it is utterly untenable to conceive the legitimacy of international claims by insurers or their home States when the insurer and insured have different nationalities.

With these general observations in mind, it is possible now to examine some of the national and international investment insurance programmes.

3. National programmes of investment insurance against political risks

(a) Motivation

Several capital-exporting industrialized countries[32] have adopted national programmes providing insurance for their nationals' investments abroad. All have the same general purpose and format. They provide insurance against three basic types of risk: expropriation; damage resulting from war, revolution or insurrection; inconvertibility or non-transfer of funds. They all struggle with the problem of trying to attain two potentially conflicting purposes: aiding the economy of the host country, and furthering their own national commercial interests.[33]

The degree of emphasis given to each purpose varies considerably from one programme to another, but it is generally said that aid considerations are being sacrificed to national commercial interests.[34] The older programmes, like the American and German, which started out mainly as instruments of government foreign aid, have over the years become more commercially oriented. Most of the recent programmes came out as a direct result of pressure from the business community and were commercially oriented from the beginning.[35]

There is no doubt that national investment insurance achieves for capital-exporting countries many political and economic advantages. By increasing the amount of investments under the insurance programme a capital-exporting country will enhance its political prestige on the international plane. It will also secure a reputable monopoly in international trade, obtain new markets and the necessary raw materials for its national industry. Thus, Japan, more dependent than most on outside sources of raw materials, has been reported to have included a special provision in its political risk insurance scheme[36] granting coverage to portfolio investments, the purpose of which is the development of mineral resources to be imported to Japan.

(b) The United States investment insurance programme

The United States investment insurance programme is the oldest, and by far the most important national programme of insurance of investments abroad. This is true both in terms of volume of insurance issued and geographical scope.[37]

The administration of the programme is now entrusted to the Overseas Private Investment Corporation (O.P.I.C.),[38] an agency of the United States under the policy guidance of the Secretary of State.

(i) *History and development*

The present United States investment insurance programme found its origin in the Economic Cooperation Act,[39] 1948 under the Marshall Plan which aimed at reconstructing the destroyed economies of the Western European countries after the Second World War. At that time, the insurance programme guaranteed only new investments in Europe against nonconvertibility into dollars. In 1949, coverage became available for expanded investments, modification and development of existing enterprises. In 1950 the range of risks was extended to include expropriation and nationalization. In 1951, the Mutual Security Act[40] extended the geographic coverage of the programme from Europe alone to any area receiving aid from the United States, and the Mutual Security Act of 1953[41] extended the programme to countries which concluded investment guaranty[42] agreements with the United States. In 1956, coverage under the programme was extended to cover losses resulting from war. In 1959, the application of the programme was restricted only to less developed countries.[43] This new trend constituted a functional restriction with regard to the criteria of eligibility and in the end it led the programme to be utilized in transferring the United States negligible technical assistance into a massive capital transfer programme in the 1960s. From that date, the guaranty programme itself was used tremendously as a private capital transfer vehicle and associated with the flow of public capital into the less developed countries.[44] The investment guaranty programme was further modified by the Foreign Assistance Act of 1961,[45] and its administration was transferred from the International Co-operation Administration, which had administered it since 1956, to the Agency for International Development (A.I.D.).[46] The latter was succeeded by the Overseas Private Investment Corporation in 1969,[47] which has administered the programme since that date until today.

(ii) *The Overseas Private Investment Corporation* (*O.P.I.C.*)

Before discussing the substantive operation and mechanism of the present American investment insurance programme, it is important to make some observations on the function and practice of the O.P.I.C.

The purpose of establishing the O.P.I.C. as a public corporation, rather than as an ordinary administrative governmental unit, was to confer on it the characteristics of the corporate management. This is preferable for an institution predominantly of a business nature and which is revenue-producing and potentially self-sustaining. This involves numerous transactions with the public and requires greater flexibility than the governmental annual appropriation budget would concede.[48]

The principal mandate of O.P.I.C. was the mobilization and facilitation of American private capital and skills in the economic and social progress of less developed friendly countries and areas, 'thereby complementing the development assistance objectives of the United States'.[49] According to its legislative mandate,[50] O.P.I.C. was to undertake, *inter alia*:

(a) to conduct financing operations on a self-sustaining basis, taking into account the economic and financial soundness of projects and the availability of financing from other sources on appropriate terms;...

(d) to conduct its insurance operations with due regard to principles of risk management including, when appropriate, efforts to share its insurance risks;...

(i) to further to the greatest degree possible, in a manner consistent with its goals, the balance-of-payments objectives of the United States;

(j) to conduct its activities in consonance with the activities of the agency primarily responsible for administering part I and the international trade, investment, and financial policies of the United States Government; and...

The programmes established by the O.P.I.C. were intended to be as follows:

Insurance of private United States investments in less developed countries against the risks of inconvertibility, expropriation, and war, revolution or insurrection;

guarantees of United States private loans to projects in less developed countries (usually from institutional lenders such as insurance companies, pension funds and commercial banks) against commercial as well as political risks;

direct dollar loans from the corporation's capital, repayable in dollars, or foreign currency loans, to assist in financing private projects in these counries;

financing of investment surveys and feasibility studies to develop projects, in selected fields and countries, especially small business and agribusiness opportunities; and

guarantees of local lending under the experimental productive credit guarantee programme to test whether Government guarantees can make more local bank and specialized credit accessible to poor people for farming and business development.[51]

From the above, it is apparent that the operations of O.P.I.C. comprised two essential activities: political risk insurance, which is by far the largest part of O.P.I.C. operations, and development financing. This book is concerned only with the first part of O.P.I.C.'s activities.

Generally, the O.P.I.C. investment insurance is available against three basic types of risks: inconvertibility, expropriation, and war, revolution or insurrection. The magnitude of the insurance portfolio varied in relation to each risk. Thus, it has been reported that on 30 June 1974, O.P.I.C. had undertaken inconvertibility insurance amounting to $3.2 billion, which was available in seventy-seven countries.[52] On the other hand, by the end of the fiscal year 1974, insurance contracts in force against expropriation were estimated to be about $3.5 billion obtainable in seventy-nine countries. As regards coverage against risk of war, revolution and insurrection, this was, by the end of June 1974, available in seventy-five countries and amounted to $3 billion.[53]

However, one basic characteristic of O.P.I.C. investment insurance operations is that by far the greatest part of the political risk insurance has been issued to large multinational corporations. The justification for this policy is that that experience has shown that these institutions are usually willing to assume unusual risks, because they have the ability and resources tremendously to contribute to developmental projects in developing countries.

Though historically O.P.I.C. has been oriented towards economic development of the host countries, yet the investment insurance programme seems to pursue national objectives. The overriding consideration of the Congressional Legislative Mandate of 1969 is that O.P.I.C. has to conduct its investment insurance operations with due regard to principles of risk management. The selectivity required by that mandate and the growing economic nationalism in the developing countries have led to the decline in the volume of investment insurance. In addition, in some instances, there is decline in investment opportunities, as some host countries have developed a tendency to appropriate for themselves the best investments, particularly extractive industries. This had led to lessening the investment insurance geographical scope.[54] All these factors have caused the orientation of O.P.I.C. insurance operations shift from stress on economic development mission to low risk project. This new attitude has been strengthened, furthermore, by the need to take into consideration the economic needs of the United States such as the balance-of-payments and employment.[55] Thus, the operative legislation under which O.P.I.C. is now conducting its operations requires it to function on a self-sustaining basis, with due regard to risk management, including efforts to share its insurance and reinsurance risks.[56]

O.P.I.C. pursues and administers the investment insurance programme in accordance with yardsticks spread in certain guidelines and regulations[57] designed to fill in the gaps in the main legislation constituting the corporation. These instruments provide the criteria to be applied in each particular case. The guidelines are not intended to be administrative regulations, which O.P.I.C. could not modify or waive for good reason, but are to be interpreted liberally to carry out the main purpose for which institution was established. To smooth its activities in a consistent and systematic instrumentality, O.P.I.C. framed standard form insurance contracts, each to suit a certain type of investment to be covered by the insurance. Each contract is usually accompanied by suitable 'Special Terms and Conditions'.[58]

(iii) *Eligible investors*

Investors who qualify for buying insurance policies under the present American investment insurance programme are strictly defined in Public Law 93–390[59] in three categories.

The first category includes 'United States citizens', i.e. natural persons. In this respect the rules of nationality and citizenship apply.

The second category is that of 'corporations, partnerships, or other associations, created under the law of the United States or any State or territory thereof and substantially beneficially owned by United States citizens'. This means that the fact that a corporation or other legal person has been established under the laws of the United States does not suffice to make such a person an eligible investor. It must be 'substantially beneficially owned by the United States citizens', i.e. by natural persons having United States nationality. The question is: what amount of substantial beneficial ownership should be possessed by United States citizens to qualify them to be eligible investors for investment insurance? The answer is given by O.P.I.C. regulations and the contracts of insurance.

O.P.I.C. regulations provide that, 'ordinarily, a corporation organized under the laws of the United States or of any State or territory of the United States will be considered substantially owned by United States citizens if more than 50% of each class of its issued and outstanding stock is owned by United States citizens whether directly or beneficially'.[60] Meron argues that where shares of stock of a corporation with widely dispersed public ownership are held in the name of trustees or nominees with addresses in the United States, the presumption is that they are owned by citizens of the United States unless the investor has knowledge of the contrary.[61] If it appears from the circumstances of the case that foreign creditors can exercise effective control over the United States corporation, O.P.I.C. may consider that corporation as ineligible, despite its being substantially beneficially owned by United States citizens.[62] The eligibility test must be traced through and applied to the ultimate beneficial owners. Thus, Article 2.01 of the contract of insurance[63] provides that:

> Beneficial ownership of an entity shall be determined by tracing through any intermediate owners to the natural persons who are the ultimate owners of the beneficial interests therein.

The third category of eligible investors is

> foreign corporations, partnerships, or other associations wholly owned by one or more such United States citizens, corporations, partnerships, or other associations, provided, however, that the eligibility of such foreign corporations shall be determined without regard to any shares, in aggregate less than 5 per cent of the total of issued and subscribed share capital, held by other than the United States owners.[64]

Accordingly, a foreign corporation (i.e. a subsidiary of a United States corporation) has to be wholly United States owned except for the aforementioned five per cent. If such a foreign corporation is wholly owned by United States legal persons, rather than natural persons, then Article 2.01 of the Contract of Insurance makes it clear that such legal persons must be 'substantially beneficially owned by natural persons who are nationals of the United States'. This means that a foreign company which is a subsidiary of a United States company is eligible for O.P.I.C. insurance if 95% of the stock of the subsidiary is owned by the parent company and if 51% of the stock of the parent company is owned by nationals of the United States.

From the above, it appears that the general criterion for the issuance of O.P.I.C. investment insurance is 51% of beneficial ownership by United States citizens rather than the place of incorporation of the company. As observed by Metzger,[65] the United States does not follow the holding in the *Barcelona Traction* case, on the *jus standi* of the Company's national State (rather than the national State of the shareholders).

It is worth mentioning that the United States criterion for the issuance of insurance is basically the same as that applied to the espousal of claims by the American Government.[66]

If a company is substantially beneficially owned by United States citizens, then, under O.P.I.C. legislation, O.P.I.C. may insure the entire foreign investment of that company, including the 49% non-United States owned minority interest in the investing company.[67]

The strict eligibility rules of O.P.I.C. are modified to some extent by section 234(a)(2) of Public Law 93-390. Under this new provision, where there is multinational participation, in the framework of arrangements with other Governments, multilateral organization or multilateral institutions, O.P.I.C. may issue insurance to investors not otherwise eligible. The purpose of this modification is to share insurance liabilities which may not exceed the proportionate participation by eligible investors in the total project financing. However, this new trend would cause some difficulties with regard to diplomatic protection (see *post*, pp. 293–9). It is not clear how the United States could represent, in case of serious investment disputes, all of the participating parties or the multinational investors should they be covered by O.P.I.C. insurance policy. Neither is it certain that the United States could, under international law, espouse in all circumstances the minority United States owners participating in the multinational enterprise.

(iv) *Eligible investments*

Section 238(a) of Public Law 93-390 defines the term 'investment' as follows:

the term 'investment' includes any contribution of funds, commodities, services, patents, processes, or techniques, in the form of (a) a loan or loans to an approved project, (2) the purchase of a share of ownership in any such project, (3) participation in royalties, earnings, or profits of any such project, and (4) the furnishing of commodities or services pursuant to a lease or other contract. (See *ante*, pp. 19–29.)

This definition is so wide that it includes various forms of contemporary investment, such as the provision of modern technology, loans, sharing of royalties, earnings or profits, and contracts pertaining to the provision of commodities and services, such as licensing of patents, process or techniques, or granting of technical and managerial assistance. Such forms of investment are of particular appeal to Saudi Arabia and the Sudan. Indeed, the structuring of the investment is very important for the accessibility of the investment to the host country and the reduction of the danger of expropriation. As pointed out before, new investment techniques embrace joint ventures, fadeout arrangements, and non-equity management, production-sharing and royalty undertaking agreements. The Sub-committee on Foreign Economic Policy of the House Committee on Foreign Affairs has recently recommended that 'O.P.I.C. should concentrate on encouraging "new modes" of investment, such as non-equity investments, joint ventures, minority United States interest, multinational investments, and projects which have fadeout provisions'.[68]

It is not enough for an investment to satisfy the eligibility test for insurance to fall within the categories envisaged by the above statutory definition. There are other basic conditions postulated by section 231,[69] which lays down the purposes of the establishment of O.P.I.C. and the policy which it should carry out. Accordingly, O.P.I.C. has been given considerable discretion in determining which investments are eligible, and which are not. Under the legislative guidelines laid down in section 231, the following investments are qualified for O.P.I.C. insurance:

(a) Investment projects involving business of not more than $2.5 million net worth or with not more than $7.5 million in total assets;
(b) investments which are sensitive and responsive to the needs and requirements of local economies;
(c) investments that have effect on the United States balance-of-payments and its employment objectives.

In addition to the above basic eligibility requirements there are, equally, other conditions which should initially be satisfied. Thus, there must be a bilateral agreement between the United States and the investee State that the investment will be covered by the insurance programme. The investor must secure the approval of the issuance of insurance of the specific investment project by the Government of the investee State before an insurance contract may be issued by O.P.I.C.[70]

A non-statutory condition for the eligibility of an investment is that the investment must be new. This means it must be in a new project, which may, however, consist of a significant expansion, modernization or development of an existing enterprise.

To be eligible for insurance an investment must generally be expected to remain in the foreign enterprise for at least three years. The legal time-limit on investment insurance contracts is twenty years.[71]

Additionally, the investor must provide O.P.I.C. with considerable specific information.[72] This seems to include the developmental effect of the project, local investment and expansion, ecology, the estimated amount of local capital and new materials to be used in the project, protective tariffs etc. Usually, an investment project will not be approved for insurance, unless favourably recommended by the United States Embassy in the host country.[73]

Perhaps the most important consideration for determining whether or not an investment is eligible for O.P.I.C. insurance is that it should make a useful contribution to the economic development of the host country. For projects involving one million United States dollars or more of O.P.I.C. insured investments, O.P.I.C. staff must submit detailed developmental effect statements. This procedure aims at evaluating and analysing the investment project in accordance with the guidelines and policies of O.P.I.C.[74] This, in practice, has led O.P.I.C. to reject many applications for various reasons.[75]

(v) *Coverage*

The risks insurable under section 234 of Public law 93-390 are:

(a) inability to convert into United States dollars other currencies, or credits in such currencies, received as earnings or profits from the approved project, as repayment or return of the investment therein, in whole or in part, or as compensation for the sale or disposition of all or any part thereof;
(b) Loss of investment, in whole or in part, in the approved project due to expropriation or confiscation by action of a foreign government; and
(c) Loss due to war, revolution, or insurrection.

Each of these will now be discussed under headings 1, 2 and 3.

(1) *Inconvertibility*

This coverage is relevant when the investor is refused the right to convert into the United States dollars the local currency received as earnings on the original investment or the capital eligible for repatriation. The practice has shown that O.P.I.C. insures that the investor will receive dollars if the central bank of the host State refuses to transfer the investor's locally-held fund.[76] Before obtaining the inconvertibility coverage, the investor has to show that the host Government is willing to permit the remittance of earnings and the repatriation of the capital.[77] It should be emphasized that the insurance does not protect the investor against devaluation losses or exchange fluctuations. Neither does it protect him from any exchange regulations which are in force at the date of the insurance contracts. So, if the Sudanese Government repeals the prevailing investment laws to the extent that repatriation of capital and profits is no longer allowed, a potential American investor who intends to invest in the Sudan will not be eligible to buy insurance coverage of inconvertibility under the insurance programme of O.P.I.C.[78]

Before being paid by O.P.I.C., the investor must deliver to O.P.I.C. cash or a draft drawn to its order for the amount of local currency for which transfer is requested.[79]

When a claim is approved, the investor receives from O.P.I.C. 99% of the local currency involved, according to the 'Reference Rate of Exchange'.[80] The blocked local currency is turned over to O.P.I.C. by the investors in consideration of the repayment of their claims, and O.P.I.C. sells such local currency to the United States Embassy in the host country.[81]

The practice of O.P.I.C. with respect to inconvertibility claims is well illustrated by the claim of *William H. Atwell* against *O.P.I.C.* (Kenya 1974).[82] In this case Atwell applied to the Central Bank of Kenya for transfer into dollars of 1,050,000 Kenyan shillings, which represented the proceeds of the sale of the foreign enterprise by the investor. The Central Bank of Kenya approved for transfer only a portion of the proceeds of the sale and denied the transfer of the rest, ordering that it should be placed in a blocked account. The investor took all reasonable steps required to effect such a transfer under Government of Kenya regulations and law. As such local currency was eligible for transfer under the contract of guaranty, O.P.I.C. paid the investor the $55,917.75 by way of compensation in accordance with the reference rate of exchange (99% of the exchange rate).[83]

(2) *Expropriation*

As noted before, it is very difficult to arrive at a definition of the controversial term 'expropriation'. However, section 234 of Public Law 93-390 defines 'expropriation' as including, but not limited, to 'any abrogation, repudiation or impairment by a foreign government of its own contract with an investor with respect to a project, where such abrogation, repudiation, or impairment is not caused by the investor's own default or misconduct, and materially adversely affects the continued operation of the project'.

As this definition usually does not accommodate all contingencies, the contract of insurance[84] supplements the legislative definition by providing a detailed definition of 'expropriation' in the following terms:

Any action taken, authorized, ratified or condoned by the host Government, with or without compensation, commencing during the insurance period which, for a duration of one year directly results in preventing:

(i) the investor from receiving when due payment in the currency specified, which the enterprise owes the investor a payment in respect of the securities;
(ii) the investor from effectively exercising his fundamental rights with respect to the foreign enterprise either as a shareholder or as a creditor;
(iii) the investor from disposing of the securities or rights accruing therefrom;
(iv) the foreign enterprise from exercising effective control over the use or disposition of a substantial portion of the property, or from constructing or operating the project;
(v) the investor from repatriating and from exercising effective control in the host country over investment earnings or return of capital.[85]

However, measures of the types enumerated above would not be considered expropriatory in certain specified conditions, particularly:

(i) When the host Government adopts any law or administrative action which is not by express terms for the purpose of nationalization, confiscation, or expropriation is reasonably related to constitutionally sanctioned governmental objectives, is not arbitrary, is based upon a reasonable classification of entities to which it applies and does not violate generally accepted principles of international law.[86]
(ii) When the investor or the foreign enterprise fails to take in the host country all reasonable measures including administrative and judicial procedures to prevent or contest such action (exhaustion of local remedies).[87]
(iii) When the action is in accordance with any agreement voluntarily entered into by the investor or the foreign enterprise.[88]
(iv) When there is provocation or instigation by the investor or foreign enterprise.[89]

The above provisions disclose a realistic approach on the part of O.P.I.C. for determining which actions of the host Government are expropriatory and which are not. Special emphasis is put on the actual deprivation of the investor by the host Government of the use or enjoyment of the foreign enterprise for a period of one year.

The question of the definition of expropriation was considered in the *Matter of the Arbitration between Valentine Petroleum & Chemical Corporation and Agency for International Development*[90] in 1967, under earlier legislation. This case concerned a contract of concession for the construction of an oil refinery in Haiti. The arbitrators decided the controversy 'pursuant to the terms of the Contract of Guaranty in the light of the federal statute evidencing conditions for claims against the United States under the Investment Guaranty Programme'.[91] A.I.D. contended that the term expropriation or expropriatory action required the taking of property. This contention was rejected by the arbitrators who held that the annulment of the contract of concession by a Decree Law, granting a similar concession to another party, and the detention and expulsion of the investor from Haiti, constituted an expropriatory action. Similar results were obtained in other arbitration awards.[92]

As soon as an expropriatory action takes place, an insured investor must notify O.P.I.C. in writing, describing the circumstances of the action that in his view is expropriatory. He must take all reasonable measures available to preserve and pursue his remedies against the host Government and maintain and preserve the assets of the foreign enterprise. If the remedies available fail, the investor can claim payment from O.P.I.C., which, if it pays the claim, has the right as subrogee to require the investor to transfer to it all of his rights, titles and interests in the insured investment. Having paid the claim and become subrogated to the rights of the investor, O.P.I.C. may attempt to recover from the host Government some compensation for the expropriated property.[93]

The obligation of the investor towards O.P.I.C. does not end by the assumption by it of the insured interest and the payment of the claim. He has an ongoing contractual obligation to co-operate with the United States Government in the prosecution of the claim, the administration of any property assigned to O.P.I.C. and the provision of necessary information, personnel etc.[94] The policy of O.P.I.C. in this respect is to avoid direct confrontation with the host Government and keep the individual investor in front.

(3) *War, revolution and insurrection*

These terms are not statutorily defined concretely. However, Article 1.07 of the Contract of Insurance[95] defines the term 'damage' in relation to this coverage as meaning

> injury to the physical condition, destruction, disappearance or seizure and retention of covered property directly caused by war (whether or not under formal declaration and thus encompassing any hostile act by any national or international organized force) or by revolution or insurrection and includes injury to the physical condition, destruction, disappearance or seizure and retention of covered property as a direct result of actions taken in hindering, combating or defending against a pending or expected hostile act whether in war, revolution or insurrection. The term does not include injury to the physical condition, destruction, disappearance or seizure and retention of covered property directly caused by civil strife of a lesser degree than revolution or insurrection.

The above detailed contractual provision raises many issues. In the first place, the losses caused in the course of civil strife of a lesser degree, such as riots and looting, would be excluded from coverage. These would normally be considered terrorist acts unless the group which carried out the acts could be considered an organized revolutionary or insurgent force. Accordingly, the hostile activities which had been practised in the south of the Sudan by the Anyanya guerrillas before the Peace Settlement of 1972 (see *ante*, pp. 9–10) seemed to be included by the coverage. Secondly, the scope of the coverage under this heading is very narrow with regard to the exclusion of securities, documents and bullion by confining the coverage only to tangible property.[96]

As domestic insurance companies usually do not undertake insurance in cases of riots and civil strife, the exclusion of these items also by the investment insurance programme is a serious shortcoming which should be rectified. It should be observed that this aspect of the problem calls for special consideration in a developing country like the Sudan where the potentiality of these contingencies is very likely to take place.

An investor claiming under this coverage must promptly notify O.P.I.C. in writing of any action which may cause or which has caused damage.[97] He has no claim if the amount of compensation does not exceed the lesser of $10,000 or 1 % of the total of the current insured amount under the coverage.[98] In assessing the compensation, special consideration will be given to the original cost of the property, earnings and losses of the investment, etc. (see *post*, pp. 204–8). If, because of the conditions in the host country, agents of O.P.I.C. cannot make an on-site inspection to determine the amount of damage caused to the property, the amount of damage will be presumed to be 60 % of the covered value of the tangible property, unless the investor proves otherwise.[99]

As in the previous coverages, the investor must, prior to the receipt of compensation, assign to O.P.I.C. any claims, causes of action or rights or compensation from other sources for the damage caused to the property.

(vi) *Premiums*

Investors who bought investment insurance policies from O.P.I.C. have to pay annual fees which range within 4–10 %. The fees are subject to review periodically in the light of the volume of business, experience in claims and other factors.[100]

(vii) *Eligible host countries and investment guaranty agreements*

Under the American investment programme, countries have to be both less developed and friendly to the United States to quality for O.P.I.C.'s involvement.

Both as regards the level of development and the degree of friendly relations with the United States, O.P.I.C. is guided in practice by the advice of the Department of State.[101] However, section 231(1) of Public Law 93-390 requires O.P.I.C. to give preferential consideration to friendly countries which have *per capita* of $450 or less.

There are two other legislative provisions bearing on the eligibility of host countries to O.P.I.C. investment insurance. In the first place, there should be a bilateral agreement between the United States and the host country.[102] Secondly, O.P.I.C. has to determine that suitable arrangements exist for protecting its interest in connection with any insurance, guaranty or reinsurance issued. This will include arrangements concerning ownership, use, and disposition of the currency, credits, assets, or investments on account of which payment under such insurance, guaranty, or reinsurance is to be made.[103]

Meron, supporting the view of the House Committee on O.P.I.C., has advocated that 'bilateral agreements should not always be an invariable precondition to insuring projects in a particular country'. He goes on to say: 'a certain measure of flexibility is desirable to suit the circumstances in every host country'. Nevertheless, as a general principle, Meron concedes that a bilateral agreement should precede the issuance of insurance by O.P.I.C. for a particular investment. He is of the opinion that such an agreement may be helpful in assuming subrogation rights and provide for a binding obligation. Moreover, he believes that the bilateral agreement may make less likely the charge of economic imperialism.[104] This is a paradoxical statement as it apparently does not coincide with its premise. How can one reject an idea and support it at the same time? However, it is inconceivable to implement any investment project without the consent of the host country. An express provision to that effect has been inserted in the United States–Sudan Investment Guaranty Agreement of 1959,[105] discussed below. Such an umbrella agreement would provide an emphatical assurance of subrogation and binding procedure for settling investment disputes (see ch. 10).

(1) *The Agreement between the United States and the Sudan Relating to the Guaranty of Private Investments*, 1959 (referred to hereinafter as the United States–Sudan Investment Guaranty Agreement)

Historical background

Being considered as an eligible country for the United States investment guaranty programme, the Sudan concluded this agreement with the United States in March 1959. As usual, the agreement was concluded through the technique of exchange of notes. Though it has been operative for nineteen years, the agreement has not been fully implemented with respect to American investments in the Sudan, except in only one instance.[106] There were two main reasons. First, the American enterprises[107] affected by the Sudanese nationalization measures in 1970 did not buy investment insurance policies under the applicable programme. Secondly, due to the involvement of the United States in the Middle East war in 1967, a common hostile policy was adopted against it by the Arab countries, which eventually culminated in severance of diplomatic relations between the Sudan and the United States. This led to the suspension of American foreign aid to the Sudan under the Foreign Assistance Act, 1961. Under these circumstances, the investment guaranty had been dormant; albeit not formally renounced. The American practice in these situations is that the O.P.I.C. and its predecessor (A.I.D.), following the guidance of the Department of State, would suspend or terminate operations in case of cut-off of foreign assistance or severance of diplomatic relations. In such cases, although new insurance is not issued, existing insurance contracts are not affected.[108]

Content

The United States–Sudan Investment Guaranty Agreement is characteristic of the traditional guaranty agreements usually concluded by the United States with developing countries. It generally reflects the American legislation in force at the time of its conclusion.

It establishes the need for the Government of the Republic of the Sudan and the Government of the United States to consult respecting investments in the Republic of the Sudan proposed by nationals of the United States with regard to which guaranties under Section 413(e)(4) of the Mutual Security Act of 1954,[109] as amended, have been made or are under consideration.[110]

Only investments approved by the Government of the Sudan will be guaranteed by the Government of the United States.[111]

The agreement provides for subrogation[112] in an appropriate form. Sudanese pound amounts acquired by the United States Government following subrogation arrangement may be used for local administrative expenditures.[113] Such amounts must be accorded treatment not less favourable than that accorded to private funds arising from transactions of the United States nationals which are comparable to the transactions covered by such guarantees.[114]

It is worth mentioning that this agreement provides for the standard of treatment to be accorded to American investments if the United States issues guarantees to cover losses, by reason of war, to these investments. This standard of treatment must not be less favourable than that accorded to Sudan nationals or nationals of third countries 'with reference to any reimbursement, compensation, indemnification, or any other payment'.[115]

It should be observed that as the American investment guaranty agreements usually reflect the changing legislative mandate and the international investment climate (see *ante*, pp. 1–6), the United States–Sudan Investment Guaranty Agreement is reported to be under extensive review,[116] although letters of registration have been issued to some American companies embarking on heavy investments, especially in petroleum extraction.

To elude regional arrangements such as the Andean Foreign Investment Code,[117] and to reflect the changing international investment climate, a new trend has emerged. Recent American investment guaranty agreements contain, in addition to a subrogation clause, a provision that if the laws of the host Government do not permit subrogation by the United States Government, the host Government should permit the investor and the insuring Government to make appropriate arrangements so as to transfer the subrogated interests to an entity permitted to own them under the laws of the host government.[118]

The United States–Sudan Investment Guaranty Agreement covers the three insurable risks, namely, inconvertibility; expropriation; war, revolution and insurrection. The finance contemplated by American investors consists mainly of loan guarantees, direct loans and extensions or modernization of pre-investments. It is anticipated that the review of the agreement would extend the coverage to other forms of investment as envisaged by the operative American legislation on the subject.

(2) *The Agreement on Guaranteed Private Investment between the Government of the United States of America and the Government of the Royal Kingdom of Saudi Arabia, 1975*[119]

This agreement is unique. It is expressed in general terms. Under Article 1, in order to increase participation by United States private enterprises in projects bringing new technology to Saudi Arabia, persons eligible under applicable United States legislation may be issued guaranties by the United States Government against loss due to specified risks relating to contracts or investments in Saudi Arabia which are approved by the Government of Saudi Arabia. And the contract or investment shall be deemed approved only if entered into with the Government of Saudi Arabia, or an agency thereof, or otherwise approved in accordance with the applicable laws and regulations of Saudi Arabia. This article raises the doubt that not all American investments are eligible for guaranty in Saudi Arabia. Thus it is unknown whether or not investments within the private sector would be covered. Another problem pertinent to this Article is that the risks to be covered are not specified, but are left to be determined by the Government of Saudi Arabia. Though it is untenable to envisage a guarantee against inconvertibility in Saudi Arabia, yet it is possible to concede a guaranty against war, revolution, insurrection or expropriation after the Mecca incident in 1979. The agreement also deals in Article 2 with subrogation of O.P.I.C. to the rights of the guaranteed person or firm. Settlement of disputes is governed by Article 3 which we shall discuss later.

(viii) *Assessment*

Though the United States investment insurance programme has been applied for nearly thirty years, it has been criticized for various reasons. From the investor's viewpoint, it has been argued that such guaranty shifts the burden of fulfilling the capital-importing states' obligations to the capital-exporting states and, by failing to punish the former state's unfair treatment of foreign investors, tends to encourage them in the wrong direction.[120] This has been succinctly stated in a report as follows: 'Guarantees offered by the United States against occurrences which are the result of policies pursued in other countries would tend to encourage rather than discourage unsound policies, and to promote the very thing which the businessman is afraid of'.[121] Moreover, the risk normally associated with any economic venture is now borne by the American taxpayers and not by the investors, despite the fact that O.P.I.C. was anticipated to be self-sustaining. Among business circles, there has been also some resentment against the possibilities for government interference inherent in the provisions on approval of investments. This created a general reluctance to disclose the requested information on the policies and operations of the enterprise concerned.[122] Finally, the eligibility of new investments only for the American investment guaranty has been criticized as an unwarranted discrimination between old and new investments.[123]

From the point of view of the Congress, it has recently been alleged that O.P.I.C. tended to increase the involvement of the United States Government in the affairs of the developing nations, that it has only a marginal influence on the development of such countries and that inherent in it was a conflict between the achievement of public policy goals and sound insurance principles.[124] For these reasons it has been suggested that insurance of investments should be a function of the private insurance industry or of international multilateral institutions, and the development-oriented functions of O.P.I.C. should be handled by the United States foreign aid programme. Both the Senate and the House of Representatives are of the opinion that O.P.I.C. must turn over its function as insurer to the private insurance industry and assume, instead, the function of the reinsurer.[125]

These are radical proposals which overlook the valuable functions of O.P.I.C. in encouraging American investments abroad and contributing to settling investment disputes. Additionally, to cast the task of insuring investments abroad on private insurance companies would lessen the scope of the insurance coverage, especially with regard to the risk of war and revolution which private insurance companies are very reluctant to insure against. The private insurance industry is still in its inception in this area and even if it developed, high premiums would be charged. As regards the prospect of assuming the function of insuring foreign investments by multilateral organizations, as will be shown, it is very difficult to achieve any arrangement of that sort in the present state of the international investment climate.

From its application, the United States investment insurance programme has performed – and would perform – a major role in fostering investments in developing countries, if the American companies refrain from interfering in the internal affairs of the countries in which they operate. More importantly, the American programme has also served as a source of experience for other countries' insurance programmes.

(c) The German Investment Guaranty Programme[126]

This programme has been in operation since the latter part of 1959. It was first introduced by the Budget Law of 1959.[127] It is operated by two state-owned banks – Hermes Kreditversicherungs A.G. and the Deutsche Revisions und Treuhandel A.G. The programme is closely related to the export credits guarantee programme which had been operating for several years through these two institutions.[128]

Though the German investment guaranty programme follows generally the American model, it offers more extensive protection and greater flexibility. It can be examined briefly as follows:

(i) *Geographical scope*

Guarantees may be granted for capital investments to be made in countries which have concluded bilateral investment treaties with West Germany. Guarantees may be granted even in the absence of such treaties, if the particular country adequately protects foreign investments through general legislation or other means, such as concession contracts.[129] As mentioned before, the Sudan, like several developing countries, concluded an investment protection treaty with West Germany in 1963.[130]

(ii) *Investment protection treaties*

Unlike the United States agreements, the German counterparts are fairly elaborate. Thus, in addition to provisions on the subrogation of the Federal Republic of Germany to the claims of German investors who have received payments under guarantee contracts,[131] and those dealing with settlement of disputes,[132] the Sudan–German Investment Protection Treaty contains certain substantive provisions. As stated earlier, it provides for non-discrimination,[133] for payment of adequate compensation in case of expropriation,[134] and the right to remit profits and repatriate capital.[135]

The guarantees under the West German bilateral treaties may in exceptional cases be retrospective, having application to investments which have been made prior to the date of the treaty or agreement. The agreements are of stated duration and normally continue to be operative, for a specified period after their termination, for investments made before the termination date.[136] Thus, the Sudan–German Treaty will continue for twenty years after the date of its termination, in relation to investments made prior to that date.[137]

(iii) *Eligible investors*

Guarantees may be purchased by German nationals and by companies having their domicile or place of business in Germany which invest abroad. Special priority is given to those investing in developing countries.[138]

(iv) *Eligible investments*

Guarantees are granted for future (new) investments which are deemed to merit encouragement, particularly those which strengthen Germany's relations with the less developed countries. Guarantees are intended primarily for enterprises engaged in production, extraction or marketing of goods or in transport.[139]

Investment may be in the form of equity, a long-term loan of an investment type or capital provided to an overseas branch, and may be made in cash or in non-monetary form. Earnings from equity investments or long-term loans are eligible for guarantee if their coverage is sought when application is first made for the guarantee; protection extends to dividends declared but not paid and earnings in process of transfer.[140]

This categorization seems to delimit the scope of the German guaranty to the types of investments mentioned above only. As explained before (see *ante*, pp. 22–3), under the Sudan–German Treaty the term 'investment' is widely defined as to comprise many kinds of property.[141] The restrictive categorization may imply that certain German investments in the Sudan may not qualify to meet the insurance eligibility criteria.

Furthermore, to qualify for the German guaranty, the investments have to be 'worthy of promotion'. The investor's applications are examined by a committee composed of the representatives of the Federal Ministries of Economic Affairs, Finance and Foreign Affairs, which decides in each particular case whether or not to grant a guarantee.[142] There is no formal requirement of specific approval by the Government of the investee country, as in the case of the United States programme. But the investor is expected to have obtained all necessary permits prior to the grant of the guaranty and to observe all relevant regulations, both in the country of investment and in the Federal Republic of Germany.[143]

(v) *Guarantee contingency*

The risk-coverage of the German investment guarantee programme is more extensive than that of the United States. The guarantees are designed to cover risks of loss by reason of the following actions by the government of the investee country:

(a) nationalization, confiscation or measures equal to confiscation in their effect (confiscation contingency);
(b) war or other armed conflict, revolution or insurrection (war contingency);
(c) blockage of payment or moratoria (moratorium contingency). This is conceived to include monetary devaluation when occurring in conjunction with the imposition of exchange restriction.[144] This is a novelty of the German programme, as usually the insurance guarantees of other States do not cover the risk of currency devaluation;
(d) impossibility of conversion or transfer (C.T. contingency).

The coverage offered is a blanket coverage; the investor cannot purchase protection against a single risk or combination of risks.[145]

(vi) *Duration of guarantee*

A capital investment may be guaranteed for a maximum period of fifteen years; in exceptional cases the term may be twenty years. Renewal or further extension is not permitted. The guarantee becomes effective and the term begins to run when a 'notice of guarantee' is delivered to the investor; coverage does not begin, however, until the investor has made the investment which is subject to the guarantee. Earnings are protected for a term of years which may, in specified circumstances, be extended so long as the term, so extended, does not run beyond the term of the capital guarantee.[146]

(vii) *Amount of coverage*

The maximum amount of coverage for capital is the original book[147] value of the investment. Any increment in value is thus not protected, although an expansion of the original undertaking by the investment of the additional capital may be covered as a new investment. Normally, beginning with the fourth year of the guarantee, the maximum amount of coverage is automatically reduced at the end of each year by an amount stated in the notice of coverage, determined after taking account of the expected return on investment and duration of the guarantee. Coverage is also proportionately reduced by a reduction in the original investment, as by a repatriation of capital. The maximum earnings coverage is an aggregate, over the term of the earnings guarantee, of 24% of the original book value of the investment, and no more than 8% in any one year. There is no automatic and progressive reduction of the maximum coverage for earnings.[148]

(viii) *Premium*

The annual fee to be paid by the investor varies from 1.0 to 1.5% of the investment according to the duration of the coverage. This fee is payable only after the investment is completed. Certain other relatively minor fees are also to be paid, such as a fee for consideration of the application and an annual fee for the period after the grant of the guarantee. This also would be before the completion of the investment.[149]

(ix) *Operation of guarantee*

The guarantee becomes operative when a capital investment is wholly or partially lost by reason of a confiscation or moratorium contingency, or when the assets of the enterprise in which the guaranteed investment was made have been destroyed totally or substantially.[150]

(x) *Amount of loss*

When the guarantee becomes operative, the amount of loss will be fixed at the D.M. value of the investment at the time of the guarantee contingency. In the case of partial loss of an equity interest or a long-term loan, the amount of loss will be the difference between the value of the investment immediately prior to the guarantee contingency and its value following that event.[151] In the case of an earnings guarantee, the amount of loss will be the unpaid amount of earnings distributed during the term of the guarantee.[152]

(xi) *Compensation*

If the amount of loss does not exceed the maximum coverage applicable when the guarantee contingency occurred, the loss figure will serve as the basis for compensation; otherwise the maximum coverage is determinative. Any payments or benefits received by the insured investor from the host Government, the enterprise or other sources subsequent to the guarantee contingency will be deducted. The investor is required to be a self-insurer for 20% of any loss sustained, and may not insure this portion elsewhere.[153] Compensation will be paid for the balance remaining after application of these ceilings and deductions, unless by the notice of guarantee the Government has exempted itself from liability for claims of less than a specified amount and the claim in question falls below that amount.[154]

(xii) *Subrogation*

Upon payment of compensation, the Federal Republic of Germany is subrogated to the investor's rights in the investee State.

With respect to the operation of subrogation in relation to German investors in the Sudan the governing provision is Article 5 of the Sudan–German Investment Protection Treaty. Under this article:

> If a Contracting Party makes payment to any of its nationals or companies under a guarantee it has granted in respect of an investment, the other Contracting Party shall, without prejudice to the rights of the former Contracting Party under Article 11, recognize the transfer of any right or title of such national or company to the former Contracting Party and the subrogation of the former Contracting Party by virtue of law or of legal transaction to any such right or title (devolved interest) which the former Contracting Party is entitled to exercise to the same extent as its predecessor in title. As regards the transfer of payments to be made by virtue of the devolved interest to the Contracting Party concerned, paragraphs 2, 3, 4 and 5 of Article 3 as well as Article 4 shall apply *mutatis mutandis*.[155]

If a German investor is granted guarantee to his investment in the Sudan by the Government of West Germany under the prevailing guarantee programme, he may be compensated by the latter if the risk guaranteed takes place in the Sudan. The compensation to be paid by the German Government will be recovered from the Sudan through the process of subrogation, whereby the Sudan Government must recognize the transfer of any right or title of the aggrieved German investor to the West German Government. This subrogation may arise by operation of law or by contract. By this arrangement the German Government would be able by virtue of the devolved interest to exercise the same titles and rights as its predecessor in title (German investor in the Sudan) would have exercised. However, this arrangement will not prejudice the right of the German Government under Article 11 of the treaty which stipulates for settling investment disputes through arbitration (see ch. 10).

(d) Disadvantages of national investment insurance programmes

The application of the United States and the German guaranty programmes cannot always be considered as effective mechanisms for protecting and encouraging investments abroad in all cases. Their disadvantages are evident. In both of them, only 'national' investments are protected. Even then, protection is afforded in specific countries with which the United States and West Germany have concluded bilateral agreements.[156] Moreover, guarantees are available only for certain specific investments: in the United States, only for new investments in developing countries.[157] The premium cost is considered high in both programmes. In the case of the United States, the programme is considered prohibitive for some investors.[158] They maintain that it is not worth the time and effort it takes to obtain the guarantee.

German investors object to the provision requiring self-insurance up to 20% or more of the loss incurred.

Perhaps the most significant criticism that can be launched against national investment insurance programmes is that they are impractical for insuring multinational consortia or projects which involve companies from different countries. These cannot be uniformly insured under several diverse insurance systems.

For these and other reasons, the idea of forming a multilateral investment insurance agency has stimulated abundant proposals.

4. A multilateral investment insurance agency

The idea of establishing a multilateral insurance agency for insuring foreign investments against non-commercial risks has been the subject of study by different international organizations and individuals since 1957.[159] They all share the idea of creating an international independent agency which would undertake the function of furnishing insurance to foreign investments regardless of nationality. All countries would be parties to the multilateral agency which conducts its operations freely without any influence from the participating countries. Of course, there are various differences among the proposals on the substantive and procedural provisions that would be contained in the multilateral convention constituting the investment agency. There are more than sixteen proposals[160] on the subject which cannot be examined here in detail. It is intended to discuss in this chapter only the Inter-Arab investment scheme and the World Bank proposal for an international investment insurance agency.

(a) The Inter-Arab Investment Guarantee Corporation: a regional scheme[161]

(i) *Origin and policy*

This is a regional scheme sponsored by some Arab countries with a view to encouraging investments of their nationals to be directed to other poor countries. Viewed as one group, the Arab countries present an ideal field for a regional application of an investment guarantee programme. Although they are all underdeveloped in various degrees, not all of them fall under the typical description of 'have-not nations'. In fact, countries like Saudi Arabia, Libya and the United Arab Emirates are among the world's richest *per capita* and accumulate capital surpluses beyond the present absorption capacity of their economies. Most other Arab countries remain, however, in dire need of new investments.[162] Instead of the outflow of surplus capital from the rich Arab countries to their neighbouring countries, most of this capital has been invested in the more advanced Western economies. This is due mainly to the rather unstable investment climate in the poorer Arab countries which have a suspicious outlook towards private foreign investments. There is a growing awareness of the important role to be played by Arab capital in financing the development of these countries. This thesis has a special concern for the Sudan which is described, as noted before (p. 8), as the food-basket of the Arab World.

Little effort has been made, however, to alleviate the fears of Arab investors of political risks in other Arab countries. On their part, the national governments of potential investors have not adopted national guarantee programmes. Investee Arab countries, on the other hand, have behaved hostilely to receiving foreign private capital.[163] The cases of the Sudan and Egypt in the 1950s are illustrative. The instability of governments adds to the complexity of the problem. In such a situation, an inter-Arab investment guarantee corporation may effectively bring forth a positive influence. By assuring potential Arab investors of guarantees against such non-commercial risks as would meet their investments in other Arab countries, the Corporation would be alleviating the major obstacle facing these investors at present. Moreover, it would achieve this significant objective without adversely affecting the 'economic sovereignty' of the receiving Arab States.

The formation of the Arab Investment Guarantee Corporation was first proposed in the Arab Industrial Development Conference held in Kuwait in March, 1966.[164] The idea was well supported in the Conference which requested the Government of Kuwait to prepare the necessary study. Kuwait conferred this task on the Kuwaiti Fund for Arab Economic Development. The Fund, while welcoming this opportunity for playing an active role in improving the investment climate in Arab countries, first took the view that the question of financial guarantees could not be tackled in isolation from other substantive and procedural safeguards.[165] Consequently, it issued a report comprising an outline of suggested agreements on three subjects: (1) an inter-Arab investment code, (2) a regional machinery for the settlement of inter-Arab investment disputes, and (3) an Arab investment guarantee programme.[166] The report was approved by the First Meeting of Arab Financial Experts in 1967[167] which in turn asked the Fund to prepare the necessary agreements. For logical and practical reasons the investment guarantee programme figured, among the three plans, as one deserving immediate concern. As a result, a draft convention for the creation of the Arab Corporation for Investment Guarantee came into being, which was approved by the Council of Arab Economic Unity,[168] with slight modifications. On 27 May 1971 the Convention was signed in Kuwait by Jordan, Sudan, Syria and Egypt, and was later ratified by the Sudan[169] and Jordan. Later on, all the Arab League's States, except Bahrain and Djibouti, became parties to the convention.

The operative articles of the convention can be briefly discussed under the following headings:

(ii) *Institutional and financial structure of the Corporation*

The Corporation is envisaged as a multinational public enterprise created by Arab States without distinction between the capital-importing and the capital-exporting.[170] It would be endowed with a share capital of its own and with the authority to conclude contracts of guaranty bearing itself the financial risk of such gurarantees.[171] A contracting party may choose to be a member of the Corporation or may designate for this purpose one of its public agencies.[172]

The drafters of the Arab Corporation Convention chose the institutional pattern of a financial and administrative entity in order to easily acquire the much needed confidence of its potential clients. These clients look, above all, for a direct and ready method of compensating their non-commercial losses. This advantage could not have been obtained if the Corporation operated only on behalf of its member governments.[173]

The share capital of the Corporation was initially 10 million Kuwaiti dinars ($28 m.) divided into 10,000 nominal shares.[174] One-half of the value of each share is to be paid in five equal annual instalments while the balance remains subject to call.[175] All capital must be paid in Kuwaiti dinars (K.D.) at their present official gold parity or in equivalent freely convertible currencies.[176] A state suffering from an exceptional balance-of-payments crisis may, however, pay part of the callable capital, not exceeding 25% of the requested amount, in its local currency. Such a payment can only be authorized by the special permission of the Council of the Corporation and subject to the undertaking of the paying member to re-purchase the same by transferable currencies as soon as the circumstances permit.

In view of the positive objectives of the Corporation, the initial capital of K.D. 10 million was surely very small. It was decided upon to facilitate the actual implementation of the project in the hope that the initial success of the Corporation would ordinarily lead to an appropriate capital increase. This increase could either be achieved by increasing the annual instalments or by admission of new member countries.[177] And as of January 1979 the capital has been increased to more than K.D. 20 million.

From the above descriptive account, it is apparent that the inter-Arab investment insurance project adopts a subscription financing system, under which every member of the Corporation is also a shareholder. At the same time, the Corporation relies mainly on its own capital to meet its obligations. One obvious advantage of this system is that there will be no need here to draw the distinction, maintained in many other projects,[178] between capital-importing and capital-exporting countries in the process of loss financing. This distinction, often difficult to apply, becomes necessary when overwhelming reasons require that only one of the two groups assume the financial burden of the programme. There are no such reasons for this discrimination in the Arab project. The richer Arab countries, unlike the developed industrialized countries, seem to have no particular economic interest in encouraging their nationals to invest in their less fortunate neighbours. Participation of the capital-importing countries in the financing of the project helps, to a great extent, to make them financially interested in avoiding the events which give rise to losses guaranteed by the Corporation. However, in order that the requirement of their participation may not prove self-defeating, it should not be effected in such a manner as to discourage altogether subscription by these countries in the project. This could perhaps be ensured by applying the criterion of ability to pay in establishing the percentage of capitalization to be subscribed by each member. Such a criterion is actually ignored in the Arab project, which requires only a minimum contribution from each member (5% of capital). As all capital-importing Arab countries which have so far signed the Convention have limited their declared subscription to the bare minimum, the project will not be effectively implemented unless richer members subscribe in larger percentages, and thus bear a greater share of the risks involved.

Under the subscription financial system of the Arab Corporation, the voting structure ties the number of votes of each member to the amount of his subscription in the share capital. This is ensured by the standard formula allowing each member a minimum number of votes (500) plus an additional quantity based upon the number of its shares (one vote for every two shares).[179]

The Convention does not adopt the standard of institutional structure distributing administrative powers between a general assembly and a board of directors. Having regard to the limited number of participating members, it sets up one organ (the Council) to act simultaneously as the general assembly and the executive board.[180] To offset possible disadvantages of this arrangement, the Convention provides for large powers for the director-general and establishes a supervisory committee over the Corporation's Management.[181] The Council is composed of one representative of each member and exercises all powers not explicitly granted to the director-general and the supervisory committee. It is endowed in particular with the power of interpretation and modification of the constituent convention. This latter power ensures for the corporation both independence and flexibility, 'elements proved by practice to be of special importance for the sound functioning of international economic agencies'.[182] With the exception of certain prescribed decisions which must be passed by a special majority of two-thirds, all other decisions of the Council are taken by the simple majority of the required quorum (three-quarters of the total votes, or, if this quorum does not obtain, two-thirds of the total votes at a subsequent meeting).[183]

(iii) *Risk coverage*

Risk coverage is confined to three designated types. Each of them is defined in the convention in a rather broad language followed by appropriate examples, while it is categorically emphasized that more specific terms must be used in the contracts of guaranty. The corporation is thus authorized to provide guarantees against all or part of a loss resulting from one or more of the following types of risks:

(a) Measures of the public authorities of the host country, whether taken directly or through an intermediary, which deprive the investor of substantial rights over his investment. Such measures include, but are not limited to, expropriation, nationalization, confiscation, seizure and sequestration. They also include the deprivation of a creditor from collecting or disposing of his credit as well as moratoria imposed on foreign debts for unreasonable periods.[184]

(b) New measures taken, directly or indirectly, by the public authorities of the host country which substantially limit the investor's ability to transfer abroad the principal, the income or the depreciation allowances of his investment. This also includes the adoption in the host country of obviously discriminatory rates of exchange on transfers and the unreasonable delays in granting transfer permits. They do not include, however, the risk of devaluation or depreciation of currency.[185]

(c) Any military act or civil disturbance, including revolution, rebellion, insurrection and general mob violence, which directly affects the material assets of the investor.[186]

The Convention adds three requirements, all negative in character, which further limit the scope of insurable risks. First, the risk must be such as could not be insured through normal commercial channels at reasonable rates.[187] Secondly, the investor must not have agreed to, or have directly been responsible for, the risk involved.[188] And thirdly, the insurable risk cannot be merely a reasonable non-discriminatory measure taken by the host government in the course of its regulation of economic activities in its territories.[189]

Though the last of the above-mentioned requirements is obviously justified, it may raise tremendous difficulties in practice. For it is a subtle line, indeed, that separates such 'reasonable measures' from the less justifiable ones which may amount to a creeping nationalization. To solve this problem, a more definite criterion will probably have to be developed in the guaranty contracts in order to ensure for each investor some certain knowledge of the limits of his coverage. One scholar[190] asserted that 'the corporation should rather be able to provide guarantees against any form of actual "taking of property" with the exception of confiscation ordered by a court of law after a fair trial'. I think this is too general an assertion, which tends to fetter the sovereign right of a State to regulate the economic activities within its territory.

(iv) *Nationality of investor*

The guarantee under the Arab Corporation is limited to investments in contracting countries represented by assets which belong to other contracting countries or their nationals. A broader view allowing the corporation to cover, in exceptional cases, other foreign investments was suggested in the draft prepared by the Kuwaiti Fund, but was later rejected by the Conference of Arab Financial Experts.[191] The more restrictive attitude adopted in the final text may be justified by the contention that the project should serve only the economies which participated in its finance. This contention fails, however, to consider the wider interests of the receiving States, and may conceal in fact reservations towards non-Arab investments based on non-economic factors.

The Convention maintains, however, a distinction between the nationality of individual investors and corporate bodies. Whereas the former must be 'nationals of the contracting countries',[192] the latter may simply be corporate persons whose shares are substantially owned by one of the contracting countries or their nationals and which have their seat (*siège sociale*) in one of these countries.[193] This implies that an eligible corporate investor must be under the substantial control of nationals of the contracting countries, but it does not necessarily mean that it must have the nationality of a contracting party. A corporation owned by nationals of one member country and having its seat in the territory of another member might nevertheless enjoy the nationality of a non-member, e.g. by having its business in that latter country. The distinctions maintained in the convention equally serve the important purpose of allowing the guarantee of joint Arab enterprises (joint ventures) between member countries or their nationals. Such a phenomenon, as elucidated before, is of special concern to the Sudan where several joint ventures have been established.

The condition of nationality must be satisfied both on the conclusion of the guaranty contract and at the time of claiming indemnification of the guaranteed loss. In case the investor has two or more nationalities, the nationality of a contracting party would prevail over that of a third country, and the nationality of the investee country would prevail over that of any other party.[194] In all cases, the Corporation cannot provide insurance to a national of the host country. If this latter limitation is justified by the purpose of the corporation (encouragement of foreign investment), it probably has exceeded its objective. An investment may be foreign in economic terms, i.e. represented by additional assets transferred from abroad to the economy of the investee country. By limiting the condition of foreignness to the 'investment' rather than the 'investor', the convention could really have encouraged the return, under the Corporation's guarantee, of the large amounts of capital which had previously fled the Arab countries to more stable markets abroad.

(v) *Eligible investments*

Almost all types of investment are eligible for guarantee under the Arab programme. Only loans must exceed at least a three-year maturity, unless the Council authorizes the Corporation to waive this limitation.[195]

Pre-existing investments cannot be guaranteed, however, as 'only new investments whose execution follows the conclusion of the insurance contract' are eligible.[196]

Re-investment of earnings from existing investments is considered, on the other hand, as a new investment and therefore eligible.[197]

Apart from its newness, an eligible investment must be approved by the host country, both for execution in its territory and for the purpose of guarantee against the designated risks.[198] This double approval may prove to be a cumbersome and lengthy procedure that puts off an investor from ever trying, in view of the bureaucracies of Arab governments. The Corporation should, therefore, be able to work out some formula with the appropriate authorities of host governments so as to simplify this procedure.

Investments need not, on the other hand, be privately owned in order to be eligible for guarantee. The convention categorically authorizes coverage of 'private investments' as well as other mixed and public investments operating on commercial basis. This is a new approach not adopted in any other investment guarantee project.[199] It guards against discrimination against some Arab countries which have a public sector type of economy.

There are certain priorities for investments which promote inter-Arab economic co-operation, and in particular joint Arab ventures; for investments considered by the corporation as instrumental in strengthening the productive capabilities of the host country; and for investments which may not be carried out without the Corporation guarantee.[200] The order of these priorities is not conclusive. The convention does not seem to create a legal duty on the Corporation to respect such priorities in the course of drawing up each guarantee contract. They should only be generally reflected in its operational policy.

(vi) *Range of coverage*

The compensation to be paid to the guaranteed investor should not exceed the lesser of two amounts, the losses actually sustained or the agreed amount of guarantee.[201] This follows from the nature of the guarantee contract as a contract of indemnity.[202] The Corporation's Council must set the maximum limit for the total value of all insurance operations provided it does not exceed at any given moment five times the Corporation's capital and reserves.[203] The amount of guarantee in any one single operation must not exceed 10% of capital and reserves, or 20% if the investment is an inter-Arab joint venture.[204] The Council must ascertain that guarantee operations are distributed among contracting parties. This is obviously meant to diversify the directions of investible funds in order to maintain some geographic equilibrium in the flow of inter-Arab investments, as well as to avoid excessive exposure of guaranteed investments.[205]

(vii) *Premiums and charges*

The Corporation is authorized to receive fees for examining the investors' applications and premiums for coverage of each type of risk. Such fees and premiums are not meant, however, to fully finance the Corporation's costs. The Corporation is meant to encourage the flow of inter-Arab investments by placing the cost of non-commercial risks which may face them mainly upon member countries, not on the investors themselves. Charges and premiums are only required, as the convention explicitly suggest, for the more modest purpose of (meeting administrative expenses of the Corporation and, to the extent feasible, providing suitable reserves).[206] They also ensure the seriousness of applications so that the Corporation's limited resources may be allocated to the investments which need them most.

The Convention permits a differentiated premium of each type of risk. It prohibits, however, discrimination among contracting parties in the premiums required from investors in the territory of each.[207] The policy behind this seems to be that discrimination would involve the Corporation in the embarrassing and uncalled-for situation of adopting prejudged views about investment climates in the different member countries, branding some as more risky than others.

To further encourage potential investors to seek the Corporation's guaranty, the Convention authorizes it to enter into special agreements with host countries in which the latter may undertake to share in the cost of, or even to pay fully, such charges and premiums as may be required from investors in their territories. This has been described as 'the only gesture in the convention suggesting the underlying assumption that the guarantee programme serves the interests of host countries more than those of the capital-exporting members'.[208]

(viii) *Time of presentation of the investor's claim for compensation*

The moment at which a contracting investor becomes entitled to claim compensation from the Corporation is not categorically indicated in the convention. In theory, this may be one of many possible moments beginning with the date of the realization of the particular risk covered by the contract until the inexecution by the host country of such arbitral award or judicial decision as the investor may finally obtain against it. However, in the absence of a contractual provision determining such a moment, it may be safely assumed that the investor can legitimately present his claim to the Corporation as of the date of definitely sustaining the guaranteed loss. But the question is: how is it possible to determine this particular date? If the Corporation requests the investor to exhaust first all local remedies, it would defeat its purpose by restricting the scope of its guarantee to the one risk of the failure of the host government to arbitrate. On the other hand, the aggrieved investor is reasonably expected to exert a minimum effort by using such remedies as may be readily available to him in the host country.[209]

(ix) *Subrogation*

Under the convention, contracting countries expressly accept the transfer to the Corporation of the rights and claims of the investor whom it indemnifies or agrees to indemnify.[210] The particulars of such a subrogation will be specified by individual contracts of guaranty which will undoubtedly be subject to many differences in national legal systems. Two important questions are posed in relation to subrogated rights of the Corporation over the assets: would the immunities[211] accorded by the convention to the Corporation's property extend to such assets? And must the Corporation exhaust all remedies previously available to the investor before it resorts to international methods of settlement of disputes with host countries? Unfortunately, the convention provides only partial answers to these questions. It is explicitly provided, for instance, that funds accruing to the Corporation as successor to investors will not enjoy immunity from exchange restrictions merely by virtue of its subrogation to them.[212] But the convention mentions in general terms that host countries will accord the Corporation suitable facilities to enable it to benefit from the rights to which it may be subrogated.[213] This may prove to be a particularly useful provision, especially as the Corporation could eventually receive from host countries large sums of local currencies which it may not otherwise be able to use in pursuing its purposes.

The requirement of exhaustion of local remedies by the Corporation, on the other hand, is not mentioned at all. The convention and its annex specify direct methods for the settlement of disputes between the Corporation and member countries. It may be argued that by agreeing to these methods of settlement host countries waived the requirement of exhaustion of local remedies (see *post*, pp. 296–7) in relation to the Corporation as subrogee to the rights of the indemnified investors.

(x) *Law to be applied by the Corporation*

The convention has attempted to establish a special legal order for the Corporation. In the absence of an applicable provision in the convention and the regulations issued by the Corporation's Council, 'common principles in the laws of contracting parties and recognized principles of international law'[214] will be applied to the case in hand. This formula has its value in insulating the Corporation's activities from the sphere of the domestic law of any particular member. But it is hardly possible to balance this negative aspect by the suggested alternative of applying common domestic principles and recognized international rules in a field where precedents and unanimity are very rare.

(b) The Proposed International Investment Insurance Agency (the World Bank Programme)

(i) *Background*

It has already been pointed out that the national investment insurance programmes are normally based on the notion of subrogation. But the difficulty with the entire operation of subrogation is that the host State might refuse to recognize the principle and object to the transfer of the claim from the individual investor to his national State. Indeed, past experience has indicated that certain developing countries, and particularly Latin American States object in principle to the operation of subrogation with respect to foreign investments on their territories. They consider subrogation as contrary to their sovereignty and as politically dangerous in that it transforms a dispute between a state and a foreign investor into a dispute between two sovereign states.[215] Also, they may argue that the principle of subrogation is incompatible with Article 2 of the Charter of Economic Rights and Duties of States.

In view of such difficulties, given the public interest in facilitating the flow of investment capital from developed to developing countries, and the fact that private insurance is neither available nor adequate to provide the necessary coverage[216] against non-commercial risks to foreign investments, the establishment of an international investment insurance institution has become very essential. However, among the various proposals towards this goal which are of particular concern to the Sudan is that sponsored by the World Bank. Indeed, the Bank had undertaken such a study as early as 1965, following a request of the Organization for Economic Co-operation and Development (O.E.C.D.)[217] which sent to the Bank a Report on the Establishment of a Multilateral Investment Guarantee Corporation. Consequently, Draft Articles of agreement for an International Investment Insurance Agency (I.I.I.A.) were prepared in 1966, 1968[218] and most recently in 1972. The 1972 draft together with a Staff Memorandum on Principal Outstanding Issues were circulated to the Executive Directors of the Bank by its President on 16 April 1973. But since that time not enough interest has been shown by the developed or by the developing countries in going further in establishing such an important agency.

(ii) *General survey of the Draft Articles of Agreement of the International Investment Insurance Agency*[219]

It is proposed in the Draft Articles of Agreement to extend the membership of the Agency to all States of the World Bank (I.B.R.D.) and to any other State which has been invited to sign the agreement.[220] The Agency will not have legal personality like the Arab Corporation, but will conduct its operations as the agent of, and for the account of, its members.

With regard to insurable risks, it is noteworthy that the Draft Articles follow the usual categories of political non-commercial risks which are usually insurable under the national insurance programmes, namely: expropriation, inconvertibility of currency, and armed conflict or civil unrest.[221] It is very interesting that the

Board of Directors of the Bank is empowered under the Draft Articles to decide by a weighty vote to insure other non-commercial risks which discourage international investment.[222]

To be eligible for the Agency's insurance, investments have to satisfy five tests under Article 2 of the Draft Articles. These are: the investment must be made by a private investor; it has to be 'sponsored for insurance' by a member State; it has to be made in the territory of a developing country which is not the sponsoring country; and it must have been approved for the purpose of insurance by the developing country in which the investment was to be made. A further, fifth test for the eligibility of investments for insurance is that they must be new.

As regards sponsorship, Article 3 provides that a member State may sponsor for insurance investments made by investors of any nationality, provided only that another member State did not object on the ground that the investor was its national, and may sponsor for insurance investments made by investors of more than one nationality. Such provisions reflect and emphasize the multilateral character of the proposed Agency.

To co-ordinate the operations of the Agency with those of the existing national programmes, Article 5 provides for the possibility of reinsurance by the Agency against all or part of the loss resulting from a risk covered by investment insurance or guarantee programmes of member States.

Article 6 deals with premiums to be charged for each type of risk or combination of types of risks.

The most important Article of the draft is Article 9 which governs the principle of subrogation. Thus, under paragraph (a), upon payment in accordance with the contract of insurance, the Agency is subrogated to all the rights and assets of the insured in relation to the loss suffered, and conversely, states who are members of the Agency must recognize such subrogation. The provision will be applicable in particular to the host state, whose duty to recognize subrogation is qualified by paragraph (b), by giving precedence to an arbitral settlement agreement between the insured investor and the host state under the International Centre for Settlement of Investment Disputes (I.C.S.I.D.)[223] auspices and avoiding the elevation of the dispute to an inter-governmental level. Meron in commenting on this provision observed that 'Thus, the host State need not recognize subrogation if it has agreed to submit the dispute to I.C.S.I.D. for arbitration, except if the dispute does not lie within I.C.S.I.D.'s competence, as determined by its Secretary-General or the arbitral tribunal, or if the host State fails to abide by or comply with the arbitral award'.[224]

The principle of subrogation was opposed by the Board of Directors of the Bank on the ground that it would ultimately lead to a confrontation between the Agency and a member country. However, this objection would seem to apply to the essence of a multilateral insurance institution. Furthermore, the opponents of subrogation argued, that subrogation might encourage the Agency to pay claims under insurance contracts in anticipation of recovery from the host country.[225]

Article IV provided for the financing of the Agency, which envisages formulae for sharing of administrative expenses, premium income and losses.

It is a pity that no consensus was reached by the Board of Directors of the Bank on several principal issues when they discussed the establishment of the I.I.I.A.[226]

(c) Difficulties facing the establishment of a multilateral insurance agency

There are several factors which are making the international investment climate, at present, less attractive than ever for establishing an international investment insurance institution.

In the first place, the majority of the capital-exporting countries are apathetic about delegating the task of insuring investments abroad to such an institution, because they have already established their own national insurance programmes. So far, most of them consider these national programmes successful. An international investment insurance agency would be a potential rival.

Secondly, there is the problem of the scepticism of several key developed countries, especially Germany and Japan, which do not believe that a multilateral insurance agency can serve their investors as reliably or cheaply as their national agencies. Yet some are reluctant to pool risks with the United States.[227]

Thirdly, considerations of language, location and national foreign investment policy require the continuation of national insurance programmes. For this reason, West Germany has opposed the creation of the International Investment Insurance Agency under the World Bank out of fear that German investors would have to deal with an organization in Washington whose language was English. This means using foreign contractual forms and not being guided by German political or economic interests.[228]

Most importantly, if a multilateral investment insurance agency or institution is to come into being, compulsory arbitration of disputes and subrogation must apply. But, as pointed out before, these principles are not acceptable to some developing countries, especially the Andean Pact countries.

A further difficulty is how to elect the board of directors and how voting rights are to be divided in the Council of the Agency.

In view of the above, it seems that the establishment of any multilateral investment insurance institution is far from obtained in the near future. With the demise of the World Bank's proposals, no further suggestions have been made for the creation of a multilateral investment insurance scheme, though there are some proposals for creating regional schemes.[229]

5. Concluding observations

Capital-exporting countries both developing and developed may encourage private investments abroad by facilitating investment insurance programmes. By so doing, the investor whose investment has been expropriated, or destroyed by war, or who has been refused permission to repatriate his capital or remit profits, will be enabled to receive compensation from his insurer without necessarily having to obtain a prior determination that a breach of international law has been committed by the host country. But these national programmes provide only a partial therapy for the problem, because they apply to national investments.

The establishment of an international investment insurance agency is desirable and should be welcomed. But the conflict of interests and the prevailing international investment climate do not seem to be favourable to that end.

Theoretically, the existing Sudanese investment laws furnish sufficient protection against expropriation and inconvertibility, but they fall short of providing any protection against war risks, which are pertinent to the Sudan at present. Experience has shown that the occurrence of civil disturbance and strife are not unlikely to take place in view of the repeated military coups in the last ten years, in addition to the stormy political situation in the Southern Region. These reasons, *inter alia,* impel the Sudan to support any move towards establishing an international investment insurance agency on the model of the World Bank Draft Articles of Agreement. On the other hand, such a suggestion may not be so appealing to Saudi Arabia despite the isolated sign of instability witnessed in the Mecca incident in November 1979.

The Arab Guarantee Programme has probably covered all the basic issues involved in the creation of a multilateral investment guarantee programme. However, since it will be the first experience of its kind on the international scene, unexpected legal problems may nevertheless arise in practice. Relevant precedents will ordinarily be found in the work of different national investment guarantee programmes such as that of the United States, which, foremost, seems to receive international recognition, in view of the great number of developing countries which are at present involved in it.

In the absence of an international investment insurance agency, it is advantageous to secure bilateral arrangements whereby national investment insurance programmes could be undertaken in respect of foreign investments. Of special relevance are the United States, the West German and the British investment insurance programmes. The latter has been recently introduced on a large scale by the Overseas Investment and Export Credits Act, 1972.[230] Strangely enough, though many British firms had been substantially hit by the Sudanese nationalization measures in 1970, yet, so far, no investment insurance policy has been issued with respect to any British investment in the Sudan. There has been only negligible application of export credit guarantees sponsored by the Export Credits Guarantee Department before the introduction of the existing British investment insurance programme. In relation to the Sudan, only one company[231] was reported to have benefited from that export credit guarantee. It is alleged that British investors are reluctant to buy investment insurance policies from the Export Credits Guarantee Department for three reasons. In the first place, the British investment insurance programme is very expensive. The investor has to pay a high premium – double the German and the American counterparts. Secondly, there is no selectivity at all in risks coverage; the investor must insure against all risks. Hence, it is pointless to buy investment insurance policy against inconvertibility in Kuwait or Saudi Arabia. Thirdly, the process of obtaining the insurance policy takes a long time, not less than six months, which is dramatically resented by the British business community.[232]

As the majority of investment insurance programmes, whether national or international, are effected through treaties, the observations made in chapter 6 on the legal character of treaties generally, apply with equal force to this chapter.

8

ASSESSMENT OF COMPENSATION

As pointed out in chapters 5 and 6, in the Sudan and Saudi Arabia foreign investors are given legal assurance, by the local laws and often by treaty, that their investments will not be expropriated or nationalized except for a public purpose and on payment of fair or just compensation. As expropriation and nationalization can never be wholly excluded for the future, what is left to foreign investors in the end is the right to compensation. The existence of such a right under international law is well established. It is supported by existing case-law of international tribunals, state practice and by legal opinion. Though the Communist states have sought to deny the existence of the right of compensation in case of nationalization or expropriation, they have actually awarded compensation by special lump-sum agreements to the western enterprises.[1]

As nationalization is a relatively recent phenomenon, international law has not evolved a clear or satisfactory standard of valuation of the nationalized property for the purpose of compensation. Because of this uncertainty, it has become important to foreign investors to have some assurance of favourable techniques and procedures that would secure to them a high scale of compensation. Neither the investment laws nor yet the treaties normally contain detailed rules in this respect. They simply provide general descriptions such as 'adequate', 'prompt', 'effective', 'equitable' or 'just' compensation. This state of affairs takes the inquiry to the practice of states, to see whether it is possible from that practice to fill in the gap.

1. Reparation, compensation and restitutio in integrum distinguished

Before embarking on an examination of the controversial issue of compensation, it is important to distinguish it from other two terms, namely, reparation and *restitutio in integrum*. This involves, practically, the distinction between lawful and unlawful expropriation. As noted earlier, measures taken in violation of treaty commitments or in pursuit of no public purpose, or measures discriminatory against foreigners, are unlawful under international law. Lawful measures, on the other hand, are those which are taken for public purposes and do not otherwise violate international law. This distinction is of considerable practical importance because it corresponds to a difference in the manner in which the compensation is to be calculated. It is noteworthy that though the term compensation is considered as one form of reparation for an international wrong,[2] it is not used here as a term of art, but as a generic term to cover all compensatory remedies. With respect to unlawful expropriation, compensation constitutes reparation for an international tort and has, therefore, a mixed punitive and compensatory character.[3] Such compensation aims at restoring the exact *status quo ante*, at least in financial terms. The Permanent Court of International Justice in the *Chorzow Factory*[4] case declared:

> It is a principle of international, and even a general conception of law that any breach of an engagement involves an obligation to make reparation.

The obligation is an immediate and automatic consequence of breach of an international duty.

(a) Meaning and origin of restitutio in integrum

On the other hand, it has been widely held in the theory of international law[5] that *restitutio in integrum* is the principal mode of reparation of a material wrong, pecuniary compensation being subsidiary in character, and applicable only when *restitutio in integrum is* not possible or not claimed.[6] But what is the exact meaning of *restitutio in integrum*? Unfortunately, the decisions of international tribunals are of very little help on this point. They speak of this remedy without indicating its precise meaning; they just refer to restitution in kind. Some common lawyers[7] on occasion seem to use *restitutio in integrum* as meaning 'specific performance', which is very confusing. Admittedly, this view may prima facie be quite sound when the international wrong emanates from breach or arbitrary abrogation of contract, either by nationalization or otherwise, yet one doubts the applicability of this interpretation to accommodate all cases of illegal taking of foreign private investment. Thus, it is untenable to equate *restitutio in integrum*[8] with 'specific performance' in the case of expropriation of a factory or bank.[9] Actually the distinction is very subtle, and the two concepts may coincide in the end in the same result.

To explore the exact meaning of *restitutio in integrum* it is essential to have recourse to Roman Law, the system from which the term is borrowed.[10] Buckland,[11] who investigated the classical Roman jurisprudence, observed that, '*restitutio in integrum* was the exercise of the Praetor's *imperium* by which, in effect, he caused to be treated as non-existent some event which had prejudiced a person's legal position. To base a claim in Roman Law on *restitutio in integrum*, there must be shewn an *interesse* i.e. injury to a man's property rights resulting from a transaction, or an event. Any property loss sufficed, either *damnum emergens* or *lucrum cessans* and it might be a realised loss e.g. a transfer of property or a liability incurred, an obligation or the like.'[12]

(b) Restitutio in integrum as reparation under international law

The most authoritative recognition of the Roman-orientated term of *restitutio in integrum* in the domain of international law, as a form of reparation for an international tort, is the dictum of the Permanent Court of International Justice in the *Chorzow Factory* case; albeit the Court did not use the same Latin terminology, when it stated:

> The essential principle contained in the actual notion of an illegal act – a principle which seems to be established by international practice and in particular by the decisions of arbitral tribunals – is that reparation must, as far as possible, wipe out all the consequences of the illegal act and re-establish the situation which would, in all probability, have existed if that act had not been committed. Restitution in kind, or if this is not possible, payment of a sum corresponding to value which a restitution in kind bears, the award, if need be, of damages for loss sustained which would not be covered by restitution in kind or payment in place of it – such are the principles which should serve to determine the amount of compensation due for an act contrary to international law.[13]

The purpose of reparation should certainly be to wipe out all the consequences of the unlawful act. This can be achieved if reparation takes the two forms explicitly mentioned above, namely, restitution in kind and pecuniary compensation. In the above judicial pronouncement, restitution in kind is explicitly made contingent on whether it is 'possible' to implement it. In reality, *restitutio* is seldom practicable. Sometimes it is not possible for purely material reasons, as when property of which the alien in question was unlawfully deprived has been destroyed. At other times it is not possible for legal and constitutional reasons, since it is very doubtful whether a state can rescind a legislative measure or set aside a decision pronounced by the courts,[14] especially when the nationalized assets have been integrated in the national economy under a new business and economic set-up. However, an exception may be exemplified by the Libya–Oil Companies Arbitration Award, which is the first incident in the history of international arbitration relating to economic development agreements; an arbitral tribunal held that the injured parties were entitled to *restitutio in integrum* and that the sovereign State was obliged to perform specifically its contractual obligations with private foreign investors.[15] It should be observed that the practicability of *restitutio in integrum* in such cases is dubious.

Even if *restitutio* is legally and practically feasible, it might still be completely futile, as it does not wipe out all the consequences of the illegal act or re-establish the situation which would in all probability have existed if that act had not been committed. A striking example of this is when a claim is made on the basis of loss of profits. In this case, the mere restitution of the property or rights is not sufficient, and hence the payment of an indemnity is the appropriate remedy either in lieu of or as a supplement to restitution. This means in simple terms that restitution of a thing *in specie* is often not enough; for complete restitution what is required is more than giving back a factory or thing illegally taken. Thus, in the wake of the sweeping confiscation of private enterprises by the Sudanese dissolved Revolutionary Command Council, Amedco Creslenzi,[16] an Italian national, refused to receive compensation for his confiscated firm in the form of restoring to him only the original assets, which were express buses. He alleged that the buses had been absorbed into the National Transport Corporation, a government-owned corporation, which had always run the confiscated firm at a loss, because of mismanagement; and that the bus service had become valueless. In the end, the claimant was compensated in monetary terms and allowed to reinvest in the same venture, though in certain specified areas.

(c) Theory and practice

Thus, in case of unlawful nationalization or expropriation, the first requirement is not pecuniary compensation, but 'restitution in kind'. In cases of lawful nationalization, a State is not under an obligation to restore. In reality, *restitutio in integrum* is possible only in exceptional cases. In the majority of cases, the responsibility of the State is discharged by the payment of compensation. This view is supported by the case-law of international tribunals, as well as prevailing diplomatic practice and the opinion of jurists. It has been recently reaffirmed by the International Court of Justice in the *Barcelona Traction* case.[17] This trend results in contradiction between actual practice and the theory of *restitutio in integrum*. For the practice follows a pattern which is exactly the opposite of the latter theory. In practice compensation constitutes the principal remedy, *restitutio* being clearly an exceptional one.

2. Orthodox view on compensation

The classical view required 'prompt, adequate and effective' compensation.[18] This derives from nineteenth-century ideas of private property ownership. The view was clearly articulated at the time of the Mexican nationalization of 1938 by the United States Secretary of State, Hull, in the following terms:

> The Government of the United States readily recognizes the right of a sovereign State to expropriate property for public purpose...the right to expropriate is coupled with and conditioned on the obligation to make adequate, effective and prompt compensation. The legality of an expropriation is in fact dependent upon the observance of this requirement.[19]

This traditional approach has been uniformly embodied in the draft multilateral codes suggested by capital-exporting countries for the protection of foreign investment.[20] It will be useful now to consider each element of this classical formula in turn.

(a) Prompt

In order to be prompt, compensation must be paid either before the taking or within a short time thereafter. If payment is delayed, the usual practice is to determine an appropriate rate of interest so that the claimant will not suffer any additional loss through delay.[21] Some municipal laws stipulate that compensation should be paid prior to the act of nationalization.[22] International tribunals have used various expressions to indicate the proper moment for payment of compensation. Thus, in the *David Goldenberg* case,[23] the arbitrator has ruled that compensation be paid 'as quickly as possible', while in the *Norwegian Claim* case,[24] compensation was to be paid in 'due time'.

Under the Sudan–German Investment Protection Treaty, compensation must be paid without undue delay.[25] The same formula has been adopted in the Sudan–Swiss Treaty.[26]

In actual practice, the term 'prompt' seems not to have been defined by rigid formula. Its meaning depends on the peculiarities of each case. As a distinguished rapporteur to the United Nations International Law Commission at one time observed:

> It is clear that the time-limit for the payment of the agreed compensation necessarily depends on the circumstances in each case and in particular on the expropriating State's resources and actual capacity to pay. Even in the case of 'partial' compensation, very few States have in practice been in a sufficiently strong economic and financial position to be able to pay the agreed compensation immediately in full.[27]

In most recent actual instances of nationalization measures, the payment of compensation provided has been by instalments spread over a number of years. This would be much affected by several factors, such as the extent of the nationalized property, the amount of compensation and the expectation of future commercial relations.[28] Examples are found in the Mexican nationalization of American property whereby Mexico paid compensation to the United States over a period of nine years,[29] whereas Poland paid compensation to France over a period of fifteen years.[30] In some compensation agreements, it has been agreed that compensation will be paid in a fairly large amount of cash and the remainder spread over a number of years. This was the case, for example, in the compensation agreements between Britain and Yugoslavia of 1948, Switzerland and Czechoslovakia of 1949, and Norway and Bulgaria of 1955.[31]

(b) Adequate or partial compensation

To be adequate, compensation should correspond fully to the value of the foreign investment affected by the nationalization. Ordinarily, the foreign investor's actual loss will correspond to the State's gain. By calculating the latter, the former is determined.[32] The recent practice of States, however, has shown that compensation has seldom been adequate and in most cases the indemnity paid has been partial. This is clearly demonstrated by the agreements between the socialist States of Eastern Europe and the Western countries, where the lump-sums awarded were not equal to the total of the individual claims. In fact, the difference between the two seems to have been considerable in the great majority of cases.

The practice of partial compensation has received theoretical support from several jurists, though the majority of writers on the subject reject it. The main agreement put in support of the view of partial compensation is its economic necessity, which means that if full compensation had to be paid, the nationalization measures would have been impossible or the nationalizing state would have fallen into bankruptcy. Judge Sir Hersch Lauterpacht maintained that the financial capacity of the expropriating State limits the obligation to pay full compensation in case of fundamental social reforms. He argued pragmatically that full compensation could in effect nullify the proposed reform and saw justification for payment of less than full compensation. He stated:

> The rule is clearly established that a State is bound to respect the property of aliens. This rule is qualified, but not abolished...(a) modification must be recognized in cases in which fundamental changes in the political system and economic structure of the State or far-reaching social reforms entail interference, on a large scale, with private property. In such cases, neither the principle of absolute respect for alien private property nor rigid equality with the dispossessed nationals offer a satisfactory solution of the difficulty. It is probable that, consistently with legal principles, such solution must be sought in the granting of partial compensation.[33]

Katzarov and other Eastern European writers suggest that compensation for claims arising from nationalization be fixed by 'new criteria'.[34] Relying on practices of States and many constitutional and legislative materials, Katzarov concludes that there is no place for 'full' compensation but only for 'equitable' compensation. To him equitable compensation comprises a number of elements involving a subjective appraisal. He thinks that four factors do in fact affect the amount of compensation in municipal as well as in international law. These are:

the nature of nationalized property, the expediency and social necessity of the nationalization, the financial capacity of the nationalizing State to pay compensation, and finally the way in which the property was acquired.

The determination of compensation on the basis of the above criteria according to Katzarov will to a great extent allow the equity which is sought to be attained. This new orientation can be found in legal theory expounded by some western writers, after the Second World War.[35] This modification to the traditional view on compensation is not due only to the influence of socialist philosophy; but also, and perhaps primarily, can be explained on the basis of the visible imbalance between poor and rich nations, compelling the former to achieve social and economic reforms within a minimum period of time. If nationalization is to be governed by traditional compensation standards, the dominant capital-exporting countries could exercise a veto power over legitimate attempts of poorer nations to achieve fundamental economic and social reform. Khun rightly has urged that the traditional doctrine of compensation must, *inter alia*, yield to 'consideration of the debtor's political instability or its capacity to pay'.[36] He concludes that 'a compromise in the method of compensation is not a compromise in the principles of international law'.[37] On the other hand, Francesco Francioni supports the new doctrine of 'equitable compensation'; though he justifies it on the principle of unjust enrichment.[38] In his view, this will not be applied in cases of individual expropriation, because the enrichment attained by the expropriating State is not *sine causa vis-à-vis* the dispossessed owner. Moreover, *vis-à-vis* the State of the dispossessed owner, the monetary value of most individual expropriations could not reasonably involve an impoverishment of the investor's community at large, so as to invoke the concept of unjust enrichment at inter-State level.[39] After condemning the assimilation of the concept of unjust enrichment to the idea of full damages, Francioni comes to the conclusion that compensation can be fixed by taking into consideration past profits gained by foreign investors under privileged conditions which allowed them a high rate of profits. He puts this view in the following words:

> Only by going back to the equitable root of the principle of unjust enrichment can we achieve a fruitful application of such a principle in nationalization situations. To this effect, we need to take into account all the elements of the specific situation in which the nationalization measure applies as well as the concrete character of the bilateral relationships involved. The notion of equity which thereby has to be applied – far from being a fluid and subjective criterion of general justice and fairness – will have to provide a tool for balancing over a reasonable period of time, the claims of the dispossessed owner with the profits and advantages that he enjoyed prior to nationalization.[40]

Depsite the justification for this 'equitable' view, which tends to dominate the recent practice of States,[41] the view does not escape criticism. First of all, it is undermined by the objective that it would run counter to the general principle of non-retroactivity of laws. In most cases the nationalization measure is not intended to apply retrospectively, and it is inconceivable to stretch its application as to seize profits gained by foreign investors under a privileged or favourable regime without express provision to this effect. Furthermore, the 'equitable' view will also contradict the doctrine of 'acquired rights' which seems to be firmly established in many legal systems as to attain the status of a general principle recognized by civilized nations, and hence a source of international law. The application of the 'equitable' view rests on the assumption that foreign investors would always gain profits under a privileged regime. This theory may fail to take proper account of the fact that gaining profits may not be achieved due to economic reasons. Not only this, but also that nationalization may take place where there has been no privileged treatment of foreign investment. Nationalization may be dictated by economic reform aiming at State economy in pursuit of an economic policy sponsored by a leftist regime. Also the partial application of the doctrine to large-scale nationalization is difficult to sustain. There may be an individual instance of nationalization which might impoverish the community of the home State of investors, especially in a multinational corporation, where the distinction of size and quantity is very difficult indeed to maintain. But, the main objection to the 'equitable' view is that its application destroys at a stroke the future of the investment incentives, which are thereby nullified. Despite this criticism the 'equitable' doctrine offers a useful theoretical justification for the recent practice of States on partial compensation.

(c) Erosion of the traditional rules

As described in chapter 6, a recent development concerning compensation arises from recent pronouncements of the General Assembly of the United Nations. Under resolution 1803 (XVII) adopted in December 1962,[42] in the event of nationalization, 'appropriate' compensation must be paid. That all the western developed countries, except France, voted for the resolution suggests that they waived their insistence on the standard of 'prompt, adequate and effective compensation' in favour of the term 'appropriate'. In fact, the classical formula seems to be little more than a preference assumed for bargaining purposes.

But the crucial question in international law has always been: how is the adequacy or appropriateness of compensation to be determined, and under what guiding principles? The G.A. Resolution 1803 (XVII) gives a rather vague answer. Appropriate compensation should be made 'in accordance with the rules in force in the State taking such measures in the exercise of its sovereignty and in accordance with international law'. This would not be a satisfactory criterion for some traditional international lawyers. Apart from the generality presented therein, there might be a conflict between the municipal law of the nationalizing State and the international law rules concerning the appropriateness of compensation. Robin C. A. White states that 'in the 1970s G.A. Resolution (1803 (XVII)) has become the developed nations' view of the conditions permitting expropriations'.[43] In the debate on the latter resolution the United States delegate asserted, and submitted an amendment, that 'appropriate compensation...in accordance with international law' means 'prompt, adequate and effective compensation'.[44]

The controversy has been recently widened by the Charter of Economic Rights and Duties of States (see ch. 6, pp. 127–41). The whole problem of nationalization and compensation has been shifted from the arena of international law to the municipal law of the nationalizing State. Thus paragraph 2(c) of Article 2 of the Charter does not categorically provide for compensation for nationalized foreign investments under international law. Instead, it provides that compensation may be paid under domestic law – thus, in effect, encompassing its antecedents in Latin American practice of the *Calvo* clause.[45] As mentioned before, the right to compensation is incorporated in the national legislation and even constitutional instruments of many developing countries. Moreover, the host State may consider itself bound by the norms of customary international law, and may submit to arbitration or other international means of settling disputes.

By restricting all matters of compensation for nationalization of foreign-owned property to the jurisdiction of the host state, Article 2 of the Charter does, in effect, raise the question whether there is a right to compensation. Also apart from the right of compensation, Article 2(2)(c) is problematic with respect to the terms of compensation. The criteria required by international law are not specified. During the discussion in the Second Committee an amendment was proposed in an attempt to lessen the rigour of this article. The proposed amendment formulated the right to nationalize foreign property in the following words:

> Each State has the right...to nationalize, expropriate or requisition foreign property for a public purpose, provided that just compensation, in the light of all relevant circumstances, be paid.[46]

The amendment was defeated by an overwhelming majority. Though the developed countries regard the Charter as devoid of any legal force, and not binding at all, it is not feasible to concede that, with a consensus of at least 104 States in favour of the new standard on compensation, the existence of any requirement of just compensation is a pre-condition to the legality of expropriation.[47]

(d) Effectiveness

'Effectiveness' usually refers to the exact form of the indemnity, and especially to the possibility of its immediate utilization by the recipient. This in practical terms turns on the currency in which compensation should be paid. This means compensation must be paid in hard currency. Under the German[48] and Swiss[49] treaties concluded by the Sudan, which represent the orthodox view, compensation must be freely transferable and settled in the currency of the country of origin of the investment. The same view has been adopted in the Sudanese investment laws (see *post*, pp. 222–3). In the *Wimbledon* case, the Permanent Court of International Justice considered this problem when specifying the compensation to be paid by Germany. The court said:

> Payment shall be effected in French Francs. This is the currency of the applicant in which his financial operations and accounts are conducted, and it may therefore be said that this currency gives the exact measure of the loss to be made good.[50]

This was, by one authority, thought even sometime ago to be in accord with the majority of cases decided by international tribunals.[51]

However, it is possible that payment of compensation may be in the nationalizing State's currency as was the case in the compensation agreement between the United Kingdom and Greece in 1929. The latter paid the former in drachmas. Other forms of payment may be utilized, such as the use of frozen assets[52] of the nationalizing State in the other State or the delivery of specified raw materials or other goods.[53]

From the foregoing, it is clear that neither the orthodox view on compensation that requires prompt, adequate and effective compensation, nor the modern view that seeks to delimit the whole issue within the arena of municipal law, does in fact correspond to the realities of the situation. Under the former view, there is a close relationship between the three requirements. The State and aliens involved have to choose between alternative forms and amount of compensation. The value of each of them depends on circumstances. Thus, when a debtor State is under a socialist regime, effectiveness would be the basic consideration. This is because there will be no other investment opportunities in that State to absorb the capital paid to the foreign investors. On the other hand, devaluation of currency or governmental instability may increase the value of promptness, while in a capitalist State of relative economic stability, it is the amount of compensation that counts.

3. Methods of valuation

State practice has developed certain methods of valuation of nationalized property for the purpose of fixing compensation. Even so, no simple solution is offered and no permanent and stable criteria may be used to determine the measure of compensation in all instances. In their place, there are several factors whose presence, extent, form or quality plays an important role in the determination of the amount of compensation. The importance of each variable is not the same in each case, nor are the same criteria always used. These factors are as follows.

(a) Market value

The municipal laws of some States assess compensation to be paid in the case of a lawful taking of private property on the basis of the market value of such propety.[54] This standard is also used in international law, when the property involved is such as to make the determination of its market value possible. But international judicial decisions have shown that the market value can only be determined with a fair degree of precision where the State measures involved were concerned with an individual enterprise (in which case they risk being discriminatory).[55] But at present, State measures involved are, as a rule, general in character, affecting the whole sectors of the economy. They usually result in a radical change of the country's economic structure, which in its turn, affects the value of the particular interests involved. This makes the market value of enterprises very difficult to determine, especially in cases of those enterprises functioning through concession contracts (see ch. 11). Also this method implies the existence of a perfectly competitive market free from external controls and internal monopolistic arrangements. These are very stringent requirements which are unlikely to be met with in most actual situations, especially in cases of general nationalization; specifically when the appropriate assets are unique thus precluding even the existence of a market. In this method, the claimant is confronted with the problem of obtaining reliable evidence which might be available as regards houses and other real property and some kinds of equipment and machinery. Even when perfectly competitive markets exist for the identification of these physical assets, however, it is by no means certain that market price is the appropriate measure of their value.[56]

(b) Value based on some measure of cost

Under this method, valuation of assets will be based on original cost, book value or replacement cost. It may be that this method is appropriate in some instances;

yet it has the obvious defect of being unable to reflect accurately the market conditions and technology that can change between the time when an asset is put into operation and the time of valuation.[57] If such changes take place, it is unnecessary to contemplate any relationship between original cost, depreciated original cost, or replacement cost, on the one hand, and value on the other.

In like manner, the value of an investment that has been nationalized may be seen to bear no necessary relation to the original cost, book value, or replacement cost. Usually the real cost of nationalization to the investor is the loss of opportunities foregone, and ordinarily he cannot reclaim them by replacing the lost assets. Alternatively, the nationalized investment may not be profitable or technology may make its assets obsolete, and hence its value would not be worth what it would cost to replace them.[58] This means that valuation based on some measure of cost, bears no relation to the real cost of nationalization, especially in the case of direct foreign investment.

(c) Value based on expected earnings

Before indulging in the discussion of this controversial method of valuation, it is important to distinguish between two issues, namely direct and indirect damages under international law. Direct damages will include all capital already invested by the foreign investor, e.g. in factory plants, offices or machinery. They will also include any stocks of raw materials or goods taken along with the investment enterprise. Indirect damages include intangible assets of the enterprise involved, such as goodwill and prospective profits of the investor. Which of these elements will be included in the compensation in any particular case depends on several factors, the most important of which is the lawfulness or unlawfulness of the measures involved.[59]

The validity of the method of expected earnings as a criterion for evaluating nationalized investment for fixing compensation therefor is very doubtful in legal theory. There exists in international law a dispute of long standing regarding the existence of an obligation to compensate for indirect damages.[60] One category of these indirect damages which presents serious problems is that of prospective profits (*lucrum cessans*). In the *Oscar Chinn* case,[61] the Permanent Court of International Justice held that '"the possibility of making a profit", cannot be considered a vested right of the owner of an enterprise.' When nationalization is lawful, the accepted view is that compensation aims at elimination of the alien's loss (*damnum emergens*) and not at the restoration of the *status quo ante*. The question of *lucrum cessans* should not arise except in the case of unlawful nationalization, since the State in such a case is bound to restore the *status quo ante*.[62]

Lucrum cessans is criticized as remote, speculative, contingent and incapable of ascertainment. It certainly leads to practical difficulties.[63] Thus, the lost profits in the *Anglo-Iranian Oil Company* case, for example, would amount to huge sums, many times higher than the value of the original investments, the factory plants and any other concrete assets or the enterprise in question. But surely the measure should be for a number of years – not the whole term of the concession. Actually, loss for *lucrum cessans* in all cases of radical nationalization would render the cost of such a measure prohibitive to most States.

However, international tribunals have on many occasions awarded damages for *lucrum cessans* where the circumstances so justify.[64] But it seems that this would be familiar in cases of breach of economic concessions, because the value of the agreement to the private investor is the profit which he expects to make during the duration of the contract. This will be discussed in chapter 9.

Thus, it would seem that the method of expected profits gives rise to practical difficulties in determining compensation for nationalized investments. Despite the strong opposition it encountered, Weigel and Weston[65] are of the opinion that valuation of an enterprise is best approached by using expected earnings methods. They believe that 'the value to the owner of an appropriated foreign enterprise is dependent on the expected annual earnings of that enterprise, i.e. total sales less total cost and taxes'.[66] This view seems to ignore the practical factors which may persuade the aggrieved investor to relinquish his claim for expected earnings. Thus, for instance, in the course of negotiations leading to the agreement on compensation for the nationalization by Egypt of the Universal Suez Maritime Canal Company, the representatives of the latter's shareholders abandoned their claim to compensation for the loss of revenue expected during the remaining years the concession had to run.[67]

(d) Latest tax declaration

This method bases the amount of compensation on the valuation of the properties involved by the investors themselves in their latest tax declarations. It was applied in the Mexican land expropriation and in the compensation for the landholdings expropriated under the 1959 Cuban Agrarian Reform law.[68] This method is applied because it creates a kind of estoppel against foreign investors who had declared under previous regimes false values for their investments in order to pay lower taxes. Foreign investors should be held to the same standard of good faith to which the host government is held. However, this method is applicable only when tax valuation is made by foreign investors themselves and not made by the expropriating government.

(e) Capitalization of net maintainable revenue

This method was followed in some of the British postwar nationalizations.[69] Under this method, the value of the enterprise concerned can be calculated on the basis of its average annual net earnings. Thus, if for some period of time prior to nationalization a company was netting £200,000 a year, conventionally, its value is determined by capitalizing projected earnings upon a risk–yield appraisal. If one chooses a 10% appraisal figure, the company is worth £2,000,000. Accordingly, if this company is nationalized, the owners are entitled to receive £2,000,000 as just compensation, which seems to be sensible.

(f) Price of shares of capital stock

The application of this method is particularly favoured in relation to enterprises of great size operating under concessions. The compensation here is assessed on the basis of the price of the enterprise's shares of capital stock. This method was adopted in many recent nationalizations, especially those effected within the western world. Under appropriate situations, the method is fair and practical, since the shares of stock have usually a market, namely, the Stock Exchange where the market price of shares is usually quoted. And, undoubtedly, rumours of nationalization will have a direct effect on the price of shares quoted by the Stock Exchange.

Since there is no single permanent price of shares, but rather a series of successive prices, the question is which price will be selected as the one on which the calculation of the company's value will be based.[70] In this respect, the situation in the Stock Exchange at various times before the taking of the measures in question has to be taken into consideration.

(g) Amount of insurance in force on property at the time of nationalization

This method was employed by the British Foreign Compensation Commission in the valuation of property in Eastern Europe. Thus, in the Application of Mary Ernestine Eagle (1964) the Commission held that:

> In the absence of any other evidence of value, such as the rental value in 1939, and the applicant had not refuted the valuation suggested by the Legal Officer, the Commission determined the value at 1,200,000 Lei which was the figure for which the property was insured in 1939.[71]

As most insurance policies are based upon the insurable value of the building alone, the Foreign Compensation Commission normally increased the figures by 10–35% to cover the uninsured parts such as foundations and site.[72]

(h) Valuation on the basis of site

This was also adopted by the British Foreign Compensation Commission to determine the value of buildings. It is usually based upon the assessed valuation of the site, by increasing this value by a certain multiplier in order to obtain a fair estimate of the value of the building as well. The location of the site and the type of buildings there would make a substantial difference in this case.[73]

The above survey of methods adopted in the practice of States shows that there is no single valuation formula that can be applied with mathematical certainty in every instance. There are other methods to be invented to suit new situations and there were other methods which had been applied in particular situations at different times. Indeed, in view of the various methods of valuation of property which exist in many States, it seems sound to conclude that the process of establishing an international standard will have to start with a study on a comparative basis of the municipal systems of valuation. Nevertheless, the validity of this thesis has been to a great extent undermined by the International Court of Justice in the *Barcelona Traction* case.[74] The court stated:

> Also distinct are the various arrangements made in respect of compensation for the nationalization of foreign property. Their rationale too, derived as it is from structural changes in a state's economy, differs from that of any normally applicable provisions. Specific agreements have been reached to meet specific situations, and the terms have varied from case to case. Far from evidencing any norm as to the classes of beneficiaries of compensation, such arrangements are *sui generis* and provide no guide in the present case.

This judicial pronouncement should be confined to the particular facts of the case which had been disposed of on a preliminary objection of the competence of Belgium to claim protection on behalf of Belgian shareholders in a Canadian company. It is true that compensation agreements are *sui generis*, as they are designed to deal with specific situations under varying economic, political and social conditions. But still, they serve as momentum to stimulate consensus among States on the controversial issue of the standard of compensation.

Having this background in mind we proceed to examine the Sudanese practice on the assessment and payment of compensation in cases of nationalization of foreign private investments.

4. Standard of valuation under Sudan municipal law and practice

(a) Compensation paid to the nationalized banks and companies in 1970

As has been pointed out earlier, Nimeiri's regime, in its early period in 1970, adopted a socialist policy aiming at complete social and economic reform, and nationalized all commercial banks and some leading companies. These nationalization measures. were general in character, including national and foreign enterprises as well. In this respect, they were consonant with the general rules of international law. What is important for the purpose of this chapter is to evaluate the *quantum* of compensation awarded on these occasions to see to what extent the Sudanese practice has been in conformity with the practice of other states. The evaluation is also important in relation to the Sudanese investment laws which have never yet been invoked, because there have been no nationalizations since they came into operation.

Before the nationalization measures in 1970, the operative investment law was the Organization and Promotion of Industrial Investment Act, 1967 (repealed). Under section 14 of this Act, the Government had the right to acquire anything owned by the industrial enterprises in time of emergency or for strategic reasons, provided that it paid just compensation and gave permission for the transfer of such compensation abroad in the currency in which the capital was imported. This Act was only partially relevant to the 1970 nationalization measures, as it dealt only with industrial enterprises, whereas the nationalization laws, namely the Banks Nationalization Act, 1970,[75] and the Companies Nationalization Act, 1970[76] were applicable to commercial banks and companies, in different sectors of the economy.

(i) *Constitution and terms of reference of Valuation Committees*

The net value of the nationalized banks and companies was fixed by Valuation Committees; each consisted of three members pursuant to section 4 of the Banks Nationalization Act, and section 3 of the Companies Nationalization Act. In the case of banks, the Committees were constituted by Presidential Decrees, which also determined their terms of reference and duties. On the other hand, the Minister of Finance and National Economy constituted the Valuation Committees for nationalized companies. Every Valuation Committee has to give its decision on valuation within a period not exceeding six months from the date of its constitution.

The Valuation Committees had to discharge a technical function involving lengthy examination of detailed facts and documents, complex accounts and extensive computations. In the wisdom of the Sudanese legislature, all these matters had to be entrusted to different bodies of independent experts with a background of recognized experience and skill in their specialized fields. This was considered essential to enable them to apply objective standards for the valuation of compensation. Accordingly, the membership of these committees, though based on a personal selection basis, has in fact included lawyers, economists and accountants.

The terms of reference empowered the Valuation Committees to examine any register, or private or public documents, in addition to the rights of discovery, and to collect information from whichever source. They were also given the right to seek the help of any official or semi-official authority or any person. They might, with the consent of the Minister of Finance and National Economy, form any sub-committees for certain purposes if this was deemed necessary for carrying out their functions.

(1) *Preliminary stages*

To co-ordinate and standardize the proceedings of these Valuation Committees a Central Committee was set up under the auspices and direct supervision of the Minister of Finance and National Economy. To achieve uniformity and systematic methods, the Central Committee had drawn up certain general guidelines, mainly of an accounting nature, setting out the methods and proceedings to be followed by all Valuation Committees throughout the process of valuation. The valuation processes under these guidelines have been accomplished in three stages. Stage one was a preliminary investigation aiming at identifying the relevant documents and particulars which were necessary to determine the net value of the nationalized property in each case. This helped to ascertain the assets of the company and verify the book value, and consequently to show the financial position of the company before nationalization.

In this stage, each Valuation Committee had to embark upon a data-collection process. Thus, it had to acquire a balance sheet showing all the assets of the company before nationalization. This included movables or immovables, goods stored; all contracts; goods despatched to agents, or *en route* to be exported; statements from banks, and cheques under collection; letters of credit; taxation position indicating all liabilities, etc. After collecting all the data and informations, each Valuation Committee had to sort out the documents collected in order to make sure that the documents of title and possession were in order. Finishing that, the Valuation Committees had to inquire about mortgages and cautions on all real property of each nationalized company. Then, it had to test the regularity of all licences and permits from appropriate authorities.

After this lengthy stage was accomplished, the Valuation Committees embarked upon stage two of the valuation process, which was in fact a revision of the first stage in an attempt to develop the correct procedure to be adopted in the technical valuation of every type of asset according to the latest results obtained.

The most important of all preliminary stages for legal purposes was stage three, which was the last step towards actual valuation. In this stage, the criteria and basis for valuating the assets and liabilities had been identified, and determined systematically as a final step towards determining the fixed assets on one side, and the obligations on the other side. The difference between the two would be the net value of the nationalized company or bank, as the case would be. This procedure had been systematically adopted by all Valuation Committees in order to maintain some sort of conformity and consistent adherence to the guidelines to avoid any discrimination or inequities that might result from applying a different procedure; which would, undoubtedly, influence subjective valuation, and inevitably affect the *quantum* of compensation to be awarded in each case.

(2) *Methods applied for valuation*

The nationalization laws, however, made no provisions with regard to the measure or the basis of calculation of compensation. The Sudanese legislature, by virtue of the nationalization laws, left such compensation to be fixed by the statutory Valuation Committees.

In fixing the amount of compensation to be paid to the nationalized banks and companies, the Valuation Committees had not systematically followed a single method of valuation in all cases. Like any other national Claims Commissions, the choice of method depended on the nature of the property to be valued. However, the Sudanese Valuation Committees had adopted the following methods:

Valuation of fixed assets

The calculation of the Valuation Committees of the nationalized companies' fixed assets proceeded on the basis of the actual cost price of such assets, less an amount of depreciation worked out with Business Profit Tax Schedules.[77] An obvious flaw of this formula is that it makes no allowance for normal fluctuation of prices from the date of purchase of the asset and the date of acquisition; nor does it give regard to the drop in the value of money, a fiscal feature which is international in character and not peculiar to the Sudan. Another serious flaw of the formula is that it takes no account of the duration of time in business of the nationalized industry in question, the degree of stability it achieved, or the earning capacity it attained.

Despite this criticism, the Valuation Committees considered this method as being equitable and reasonable. Though the method has been applied by the

British,[78] Canadian[79] and United States[80] courts on many occasions, it cannot be an ideal method of reflecting accurately the market value of fixed assets such as premises, hotels, agricultural lands, etc. In the case of goods, the purchase price and incidental expenses till delivery, according to the prevailing conditions of the market at the time of nationalization, were taken to represent the net value of all stored goods.

Indeed, the market value of the fixed assets of nationalized banks and companies had profoundly increased by the time of nationalization to more than ten times their original cost value, especially buildings and agricultural lands.

In determining the net values of nationalized fixed assets on the basis of the original cost less depreciation, the Valuation Committee took into consideration all the relevant and incidental expenses incurred in registering and adapting these assets for use. The rate of depreciation formula applied all through did not exceed 5% in each case. This added to the inequities which resulted from the utilizing of this method of valuation, which proved to be unjust in all cases. Consequently, all valuations by this method were subject to appeals, whereby the amount of compensation has been considerably increased as will be indicated below.

Valuation of shares

Shares were excluded from the items of fixed assets and classified into three categories as follows:

Shares in service companies

Shares in companies in the services sector such as hospitals and health centres were valued on normal value amounting to only one Sudanese pound per share; the reason being that they were not considered investment enterprises. This is absurd. Some of these service companies had been continuously employed as investment projects generating profits to their owners.

Shares in holding companies abroad

In these cases, three subsidiary arrangments were adopted. In the first place, shares validly transferred at the time of nationalization to the nationalized company or to the public corporation which succeeded it were valued on the basis of their book value or on the aggregate of their quotation in the Stock Exchange in the last week preceding the nationalization, whichever was the less. Secondly, shares which were proved to be validly transferred after nationalization were valued on the basis of their book value. Thirdly, shares which were proved by cogent evidence to be eligible for transfer to the public corporations which replaced the nationalized companies were completely excluded from valuation.

Other shares and debentures

In this case, the same procedure adopted in evaluating shares in holding companies abroad was applied, i.e. on the basis of book value or quotations in the Stock Exchange, whichever was the less.

Internal shares and debentures were valued on the basis of nominal value or original cost whichever was less. The cash asset was acknowledged on the basis of banks' certificates expressed in statements of account.

As the valuation of the assets of nationalized banks involves some technicalities, special general principles were embodied in a general memorandum. They were, in substance, the same as those followed in the valuation of nationalized companies' assets, except to the extent that it was considered necessary to adopt a special rule pertinent to banking business, such as local and foreign currency and promissory notes.

(3) *Appeals against Valuation Committees' decisions*

The above methods applied by the Valuation Committees proved to be inadequate devices to arrive at an acceptable amount of compensation; and the nationalized banks and companies were not satisfied at all with the decisions reached in all cases. Many petitions were lodged, by way of appeal to the appellate authority, which was a minister and not a judicial organ.[81]

Procedure of appeal

After a Valuation Committee finishes its work and fixes the net value of a nationalized company, it has to notify the Minister of Finance and National Economy of the gist of its decision, before notifying the interested party. On receiving the decision of the Valuation Committee, the interested party has the right to appeal to the Minister within thirty days from the date of notification of the decision of the Committee. The practice which was followed in all cases was that the Minister, before disposing of the appeal, used to refer the appeal to the Nationalized Companies Appeals Advisory Committee[82] for advice. The Advisory Committee, after consultation with the Valuation Committee which had originally examined the claim, would advise the Minister on all relevant issues legal or non-legal. Though the recommendation of the Advisory Committee is not binding on the Minister, the practice has shown that he usually gave them much weight in rendering his decision, which he had to deliver within three months from receiving the appeal.[83] The decision of the Minister is final, and cannot be overruled by the Sudanese courts.

Content of appeals

Not all the owners of the nationalized banks and companies were content with the *quantum* of compensation reached by the Valuation Committees. Their petitions of appeal to the Minister of Finance, as a final appellate authority, were mainly founded on the following grounds.

In the first place, they frequently contended that the compensation was not in consonance with the classical formula of 'adequate, effective and prompt' compensation. This was a natural result, as the majority of the foreign firms affected by the nationalization measures were of Western European and American origin, which have notoriously stood firm on the classical formula on compensation. In this respect, their petitions were mainly directed against the methods applied in the valuation. They claimed that the valuation of fixed assets should have been based on the market value at the time of valuation.[84] Some petitions claimed the amended book value, while others added considerable sums thereto, so as to reflect the market value for many reasons. Among these were: (a) they claimed that the revaluation was prompted by fluctuation of market prices; (b) that the revaluation was accomplished by qualified and expert technicians in the field of valuation; (c) that the revaluation was approved by the Sudanese competent authorities and acknowledged in the balance sheets of the nationalized companies before nationalization; (d) that the value of the fixed assets had considerably increased at the time of nationalization more than the book value, due to the rapid increase in the market prices generally; (e) that the Valuation Committees did not take into consideration the earning capacity of the nationalized companies.[85] This means that they claimed compensation for future profits; (f) some of them, especially the British firms, claimed compensation for goodwill. Thus the Tunnel Cement Company presented its claim for goodwill in the following terms:

> The Company has maintained the highest degree of industrial and administrative efficiency. At the time of take-over, the factory, quarry and all associated operations were in excellent working order and with every respect of enjoyment of a prosperous future.
>
> We are confident that this fact will be borne out by our successors, who have now taken over the factory as a long established and successful going concern...
>
> ...our nationalized company presents special features, and therefore, falls into a special category, which justifies its case being considered and treated on its own particular merits. The most important of these considerations is the fact that the company was carrying out one of the most essential industries and not merely ordinary commercial activities. As such, we consider that our company constituted one of the most important cornerstones in the economic development of the Sudan.
>
> For a period of over 23 years, our company was the only cement factory in the country and actually succeeded in providing a substantial proportion of its requirements of cement.[86]

Barclays Bank (International) claimed that they were entitled to be compensated for their firmly-established business, fifty-seven years old, the benefits of which have, since nationalization, accrued to the Sudan Government. They computed the goodwill of their twenty-three branches in the Sudan on the basis of ten times profit less an allowance for interest on the capital employed, totalling £S 6,569,563, on the grounds that the average return of profits to the Bank of Sudan for the years 1967–69 was £S 607,374.

Furthermore, Barclays Bank alleged that declared dividends should not be included in the valuation of the fixed assets and should be paid immediately, as the reason for not repatriating them was the failure of the Bank of Sudan to provide the required hard currency. Here, interestingly, it was alleged that declared dividends were beyond the reach of the nationalization laws, on the ground that, by their being declared, they were no longer considered properties of the nationalized banks and companies. The nationalization laws explicitly stated that they were applicable to the assets of the nationalized banks and companies and not the assets of the shareholders thereof.

Some companies objected to the method of payment as being inequitable. They also challenged the rate of interest applicable to deferred payments which had initially been fixed at 4%, whereas the average prevailing rate was 8%. This was alleged to considerably reduce the compensation.

Disposing of appeals

Surprisingly enough, the above objections raised in the appeals were dismissed summarily *in toto*. In disposing of these appeals, the appellate authority referred all petitions to the Advisory Committee, which examined them *en bloc* without disposing of each case on its own merits. It then rendered a general advice to the Minister (the appellate authority) refuting all the arguments put forward in support of the appeals. This approach seemed to be dictated by the economic policy not to increase the *quantum* of compensation fixed by the Valuation Committees, so as not to open the door to preferential or special treatment. The Advisory Committee usually referred the individual appeals to the original Valuation Committees which examined the claims initially. The purpose of this procedure was to give the Valuation Committees an opportunity to revise their decisions in the light of the particulars of the appeals. Theoretically this in itself is a vindication of the right of appeal by way of revision. But actually the Valuation Committees stood firm in their original decisions, which were subsequently confirmed by the Minister on the recommendation of the Advisory Committee. However, the arguments put forward by the Committees against the appeals centred mainly on the following points.

In rejecting the market value as a basis for valuation, it was contended that this method was inapplicable in the actual situation, because the rise in the market prices is usually the result of supervening economic reasons unconnected with the activities of the nationalized banks and companies.[87] It had been the view of the Advisory Committee that the methods adopted by the Valuation Committees were just and equitable because they maintained equality of treatment to all claimants, as the market value is very difficult to determine and even then depends on many variables and subjective assessment in each case at different times.

The Advisory Committee also rejected the contention that the revaluation should be taken as a basis for evaluating fixed assets. In its view, these revaluations had been prompted by the Egyptian Revolution in 1952 and the Sudanese October Revolution of 1964, as precautionary measures against probable nationalization that might have taken place as a consequence of these political events. This argument could be challenged on the ground that the initial acceptance of the revaluations by the previous Sudanese authorities would amount to estoppel against the Government contesting these revaluations. However, this line of argument could hardly be sustained. President Nimeiri's regime declared itself not bound by the acts of the previous regimes. Indeed, the nationalization laws were specifically designed as revolutionary measures to achieve overall economic and social reform, and to correct the errors of the past. In this connection, the Sudanese practice of valuation may be considered as a clear application of the 'equitable' theory on compensation as propounded by Francioni (see *ante*, pp. 201–2).

On the controversial issue of 'goodwill', the Advisory Committee alleged that a claim under this item could not be substantiated, for many reasons. Such reasons were, *inter alia*, that, upon being nationalized, the names of the banks and companies were altered. Thus, for example, Barclays Bank's name was first altered to 'State Bank for Foreign Trade', and the latter adopted its new name on the first business day after nationalization. So there was no benefit on advantage of the good name, reputation and connection of business. Also the element of competition, in which profit-making had been the dominant factor, had been eliminated. Nationalization introduced a different structural re-organization of all commercial banks and companies. A new style has been adopted in the management and purpose of the nationalized enterprises. This involved amalgamation, specialization and transfer of staffs from one bank or company to another; thus a new set-up has emerged. It has also been rightly alleged that the objective of the nationalization laws is not merely to acquire the benefit and advantage of the good name of the banks and companies, but to create a strong public sector which is anticipated to participate effectively in the development of the social and economic reforms. In addition, the claim of compensation for goodwill, was summarily dismissed, because of the change of external customers as a result of severance of connection with banks' and companies' headquarters. Indeed, it is true to say that goodwill may be more valuable than the net worth of the business itself, for instance where its is operated for the manufacture of a small and inexpensive commodity with a low wage bill and large profits.[88]

The practice of States on compensation for goodwill is at variance. The Canadian and English courts do make allowances for goodwill when calculating compensation. English courts generally measure goodwill by 'certain number of years' purchase according to the nature of the particular trade or business',[89] On the other hand, the Foreign Claims Settlement Commission (F.C.S.C.) of the United States has excluded totally compensation for goodwill. This is against the British Foreign Compensation Commission practice[90] which has taken goodwill into account in many instances.[91]

Relying on the advice of the Minister of Justice (now Attorney-General), the Advisory Committee rejected all claims to the declared dividends. Strangely enough, the Minister of Justice, interpreted the net value of the nationalized banks and companies, under the nationalization laws, as to including declared dividends as well, which had not been repatriated to the headquarters of these banks and companies.

5. Compensation agreements

The summary dismissal of appeals was resented by all claimants. The compensation fixed by the Valuation Committees had in fact fallen far short of the estimated amounts claimed. One difficulty in assessing compensation is that international claims are usually presented in greatly exaggerated amounts. It is a well known fact even in municipal law that a claimant seldom underestimates his claim. In a claim for compensation for properties of United States citizens nationalized in Yugoslavia, the claims originally submitted to the United States Foreign Claims Settlement Commission amounted to $148,472,773, out of which the Commission allowed only $18,817,409.89.[92] In this respect, the Sudanese experience runs counter to that of other States. For there had been no gross exaggeration in the amounts claimed by the owners of the nationalized banks and companies, if compared with the compensation fixed by the Valuation Committees. In the majority of cases, the suggested compensation corresponded at least to 60% of the amount claimed. Even then, the Government considerably increased the compensation, but the claimants were adamant and asked for full payment of their claims. As indicated in Table 3, the average percentage of the amount of compensation agreed upon to the amount claimed is roughly 82%.

During his State visit to Britain early in 1973, President Nimeiri had talks with

Table 3. *Samples of compensation paid to foreign nationalized banks and companies pursuant to the Sudanese nationalisation laws, 1970**

(Amounts in Sudanese pounds, unless otherwise indicated)

Name of nationalized bank or company	Nationality of Investors	Amount of claim presented	Compensation fixed by the Valuation Committee	Compensation paid	Percentage of compensation paid to amount claimed	Percentage of compensation fixed by committee to amount claimed
Gellateby Hankey & Co.	British	1,900,000	1,500,000	1,700,000	89.47%	78.9%
Imperial Chemical Industries	British	70,000	65,000	50,000	71.42%	92.8%
Sudan Mercantile	British	1,519,057	1,098,293	1,300,000	85.56%	72.30%
Barclays Bank International	British Also some American[1] interest	3,141,487	1,657,771	2,850,000	90.27%	54.21%
Portland Cement	Majority Shareholders: Swiss[2] and British;[3] Minority: different nationalities[4]	3,500,000	1,630,018	2,498,025	90.72%	72.3%

Bata Co.	British	1,600,000	1,200,000	1,150,000	71.8%	75.0%
The Mitchell Cotts Group of Companies	British	3,000,000	1,820,645	2,250,000	75.0%	66.0%
National Cash Register (N.C.R.)	American	80,000	45,000	55,000	68.75%	46.25%
Claims of certain individuals	Egyptian	53,900	53,900	53,900	100%	100%
	British	598,051	459,091	598,051	100%	78%

* Information and figures obtained from the Ministry of Finance and National Economy, Affairs of nationalized companies. Due to non-availability of sufficient correct data the writer is content with these figures.

[1] 3% of the stock shares of Barclays Bank International are owned by the Bank of America: 2 *I.L.M.* (1972), 106.

[2] Schmidheiny, Swiss, received 1,258,631 which comprised compensation to minority shareholders.

[3] The Tunnel Group, who received 1,258,631.

[4] Nationalities of Minority shareholders are as follows:

a. Sudanese 11 owning 11 shares
b. Egyptians 14 owning 12,990 shares
c. British 3
d. Swiss 3 owning 120 shares
e. Norwegian 1
f. Danish 1

N.B. 1. The average percentage of amount paid to compensation claimed was approximately 82.4%.
2. The average percentage of compensation fixed by Valuation Committees to amount claimed was approximately 67%.

the British Government about the question of compensation for the assets of British firms nationalized in the Sudan. There had also been talks between the Sudanese representatives and representatives of the majority of the firms on the terms of payment of compensation. A final agreement thereon was reached. It was expressed in general terms leaving the details to be spelt out in separate agreements with individual firms. The main agreement had generally set out the skeleton on methods and duration of payments, rate of interest payable, time of exchange rate, and sanction for delay or default.

(a) Pattern and characteristics of compensation agreements

In accordance with the general terms agreed upon in the Main Agreement, the Sudanese Government concluded separate compensation agreements with the claimants of nationalized assets. Formally, these agreements were formulated in standard form instruments with little variation. Particularly, they generally dealt with the following issues.

In the first place, they acknowledged the effect of the nationalization laws in vesting title of the nationalized banks and companies in the State from the date of nationalization.

Secondly, each agreement stated unequivocally that a certain *quantum* of money, described in specific figures, must be paid by way of compensation in the manner set out under the particular arrangement: this compensation to be in full and final satisfaction of the net value to each firm, and of all claims by either party against the other resulting from or arising out of the nationalization laws. The payment of compensation is undertaken to be made by annual instalments ranging from four to six years in sterling convertible at the rate of exchange prevailing at the time of nationalization as certified by the Bank of Sudan. No instalment or down payment whether of principal or interest was to be subject to any deductions of whatever nature. If any instalment or interest thereon were not paid within thirty days from the date on which it became due in accordance with the terms of the particular agreement, the balance of the compensation with interest at the specific rate was forthwith to become due, and payable on demand by the claimant. With regard to the British firms, all payments were to be made to the Bank of England as a paying agent. Furthermore, the Government undertook and warranted to the claimants that the Bank of Sudan would provide sufficient foreign exchange for paying all the sums as and when payable under the specific arrangements stipulated in the respective agreements.[93]

Thirdly, all instalments were secured by promissory notes in specific forms annexed to each agreement, and to be issued by the Government to the claimant contemporaneously with the execution of the agreement. The acceptance of such promissory notes would be by way of collateral security only and not as a satisfaction of the agreements or as accelerated payments in cases of default.[94]

Fourthly, it was agreed that interest would be calculated from the date of nationalization down to three years, at the rate of 4% per annum. This interest would become an additional sum payable at the due dates, be added to 'the residual sum', and be paid to the claimants by instalments as stipulated in each agreement.

Additionally, the Government agreed to pay interest on the accumulated sums at the rate of 6% per annum from the date of concluding the particular agreement until the final settlement.

Some nationalized British firms had before nationalization adopted Provident Fund schemes. As these firms were transformed into public corporations after nationalization, the previous staff were automatically absorbed in the new corporations. For this reason, it was stipulated in the compensation agreements[95] that the entitlements of the staff in the Provident Fund would be deducted from the compensation to be paid in each particular case. Consequently, the Government agreed to indemnify the claimants against all claims and demands of whatsoever kind which might be made against any of them by any member of their Sudanese staff serving on the nationalization date. This would cover all claims arising from pensions or contracts of employment or redundancy.

There were certain agreements of a peculiar nature owing to particular situations. Thus, under the Agreement with Schmidheiny and Tunnel Cement[96] (referred to hereinafter as the Tunnel Agreement), the compensation was paid immediately by special arrangement. In order to obtain the agreed compensation, Tunnel and Schmidheiny had to provide two middle-term loans to the Sudanese Government through Kleinwort, Benson Ltd, London, and the Union Bank of Switzerland, to cover the total compensation of £S 2,498,825 due to them in accordance with the agreement. The terms of the two loans were agreed upon between the Government and the two banks. The arrangement was that the two lending banks should pay, on behalf of the Government, the compensation due to the two claimants.

The Tunnel Agreement also has another peculiar feature. Tunnel and Schmidheiny agreed that the compensation due to the minority shareholders be included in their compensation. In return, they promised to indemnify the Government for any claims or demands of whatever kind resulting from or arising out of the nationalization of the Sudan Portland Cement Company. Owing to these unique arrangements, the Tunnel Agreement can be described as a typical package deal.

This technique of linking the question of compensation with the idea of procuring a loan of hard currency to provide the necessary funds for paying the compensation was raised in the course of the official negotiations between the Sudanese representatives and the British authorities during the State visit of President Nimeiri to Britain in 1973. The idea was completely rejected by the British Government on policy grounds. It was alleged that this would encourage the nationalization of British interests in other countries, which is against the British policy of encouraging private investment abroad. It was also contended that giving the Sudan a loan for paying the compensation would be resented by the British Parliament. The Sudanese delegation also unsuccessfully suggested diminishing the agreed compensation in exchange for giving the British companies opportunities of re-investment in the Sudan in new activites other than thoe sectors affected by nationalization.[97]

6. Practical problems

The implementation of the compensation agreements has created many practical, financial and legal problems. According to the Banks and Companies Nationalization Acts, 1970 the net value of the nationalized banks and companies must be converted to nominal bonds on the State for fifteen years with a 4% interest per annum. The State may, after ten years, redeem these bonds wholly or partially for the nominal value. At first, it was thought that the period of fifteen years would be sufficient to provide the required funds for redeeming the nominal bonds. Because of pressure exerted by the owners of the nationalized assets, who were not pleased with the methods and duration of paying the agreed compensation, the Government agreed to effect payment in a shorter period on special terms not provided for by the original nationalization laws. Accordingly, the Companies Nationalization Act was amended in August 1973,[98] whereby it was made possible for the Government to pay the compensation for nationalized firms by agreements by any methods in a short time, if this would be in the public interest. It was only through this legislative amendment that compensation agreements were made legally possible.

The discharge of obligations arising out of the compensation agreements subsequently caused acute financial difficulties relating to the availability of funds necessary for paying the compensation. Many proposals were put forward to solve the problem, but proved to be unworkable because of financial technicalities. According to the advice of the Attorney-General, it was thought better to re-amend the Companies Nationalization Act[99] to such an extent that the compensation due to any nationalized company should be considered as a loan from the Bank of Sudan to the particular corporation which succeeded that company. This loan ought to be paid in fifteen years, leaving an interest at the rate of 4% per annum as from July 1975. Under the amendment, each corporation was to pay the loan by equal instalments and the Government guarantee was to the Bank of Sudan for repayment of all loans. If any corporation for one reason or another failed to repay the prescribed instalments, the Government had to pay on receiving a notice therefor from the Bank of Sudan. It is believed that this amendment serves to cure all internal technical irregularities that might result from the implementation of the compensation agreements, as it helps the Government to allocate the necessary foreign exchange for paying compensation due to the nationalized firms, which was estimated to be £S.16 million to be paid by the Bank of Sudan.

As regards the compensation to nationalized banks, the problem was not considered as complicated as it seemed to be in the case of companies. This was because under Section 3(1) of the Banks Nationalization Act, all of the nationalized banks were transformed into sharing companies, the shares of which are owned by the Bank of Sudan. Owing to this statutory title, the compensation due to the nationalized banks is to be paid by the Bank of Sudan on behalf of the Government in accordance with the compensation agreements in each case, though there is no express provision to this effect in the Banks Nationalization Act, 1970. For this reason it was decided, as a matter of prudence, and on procedural grounds, to amend the Banks Nationalization Act in such a way as to legalize all past and future payments made by the Bank of Sudan in the implementation of the compensation agreements with the headquarters of the nationalized banks. It has been asserted that the acquisition by the Bank of Sudan of all the shares in the nationalized banks which have been transformed into sharing companies would be in consideration for the compensation it paid or will pay to the claimants thereof, on the request of the Government in accordance with the methods prescribed in each case.[100]

There are other incidental legal issues that ensued during the preliminary discussions leading to the conclusion of the compensation agreements. Most important of these was the question of the currency in which payment was to be effected. The issue was discussed at length and ultimately it was rightly resolved that compensation should be paid in hard currency, which is taken to refer to the currency of the home State of the claimant or the origin of the investment. This was decided on the authority of the *Wimbledon* case decided by the Permanent Court of International Justice and the opinion expressed by Fatouros,[101] and seems to satisfy the classical requirement that compensation must be 'effective'.

There have been queries by some British lawyers[102] on the precise effect of the Companies Nationalization Act. They asked whether the undertakings of the nationalized companies were acquired or the shares therein taken over? If it was the undertakings which were acquired, to whom was the compensation payable, i.e. (i) was it the companies whose undertakings had been taken over, or (ii) the shareholders in these companies at the date of nationalization, or (iii) the shareholders in these companies at the date the compensation agreements were signed, or (iv) the shareholders at the time when the compensation was assessed?

These questions were asked by way of precaution, in anticipation of the presence of more than one claimant to the compensation: a situation which can arise as a result of transfer of shares taking place subsequent to nationalization.

The situation was clarified by the advice of the Attorney-General, to the effect that under Section 2 of the Companies Nationalization Act, 1970, as amended in 1971,[103] the undertakings of the companies were nationalized and not the shares therein. The Attorney-General went on to say that according to section 3 of the said Act the compensation was payable to the nationalized companies, i.e. the shareholders in those companies at the date of the nationalization. This is understood as rejecting any claim other than by the original shareholders at the time of nationalization, and that under no circumstances would subsequent transfer of shares entitle the new shareholders to claim compensation. How to ascertain the eligibility of a shareholder to claim compensation for his nationalized shares was also settled by a previous advice, that under section 25 of the Companies Ordinance 1925 every share certificate duly stamped by the company, indicating the nature of the shares therein, was to be considered as conclusive evidence of the entitlement of the holder to the ownership of the nationalized shares. This would automatically qualify the holder to the compensation.

7. The Technical Committee for Revising the Confiscation Measures

As has been mentioned before, many private interests were sweepingly confiscated in 1970. However, this action caused severe disruption and repercussions in the Sudanese economy. As a result, it was decided to reverse these measures in order to encourage private investment. A top-level committee[104] was formed by a Presidential Order,[105] to revise all confiscation measures affecting Sudanese nationals only. Later on, the terms of reference were amended in order to consider some cases of aliens as well.

The method adopted by this committee with regard to valuation of confiscated assets, differed conceptually from those adopted by the Valuation Committees for valuation of nationalized assets described above. The Technical Committee's valuation was based on the book value of the confiscated assets at the time of confiscation. Assisted by subsidiary committees and advisers,[106] it fixed the net value of the confiscated assets on the basis of the last taxation declarations as shown in the balance sheets and the duly audited budgets of the confiscated firms at the time of confiscation, without deducting any depreciation. The terms of reference of the Technical Committee were indeed very wide. It could make any recommendation it might think suitable to the President, and in fact its deliberations disclosed that it had assumed a quasi-judicial function in investigating the confiscation measures. In doing so, the committee had examined all evidence for and against respective claimants in an attempt to ascertain whether or not the accusations levelled against them were true or false. Such a procedure could rightly have been followed prior to confiscation measures which were unfounded, and taken without giving the dispossessed owners the right to defend themselves. Actually, it had been publicly proclaimed that the confiscation was dictated by the desire to punish these dispossessed owners for the irregularities they committed and restore to society the ill-gotten gains they obtained under the previous regime. Surprisingly enough, it was proved to the Technical Committee that many of these accusations had been ill-founded and it consequently recommended the restoration of the confiscated assets to their original owners. In a few cases some of the accusations were proved to be true, to the satisfaction of the committee, which then had to recommend that only partial restoration was possible by way of penalty for the established irregularities. But in very few cases was the committee convinced by cogent evidence to confirm the confiscation measures.

The technique adopted by the Technical Committee was unique, if compared with that of the Valuation Committees, both in concept and function. In the first place, though the Valuation Committees were statutory organs like the Technical Committee, yet their function was only to value the nationalized assets as a step toward fixing the compensation to be paid in each case. In the case of the Technical Committee, a heavy job was assumed and carried out. This involved not only assessing the compensation, but also checking the legality of the measures themselves. In this respect, the Technical Committee entertained a revisionary jurisdiction and worked as a fact-finding committee, as well. In the case of Valuation Committees, the legality of nationalization has been implemented through legislation which acknowledged the right to compensation. The measure was prompted by the necessity of achieving economic and social reform, and not by way of punishment for contravening any laws or regulations as is the case in confiscation, which had initially denied the right to compensation.

The decisions of the Valuation Committees were formalized, with modifications in various degrees, in compensation agreements as described above. In the case of the Technical Committee, its recommendations were confirmed by Presidental Orders restoring the confiscated assets to the original owners. As many of the public corporations which succeeded the confiscated firms have been run at a loss, the Government had to compensate their owners for these losses. This actually entailed the payment of the difference between the net value of the confiscated firms at the time of confiscation and that at the time of the decision of restoration.

The payment was usually decreed to be made by instalments within shorter periods than under the compensation agreements with nationalized banks and companies. This disparity is due to the amount and nature of compensation in the latter case, whereby the State is taking over all the assets of the nationalized banks and companies. This presupposes the payment of large amounts of money, the payment of which has to be made in hard currency, thus having severe adverse effects on the balance-of-payments. At the present time, the Government is unable to honour its obligations under the compensation agreements by paying all the instalments as initially agreed upon. To solve the problem, negotiations are progressing for rescheduling these instalments.

8. Comparative evaluation

Though the Sudanese nationalization laws do not contain any provisions with regard to the measure of the basis of calculating the compensation, as is the case in some countries[107] which entrust this task to statutory commissions, yet the method so far adopted by the Valuation Committees and the Technical Committee has resulted in paying adequate compensation. It is true that the conclusion of the compensation agreements was accelerated by diplomatic efforts and lengthy negotiations between the Sudanese and British authorities on the one hand, and the representatives of the nationalized firms on the other. Still, this did not disturb the premise that the work of the Valuation Committees had established the basis of the negotiations without which the task would have been very difficult. If their deliberations and recommendations are compared with their counterparts in other countries, it appears that their decisions in fixing the net value of the nationalized assets were far ahead. Albeit their methods had conceptually been much criticized and condemned as not reflecting the realities of the international economic situations and disregarding the increasing rate of inflation, yet the outcome is encouraging. The compensation awarded in all cases could theoretically be elevated to the classical formula of being 'adequate, effective, and prompt'. The instalments are payable in short periods of not more than six years. If this is compared with the practice of other States,[108] it is undoubtedly far less than the period usually contemplated for paying the compensation.

The conclusion that can be drawn is that compensation for nationalized property in the Sudan has been settled by mutual agreement. However, one may go further, and say that the Sudan Government has in fact bought out, and not nationalized the banks and companies covered by the nationalization laws, in view of the amount agreed to be paid for them, in comparison with contemporaneous international practice. In the majority of cases the difference between the awarded and claimed amounts is, indeed, negligible, and ultimately has been relinquished by the claimants.

If the Sudanese compensation agreements are compared with those which had been concluded after the Second World War between the Eastern European and the western powers, it can clearly be shown that the pattern and content differ in important respects. The latter envisaged the setting up of mixed commissions composed of the representatives of the contracting States 'to determine the amount of compensation to be paid by the nationalising State.'[109] In the Sudanese counterpart, the compensation was unilaterally determined by statutory Valuation Committees, the creation of which resulted not from an international agreement or treaty, but by the voluntary act of the State as expressed in the original Nationalization Laws under which also the claims were made. Viewed from that perspective, therefore, the Valuation Committees are impartial quasi-judicial tribunals, international in scope, but domestic. Speaking of a similar case, the United States Assistant Attorney-General Holtoff said:

> the arbitration was unique in that, instead of being brought about as the result of a treaty or convention between the powers in question, it was the result of an Act of Congress [*analogous to the Sudan Nationalisation Acts*] by which a special tribunal [*analogous to the Sudan Valuation Committees*] was entrusted for the hearing of such claims against the U.S. Thus we are confronted with the unusual spectacle of a power against whom the claims were asserted, and establishing of its own accord a special tribunal for the determination of claims. It was consequently an arbitration international in scope but conducted before a domestic tribunal.[110] (My italics.)

It is interesting to note that the the Sudanese compensation agreements were in the main concluded between the individual companies and banks, whereas in the case of the postwar agreements they were made between two sovereign States with equal negotiating powers.[111] Despite this difference in the capacity of the parties, the former resulted in generous terms better than the latter with respect to the adequacy, promptness and effectiveness of compensation.

The question is: how far will this favourable practice be applied in assessing the compensation systematically in the future? Indeed, the certainty of this would no doubt assure foreign investors in the Sudan that they would be awarded compensation equivalent to the net value of their investments in cases of nationalization. Though there is no guarantee that the previous standards of valuation would always be followed in the future, yet they will definitely have their impact in stimulating an acceptable formula. In the writer's view, the assessment of compensation by Valuation Committees might reasonably have taken into consideration the financial capability of the State to honour the obligation arising from the compensation agreements. Otherwise the Government might find itself at the mercy of the transnational corporations owning subsidiaries in the Sudan, which might be nationalized if the economic strategy required it.

9. The existing standards of compensation

Under the previous Sudanese investment laws,[112] the private investor had to be given a just compensation after valuing his investment according to the current price at the time of nationalization. The valuation had to be made within six months from the date of nationalization and the value of compensation had to be paid in annual instalments not exceeding five years, in the same currency or currencies brought for the purpose of investment.[113]

In case a dispute arose as to assessment of the value of compensation, the investor was entitled to request the submission of the dispute to a committee of arbitration to be constituted of one member representing the investor, another representing the Government and the third the Chairman of the Committee of Arbitration agreed upon by the two members referred to, or on their failure to agree thereto, to be appointed by the President of the Supreme Court (now the Chief Justice) of the Sudan.[114]

Under section 19 of the Encouragement of Investment Act, 1980 the investor is assured of just compensation, which also must be fixed within six months from the date of nationalization, but the value of compensation must be paid outside the Sudan in instalments to be agreed upon, in the same currency or currencies brought for the purpose of the investment, unless otherwise agreed upon. Though this new provision does allow some flexibility as regards the duration of paying the instalments, yet it is rigid in requiring that the compensation must be paid outside the Sudan as this would prevent re-investing the compensation in similar or related ventures allowed by the Government.

The above legislative provisions indicate in clear terms how the previous experience in valuating compensation is given legislative recognition with substantial modifications to achieve a better procedural arrangement. Instead of leaving the fixing of the *quantum* of compensation to the sole judgment of a one-sided committee, this function under the previous legislation was entrusted to a Statutory Committee of Arbitration representing both sides of the claim, under an impartial chairman acceptable to the other two members. It is noteworthy that the Encouragement of Investment Act, 1980 does not indicate how the nationalized investment would be valued. Presumably this will be done by the Valuation Committee, and if there are disputes on the *quantum* of compensation, they will be settled by arbitration in accordance with section 32 of the Act, which we shall examine later in chapter 10.

The new legislative provisions also establish that the method of payment of compensation is to be in hard currency which is to be the same as that brought for the purpose of the investment. Viewed in this perspective, compensation to be paid to potential investors will in theory be effective. In this respect, the investment laws are in conformity with the German and Swiss investment treaties concluded by the Sudan, which require that compensation must be effective.

As to the adequacy of compensation, the previous and new Sudanese investment laws are not specific, save that the compensation must be just and according to the current market price at the time of nationalization. How to determine the exact amount of compensation according to this criterion is very difficult. The determination of the market value is also very difficult, and as such is not a guiding yardstick which can be considered as a step forward for improving the municipal standard of valuation of nationalized property. It is not clear whether or not the arbitration committees will award compensation for speculative items such as goodwill and future profits. The success of such claims will depend on the merits of each case.

There seems to be an apparent conflict on the *quantum* of compensation contemplated by the investment laws and the Constitution on the one hand, and the treaties on the other hand. While the investment laws provide that the compensation must be 'just', Article 34 of the Constitution provides that it must be 'fair', whereas the investment treaties demand that the compensation must be adequate, which, as explained before, must represent the exact value of the nationalized assets. To reconcile these standards, under the Sudanese municipal law, one should take into consideration the hierarchy of the three legal instruments in relation to each other. Obviously, in Sudanese municipal law, the constitutional provision must prevail over the other two,[115] and hence compensation must be fair, and neither 'adequate' nor 'just'. What is the difference between 'just' and 'fair' is a question of linguistic taste. There seems to be no practical difference. But still, there must be a uniformity in the drafting to avoid conflicting interpretation. Concerning the relation between treaties and investment laws under Sudanese municipal law, it has already been stated that the later in time prevails. But on the international plane, neither the constitutional nor the legislative provisions will relieve any State from treaty obligations, and consequentially in international litigation the treaty standard of adequate compensation prevails to determine the *quantum* of compensation to be paid to the German and Swiss investors in cases of nationalization as has been promised by the Sudan in the respective bilateral investment treaties with Germany and the Swiss Confederation.

However, the new Sudanese standard of *just* compensation can be considered as a compromise between the classical view and the Charter of Economic Rights and Duties of States, which provides for 'appropriate' compensation; which represents a *de lege ferenda* rule.

There should be amendments in the existing laws in such a way that there should be conformity between the Constitution and the international obligation of the Sudan. This would avoid any discrepancy both in the international and external arenas.

As to Saudi Arabia, the applicable law for assessing compensation is Islamic law which, in principle, entrenches the classical formula. But materials on this point are scarce and difficult to obtain. Furthermore, as indicated before, the experience of nationalization is not conceivable under the Saudi law, apart from Aramco, which is a fading-out process rather than nationalization in *stricto sensu.*

10. Conclusions

The real issue has almost been not whether compensation would be paid, but how much? What formula should be applied to determine value in gross will in fact depend on the policy towards foreign investment in each country. The debate over the amount of compensation to be paid when a country nationalizes foreign investment is still going on. This controversy arises because international law has no specific rules of its own on the standards to be applied in all cases at all times. According to international law, compensation is procedural and not of a substantive nature. Much depends on the *situs* and quality of the property to be valued in each case.

Though certain methods have been adopted in the past, it is not certain that they will be followed in the future. The Western developed countries, especially the United States, adhere to the classical formula of 'adequate, effective and prompt' compensation. In practice, the formula has seldom been applied. In most cases partial compensation has been accepted in full satisfaction. In fact, a decision to accept less than 'prompt, adequate and effective' compensation is, indeed, a political decision. The current practice of States is in favour of the criterion of compensation agreements which presupposes the existence of lengthy negotiations. This pragmatic process would encourage package settlements that take advantage of both the nationalized firm's expertise and the host country's economic and political needs. Thus, under this arrangement compensation may be awarded in kind such as coal,[116] crude oil[117] or other exports of the nationalizing state.[118]

The desirability of achieving an international standard of assessing compensation in cases of nationalization has been to a great extent made difficult to obtain in view of the Charter of Economic Rights and Duties of States, which denies the existence of any international law standard, and confines the whole issue to the national law of the nationalizing State. As a result of this new development, the national standard on compensation has assumed a special importance for foreign private investors. The more generous and popular the national standard is, the more foreign investors feel able to undertake the adventure of investing in a particular country. For this reason, it has become very important for a developing country desirous of encouraging foreign investment in its territory to provide an equitable standard for assessing compensation in cases of nationalization. In this respect, the Sudanese practice has been in the lead among the Third World countries, yet proved unrealistic in the critical situation of the ailing Sudanese economy.

9

ECONOMIC DEVELOPMENT AGREEMENTS

1. Introduction

The investment of foreign private capital in a state may be effected by contractual arrangements in three major ways:

(a) contracts between nationals (including companies) of the host State and foreign private investors, which contracts are governed by rules of private international law;
(b) inter-State agreements, i.e. treaties governed by principles of public international law (see chapter 6);
(c) contracts between States and foreign private investors. It is this last type of agreement that has been the subject of extensive study by scholars. The present chapter is devoted to the legal problems pertaining to such contracts.

First, this chapter will examine the nature and functions of economic development agreements, then discuss critically and analytically their legal effect, and try to ascertain to what extent they provide protection to foreign private investments. As there is some dispute about the international rules governing economic development agreements, some attention will be given to the practicalities of the matter, besides the views of scholars, the practice of States, and decisions of international and national tribunals.[1] The arbitration award between *Turriff Construction* (Sudan Ltd) and the Sudan[2] assumes a special place in this connection.

2. Nature and functions of economic development agreements

(a) Form and characteristics

There is no established legal definition of the term 'economic development agreement'. It is said that the term itself contains a functional description of an economic rather than a legal character.[3] The best view is that the term has replaced the traditional 'concession', which during the nineteenth century had become the standard denomination of agreements for the exploitation of natural resources. Thus, in the words of Nwogugu:[4] 'formerly, the term "concession" or "economic concession" was employed to describe all contracts for the investment of private foreign capital in developing the resources of a State, with the exception of loan agreements'. According to O'Connell,[5] an economic concession is usually: 'A licence granted by a State to a private individual or corporation to undertake works of a public character extending over a considerable period of time, and involving the investment of more or less large sums of capital. It may also consist in the grant of mining or mineral and other rights over State property.'

More recently, the term 'concession' has been identified as a contract by René-Jean Dupuy, the sole arbitrator in the Libya–Oil Companies Arbitration Award. In examining the legal nature of the Deeds of Concession in dispute, the Arbitrator asserted that:

> The tribunal must consider this question in the light of the general principles of law and the teachings of comparative law: a contract is defined as an agreement of one or several wills for the purpose of creating legal obligations. It appears therefore that, from a formal point of view and *prima facie*, the Deeds of Concession in dispute were of a contractual nature since they expressed an agreement of the wills of the conceding State and of the concession holders. Furthermore, the contractual nature of the Deeds of Concession corresponds to the standard accepted both by international practice and by international theory.[6]

Recent writers[7] have objected to the use of the term 'concession' in this respect, because it conceals the essentially bilateral character of the transaction. Thus, in the opinion of Lord McNair,[8] it could best be described as an 'economic development agreement'. This new term is preferable to the previous one, for two reasons. First, it clearly expresses the object of the agreement, i.e. the economic development of the country. Secondly, it stresses the dependence of such development projects on agreement or contract between the State and the foreign private capital owners. In the opinion of Nwogugu,[9] 'as the use of "concession" implies in most cases a unilateral grant by the State, the new term removes all doubts about the true relationship of the parties'.

Whatever the terminology employed, the form of the particular legal instrument is not important. What is important is the content. As far as the Sudan is concerned, the term 'concession'[10] is not favoured and 'economic development agreement' is used instead. It is, and has been, the practice to use the terms 'contract' and 'agreement' interchangeably. Whether the legal instrument be termed economic development agreement, contract or concession, all these instruments are in essence contracts between States and foreign private investors. It will be assumed here, therefore, that the terms 'concession' and 'economic development agreement' are merely alternative names for the same kind of bilateral agreement.

It is a purpose of economic development agreements to create a suitable legal climate for foreign long-term private investments in developing countries. These are of the following different kinds:

(1) agreements concerning transport and public utilities;[11]
(2) agreements for the exploitation of natural resources such as oil[12] and minerals;[13]
(3) agreements concerning manufacturing,[14] commercial[15] and agricultural activities;[16]
(4) guarantee contracts for loans and credit facilities to governmental departments and public corporations from private international banks and other financial institutions. The guarantees are usually furnished by the Bank of Sudan,[17] the commercial banks,[18] and the Ministry of Finance and National Economy;[19]
(5) management services agreements.[20]

These economic development agreements contain intricate networks of reciprocal rights and duties between the foreign investors on the one hand and the State on the other.[21] The rights and obligations of each party are well defined, so as to constitute a standard of conduct governing the performance of the contract. With the partial exception of the guarantee contracts, the economic development agreements share common features and characteristics. Lord McNair[22] conceded that the following characteristics are attributed to them:

(a) They are concluded between a government and a foreign individual or corporation belonging to another legal system.
(b) They are normally contracts for some long-term exploitation of natural resources involving the expenditure of capital in setting up permanent installations for the duration of the agreement.
(c) The rights created are not purely contractual, but are more assimilated to rights of property.[23]
(d) They confer extensive incentives to foreign investors, such as complete freedom from export and import duties, exemption from taxation and, in some cases, special facilities with regard to foreign exchange and exemption or reduction in rates.[24]
(e) Many of these development agreements are governed partly by public law and partly by private law.[25]
(f) There need not be any close connection between the host State and that of the investor, though the latter State usually lends its good offices in the early negotiations before concluding the agreement.
(g) In the majority of cases, economic development agreements make provision for arbitration in the event of dispute.[26]

(b) The legal nature of economic development agreements

The legal nature of economic development agreements is controversial and confused. Superficially, they look very similar to treaties, both in their negotiation and drafting. But despite this formal similarity between the two instruments, economic development agreements, being agreements between subjects and objects of international law, cannot properly be regarded as treaties.[27] This view was authoritatively stated by the International Court of Justice in the Anglo-Iranian case, when rejecting the British contention that the 1933 Concession Agreement had a double character – both as a concession agreement and a treaty. The court said that the agreement:

was nothing more than a concession agreement between a government and a foreign corporation. The United Kingdom Government is not a party to the contract: there is no privity of contract between the Government of Iran and the Government of the United Kingdom. Under the Contract the Iranian Government cannot claim from the United Kingdom any rights which it may claim from the company nor can it be called upon to perform towards the United Kingdom Government any obligations which it is bound to perform towards the Company. The document bearing the signatures of the Iranian Government and the Company has a single purpose; the purpose of regulating the relations between the Government and the Company in regard to the concession. It does not regulate in any way the relations between the two governments.[28]

On the other hand, economic development agreements are not simply private contractual agreements, since the other party is a sovereign State. The State of the individual or corporation is also frequently involved directly or indirectly.[29]

One scholar[30] classifies economic concessions as quasi-international agreements, because they are concluded between a State and a foreign corporation *inter pares.* They are neither contracts, governed by municipal law of some States, nor are they international treaties. This new trend has received recognition in the Libya–Oil Companies Award in the following words:

While the old case law viewed the contract as something which could not come under international law because it could not be regarded as a treaty between States, under the new concept treaties are not the only type of agreements governed by such law. And it should be added that, although *they are not to be confused with treaties, contracts between States and private persons can under certain conditions, come within the ambit of a particular and new branch of international law: the international law of contracts.*[31] (My italics.)

Contemporary writers such as Fatouros[32] and Cattan[33] have argued that development agreements cannot fit under either public international law or municipal private law; they are agreements *sui generis.* Cattan remarked that:

the contract is thus constituted in the first instance under public law, but it gives rise to rights of a subjective private nature. Although it is at times difficult to decide whether it is the public or the private aspects of a concessionary contract which are predominant, there is little doubt that the interest which the concessionaire acquires is one governed and protected by private law.[34]

Furthermore, in *Aramco* v. *Saudi Arabia,*[35] the Arbitration Tribunal was of the opinion that economic concessions may vary in their object, type and legal nature. This signifies that economic concessions cannot be subsumed under a common concept. The operative part of the award of the tribunal reads as follows:

the concept of the concession is very wide and varied; it may extend, according to the legislation and the doctrines concerned, from the grant of titles of nobility or of a burial ground to that of public functions...

Even the legal nature of economic concessions is not the same in the case of public service concessions, or of public works concessions, or of concessions for the occupation of the public domain or the exploitation of State resources, or of port concessions, or of concession of water works or of land, for instance in the colonies, or, lastly, of mining concessions. It does not seem possible to subsume all these various concessions under a common concept; this was recognized by the French Conseil d'Etat in its opinion of 19 and 26 December, 1907 about various questions relating to mining concessions. Finally, the legal nature of the concession is not the same in the different systems of law.[36]

In view of the recent developments in international economic relations, where tremendous and long-term development projects have been undertaken or are to be undertaken by transnational corporations in developing countries, there is now a tendency to internationalize development agreements. Accordingly, neither the *obiter dictum* in the *Aramco Award* nor the contentions of Cattan and Fatouros are tenable. Development agreements between States and foreign investors are international – or at least quasi-international – agreements. The question of their nature touches upon the fundamental aspect of the problem, viz. the law which governs the contractual relations which a state may establish with a private investor. However, the legal nature of the agreement will, to a great extent, have a direct bearing on the law to be applied, whether it be international law, the municipal law of the investee State or any other law (see *post*, pp. 238–52).

3. Validity of economic development agreements

Initially, as in the case of any agreement, the question of essential and formal validity is presented. Because of their hybrid character, the essential validity of the development agreements depends in part upon the authority of the parties to make the kind of contract involved.[37] However, in the opinion of Ray,[38]

> the State's authority will depend upon the law of the State; the company's authority will depend usually upon the law of the State of incorporation, or, as in the civil law, upon the *siège sociale*. Even if the representatives of the parties have authority to sign contracts on behalf of their principals, the contract must be of a kind not prohibited by the law of the State; and if permitted there, its implementation also must be permitted by the laws of the State where it is implemented.

In the view of this writer, this opinion is defective in two respects. In the first place, economic development agreements, as pointed out above, are at least quasi-international agreements, and hence private and public international rules may both be applicable. Thus, their validity may be determined by the principles applicable to the validity of international agreements.[39] As a State is a party to the agreement, rules of general international law shed light on its status. Consequently, such agreements must not provide for performance inconsistent with international standards of conduct or in conflict with the Charter of the United Nations. A choice of law or terms by the parties to an economic development agreement could not validate an agreement that ran counter to those international limitations.[40]

Secondly, the domestic law of the State party to the agreement will determine the authority of a person, and not the State itself, to conclude a particular agreement.[41] Thus, all economic development agreements in the Sudan must be concluded by different persons in accordance with certain directive financial circulars issued by the Sudanese Government.[42] The status of the signatory depends on the size and importance of the contract. In the case of mining,[43] petroleum[44] and large-size construction agreements, the authority to sign such agreements is conferred on ministers on the approval of the President.[45]

A very intricate question can be raised in relation to the validity of a contract concluded by the official of a State: can the State repudiate the contract on the grounds that it is *ultra vires*, because the official lacks the real authority to sign the contract?

The early international arbitrations applied solely the restrictive domestic law rules and, therefore, rejected claims arising out of the repudiation of *ultra vires* contracts.[46] But the recent arbitral awards have displayed a more liberal attitude. They have proceeded to establish the responsibility of the State for the repudiation of an *ultra vires* contract completely independently of the domestic law of the contracting State.[47] They have based their decisions either on general principles recognized by civilized nations,[48] or on customary rules of responsibility of State for injuries to aliens.[49] This latter view has rightly been supported by Theodor Meron[50] in the following terms:

> It is submitted that the soundest theory expounded by the tribunals is that under which conduct of the State in repudiating a contract made between an alien and an official acting within his apparent authority is considered as internationally wrongful. Certainly, the security of international trade and investment can be considerably fostered by holding States bound internationally by the apparent authority which they themselves have conferred on their officials.[51]

Since, under both international and domestic law, a person may be held out to another as having an apparent authority to conclude an agreement when in fact there is no actual authority, an economic development agreement concluded in such circumstances may be valid as to both the State and the alien.[52] This statement is subject to the qualification that the other party neither knew of, nor was reasonably chargeable with knowledge of an absence of actual authority.[53]

4. Law governing economic agreements

This is the most contentious issue in this area of international law. Various laws and principles have been propounded as being applicable to contracts between States and aliens. But there is no general consensus. Some proclaim the application of the *lex contractus*, while other entrench the application of the municipal law of the contracting State or the principles of law common to the parties, or the principles of law recognized by civilized nations, or international law, or administrative law. The Sudanese practice in this respect is not uniform in the sense of adopting a single body of law to govern all development agreements. Thus, in some agreements Sudanese law applies, while in others general principles of law recognized by civilized nations, or principles of law common to the parties, apply. On the other hand, the recent Saudi practice has became uniform in subjecting the whole contractual regime to Saudi law. Because of this difference, it is advisable to examine briefly the extent of the applicability to economic development agreements of these various laws and legal principles which have been proposed as constituting the proper law of the contract.

It is not proposed to discuss the rules of private international law which may call for the application of the *lex situs*, *lex loci contractus* or the *lex loci solutionis* to determine the choice of the proper law of the contract.[54]

(a) The lex contractus

It has sometimes been suggested that the terms and conditions of an economic development agreement itself constitute the law which governs the relationship between the parties. But it is difficult to conceive of a law for the parties that is not related to some complete system of law. Of course, every legal system recognizes the binding effect of the terms and conditions of contracts.[55] Some legal systems expressly declare the contract to be the law *inter partes*. In Sharia law, there is an established rule expressed in the maxim: 'The contract is the law of the contracting parties,' which is systematically applied in the Middle East.[56] Here, the Sharia is the proper law of the contract. Section 4 of the Sudanese Contracts Act, 1974[57] provides that a contract is a legally binding agreement. The provisions of the Act are applicable to all contracts.[58]

Nevertheless, commenting on oil concessions in the Middle East, Professor Carlston says something rather different. He goes so far as to assert that:

> An examination of concession agreements relating to the production of oil in the Middle East will reveal the comprehensive character of a modern concession agreement. Such an agreement becomes the fundamental or constitutive law of the joint enterprise of the government and the concessionaire.[59]

Some writers have carried this idea so far as to advocate that the *lex contractus* regulates the relationship between the contracting parties quite independently of another legal order. Professor Verdross stated:

The contract, created by a quasi-international agreement, is an independent legal order, regulating the relation between the parties exclusively. Nationally, the *lex contractus* may refer, for its interpretation or the filling up of eventual gaps, to the legal order of the contracting State, or of the other Party, or to international Law. But these legal order can only be applied in as much as they are delegated by the *lex contractus*, because it is the mutual rights and duties of the parties.[60]

This is an extreme view which has been much criticized by the majority of writers.[61] It is correct to assert that an agreement may be considered as constituting the law which governs the relationship between the contracting parties, but it is very dubious to suggest that an agreement can 'exhaustively' regulate the relationship between the parties independently of a legal order. No contract can exist *in vacuo*, i.e. without being based on a legal system. Lord McNair observed:

It is often said that the parties to a contract make their own law, and it is, of course, true that, subject to the rules of public policy and *ordre public*, the parties are free to agree upon such terms as they may choose. Nevertheless, agreements that are intended to have a legal operation (as opposed to a merely social operation) create legal rights and duties, and legal rights and duties cannot exist in a vacuum but must have a place within a legal system, which is available for dealing with such questions as the validity, application and interpretation of contracts and, generally, for supplementing their express provisions. Often such contracts may give some indication of the legal system within which they, or some part of their provisions, are intended to operate.[62]

Mann[63] also has criticized the proposition that a contract can constitute the law for the parties independently of a legal order. Such an idea, according to him, is 'doctrinally so unattractive, so impractical, so subversive of Public International Law', and it hardly requires emphasis that every legal relationship in general and every contract in particular must be governed by a system of law and is otherwise 'unthinkable'.

There is a distinction between the 'law which governs the contract and the legal order from which the binding nature of the contract stems'.[64] This distinction has been overlooked by Professor Verdross. Even Islamic Law, which maintains the principle of *lex contractus*, requires that the contract must be in conformity with the general principles of Islamic law as established by the Koran, the Sunna and the writing of Moslem jurists[65] over the years.

However, the acceptance of the *lex contractus* as governing State contracts with foreign investors assumes a special place in regard to the sanctity of development agreements in Saudi Arabia, and the Sudan. It is interesting to note that it is the declared policy of the present Sudanese Government to Islamize all laws pursuant to Article 9 of the Permanent Constitution which provides that 'the Islam and Custom shall be the main source of legislation'.

(b) Municipal law

According to the traditional international lawyers contracts between States and aliens were governed by municipal law. This orthodox view reflected the dogma of traditional international law which maintained that international law is a system of law applicable only to inter-state relations, *jus inter gentes.*[66] Since the alien party to a development contract is not a State, then such a contract, so the theory runs, cannot be governed by international law.

This traditional view was emphatically stated in the celebrated case of the *Serbian Loans*,[67] where it was said that 'Any contract which is not a contract between States in their capacity as subjects of international law is based on the municipal law of some country.' In determining the proper law of the loan agreement, the Permanent Court of International Justice observed:

> In this case it is the sovereign State which cannot be presumed to have made the substance of its debt and the validity of the obligations accepted by it in respect thereof, subject to any law other than its own.[68]

The accepted interpretation of this statement is that in the absence of a specific law there is a rebuttable presumption in favour of the law of the contracting State. Otherwise, the pronouncement would negate the generally accepted view that parties to a contract are free to choose the law to govern their contractual relationships. It has been observed that all legal systems apply the principle of the autonomy of the will of the parties to international contract.[69]

In the overwhelming majority of the development agreements concluded by the Sudan Government with foreign investors, Sudanese law has been chosen by the parties to govern the agreement. Examples are abundant. Thus, in the Contract between the Government of the Sudan and Turriff Construction (Sudan), 1962,[70] it was expressly stated that the Sudanese law be applicable to the contract; and the *ex parte* award against the government was rendered according to that law.

More recently, the choice of law clause in the Rahad Irrigation Project Supply Contract between the Democratic Republic of the Sudan and McDonald & Partners, 1974[71] reads:

> The contract shall be and be deemed a Sudanese contract and shall accordingly be governed and construed according to the laws of the Sudan.

Similar provisions are prescribed in mining contracts. Thus, the Agreement between the Democratic Republic of the Sudan and the Japanese Group of 1976 explicitly states in clause 12:

This Agreement shall be governed by and construed in all respects in accordance with the law of the Sudan. Sudanese courts shall have jurisdiction to determine any matter arising from the Agreement.

In a very few cases the law of the State of the foreign investor is chosen as the law applicable to the contract between the State and the foreign investor. Thus, Article 7 of the Financial Agreement between the Sudan Government and the Belgian Bank of Banque Lambert, 1978[72] postulates the application of Belgian law in the construction and interpretation of the contract.

In Saudi Arabia, there is a systematic policy that in all contracts between foreign investors and government departments or institutions Saudi law should be the law of the contract. This has become a settled practice familiar to all transnational corporations embarking on huge investment projects in the Kingdom. Some investing companies, such as Bechtel, went so far as to include the practice in their contract manuals all through their dealings with the Saudi government.

The chain of contracts described above demonstrates the prevalence of the autonomy of the will of the parties to choose the law applicable to their contract.

It is noteworthy that the selection of the municipal law of the contracting State as the proper law of the contract presents certain difficulties pertaining to the meaning of that law. Will it be the law when the contract was signed and acted upon, or the law when the dispute arises?[73] The contracting State may disappoint the expectation of an alien contractor in a number of ways. It may refuse to honour obligations owed even according to the local law. But the difficult case arises where the State has itself changed the law; for since the contract is created in the local municipal law and subsists in that law, it follows that the State can, by the exercise of its sovereignty, alter the local law.[74] In this way, a State may end its obligations under the contract before the period has run. This has been usually catered for by a 'stabilization clause'[75] in the economic development itself. Perhaps the best-known example of a stabilization clause is that stipulated by Article 41b of the Iran Consortium Agreement of 1954 which provides:

No general or special administrative measures or any other act whatsoever...shall annul this agreement, amend or modify its provisions or prevent or hinder the due and effective performance of its terms. Such annulment, amendment or modification shall not take place except by agreement of the parties to this agreement.[76]

Similarly, Article XVIII of the Petroleum Production-Sharing Agreement between the Democratic Republic of the Sudan and Chevron (Sudan) Co. Inc.[77] provides that:

The law of the Sudan and regulations shall govern the Agreement, *provided that such laws and regulations shall not be contrary to or inconsistent with the provisions of this Agreement.* (My italics.)

A similar clause is incorporated in the Exploration and Development Agreement of 1974 concluded by the Chevron Exploration Corporation with the Sudan Government for extracting copper, uranium and gold in the Hofrat En Nahas project.

How far such stabilization clauses are binding on the host State is very controversial, and this problem will be discussed below. To ensure stability in the contractual relationship of the parties, it is submitted that in all cases where an investment contract or agreement is governed by the law of the investee State, that law should be construed as to refer to the law when the contract was actually concluded.[78] In the *Alsing* case,[79] the umpire held that the supply contract between the Greek State and the Alsing company was governed by Greek law. This law was regarded as the law in force when the contract was signed rather than the new Greek Code of 1940.[80]

(c) The applicability of the principles of law common to the parties

A good illustration of this trend is Article 46 of the Consortium Agreement with Iran of 1954 which provided:

In view of the diverse nationalities of the parties to this Agreement, it shall be governed and interpreted and applied in accordance with principles of law common to Iran and the several nations in which the other parties to this Agreement are incorporated, and in the absence of such common principles, then by and in accordance with the principles of law recognized by civilized nations in general including such of those principles as may have been applied by international tribunals.[81]

Similarly, for the purpose of arbitration, Article XXIII of the Sudan–Chevron Petroleum Production-Sharing Agreement provides:

The signatories base their relations with respect to this Agreement on the principles of goodwill and good faith. Taking into account their different nationalities, this Agreement for such arbitration shall be given effect and shall be interpreted and applied *in conformity with principles of law common to the Sudan and the U.S.A., and in the absence of such common principles, then in conformity with the principles of law normally recognized by civilized nations in general, including those which have been applied by international tribunals.*[82]

Thus, in the event of arbitration under such Iranian and Sudanese agreements, it may be necessary to determine the common principles existing among different systems of law including Islamic law, civil law and so on. Such provisions can, at least, help to ensure that the parties do not misunderstand the legal effect of their agreement and the exact scope of their rights and duties.

(d) International law of contracts?

(i) *Express choice*

It has been suggested by Mann that contracts between States and aliens can be governed by international law, if that law be chosen by the parties to be the proper law of the contract. He expressed his view in the following terms:

It is possible, however, for contracts between parties only one of whom is an international person to be subject to public international law... (a) According to the theory referred to, a contract could be 'internationalized' in the sense that it would be subject to public international law *stricto sensu*, that, therefore, its existence and fate would be immune from any encroachment by a system of municipal law in exactly the same manner as in the case of treaty between two international persons; but that, on the other hand, it would be caught by such rules of *jus cogens* as are embodied in public international law.[83]

Mann has elaborated his thesis recently in an article in a foreign journal[84] which has been translated and applied by Professor Dupuy in the Libya–Oil Companies Award.[85] The English text is:

Although normally the law of a given State will govern the State contract precisely, years ago another possible solution was suggested. It was said that a contract between a State and an alien private person could be 'internationalised' in the sense of being subjected to the only other legal order known to us, namely public international law. This does not mean or was ever intended to mean that the State contract should be considered to be a treaty or should be governed by public international law in the same way as transactions between States. It simply means that by exercising their right to choose the applicable legal system the parties may make public international law the object of their choice. Certainly French law is designed normally to apply to French people or French transactions. Certainly public international law is designed to apply as a rule to States and the transactions between them. But nothing prevents a contract between the German State and a Dutch firm to be submitted to French law. Similarly, the fact that one party is not a State should not prevent the contract from being submitted to public international law. It would thus become subject to the mandatory rules of public international law. No mandatory law of any national system as such could touch it. If the parties desire this, why should we put any obstacle in their way?

In the Libya–Oil Companies Award, the Sole Arbitrator was to consider the following choice of law clause provided by Clause 28 of the Deeds of Concession in dispute:

This concession shall be governed by and interpreted in accordance with the principles of the law of Libya common to *the principles of international law* and in the absence of such common principles *then by and in accordance with the general principles of law*, including such of *those principles as may have been applied by international tribunals.*[86] (My italics.)

Thus, a complex system to determine the law applicable has been provided by the contracting parties involving a two-tier system:

the principles of Libyan law were applicable to the extent that such principles are common to principles of international law;
alternatively, in the absence of such conformity, reference was made to the general principles of law. This latter criterion of choice of law was made subsidiary, because it operated only where Libyan law and international law were not in conformity, but it was a sufficient criterion for the internationalization of the contract; and recourse to such general principles was justified by 'the need for the private party to be protected against unilateral and abrupt modifications of the legislation in the contracting State'.

The Sole Arbitrator, after tracing the origin and content of the relevant Libyan law, found it in conformity with the principles of international law, and consequently applied the choice of law clause in dispute.

However, the authority of this award may be questioned for two reasons. In the first place, the award was *ex parte* the Libyan Government as the Libyan Government did not appear at all throughout the proceedings, except for a diplomatic memorandum objecting to the arbitration in principle. Secondly, the parties had chosen the law applicable to the Deeds of Concession as it appeared in clause 28 which included international law as a legal order with which the Libyan law had to conform. For this reason, it might be argued that the award would only be narrowly applicable, and not of general application in cases where the parties did not designate by their own choice that international law will be applied to their contract.

Nevertheless, it should be observed that the award is innovatory and illuminating. It touched upon the very controversial issue which should be investigated thoroughly by international lawyers. This is the subjection of municipal law, as the proper law of the contract between States and foreign investors, to international law. And indeed at some point that international law must be superior over the municipal law,[87] if there is to be security of transactions and protection of contractual rights of foreign investors under the development agreements which they conclude with host States. In the words of Professor R. Y. Jennings:

The first step then, if matters are to be improved, is to establish a legal bridge between the contract and international law. An effective link must be forged between the principles of international law and the relevant municipal law, so that these two systems interact. We may find ourselves, for example, wishing to say that, even in the cases in which the contract is governed by the local municipal law as its proper law, certain overriding principles of international law impinge upon the contractual relationship itself. We can imagine a situation in which the principle of *pacta sunt servanda* or the *notion of acquired rights* or something of that sort operates so as to invalidate an apparent dissolution of the contract by municipal law.
... The relationship between international law and municipal law must be regarded as a monist system and no longer can be explained on the basis of a dualist theory that international law and municipal law operate on different planes and 'never the twain shall meet'.[88]

(ii) *Application of international law by inference*

Internationalization of contracts entered into between States and foreign private persons can result from various forms, though the parties may not say so expressly.

(1) *General principles of law*[89]

The reference made in a contract, in the clause concerning the governing law, to the general principles of law, may lead to the inference that the contract has been internationalized i.e. governed by international law. These general principles, being those which are mentioned in Article 38 of the Statute of the International Court of Justice, are one of the sources of international law. They may appear alone in the choice of law clause, or jointly with a national law, particularly with the law of the contracting State. A typical Sudanese example in this respect is Article XXIII of the Petroleum Production-Sharing Agreement with the Chevron Co. which, as mentioned before, envisages the application of the 'principles of law common to the Sudan and the U.S.A.', and in the absence of such common principles, then, 'the principles of law normally recognized by civilized nations in general, including those which have been applied by international tribunals'.

In the Libya–Oil Companies Award, general principles of law have a subsidiary role (like the Sudanese choice of law clause), in the governing law clause, and apply in the absence of conformity between the principles of Libyan law and the principles of international law. But the expression 'principles of international law' is of much wider scope than 'general principles of law', because the latter contribute, with other elements (international custom and practice which is accepted by the law of nations),[90] to constitute what is called the 'principles of international law'. These principles of international law were held to be the standard for the application of Libyan law in the Libya–Oil Companies Award, since it is only if Libyan law is in conformity with international law that it should be applied. The Sole Arbitrator concluded:

> Therefore, the reference which is made mainly to the principles of international law and, secondarily, to the general principles of law must have as a consequence the application of international law to the legal relations between the parties.[91]

The Sudanese agreement with Chevron will not be governed by the Sudanese law common to the principles of international law, as is the case in the Libyan counterpart, but by those principles of law which are common to the Sudan and the U.S.A. Is there any difference between the two provisions, and if there is any, what is the legal impact of this on the standard required for the protection of the contractual rights of the foreign investors?

Apparently, there is a basic difference between the two provisions. In the Libyan Deeds of Concession, the Libyan law would not be applicable unless it is – and has been found to be – in conformity with international law. But in the Sudanese provision, Sudanese law will not apply automatically, unless it conforms with the principles of law common to the United States; so the parties here have chosen the conformity with the law of the United States to be the standard criterion for applying Sudanese law. This implies that international law will not be applied if the laws of the Sudan and the United States coincide. The justification for this attitude towards Sudanese law can be explained in terms of policy. The parties did not intend to subject Sudanese law first to international law, because it was not conceived at the time when the agreement was concluded that there will be any major difference between the laws of the United States and the Sudan. Both stemmed from the same origin, i.e. common law. In the case of the Libyan Deeds of Concession, the parties elected to subject, from the outset, the Libyan law to international law on the assumption that both the Libyan law and the American law originate in different legal systems. The Libyan law originates in the civil law and Islamic law, whereas the United States law stems from the common law.

Nevertheless, this difference in the choice of the applicable law does not make any significant effect on the standard required for the protection of the contractual rights in the case of foreign investors. In any case, international law will come into operation, especially if Sudanese law and United States law do not agree on the issue in dispute. But international law will come into the scene later, while in the Libyan Deeds of Concession it will come immediately because the applicable Libyan law is determined by reference to international law, and as such, would not apply unless it initially coincides with international law.

International arbitration case law confirms that the reference to the general principles of law is always regarded as a sufficient criterion for the internationalization of a contract. The majority of these cases deal with oil concessions.[92] Perhaps the most influential exposition of the idea that economic development agreements can be governed by general principles of law was that by Lord McNair. He maintained that the system of law governing such contracts cannot be international law *stricto sensu*, since these contracts are not inter-State contracts and do not deal with inter-State relations. He suggests that the system of law most likely to be suitable for the regulation of these contracts and the adjudication of disputes arising under them is 'the principles of law recognized by civilized nations'.[93]

The body of law represented by the general principles of law recognized by civilized nations has received different names: 'transnational law', 'common law of nations', 'a modern law of nature'.[94]

Many doubts have been expressed as to whether such general principles of law or 'transnational law' constitute a law or a legal system.[95] Thus, Mann has said on this point that:

It is impossible, or would at any rate be inexact to speak of the application of the general principles of law recognized by civilized nations. The general principles are not a law or a legal system that can be applied or referred to...Lord McNair...somewhat surprisingly considers the general principles as affording, in certain cases, 'the choice of a legal system', and, indeed, describes them as a 'system of law'. Yet it is hardly open to doubt that, unless they are equiparated to public international law, the general principles are not a legal system at all, and Lord McNair clearly refuses to equiparate them. For he submits that the contracts he has in mind are not 'governed by public international law *stricto sensu*', but 'should be governed by the general principles of law recognized by civilized nations'.[96]

However, the general principles of law recognized by civilized nations have received such recognition that it seems now almost immaterial whether such principles are described as a 'system of law' or as a 'source of law'. Their recognition as a distinct body of legal rules in the international scene was their inclusion in Article 38 of the Statute of the International Court of Justice as one of the sources of international law. No precise definition of the general principles of law exists as yet, though their structure has been outlined in broad terms. Friedmann has observed that an examination of these general principles means a pragmatic attempt to extract from the major legal systems of the world the maximum measure of agreement on the principles relevant to the case in hand.[97]

This approach was followed in the *Abu Dhabi* case,[98] by Lord Asquith, whose aim was to use comparative law as a guide to the principles that, in the circumstances of the case, are most appropriate and equitable. The oil concession which gave rise to this arbitration, contained a declaration by the parties 'that they base their work in this agreement on goodwill and sincerity of belief and on the interpretation of this agreement in a fashion consistent with reason'. Lord Asquith held that, since no relevant law could be found in the State of Abu Dhabi, the proper law of the contract consisted of 'principles rooted in the good sense and common practice of the generality of civilized nations – a sort of "modern law of nature".' The arbitrator found that 'the Sheikh administers a purely discretionary justice with the assistance of the Koran (sic); and it would be fanciful to suggest that in this very primitive region there is any settled body of legal principles applicable to the construction of modern commercial instruments'.[99] But that is not true. There are scores of volumes on the Islamic law which have a lot about contracts. After all, Lord Asquith sat in Paris and was addressed only by two counsel: one English and one Jewish (Waldock and H. Lauterpacht)! What would they know about Islamic law?

This process of reasoning employed by Lord Asquith is reported to be of basic and utmost importance. It has been quoted with approval as representing a major advance, *inter alia*, by Jessup, McNair and Mann.[100] By using the term 'modern law of nature', Lord Asquith was meaning a shorthand description of the principles, to be selected either from international law or from any of the several national systems of law, applicable to the circumstances of the agreement in issue, and to the equities of the situation. As a matter of fact Lord Asquith was seeking a way of applying the English law of contract, which was the only law he knew.

By a similar token, the Arbitrator in the *Ruler of Qatar* v. *International Marine Oil Company Ltd.* again found that the law of the host State (Islamic law) could not be considered as the proper law of the contract, because it did not embody legal principles applicable to oil concessions. Therefore, the agreement was governed by the 'principles of justice, equity and good conscience'.[101]

In the view of the writer, these cases were decided on a misconception of the content of Islamic law, which recognizes the sanctity of the contract generally. Under Islamic law the parties to the contract must carry out their obligations fully and in good faith (*pacta sunt servanda*): 'Pacts are binding'. It does not make any difference whether one of the parties is the state or a foreigner. This is a basic tenet of Islamic law which does not require any investigation. The real difficulty is that there was no body of legislation one could point to. But this negative aspect has been catered for at present, in some Arab countries by modern legislation, which more or less follows Islamic law (figh).

Furthermore, in the *Sapphire–N.I.O.C. Arbitration*, the Arbitrator held that Article 38 of the Concession agreement, to the effect that 'the parties undertake to carry out its provisions according to the principles of good faith and good will, and to respect the spirit as well as the letter of the agreement', was scarcely compatible with the application of the municipal law of a particular country, and it called for the application of the general principles of law recognized by civilized nations.

(2) *The arbitration clause*

It is possible to suggest that a contract can be internationalized if the contract contains a clause providing that disputes are to be adjudged by an international court or arbitration.[102] Such a clause has a twofold consequence. On the one hand, the institution of arbitration must be that established by international law. On the other hand as regards the law applicable to the merits of the dispute itself, the inclusion of an arbitration clause leads to a reference to the rules of international law.[103]

Even if the arbitration clause cannot by itself be a conclusive factor in indicating the application of international law, yet it may be considered as one of the elements from which to draw that inference. Thus, the arbitration clause was relied on in the *Sapphire–N.I.O.C. Arbitration* case[104] to dismiss the presumption in favour of Iranian law. Professor Dupuy put it bluntly in the following words:

It is...unquestionable that the reference to international arbitration is sufficient to internationalize a contract, in other words, to situate it within a specific legal order...*the order of the international law of contracts.*[105] (My italics.)

(3) *Policy-oriented reasons*

It has been suggested that certain types of contract, i.e. economic development agreements, must be internationalized[106] for several reasons. In the first place, their subject matter is particularly broad: they are not concerned only with an isolated purchase or performance, but they are used as effective vehicles to channel to a developing country investments and technical assistance, especially in the field of research and exploitation of natural resources, or in the construction of factories. Thus, they assume a distinct function in the development of the host country.[107] It is worth mentioning that the importance of the obligations assumed by the American and Japanese companies in training Sudanese personnel should not be ignored.[108] The foreign investor contracting with the host State is assumed to be associated with the realization of its economic and social progress.

Secondly, the long duration of these contracts calls for close co-operation between the host State and the foreign investor for their mutual benefit. Because of this co-operation and the magnitude of the investments invited by the State, the contract must bring about an equilibrium between the interests of the two contracting parties. The contract must also ensure to the foreign private investor a certain stability, which is justified by the considerable investments which he makes in the country concerned. He needs in particular to be protected against legislative uncertainties such as the risks of modification of the municipal law of the host country, or against any government measures which would lead to an abrogation or rescission of the contract. This is usually catered for by stabilization clauses. The effect of these clauses is to remove all or part of the agreement from the internal law and to provide for its correlative submission to *sui generis* rules, as stated in the *Aramco* case, or to a system which is properly an international law system. The best exposition of the policy-oriented view was stressed in the Sapphire Award in the following words:

Such a solution seems particularly suitable for giving the guarantees of protection which are indispensable for foreign companies, since these companies undergo very considerable risks in bringing financial and technical aid to countries in the process of development. It is in the interest of both parties to such agreements that any disputes between them should be settled according to general principles universally recognized and should not be subject to the particular rules of national laws, which are very often unsuitable for solving problems concerning the rights of the State where the contract is being carried out, and which are always subject to changes by this State and are often unknown or not fully known to one of the contracting parties.[109]

(4) *Validity and invalidity of internationalization of contracts*

The view that contracts between States and aliens should be governed by some form of international law is not without theoretical difficulties. It has been opposed by Wolff, Fawcett and Friedmann.[110] Their argument against that view is that the 'internationalization' of a contract would not, in practice, be carried out, because international law has allegedly not yet succeeded in developing, or sufficiently developing, the necessary legal rules.

But the real dilemma facing the internationalization of contracts is not merely the insufficiency of the traditional international rules on the matter, but the impossibility and inability of these rules to accommodate any notion of reciprocal obligations arising at international law between a State and an individual from their contract. Under classical international law, only States are subjects of international law, while individuals are not. Nevertheless, this classical view starts to give way to a new trend. Thus, Professor Jennings asserted:

> In modern international law the notion that only States are the proper subjects of international law has so far been changed that we see, at any rate in some parts of the world, the possibility for an individual to bring an action before an international tribunal for breach of international human rights against his own government.[111]

The classical rules of international law, particularly those relating to State responsibility were laid down in the nineteenth century when the dogma about the question of international subjects was considered as unassailable. But the circumstances have changed now, because of the rapid economic and social progress and international co-operation which led to huge transactions between States and individuals. It is considered as established today that international legal capacity is not solely attributable to a State and that international law encompasses subjects of a diversified nature. If States, the original subjects of the international legal order, enjoy all the capacities offered by the latter, other subjects may enjoy only limited capacities which are assigned to specific purposes.[112] In this respect, the International Court of Justice stated in its Advisory Opinion on Reparation for Injuries Suffered in the Service of the United Nations, 1949:

> the subjects of law, in any legal system, are not necessarily identical in their nature or in the extent of their rights and their nature depends on the needs of the community.[113]

To avoid misunderstanding and to limit the meaning of internationalization of a contract, it should be observed that it neither means that the foreign private party is assimilated to a State nor that the contract entered with it is assimilated to a treaty. The private contracting party will have a specific and limited international capacity for the purposes of interpretation and performance of the contract.[114]

Furthermore, the internationalization of a contract is difficult to obtain in the absence of a contractual form of action under traditional international law. The remedy was always expressed in delictual form, though contractual in substance. For the protection of the individual, the introduction of the protecting State was necessary. Therefore, there had to be a transformation of the claim out of the realm of obligations fixed by the parties in contract, to the realm of general duties owed by one State to another.[115] Consequently, this led, in effect, to the transformation of the form of claim from the realm of contract to the realm of tort or delict. This has been observed as a fundamental reason why the traditional law accepted almost as a dogma the idea that the mere non-performance by a State of its obligation under a contract with an alien individual does not in itself necessarily give rise to international responsibility.[116]

Nevertheless, it is feasible for international law to have a law of contract, even though it may be disguised in the interests of the traditional delictual remedy. There is nothing in the structure of international law which inhibits the recognition of remedies which relate directly to the contract.[117] Even in the common law the remedies for breach of contract appeared first as aspects of the writ of trespass, i.e. as remedies essentially tortious in form.

(e) Applicability of administrative law

Some writers[118] suggest that economic development agreements or contracts are governed by administrative law. This law, in the sense of *droit administratif*, as understood in French law and in countries which adhere to the French legal system, is a separate and autonomous branch of law. It covers a wide field that includes administrative contracts, acts and powers, administrative courts and State liability.

The concept of *contrat administratif* (administrative contract) is characterized as a contract between the State and a private person, concluded for the sake of the functioning of a public service. It contains provisions which differ from those found in private law contracts. Since all these elements should be present, it is evident that not all contracts concluded by Governments are administrative contracts.

The fundamental character of an administrative contract is the recognition of certain unilateral powers of control by the State in the public interest. The public interest requires that the State authority be empowered to carry out continuous supervision over the execution of the contract. The State is also granted certain unilateral powers: to suspend, modify, or even to terminate the contract without prior recourse to the court.

The private party to the administrative contract is entitled to compensation for any damage suffered through the direct or indirect modification of the contractual terms of the contract.

According to Cattan, an oil concession in the Middle East has always been treated as a contract between the State and the concessionaire which is governed by ordinary rules of contract.[119] It is not *contrat administratif* and is not subject to *droit administratif*. It possesses a basically contractual character and no change is made in its terms except by common consent of the parties. Only one case was the contractual character of an oil concession questioned as to its linkage to *droit administratif*. In the *Aramco* case, the Government of Saudi Arabia argued for the application of the *droit administratif* to the concession agreement in question and was ruled out by the Arbitration Tribunal. The same result was obtained in the Libya–Oil Companies Award, though the issue was not raised, but considered and decided upon by the Sole Arbitrator on his own motion.

It should be observed that the concept of the applicability of administrative law to State contracts with aliens is peculiar to the French system, and hence it could not be characterized as a general principle recognized by civilized nations.[120] Consequently, its application as a proper law of the contract is untenable. Nevertheless, there is nothing which prevents the parties, if they so wish, in a country which adheres to the concept of *droit administratif*, to confer on their agreement the attribute and characteristics of a *contrat administratif*. In Algeria, for example, the oil concessions envisaged by the Sahara Petroleum Code of 1958 were said to fall within the territory of *contrat administratif*.[121]

5. The legal effect of economic development agreements

Having established that international law is applicable to economic development agreements, it is important to ascertain its rules on the matter. The investigation will be directed towards exploring the legal nature of these instruments, whether they are binding, and the principles of law which uphold their binding force. The determination of these issues with precision is, indeed, very difficult, owing to the absence of any consensus on settled and universally accepted international rules in this field of State responsibility. The difference of opinions extends not only to the *de lege lata*, but also to the *de lege ferenda* rules.

(a) Classical theory

In the early nineteenth century, States' practice disclosed a general reluctance to espouse claims of their nationals against foreign States, when such claims were founded on contracts. The reason was that such contracts were concluded at the contracting individuals' risk and such individuals had no right to expect the support and intervention of their States of nationality on their behalf.[122] This was the situation when the export of capital was not encouraged, because of the pressing needs for domestic investment.

But economic conditions had changed in the latter part of the last century and foreign investment began to be considered with increasing favour by the governments of the Western industrialized countries. Accordingly, their position on the international law on the matter changed. It came to be accepted that contractual claims could form the basis for a State intervention in support of its nationals, though under certain conditions. The chief condition was that a denial of justice should be proved. This means, before a claim could be raised, it should be shown that the alien had been denied the judicial and other remedial processes under local law through which he might obtain reparation for injury to his interests. This view, with certain qualifications, is considered as the 'classical' international law theory.[123]

Under this classical theory of international law, a breach of contract by a State is still not considered, by itself, as internationally unlawful. It is not the breach of contract, but the denial of justice which follows it, that constitutes the internationally tortious act. This expresses rather the traditional conception of international law as the law governing the relations between States. This view, as demonstrated before, is not acceptable to some international lawyers today. Moreover, the classical theory was adequate when there was general agreement between capital-exporting and capital-importing countries on the value of the institution of private property and the necessity for its protection.

At present, there is no longer any general agreement on the standard of treatment to be accorded to private property and the rights connected therewith. Much criticism has been levelled against the classical theory on the protection of contractual rights of aliens.[124] Several scholars now consider it as insufficient and outdated, with no relevance to modern legal and economic conditions. They argue that States should be held responsible for an international tortious act whenever they violate, directly or indirectly, their contracts with aliens.[125] There is no need to prove a denial of justice and, accordingly, it is not necessary to satisfy the prior requirement of the exhaustion of local remedies. It should be observed that such criticism of the classical theory is valid in view of the latest developments which have their impact on the old rules. However, the tenets of these modern views will be discussed below.

(b) Contemporary developments

(i) *The binding force of contracts on States and the concept of sovereignty*

It is argued in some quarters that agreements between States and foreign private investors cannot be recognized as binding on these States. This argument rests on two reasons.

Principally, it is alleged that, as a State possesses a sovereign and independent status, it cannot contract away its powers of taking unilateral action in the future.[126] The justification is that the State, being the guardian of the public interest, has power to take any action in furtherance or protection of that interest, and this power should not be fettered. Since the State is concerned with the economic welfare of its citizens, it cannot bind itself to relationships with individuals that might in time derogate from that welfare. Accordingly, whenever the State considers that the public interest requires the repudiation of a contract with a foreign individual, it may lawfully do so, despite a contractual provision to the contrary.

Secondly, it is alleged that development agreements between foreign private investors and States have no international status, because individuals are only objects and not subjects of international law, and hence their agreements with States cannot strictly be equated to treaties. It is submitted that both arguments are untenable. As regards the second, it has been already observed that there are considerable authorities which support the opinion that individuals may have limited international capacities to enjoy and exercise their rights under international agreements.

With regard to the first argument, it is accepted today that the sovereignty of the State is not incompatible with its power to bind itself by a contract with an individual as regards its future action in furtherance or protection of the public interest and welfare.[127] A State may legislate within its territory even in violation of its contracts. The basic question is not one of fettering future legislative powers, but the nature of obligations arising out of a contract with a foreigner. Whether or not there are limitations on the legislative authority of the legislature of a State depends on its constitutional law and practice.

When a State, in the exercise of its sovereignty, contracts with foreigners, it undertakes well defined obligations, the most important of which is to respect and perform the agreement. If the contract is abrogated by any future act of the State, then there is a violation of this obligation. The binding character of economic development agreements rests primarily on the obligation in international law to respect such agreements. The breach of this obligation will give rise to an obligation to make reparation. If the State contracts with an alien, it acquires substantial benefits and should take corresponding obligations.

Sovereignty does not prohibit the effectiveness of such obligations or the grant of irrevocable right. It was held that a State when contracting with an alien is putting a limitation in the exercise of sovereignty and this very act is an affirmation, rather than a negation, of national sovereignty.[128] It restricts its sovereignty temporarily only for the period of the development agreement. Thus, in the Aramco case, it was held that:

> The concession has the nature of a constitution which has the effect of conferring rights on the contracting parties. By reason of its very sovereignty within its territorial domain, the State possesses the legal power to grant rights which it forbids itself to withdraw before the end of the concession... *Nothing can prevent a State in the exercise of its sovereignty, from binding itself, irrevocably by the provisions of a concession and from granting to the concessionaire irretractable rights.* It (the government) has guaranteed to the company that it would not exercise its sovereignty in any way contrary to the obligations it has undertaken towards Aramco and to the rights it has granted.
>
> *The sovereignty of the State is not limited by some exterior cause; it is the State itself which undertakes the (negative) obligation not to impede the grantee's exercise of its rights... The exclusive right of Aramco can no longer be modified without the Company's consent.*[129] (My italics.)

This authoritative arbitral pronouncement has been quoted with approval by many authorities.[130] In the Libya–Oil Companies Award, the Sole Arbitrator in upholding the binding force of a stabilization clause in the Deeds of Concession in dispute applied the rule in the *Aramco* case and held that the abrogation of the Deeds of Concession by nationalization measures by the Libyan Government was unlawful under international law, because it was contrary to the stabilization clause. Under that clause, the Libyan Government agreed to restrict its sovereignty, not to take any measure which would interfere with the Deeds of Concession throughout its duration without the consent of the concessionaire. The Arbitrator did not question the right of Libya to nationalize, but he denied its right to that effect if this is contrary to specific commitments towards the concessionaire. This in reality amounts to considering nationalization in such cases illegal *per se*, which is difficult to accept as it deprives the State of the right to regulate its economy to offset adverse changing circumstances.

(ii) *Effect of the resolutions of the General Assembly on Natural Resources and the Charter of Economic Rights and Duties of States on the Binding Force of State contracts*

Does a State need to invoke its right of permanent sovereignty over natural resources as a supreme principle justifying nationalization in every case? Furthermore, is the principle of permanent sovereignty over natural resources, which has been affirmed by the General Assembly of the United Nations since 1952, a standard of *jus cogens*? This was exactly the situation faced by the Arbitrator in the *Libya–Oil Companies* case, where the Libyan Government refused to submit to arbitration, because that would be contrary to its permanent sovereignty over its natural resources and its sovereign right to settle the dispute within its own municipal sphere, as confirmed by the United Nations resolutions. The Arbitrator rightly answered both questions in the negative. He observed that the notion of permanent sovereignty can easily be reconciled with the contractual obligation of a State towards the foreign national. He asserted that a distinction should be made as to the 'enjoyment' and 'exercise' of permanent sovereignty. In his view, the State granting the concession retains the permanent enjoyment of its sovereign right; it cannot be deprived of the right in any way whatsoever.[131] The contract which it entered into with a private company cannot be viewed as an alienation of such sovereignty, but as a partial and temporary exercise of sovereignty.

Furthermore, the Arbitrator observed that the resolutions of the General Assembly on permanent sovereignty over natural resources have only political and moral force, and, as such, they are not binding on member States, because they are only recommendations and some of them have not been unanimously adopted and have even attracted negative votes; especially Article 2 of the Charter of Economic Rights and Duties of States dealing with nationalization. Accordingly, the positive international law in this respect has undergone no change at all as a result of these resolutions. The principle of permanent sovereignty does not affect the binding force of State contracts with aliens. More specifically, resolution 1803 of 1962 provides in paragraph 8 that 'foreign investment agreements freely entered into by or between sovereign states shall be observed in good faith'. This resolution is strong evidence for the view that foreign investment agreements have a status internationally superior to that of other State contracts.

(iii) *The legal effect of unilateral abrogation and a stabilization clause*

According to the *Aramco* case, when a State renounces in its contract the right to repudiate or interfere by future measures with the contract, that obligation is binding. The validity of this principle finds support in decided cases and many development agreements.[132] Of particular interest in this respect is clause XXIII of the Petroleum Production-Sharing Agreement between the Sudan and the Chevron Co., under which the Government renounces the right to enact laws or regulations which may be inconsistent with the provisions of the agreement. However, from a nationalistic and political point of view this clause might be attacked as impinging on the national sovereignty and fettering the legislature from enacting laws in the future to regulate the petroleum industry. However, from a constitutional point of view, nothing in the agreement can prevent the legislature from exercising its usual function in the future in enacting laws or regulations in the Sudan on whatever matter. But the practical effect of such a stabilization clause is that if future laws or regulations contradict the provisions of the agreement, the clause may be pleaded on the international plane to substantiate the claim against the Sudan Government, provided that all the procedural requirements are satisfied.

Municipal courts, though, almost inevitably uphold the sovereign status of the States, have on certain occasions accepted the obligations of a State to respect its contracts. This was stated unequivocally by the United States Supreme Court in *Perry* v. *U.S.*[133] in the following terms:

> The United States are as such bound by their contracts as are individuals. If they repudiate their obligations, it is as much repudiation with all its wrong and reproach that term implies, as it would be if the repudiator had been a State or a municipality or a citizen.

A similar approach has been taken in English courts.[134] It has been always the practice of the Sudanese courts to uphold the binding force of State contracts and to pass judgments against the Government if it wrongfully repudiated its contracts with private persons, whether nationals or foreigners.[135]

A long time ago, many international tribunals held that the unilateral abrogation by a State of its contract was an unlawful act for which adequate reparation was due. In the *Shufeldt* case,[136] an American citizen was the assignee of a concession for ten years, granted by the Government of Guatemala for the extraction of chicle. After the expiration of six years, the Government abrogated the concession by a legislative measure. The Arbitrator found that the abrogation of the concession gave rise to an obligation to make adequate compensation.

Another case in point is the *El Triunfo* case,[137] where the Government of El Salvador made a concession contract with the El Triunfo company which was owned by an American Corporation. The concession was to run for twenty-five years and authorized the concessionaire to establish steam navigation in the port of El Triunfo and to carry on coasting trade with adjacent ports. The Government of El Salvador abrogated the concession by an executive decree. The arbitrator held that the Government was responsible for arbitrary destruction of the concession and awarded damages for loss suffered by the company. The award stressed the mutuality of rights and obligations in contractual arrangements.

The unilateral abrogation of a contract by the State can best be illustrated by the repudiation of the Sudan Government of a concession which it had granted to the Sudanese Minerals Co. Ltd., a Sudanese company whose stock ownership was nationalized in June 1970. Sudanese Minerals Ltd. held certain exclusive prospecting licences convertible into mining leases covering Atlantis II Deep in the Red Sea, in the area which is repoted to comprise several minerals (sea brines) in the continental shelf between the Sudan and Saudi Arabia. Sudanese Minerals entered into an operating agreement with an United States company called the International Geomarine Corporation, under which the latter would provide the necessary funds and management for exploration and exploitation of the minerals in return for a specified percentage of the net profits, if there were any. International Geomarine subsequently entered into a series of agreements with Preussage A.G. of West Germany to share the responsibilities and benefits of the operating agreement.[138] Though the original operating agreement was modified through negotiation between these companies and the Sudanese Government, which issued a non-exclusive concession over much of the rest of the Red Sea opposite its coast, the agreement was thwarted by extraneous factors: the claim of Saudi Arabia that the Red Sea brines lie within its continental shelf according to its law relating to the Acquisition of the Red Sea Resources, 1968,[139] which provides that hydrocarbons and minerals 'in the strata of the high sea bottom with respect to an area of the Red Sea, extending below the high sea and contiguous to the continental shelf of Saudi Arabia', appertain to the Kingdom.

It was argued that the Red Sea brines must be regarded as being on the continental shelf of the Sudan, as they are situated west of the median line between the Sudan and Saudi Arabia. The view is based upon the equidistance rule in Article 6(1) of the Geneva Continental Shelf Convention[140] which the Sudan has ratified. But Saudi Arabia is not a party to the convention and, in such circumstances, the use of the equidistance method of delimitation has no element of obligation on coastal States. It would, therefore, appear as a consequence of the *North Sea Continental Shelf* cases,[141] that the Sudanese argument based upon the median line is far from being decisive.

The dispute was settled by special agreement,[142] whereby a joint commission was set up to undertake and administer the exploitation of the natural resources in the common zone in the continental shelves and seabed appertaining to the Sudan and Saudi Arabia. The expense of the exploitation of these resources is to be paid by the kingdom of Saudi Arabia, which will recover such funds expended from the return of the production of the common zone and in a manner to be agreed upon between the two countries.

The operative Article of the Agreement is Article XIII which reads as follows:

> Whereas the Government of the Democratic Republic of the Sudan has concluded on May 15th, 1973, an Agreement whereby it has given exploration licences to Sudanese Minerals Limited and the West Germany Company of Preussag *which Agreement has created legal obligations on the Government of the Democratic Republic of the Sudan*, the two Governments have agreed that the joint Commission shall decide on this matter in such a manner as to preserve the rights of the Government of the Democratic Republic of the Sudan and in the context of the regime established by this Agreement for the common zone. (My italics.)

Pursuant to the Article of the Agreement, the joint commission reached agreement with the concessionaires, whereby the original exploration licences (concessions) were repudiated, and a new contractual arrangement established.

Had the concessionaires not consented to the abrogation of the exploration licences, the abrogation decision could have engendered the international responsibility of the Sudan as regards the German company. Thus, a typical case could have been created similar to that of the *Aramco* case. Assuming that the German company had not consented to the repudiation of the exploration licences before their expiry period, it might have been argued that, as in *Aramco*, the rights of the concessionaires had been interfered with, and their vested rights in exclusively exploring the resources of the Red Sea destroyed by employing other parties to carry out the exploration. The only difference between the two cases is that, in the *Aramco* case, the concession was not abrogated, but only interfered with. In the German company's case, the Sudanese Government not only interfered with the exploration licences, but repudiated them completely, but with the consent of the concessionaire.

(c) Principles upholding the binding nature of development agreements

Why are development agreements between States and aliens binding? The answer to this question has strong roots in international legal principles relating to the protection of private property. These principles can be identified as follows.

(i) *Vested rights*

The concept of 'vested' or 'acquired' rights deals specifically with the sanctity of property rights obtained under a particular legal system which is threatened by a change of the *lex situs*. Once property rights have been acquired under the existing law, they cannot validly be arbitrarily destroyed by a later change of that legal system without obligation to make adequate reparation.[143]

But not every right to property can be correctly classified as being 'vested right' or 'acquired right'. For this reason the principle of acquired right was described as one of those question-begging principles of international law, because it does not, of itself, indicate which rights can be regarded as acquired or vested rights.[144] Nevertheless, it is a useful, instructive, and authoritative way of asking which rights international law will protect. Its importance lies in the fact that it expresses so well the nature of the link between international law and municipal law. Thus, the right acquired, though recognized and protected by municipal law, is also within the purview of international law.[145]

The rights derived by foreign private investors under economic development agreements are property rights which are acquired or vested and so entitled to international protection. The principle of acquired rights has been recognized as among the most established international legal principles and is 'applied by international tribunals'.[146] It is well to recall that this principle was applied to render ineffective in law a purported subsequent concession by awarding a contract to another concessionaire. Thus, in the *Aramco* case the arbitral tribunal observed:

> In its capacity as first concessionaire, Aramco enjoys indeed exclusive rights which have the character of 'acquired' or 'vested' rights and which cannot be taken away from it by the government by means of a contract concluded with a second concessionaire, *even if that contract were equal to its own contract* from a legal point of view. The principle of respect for acquired rights is one of the fundamental principles of both public international law and of the municipal law of most civilized States.[147] (My italics.)

Accordingly, a State cannot derogate from its previous agreement by making another contract with a second concessionaire.

(ii) *Pacta sunt servanda*

The most important and persuasive principle for holding States internationally responsible for abrogating or breaching their agreements or concessions with aliens is the principle of *pacta sunt servanda.* As has been stated in chapter 6, in accordance with this principle, it is universally agreed that under international law, States are bound to perform their treaties with other States and to carry out in good faith the obligation assumed thereunder. It has been generally confirmed that *pacta sunt servanda* is part of customary international law as well as one of the general principles of law recognized by civilized nations. No arbitral tribunal has ever rejected this principle or even thrown doubt on it.[148] In the opinion of Kelsen, '*pacta sunt servanda* is the basic norm (*Grundnorm*) of the whole system we call international law'.[149] This is well brought out in the works of several jurists[150] and there is no need to dwell further upon it here.

The crucial question here is whether this same principle should be applied to a contract between States and aliens.

There seems to be a strong support for the proposition that *pacta sunt servanda*, as a principle of international law, applies to contracts between States and foreign nationals.[151] In its memorandum to the Permanent Court of International Justice in the *Losinger and Company* case, the Swiss Government contended that:

> the principle of *pacta sunt servanda*... applies not only to agreements directly concluded between States, *but also to those between State and foreigners*... A State may not invoke any provisions of its private law or of its public law in order to evade the performance of valid contractual obligations.[152] (My italics.)

Professor Wehberg, after dealing with the origin and sanctity of *pacta sunt servanda* principle, concluded that: 'the principle is valid exactly in the same manner, whether it is in respect of contracts between States or in respect of contracts between States and private companies...the principle of sanctity of contracts must always be applied'.[153] And it is interesting to note that this principle is also well entrenched in Islamic jurisprudence.

Professor Jennings, quoting Wehberg, agreed that the principle of *pacta sunt servanda* could be applied to State contracts, but added that it is too general to be serviceable without further definition in relation to particular classes of situations. In this opinion, this can best be achieved by qualifying the principles as not to be strictly applied in all cases. Some legislative changes must be permissible such as currency legislation, police power and so on. Professor Jennings advocates that the principle of *pacta sunt servanda* needs to be linked with the principle of 'acquired rights' if it could be given any content. In his view, 'it will never gain strength if it is allowed to be used as a mere incantation'. Its meaning should be determined by international law, even in the case of a contract whose proper law is the municipal law of the contracting State.[154]

The principle of *pacta sunt servanda* was applied by an arbitral tribunal in the case of *Czechoslovakia* v. *the Radio Corporation of America*.[155] The arbitrators in interpreting the concession agreement in favour of the concessionaire, held that Czechoslavakia 'has not the right to establish a second direct radio telegraphic link', and that it must specifically perform. The government had argued that the public law not private law concepts were applicable. Even conceding this, said the tribunal, 'in public law the sentence *pacta sunt servanda* will also apply, just as public interest requires stability as regards any arrangements legally agreed upon'.[156]

(iii) *Estoppel*

This is another important rule of law which can in certain circumstances help to secure the binding effect of contracts. It requires that a party who by word or conduct wilfully causes another to act to his detriment or to the benefit of the party by whom the statement is made, cannot deny the truth and validity of his representation before a judicial tribunal.[157] This principle is based on the principles of good faith and common justice. It seeks to ensure that there is consistency in the actions of every party to a transaction. It is conceded that the *rationale* of estoppel is expressed in the maxim '*allegans contraria non audienda est*'.[158] Its essential aim is to preclude a party from benefiting by his own inconsistency to the detriment of another party who has, in good faith, relied upon a representation of fact made by the former party. It is a useful device for limiting the powers and assuring the *bona fide* conduct of States in connection with their contractual obligations with aliens.

The principle of estoppel is common to most legal systems and has been recognized as a general principle of international law by international tribunals.[159] Thus, a State will be estopped from asserting the invalidity of a concession if it has treated it as valid for some time and has profited from the other party's fulfilment of its obligation under the contract. A case very much in point is the *Shufeldt* claim, in which the United States contended that Guatemala, having for six years recognized the validity of the claimant's contract, and received all the benefits to which she was entitled thereunder, and having allowed Shufeldt to continue to spend money on the concession, was precluded from denying its validity. The Arbitrator held that the contract was valid and that this contention is 'sound and in keeping with the principles of international law'.[160]

The principle of estoppel was argued successfully in *Turriff* Case.[161] The dispute arose from the following facts. In 1959 the Sudan Government made an agreement with the Government of the United Arab Republic for the full utilization of the Nile waters. Under this agreement, the Government of the United Arab Republic were to build the High Aswan Dam, and by clause 7 the Government of the Sudan undertook to move the people of Wadi Halfa and other Sudanese whose lands would be inundated by the pile-up of the water behind the dam, before July 1963. From this agreement stemmed the need for the Sudan Government to carry out a major housing scheme in forty-four months only. After protracted negotiations.[162] and inquiries which took more than thirty-three months, a contract was concluded on 16 October 1962 with Turriff Construction Ltd (an English Company), to build 33,000 houses in eight months. It is apparent that if any substantial part of the scheme was to be completed in time, Turriff was required to work with great speed. This would depend on the Government providing Turriff with drawings, raw materials and layouts for the commencement of the works as postulated by the contract. The Government failed to carry out this obligation. Complaints soon began to be made by each of the parties to the other. The Government complained of delay on the part of Turriff, which in turn complained that they were unable to proceed faster because of changes in decisions, lack of drawings, raw materials, transport facilities and similar necessary infrastructure.

The Government exercised its right under clause 66 of the contract which empowered it to notify Turriff of its intention to enter upon the site and to employ other contractors to complete the work if Turriff failed to fulfil their obligations under the contract. Turriff disputed the Government's right to take this action, but the Government maintained its position. Turriff then alleged that the Government had repudiated the contract and that it accepted the repudiation.

Pursuant to clause 70 of the contract, the parties agreed to submit the dispute to arbitration under the auspices of the Permanent Court of Arbitration at the Hague. The main issue to be decided by the arbitral tribunal was the question of interpretation as to which of the parties had repudiated the contract. The Government's measure was alleged to be in the exercise of its contractual right under clause 66 of the contract. Later on, the Government raised the issue of the invalidity or voidability of the contract for mistake and misrepresentation, on the ground that Turriff had represented to the Government that it had no connection whatsoever with South Africa nor that the contract was financed by South African nationals, which was untrue. Ultimately, the Government, relying on this South African issue, withdrew from the arbitration for political reasons: Turriff replied that the Government was estopped by the recitals to the submission to arbitration from alleging that the contract was void or voidable for mistake. The arbitral tribunal decided in favour of Turriff in an *ex parte* award as the Government withdrew from the proceedings before the hearing. The tribunal ordered that the Government should pay damages to Turriff for breach of contract. The award was rendered only on the documents presented by Turriff and the issues had not been fully argued and decided upon. No authorities were cited. Significantly, the award was rendered according to Sudanese law as this had been initially chosen by the parties to govern the contract. For these reasons, the import of the case in international law is not of direct consequence. The situation could have been otherwise had the Sudan Government continued in the proceedings up to the rendering of the award, for in that case, certain international aspects of the case could have been raised and argued. However, the dispute was settled by a special compensation agreement which will be examined below.

(iv) *Unjust enrichment*

The obligation of a State to honour its contracts with aliens is also supported by the application of the principle of unjust enrichment.[163] According to this principle, a party unjustifiably enriched at the expense of the other is bound to make just reparation to the injured party. For invoking the principle of unjust enrichment, two basic conditions must be satisfied. First, the respondent in the action must have been enriched and second the plaintiff impoverished. Both incidents must arise from the same transaction. Thus, where an investor establishes a business enterprise in the Sudan or Saudi Arabia in consequence of a contractual arrangement, and the enterprise is seized or lost by abrogation of the contract, there is a resulting enrichment to the state and loss to the private investor.[164] Secondly, the enrichment must be *sine causa*, i.e. not justified by any legal principle. In the opinion of Nwogugu,[165] such a legal justification must be judged by the standard of international law and cannot be approved merely because it is accepted by the municipal law of the enriched State.

The principle of unjust enrichment has developed in the continental systems as an important and flexible principle of justice and has been embodied in the civil codes of Germany, Switzerland, Italy and Spain.[166] In the Anglo-American jurisprudence the term unjust enrichment is not normally used, though its tenets can be found in the notion of restitution, and the fundamental principles of the rule appear in actions for *quantum meruit* and the enforcement of constructive trusts. Friedmann[167] advocates that the principle of unjust enrichment should be regarded as a general principle of law recognized by civilized nations. Perhaps the best case of the application of this principle is the *Lena Goldfield Arbitration.*[168] A British company invested huge capital in gold mining on Soviet territory on the strength of an agreement with the Russian Government. Following a change of Soviet economic policy, the company's operations were harassed and its property seized. The arbitral tribunal decided that:

> The conduct of the Government was a breach of the contract going to the root of it. In consequence Lena is entitled to be relieved from the burden of further obligations thereunder and to be compensated in money for the value of the benefits of which it has been wrongfully deprived. On ordinary legal principles this constitutes a right of action for damages, but the Court prefers to base its award on the principle of '*unjust enrichment*' although in its opinion the money is the same.[169]

It would seem that the principle of unjust enrichment is more relevant to determining reparation for an unlawful act which amounts to a breach of a State's international obligations. Such a principle is, indeed, relevant to the contractual relations of a State with private investors, for when the State abrogates its contract and thereby enriches itself, there is an international obligation to make adequate reparation. Thus, Turriff also invoked this principle to claim compensation from the Sudan Government for its breach of contract and the seizing of the company's machinery and equipment; and the arbitral tribunal rightly ruled accordingly.

(v) *Abuse of rights*

The binding force of a development agreement may be justified also by invoking the principle of abuse of rights (*abus de droit*). This principle requires rights to be exercised honestly and loyally in accordance with their social and economic purposes.[170] Any fictitious exercise of a right for the purpose of evading either a rule of law or a contractual obligation constitutes an abuse of right, and is prohibited by law. The *rationale* of this concept is said to be to restrict the arbitrary and capricious use of a right to the substantial detriment of other parties. It is a common principle in most continental legal systems, and it seems to be recognized as a general principle of international law.[171]

Some jurists have cast doubts on the place of abuse of rights as a general principle of international law, because of its vagueness and uncertainty.[172] This criticism was not accepted by Nwogugu who advocated that the concept is fashioned to be flexible to suit various situations in which injustice will otherwise result. He said that its application is left to the capable hands of judicial tribunals.[173] Gutteridge, after considering the application of the principle of abuse of rights in different legal systems, came to the conclusion that the arguments against the doctrine are inapplicable where 'a proprietary right is being exercised from a wholly improper motive'.[174] According to Wortley,[175] 'only theorists who consider that a right is something absolute can object to the suggestion that even a legal right may occasionally be abused, that is misused or used to effect improper oppression or injustice or to accomplish a piece of chicanery'.

International tribunals have refused to presume an abuse of right and insist that the party alleging that an abuse has been committeed must prove it.[176] Indeed, the wide legislative powers enjoyed by a State within its territorial competence and the importance of private property rights in international law demand the existence of limitations on the ways in which such powers can be exercised.

As State contracts are usually quite extensive and detailed, both parties to them may act in a manner which, without being in direct breach of the contract, may still constitute an abuse of the party's right under the contract. Thus, in the *Turriff* case, the Government had the right under clause 66 of the General Conditions of the Contract (forfeiture clause) to enter upon the site of the work and expel Turriff therefrom and complete the work after giving the company two weeks' notice on the certificate of the Consultant Engineer that Turriff failed to execute the work as agreed upon under the contract. The Government, in exercising its contractual right, entered upon the site and expelled Turriff and employed local contractors to accomplish the work. The question was whether the Government was entitled to exercise its right under clause 66 in the particular situation and enter upon the site and expel Turriff from the work. Though the principle of abuse of right had not been pleaded expressly, it seemed that the *ex parte* award was based on this principle. This same opinion was reached by Sayed Mahdi Shareif who was the Attorney-General at the time of the conclusion of the contract. He advised the Government that clause 66 did not empower it to expel the contractor from part of the works only and that, accordingly, the exercise of the power of forfeiture by the Government was abused, and wrongful.

It is therefore essential, so far as the property rights of investors are concerned, that a State should exercise its sovereign rights in good faith and in accordance with obligation undertaken in a contract. This prohibition against abuse of rights condemns and restricts the legislative or administrative powers to annul economic development agreements unilaterally. Importantly, the principle of abuse of rights would be used as an effective yardstick to ascertain the genuineness of the exercise of certain rights and powers attributable to a State party to the contract in view of certain purposes. The employment of such rights and powers by the State in pursuit of other ends would constitute a 'misuse of power'. This would occur, for instance, if the reasons of public interest invoked by a State when taking measures affecting contractual rights of aliens were manifestly false, or non-existent.[177]

(vi) *Policy grounds*

Some commentators argue that a State's unreasonable interference with economic development agreements must be internationally unlawful for policy considerations. They suggest that the acceptance of this view is indispensable to the security of international investment. There would be no increase in private investment without such security. Thus, one writer[178] explains this policy as follows:

> The interest in a maximum flow of international capital and trade is, as a matter of economic fact, and as between borrower and investor, buyer and seller, wholly mutual. International contracts are a primary means of implementing that interest. Unilateral repudiation or alteration by States of their contracts with aliens hardly promotes that interest or the conclusion of contracts.

Apparently, it is to the interest of the capital-importing countries to adopt a similar view on the existing law. This is evidently a question of policy, rather than law, an expression of *de lege ferenda* rather than *de lege lata*.

Schwebel[179] even goes so far as to assert that 'If States were to be deemed to have reserved a legal right to invalidate their international contracts, the foreign investor would conclude no contracts at all.'

The interdependence of the world is often given as a reason why concessions should be inviolable. As Carlston advocates, 'the image of international society as a society of separate and independent nations, an image still held by the systems of public and private international law, no longer adequately reflects the true nature of society'.[180] This statement ignores the peculiar economic problems and interests of the developing countries. The community of interest between developed and developing nations does not always coincide, at least in their short-term economic interests.

6. Alteration or abrogation of development agreements

In the absence of express provision to the contrary, an economic development agreement may be legally abrogated or modified in the following instances.

(a) Abrogation within the general limits of the contract

The contracting parties may expressly confer on the State power to modify or abrogate the agreement under certain conditions. In such cases, the power of abrogation or modification is an express term of the contract. If it is exercised in accordance with the stipulated conditions of the contract, the private contracting party cannot challenge its validity. In the *International Fisheries* case (*U.S.* v. *Mexico*)[181] the contract between a private fisheries company and the State of Mexico contained a clause permitting the State to cancel the contract if the company failed to fulfil certain obligations within a specified period of time. The arbitral tribunal upheld the non-performance of the stated obligations as good ground for annulling the contract.

Usually, the existence or absence of a breach of contract will depend on the interpretation of the contractual provisions. The court will have to decide on the correctness and the good or bad faith of the parties' conflicting interpretations. States, in abrogating or otherwise interfering with their contracts with aliens, have maintained that they were exercising a contractual right based on the provisions of the contract involved. Such claims are usually settled before the courts of the capital-receiving State. Thus, in the *Sudan Government* v. *Brown International Inc.*, the Sudan Government made, on 13 October 1962, a contract with Brown International for the construction of two berths and works in connection therewith in Port Sudan harbour. Under the construction contract, the Government had the right to terminate the contract by giving the company two weeks' notice for failure in completing the contract within the specified time and to enter upon the site and complete the work. The Resident Engineer gave the company one week's notice contrary to the contractual provision. The Government argued that the issue of the duration of the notice was of no importance and would have no effect on the basic issue of the failure of the contractor in executing the work as agreed upon. According to clause III the dispute was referred to arbitration.

The arbitration board rendered an award against the Sudan Government, whereby it was ordered to pay the aggrieved company a generous compensation in United States dollars. The decision of the District Court in accepting filing the award was upheld by the Court of Appeal, and judgment was passed against the Government for breaching the contract. Later on, the dispute was settled by agreement whereby the claimant accepted only £S250,000 by way of damages in full satisfaction.[182]

(b) Interfering with contract for public interest

Although investment contracts are legally binding and protected by international law, it seems to be accepted that there are situations in which a contracting State is entitled to disturb the contractual relationship. States possess the right to pass legislation for the protection of the public interest, such as public health, public safety or general welfare of the subjects.[183] These measures may affect the contractual right of the foreign investor, having the effect of abrogating the contract altogether. One of the most notorious incidents of these State legislative measures, which have the effect of destroying the contractual rights of aliens, is nationalization, which applies in the same degree as it does in the case of property rights.[184] Under classical international law a State may interefere with contractual rights of aliens when: (a) its measures are taken in the public interest and (b) they are not discriminatory against aliens as such, in the absence of denial of justice.[185] How to determine this public interest is very difficult as indicated in chapter 5. If State measures are taken in good faith and for the public interest, they are not regarded as wrongful taking, but merely as regulation of property. It is usually contended that property rights under a contract with a State are subject to the power of eminent domain. But the power of regulating property in a State for public welfare may be misused as a smoke-screen for seizing foreign-owned property.[186] When this takes place, the action may amount to an unlawful repudiation of contractual obligations.

(c) Punitive measures

A State may interfere with investment contracts by taking confiscatory measures to punish criminal offenders under its penal laws. This is a question of territorial competence of a State which gives it the right to declare certain acts within its territory as criminal and subject to punishment. As demonstrated earlier, these include offences relating to customs, currency regulations and offences punishable under the State Security Act, 1973 (see *ante*, pp. 94–6). These are usually listed under State policy powers.[187] When a foreign investor engages in acts declared criminal by the host State, or uses the investment property for that purpose, the punishment may involve the confiscation of his property. If the investment was undertaken under a contract, the contract may be altered or cancelled in punishment of the offence. Whether such punishment is acceptable to other States will depend on its being known to international law or the customs of States. Nwogugu[188] has asserted that the punishment must be reasonable according to civilized standards and proportional to the offence committed. This is an extreme assertion which is difficult to support in view of the sovereign right of a State to declare any acts within its territory as criminal.

(d) Change of circumstances (clausula rebus sic stantibus)

In international law, the principle of *clausula rebus sic stantibus* provides that a vital change of circumstances after the conclusion of a treaty may lead to its dissolution. The principle is a counterpart of the common law concept of frustration. The principle of *clausula rebus sic stantibus* has been pleaded in several cases before the World Court. On each of those occasions the Court found that it was not applicable on the particular facts.[189] However, the automatic application of the principle unilaterally by either party of the contract must in any event be excluded. If there is a need to alter or abrogate the agreement because of an alleged change of circumstances, this must be obtained by agreement of the parties. Failing that, the dispute should be submitted to an impartial tribunal.[190] The change of circumstances must fundamentally affect the enforcement of the contract in its original form.

The problem of alleged change of circumstances may in the case of economic development agreements be avoided by express provision for periodic review of such agreements. Usually long-term investment contracts carry with them what Professor Charlston[191] has called the 'living law' of re-negotiation. This was affirmed by Schwebel in the words: 'As a matter of international practice, it is the fact that aliens and States renegotiate their contracts in the light of unfolding events and equitable consideration.'[192]

In the light of this realistic approach one would question the desirability of the stabilization clause stipulated in the Production-Sharing Agreement between the Democratic Republic of the Sudan and Chevron Co. which has totally ignored any future change of circumstances in the petroleum industry, which it is hoped will play an active role in the development of the country.

(e) Force majeure

Usually long-term investment agreements, especially those pertaining to mining and petroleum extraction, contain clauses on *force majeure*. Under such clauses the non-performance or delay in performance by the Government and concessionaire, or either of them, of any obligation under the agreement shall be excused by *force majeure*. The clause provides in normal circumstances that the period of any such non-performance, or delay, together with such period as may be necessary for the restoration of any damage done during such delay, shall be added to the time given in the agreement for the performance of such obligation and for the performance of any obligation dependent thereon and to the duration of the agreement.[193]

But the dilemma is to know how *force majeure* can be determined. In Most cases the agreements themselves enumerate certain events, indicating incidents of *force majeure* such as Act of God; fire; unavoidable accidents; act of war or conditions arising out of or attributable to war; laws; rules, regulations and orders by any Government or Governmental agency; strikes, lockouts and other labour disturbances; delays in transportation; floods, storms and other natural disturbances; insurrection, riots and other civil disturbances, or any other cause not due to the fault or negligence of the concessionaire: provided that any such cause is beyond the reasonable control of the Government or concessionaire.

7. The nature of breach of contract

The preliminary question of whether or not there is a breach of contract is to be determined by the proper law of the contract. If this is accomplished, it will be comparatively easy to link the breach of contract with a violation of international law.[194] The idea of submitting questions of breach of contract between individuals and States to the proper law was adopted in the 1961 Harvard Draft Convention on the Responsibility of States.[195] Article 12(1) provides:

> The violation through an arbitrary action of the State of a contract or concession to which the central government of that State and aliens are parties is wrongful. In determining whether the action of the State is arbitrary, it is relevant to consider whether the action constitutes:
>
> (a) a clear and discriminatory departure from the proper law of the contract or concession as that law existed at the time of the alleged violation;
> (b) a clear and discriminatory departure from the law of the State which is a party to the contract or concession as that law existed at the time of the making of the contract or concession, if that law is the proper law of the contract or concession;
> (c) an unreasonable departure from the principles recognized by the principal legal systems of the world as applicable to governmental contracts or concessions of the same nature or category; or
> (d) a violation by the State of a treaty.

The choice of law rule formulated above does not affect the international aspect of the contractual right. Even where an economic development agreement is governed by municipal law, the right originating under the contract is an international right which the home State of the investor is entitled to protect.[196]

8. Remedies for breach of State contract

(a) Restitutio in integrum and specific performance

As stated before it is a well-recognized principle of international law that any wrongful act committed against the property of aliens should be accompanied by adequate reparation. The measure of such reparation is restitution in kind or payment of pecuniary compensation of equal value. The purpose is to put the injured party in the same position as he would have been if the wrongful act was not committed: restitution of the *status quo ante* (see *ante*, pp. 195–6).

Equally, when there is a wrongful breach of a contractual obligation, the appropriate international law remedy is to restore the *status quo ante*, either by making restitution in kind, or if this is impossible or inadequate, by paying pecuniary damages in fair, adequate and effective manner to the party who has suffered the loss.[197]

Where restitution in kind is made there are no major problems, but, as stated before (see *ante*, pp. 196–7), its implementation is impracticable, if not at all impossible, if the contract is abrogated as a result of change of an overall and radical economic policy aiming at establishing a State economy antagonistic to private property, especially in cases of nationalization. Though Professor Jennings rightly conceded that nationalization of property implies the power to dissolve the contractual relationship against payment of damages, yet relying on the *obiter dictum* of the Permanent Court of International Justice in the *Chorzow Factory* case,[198] he asserted that the power of nationalization may be qualified by awarding actual restitution (*restitutio in integrum*) as a proper remedy in economic development agreements with long-term arrangements. He puts his thesis in the following terms:

> Thus, there may be no difficulty in holding that restitution should be an appropriate remedy where the power to nationalize or expropriate property or to abrogate the contract has been waived expressly by the State, whether by treaty as in the *Chorzow Factory* case or by the contract itself as in the *Anglo-Iranian* case. Again, it would seem the appropriate remedy in all those long-term arrangements – commonly called 'economic development contracts' – where a period is set to the contractual relationships and where, by an arbitration clause or a proper law clause referring to international law or general principles of law or in some other way, the contract is given a particular international rather than local emphasis.[199]

This view is very difficult to apply in long-term economic development agreements. As these agreements usually have a direct effect on the economic development of a developing country, it will be unrealistic to attempt to fetter its power to accelerate its economic growth as it thinks fit for the welfare of its citizens, especially in cases of mining and petroleum resources. Furthermore, the company or corporation may by nationalization be amalgamated or merged with another national firm to form a public corporation. Not only that, but also the marketing policy of the product of the concession may change and cause a direct commitment to the nationalizing State and hence *restitutio in integrum* may become out of hand – if not completely impossible. To reverse the nationalization measures may constitute constitutional problems, such as cancelling a decision of a court which has become final, or the destruction of the subject-matter of the contract. Though the Sole Arbitrator in the Libya–Oil Companies Award favoured the remedy of *restitutio in integrum* and ordered accordingly, he realized the difficulty in implementing it, which had not been specifically brought to his knowledge, because of the abstention of the Libyan Government all through from the arbitration proceedings. He observed that:

> the tribunal does not lose sight of the consideration that the solution in principle which is constituted by *restitutio in integrum should be discarded when there is absolute impossibility of envisaging specific performance, or when an irreversible situation has been created. This does not seem, at least until further information is available, to be the case here*: so far as this Tribunal can determine, the performance of its obligations by the defendant seems to depend on the defendant itself and it should, in all likelihood, be possible for the Libyan Government to take the necessary measures to restore the situation as postulated by the application of legal principles. If, for reasons which should have been brought to its knowledge, a situation irreversible and beyond the will of the parties has been created, this Tribunal can only regret that this has not been brought to its knowledge. The Tribunal must note that only the defendant could have been in a position to bring forward information tending to establish that there was an absolute impossibility, beyond its control, that eliminated the possibility of restoring things to the previous state and the Tribunal can only regret, once again, the default in which the defendant seems to have thought it necessary to take shelter.[200] (My italics..)

Needless to say, the situation might have been different had the Libyan Government appeared and argued the case on its merits. It is to be observed that, to say that *restitutio in integrum* must always be awarded when economic development agreements are abrogated by nationalization measures, is virtually to ignore the realities and to neutralize the right of a State to nationalize at all. *Restitutio in integrum* is presumably used by Professor Jennings not to mean restitution in species, but the amount of loss suffered by the contractor. In this respect, its relevance is significant to determine the amount of reparation, which should be higher than when the abrogation or interference with the contract is permitted by international law for public purpose, and indiscriminatory.

As mentioned before, Mann[201] distinguished '*restitutio in integrum*' from the common law remedy of 'specific performance'. Ironically, he advocated: 'there is no reason at all why an international tribunal should not be able and entitled to make a decree of specific performance for the benefit of the plaintiff State which grants diplomatic protection to enforce a contract between a State and a foreign national'. One doubts the practicability of this argument, which ignores the realities of the present situation of international law which lacks an effective enforcement machinery that could compel a recalcitrant State to execute the decree of specific performance, as understood in the common law.[202] It also ignores the fact that such a step may be politically, even if not economically, quite out of the question for the defendant State.

(b) Pecuniary damages

In the words of Nwogugu:

When there is a wrongful breach of contractual obligation the appropriate international law remedy is to restore the *status quo ante* either by making restitution in kind or if this is impossible or inadequate to pay pecuniary damages in *fair, adequate* and *effective* manner to the party who has suffered a loss.[203]

Suffice it to say that how to assess adequate, fair and effective damages is far from being certain in any case. For this reason, the observations made in the preceding chapter on assessment of compensation in cases of nationalization and expropriation are, to some extent, applicable here. The nature, and extent, of pecuniary damages, which could be a substitute for restitution, is complicated and requires further clarification. If pecuniary compensation is to restore the injured party to the position he would have occupied but for the abrogation of his contract, then such compensation must cover the entire loss suffered including the prospective profits. In the case of *Messrs. Punchard, McTaggart, Lowther* (*Britain* v. *Colombia*) the arbitral tribunal said:

The damage caused to one party by the illegal breaking of the contract comprises, as a rule, all the expenditure which it has made uselessly in carrying out its contractual obligations (*damnum emergens*), on the one hand, and, on the other hand, all the profits which the regular performance of the contract would have brought it (*lucrum cessans*).[204]

(i) *Damnum emergens*

The breach of an economic development agreement by a State usually results in substantial loss of property rights to the foreign investor. International tribunals have constantly upheld the rule requiring the respondent in a breach of contract case to pay for *damnum emergens* which ensues from his act.[205] The major basis of the claim is the value of actual property lost as a consequence of the breach. This usually comprises the cost of machinery and equipment, labour, and other expenses incurred in performing the contract up to the time of breach. One of the most reliable methods of assessing the real value of machinery and equipment so lost is by determining their market value at the time the wrongful act was committed.[206] This had been partially employed by the Sudan Government in the *Turriff* case to reach settlement on the arbitration award. The Government employed the English firm of accountants, Cooper Brothers & Co.[207] They assessed the value of the machinery and equipment left behind by Turriff, together with work done and labour, as amounting to £3,000,000, in contrast to Turriff's claim, which was for £4,730,000, to which had to be added approximately £1,270,000 as interest, making a total claim of the order of £6,000,000. Actually, the arbitral tribunal awarded Turriff £6,186,070, including interest in addition to costs and fees.

However, Turriff agreed to a settlement in 1972 on a *quantum meruit* whereby it was compensated for the cost of work done as well as machinery, equipment and materials left behind and taken over by Sudan Government. The Company agreed to accept only £3,300,000 in full satisfaction of the award. This agreed sum was to be paid in sterling in London in six annual instalments, and in each case, against the surrender of the appropriate promissory note. An initial payment of £900,000 was paid before the commencement of the payment of the instalments. Under clause 5 of the Agreement, if any instalment is not paid on the date agreed upon, such unpaid instalment shall bear interest at the rate of 6% per annum from the due date until actual payment, and if not paid within thirty days of the date on which the same becomes due, all the remaining instalments together with interest at the rate aforesaid shall forthwith become due and payable in sterling in London on demand by Turriff. All amounts payable by the Sudan Government under the agreement shall be paid in gross without any deductions of whatsoever nature and kind. The agreement stipulated further in clause 7, that, if the Sudan Government effected all payments, Turriff would treat the obligations of the Government under the Arbitration Award as being ended, and neither party would have any claim of any kind or of whatsoever nature against the other.

The compensation agreement is unique in three respects. First, it shows how far the Sudan is prepared to abide by an arbitration clause prescribed in a contract with a foreign investor. This attitude by itself is sufficient to reflect the Sudan's genuine desire to settle investment disputes amicably. Second, though the agreement is *sui generis*, and hence engendering no positive rules on the contentious topic of international responsibility of a State, yet it will establish a persuasive precedent. Third, the agreement signifies how an *ex parte* award can be expediently employed as a starting point for negotiating a final settlement. Thus, before the conclusion of the agreement, though the Sudan Government had withdrawn from the arbitration proceedings at an early stage, and despite its systematic formal denial of giving the award any binding effect, it has not actually, all through the pre-negotiation stages, ignored its practical implications. The explicit stipulation in the agreement itself that Turriff should renounce its claims under the award when fully executed is indicative of the effect of the award as a pressure and background for the agreement. Fourth, and most important, is that the agreement elucidates, in very practical terms, the damages in such cases, where market value is not easy to determine or not obtainable at all costs. International tribunals usually seek the assistance of experts to fix the probable value of the property to the owner at the time when the contract was made. In this respect, it is necessary to take into account all relevant facts which may reduce or increase the value of the property so as to avoid unjust enrichment of the injured party.

(ii) *Lucrum cessans*

Though it is generally agreed that loss of property must be accompanied by payment of *damnum emergens*, it has been doubted whether the party in breach is also liable for loss of future profits. Critics of *lucrum cessans* (future profits) as a basis for damages, regard it as always remote, speculative, contingent and incapable of ascertainment. But international tribunals have been in the habit of awarding some damages for prospective profits where the situations so justify.

The award of pecuniary damages for contingent profits is particularly important in cases of breach of economic development agreements, because the value of the agreement to the private investor is the profits which he expects to make within the duration of the contract. If, therefore, a contract between a State and a private investor is terminated before its expiry date, there is a strong case in favour of a claim for future profits.[208] But the crux of the matter is how to prove that future profits would have been made if the wrongful breach had not been committed.

For any claim for future profits to succeed, it must be supported by proof that the loss sustained arose out of a valid contract which by commercial practice and experience usually produces profits in the future. When a clear wrong is committed against such a substantial source of profit, then a good case for a claim will arise. In the *Rice* case,[209] the arbitrator stated this cardinal rule in the following words:

> There must be a manifest wrong, the effect of which prevents the direct and habitual lawful pursuit of gain, or the fairly certain profit of the injured person, or the profit of an enterprise judiciously planned according to custom and business.

Additionally, international tribunals require any claim for prospective profits to be 'the direct fruit of the contract and not too remote or speculative'.[210] Two tests are required to be satisfied in determining the remoteness of future profits. In the first place, there must be a close connection between the cause and effect. The loss must have resulted from the wrongful act of breach and not from any other extraneous cause. Secondly, such profits should be within the resonable expectation of the contracting parties. This rule was applied in the *Brown International* case where the Sudanese courts endorsed the arbitration award which awarded the claimant damages for loss of profits which could have been gained had the Government not broken the contract. The same result obtained in the *Turriff* case where the arbitral tribunal awarded the claimant damages including loss of prospective profits, though in the latter case the award is of less importance as it was *ex parte* the Government and, hence, the issues had not been argued on their merits. However, in such cases the proof of profits is easy, because by their very nature the construction contracts are service contracts and the profits could be determined initially, except when the costs of labour and materials increase remarkably so as to negate the potential of profits in any case. But the real difficulty would be in development agreements for exploitation of petroleum and mineral resources, especially when the agreement is abrogated early before production, and to assess the return from the project so as to ascertain the profits therefrom is very difficult indeed.

However, to determine what has been in the expectation of the parties, it is usual to apply the objective test of the reasonable man which is applied by international tribunals.[211] In the *Shufeldt* claim[212] the arbitrator in awarding damages for loss of future profits observed that:

> Such profits are the direct fruit of the contract and may reasonably be supposed to have been in the contemplation of both parties as the probable result of a breach of it.

To award damages for prospective profits, the tribunal will weigh all the evidence for and against. It will be guided in each case by a full review of all necessary capital and other expenditure and other past losses to ascertain if such profits could have been made.[213] Even where it is proper to award contingent profits, only net profits will be allowed. All deductions must be made, such as charges for freight, storage, insurance, fees, duties and all other probable expenses which are to be met before the profit accrues. According to Whiteman[214] other relevant factors which may be taken into account in computing future profits are the claimant's business ability, the condition of the property to be used in the acquisition of future gains, the general prevailing conditions in the area where the profits were to be obtained and the attendant risks.[215]

It is also logical to expect the concept of mitigation of damages if the circumstances of the case were that the loss of profits could be avoided. Thus, if a State pays prompt and adequate compensation to the injured private investor for breach of contract, and at the same time offers him an alternative good opportunity for investing the compensation received within the State, this will mitigate or even eliminate any claim for profits.[216] This is what had taken place with respect to the British investors who were adversely affected by the Sudanese nationalization measures in 1970. During their negotiations with the Sudanese Minister of Finance for settling the compensation due, the prospects of re-investing in the Sudan were taken into consideration in some cases, though not expressly, to lessen the amount of compensation initially claimed by the nationalized British firms.

The most authoritative elaboration on the measure of damages for breach of concession contract was the *Lighthouse Arbitration*[217] between France and Greece. The arbitration tribunal observed that the probable profits should be computed by taking into consideration the average annual net profits earned from executing the contract during the preceding years before breach for the unexpired period of the contract.

Another method of computing lost profits adopted by international tribunals is to use the earned income of a similar enterprise to the one injured during the unexpired period of the contract. This was followed in the *Norwegian Shipowners Claim*.[218]

In some cases international tribunals resort to capitalization of probable income by finding out what could be sold as a going concern to a willing purchaser at the time when the contract will terminate. This was applied in the *Delagoa Bay Railway Co.* case.

From the above, it is apparent that no absolute criterion can generally be applied in all cases for computing the probable profits lost for every breach of contract. No pre-condition, in any attempt to assess the value or *quantum* of profits, can always be required to be satisfied. Each contract has its own purposes and facts which warrant different devices for ascertaining a claim for profits.

9. Conclusions

Economic development agreements or investment contracts between the State and foreign private investors assume special concern for the economic development of a developing country. Not only do they serve as vehicles for channelling foreign capital, but also they are useful and effective instruments for transferring technology, expertise and know-how. Foreign capital can possibly flow to a developing country by other means, namely, public foreign aids in the forms of credit facilities and loans, tools and machinery, but there will be no qualified personnel to administer, or technicians to execute and even supervise the development projects financed by foreign capital. Hence, this adds to the importance of the development agreements or contracts, even in Saudi Arabia, one of the richest countries in the world, let alone the Sudan.

In whatsoever form they may be drafted, and for whatsoever purposes they are designed, and whether or not they incorporate the investment laws by reference, development agreements contain reciprocal rights and duties and their implementation depends, to a large extent, on the co-operation of the two parties.

Furthermore, development agreements are, by their very nature, international instruments, and accordingly they are governed by international law, though they are not treaties in *stricto sensu*. International law comes into play either by the express choice of the parties or by implication if the parties include in their agreement an arbitration clause or refer to general principles of law as to be the proper law of the contract. Even if the parties choose the municipal law of the contracting State, international law will be the legal order within which the municipal law must operate and conform.

Though it was the dogma of traditional international law that individuals were not subjects of international law, there seems to be, at present, considerable authority to the effect that individuals can be for particular purposes subjects of international law. With respect to development agreements, foreign investors may have limited international capacities to enjoy their rights thereunder.

Under classical international law, the breach of contract by itself would not create international responsibility unless there is a denial of justice, and liability in this case was characterized in delictual form, though it is contractual in substance. This classical theory is outdated and not suitable to the realities of the current economic developments. It is tremendously urged by some writers to hold States directly responsible for their breach of contracts with foreign investors under the international law of contracts, subject to certain exceptions. States' obligations under these contracts can be justified on the general principles of international law of *pacta sunt servanda*, 'estoppel', respect for acquired rights, rules against abuse of rights and security of transactions.

In principle, if the State contract with the foreign investor contains a stabilization clause, whereby the State waives its right to take nationalization or any other measure which may interfere with the contract, this clause should be upheld. Thus, if the Democratic Republic of the Sudan takes nationalization measures or promulgates law that run contrary to the stabilization clause of the Petroleum Production-Sharing Agreements concluded with Chevron and the other companies, it will commit an internationally wrongful act which entails its international responsibility to make adequate reparation. But from a constitutional law point of view, nothing can prevent nor, indeed, perhaps *should* prevent, the State from legislating contrary to the provisions of the agreement. To avoid such a paradoxical situation, it is prudent to replace the stabilization clause with a periodic revision clause, which gives the contracting parties the right to revise their contractual terms in the light of new circumstances, especially in the petroleum and mining industries.[219]

If a State is held responsible for breach of its contract with a foreign investor, it has to make adequate reparation which, as a matter of principle, may be designated as a *restitutio in integrum*. If the situation is irreversible and it is not within the State's power to restore the *status quo ante*, compensation is the alternative remedy. But in practice reparation takes, and should take, the form of compensation which represents the actual value of the property (*damnum emergens*). It may also include some sum representing loss of future profits directly connected with the breach of the contract and in the reasonable expectation of the parties.

PART THREE

REMEDIES

10

SETTLEMENT OF INVESTMENT DISPUTES

1. Introduction

The previous chapters demonstrate that the investment of foreign private capital in the Sudan and Saudi Arabia is regulated by municipal laws, treaties, contracts and other similar instruments. These regulatory instruments grant extensive incentives and concessions to foreign investors. Occasionally, disputes may arise from the practical application of these incentives or in the interpretation of the rights and obligations of the parties. In order to maintain and preserve good relations among the parties, it is essential to have an independent and impartial body capable of settling such differences, and which can, when called upon, define the rights and duties of each party, thereby adding great effectiveness to the relationship of the investor and the investee State.

Judicial settlement of commercial disputes between States and private investors is beset with tremendous difficulties which result principally from the difference of status between the parties – one a sovereign State and the other a private individual or corporation. Traditionally, this difference was reflected by regarding States as subjects of international law and individuals as mere objects. But there are ample recent authorities for endowing individuals with limited international capacity. The major task, however, in the settlement of investment disputes is to secure juridical equality for both parties. It is axiomatic that one important principle of justice is that both parties must be equal before the tribunal (*auditur et altera pars*),[1] so that each party is able to appear before the tribunal and to present his case without hindrance. The tribunal is also under a duty to listen to both parties. In disputes between States and individuals, this equality has not been fully attained in all cases. It is sometimes alleged, and indeed held, that States enjoy immunity from judicial proceedings in the courts of some foreign

States or even in their own courts, and the private investor may find it difficult to bring action against the investee State in many municipal courts.[2] On the other hand, there is authority for the view that the sovereign character of a State does not *in principe* relieve it from responsibility to other States for actions affecting other States or their nationals. This point was well illustrated in the opinion of the arbitrator in the *Shufeldt* case as follows:

> The Guatemalan Government contend further that the decree of the 22nd of May 1928 was the constitutional act of a sovereign State...and is not subject to review by any judicial authority. This may be quite true *from a national point of view but not from an international* point of view, for *it is a settled principle of international law that a sovereign cannot be permitted to set up one of its own municipal laws as a bar to a claim by a sovereign for a wrong done to the* latter's subject.[3] (My italics.)

It is true that sovereignty may raise procedural obstacles to the redress of a wrong. But a wrong is not made right by the single fact that it was done in the exercise of sovereign power. The acceptable view seems to be that whenever there is a wrong, there should be a remedy.[4] Additionally, the rigours of sovereign immunity may be ameliorated by the distinction of the acts of the foreign sovereign whether they are acts *imperii* or acts *gestionis*; thus the latter will be reviewable by the courts.[5]

Furthermore, individuals are generally not given the right to bring actions against States before the principal international tribunals, save as special international or regional tribunals or centres recently created by treaties purposely to settle investment disputes which will be examined below. Although the parties to an investment dispute frequently resort to arbitration, difficulties may arise from the inability to enforce an award. This chapter is devoted to an examination of these and other relevant matters, with the main emphasis on how foreign investment disputes in the Sudan and Saudi Arabia can be settled. First, it is intended to examine the remedies, if any, available under Sudanese and Saudi municipal laws, and then discuss other methods under international law such as diplomatic channels, good offices, mediation and adjudication by an arbitral tribunal. Failing to respect the observance of the undertaking given to foreign investors may call for international litigation and in this respect the role of the International Court of Justice is not to be ignored.

The term 'remedy' is not used in this part of the book in its strict legal sense to denote the kinds of remedies, such as compensation, nullity, declaration or *restitutio in integrum*, but to describe the forums in which the remedies themselves are obtained.

2. Settlement under municipal laws

(a) Under Sudanese law

Before the enactment of the Encouragement of Investment Act of 1980, foreign investors had alternative courses of action before the Sudanese courts to seek redress for injuries to their investments: they might either institute legal suits before the Supreme Court, or before courts of appeal. The first is a constitutional action to be resorted to when a fundamental constitutional right is in question, or has been infringed; while the latter consists of a judicial review of administrative decisions. From this classification, it is apparent that the nature of actions or measures complained of is unique. For this reason, it is important to deal with the issue under the following sub-headings.

(i) *Action for protection of constitutional right*

As has been stated in chapter 5, under Articles 33 and 34 of the Permanent Constitution of the Sudan, 1973 the right of private ownership is guaranteed and protected against expropriation except for a public interest, in accordance with the law, and on payment of a fair compensation. Suppose that any of these requirements has not been observed, what will be the remedy to a foreign investor before the Sudanese courts? The answer seems to be very simple. He can institute a constitutional suit before the Supreme Court under Article 58 of the Constitution which reads:

> Subject to Article III[6] hereof, any person aggrieved by any law passed by any legislative authority may institute a civil suit before the Supreme Court to declare such law void on the ground of its violation of the freedoms and rights guaranteed by this constitution.

The procedure to obtain such a constitutional remedy is set out in chapter 5 of part XII of the Civil Procedure Act, 1974 as amended recently.[7] The procedure can be summarized as follows.

The suit to determine the constitutionality of any law or legislative provision may be instituted in the Supreme Court by a petition which must include, in addition to the general particulars required in the plaint, a statement of the law or legislative provision the subject-matter of the petition, the grounds for alleging its contravention of the Constitution and right or interest of the petitioner which is directly affected thereby.[8]

If a plea of the unconstitutionality of any law or legislative provision is raised before any court, and such court is satisfied of the genuineness of the plea, it must fix a time within which the party interested may institute a suit in the Supreme

Court.[9] If a suit is instituted within the time so fixed, the court before which the plea is raised must stay the proceedings pending the final disposal of the suit in the Supreme Court, and if no suit is instituted within the time so fixed, the plea must be considered as nugatory.[10]

This constitutional remedy is limited to cases where the applicant has exhausted all remedies whether by way of appeal or other civil or criminal proceedings.[11]

As regards the disposal of the suit, the Supreme Court has to follow the ordinary procedure for ordinary suits, except for minor special provisions of a usual kind.[12]

It is clear, therefore, that the constitutional remedy is limited to State measures which may adversely affect foreign private investments through laws or legislative provisions. The usual measures are expropriation or nationalization. However, this constitutional limitation entails the importance of differentiating between the legislative and executive measures of the President under the Constitution. This process postulates a careful examination of the provisions of the Constitution and the other laws which endow the President with the power to take action which has the force of law and hence be equated with 'laws and legislative provisions' as envisaged by Article 58 of the Constitution and the Civil Procedure Act so as to fall within the ambit of the constitutional powers of the Supreme Court to have them declared null and void. No definitive answer is given beforehand by the Constitution itself or any other law. Much depends on the nature of the measure taken by the President in each particular case. There are certain Presidential Orders which are by their very nature considered as laws, while the great majority are exercises of the executive function which is peculiar to the Sudanese Constitution, like most other presidential systems. Thus, Provisional Orders issued by the President under Article 106 of the Constitution are laws if they are ratified by the People's Assembly, and hence can be subject-matter of constitutional suits before the Supreme Court. Similarly, Republican Orders ratifying treaties are considered as laws, as mentioned before (pp. 145–7). The same criterion applies to orders declaring a state of emergency under Article 111 of the Constitution which are not subject to be reviewed by the Supreme Court. However, the obvious conclusion to be drawn is that any order which is in the exercise of the executive function is outside the orbit of the constitutional remedy, and accordingly fall within the judicial review of the administrative decisions. But this is begging the question.

(ii) *Judicial review of administrative decisions*

If the measure or action complained of by the foreign investor is not a law or legislative provision contravening the Constitution, the only remedy open to him before the enactment of the Encouragement of Investment Act of 1980 was to apply to the competent Court of Appeal to review that measure or action if it were *ultra vires*. The procedure to be followed in this case is outlined in chapter 2 of Part XII of the Civil Procedure Act, 1974, which can be summarized as follows.

The application to review an administrative decision will lie to the competent Court of Appeal and must be in the form of a petition which includes, in addition to the general particulars required in the plaint, a statement of the nature of the decision subject to review and the grounds thereof.[13] Where the decision required to be reviewed is appealable to a competent administrative authority, the application must specify the result of such appeal and the date thereof.[14] The application must be accompanied by a copy of the decision required to be reviewed.[15]

The application for review must be made within sixty days from the publication of the decision in the Gazette or in departmental circulars, or from the date of communication to the parties interested, whichever is earlier.[16] The application for review must not be accepted:

(a) where the applicant has no personal interest;
(b) where the applicant has not exhausted all the modes of redress available to him by law;
(c) unless the application is based on incompetence or an abuse of authority or a defect in form of a departure from the law or a mistake in the application or interpretation of law.[17]

The competent court is to decide upon claims for compensation for damages arising out of an administrative decision without limit as to value and whether the claim was submitted as an original claim or incidental to a claim for setting aside the administrative decision or order.[18] This is a novel provision which is far ahead if compared with the English law, which has not recognized the award of compensation in judicial review of administrative decisions until recently.[19] However, a decree setting aside an administrative decision or the award of damages will not be executed until it becomes final on exhaustion of available modes of objection or where the time for such objection has expired.

On the face of it, the above procedure is sufficient for redressing grievances resulting from arbitrary and *ultra vires* administrative decisions. But when it comes to operate in reality, it is marred by several difficulties which tend to negate the whole remedy. Thus, suppose that an investor obtained a licence under the Industrial Investment Act to establish a certain industry; suppose that his licence was revoked by the Minister under section 14 of the same Act for any of the reasons mentioned therein; what, then, is the remedy for this investor against the decision of the Minister? Obviously, he has the right to appeal against the decision, but to whom can the appeal be addressed? Under the Industrial Investment Act, 1974 the appeal lay to the same Minister, by way of application for the revision of such a decision. The Minister must make his decision within a maximum period of one month from the date of presenting the application, provided that the decision will be final and not to be challenged by any court.[20] This provision has been resurrected in section 23 of the Encouragement of Investment Act of 1980, only with the difference that the appeal against the decision of the Minister lies to the Ministerial Committee whose decision is final. Such ouster clauses deprive the private investor of a remedy against the cancellation of his investment licence. It is also not clear what will happen if the Minister does not give his decision within the prescribed period of one month. Can the aggrieved investor challenge the inaction of the Minister before the Sudanese courts by arguing that the ouster clause is applicable only when there is a decision by the Minister? The answer to this question is very difficult indeed. The aggrieved investor has the right to apply to the competent court to have the decision reviewed, but in this hypothetical case no decision is normally forthcoming, and if it is rendered, the Sudanese courts are explicitly prevented from challenging it. In conferring the power on the Minister to revise his own decision, or as recently on the Ministerial Committee, to the exclusion of the courts to do the same, the Sudanese legislature intended that the executive should be allowed to be the final judge of the extent of his own powers; a result which is indeed undesirable. One may wonder whether in any event the Sudanese courts would be as zealous to refuse to apply ouster clauses, and to refuse to vindicate *ultra vires* administrative decisions, as the English courts, for example in the House of Lords case, *Anisminic Ltd* v. *Foreign Compensation Commission*,[21] when the House confirmed the inherent powers of the English courts over statutory authorities and held that statutes which forbid recourse to the courts should not protect an action which is clearly *ultra vires*.

But experience suggests that the Sudanese courts are very reluctant to review an ouster clause in a statute which expressly inhibits them from exercising jurisdiction in relation to a specific matter or any issue related thereto. There have been very many cases where the Sudanese courts have declined to exercise jurisdiction pursuant to section 3 of the Unregistered Lands Act, 1970[22] which is intended to prevent the courts from entertaining suits related to claims to lands which are at the time of the suit not registered in the name of any person. Not only that, but also the courts have been directed to stay proceedings in pending suits.

In the light of the above, the previous Sudanese laws did not provide an effective remedy against the ministerial decisions cancelling investment licences, incentives and guarantees. The situation is aggravated, furthermore, by another ouster clause which has a general application in relation to the doctrine of 'act of State' which is explicitly endorsed in section 6 of the Judiciary Act, 1973[23] to the effect that the Sudanese courts have no jurisdiction directly or indirectly over acts of State. What these acts of State are under Sudanese law is not clear. No positive definition is given. None the less, there is an incomplete and obscure general definition which helps very little. Thus, Sayed Khalaffalla El Rasheed, the previous Chief Justice of the Sudan, rendered an advice to the Council of Ministers, when he was Advocate-General, to the effect that 'acts of State' are those which are expressed by Republican Orders and do not embrace decisions of the Council of Ministers. The advice related to the power of the Council of Ministers to deprive an individual of his nationality under the Sudanese Nationality Act, 1957.[24] It should be observed that this advice is not convincing, as it lacked authority, and that it is general in character, because it confers on all Republican Orders a sacrosanctity that gives an impression that all Republican Orders are beyond the reach of the courts, which was not the intention of the legislature at all. Under the Constitution, as indicated above, the aggrieved investor can apply to the Supreme Court to declare a law or a legislative provision null and void if it encroaches on his fundamental rights. It has been established also that many Republican Orders are laws or have the force of law. The only type of Republican Orders that have been expressly removed from the jurisdiction of the courts are those envisaged by Article 111 of the Constitution which deals with declaring a State of Emergency.

The difficulty facing the Sudanese courts with regard to the definition of 'acts of State' is apparent in cases of the Republican Orders which are executive in nature. They would presumably be subject to judicial review as administrative decisions. But suppose that the President has issued a Republican order imposing additional taxes on a certain investing foreign company which has been accorded tax exemption pursuant to any of the investment laws, can this company apply to the competent Court of Appeal to have this Republican Order reviewed and claim compensation for the damages resulting therefrom? In theory, there is no reason why such a company cannot pursue this line of action. But suppose that the court is faced with a preliminary objection that the Republican Order is an 'act of State' and the court is not competent to exercise jurisdiction in relation to the effect of this Republican Order, will the court sustain or overrule the objection? No definite answer can be given. So far, there is no Sudanese case where the issue has been raised; though there have been many potential Republican Orders of a similar nature, no adjudication has materialized. The justification may partially either be attributed to the sanctity accorded to Republican Orders issued by the President or to the ignorance of the litigants of the extent of their rights to contest the validity of these orders in the courts. In any case, it is hardly possible to concede that any Sudanese court could venture to challenge any Republican Order or Decree in view of the procedure usually adopted in appointing, promoting and sacking judges which are always effected by Republican Orders.[25] In such a dramatic situation, it is noteworthy that the independence of the judiciary is at stake.[26]

As there is neither a Sudanese statutory nor judicial definition of the doctrine of 'act of State' it is worthwhile to have recourse to English law. It has been the practice of the Sudanese municipal courts to apply English law when confronted with the absence of a provision governing the issue at hand. An English case in point is the *Attorney-General* v. *Nissan*[27] decided by the House of Lords. Lord Reid held that a British subject can never be deprived of his legal right to redress by any assertion of the Crown that the acts complained of were 'acts of State'. He elaborated further by stating that:

> I think that a good deal of the trouble has been caused by using the loose phrase 'act of State' without making clear what it meant. Sometimes it seems to be used to denote any act of sovereign power or of high policy or any act done in the execution of a treaty. This is a possible definition, but then it must be observed that there are many such acts which *can be subject of an action in court if they infringe the rights of British subjects*. Sometimes it seems to be used to denote acts which cannot be made the subject of inquiry in a British court. But that does not tell us how to distinguish such acts: it is only a name for a class which has still to be defined. One definition which has been accepted in some quarters is that of Professor Wade, quoted in *Halsbury's Laws of England*, Vol. VII, para. 593, p. 279:
>
> '*An act of the executive as a matter of policy performed in the course of its relations with another State including its relations with the subjects of that State, unless they are temporarily within the allegiance of the Crown, is an act of State*'.[28] (My italics.)

Lord Reid went on to comment that:

> I do not think that this is entirely satisfactory. I am not sure what is meant by 'a matter of policy'. For the definition to be complete must be added: '*or against another State or a subject of that State*'.[29] (My italics.)

Furthermore, Lord Reid elaborated on the practice of the British courts when faced with the plea based on the doctrine of the 'act of State' by stating succinctly, but with certain qualifications, that:

> It is sometimes said that the question whether an act done on behalf of or ratified by the Crown – which here must mean the Government – is an act of State, depends on the nature or quality of the act, and that it is for the court to determine whether any act is an act of State. It is true that *the Court must determine, on such facts as are available, whether the act was done in purported exercise of a legal right: if it was it cannot be regarded as an act of State. But if it was not done in purported exercise of any legal right and was done by an officer of the Crown apparently in the course of his duty, then it appears to me that it must be for the Crown to say whether it claims that the act was an act of State*. The act may appear to be of a routine or trivial character. But in a delicate situation there may be discussion and decision at the highest level about such acts, and the decision to do such an act may be a decision of high policy. *If the Crown claims that such an act was done as an act of State I do not see what right the court can have to reject that claim: the court cannot inquire into or ask the Crown* to disclose the reason why the act was done.[30] (My italics.)

According to this judicial pronouncement, it would seem that the English courts regard the doctrine of 'act of State' *stricto sensu* as falling within the questions of high policy of the executive, like the question of recognition and other similar issues regarding foreign relations. Consequently, if the British Government deprives a foreign national of a certain property right, the obvious inference to be drawn from the above judicial statement is that an English court will not question the measure of the Government if a plea of 'act of State' is raised, while this result is not obtainable if the aggrieved person is a British subject.[31]

If a Sudanese court is to apply the above judicial precedent to fill in the gap in the Sudanese law presented by the absence of any legislative or judicial authority on the 'act of State' doctrine, it would seem that there should be a distinction between those acts done in the exercise of legal rights and those not based on any legal right. According to Lord Reid's view the first category will not be considered as 'acts of State', and hence are subject to be reviewed by the Sudanese courts. These may be the rights of the Taxation Department, the Exchange Control, the Ministry of Commerce and Supply and the Customs Department in imposing taxation, exchange control, export and import restrictions and customs duties, or similar measures which depend on the exercise of discretionary powers under certain statutes. Undoubtedly, these will be subject to judicial review by the Sudanese courts on the application of aggrieved foreign investors. The form of the measure is irrelevant, whether it be carried by a ministerial decision or Republican Order; still, it must be considered as an administrative decision so long as it cannot be regarded as a law or legislative provision.[32] It all depends on the nature of the decision regardless of the authority which took that decision.

On the other hand, when there are acts which are no done in purported exercise of any legal rights and were done by a public officer, Minister or the President at their discretion in the course of their duties, it must be for the Government to say whether it claims that those acts were done as acts of State, provided that they are consonant with the Constitution. I think the prudent approach to be pursued by the Sudanese Government is to restrict the plea of 'act of State' to those cases where the security and sovereignty of the State are at stake, such as the declaration of war or of a state of emergency, passports, nationality, and similar matters. Otherwise, foreign investors will be deprived of any remedy to challenge administrative decisions which may impinge on their investments in the Sudan. Any wider interpretation of the scope and application of the doctrine of 'act of State' will defeat the purpose of the Constitution, which entrenches the supremacy of the Rule of Law[33] and will be incompatible with the declared policy to encourage the flow of foreign investment to the Sudan.

(iii) *Action for breach of contract*

A foreign investor who concluded an investment contract (development agreement) with the Sudan Government has the right under the Civil Procedure Act to bring an action for breach of contract before the competent court having jurisdiction. This is an ordinary procedure like any action brought by a Sudanese national if there is a breach of contract by the Government. However, in all suits against the Government a notice has to be served to the Attorney-General in accordance with section 33 of the Civil Procedure Act.

It had been the practice of the Sudanese courts to give relief for breach of contract by the Government. There are abundant judicial decisions to this effect. The most notorious one is the case of *Sudan Government* v. *Brown International Inc.* It is also worth mentioning that the Sudanese Government has been, and would be willing to execute the judgment once it becomes final. It is very reluctant to claim immunity from jurisdiction or to raise the plea of 'act of State' in actions for breach of contract.

Unless the contract expressly provides for reference to arbitration, the Sudanese courts are apathetic about upholding an ouster clause in a contract which purported to vest jurisdiction in foreign courts if they themselves have jurisdiction for all intents and purposes.[34] Of course, assuming that the foreign investor has the right to, and does, bring his action for breach of contract before the Sudanese courts, it is inconceivable that the Government would plead the ouster clause so as to transfer the suit to a foreign forum.

But the problem may be augmented if the breach of contract resulted from the unilateral act of the Government couched in a legislative instrument duly passed by the legislature. This exemplifies the cases of nationalization where the injury to the foreign investor is caused by the application of the local law which is binding on the local courts. These courts are unable to give a remedy for an act which is not wrongful according to the law which they administer. Thus, when addressing the Council of the League of Nations in connection with the cancellation by the Persian Government of the Anglo-Persian Company's 1901 Concession, the United Kingdom's representative said that since the cancellation had been ratified by the Persian Parliament, resort to the local courts would have been in vain, as they had no jurisdiction to grant a remedy to the company.[35]

(iv) *Settlement of investment disputes under the Encouragement of Investment Act, 1980*

Under this Act it is no longer possible for a foreign investor to settle his dispute with the Sudanese Government by ordinary litigation to review an administrative decision. This is because, under section 32 of the Act, all investment disputes should be settled by arbitration which should be conducted inside the Sudan. The section distinguishes between separate procedures according to the nationality of the investor. Firstly, if the investor is a Sudanese national, the dispute will be settled by municipal *ad hoc* arbitration provided for by the Civil Procedure Act 1974. This falls outside the scope of this book. Secondly, if the private investment is an Arab investment, the dispute must be settled in accordance with the provisions of the Convention on the Settlement of Investment Disputes between Host States for Arab Investments and Nationals of Other Arab States, 1974,[36] if the arbitration procedure envisaged by that convention be applicable to the investment dispute. Thirdly, if the investment is a foreign non-Arab investment, the dispute must be settled in accordance with the Convention on the Settlement of Investment Disputes between States and Nationals of Other States 1965[37] (*the Washington Convention*), if it is applicable to the dispute. But, the new provisions ignore the situation where the investment is in the form of a joint venture between Sudanese, Arab and non-Arab nationals or companies, a phenomenon which is increasingly dominating the investment pattern in the Sudan.

Though the settlement of disputes through arbitration should be welcomed, yet the mandatory incorporation by reference of these two conventions in section 32 of the Encouragement of Investment Act, 1980 is not free from certain defects which create a lacuna in the law. First, as will be shown below, not all States are parties to the Conventions envisaged by the section, and it is unclear what will be the solution in these situations. Furthermore, as we shall explain below, under the Washington Convention, referring any of the investment disputes to the centre established by that Convention is not mandatory. Both parties to the dispute should consent in writing to the jurisdiction of the centre. The section makes it obligatory to settle all investment disputes by arbitration inside the Sudan, but only through the three arbitration processes indicated above, except for the cases where it is otherwise provided for by any other law. Even this elusive proviso will not solve the problem, as there might be no law on the point. I pointed out this loophole to the draftsmen when we discussed together the final draft of the law, but my point has not been taken into consideration in the final draft.

All in all, the incorporation of institutionalized arbitration in the law of the Sudan discloses a monist approach which must be encouraged and enhanced, as it is consistent with Article 2 of the Charter of Economic Rights and Duties of States, which, as mentioned before, calls for settling investment disputes inside the territory of the investee State. However, to improve the venues for settling investment disputes in the Sudan, section 32 of the Encouragement of Investment Act, 1980 should be amended in such a way as to permit *ad hoc* arbitration, where institutionalized arbitration is not viable. Also, consideration should be given to the mutuality of the parties to agree on any other procedure for settling their disputes, provided that the proceedings should always be conducted inside the Sudan.

(b) Under Saudi law

Disputes between private investors are usually settled by the Board for the Settlement of Commercial Disputes. This board consists of three judges and it follows a procedure of its own. Litigation before it is a long, time-consuming process. For this reason, it is advisable for foreign investors entering into joint ventures with Saudi nationals to include in their agreements an arbitration clause so as to obtain a quick result.

As regards disputes between foreign investors and the Saudi Government or its agencies, they fall within the jurisdiction of the Grievances Board which has been established by special regulations.[38] The verdict of the Board is final and binding. This means that no further action is contemplated in the Saudi municipal legal system, as there is no procedure for appeal in this respect. And under section 10 of the Foreign Capital Investment Law 1979, the jurisdiction of the Grievances Board extends to considering appeals against the decision of the Minister of Industry and Electricity to revoke investment licences and guarantees granted under that law.

Though traditional Islamic law would not prevent a Saudi agency, whether public or private, from agreeing to international arbitration, nevertheless the Council of Ministers issued a decision in 1963 which restricts the ability of government agencies to settle their disputes with foreign investors. According to that decision a government may not make a contract which has the effect of subjecting it to a foreign court or judicial body. This policy has been recently emphasized, furthermore, by a ministerial circular, obligating foreign companies not to stipulate in their investment contracts provisions which have the effect of settling disputes outside the Kingdom.

(c) Settlement of disputes under foreign municipal law

It is possible for an aggrieved foreign investor to have recourse to local remedies within his home State. In the absence of any inhibiting legal principle, the private investor might move to indemnify himself through such means for the wrong allegedly done to him by proceeding against assets belonging to or derived from the Sudan, but located within the home State. One obvious bar to such action for obtaining compensation is the doctrine of sovereign immunity of states which is illustrated in the *Chemical Natural Resources* v. *Republic of Venezuela* case.[39] Another formidable bar to such action is the doctrine of 'act of state' which was first acknowledged by the United States Supreme Court in the *Underhill* case. Chief Justice Fuller stated the doctrine in the following words:

> Every sovereign State is bound to respect the independence of every other sovereign State, and the courts will not sit in judgment on the acts of the government of another done within its territory. Redress of grievances by reason of such acts must be obtained through the means open to be availed of by sovereign powers, as between themselves.[40]

In the *Sabbatino* case,[41] a United States Court of Appeal held that since a Cuban decree of nationalization not only failed to provide adequate compensation, but also was punitive in purpose and discriminated against United States nationals, it was in violation of international law. On appeal, the United States Supreme Court reversed the decision and held that in the absence of a treaty or other agreement, American courts would not question the taking of property within its own territory by a sovereign Government recognized by the United States.[42] This led to remand of the case to the district court, to congressional legislation, and to a new decision in 1965.

However, resulting from the disfavour that has been evident regarding the decision of the Supreme Court, both in the United States and abroad, the Foreign Assistance Act has been subsequently amended. The amendment, known as the Hickenlooper Amendment[43] incorporated in section 301(d) of the Act, directed that no American court shall decline, on the ground of the federal 'act of State' doctrine, to determine on its merits a case in which a claim of right by any party is based on confiscation by a foreign State, in violation of international law occurring after 1 January 1959. But the doctrine was made inapplicable in cases with respect to which the President determines and so informs the court that United States foreign policy interests require application of the act of State doctrine.[44]

The application of the doctrine of the 'act of State' by the courts of other States cannot be predicted with any precision. Much will depend on the nature of the action pursued and the juridical form of the right sought to be protected. Furthermore, the nationality of the claimant will have its impact.[45] The general tendency in recent years is towards restricting the scope of the doctrine.

3. Diplomatic intervention, good offices and mediation

(a) Diplomatic intervention

(i) *Extent of application*

States are in the habit of intervening diplomatically to protect property situated abroad which belongs either to the State, to the Government or to its nationals, against threatened or actual injury at the hands of a foreign Government. This protection also covers injury to the person of a national without regard to his material property, but this book is concerned primarily with the circumstances and conditions under which a State can protect investments of its nationals abroad against loss caused by or threatened by a foreign Government.

Investors belonging to a special group in extreme cases raise this question of diplomatic protection of their home States when other sources of protection are ineffective. Actually, the majority of present-day businessmen would much prefer to avoid such a course, as sovereign relations with host Governments are governed by many political considerations. The home Government is usually reluctant to disturb its relation with the host Government. For this reason, a foreign investor would be content only with the quiet form of his home State's 'good offices'. Legally, according to the Permanent Court of International Justice:

> It is an elementary principle of international law that a State is entitled to protect its subjects, when injured by acts contrary to international law committed by another State, from whom they have been unable to obtain satisfaction through the ordinary channels.
>
> By taking up the case as one of its subjects and by resorting to diplomatic action or international judicial proceedings on his behalf, a State is in reality asserting its own rights – its right to ensure in the person of its subjects, respect for international law. Once a State has taken a case on behalf of one of its subjects before an international tribunal, in the eyes of the latter, the State is sole claimant.[46]

Diplomatic intervention by a State for the protection of private property situated abroad is allowed in international law if two basic conditions are satisfied, namely nationality of claims and exhaustion of local remedies.

(1) *Nationality of claim*

Natural persons

Not ever individual can claim the protection of a State. In the *Panevezys-Saldutiskis Railway* case[47] the Permanent Court of International Justice authoritatively laid down the rule that a State's right of diplomatic protection 'is necessarily limited to intervention on behalf of its own nationals because, in the absence of a special agreement, it is the bond of nationality between the State and the individual which alone confers upon the State the right of diplomatic protection'. For a State to intervene lawfully in property disputes abroad, the individual owner, on whose behalf the State claims to act, must be its national from the time of injury up to the presentation of a claim by the State.[48] It is not sufficient merely to be a national at one of the relevant moments.

As pointed out before, the question of nationality is determined by the municipal law of each State.[49] Even then, the right of a State to use its discretion is nevertheless restricted by international obligations it may have undertaken towards other States.[50]

In the case of protection of persons with double nationality, the accepted view adopted by international tribunals is that the effective nationality prevails.[51]

The protection of companies

As established earlier (see *ante*, pp. 16–19, the nationality of a company can be determined by applying three theories, namely the *siège sociale*, the law of the place of incorporation and the nationality of the majority of the shareholders (control test).

The accepted principle in international law is that only the State of the nationality of the company, and not the State or States of shareholders, can exercise the right of diplomatic protection against a foreign country.[52] According to the report of the League of Nations Committee of Experts on the Nationality of Commercial Corporations and their Diplomatic Protection:[53] 'The right of diplomatic protection and intervention on behalf of commercial companies shall belong to the State of which they are nationals.'

This principle has been recently confirmed by the International Court of Justice in the *Barcelona Traction* case.[54] The Court, in considering the right of Belgium to exercise diplomatic protection of Belgian shareholders in a Canadian company with respect to measures taken in relation to the company by Spain, rather than the shareholders, insisted on a clear distinction between a direct injury to the company and injury to simple, economic interests of the shareholders, regarding only the former, and not the latter, as involving the international responsibility of a State.[55] The Court was of the opinion that consideration of equity required no more than the possibility for one protector State to intervene, primarily the national State of the company, and secondarily, the national State of the shareholders.[56] This means when a corporation or company suffers loss through the action of the Government of the country where it operates, the first right of diplomatic protection belongs to the State whose nationality it possesses. But it is generally accepted that in exceptional cases the home State of shareholders has the right to protect their interests in a foreign country.[57]

However, there are three situations where neither the company nor its home State provide effective protection for the property of the company:[58]

- (i) if the company becomes defunct or goes into liquidation so that it cannot look after its interest, or
- (ii) the home State of a company may be itself guilty of suppressing it,[59] or
- (iii) where a company which possesses the nationality of State A is injured by the government of State B, State A may refuse to accord it diplomatic protection, as it is an established principle that the exercise by a State of its right of diplomatic protection is discretionary.[60]

It has been the practice of States to present diplomatic protests against actions of foreign governments for the injury of the economic interest of their nationals even when these nationals are only shareholders in multinational corporations. What is relevant here is the nationality of the persons who have the final economic interest.[61] Such a practice was not much evident in the practice of States whose nationals' investments had been nationalized or confiscated by the Sudanese Government in 1970.

These traditional rules on nationality of claims discussed above are rather elementary, archaic and outdated. They were evolved in the nineteenth century when the modern investment patterns were unknown. The old cases dealt with individuals, but the problem today virtually arises with multinational corporations and joint ventures which are increasing phenomena particularly in the Sudan and Saudi Arabia.[62] This requires the adaptation of the traditional nationality of claims rules which were designed for rather different circumstances. Of equal significance in this respect are the local rules that require investors to incorporate their companies under the local law; thereby these companies are to acquire the nationality of the host country. In such situations the nationality of claims rules would be illusory if the host State were to destroy the investment sponsored by the locally-incorporated company. However, this presents no problem in the Sudan. As depicted before, a foreign company would be registered in the Sudan as a subsidiary of a foreign holding company. Except in the petroleum sector, it is not mandatory on a foreign company to be incorporated under the Sudanese law (*see ante*, pp. 32–3).

(2) *Exhaustion of local remedies*

Another cardinal pre-condition for the effective exercise of diplomatic intervention is the exhaustion of local remedies. It is a well-established principle of international law that before an alien, who is injured in a foreign country, can invoke the assistance of his home State, he must exhaust all the available local remedies.[63] Once the local remedies have been explored without satisfaction, a State can present a claim on behalf of its national to an international tribunal. To exhaust local remedies, redress must have been sought in the highest tribunal of the land by appeals or other procedures. In the case of *Electricity Company of Sofia and Bulgaria*,[64] the Permanent Court of International Justice held that:

> The local remedies rule contemplated . . . implies the exhaustion of all appeals, including appeals to the court of Cassation, a decision by which alone renders the judgment final.[65]

This would presumably include all remedial processes, judicial and administrative as well.

However, there are well recognized exceptions to the local remedies rule. In these cases, a State can take action on international level to protect the property of its national situated abroad where the latter has not exhausted the local remedies. There are three known exceptions relevant to the present study:

(a) Where the highest judicial tribunal of the land is controlled by the executive which committed the alleged injury, any effort to obtain local remedy will be futile, because there will be no chances for the court to do justice to the complainant. This is really a denial of justice – which of course does not require exhaustion of local remedies.[66]

(b) If the decision on which an appeal could be made to the highest court is based on an express and mandatory municipal legislation so that on appeal the same statute will be applied, there is no need to exhaust local remedies because by definition there are none.[67] Municipal courts are often bound to apply local legislation even when this results in direct injury to an alien.

(c) According to Oppenheim, the local remedies rule becomes inapplicable 'when the injury to the alien is the result of an act of the government as such'.[68] Nwogugu[69] explained this exception by a hypothetical case, that if a government which has nationalized or expropriated foreign-owned property makes no provision for compensation or denies the property owner access to the courts to contest the legality of the measure or adequacy of compensation, there are no local remedies to be exhausted.

(ii) *Nature of diplomatic intervention*

Basically, a State goes to the assistance of its nationals injured abroad by lodging a protest. This could be followed later by other international means of challenging a breach of international law, e.g. resort to arbitration or other international tribunal, retortion or retaliation. These will be examined below.

According to Oppenheim:[70] 'Protest is a formal communication from one State to another that it objects to an act performed, or contemplated, by the latter. A protest serves the purpose of preservation of rights, or of making it known that the protesting State does not acquiesce in, and does not recognize, certain acts.' Accordingly protests are a recognized international device by which a State can lodge its immediate objection to an act whether contemplated or executed by another State. However, there are two established occasions when protests can be effectively employed. The right of protest can be exercised when there is a threat of loss to the property of nationals situated abroad. As MacGibbon[71] observed: 'It is clear, however, that States are under no obligation to refrain from protesting until an actual violation of their rights has taken place.' Such a protest indicates to the respondent State the objection of the protesting State to its contemplated action as contrary to international law and injurious to foreign interests. This anticipatory protest is regularly used by States.[72]

Protests are also employed for protection after loss or injury has actually occurred to the nationals of a State in a foreign country. The majority of the cases of the use of protest are of this kind.[73]

(iii) *Effect of diplomatic intervention*

Assuming that no local remedies are available and that all the requirements for diplomatic protection are satisfied, what then is the effect of this practice? If the home State of the private investor agrees to espouse his claim officially, the issue will lie between two sovereign and equal States, whose relations with each other are governed by international law. Henceforth, the private claim is transferred into a public claim, viz., the claim of the home State of the private investor. This has been confirmed, as mentioned before, by the Permanent Court of International Justice in the *Mavrommatis* case.

There are certain important consequences which flow from this transfer of claim to the inter-State level, some advantageous to the private investor and some disadvantageous. One of the advantages is that the espousal by the home State of the claim of the foreign investor removes the disparity between the parties and opens possible remedies under international law, which the private investor could not pursue directly. Furthermore, the foreign State may find the home State has arguments and inducements, legal and meta-legal, which were not available to the private investor and which the foreign State cannot afford to ignore.[74]

On the other hand, the obvious disadvantage to the private investor is that he loses control when his claim is transferred into a State claim. The home State assumes exclusive control over the claim. This entails that the method of settlement, the arguments to be used, the relief to be sought are for the State to determine. Owing to certain circumstances, a State may at its discretion abandon or compromise the claim, while the private investor will be forced to accept any settlement obtained by it.[75]

Despite all the home State persuasions, diplomatic intervention may fail to produce either a settlement or an agreed recourse to judicial or arbitral proceedings. Suffice it to observe that the Sudanese Government is responsive to solving investment disputes through diplomatic channels as experience has shown (see *ante*, pp. 217–20).

From a practical point of view, private foreign investors prefer to obtain a direct settlement with the investee State than to have recourse to the diplomatic protection of their home States. Diplomatic protection entails presentation of enormous documents and lengthy proceedings which are considered time-consuming. Additionally, the outcome of the settlement is always considered unsatisfactory, usually securing only one-third of the amount claimed. Conversely, investee States dislike settling disputes directly with foreign investors; they usually insist that negotiations leading to the settlement should be conducted through the national governments of the aggrieved investors. The *Turriff* case and the *Marcona* case are typical incidents.

(b) Good offices and mediation

Good offices and mediation have been recognized as devices or modes of settling international disputes. Under Article 33 of the United Nations Charter[76] 'the parties to any dispute, the continuance of which is likely to endanger the maintenance of international peace and security, shall, first of all, seek a solution by negotiation, inquiry, mediation, conciliation, arbitration, judicial settlement, resort to regional agencies or arrangements, or other peaceful means of their own choice'. Furthermore, under the same article, the Security Council shall, when it deems necessary, call upon the parties to settle their dispute by such means. However, there is a theoretical distinction between good offices and mediation. Thus, while the former consists of acts intended to bring the disputing parties together to negotiate, mediation involved actual conduct of the negotiations on the basis of proposals made by the mediator.[77] In practice, both methods have a basic common feature – the assistance of a third party in the settlement of a dispute. Perhaps the most important international organization that used to lend its good offices for settling investment disputes is the World Bank. It has been involved, on several occasions, in the settlement of investment disputes arising from the destruction of the investments of nationals of one State in another. A clear example of the situation is the nationalization of the Suez Canal Company in 1956. On that occasion, the affected States – Britain, France, and Egypt – failed to resolve their disputes over the Egyptian nationalization measures by peaceful means. In the end, the three States requested the good offices of the World Bank. The Bank was very effective in the negotiation of a settlement between the Suez Canal Company and Egypt and agreed to perform some important functions in the execution of the final agreement.[78] Subsequently, the Bank's President mediated in the financial agreement between the United Kingdom and Egypt.[79]

In addition to the role of international organizations such as the World Bank as exemplified by the Suez Canal case above, foreign investors in the Sudan and Saudi Arabia can settle their disputes with the Sudanese and Saudi Governments through the good offices of the regional organizations. Of particular importance in this respect are the Organization of African Unity and the Arab League.[80] The relevance of the role to be played by these two regional organizations will be enhanced when the foreign investor is of African or Arab origin. So far, there is no case where either of the organizations has intervened positively to settle an investment dispute.

4. International Court of Justice

When the property of a national situated abroad is injured by the action of the government of the *situs*, the home State of the individual may be willing to pursue his claim against the respondent State. As indicated above, this may take the form of diplomatic claim or the institutions of proceedings before an international tribunal. As is the case in diplomatic intervention, it is an established principle of international law that there is no obligation on a State to espouse the claim of its national against a respondent State before the World Court.[81] Whether or not a State is zealous to pursue the claim depends mainly on the relation between the home and the respondent States. In this respect, the foreign investor may find himself without a remedy.

By article 34 of the Statute of the International Court of Justice 'only States may be parties in cases before the court'.[82] Consequently, the claim of an individual against a foreign State may only be brought before the International Court of Justice by his home State which may decline to do so in the particular situation. In the *Serbian and Brazilian Loans* case,[83] claims of the French bond-holders arising from Serbian and Brazilian loans issued in France were brought before the Permanent Court of International Justice by the French Government. This exclusive jurisdiction of the Court has been extended to its advisory opinions in which individuals are involved. Disputes are usually referred to the Court by the parties concerned in three different ways: (1) if the parties agree to submit a dispute to the Court; (2) if both parties have previously agreed to the 'compulsory jurisdiction' provision of the Court's Statute and one of them refers the dispute to the Court; (3) if both parties have previously concluded a treaty which makes provision for utilizing the Court to resolve different interpretations of the treaty and one party submits the problem to the Court.[84]

In appropriate situations, States have brought the claims of their nationals before the World Court and its predecessor. The success of the claim in each case would depend on the extent of the acceptance of the jurisdiction of the Court. In many cases claims were dismissed on preliminary objections relating to lack of jurisdiction, and consequently, the Court did not have to rule on the merits.[85] This usually emanates from the practice of States in entering reservations to accepting the compulsory jurisdiction of the Court.

On 2 January 1958, the Republic of the Sudan deposited with the Secretary-General of the United Nations a declaration accepting the compulsory jurisdiction of the International Court of Justice under Article 36(2) of the Statute of the Court. Following the example of the 'Connolly Amendment' reservation of the United States, the Sudan excluded from its acceptance,

(ii) disputes in regard to matters which are essentially within the domestic jurisdiction of the Republic of the Sudan *as determined by the Government of the Republic of the Sudan.*[86] (My italics.)

This subjective form of reservation has been described by Judge Lauterpacht as 'automatic' because once a defendant Government made a decision that a particular matter was essentially within its domestic jurisdiction, then:

the function of the Court is confined to registering the decision made by the defendant Government and not subject to review by the Court.[87]

Juristic as well as judicial opinion had challenged the validity of 'automatic reservations' like the one mentioned above which, strangely enough, the Sudan is still keeping despite the strongest opposition it has encountered by academic as well as judicial authorities inside[88] and outside the Sudan. Professor Waldock took the position that a declaration to which an 'automatic reservation' was appended has no legal force as a declaration under the optional clause because of its incompatibility with Article 36(6) of the Statute of the Court which confers on the Court itself the competence to decide whether or not it has jurisdiction in the event of a dispute.[89] He further contended that:

the reservation of what appears to be a general right to exclude from the scope of the declaration any dispute at any time at the will of the State concerned can scarcely be regarded as a genuine 'recognition' of the Court's compulsory jurisdiction within the meaning of the Optional Clause.[90]

The 'automatic reservation' attached to the Sudan's declaration would be destructive to its own vital interests, for it might be invoked by a respondent State to exclude the jurisdiction of the Court through the application of the principle of reciprocity as explained by the Court in the *Interhandel* case in the following words:

Reciprocity in the case of Declarations accepting the compulsory jurisdiction of the Court enables a Party to invoke a reservation to that acceptance which it has not expressed in its own Declaration but which the other Party has expressed in its Declaration.[91]

As a matter of policy, to encourage foreign investment, the Sudan would be well advised to replace its present declaration by one appended by an objective domestic jurisdiction reservation, if it is necessary to make any reservation.

The question posed is: as long as the present automatic reservation is in force, will the Government of the aggrieved foreign investor be precluded from invoking the compulsory jurisdiction of the Court on the objection by the Sudan Government that the investment dispute is essentially within its own domestic jurisdiction? The possibility of raising such a defence is persuasively strengthened by Article 2 of the Charter of Economic Rights and Duties of States if the matter in dispute relates to the payment of compensation for a nationalized investment. To start with, it would seem unlikely that the Sudan would succeed on the latter point, as it has been already established that the Charter has no binding force, and hence it has no positive effect on the positive international law rules on the issue under discussion. However, as will be mentioned below, under the operative Sudanese investment law, investment disputes will be settled by arbitration. If the matter is taken by the home State of the investor to the World Court before exhausting this local arbitral remedy, the Sudan would have a strong defence based on the pleas of non-exhaustion of local remedies and the 'automatic' reservation appended to the Optional Clause. But if the statutory arbitration committee's award is not honoured by the Sudan Government there is no chance for it to allege that the dispute lies 'essentially with its domestic jurisdiction', as the issue will then be of an international wrong to be decided in accordance with international law by the International Court of Justice.

Though Saudi Arabia is entitled to appear before the court, because it is an original member, it has not as yet signed the optional clause.[92] So, the provisions of the Statute of the Court and its Rules will determine the jurisdiction of the court in cases in which Saudi Arabia is involved.

The present incapacity of individuals to use the World Court has been criticized.[93] The most notorious statement criticizing Article 34 of the Statute of the Court in this respect is that of the late Judge Lauterpacht during the Institut de Droit International discussion on the amendment of the I.C.J. Statute in 1954. He commented:

> I submit that in connection with article 34 of the Statute consideration may be given to the question whether that article ought to be maintained in its present rigid form... But is there a good reason, other than the persistence of certain traditional modes of thinking, why the Court should not be able to adjudicate upon a dispute which involves a question of international law and in which one party to the dispute is a State – provided that that State agrees in the specific case to the exercise of jurisdiction by the Court?[94]

The amendment of the I.C.J.'s Statute, in principle, is desirable as it includes the jurisdiction to entertain commercial disputes between States and individuals. Such a suggestion is appealing to foreign investors who are obsessed by the idea that the International Court of Justice is the best forum for redressing their grievances. In actuality this is a misconception. The litigation of the World Court is time-consuming as it involves application of rigid procedural complexities. Furthermore, the Governments prefer other means of settling investment and commercial disputes to avoid the publicity which usually characterizes the World Court's decisions.

Even if one favours the desirability of amending the Court's Statute to allow for the individual's direct recourse to the Court without the aid of his home State, the amendment is very difficult to obtain in view of linking the amendment of the Statute with that of the Charter of the United Nations.[95] Such a measure is far from being achieved at the present stage of a world divided on every issue, especially in the area of international economic co-operation, as exemplified by the Charter of Economic Rights and Duties of States and similar documents.

5. Arbitration

(a) Advantages

It is rightly stated that arbitration provides flexible and effective machinery for the settlement of commercial disputes. It has several advantages; only a few of them can be mentioned here. In the first place, arbitration is much less cumbersome and time-consuming than the complexities of adjudication. Decisions, except in very few cases, are rendered in shorter time. Another important factor is the care which arbitrators take to avoid any kind of publicity for the disputes which have led the parties to have recourse to arbitration, or for the discussions which precede and pave the way for arbitral awards. However, this depends, more or less, on the terms of the *compromis*. Flexibility is another crucial consideration. The parties to the dispute are free to select the arbitrators themselves or, alternatively, to choose the method of selection. They define the issues between themselves and agree on a site of arbitration to suit their mutual convenience. Both parties agree in advance that the award of the arbitration will be lasting and binding, thus avoiding the complexities of judicial appeal, which usually takes a long time.[96]

More significant is the problem of technical expertise. Since most commercial conflicts raise issues of fact rather than of law, a layman who has training and experience in a particular field or business is likely to be in a better position to resolve a conflict of this nature than is a judge who has not this background. In many cases, arbitrators are required to decide a case *aequo et bono* instead of applying the strict letter of the law.[97] International disputes raise further problems, since laws and procedures vary from one country to another; some apply the common law while others adopt civil law. In these circumstances, it is said that, arbitration can bridge the gap between different legal systems.[98] The validity of this view is dubious as in the end the arbitral tribunal may be forced to apply the law chosen by the parties which may fall inside or outside either legal system.

Arbitration is particularly useful for settling investment disputes, because it may make it easier to limit the claim of sovereign immunity which constitutes a hindrance in suing a foreign State. In the *Lena Goldfield* case[99] there was no reference to the sovereign status of the Russian State. But the authority of this case in this respect is weak as it was, after all, an *ex parte* arbitration, though the Russian Government in the end agreed to compensate the aggrieved company.

The justification for adopting the arbitral concept in oil concessions was noted by the Organization of Petroleum Exporting Countries' former Secretary-General, who said:

> in general, there is considerable international support for the opinion that for the settlement of trade disputes arbitration is preferable to judicial procedure even where domestic differences are concerned, for reasons which seem to be universally recognized; arbitration is less rigid, less costly, and less dilatory than the normal judicial procedure. Furthermore, persons who invest capital on a large scale in a foreign country feel more secure on having an assurance that, if a dispute arose between them and the host country, they would not be subject to the strict legal system of the country, of which they are often ignorant, and which they may fear may be applied with less than complete impartiality in cases involving foreigners.[100]

As regards the advantage of arbitration of being 'less costly' as stated above, one would wonder whether or not this is correct. The whole expenses of the International Court of Justice are on the United Nations budget.[101] Conversely, in arbitration the parties usually share the entire cost, and in some cases only one party has to pay all costs and fees.[102]

(b) Types of arbitration

Arbitration may be classified into two major categories, namely *ad hoc* and institutional arbitration. The first category may be subdivided, according to its nature and purpose, into national and international arbitration, according to the instrument giving rise to the arbitration, viz. law or treaty. As regards institutional arbitration, it is proposed to deal only with arbitral institutions which are directly relevant to settling investment disputes in the Sudan and Saudi Arabia. This may take place either by express reference to a particular arbitral procedure of a certain trading organization or by reason of the two countries' membership in multilateral conventions establishing international arbitration centres. It is not intended at all to dwell on other foreign arbitration centres.[103] Specifically, the emphasis will be focused on four international institutional arbitration centres, namely the International Chamber of Commerce, the Permanent Court of Arbitration, the International Centre of Investment Disputes and the Arab Board for Settlement of Investment Disputes. With regard to *ad hoc* arbitration, it will be examined with special reference to investment laws, investment bilateral treaties, investment insurance programmes, and economic development agreements.

(i) *International institutional arbitration*

(1) *International Chamber of Commerce (I.C.C.)*

One of the I.C.C.'s main activities is to provide, under its arbitration clause,[104] international facilities for avoiding or resolving business disputes. The clause provides as follows:

> All disputes arising in connection with the present contract shall be finally settled under the Rules of Conciliation and Arbitration of the International Chamber of Commerce by one or more arbitrators appointed in accordance with the Rules.[105]

It would seem that the parties can agree to submit a dispute to I.C.C. even when the contract does not contain the I.C.C. clause. The I.C.C. offers its good offices to any party desiring to avail itself of them, without exception.[106] The clause is applicable not only between firms which are not members, but also between Governments and individuals in different parts of the world.[107]

Disputes referred to I.C.C. arbitration must be 'business' disputes which are given a broad meaning, to include various transactions. Particularly, this would include transactions and operations involving international trade and economic co-operation in public works agreements for developing areas and investment contracts.[108]

The I.C.C. has an international Court of Arbitration which is composed of lawyers and businessmen of international reputation. This Court does not itself hear cases, but appoints arbitrators. In normal cases, there will be either a sole arbitrator appointed by the Court or three arbitrators, two of whom are appointed by the parties concerned and the third, the chairman, by the Court. Unless otherwise agreed by the parties, the nationality of the sole arbitrator or the chairman of the three-man arbitral tribunal is different from that of the parties to the proceedings.[109]

Some economic development agreements concluded recently by the Sudan Government have stipulated recourse to I.C.C. arbitration. These will be examined later in this chapter. The same practice finds parallels in other developing countries.[110] In Saudi Arabia the I.C.C. arbitration machinery is seldom utilized, and is not expected to be utilized, as the result of the new policy towards domestic *ad hoc* arbitration and enlarging the jurisdiction of the Grievances Board to undertake the task of settling all investment disputes between the government agencies and foreign investors.

As to the actual conduct of the arbitration in accordance with the Rules of Arbitration of the I.C.C., when the files have been prepared, the case is passed to the arbitrator or arbitrators for decision. After investigating the case, the arbitrator submits his award, which is in all cases final. A party against whom an award is rendered must carry it out promptly.[111]

(2) *The Permanent Court of Arbitration*

The Permanent Court was an offspring of the Convention for the Pacific Settlement of International Disputes signed at the Hague on 29 July 1899. This convention was revised and replaced by the 1907 convention of the same title concluded at the Second Peace Conference at the Hague.[112]

The Permanent Court of Arbitration is actually neither a court nor a permanent institution. It is merely a panel of arbitrators, members of which may be called to act as an arbitral tribunal. It has no regular sessions, and it meets only when a dispute takes place and some of its members are chosen to adjudicate it.[113] Basically, the machinery of the Permanent Court is for the settlement of inter-State disputes. However, in 1962 the Bureau of the Court established new rules for organizing arbitration proceedings between States and public international bodies on the one hand and companies or individuals on the other.[114] This positive step opened possibilities which may deserve to be considered when questions of arbitration proceedings between a State and a private investor arise.

The new Rules of Arbitration contain general rules for the constitution of the tribunal and rules of procedure. The State party to the dispute to which the machinery of the Court is open under the new rules, must be a contracting party to the Convention of 1907. Unless the parties decide otherwise, the *ad hoc* tribunal to settle their dispute is to consist of three arbitrators. In case the parties fail to agree on the arbitrators, they could seek the assistance of the Permanent Court's Bureau who will present each party with a list of arbitrators. From this list the tribunal may, with the agreement of the parties, be constituted. If this does not provide a solution, the parties could authorize the Secretary-General of the Court to nominate the arbitrators or the umpire. The arbitral tribunal once constituted is to sit at the Peace Palace of the Hague, unless the parties agree otherwise. The cost of the arbitration will be borne by both parties to the dispute.

The Permanent Court of Arbitration was utilized in the *Sudan–Turriff Arbitration*.[115] On 21 October 1966, at the Peace Palace, the Hague, a Submission to Arbitration was signed by the Sudan Government and Turriff. By this submission the parties referred to the Arbitral Tribunal, then consisting of the Honourable Charles Cameron of Ottawa, Sayed Mohammed Yousif Mudawi of the Judiciary, Khartoum, and Roger J. Parker, Q.C., of London, disputes described in the recitals to the Submission as:

> Disputes arising out of or in connection with a contract entered into by the Government and Turriff on the 16th October 1962 under which Turriff was to carry out a housing scheme in the Irrigation Area of the Khashm-el-Girba Dam subject to the contract documents attached to the said contract.

The International Bureau of the Permanent Court of Arbitration agreed to and did from the time of the Submission place its premises and organization at the Peace Palace at the disposal of the parties for the purposes of the Arbitration in accordance with Article 47[116] of the Convention for the Pacific Settlement of International Disputes, 1907.

The Submission to Arbitration adopted, with slight modifications, the model rules for arbitral procedure prepared and published by the United Nations International Law Commission in 1958.[117] Accordingly, the Submission conferred on the Tribunal wide powers which included, *inter alia*, power:

(i) to interpret the submission and to judge its own competence to decide any matter in dispute referred to it as provided in the Submission;[118]

(ii) notwithstanding any failure of one of the parties to attend any session of the Tribunal (without having previously shown to the Tribunal what the Tribunal should consider to be good and sufficient cause for absence) to proceed with the hearing of the Arbitration in the absence of that party and to make any such order or award as it should think fit.[119]

It was on the faith of this latter clause that the arbitral tribunal rendered an *ex parte* award against the Sudan Government which withdrew from the arbitration, before the hearing, for political reasons relating to the connection of Turriff with South Africa. Though the award had not been fully executed, and hence it had less importance as regards the amount of the claim, nevertheless it had a practical value for it paved the way for the final settlement. The award of this arbitration also strengthens the assertion that the use of the facilities of the Permanent Court of Arbitration would make available suitable premises, an excellent library, an atmosphere of peaceful settlement and a trained administrative staff to handle the details of an arbitration. More significantly, the Permanent Court would provide a speedy machinery for appointing the arbitrators in cases of disagreement of the parties or if one party withdraws its arbitrator during the early stages of the proceedings before judgment, as had been the case in the *Turriff Arbitration*, where the Sudan Government withdrew its arbitrator and refused to appoint an alternative.

(3) *The International Centre for Settlement of Investment Disputes (I.C.S.I.D.)*

This centre has been established by the Convention on the Settlement of Investment Disputes between States and Nationals of Other States which came into force on 14 October 1966,[120] prepared by the World Bank. This is not surprising, as the question of foreign private investment and legal guarantees has attracted the attention of the World Bank to encourage the increase of flow of private capital to developing countries which is, indeed, the primary purpose of the Bank. Furthermore, the international status of the Bank, its reputation for integrity and impartiality, are trusted to a considerable extent by all governments connected with foreign investments. This is witnessed by the tendency of the several proposed investment guarantee programmes to link any programme with the Bank.

Having acquired accumulated experience in settling disputes associated with international investments, the World Bank was well placed to develop permanent machinery for settling investment disputes. The reasons which in 1962 prompted the Bank to step into the breach are set out in the Report of the Bank's Executive Directors on the *Convention on the Settlement of Investment Disputes between States and Nationals of Other States*, 1965.[121]

The Convention established an international remedial organization entitled the International Centre for Settlement of Investment Disputes (I.C.S.I.D.) structurally linked with the Bank,[122] though having a juridical personality of its own.[123] It was designed to strengthen the partnership between countries in the cause of economic development by facilitating the settlement of disputes between States and foreign investors, and thus promoting an atmosphere of mutual confidence and stimulating a large flow of private international capital into the countries which wish to attract it.[124] The Convention was based on the understanding that the parties to investment disputes frequently do consider it in their mutual interest to settle their disputes by resort to international methods of settlement.[125]

The Convention can be descriptively and critically examined under the following sub-headings.

Structure and administration

The Convention vests the policy-making power in an Administrative Council composed of one representative from each contracting State.[126] The Council's chief functions are to adopt regulations governing the conciliation and arbitration procedure of the Centre and to approve the financial regulations and the annual budget for the Centre. The President of the World Bank is to be the Chairman of the Council, but he will sit without voting power.[127]

The membership of the Centre will be confined only to the contracting States. A State will be eligible to be a party if it is a member of the World Bank. Additionally, any State party to the Statute of the International Court of Justice will be eligible to sign the Convention and be a party to the Centre if it is invited thereto by two-thirds of the Administrative Council.[128] This is an unwarranted restriction which would exclude many States from membership of the Centre and, in essence, is partially self-defeating in this respect. It will be in the interest of the international community to make the facilities of the Centre open to as many States as possible as this would, in the end, achieve uniformity in arbitration rules and procedure on a worldwide scale. For these reasons, I think it would be better to allow any State to adhere to the Convention by a one-third majority of the Council instead of two-thirds.

The day-to-day administration of the Centre is conducted by the Secretariat, which is headed by a Secretary-General and staffed by one or more Deputy Secretaries–General, all of whom are to be elected by a two-thirds vote of the Administrative Council.[129] To secure administrative impartiality in the course of contact with many governments and member States, the Convention specifically provides that 'the offices of the Secretary-General and Deputy Secretary-General shall be incompatible with the exercise of any political function'.[130]

The panels consist of counciliators and arbitrators, to each of which the contracting State may designate four persons (who may, but need not be, its nationals), and to which the chairman of the Administrative Council may designate ten persons, each having a different nationality.[131] Of significant interest is the setting forth of the qualifications necessary for designation as an arbitrator or conciliator. Article 14 lists 'high moral character, recognized competence in the fields of law, commerce, industry or finance', and the Centre seeks a person 'who can be relied upon to exercise independent judgment'. It is noteworthy that throughout the Convention there is special emphasis on formal law. Thus, Article 14(1) concludes with the direction that 'Competence in the field of law shall be of particular importance in the case of persons on the Panel of Arbitrators'. This leads to the inference that the same criterion will not be applicable in the case of persons on the Panel of Conciliators. However, in exercising his power of designation, the Chairman of the Administrative Council must take into consideration the importance of assuring representation on both panels of the principle legal systems of the world and of the main forms of economic activity.[132]

Jurisdiction of the Centre

The most problematic article is Article 25 of the Convention which confers power on the Centre to lend its offices to settle an investment dispute in accordance with the Convention. This article establishes jurisdiction over:

> any *legal dispute* directly arising out of an investment, between a *contracting State* (or *any constituent sub-division or agency of a* contracting State designated to the Centre by that State) and a *national of another contracting State*, which the parties to the dispute consent in writing to submit to the Centre. *When the parties have given their consent, no party may withdraw its consent unilaterally.*[133] (My italics.)

This broad grant of jurisdiction rests on three assumptions, namely, the nature of the dispute, the parties to the dispute, and the consent to refer the dispute to the jurisdiction of the Centre.

The nature of the dispute

The Convention requires that the dispute must be a 'legal dispute directly arising out of an investment'. This would presumably exclude disputes which are political in nature or those arising from differences in interests between the parties in the jurisdiction of the Centre. This uncertainty is caused by the absence of any definition of 'legal disputes' in the Convention. However, the Report of the Bank's Executive Directors has stated that the expression 'legal disputes' has been used to make it clear that while conflicts of rights are within the jurisdiction of the Centre, mere conflicts of interests are not.[134] The dispute must concern the existence or scope of legal right or obligation, or the nature or extent of the reparation to be made for breach of a legal obligation.[135] Such a general explanation can hardly clarify the meaning of 'legal disputes'. Obviously, the expression 'legal disputes' is sufficiently controversial to call for a more exact definition in a Convention which is intended for parties the great majority of which have but recently acquired a direct access to international law.

Where the issue is exclusively of a legal nature, there has been less hesitation, though not much eagerness, to obtain a solution by arbitration.

Furthermore, the jurisdiction of the Centre is obscured by the absence of the definition of 'investment' in the Convention. This omission was intentional, according to the draftsmen. It was predicated upon the desire to allow some discretion to the conciliation commissions and arbitral tribunals.[136] It is possible that the conciliators and arbitrators will adopt a liberal definition of 'investment' in order to open the doors of the Centre to a wide range of important international economic agreements (see *ante*, pp. 19–23).

The parties to the dispute

Article 25 makes it clear that the services of the Centre are not available in connection with disputes between private individuals, between States, or between a State and its own nationals. This limitation on the Centre's jurisdiction has been appraised as good to confine the jurisdiction *ratione personae*.[137] Disputes between private individuals can be settled through municipal systems of law. Disputes between States and their own nationals fall outside the scope of an international convention intended to deal with foreign investment. Disputes between States may be settled under traditional international law.

One party to the proceedings under the convention must be a Contracting State, or one of its constituent sub-divisions or agencies. The question is: when, then, does a State become a 'Contracting State'? The term is not defined in the convention, but Article 68 provides that the convention enters into force for each

State thirty days after the deposit of its instrument of ratification, acceptance or approval of the Convention. There can be no doubt, therefore, that a State becomes a Contracting State thirty days after it has deposited its instrument of ratification, acceptance or approval. This provision cannot be waived by agreement between the parties to a dispute. Thus, it is insufficient if a State, instead of signing, ratifying and depositing its instrument of ratification, merely authorizes the *ad hoc* submission to the Centre of a particular dispute or a class of disputes to which it is a party.

Still, there are several other questions which have been left unresolved by the Convention. Thus, it is not clear at what time the State party must be a contracting State for the jurisdiction of the Centre. Will it be at the time of a request to register for conciliation or arbitration or when the Secretary-General takes the request into consideration? Amerasinghe preferred the former date.[138]

Furthermore, the term 'constituent sub-divisions or agencies' may be subject to many interpretations. Since, according to Article 25(1), constituent sub-divisions and agencies must be designated to the Centre by the Contracting State in order to have *locus standi* before the Centre, it would seem that the importance of establishing precise definitions for these terms is greatly reduced. The question is whether the entity satisfied the jurisdictional requirements of the Convention so as to be able to have *locus standi* in a position which would otherwise be taken by a State.

Another difficulty might arise in relation to the designation of the sub-division or agency by the Contracting State to the Centre. It is not clear from the Convention whether or not the designation be limited in some way. Another relevant question is whether the designation of a sub-division or agency must be officially and formally notified to the Centre by the Contracting State concerned. Also the Convention is silent on the specific time at which the designation to the Centre should be made. I think technically the 'notification' of the designation to the Centre can be executed even after the dispute has arisen, but before a request for conciliation or arbitration is filed.

With regard to the eligibility of a private person to the jurisdiction of the Centre, there are numerous questions pertaining to nationality. In the first place, it is not clear whether the jurisdiction would be confined only to purely privately-owned investment. Broches was reported to have observed that, despite the fact that the first preambular clause of the Convention speaks of 'private international investment', a national (a juridical person) of another Contracting State need not be a privately-owned entity, and that mixed economy companies or even government-owned corporations should not be disqualified unless acting as an agent for the Government or discharging an essentially governmental function.[139] Second, it is not clear from the Convention whether or not the same criteria of determining nationality in cases of diplomatic protection as articulated in the *Nottebohm* and *Barcelona Traction*[140] cases be applied to determine the jurisdiction of the Centre. Rightly, Amerasinghe[141] is of the opinion that there should be a distinction of the application of nationality as applied to diplomatic protection and the jurisdiction of the Centre, by allowing flexibility and relaxation in the latter situation.

Perhaps the more obvious defect in the Convention is that it is incompatible with the doctrine of subrogation under the foreign investment programmes discussed in chapter 7. In this case, there should be a distinction between three cases. In the first place, if the insurer is a private entity and is a national of another Contracting State, nothing in the Convention, and, specifically, in Article 25, would adversely affect the operation of the arbitration clause if the insurer is subrogated to the rights and claims of the insured investor. Broches points out that the Convention is silent 'as to the assignability of I.C.S.I.D. arbitration agreements and there is no reason to consider that assignment is not permitted', as long as the assignee or successor has the status required by the Convention.[142] Secondly, if the insurer is an agency or an institution of the State, difficult questions arise. A State cannot under Article 25 of the Convention be a party to the arbitral proceedings against another State. The subrogated State could not avail itself of the agreement to arbitrate, because of the explicit and strict jurisdictional limits laid down in the Convention. Thirdly, if the insurer is a mixed public–private institution, with a different type of charter and organization, it seems that it will be qualified to benefit from the arbitration clause as subrogee under the Convention. The financial interest of a State in the insurance organization should not disqualify the latter from being a party to an I.C.S.I.D. arbitration. In the opinion of Broches[143] the guiding criterion should be the juridical organization of the insurer; if it is organized so as to be independent of the State, as a separate legal entity, in the way in which private entities are organized, it should qualify as a party, except where the relations between the State and the insurer are such that the latter is in effect dependent on the former.

Consent to the Centre's jurisdiction

The Convention stresses consent in establishing jurisdiction. The draftsmen of the Convention state: 'Consent of the parties is the cornerstone of the jurisdiction of the Centre.'[144] The consent is to be written, that is, an arbitration clause, a submission, or the result of a *compromis*. Nothing in the text of the Convention speaks of the timing of this consent. This omission would give the Centre broad authority to find consent to some very particular and detailed formula of settlement. The consent once given cannot be withdrawn unilaterally.

The legal consequences of consent to arbitration under the Convention are far-reaching. Unless a Contracting State has reserved its right to require the prior exhaustion of local remedies, the issue is taken out of its own jurisdiction.[145]

Correspondingly, the Contracting State whose national is involved in the dispute must refrain from giving diplomatic protection to its national (otherwise than by informal diplomatic exchanges for the purpose of facilitating a settlement of the dispute) or from bringing an international claim in the matter against the other Contracting Party.[146] The purpose of this provision was to assure a host State which has agreed to the jurisdiction of the Centre that it will not be exposed in the alternative, or cumulatively, to an international claim put forward by the investors' national State in the exercise of diplomatic protection. The only exception to this renunciation by the Contracting States of their traditional right to exercise diplomatic protection is when the host State fails to abide by and comply with the arbitral award, in which case the right becomes operative again.

Settlement proceedings

The settlement proceedings provided by the Convention allow for both conciliation and arbitration of investment disputes. The conciliation procedure calls for an attempt by a conciliation commission selected by the parties to mediate the dispute between them.[147] If the parties fail to agree on a method of selecting their commission, each party must appoint one conciliator and the third will be appointed by the two appointees.[148] But should the conciliation commission not be constituted within ninety days after notice of the request for conciliation has been dispatched to the opposing party, the Chairman of the Administrative Council is to appoint the conciliator or conciliators not yet appointed.[149]

The most important settlement facilities established by the Convention are the arbitral tribunals. An arbitral tribunal, as distinguished from a conciliation commission, must reach a decision on the merits of the dispute, and under the Convention that decision is binding on both parties.[150] Each Contracting State may appoint four members to a Standing Panel of Arbitrators. As mentioned above, the parties to a dispute may designate their arbitrators from persons not members of the Panel.[151] If an arbitral tribunal has not been constituted within ninety days after the opposing party has received notice of the dispute, the Chairman of the Administrative Council will appoint from the Panel the arbitrator or arbitrators not yet appointed.[152] However, he may not choose any arbitrators whose nationality is that of either the State or the private party to the dispute.[153]

Article 42 limits the freedom of the arbitral tribunal with respect to the applicable law, directing that:

> the Tribunal shall decide a dispute with such rules of law as may be agreed by the parties. In the absence of such agreement, the Tribunal shall apply the law of the Contracting State party to the dispute (including its rules on the conflict of laws) and such rules of international law as may be applicable.

From this provision it seems that, in substance, such disputes are and remain mainly disputes under municipal law. According to the draftsmen, the term 'international law' as used in this context should be understood in the sense given to it by Article 38(1) of the Statute of the International Court of Justice, with allowance being made for the fact that Article 38 was designed to apply to inter-State disputes.[154]

Nor may the tribunal avoid rendering a decision by entering a *non liquet* on the ground of silence or obscurity of the law.[155] This discretion is reinforced by Article 38 dealing with the requirement for a valid award which states, *inter alia*, that the 'award shall deal with every question submitted to the Tribunal and shall state the reasons upon which it is based'. Furthermore, the tribunal may be permitted to make an equitable award (*ex aequo et bono*), but only if the parties so agree.[156]

The parties which have consented to arbitral proceedings under the Convention are irrevocably bound to abide by the resulting award,[157] subject only to provisions such as those covering interpretation,[158] revision[159] and annulment.[160] Under Article 54, each Contracting State is required to recognize such an award as binding, and to enforce the pecuniary obligations imposed by the award within its territories as if it were a final judgment of a Court in that State. However, execution of the award against a State is limited by the extent to which the laws of that State and the doctrine of sovereign immunity are applied. In the words of the draftsmen:

> In order to leave no doubt to this point, Article 55 provides that nothing in Article 54 shall be construed as derogating from the law in force in any Contracting State relating to immunity of that State or of any foreign State from execution.[161]

There is no appeal from the award.[162] Disputes over interpretation or application of the award that are not settled by negotiation or referred by agreement to another method of settlement are to be sent to the International Court of Justice.[163] In the event of a State's failing to abide by or comply with the award rendered in a dispute with a national of another State, the latter State may have recourse to its traditional diplomatic and international law remedies.[164]

Evaluation and future of the Centre

Though a considerable number of States signed and ratified the Convention, it is unfortunate that the Latin American States have prejudice against the Convention. Their objection, primarily, rests on the ground that it gives the foreign investor, merely by virtue of his foreignness, the right to sue a foreign State outside its national territory and thus avoid the national courts. This, they advocate, is contrary to their accepted legal principles.[165]

It has been asserted that one of the most significant features of the Convention is that it provides a system-shifting device which insulates an actual or potential investment dispute from the 'realm of policies and diplomacy' and subjects the dispute to regular settlement machinery.[166] Under the Convention, once the consent of host State has been given, the investor would have direct access to the facilities of the Centre, without the intervention of his national State. In such a case, the private investor is considered to have waived the diplomatic protection of his national State, and thus his State is not entitled to take up his case. In this respect, the Convention would, indeed, contribute to the development of existing international law by removing investment disputes from the inter-governmental political sphere.

As the capital-importing States are too sensitive to committing themselves to substantive rules of international law relating to foreign investments, it is very wise that the Convention has put emphasis on procedural rather than substantive standards. Despite that, in practice, private investors are reluctant to use the International Centre for the Settlement of Investment Disputes for settling their disputes with foreign governments. It has been reported that, though more than ten years have elapsed since the Convention establishing the Centre came into force, only seven cases were registered.[167] Nevertheless, the Convention provides a viable and instrumental device for avoiding disputes and not settling them, as it provides a deterrent against adverse actions by investee States against foreign investors. The importance of the Convention lies, furthermore, in the fact that, when the parties have agreed to have recourse to the facilities under it, there will be assurance that their agreement will be given effect. This would, undoubtedly, create an element of mutual confidence which would, in turn, contribute to a healthier investment climate. Furthermore, the international status of the Centre is enhanced by its policy of entering into agreements with other international and regional commercial arbitration centres such as the Permanent Court of Arbitration, the I.C.C. Court of Arbitration, as it did recently with the Asian–African Legal Consultative Committee and the Regional Arbitration Centre (Kuala Lumpur). These agreements provide for reciprocal assistance in connection with proceedings under the auspices of these institutions, and for consultation.[168]

The first case submitted to the Centre for arbitration was *Holiday Inn's/Occidental Petroleum* v. *Government of Morocco*. The arbitration started in 1972 in Morocco but was discontinued in 1978, because the parties reached an amicable settlement. Two other cases were registered in 1977 and a third one in 1978. These are: *AGIP S.P.A.* v. *Government of the People's Republic of the Congo*; *Société Ltd. Benvenuti & Bonfant Srt.* v. *Government of the People's Republic of the Congo*, and *Guadalupe Gas Products Corporation* v. *The Federal Military Government of Nigeria.*[169]

So far, the only case in which the I.C.S.I.D. Arbitral Tribunal rendered a unanimous award was *Adriano Gardella S.P.A.* v. *Government of Ivory Coast* which was instituted in 1974. Unfortunately, the Centre has not received consent from the parties to publish the award.[170] In two other cases, namely *Reynolds Jamaica Mines Ltd and Reynolds Metals Company* v. *Government of Jamaica*, the proceedings were discontinued at the request of the parties.[171]

Perhaps the merit of the Convention lies in its flexibility: it does not designate a particular venue where arbitration should always be held. Under the convention the arbitration proceedings can take place anywhere, and most likely in the territory of the investee State, as was the situation in the *Holiday Inns* case where the proceedings were conducted in Morocco, the respondent State. This aspect of the Convention meets the needs of Saudi Arabia, which will never agree to any arbitration being held outside its territory.

However, the success of the Centre for the Settlement of Investment Disputes in the future depends on the interpretation to be given to the provisions of its constituent Convention, which has been couched in broad terms which left certain basic issues unresolved. It seems that the best approach is to apply a teleological and liberal interpretation so as to sustain the existence of the jurisdiction – *ut magis valeat quam pereat* – rather than a restrictive approach which may destroy jurisdiction.[172] And the approval of a recent proposal for the creation of an additional facility for the administration of certain proceedings which are not within the jurisdictional limits of the Convention is indeed encouraging towards widening the jurisdiction of the Centre. This new additional facility rule provides for the administration, at the request of interested parties, of certain types of conciliation and arbitration proceedings which do not meet the jurisdictional requirements of the Convention, and of proceedings limited to pure fact-finding.[173] As submission to the Centre is based on consent, it is preferred to give effect to this consent. There is every reason to concede that the effect of this consent should not be frustrated, except only in the limited situations where 'if such consent were given effect to, the result would be that the Convention would be used for purposes for which it was clearly not intended'.[174]

As of 1980 the I.C.S.I.D. has become of great interest to the Sudan. This is because, as mentioned before, section 32 of the Encouragement of Investment Act, 1980 has incorporated by reference the I.C.S.I.D. arbitration machinery, a technique which has become prevalent in the practice of the Third World countries.[175] By this device the arbitration mechanism of the I.C.S.I.D. would gain prominence over any other arbitration, whether *ad hoc* or institutionalized.

(4) *The Arab Board for Settlement of Investment Disputes* (*A.B.S.I.D.*)

This is an inter-Arab forum established by the Convention for the Settlement of Investment Disputes between Host States for Arab Investments and Nationals of Other Arab States, 1974,[176] concluded by the six member States of the Council of Arab Economic Unity.[177] As is stated in the preambular paragraphs the purpose of the Convention is to strengthen economic co-operation and integration among Arab states and to achieve the objectives of the Convention on the Investment and Transfer of Arab Capital among the Arab Countries and the Convention on the Arab Corporation for Investment Guarantees.

The A.B.S.I.D. Convention calls for the creation of a permanent institution to be called the Board for Settling Investment Disputes between Host States for Arab Investments and Nationals of Other Arab States,[178] which in many respects resembles I.C.S.I.D., if it is not indeed identical except for organizational provisions. I shall examine briefly the important aspects of this institution under various headings.

Jurisdiction of the Board

Under Article 2 of its establishing convention the A.B.S.I.D. has jurisdiction to settle any legal dispute arising directly from investments between host Arab countries or their agencies or public corporations and natural or juridical nationals of other Arab countries. Disputes between States as such are excluded from the jurisdiction of the Board.

The dispute shall first be settled by conciliation, or, failing that, by arbitration in accordance with the Convention.[179]

Administration

The administrative machinery of the A.B.S.I.D. consists of a permanent Board and a general Secretariat. The Board consists of one member or more for each member State. The Convention provides for a permanent headquarters, which, as yet, has not been established. The chairmanship is for one year by rotation among the member States.[180] The Board has, *inter alia*, to solve any dispute among the member States on the interpretation or application of the Convention. It is also the competent authority for appointing the arbitration and conciliation committees for the settling of investment disputes.[181]

Conciliation and arbitration

The Conciliation Committee shall be constituted by the mutual consent of the parties, within a prescribed period from the date of registering the application to refer the dispute to conciliation or arbitration in accordance with Article 27 of the Convention. Under that article the application by the interested party must be in writing and addressed to the Secretary-General, who has to register the application unless he considers it to fall outside the jurisdiction of the Board. After registering the application, the Secretary-General must send a copy thereof to the party, who must send his consent, in writing, to the conciliation or arbitration. If the parties did not reach agreement on the appointment of an even number of the conciliators or arbitrators within the prescribed period, the appointment will be made by the Secretary-General from the panels of conciliators and arbitrators as the case may be.[182] Each member State is entitled to designate up to six of its nationals, or nationals of other Arab countries, as conciliators or arbitrators to the panels.[183] In the same way as for I.C.S.I.D., the Secretary-General may appoint to each panel ten persons, who must be nationals of the Arab countries; however, he is not entitled to appoint more than one person from each country. In appointing the arbitrators and conciliators, the representation of the different legal and economic systems of the Arab World should be preserved.

The Convention contains detailed provisions on the procedure to be followed in the conciliation and arbitration, which are more or less in line with the ordinary practice of international arbitration. Thus, there are provisions on the conduct of the proceedings,[184] the finality of the award,[185] its interpretation,[186] review[187] and its execution, which must be carried out in the territory of a State member like any other final judgment rendered by its national courts.[188]

Exclusion of international claim

If the two parties to the disputes have agreed to settle their disputes in accordance with the A.B.S.I.D. Convention, they are prevented from resorting to any other forum unless it is provided otherwise by the Convention.[189] And as for the I.C.S.I.D., to avoid double claims against the respondent State, the member State whose national has agreed with the respondent State to refer the dispute to arbitration under the Convention will not be entitled to institute an international claim on the same dispute. The only exception to this rule is when the respondent State refuses to honour or execute the arbitration award. However, diplomatic good offices are not considered by the Arab Convention as an espousal of an international claim in the meaning envisaged by the Convention.[190]

Like the World Bank Convention on Settlement of Investment Disputes, the Arab Convention has been incorporated by reference into the Sudan machinery for settling investment disputes by section 32 of the Encouragement of Investment Act, 1980. But the defect of the latter convention lies in the fact that its scope is limited only to the member States of the Council of Economic Unity, which does not embrace all Arab countries. And, at present, there are massive investments in the Sudan from non-member States, notably Saudi Arabia and the United Arab Emirates. Also, the Board has not yet been established, and hence its constituent convention is still on paper only. However, as the general structure of the A.B.S.I.D. is similar to I.C.S.I.D., it is expected that the experience of the first institution will be of constructive guidance to the latter.

(ii) *Ad hoc arbitration*

Before the Encouragement of Investment Act of 1980, the previous Sudanese investment laws did not contain detailed provisions on the settlement of disputes. The only exception in which the Sudanese investment laws did provide for settlement procedures was in the case of assessment of compensation as depicted in chapter 8. This narrow provision was abolished by section 32 of the Encouragement of Investment Act, 1980.

Ad hoc arbitration is frequently provided for in bilateral investment treaties which provide for the settlement of disputes which may arise between the parties on the treaties' application or interpretation. They usually give precedence to consultation between Governments as a first step towards any settlement.[191] If a dispute cannot thus be settled, the treaty normally goes on to provide how the arbitrators and the umpire are to be appointed, if the parties fail to agree on the appointment. Reference is usually made to the President or Vice-President of the International Court of Justice to make the necessary appointments.[192] However, under Articlle VII of the Economic Agreement between the State of Kuwait and the Democratic Republic of the Sudan, 1970,[193] the third arbitrator (umpire) must always be appointed by the Secretary-General of the Arab League.

As treaties are instruments of international law, there is no difficulty as to the applicable law, which would presumably be international law. It is possible also for the arbitral tribunal to apply conventions and rules of common practice in commerce relating to the subject-matter of the dispute.[194]

The investment insurance programmes also provide for an arbitral procedure for the settlement of disputes which might arise after the subrogation of the State to an investor's rights. Under the United States Investment Guaranty Agreements,[195] if direct negotiations between the two governments fail to bring about a settlement, the dispute must be referred to a single arbitrator named by the parties. If they do not agree on the appointment of the arbitrator, he will be designated by the President of the International Court of Justice.

The most significant type of *ad hoc* arbitration for settling investment disputes is that which is frequently detailed in arbitration clauses in development agreements and concessions. They usually describe in detail the procedure to be followed in case of dispute. The most important arbitration clause is that which is contained in the Petroleum Production-Sharing Agreement between the Democratic Republic of the Sudan and Chevron Company. The operative clause provides as follows:

> Any disputes arising between the Government and the Contractor relating to the Agreement or with respect to the interpretation, application or execution of this Agreement and which cannot be settled amicably shall be finally settled by arbitration. The arbitration shall be held

in *Paris, France, and conducted in accordance with the Rules of Conciliation and Arbitration of the International Chamber of Commerce.* In the event of no provisions being made in these Rules in certain cases, the Arbitrators shall establish their own procedures.[196] (My italics.)

Under the same clause, if one party fails to appoint his arbitrator, the arbitrator will be appointed by the Court of Arbitration of the International Chamber of Commerce. Also, the Chamber will appoint the chairman of the arbitration if the two arbitrators fail to agree on the appointment. To achieve an impartial tribunal, the third arbitrator (chairman) must be a citizen of a country other than the Sudan or the United States of America, of which the investing company is a national. The chairman must also have no economic interest in the oil business of the Sudan or of the United States. Not only that, but he must be a national of a foreign country which has diplomatic relations with both the Sudan and the United States. The purpose of this provision is to avoid selecting an umpire who might turn out to be a national of a country which has hostile propensities against either of the two countries concerned.

One may argue that such arbitration clauses may not be permissible in the future, since conducting arbitration outside the Sudan is now statutorily prohibited under section 32 of the Encouragement of Investment Act, 1980. But such an argument is untenable, as oil agreements are outside the orbit of the Encouragement of Investment Act, 1980.

Perhaps the most cogent Sudanese case on *ad hoc* arbitration is *Sudan Government* v. *Brown International Inc.* In this case, clause 111 of the construction contract provided that all decisions of the Consulting Engineer in respect of which due notice of appeal has been given shall be referred to arbitration. This clause also provided for the procedure to be adopted in the appointment of the three arbitrators.

Differences having taken place between the contracting parties, the matter of dispute was referred to a board of three arbitrators constituted as follows:

1. James G. Tripp – for the respondents,
2. M. Abdalla Galander – for the applicant,
3. D. V. Buck – appointed as a third arbitrator and umpire by the President of the Institute of Civil Engineers in England at the request of both parties.

The board of arbitrators rendered their award, thereby ordered that the applicants should pay the respondents the sum of 1,161,942 United States dollars in complete and final determination of all claims and counterclaims arising from the contract.

The award was filed with Khartoum District Court under section 166 of the Civil Justice Ordinance, 1929 (repealed).[197] The Attorney-General failed in his application to the Court of Appeal to have the award set aside for misconduct on the part of the Board of Arbitration, and on the ground that the award exhibits errors of law and facts.

Though the import of this case in international law is doubtful, yet it indicates how far the Sudanese Government was ready to accept *ad hoc* arbitration as a forum for settling investment disputes. The case also, unlike *Turriff*, discloses the wholehearted readiness of the Sudan to honour an arbitration clause in a development agreement or contract.

In addition to this detailed procedure for conducting the arbitration, arbitration clauses, as demonstrated in the preceding chapter, are useful devices by which the arbitral tribunals will be guided in finding out the proper law of the contract, in the absence of express choice of the parties.

More significantly, the arbitration clause would relieve the foreign investor from the requirement of the local remedies if the host State refused to abide by the award or refused to arbitrate. He is free, rather, to pursue the courses open to him under international law.[198] This was the position of the United Kingdom Government in the Anglo-Iranian case before the International Court of Justice.[199]

Settlement of the investment disputes by arbitration has also been favoured by the proposals for investment codes and multilateral conventions discussed in chapter 6. The most prominent of these is the O.E.C.D. Draft Convention[200] under which any disputes concerning the application or interpretation of the Draft Convention may be submitted to arbitration in accordance with the Annex to the Draft Convention. The difference between this Draft Convention and the other proposals on the one hand, and the Convention on the Settlement of Investment Disputes between States and Nationals of other States on the other hand, is that the former contains both substantive and procedural rules for the protection of foreign investments in one instrument, while the operative convention, as mentioned before, contains only procedural rules for the settlement of investment disputes.

Recently, the United Nations Commission on International Trade Law (U.N.C.I.T.R.A.L.)[201] unanimously adopted model arbitration rules for the settlement of commercial disputes. This marked a step forward in bridging the cleavage between the developed and developing countries. These rules set out detailed procedures for conducting arbitration, from the preliminary stage of notice of arbitration to rendering the award. Under Article 1(1), their scope of application was intended to operate when the parties to a contract agreed in writing that disputes in relation to that contract are to be referred to arbitration under the U.N.C.I.T.R.A.L. Arbitration Rules, in which case such disputes had to be settled in accordance with these Rules, subject to such modification as the parties might agree in writing.

Under Article 1(2), these Rules must govern the arbitration except that where any of them is in conflict with a provision of the law applicable to the arbitration from which the parties cannot derogate, that provision shall prevail.

The importance of U.N.C.I.T.R.A.L. Arbitration Rules lies in the fact that they provide an acceptable mechanism for appointing arbitrators by an appointing authority agreed upon by the parties. If no appointing authority has been agreed upon by the parties, the Secretary-General of the Permanent Court of Arbitration at the Hague will designate an appointing authority, at the request of either party.[202] This enhances the status of the Permanent Court of Arbitration as an international forum for settling investment disputes, at least in this minor and formal point of designation of the arbitrators' appointing authority.

The Rules also provide for notice and calculation of period of time,[203] notice of arbitration,[204] presentation and assistance,[205] hearings,[206] place of arbitration,[207] statements of claim and defence,[208] how the award can be rendered,[209] etc.

In a footnote to Article 1, which contains introductory rules, the U.N.C.I.T.R.A.L. Arbitration Rules formulate a model arbitration clause which is highly recommended to be incorporated in any development agreement or investment contract. The incorporation of such a model clause,[210] which received the unanimous approval of representatives of all nations, will help very much in reaching agreement in the future on the substantive rules that should govern the whole of the foreign investment transactions.

But the apparent shortcoming of the U.N.C.I.T.R.A.L. Arbitration Rules lies in the clause dealing with the choice of applicable law to the dispute. Under Article 33 the arbitral tribunal shall apply the law designated by the parties as applicable to the substance of the dispute. Failing such designation, the arbitral tribunal shall apply the law, determined by the conflict of laws rules, which it considers applicable. There is no reference at all in the article to international law. In the preceding chapter, we established that, if the parties to a development agreement failed to designate the applicable law, the obvious inference is that international law applies. The mere submission of the dispute to arbitration leads to that inference. Consequently, the U.N.C.I.T.R.A.L. Arbitration Rules would be incompatible with the doctrine of internationalization of development agreements (see *ante*, pp. 243–50). By providing that the arbitral tribunal must apply the conflict of laws rules to determine the applicable law in solving disputes arising from these agreements, it would seem that the U.N.C.I.T.R.A.L. Arbitration Rules were intended to apply only to contracts between two private parties and not to those between States and private investors. Alternatively, this shortcoming should be remedied by providing that:

Failing designation by the parties of the applicable law, the arbitral tribunal shall apply '*international law, and in the absence, general principles recognized by civilized nations, including such of those principles as may have been applied by international tribunals'*, or the law determined by the conflict of laws rules which it considers applicable. (My italics.)

Such a model arbitration clause would accommodate both contracts between private persons and contracts between a State and foreign investors.

6. Enforcement of judgments and awards

In the absence of voluntary acceptance, the means afforded by international law to secure obedience by a State to an international judicial or arbitral decision are very limited. International tribunals have no enforcement machinery. Obviously, this is a serious weakness of international law. Improvement is not forthcoming unless States give up some of their sovereignty.

Regarding judgments rendered by the International Court of Justice, Article 94 of the Charter of the United Nations provides that each member shall comply with the decision of the court in any case to which the member is a party. It further provides that, if any party to a case fails to perform the obligations incumbent upon it under a judgment of the court, the other party may have recourse to the Security Council. The Council may then, if it deems it necessary, make recommendations or decide measures for giving effect to the judgment. Just what the Security Council could do in such a situation is not clear.[211] And the recent refusal of Iran not to execute the Court judgment which ordered the release of the American hostages despite the decisions and measures of the Security Council is indicative of the ineffectiveness of international law enforcement machinery.

For practical purposes, action or non-action by the Security Council under Article 94 of the Charter will be governed largely by political considerations. However, if the past practice of States is any indication for the future, it seems unlikely that the Sudan and Saudi Arabia will refuse to abide by a decision of the Court.[212]

As regards other judgments and awards the major difficulty in levying execution against the property of a State situated abroad is the claim of sovereign immunity. Even where a State has voluntarily submitted to the jurisdiction of a foreign court, this is not considered generally as a waiver of immunity, so far as execution or attachment of State property is concerned. In the *Duff Development* v. *Government of Kelantan*[213] case, the Court of Appeal refused to order execution against the property of a foreign sovereign who had submitted, in a contract, to the jurisdiction of English courts. As stated above, there are some States where the restrictive theory of sovereign immunity is applied. Even then, there is no unanimity on the question of execution against foreign State property. While some courts refused to extend the restrictive principle to execution,[214] others apply it to execution in all State trading activities (*jure gestionis*).[215] The restrictive view is endorsed by the European Convention on State Immunity, 1972,[216] which deals with enforcement. Under this Convention each State undertakes to comply with a final judgment rendered against it in another State, as defined in the Convention.

Enforcement of foreign arbitration awards is less problematic than that of foreign judgments. Most awards are carried out voluntarily with no need to have recourse to legal proceedings for enforcement. The reasons are said to be practical. Arbitration usually takes place between parties who do business together, and the loser usually will comply with the award because of the danger that resistance will lose a customer or source of supply.[217] It has been the practice of the Sudan since its independence in 1956 to comply with arbitral awards. *Turriff* Arbitration is an instructive illustration where, though the Sudan Government had withdrawn from the arbitration, the *ex parte* award was considered in negotiating the settlement. Before reaching a settlement, the Government was contemplating execution of the award, and hence certain precautions were taken to preserve the Government's assets and property abroad.

In the past Saudi Arabia was receptive of foreign arbitration awards and rarely elevated disputes to international fora. The *Aramco Award* was a notorious demonstration. But, at present, the Saudi courts do not automatically endorse foreign judgments. So, if a foreign investor were to obtain an award in international arbitration and reduce it into judgment in a foreign court, he would not be able to enforce the award against assets situated in Saudi Arabia. The Saudi courts would start a new hearing on the merits, applying Saudi law, before permitting execution on assets situated in Saudi Arabia. The situation is exacerbated by the new policy followed by the Grievances Board of not recognizing at all an arbitration award rendered by a non-Muslim arbitrator or arbitrators.

Furthermore, arbitration agreements are parts of contracts entered into by the parties with knowledge that awards may be rendered against them. It is said that trade organizations may apply pressure on their members to ensure that awards against them are carried out. A losing party usually prefers carrying out the award to losing his good standing in the trade association.[218]

However, difficulties may arise if the losing party in arbitration resists the award. To combat this dilemma States have entered into multilateral treaties dealing with enforcement of arbitration awards. None of these treaties has been ratified or acceded to by the Sudan and Saudi Arabia. This passiveness may be merely due to oversight, which is indeed regrettable. It is advisable that the Sudan should ratify the United Nations Convention on the Recognition and Enforcement of Foreign Arbitral Awards of 1959.[219] The scope of this Convention is outlined in Article 1 which provides that:

This Convention shall apply to the recognition and enforcement of arbitral awards made in the territory of a State other than the State where the recognition and enforcement of such awards are sought, and arising out of differences between *persons*, whether *physical or legal*. It shall also apply to arbitral awards not considered as domestic awards in the State where their recognition and enforcement are sought.[220] (My italics.)

Under this Convention, the enforcement of an arbitral award is obtained simply by filing in court the arbitration agreement and the award, whereupon enforcement follows, unless the defendant establishes any of the five specified challenges.[221] The court may, however, on its own motion deny enforcement on only two specified grounds, i.e. that the subject-matter is not arbitrable under the local law of the country in question, or that enforcement would violate the public policy of the State involved.[222]

The extent to which this Convention extends to arbitral awards concerning an individual and a State depends on the interpretation to be put on that part of Article 1 which applies the Convention to awards 'arising out of differences between persons, whether physical or legal'. Undoubtedly, public or trading corporations are 'legal persons' under this Article just as ordinary private corporations are.[223] Thus, where an investment agreement is concluded by a commercial agency of the investee State, e.g. the Sudanese Development Corporation or the Royal Commission for Jubail and Yanbu in Saudi Arabia, with foreign investors any arbitral award against either party is enforceable in the territories of States signatory to the Convention. Is the position the same where a Government department, as distinguished from a public corporation, is involved? Can the Government department in such case be regarded as a 'legal person' under the Convention? The authorities disagree on this point. On the one hand, strangely enough, Nwogugu[224] answered the question in the negative. He contended that 'the phrase "legal persons" does not cover government departments when not acting through public corporations'. He went on to say that 'if the position was otherwise, the contracting parties would have made an express declaration to that end'. I think that this view is erroneous, for under international law States are considered persons.[225] Furthermore, there is nothing in the Convention which prevents States from being regarded as 'legal persons',[226] as the phrase has not been qualified in any way. Each contracting State agreed to recognize *all arbitral awards*[227] as binding and to enforce them in accordance with the rules and procedures of the country where the award is made. This generalization strengthens, rather than restricts, the view that the word 'persons' includes States.

The execution of judgments and awards has also been of particular concern to regional organizations. And it is not a surprise that the Arab League participated in this field by concluding the Convention on the Execution of Judgments as early as 1952. This Convention was signed by only eight Arab member countries of the organization, namely Jordan, Syria, Iraq, Saudi Arabia, Lebanon, Egypt, Bahrain and North Yemen. The Sudan has neither signed nor ratified the Convention. Under this Arab Convention, judgment is defined so widely as to include arbitral awards. Generally, the provisions of the Convention are similar to the United Nations Convention discussed above, with the notable difference that the Arab Convention does not envisage execution of judgments against the country in which territory the execution is sought.[228]

Under Article 8 of the Arab Convention each member State must designate the competent judicial authority to execute the judgment, which in Saudi Arabia is the Grievances Board. Though Article 2 of the Convention prohibits the competent judicial authority which is to execute the judgment or the award from reconsidering or reviewing the case, the Grievances Board in practice conducts a fresh hearing, a process which signifies a distrust of other Arab courts' judgments.

7. Conclusions

Apart from constitutional guarantees against expropriation without compensation, there is very little remedy for foreign investors in the Sudanese courts. Though there are statutory procedures for judicial review of administrative decisions, their application is marred by the doctrine of 'act of State' and ouster clauses. The Sudanese courts are executive-minded and very reluctant to review ouster clauses in statutes; albeit they are zealous to do so in contracts. Regretfully, they automatically acquiesce in these ouster clauses and dismiss any claims if the plea based on an ouster clause is raised (see *ante*, pp. 283–9). It is to be observed that if judicial review is to have any effect in the Sudanese legal system, all ouster clauses in statutes should be repealed and the courts must be less self-restrained.

The introduction of provisions on arbitration in the new Sudanese Encouragement of Investment Act for settlement of investment disputes is constructive and secures a quick remedial process for foreign investors who disfavour ordinary litigation. Indeed, the incorporation by this Act of institutional arbitration, particularly that of the International Centre for the Settlement of Investment Disputes, established by the Convention on the Settlement of Investment Disputes between States and Nationals of Other States, is expected to secure a healthier investment climate and provide a prestigious forum for settling investment disputes. Experience has shown that the Sudan and Saudi Arabia are responsive to settling investment disputes by arbitration. It is usual to find arbitration clauses contained in either development agreements or bilateral treaties. It will be advantageous if the arbitration clauses in development agreements incorporate the U.N.C.I.T.R.A.L. Arbitration Rules by reference. Furthermore, the direct adoption of the model arbitration clause suggested by these rules in these agreements will, to a great extent, clarify and simplify the settlement procedure.

If local remedies and arbitration prove to be futile, the home State of the aggrieved investor can espouse the claim diplomatically or before the International Court of Justice. So far, there is no case where either the Sudan or Saudi Arabia has been brought before the Court. In all cases, disputes have been resolved at early stages by diplomatic or amicable negotiations.

11

UNILATERAL SANCTIONS BY HOME STATES

If the ways for settling investment disputes surveyed in the preceding chapter prove to be unsatisfactory, what sanctions can the national State of the injured private investor take to secure conformity to the rule of respect for alien-owned property? More specifically, suppose that the investee State refuses to make adequate reparation for spoliatory measures in respect of a foreign investment, or to respond to diplomatic representations, or even refuses to submit the dispute to arbitration, and that local remedies have been exhausted in vain, what action can be taken by the national State of the private investor?[1] This is, in the specific cases of Sudan and Saudi Arabia, perhaps a hypothetical question, because it has been the practice of successive Sudanese and Saudi Governments to settle investment disputes amicably or through domestic adjudication or arbitration. Nevertheless, the question is of some importance, for it must be the background against which investment is ultimately made.

It has been contended that, if diplomatic protection yields no positive results, the State whose national's investment has suffered loss may decide to adopt unilateral measures for the enforcement of international law rules on respect for private property.[2] Any valid unilateral action which can be taken must be in consonance with the Charter of the United Nations and customary rules of international law. However, with certain limitations imposed by modern international law, a State is legally entitled to employ the following unilateral measures to secure reparation from another State for the loss of investments made by its nationals in the territories of the latter.

1. Freezing of foreign-owned assets

This has been utilized by Britain and the United States as an effective weapon for exerting pressure on States which have nationalized property of their nationals without compensation. The practice involves the withholding or freezing of assets owned by the nationals and governments of the foreign nationalizing State, as a means of persuading it to pay compensation. Such a measure can only be effective when the expropriating State or its nationals have considerable and valuable assets within the territories of the claimant State.

The practice was successfully employed on a large scale in respect of the post-World-War-II nationalizations in Eastern Europe, the Middle East,[3] and Ethiopia[4] and recently, unsuccessfully, against Iran. Ultimately, the expropriating State was persuaded to negotiate terms with the British or American Government, in the form of a global settlement whereby a lump-sum compensation was paid for the entire private property then nationalized.[5] On the conclusion of a compensation agreement, the frozen assets were released.[6] These global settlements did not necessarily equal the amount originally claimed, and might indeed be considerably short of it.

The question is: to what extent is the withholding or freezing of foreign assets valid under international law? Customary international law recognizes certain unilateral measures by which a State may seek to obtain satisfaction for injury to itself or its nationals. These are principally retortion and reprisals[7] which are retaliatory measures to be invoked in reply to a prior offending action. Viewed in this perspective, and taking into consideration Article 2[8] of the U.N. Charter, it can be asserted that the taking of foreign investment without fair and adequate compensation may be an internationally illegal act against which the right of reprisals may accordingly be used. Hyde has suggested a definition of reprisals, in the following modern terms, in relation to property, as the

> act of taking and withholding of any form of property of a foreign State or its nationals, for the purpose of obtaining, directly or indirectly, reparation on account of the consequences of internationally illegal conduct for which redress has been refused.[9]

Accordingly, the freezing of foreign-owned assets remains a principal means of obtaining satisfaction for loss of property situated abroad. It guarantees to the injured State that, if no reparation is furnished, the frozen assets will meet part of the loss suffered. So far as this process is confined to property within the territory of the claimant State, it is submitted that the withholding of foreign assets to secure reparation is valid under the rules of international law and the U.N. Charter.[10]

2. Complaint to international organizations

It can be argued that a State whose nationals' investments have suffered loss may seek to enforce the rules of international law on respect for alien-owned property by lodging a complaint to an international organization like the United Nations itself. It is true that the complaint is a unilateral action of the claimant State; nevertheless, it might in theory mobilize the general support of the organization so as to persuade the recalcitrant State to make reparation.[11]

Under Article 35 of the United Nations Charter members of the organization may bring any dispute or situation likely to endanger the maintenance of international peace and security to the attention of the Security Council or the General Assembly. On many occasions disputes arising from the nationalization of investments abroad have been brought before the Security Council. Clear examples are the Anglo-Iranian and the Suez Canal crises.[12] Though the Security Council was unable to produce immediate and effective settlement of the disputes, the Council did in fact provide a valuable forum for discussions on international legal principles relating to foreign investments. Obviously, however, the political climate in the organs of the U.N. has changed radically since those days, and it is doubtful how far a complaint about a form of nationalization by a developing State would be heard with any sympathy in the U.N. today.

3. Boycott

The taking by an investee State of foreign private investments within its territories without adequate compensation may also lead to the boycotting of its goods in the home State of the injured investors. Such action may be sought to be justified as a retaliatory act to enforce the rules of international law. Perhaps the most outstanding example is the United States boycott of Cuban sugar in retaliation for nationalization of the United States' private investments by Cuba without compensation.[13]

As regards the validity of boycott under international law, it has been said that the initiation of a boycott by a State or Government against the goods of another State, or its encouragement of, and assistance to a private boycott organized by individuals, cannot *prima facie* be a source of international delinquency. Every State is free to prohibit trade with a foreign State or encourage its nationals to do so, as long as its action is not contrary to treaty obligation or the duty to protect foreign life and property from violence and wanton destruction.[14]

Nwogugu[15] has asserted that the nationalization of foreign private investments without compensation is an internationally wrongful act against which the right of reprisals may be exercised, and this may take the form of boycott. He rightly conceded that the non-observance by one party of the guarantees in investment treaties may justify the denunciation of the treaty by the other party and retaliation by boycott, which may sometimes take the form of withdrawal of commercial privileges.[16]

4. The use of armed force

Under traditional international law a State has the right to employ military force to protect the private property of its nationals situated abroad, where adequate protection is not provided by the territorial State of the *situs*.[17]

Some writers regard the use of armed force to protect private property situated abroad as illegal and contrary to the letter and spirit of the United Nations Charter.[18] Bowett[19] has submitted that the threat or use of force cannot in most cases be extended to the protection of nationals' property. In his view an actual or threatened injury to private property can rarely injure the security of the State and thus justify the exercise of self-defence. Nevertheless, Bowett[20] further argued that:

> The right of protection [by self-defence] extends to those cases where the interest of the nationals endangered, whether they be interests in personal safety or in property, are essential in the sense that their destruction involves an irremediable and serious injury directly to the nationals involved, and indirectly to the State affording them protection.

Generally, the destruction of private property, e.g. breaches of contracts or concessions, is satisfactorily met by compensation from the respondent State (see *ante*, pp. 274–7). But injury to private property would be regarded as irremedial only 'where the property is of a physical nature, corporeal in the true sense, and of especial value due to intrinsic worth or uniqueness'. Bowett, therefore, concluded that:

> The protection of [private property] within the concept of self-defence will only be justified when the property is really endangered and the destruction of the property cannot be met by *restitutio in integrum* or adequate compensation.[21]

This contention can hardly be accepted by the present international community. The use of force to settle commercial disputes, even in collection of contract debts, has been rejected since the beginning of this century, and on particular occasions this has been affirmed in multilateral conventions.[22] Furthermore, it is inconceivable that there might be occasions where the loss or destruction of private property 'would be irremedial', in the sense that an offer of compensation or other facilities would not be an adequate remedy. The recognized rule of international law on the treatment of foreign-owned property is that in case of loss caused by State measures the consequent obligation is restitution or payment of pecuniary compensation as has been depicted before. In the majority of cases, even in nationalization of valuable investments such as oil installations, the interested parties succeeded in negotiating agreements for the payment of pecuniary compensation. Accordingly, it is very difficult to accept the proposition that there can be exceptional cases where private property can be protected by the exercise of the right of self-defence.[23]

The accepted view would be that, if the respondent State fails to comply with the rule of international law to make restitution or pay compensation, the claimant State should only be allowed to resort to non-forcible unilateral measures of enforcing international law, e.g. freezing of assets, boycott or complaint to international organizations. Even in such cases the exercise of the right of self-defence must be inapplicable, otherwise it would be abused for other ends as it is based only on subjective evaluation of the national State of the investor.[24]

However, the situation may be different if the property destroyed is State-owned property situated abroad, as distinct from the property of nationals.[25] Anyway, this latter issue is outside the scope of this book. Furthermore, even if one accepts the contention that the use of force against a respondent State for destruction of private investments can be justified on the basis of self-defence, one would be confronted with the absence of the most essential requirement of proportionality which lies at the heart of the legitimate exercise of the right of self-defence. This requirement of proportionality postulates that the action should be commensurate in kind and degree, which would be entirely lacking in case of retaliation by armed force for a violation of a private proprietary right or interest.[26]

5. Suspension of economic aid

This is a measure which can effectively be employed as a sanction against a recipient country which expropriated the private investments of nationals of the State which granted the recipient State economic aid or assistance without making adequate compensation. Under section 620(e) of the United States Foreign Assistance Act, 1961 as amended in 1962, the President is authorized to suspend United States economic assistance to the Government of any country which has:

(a) nationalized or expropriated or seized ownership or control of property owned by United States' nationals or by any corporation or partnership not less than 50 percent beneficially owned by United States' citizens, or

(b) imposed or enforced discriminatory taxes or other exactions or restrictive maintenance or operational conditions which have the effect of nationalizing, expropriating or otherwise seizing ownership or control of property so owned, and such country fails within a reasonable time, not more than six months after such action, to take appropriate steps which may include arbitration, to discharge its obligation under international law towards such citizen or entity, including equitable and speedy compensation for such property in convertible foreign exchange as required by international law.[27]

This provision was implemented when the Sudan Government nationalized and confiscated American firms in early 1970. All American aid was accordingly suspended.[28]

Similar measures were adopted by Britain when investments of British citizens were nationalized in the Sudan in 1970. That action was premature as the Valuation Committees had been embarking upon the assessment of compensation due to the nationalized banks and companies. At any rate, the suspension of both American and British aid to the Sudan had in fact accelerated the negotiation of early compensation settlements. Subsequently, after the State visit of President Nimeiri to Britain in 1973, British aid to the Sudan was resumed, after the compensation agreement with the British firms had been partially honoured. Similarly, American aid has been intensified with special emphasis on private investments in all economic sectors, notably in the petroleum industry.

Additionally, the United States is empowered under certain legislation[29] to vote against loans and aids to any country which has not taken appropriate action to resolve investment disputes in a manner assuring the realization of the standard of prompt, adequate and effective compensation.[30]

Other informal United States governmental steps related to these statutory sanctions can be taken. For instance, the Overseas Private Investment Corporation insurance has been keyed to the resolution of investment disputes (see *ante*, pp. 159–71). This policy has been explained by emphasizing that a major unresolved investment dispute means that the investee country is not credit-worthy.[31]

Nwogugu[32] rightly asserted that there is nothing internationally illegal in the suspension of economic aid voluntarily given by one State to another.

6. Legality of unilateral sanctions

States may elect to take unilateral measures for the enforcement of international law rules on respect for private property if their nationals' investments have suffered loss by investee States and the other means have yielded no results. These unilateral measures have very wide ramifications. They may be in the form of freezing of foreign-owned assets, complaints to the U.N., boycott or suspension of economic aid. In no case should they extend to the use of force by way of self-defence. Self-defence cannot extend to the use of force for destruction of private property of individuals.

The problem is apparent more than real with regard to the Sudan and Saudi Arabia. None of the unilateral measures and sanctions has been employed against the Sudan, except the suspension of economic aid, which has been prematurely adopted by Britain and the United States in the wake of the nationalization and confiscatory measures by Nimeiri's regime in its early era in 1970 (see *ante*, pp. 6–7).

For a businessman all these devices for settling investment disputes are outdated. He is always eager to avoid disputes and not to seek them. It is realized that the quicker method is to conduct direct negotiations with the Government of the respondent State.[33] However, it is prudent on the part of the foreign investor to inform his home State as a matter of courtesy before initiating his negotiations. Indeed, by having the Government of his home State in the background, ready to offer its good offices at any time, the foreign investor would reach a satisfactory settlement with the Government of the respondent State. Only in the last resort will he have recourse to the diplomatic protection of his home State, a step which is really disfavoured at any level. This is because, in practice, the home State would be reluctant to challenge the political measure[34] of a friendly State, and accordingly, may refuse to espouse the claim of its national. Additionally, it has been revealed that actually diplomatic protection is time-consuming and less satisfactory than direct negotiation. Thus, the practice of the British Foreign Claims Commissions has shown that in the majority of cases only one third of the amount claimed was obtainable.[35]

12
GENERAL APPRAISAL

The possibilities of admission of foreign private capital into a developing country depend on the political system of that country. The Sudan, opting for a mixed economy and adopting an open policy, encourages foreign capital of all sources from friendly countries, provided that it is likely to contribute to the Sudan's economic and social development. This policy is entrenched further in Saudi Arabia, which has a capitalist economy. Initially, for a foreign investment to be admitted into the Sudan and Saudi Arabia, certain procedural and substantive requirements have to be satisfied. Of great importance in Saudi Arabia are joint ventures, whereby the State or its nationals acquire some control over the activities of foreign enterprises.

Foreign private investment in the Sudan is regulated by investment laws, treaties and development agreements. The same is true of Saudi Arabia, except that treaties are not usual. Under the investment laws, foreign investors in the Sudan and Saudi Arabia enjoy generous incentives and concessions such as exemption from taxation and customs duties. They are also accorded guarantees against illegal expropriation, and assured of the right to remit profits and repatriate capital in case of liquidation. But the real problem is not the *quantum* of the incentives and concessions, but the effectiveness and duration of their enjoyment. This, in the end, depends on the political stability of the Government according them. Unfortunately, foreign investors in these two countries face unnecessary procedural technicalities which constitute formidable obstacles, thus neutralizing the incentives. These requirements emanate from the deficiency of the existing investment administrative machinery which is permeated by the overlapping of jurisdictions and red-tape bureaucracy.

The consolidation of the Sudanese investment laws in the Encouragement of Investment Act, 1980, is a constructive step towards eradicating many anomalies. But the problem in the Sudan is how to implement the law. The present environment does not encourage scientific planning and follow-up. There are chronic infrastructural crises and mounting debts which actually prevent the Sudanese economy from accommodating foreign investment. And the migration of qualified and skilled Sudanese to Saudi Arabia and the other rich Arab countries has escalated the crises; for there might be no labour force to run the new investment projects. Hence, the objectives of the legal reform require an overall socio-economic reform.

In the writer's view, all investments must be formalized in contracts between the investors and the State. This instrumentality would firmly establish an effective legal regime for both parties and secure for them some sort of mutuality.

From an international law point of view, the most effective instruments for the protection of foreign investment are bilateral treaties which reaffirm, with minor reformulations, the rules of international law. They usually contain elaborate provisions on the standard of treatment to be accorded to foreign investments by the investee State. In addition, like the investment laws, they assure foreign investors of the right to remit profits and repatriate capital in case of liquidation, and to be paid adequate, effective and prompt compensation in case of nationalization, the compensation to be freely transferred in hard currency or in the same currency in which the original capital was brought.

Considered as instruments of international law, bilateral treaties, unlike resolutions of the United Nations General Assembly, are binding on States party to them. The spreading network of these instruments, concluded in similar terms, assists in strengthening international law, improving the standard of international morality, and in reducing potential friction.

Because of the emergence of economic nationalism and the challenge to the traditional rules on the protection of private property abroad (see *ante*, pp. 1–3), it has become important to insure foreign investment against the non-commercial risks of expropriation, inconvertibility and war risks. As private insurance companies are somewhat reluctant to issue insurance policies against these non-commercial risks, some capital-exporting countries have adopted insurance programmes for their investments in developing countries. By buying insurance policies under these national programmes, the investor will be able to receive compensation from his insurer without necessarily having to obtain a prior determination that a breach of international law has been committed by the host country. But these national insurance programmes provide only a partial solution to the problem, because they apply only to investments of nationals of the sponsoring States. The traditional rules on nationality of claims and diplomatic protection are fatal to extending these programmes to cover investments of other nationals in the absence of treaty arrangements (see *ante*, pp. 153–8). This shortcoming calls for the creation of an effective international programme for insuring foreign investments against non-commercial risks on the model of the World Bank Scheme for an international investment insurance agency.

The Convention establishing the Arab Corporation for Investment Guarantees, to which both the Sudan and Saudi Arabia have adhered, is pioneering the provision of a multilateral investment insurance scheme, though on a regional basis. In spite of being confined to Arab investments, the Convention can be considered as a step forward towards an international agreement on the recent concept of foreign investment insurance (see pp. 180–8).

As insurance plays a constructive part in the encouragement and protection of foreign investment, it is prudent for the Sudan and Saudi Arabia to secure bilateral arrangements for insuring foreign investments. Of significant success is the United States programme. Being the oldest, the American programme has proved effective in promoting American investments in developing countries. Through the mechanism of subrogation, the public corporation administering the programme has always been able to recover some compensation from the host country when the insurance risk occurred; though the scheme has recently been disapproved by the American business community (see *ante*, pp. 173–4).

In addition to treaties, economic development agreements between States and foreign private investors constitute effective and useful legal devices both to investee States and to foreign investors. Through these instruments foreign capital, technology, expertise and know-how are channelled to the developing countries.

Though development agreements take different forms, yet they can be characterized as international agreements. This is not to suggest that they are treaties *stricto sensu*. International law would be applicable either by the express choice of the parties or by mere inference from an arbitration clause in the agreement itself or by other circumstances. Even if the parties have expressly chosen municipal law as the proper law of the contract, international law will be the legal order within which municipal law must operate (see *ante*, pp. 243–50). But international law should be revised to accommodate the interests of the newcomers, the developing countries, who had been incapacitated from contributing in this respect in the past.

It was the dogma of the classical theory that individuals are not subjects of international law. Nevertheless, there are at present compelling reasons for allowing foreign investors to have limited international capacity to enjoy their rights under development agreements (see *ante*, pp. 243–51). Consequently, States should be directly responsible under international law for breaching their agreements with foreign investors. This direct international responsibility obliges the respondent State to make adequate reparation so as to restore the *status quo ante* (see *ante*, pp. 271–3).

Apart from constitutional guarantees against illegal expropriation and arbitration under the Encouragement of Investment Act, 1980, there is very little remedy to aggrieved foreign investors under the Sudan legal system. The Sudanese courts are somewhat executive-minded and unsympathetic to reviewing ouster clauses. This is unsatisfactory and may actually constitute a denial of justice, which would eventually entail the international responsibility of the Sudan. For judicial review to operate effectively, all ouster clauses should be repealed, and the Sudanese courts should be less self-restrained (see *ante*, pp. 284–90).

It is noteworthy that the Sudan and Saudi Arabia have been responsive to settling investment disputes through *ad hoc* and institutionalized arbitration (see *ante*, p. 294). This is manifested in their adherence to the Convention constituting the International Centre for the Settlement of Investment Disputes between States and Nationals of Other States, which may be considered as the most prestigious international institutional arbitration forum. The accession of many countries to this Convention reflects a progress towards agreement among the developed and developing countries. The insistence of the Sudan and Saudi Arabia that arbitration should be conducted inside their territorial jurisdictions is an effective device in controlling foreign investment, albeit at a later stage.

Obviously, if local remedies and arbitration provide no solution to the particular dispute, the home State of the aggrieved investor may espouse his claim diplomatically or before the International Court of Justice. In extreme cases, a State may elect to take unilateral measures by way of sanctions for the enforcement of international law rules for respect of private property abroad. These unilateral measures may be diverse; but they should not extend to the use of force, even under the pretext of self-defence.

For a contemporary businessman, all the devices for settling investment disputes are outdated and old-fashioned. He prefers to make direct negotiations with the Government of the respondent State. By having his national Government in the background, ready to offer its good offices, the investor can reach a satisfactory settlement which accommodates his interests and those of the investee State.

In theory, there must be a multilateral convention or an investment code for creating an effective international regime for the encouragement and protection of investments abroad. The convention or the code must be couched in general terms containing general principles, leaving the details to be spelled out in subsidiary instruments. In particular, the convention must regulate all aspects pertinent to foreign investment, i.e. standard of treatment; nationalization; compensation; procedure for settling investment disputes, etc. Under the proposed convention, foreign investors must be prepared to contribute to the economic development of the developing countries, which must, in return, furnish to these investors adequate guarantees according to the international standards.

The principles to be incorporated in the convention must be considered by the international community as *jus cogens* overriding any domestic law.

Unfortunately, these proposals do not seem to go so far as to transcend the theoretical barrier to actual adherence. The present state of international relations does not allow the concluding of any convention on foreign investment, as past attempts have shown. The conflict of interests and political motivations is so polarizing as not to admit of any consensus between the developed and developing countries. The Charter of Economic Rights and Duties of States reflects the extent of the rift (see *ante*, pp. 128–40). It has accentuated the predicament by confining the whole issue of nationalization and compensation to the domestic law of the nationalizing State. It has also eroded the international standard of treatment and the right to diplomatic protection. It is worth mentioning that the standard of assessing compensation adopted by the Sudan for compensating the nationalized banks and companies can be considered as the most generous, if compared with other counterparts, since the Second World War. The endorsement of such a practice in the existing Sudanese investment law demonstrates a gesture of goodwill and is encouraging to potential foreign investors (see *ante*, pp. 225–31). And the Islamic practice adopted in Saudi Arabia secures to foreign investors the best investment climate in a capitalist and rich economy.

Despite the fact that the subsequent practice of developing countries runs counter to the Charter of Economic Rights and Duties of States, the western developed countries still disapprove of it. They consider it as a fatal blow to the traditional international rules on the protection of private property abroad, as the Charter does not postulate direct reference to international law (see *ante*, pp. 130–8). On the other hand, it has been emphasized that the developing countries consider the Charter not only as reflecting only *de lege ferenda* rules, but also as generating new international norms. Though it might be legitimate to contend that the Charter is devoid of any legal and binding force under the U.N. existing system, yet it has its political and moral impetus, and may have its persuasive momentum in the future (see *ante*, pp. 132–40) and be a source of customary international law.

Indisputably, the traditional international law rules were developed in the early nineteenth century, and hence they have become unsuitable for the present international economic relations, which are characterized by new patterns and modalities of business institutions emanating from worldwide activities of transnational corporations. Thus, it would be unrealistic to give these corporations a free hand to manipulate the economy of the investee State as they wish. This calls for adopting a code of conduct to regulate all corporate practices of transnational corporations as has been aired in the United Nations and other international organizations. Admittedly, the investee State should have the sovereign right to control all the economic activities within its territories; but to attract transnational corporations to invest and transfer their technology to the developing countries, they must be accorded certain guarantees and equitable treatment.

Perhaps through a pragmatic and realistic understanding an international legal regime on foreign investment can be obtained. Inevitably, this requires the qualification of the rhetorical assertion of sovereignty which is exemplified by the two extremes of protectionism and nationalism held by the developed and developing countries. Each side should relinquish part of its claim in order to reach an agreement, which may be a forlorn hope.

The best pattern or modality of legal instruments for protecting foreign investment in the Sudan and Saudi Arabia cannot be evaluated in the abstract. It depends on the subjective assessment of the foreign investors. However, it would seem that the cumulative interaction between treaties and contracts may secure to the investor an effective pattern. The unilateral guarantees couched in the investment laws reflect only a good-faith pattern. Their legal effect is, more or less, a question of confidence in the stability and promises of the particular Government. A potential and sanguine investor may well wonder whether the willingness to pass such laws tends to stand in inverse ratio to the credit-worthiness of that Government.

APPENDIX 1

PROVISIONAL ORDER
THE ENCOURAGEMENT OF INVESTMENT ACT, 1980

In the Name of God, the Compassionate, the Merciful
The President of the Republic.
In accordance with the Provisions of Article 106 of the Constitution, hereby makes the following Provisional Order:

Chapter 1 Preliminary

Title and Commencement

1. This Provisional Order may be cited as 'the Encouragement of Investment Act, 1980', and shall come into force as from the date of signature.

Repeal and Saving

2. (1) The following Acts are hereby repealed:
   (a) The Encouragement of Investment in Economic Services Act, 1973.
   (b) The Development and Encouragement of Industrial Investment Act, 1974.
   (c) The Development and Encouragement of Agricultural Investment Act, 1976.
   (2) Not withstanding subsection (1) all licences, privileges and guarantees in force granted under the aforesaid laws shall continue to be valid and shall be deemed as if granted under this Act.

Interpretation

3. In this Act, unless the context otherwise requires:
'The Project' means any enterprise, utility or any economic activity coming within any of the fields whereby investment is allowed in accordance with the objectives of this Act and approved in accordance therewith.
'National Capital' means the capital owned by Sudanese investor which

capital is employed at the commencement of investment in the project and consists of moveable or immovable assets plus any subsequent additions thereto either in the form of moveable or immovable assets or cash or through capitalization of profits earned by the project provided that such additions are made with the consent of the Minister.

'Foreign Capital'

(a) The foreign hard currency transferred to the Sudan at the exchange price current at the time of transfer through a bank working in the Sudan for the utilization thereof in execution of a project.

(b) Imported machinery, equipment and means of transport financed from abroad and necessary for the execution of the project and compatible with the technical development suitable for the Sudan answering such specifications as prescribed by the Minister.

(c) The foreign hard currency utilized on preliminary studies, feasibility studies and foundation undertaken by the investor within the limits approved by the Minister.

(d) The profits realized by the project if capitalized with the consent of the Minister or if invested with his consent in another project in accordance with the provisions of this Act.

(e) Intangible assets, i.e. patents, trade marks, technical experience etc. registered by the foreign investor for utilization in the project.

'Ministerial Committee' means the Ministerial Committee for Investment established under section 31.

'The Minister' means the Minister of Finance and National Economy.

'The Secretary-General for Investment' means the person appointed as such by the President of the Republic.

'The Secretariat-General' means the Secretariat-General established under section 25.

'The Consultative Committee' means the Consultative Committee for investment established under section 29.

Application

4. (1) Subject to the provision appearing at the end of section 2, the provisions of this Act shall be applied to all investment projects in the Sudan.

(2) The Minister may, on recommendation of the Minister of Energy and Mining, grant to leaseholders under the Mines and Quarries Act, 1972, the privileges and facilities set forth in this Act in accordance with the provisions thereof.

Chapter II
Encouragement of Investment

Fields of Encouragement of Investment

5. (1) This Act encourages investment in agricultural, animal, mining, industrial, transport, tourism, storage and housing fields and any other economic field prescribed by the Ministerial Committee.
(2) This Act encourages investments initiated by the public sector, co-operative sector, mixed sector national and private sectors, and the foreign sector.

Objects of Encouragement of Investment

6. The objects of this Act are in general to encourage investment in projects aiming towards the achievement of the objects of the Development Plan of the Democratic Republic of the Sudan and in particular its objects are to encourage investment in projects which:
(a) contribute effectively to the increase of national income and widening of the base of national economy and the strengthening of its activity, or
(b) contribute to the removal of any bottlenecks obstructing development, or
(c) make available necessary services which contribute to the consolidation of economic and social development, or
(d) the production of which depends on local material or the establishment of which is encouraged for production of such materials.
(e) assist in the realization of self-sufficiency and creation of surpluses for export, or
(f) assist effectively in the consolidation of balance of payment, or
(g) make available directly or indirectly chances of labour for citizens, or
(h) have defence or strategic importance, or
(i) contribute to the realization of the objects of economic co-operation or integration with Arab and African countries.

No Discrimination

7. For the purposes of granting licences, privileges and facilities under this Act, no discrimination shall be allowed among the projects by reason of their being national or foreign.

Chapter III
Privileges and Facilities

Granting of Privileges and Facilities

8. (1) Notwithstanding the provisions of any other law, the Minister, subject to the provisions of this Act, may with the consent of the Minister concerned grant a project if he is satisfied that such project achieves any of the objects specified in section 6 to such an extent or aspect as may give it a distinctive economic value, all the privileges or facilities set forth in sections 9, 10, 11, 12, 13, 14, 15, 16 or any of them.

(2) The type, extent, and period of privileges and facilities shall be specified in accordance with the extent of the achievement by the project of the objects set forth in section 6 hereof and in the light of the policies and priorities determined by the Ministerial Committee.

Exemption from Business Profits Tax

9. (1) The Minister may, subject to the provisions of section 5, exempt the project wholly or partly from business profits tax for a period of five years starting from the date of the commencement of production. The determination of the period of exemption shall be in consonance with the importance of the project to the national economy and to the size of investment therein.

(2) Notwithstanding subsection (1) the Minister may, subject to the provisions of this Act, extend the period of exemption from income profits tax to a maximum period of five years with respect to integrated projects which include in addition to production basic structures like roads and other essential services or with respect to projects requiring large investments.

(3) Any loss occurring during the whole or partial period of exemption shall be deemed to have occurred within the last year of such period.

(4) A project shall be granted exemption from business profits tax only for its own benefit and for its importance to the national economy in such way that the benefit shall not return to another State.

Exemption from Duties

10. (1) The Minister may, in accordance with the Provisions of section 8, exempt the project wholly or partly from the following duties:

(a) customs duties relating to:

(i) machines, equipment, apparatus and imported spare parts necessary for the project;
(ii) imported raw, artificial or intermediary materials necessary for the project which materials cannot be found locally in the necessary quality and quantity;
(b) import duties on artificial or semi-artificial goods arising out of the project;
(c) any other duties or taxes imposed on the project.
(2) The Minister may, in accordance with the provisions of section 8, exempt the project wholly or partly from excise duties imposed on materials or commodities locally produced which are necessary for the project.

Allotment of Land Necessary for the Project

11. Notwithstanding the provisions of any other Law, the Minister may, after consultation with any authority legally concerned, allot the land necessary for the establishment of the project; he may reduce the price of such land or order that such price shall be paid in instalments subject to such reasonable terms as he may prescribe.

No Local Duties to be Imposed on Projects

12. Notwithstanding the provisions of any other law, no local duties shall be imposed on any project which has been given exemption under section 9 or 10 hereof within the period of exemption save with the consent of the Minister.

Deduction of Costs of Electricity and Transport

13. The Minister may, subject to the provisions of section 8, and after consultation with the other competent authorities grant to the project any of the following facilities:
(i) reduction of the prices of the electricity used for the purposes of the project;
(ii) reduction of transport fares imposed on the traffic of the imports and products of the project.

Protection of Project Product

14. Subject to section 8, the Minister may direct the authority concerned:
    (a) to raise the customs duties on imported commodities which compete with or act as substitutes to the products of the project during a limited period of time;
    (b) to restrict importation of such competitive or substitute products for a limited period of time.

Preferential Facilities for Regional Development

15. Subject to section 8, the Minister may grant to the project which is established in certain regions prescribed by the Minister reasonable preferential facilities for achievement of justice in allocating development programmes among the different regions and for giving regard to regions of less development.

Submission of Feasibility Study for the project

16. Privileges or facilities established by this Act shall only be granted after a technical economic feasibility study for the project has been submitted; provided that such privileges and facilities may be granted on a preliminary basis on submission of a preliminary feasibility study.

Obtaining a Licence for Establishment of a project

17. Subject to the provisions of any other law, no investor shall establish or contribute to establish a project in the Sudan except on obtaining a licence from the Minister in accordance with the provisions of this Act.

Terms and Procedure for Obtaining a Licence, Privileges and Facilities

18. (1) Applications for a licence for any project or for grant of any privileges, facilities or guarantees conferred by this Act, shall be made on the form prescribed by regulations made under this Act.
    (2) No alteration or amendment in the size of the project or the purpose for which the licence is granted and no transfer of the project from its licensed place shall be made save with the written consent of the Minister.
    (3) No transfer of the ownership or a leasehold of the whole or any part of the project shall be made save with the written consent of the Minister.
    (4) The machines, equipment, material or spare parts with respect to which

privileges or facilities have been granted under this Act shall not be used for any other purpose other than that for which the licence was granted.

(5) The land allotted for the project under this Act shall not be used for any other purpose or mortgage save with the written consent of the Minister.

(6) The owner of the project shall present every year to the Secretary General a copy of the annual accounts of the project signed by a certified accountant.

(7) The owner of the project shall provide the Secretary General every year with reports about the progress of the operation of execution of the project and the productivity of the project after commencement of production.

(8) The project shall not be liquidated within the five years following commencement of production.

Guarantee not to Nationalize, Confiscate or Acquire the Project

19. Notwithstanding the provisions of any other law, any capital invested in the Sudan shall enjoy the following guarantees:

(a) it shall not be nationalized except for the public good and by virtue of a law; and in such case the following rules shall be followed:

(i) the investor shall be granted after valuation of his property, just compensation at the price current at the time of nationalization;

(ii) the valuation shall be completed within a maximum period of six months commencing from the date of order of nationalization; payment and transfer of compensation shall be in yearly instalments within a period not exceeding five years in the same currency of capital or any other currency agreed to;

(b) it shall not be subject to sequestration or confiscation save with the order of a competent court issued in accordance with the laws in force.

Guarantee to Transfer the Profits, Interests and Foreign Capital Abroad

20. (1) All profits arising out of the foreign capital invested in the project, and all interests arising out of any loan approved in accordance with section 21, shall after all taxes, duties, dues and other obligations due to the Government are paid or fulfilled be transferable outside the Sudan in the currency in which the capital or loan as the case may be was imported or any other currency agreed to.

(2) If the project is liquidated, sold or its ownership is wholly or partially transferred, the capital invested in the project shall, after all taxes, duties

and obligations legally due to the government or other persons are paid or fulfilled be transferable outside the Sudan in the currency in which such capital was imported or in any other currency agreed to.

Chapter IV: Rules of Investment

Investor may Obtain Loans from Abroad with Consent of Minister

21. (1) The project may, in accordance with such reasonable terms as may be agreed to by the Minister borrow money from any foreign body.
(2) No foreign investor shall borrow money from banks and financial houses working in Sudan save with consent of the Minister.

Fixing and Registration of Foreign Capital

22. The foreign capital invested in the project shall be fixed and evaluated with the consent of the Minister and shall be registered with the Bank of Sudan.

Cancellation of the Licence, Privileges, Facilities and Guarantees

23. (1) The Minister may, subject to the provisions of this Act, cancel any licence, privilege or guarantee set forth in this Act in any of the following cases:
(a) If the investor has not established the project within the period specified in the licence or any extension thereto;
(b) if the investor has broken any of the terms according to which any privileges, facilities, guarantees or licences have been granted thereby;
(c) if the investor has provided any false information or used unlawful means by which he obtained a benefit under this Act;
(d) if the project, without reasonable cause, stopped;
(e) if the investor so contravenes the law as may threaten the security and safety of the land.
(2) If the privileges or facilities are cancelled, then the investor shall be compelled to restitute the pecuniary benefit he has obtained as a result of conferment of any such privileges and facilities, provided that such benefit is attributable to the cause justifying cancellation.
(3) The investor against whom an order was made under sub-section (1) may file an application with the Ministerial committee for revision of such order and the resolution of this Committee shall be final.

Contravention of the Provisions of this Act

24. (1) Whoever contravenes the provisions of section 17 of this Act, shall be punished, on conviction, with a fine not exceeding five thousand pounds.

(2) Whoever contravenes the provisions of section 18 of this Act shall be liable to a compounding of the contravention to be prescribed by the Minister by order but not to exceed five thousand pounds, in assessment of which regard shall be had to graveness of the contravention and to the extent of the unlawful enrichment by the owner of the project. A person against whom a compounding order is issued may apply to the Ministerial Committee for revision of such order and the resolution of this Committee shall be final.

Chapter V: Bureaux of Investment

Establishment and Constitution of the Secretariat-General for Investment

25. (1) There shall be established a unified bureau to be known as 'The Secretariat-General for Investment' which shall be subject to the administrative and financial supervision of the Minister.

(2) The Secretariat-General for Investment shall consist of:

(a) The Secretary-General.

(b) The Technical Secretariat which shall consist of full-time specialists to be recruited from all technical departments and scientific specializations concerned with investment and its encouragement and of a limited administrative body, and shall exercise the functions set forth in section 26.

(c) The Consultative Committee.

Functions of the Technical Secretariat

26. The Technical Secretariat shall have the following functions:

(a) to determine the abilities of investment, the need therefore, its rules and any information relating thereto, and submit the same to and propagate among investors and give advice to them.

(b) To consider applications for licences, feasibility studies and any other applications submitted by the investor and to make the necessary studies and enquiries about them so as to help investors and enable the authorities concerned to make a recommendation or decision with respect thereto.

(c) to have contacts and co-operate with all other government bodies concerned with the follow-up of investments and control of execution of projects so as to help investors and enable the authorities concerned in this Act to exercise their functions.

(d) to seek assistance from specialists, researchers or government or private bodies in the exercise of its functions in accordance with the preceding paragraphs.

Functions of the Secretary-General for Investment

27. (1) The Secretary-General shall undertake the preparatory work which consists of the technical studies prepared by the Technical Secretariat and of the recommendations issued by the Consultative Committee and of any other necessary substance or papers and shall submit the same to the Ministerial Committee or Minister as the case may be for the exercise of the powers conferred by this Act.

(2) The Secretary-General in co-operation with other concerned government bodies shall have power to consider and give recommendation to the Ministerial Committee or the Minister as to any matter which is subject under this Act to the decision or consent of such Committee or Minister, provided the consultative Committee is not competent to consider or give recommendation with respect thereto.

(3) The Secretary-General shall submit to the Ministerial Committee or Minister as the case may be any studies or recommendations made by him or by the Consultative Committee as to any application of an investor within two months of the date of the receipt of complete application.

(4) The Secretary-General shall undertake all preparatory work to the meetings of the Consultative Committee and shall make ready all preparatory and necessary materials and keep its records and submit the Consultative Committee's recommendations to the Ministerial Committee or Minister as the case may be.

(5) The Secretary-General shall have supervision over the technicians and all other employees of the Secretariat-General and shall regulate business therein.

Composition of the Consultative Committee for Investment

28. (1) The Consultative Committee shall consist of the Secretary-General as Chairman and of such members representing bodies directly concerned with investment as the president of the Republic may appoint provided that four members representing the private sector, whose tenure of membership shall be three renewable years, shall be included in the appointment.

(2) Members of the Consultative Committee shall not depute any person to attend its meetings save with the previous consent of the Secretary-General.

(3) The Members shall disclose any interest or benefits they have relating to any matter discussed by the Consultative Committee and they shall not share in any debates or recommendation relating to that matter.

(4) The Secretary-General may invite any person to attend any meetings of the Consultative Committee if he deems this necessary; provided that such person shall not have a counted vote.

Functions of the Consultative Committee for Investment

29. (1) The Consultative Committee for Investment shall have the following functions:

(a) to consider and make recommendations to the Minister with respect to applications for grant of licences for the projects and to evaluate the feasibility studies relating thereto;

(b) to consider and make recommendations to the Minister with respect to applications for grant of privileges and facilities for the projects;

(c) to consider and make recommendations to the Minister with respect to applications for increase of capital of any project out of profits.

(d) to make recommendations to the Minister with respect to compounding of the offences it deems necessary to be imposed in accordance with section 24(2);

(e) to consider and make recommendations to the Minister with respect to cancellation of any privileges, facilities or licences within the bases referred to in section 23 thereof;

(f) to make recommendations to the Ministerial Committee or the Minister to confer on the Consultative Committee any additional functions and to delegate thereto any power.

The Ministerial Committee for Investment

30. (1) There is hereby established a Ministerial Committee to supervise the encouragement of investment.
(2) The Committee shall be composed by the president of the Republic and he may reconstitute the committee as and when he deems this suitable.

Functions of the Ministerial Committee

31. In addition to any function conferred on the Ministerial Committee by any other provision in this Act, the Ministerial Committee shall have power to frame the general policy for encouragement of investment in the light of the objects set forth in section 6 hereof and shall determine the priorities in the grant of licences, privileges and facilities and shall issue all the necessary directions for the proper implementation.

Chapter VI
General Provisions

Settlement of Investment Disputes

32. (1) If a national, Arab or foreign investor obtains any privileges, facilities or guarantees under this Act, this will be regarded as a consent by him to submit to arbitration any legal dispute arising in accordance with the provisions of sub-sections (2), (3) and (4) of this section; provided that the Sudan shall be the place of arbitration. The Government of the Sudan shall be bound to make available all facilities required by arbitration.
(2) The provisions of Chapter IV of part VI of the civil procedure Act, 1974 relating to arbitration, shall apply to every legal dispute arising directly from investment of national capital in any project.
(3) The provisions of the convention on the Settlement of Investment Disputes Between Host States for Arab Investments and Nationals of other Arab States, 1974 shall apply to every legal dispute arising directly out of any of the investment to which that convention applies.
(4) The provisions of the Convention on the Settlement of Investment Disputes Between States and Nationals of Other States, 1965 shall apply to every legal dispute arising directly out of any of the investments to which the provision of that convention applies.

Power to Make Regulations

33. The Ministerial Committee may make the regulations and orders necessary for the implementation of the provisions of this Act. Without prejudice to the generality of the foregoing such regulations and orders may provide for the following:

(a) the prescription of the procedure whereby applications can be submitted for grant of licence, privileges or facilities and imposition of fees thereon;

(b) the minimum number of projects to which this Act applies and exceptional cases;

(c) the prescription of rules relating to control and follow up of projects licensed under the Act.

Made under my hand at the People's Palace on the 11th day of Jumade El Akhira, 1400 A.H. being the 26th day of April 1980.

Gaafar Mohamed Nimeiri,
President of the Republic.

APPENDIX 2

FOREIGN CAPITAL INVESTMENT LAW OF SAUDI ARABIA, 1979[1]

Article 1

For the purposes of this law, Foreign Capital shall mean any coins, currency notes, securities, machinery, equipment, spare parts, raw materials, products, transportation facilities and intangible rights, such as patents, trade marks and similar assets, where such capital is owned either by a natural person who is not of Saudi Arabian nationality or by a corporate person whose capital shareholders are not all of Saudi Arabian nationality.

Article 2

Without violation to the provisions of other laws in force, Foreign Capital investment requires a licence issued by the Minister of Industry and Electricity following the recommendation of the Foreign Investment Committee, provided that the following two conditions are fulfilled:

(a) The Foreign Capital shall be invested in development projects which, for the purpose of this Law, do not include petroleum and mineral extraction projects.

(b) The investment shall be accompanied by foreign technical know-how and expertise.

Article 3

Development projects shall be determined by a resolution from the Minister of Industry and Electricity following the recommendations of the Foreign Investment Committee within the guidelines of the Development Plan.

Article 4

A committee called 'The Foreign Capital Investment Committee' shall be set up in the Ministry of Industry and Electricity. The committee shall be composed of the following members:

The Deputy Minister of Industry and Electricity, or his substitute (in the event of his absence) to act as Chairman.
A representative from the Ministry of Planning.
A representative from the Ministry of Finance and National Economy.
A representative from the Ministry of Agriculture and Water.
A representative from the Ministry of Petroleum and Mineral Resources.
A representative from the Ministry of Commerce.

None of the representatives for the membership of the committee shall rank lower than the tenth grade. The Director of the Foreign Investment Bureau at the Ministry of Industry and Electricity shall act as Secretary to the committee and the Minister of Industry and Electricity shall appoint a legal advisor for the committee. The committee may, at its own discretion, call on certain experts during the discussion of certain subjects, but these experts shall have no voting right. The meetings of the committee shall be valid only if attended by at least four members including the Chairman; and the committee's deliberations shall be confidential. The resolutions of the committee shall be adopted by a majority of attending votes. In case of a tie, the Chairman shall have a casting vote. However, the committee's resolutions shall not become final unless approved and ratified by the Minister of Industry and Electricity.

Article 5

The committee, referred to in Article 4, shall have the following tasks:

(a) To propose the projects that will be classified as development projects.
(b) To consider Foreign Investment applications.
(c) To examine any complaints or claims submitted by foreign investors or other parties concerned arising out of questions governed by this Law; and to submit its recommendations on these matters to the competent authorities.
(d) To recommend penalties which, in the opinion of the committee, should be imposed on any project violating the provisions of this Law.
(e) To draft rules of procedure for the implementation of this Law.
(f) To consider matters, referred to the committee by the Minister of Industry and Electricity, concerning the provisions of this Law.

Article 6

The Foreign Capital Investment Bureau at the Ministry of Industry and Electricity shall supply all necessary information, clarifications and statistical data to any foreign applicant who desires to invest capital in the Kingdom. The Bureau shall also facilitate and complete necessary formalities pertaining to licensed Foreign Investments. The Ministry of Foreign Affairs and the Ministry of Interior shall grant to investors, licensed in accordance with this Law, their employees and workers' entry and exit visas and residence permits.

Article 7

Foreign Capital which has fulfilled the conditions provided for in this Law shall have the following privileges:

(a) Privileges enjoyed by national capital under the Law for the Protection and Promotion of National Industries in respect to industrial projects only.
(b) Exemption from Income Tax and Company Tax for a period of ten years to any industrial or agricultural projects, having Foreign Capital. Other projects shall be exempted from such taxes for a period of five years.
The projects which enjoy exemption at the time of the implementation of this Law shall benefit from the provisions of exemption mentioned in this sub-clause.
The pre-requisite for any tax exemption is that Saudi Capital shall not be less than twenty-five per cent of the total capital of the project and that such percentage shall be maintained throughout the period of exemption.
For industrial projects the period of exemption shall start as of the date of the commencement of production and for other projects from the start of activities.
This last sub-clause may be amended by a resolution by the Council of Ministers.
(c) Ownership of any real estate required by Foreign Investment Projects in accordance with the Law for Non-Saudi Ownership of Real Estate.

Article 8

Without violation to the provisions herein, projects benefiting from the provisions of this law shall be subject to the Labour Law, the Law for Social Insurance and other laws in force in the Kingdom.

Article 9

The provisions of this law shall not apply to the projects in which Foreign Capital is invested in the following cases:

(a) If the project was legally in existence prior to the implementation of this law. However, the operation of such projects or any increase in their capital shall be subject to the provisions of this law.
(b) If the project is authorized to operate in the Kingdom by virtue of special laws or agreements.

Article 10

Any project licensed under this Law, violating the provisions herein, shall be warned by the Minister of Industry and Electricity to abide by these provisions within a period to be specified by the Minister. Should such project not comply with the said warning, the Minister may, following a recommendation by the Foreign Investment Committee, withdraw the licence granted to that project or order its final liquidation and closure.

Following a recommendation by the said committee, the Minister may, in lieu of withdrawing the licence, deprive such project of all or part of the privileges under this law.

However, parties concerned may appeal to the Board of Grievances against the Minister's decision imposing such penalty within thirty days as of the date on which the decision has been officially notified.

The verdict of the Board of Grievances shall be final and binding.

Article 11

The rules of procedure for the implementation of this law shall be issued by the Minister of Industry and Electricity and shall be published in the Official Gazette.

Article 12

The Law shall be published in the Official Gazette and shall become effective thirty days after the date of its publication. The Foreign Capital Investment Law promulgated by the Royal Decree No. 35 dated 11.10.1383 A.H. shall be superseded as of the date this law is put into effect.

ADDENDUM

Since the submission of the draft manuscript of this book to the publisher there have been certain changes in the law and developments in the investment climate, both at the national and international levels, which have a direct bearing on the rules and policies pertinent to foreign investment. For this reason I thought it worthwhile to write this short addendum so that the reader will be acquainted, in appropriate places, with these changes and developments without disturbing the sequence of the material already examined in the preceding chapters.

The changes and developments I intend to highlight briefly could be categorized in the areas of constitutional developments; law reform; development and promotion of investment patterns; changes in the law and certain new approaches. These main issues will be examined separately as follows:

1. Constitutional developments

As I mentioned before (see *ante*, pp. 8–10) the Sudanese Government, following the Peace Settlement Agreement of 27 March 1972, has given the Southern Sudan regional autonomy by virtue of the Regional Government for the Southern Provinces Act, 1972, which has been recently modified by the Republican Order No. 1.1983, dividing Southern Sudan into three regions instead of one. Before that, in 1980, Northern Sudan had been divided into five regions by the Regional Government Act, 1980. Khartoum remains the national capital, with an independent legal status. According to this decentralization, each region has its own government, People's Assembly and a Governor who is the head of the regional Government.

Under the operative legislation the powers are divided between the central and regional Governments in such a way as to confer on the latter some degree of autonomy, by giving them certain powers in their own right, leaving the decision-making on major issues, such as defence, foreign policy, finance and strategic utilities, to the central Government only. However, in the wake of the Fourth Conference of the Socialist Union, early in 1983, more decentralization has been recommended and certain presidential measures and decrees have been issued to achieve this objective.

The effect of these developments on the investment climate in the Sudan is quite positive. Many of the anomalies and obstacles mentioned earlier (see *ante*, pp. 37–60) are expected to be neutralized. First, there is the question of political stability, the main requisite of a healthy investment climate, whereby foreign investors feel that there is a stable system of government which will not engender any antagonistic attitude to foreign investment. Second, the wide sharing of power resulting from this process of decentralization helps very much in the identification of investment projects at regional level, whereby the regional Governments are able to embark on scientific evaluation of investment opportunities and to invite investors for specific projects, especially in the agricultural sector. Third, decentralization would eradicate the lack of supervision and inefficiencies emanating from the absence of proper accountability to the administering investment agencies. Also important is the investment licensing, which has been seen to be rather prohibitive, investors having to wait a very long time before the central investment agency considers their investment applications, even for smaller projects. Decentralization has simplified the procedure. At present the regional Governments can license non-strategic projects, while projects related to crafts can be approved by the People's Councils; except where the investment project requires tax or customs relief, which must be approved by the Central Minister of Finance on the recommendation of the regional agency in the particular situation. It is significant that the Central Investment Bureau will now license only investment projects of a minimum amount of a quarter of a million Sudanese pounds. This wise distribution of jurisdiction will undoubtedly lessen the heavy burden which is put on the Central Investment Bureau, and ultimately help in securing a quick licensing of many investment projects, a process that cuts short all red-tape and delays, which are considered formidable impediments by investors (see *ante*, pp. 42–4). However, delays on the part of the land authorities are still frustrating a lot of projects for no apparent reason, except corruption and lack of planning and co-ordination between the agencies.

2. Law reform

Applied for nearly three years since its promulgation in 1980, the Encouragement of Investment Act is reckoned to have been very successful in attracting many investors to the Sudan. This is clearly indicated by the number of investments so far licensed under it.[1] However, as indicated before (see *ante*, pp. 55–9) the Act is defective in many respects. In response to the recommendations of the First Economic Conference[2] and the Fourth Conference of the Socialist Union[3] the Minister of Finance and Economic Planning has formed a committee to revise the Encouragement of Investment Act, 1980, with a view to eradicating all the defects that have been felt during the application of the Act, and, taking into consideration the new system of government, to maintain a workable co-ordination between the central and regional agencies regarding investment licensing and supervision. This is in addition to the need to reflect new government policies, such as the employment and training by foreign investors of a minimum number of Sudanese nationals in the investment enterprises. One hopes that the committee will entrench, or at least encourage, the creation of joint ventures between national and foreign investors, especially in the agricultural and construction sectors.

As this move for reform is not enough to regulate investment, another effort has been simultaneously launched to revise the company law. This is essential for organizing and modernizing business institutions so that they can run the investment projects. A group of Sudanese law officers from the Attorney-General's Chambers and the Faculty of Law, University of Khartoum, have been put under the close supervision of certain British lawyers, expert in company law, under the umbrella of the Commonwealth Secretariat, to execute the job of preparing a new draft of the Company Act. Undoubtedly, the control and supervision of foreign entities and multinationals should lie at the heart of any reform.

Though investors under the Encouragement of Investment Act, 1980, enjoy generous tax exemption for considerable periods, the existing high tax rates take away any incentive the investors receive during the tax holiday period and this situation prohibits investment. Even for national investors it is more lucrative to put their capital into savings accounts abroad, with high rates of interest, than to invest it domestically where they are within the reach of the tax collector. This necessitates adopting a steady tax-rating system, which would keep the balance between the urgent need of the State to secure a source of revenue and the encouragement of investment in the long run.[4]

3. Development in the investment climate and promotion of investment patterns

(a) Development in the investment climate

Since 1980, certain events have taken place which have left their mark on the investment climate in the Sudan and Saudi Arabia.

On the regional level, given the repercussions of the Iranian revolution, which led to the nationalization of foreign investments in Iran and the freezing of the Iranian assets in the West as a retaliatory measure during the hostage crisis, and the Iranian–Iraqi war, new attitudes towards investing the enormous wealth of the Arab oil-producing countries outside the market economies have emerged.

Furthermore, due to the joint efforts of the Arab League, the Federation of

Arab Chambers of Commerce and the Inter-Arab Investment Guarantee Corporation, Arab businessmen and investors were able to hold their first conference in April 1980 at Al-Taif in Saudi Arabia. At this important gathering they emphatically expressed their willingness and determination to direct their investment efforts towards poor Arab countries. The outcome was the decision to form a multi-million agricultural company to secure food needs to the Arab world, to be subscribed to by investors from all Arab countries.

Again, early in 1983 the Arab Agricultural and Industrial Chambers of Commerce assembled in Khartoum and adopted resolutions reaffirming the strategy announced in Al-Taif, in addition to forming another multi-million investment company with diversified objects.

I must not ignore the promotional efforts undertaken by the Inter-Arab Investment Guarantee Corporation (whose membership at present comprises all Arab countries), which, in addition to encouraging joint ventures between Arab investors and the Sudanese private sector, has also embarked upon the activity of compiling a collection of all the business and investment laws of the Arab countries and publishing investment guides to these countries.

These promotional efforts have opened the eyes of the Arab investors to the enormous investment potentialities of the Sudan. This has been reflected in the influx of many investors into the country from the Arab and Islamic countries, which has resulted in the formation of multi-million investment joint ventures, such as the Islamic Investment Company, with a nominal capital of one billion dollars; and the Arab and Islamic funds such as the Geneva-based Dar Al Mal Al Islami, which has expressed great interest in investing and financing major investment projects in the Sudan. In addition, several commercial Islamic banks, professing to adhere to strict Islamic principles in their operations, have been established.

Another factor which encourages investment of huge amounts of accumulated oil wealth is the reduction of oil prices and the decline in demand for oil, which has resulted in the present oil glut. This has engendered an atmosphere of fear that oil may lose its status as a strategic commodity and a source of energy in the future, and that it is time to explore other sources of revenue for oil-producing countries; this could only be achieved by investing the accumulated oil-wealth in the non-oil sector.

These regional developments should be accommodated within the present international economic recession, which calls for new approaches and techniques to diversify sources of income and to increase the generating capacities of the world economy. In response thereto, oil-producing countries have tightened their belts and started to reduce many of their huge developmental projects to a modest size and to adopt new policies in order to preserve national resources. Saudi Arabia is not an exception. At present national sponsorship and participation has become mandatory, especially in the construction sector.

(b) The White Nile Petroleum Company Limited

The largest investment ever to be made in the Sudan, apart from the Gezira Scheme, is the petroleum pipeline project from the Unity oil fields in south-west Sudan to the Red Sea coast, for exporting the crude oil so far discovered by the Chevron Oil Company. As I mentioned before, oil exploration by Chevron and other oil companies is regulated by production-sharing agreements concluded in accordance with the Petroleum Resources Act. Given encouraging commercial oil discoveries, the Sudan Government and Chevron, in pursuance of section 25 of the Petroleum Resources Act (Amendment), 1975 have entered into an equity joint venture for the exploitation of petroleum discovered by the Chevron Oil Company of Sudan. This equity joint venture was formalized by the agreement between the Government of the Democratic Republic of the Sudan, Chevron Overseas Petroleum Inc., the International Finance Corporation (I.F.C.) and the Arab Petroleum Investment Corporation (A.P.I.C.) in August 1981. By virtue of this agreement, the parties agreed to establish the White Nile Petroleum Company Limited as a promotion company. It has been incorporated in the Sudan in accordance with the Companies Act, 1925. According to the original Memorandum of Association the main objects of the company are:

(1) To carry on the business of preparing and co-ordinating all necessary studies and related actions in connection with the proposed construction and operation of a refinery or refineries for crude oil and the related pipeline transportation system to transport crude oil to any such refinery for processing.
(2) To erect and operate a refinery or refineries and the related pipeline transporation system to transport crude oil to any such refinery for processing.
(3) To carry on all or any of the business of transportation of crude oil and of refining crude oil into petroleum products. (Article 3 of the Memorandum of the Association of the company.)

Under the terms of the amended joint venture agreement the Sudanese Government and Chevron each hold 45% of the equity while I.F.C. and A.P.I.C. 5% hold each.

Under the present Memorandum and Articles of Association, the company is managed by a board of directors consisting of five directors, two nominated by the Government, and one each by Chevron, I.F.C. and A.P.I.C., while Chevron is entrusted with the management of the company.

It is noteworthy that the company was established with the main object of setting up and running an oil refinery at Kosti, in the Central Region of Sudan. However, as a consequence of increased oil discoveries, Chevron has advised the

Government to suspend the refinery and instead to embark on constructing a pipeline to export the crude oil. This is indeed a basic change in the investment strategy, the justification of which is due to purely economic factors, for it will help Chevron to recover its operation costs within a shorter period, while Sudan will earn income in hard currency; though Sudan will still be importing refined petroleum products which are more expensive than crude oil. However, it is alleged, from an economic point of view, that Sudan will benefit in the long run more than from the construction of the Kosti refinery, by establishing itself in the world market.[5] Consequently, Article 3 of the Memorandum of Association has been amended to that effect, as follows:

(1) To carry on the business of constructors, layers, installers and operators of pipelines of all types and sizes.
(2) To carry on the business of transporters of all types of crude oil, natural gas and petroleum products and by-products, whether refined or otherwise.
(3) To carry on the business of building, erecting, installing, maintaining, and operating marine terminals, berths, harbours, quays, boosters and pump stations, for the transportation, storage and export of petroleum and petroleum products of all types.
(4) To carry on the business of exporters, importers and storers of petroleum and petroleum products.
(5) To carry on the business of petroleum refiners and processors and to build, erect, install and operate refineries of all types.

Under the Exportation Agreement between the Government of Sudan and the Chevron Oil Company of Sudan Inc., 1983, Chevron undertakes the responsibility of exporting the Sudanese crude oil in accordance with the terms and conditions of the Production-Sharing Agreement concluded between the Government and Chevron, 1979 (Amended). Under the Exportation Agreement, Chevron, as a contractor, shall transfer custody of the Government's and its own share of crude oil to the pipeline company at the inlet to the export pipeline system.

This joint venture indicates in very clear terms how important is the involvement of the international institutions in the investment process and pattern, for what is at stake is the financial packaging and a sound contractual arrangement for the management of the newly-created entity and the international marketing outlets (see *ante*, pp. 5–6). Despite the strength of the argument in favour of the refinery option, the legal complexity of the contractual arrangements is interlocking, and in the main reflects the basic features in the current patterns and policies of the oil industry.[6]

(c) The Kuwait–American Independent Oil Company (Aminoil) Arbitration Award[7]

This is a very important arbitration award concerning disputes between the State of Kuwait and Aminoil regarding the nationalization by Kuwait of the assets of the company, which was granted a petroleum concession, as early as 1948, for 60 years. Over the years the concession has been subjected to several amendments, with the consent of contracting parties, and these amendments came as a response to the changing policies and circumstances pertinent to the petroleum industry, and the global factors which had their impact on the relationship between the oil companies and the petroleum-producing countries, especially the O.P.E.C. members. The nationalization measure by Kuwait of the assets of Aminoil was accelerated by the failure of the protracted negotiatiions between the parties to resolve their disputes on several complex issues arising from adapting the concession to a new fiscal regime, which resulted from the adaptation and application of certain formulae relating to royalties and taxes imposed by the O.P.E.C.

The Arbitral Tribunal which rendered the final award in Paris was composed of three arbitrators.

The award is very lengthy and discussed important issues relevant to foreign investment generally and to oil agreements in particular. As the Arbitral Tribunal has made vital pronouncements and scholarly observations on the many complex issues raised by the parties during the litigation, I have selected certain issues as follows:

(1) *Applicable Law*

As mentioned before[8] the question of the applicable law to any development agreement lies at the core of the nature of the agreement, which eventually touches upon the obligations and rights of the parties. The Arbitral Tribunal in this case, adopting the techniques followed by other Arbitral Tribunals,[9] had examined the provisions of the agreement and the possibilities of applying different legal systems to it and came to the conclusion that as international law constitutes an integral part of the law of the State of Kuwait, and that the general principles of law correspondingly recognize the rights of the State in its capacity of supreme protector of the general interest, the two legal systems are applicable to the agreement, thus internationalizing the agreement. In fact the task of the Tribunal in determining the law applicable to the agreement was made easy, for the parties have themselves, in effect, indicated in the Arbitration Agreement what the applicable law should be. Article III(2) of the Agreement provides that: 'The law governing the substantive issues between the Parties shall be determined by the Tribunal, having regard to the quality of the Parties, the transnational character of their relations and the principles of law and practice prevailing in the modern world.' Thus, a later arbitration agreement, which is not part of the original concession agreement, was considered by the Tribunal together with other factors to determine the applicable law to the original agreement.

(ii) *Formalities for concluding the agreement*

As we mentioned before, in concluding development agreements certain domestic formalities have to be met, such as the procedural rules designating the officials of the State who may conclude State contracts (see *ante*, p. 237). I have discussed earlier, in chapter 10 (p. 237) the legal complexities emanating from applying the doctrine of *ultra vires* and lack of authority in this respect. The Tribunal was faced with the contention that a certain Agreement of 1973, which was supplemental to the original agreement between Kuwait and Aminoil, has no legal effect, as the legal formalities were not complied with; that it was signed only by the Minister of Finance and Oil but was not ratified by the Kuwaiti Parliament, as is required by Kuwait law. The Tribunal, in rejecting this contention, said:

> It is a matter entirely of Kuwait law whether that Minister had capacity so to act, and Aminoil has correctly accepted him as duly authorized, and the Government of Kuwait has always recognized that the Minister legally bound the State. Thus this Agreement (December 1973) was always valid *ab origine*, and the Tribunal only needs to point out that it is entirely normal and useful that, in transnational economic relations, the capacity of the Minister in charge of economic matters should be presumed, as is that of a Minister for Foreign Affairs in inter-state relationships.[10]

(iii) *Validity of nationalization and the stabilization clauses*

The validity of nationalization ordained by Decree Law No. 124 issued by Kuwait lies at the core of the arbitration. The Tribunal, in disposing of this issue, had to examine the various objections which were, mainly, that the decree effecting nationalization in the particular situation did not conform to certain general requirements for the validity of an act of nationalization and that it was contrary to some precise contractual undertakings applicable in the circumstances. The Tribunal did not find it difficult to reaffirm the requirements for nationalization under international law, and reached the conclusion that the progressive nationalization by the Government of Kuwait was valid, as it was pursuing a coherent policy of nationalization to realize a programme of economic development (see *ante*, pp. 97–9).

Having upheld the validity of the nationalization measure the Tribunal discussed the legal force of the stabilization clauses. In this respect the Tribunal had to deal with the contentions put forward by the Government of Kuwait against the validity of these clauses, the most interesting being that they were a relic of the colonial past and were imposed upon Kuwait at a time when Kuwait was still a British Protectorate, and not in possession of its full sovereign powers. On this basis the Government of Kuwait contended that the stabilization clauses were devoid of any value. The Tribunal rejected this contention on the grounds that the stabilization clauses were expressly confirmed in the revision of the concession after the attainment of complete independence by Kuwait, and again in 1973 when the text of the '1973 Agreement' was put into operation.

Another contention raised by the Government of Kuwait against the validity of stabilization clauses was that these clauses were annulled by the emergence of the Kuwait constitution of 1962, registering the permanent sovereignty of the State over natural resources, or of a public international rule of *jus cogens* forming part of the law of Kuwait. The Tribunal was able to reject this contention by finding that the constitutional provisions do not appear in any way to prevent the State from granting stabilization guarantees by contract.

On the public international law plane, the Tribunal seized the opportunity to decide on the effect of the concept of permanent sovereignty over natural resources and stabilization clauses. Indeed, it has been claimed by developing countries that permanent sovereignty over natural resources has become an imperative rule of *jus cogens* prohibiting States from affording, by contract or treaty, guarantees of any kind against the exercise of the public authority in regard to all matters relating to natural richness (see *ante*, pp. 129–40). Unfortunately, the Tribunal rejected this contention *in toto* from the outset as having no foundation. As was the case in the Libya-Oil Companies Award (see *ante*, p. 256), the Tribunal embarked for a while on an examination of the legal effect of the United Nations General Assembly resolutions on permanent sovereignty over natural resources and the New International Economic Order and reached the conclusion that, even if some of the provisions of these resolutions 'can be regarded as codifying rules that reflect international practice', it would not be possible from this to deduce the existence of a rule of international law prohibiting a State from undertaking not to proceed with a nationalization during a limited period; no rule of public international law prevents it from doing so, and in this case nationalization was not expressly provided against by the stabilization clauses.

On the other side of the spectrum, the Tribunal rightly rejected the contention of the Government of Kuwait that the concession falls within the category of administrative contracts (see *ante*, pp. 251–2) which entitles the Government to modify unilaterally the terms and conditions of the concession without the consent of the concessionaire. The Tribunal recognized that the contract of concession has undergone great changes since 1945: changes which were conceded by the company. These changes have not been the consequence of accidental or special factors but rather of a profound and general transformation in the terms of oil concessions that occurred in the Middle East, and later throughout the world. These changes took place progressively, with increasing acceleration, from 1973.

After surveying all the relevant factors and developments that took place in the oil industry in the wake of O.P.E.C. policies and measures, the Tribunal came to the correct conclusion, that stabilization clauses will not prevent nationalization, provided that the nationalization is not of a confiscatory character. To hold otherwise would indeed deny the existence of deriving forces of change in the contractual regime which must always adjust the financial equilibrium of the parties and ignore the role of the State, not only as a regulator of economic activities, but also as a guardian of the welfare of the communities. Hence the Tribunal wisely ruled that the concession had become a contract under the changed regime by which the State had, over the years, acquired a special position that included the right to terminate it if such a step became necessary for the protection of the public interest, and subject to the payment of adequate compensation.[12]

(iv) *Indemnification*

This is the most important issue discussed by the Tribunal. As I indicated earlier (see *ante*, p. 194) international law had not set specific rules on the methodology of calculating the exact compensation for nationalization. Unlike the Libya–Oil Companies Award (see *ante*, p. 272) the Tribunal recognized from the outset the technical difficulties in determining the indemnification, and that *restitutio in integrum* is not a practicable relief in cases of nationalizations. By tracing the history of nationalization, and taking into account the general formulation of the United Nations General Assembly resolution No. 1903 (XVIII) of December, 1962 on permanent sovereignty over Natural Resources, the Tribunal was able to restate the general rules applicable to a lawful nationalization, which require the payment of 'appropriate compensation'. In determining the standard of compensation, the Tribunal ruled that precedents of compensation agreements do not establish valid customary rules to determine compensation on the ground of the 'net book value' of the redeemable assets, as these agreements are *sui generis* (see *ante*, pp. 220–30). Instead, the Tribunal considered all pertinent international economic factors such as international recession, inflation, the special circumstances of the case, the need to encourage foreign investment and the need to meet the legitimate expectation of the parties. For in the end the Tribunal had to secure a fundamental equilibrium between the interests of the parties.

Before embarking on any method of evaluation of compensation the Tribunal had to examine the choices of methods offered by the parties to the dispute. Such methods, like anticipated profits, book value and replacement costs, have already been discussed (see *ante*, pp. 204–5). In rejecting all these methods of evaluation the Tribunal was guided by the conduct of the parties in adopting the conception of a reasonable rate of return in their relations and negotiations.

In determining the reasonable return, the Tribunal noted that, over the years, Aminoil had accepted the principle of a moderate estimate of profits which in effect constituted its legitimate expectation.[12] After describing the notion of reasonable rate of return in the tax of Aminoil, the Tribunal skilfully indicated the principles applicable for determining the compensation due in respect of the company's assets, thus assessing the value of the undertaking itself as a source of profits, plus the totality of the assets, and adding together the results obtained.

Throughout this process the Tribunal recognized the difficulty of deciding on a single method for valuing the physical assets, as it is not possible to postulate any absolute rule. Eventually, the Tribunal succeeded in achieving this by considering the value of the assets as at the date of transfer, taking into consideration a depreciation allowance for wear and tear and obsolescence. The Tribunal observed that generally only values for proper accounting or taxation purposes can be utilized.

The novelty of this arbitral award lies in the fact that the Tribunal, in fixing the compensation to be paid to the company, had taken account of the progress of inflation generally, and in particular with reference to the price of refined petroleum products on the American market. To state general principles for preservation of the value of money in relation to the assets of the company, the Tribunal considered also the relevance of the politics of petroleum prices and the adjustment of oil revenues, as determined by the Gulf States by reference to a 'basket of Currencies'.

Given all these observations, the Tribunal proceeded to calculate the amount of indemnification due to the company from the Government of Kuwait. In carrying out this difficult task, the Tribunal availed itself of the numerous elements furnished by the parties and the joint report of the experts they had commissioned for that purpose. Where there are differences between the accounting firms which made the joint report, the Tribunal took the mean of the two totals indicated. Then after considering all statements analysed, the balance-sheet of the financial rights and obligations of the parties, their respective debts and credits, and other related factors the Tribunal was able to make a balanced appraisal of all circumstances, a technique which has allowed it to reach the exact figures of compensation.

It appears that this arbitral award is unique. Apart from one decision by the International Court of Justice,[13] the Tribunal relied very little on judicial and arbitral precedents and other authorities. This may be attributed to the fact that the arbitrators themselves, being of recent academic qualification and experience, seem to have disapproved of the existing rules and to have seized the opportunity to start afresh in devising new rules on the issues they tackled; for the changing relations between foreign investors and investee States required new norms to suit the unfolding global events, as the old rules were tailored for circumstances which are now non-existent.

(d) New approach

As I have shown, the investment patterns and climate are a reflection of economic and political waves that call for change. Now, with many of the world's economic activities computerized, and with the spread of new modes of technological advance which have led to the evolution of new attitudes and modalities, the legal rules are not static, and do not exist in a vacuum in isolation of economic and international political realities.

Given the diversity of investment in fields unrecognized in the nineteenth century, when the international arena was dominated in every respect by the colonial powers, the traditional international rules on foreign investment have become outdated and unsuitable to an environment which calls for the creating of an international economic order to accommodate a new investment process, ranging from inventing other alternatives of economic inputs to a new life-style mastered by silicon chips, biotechnology and genetic engineering. This violent change calls for all the previous data on international rules on foreign investment to be disregarded, and for a fresh start to be made with full agreement from both the developed and developing countries on the basic international norms in the interest of all. For the concept of justice itself on an international level presupposes willing co-operation and understanding by all the parties concerned.

NOTES

1. Foreign investment in politico-economic perspective

1 Alan B. Mountjoy, *Industrialization and Development*, 4th edn. (1975), p. 85; B. O. Nwabueze, *Presidentialism in Commonwealth Africa* (1974), ch. 12. It is worth mentioning that, before 1970, British investments constituted about 74.9% of the total foreign investment in the Sudan: *Multinational Corporations in World Development*, U.N. Doc. ST/ECA/190 (1973), p. 182.

2 E. I. Nwogugu, *The Legal Problems of Foreign Investment in Developing Countries* (1965), p. 4; H. G. Johnson, 'The Efficiency and Welfare Implications of the International Corporations', in John H. Dunning (ed.), *International Investment* (1972), p. 468.

3 Arthur Lewis, *The Theory of Economic Growth* (1955), p. 142.

4 Resolution 626 (VII) of 21 December 1952, *United Nations Yearbook* (1952).

5 United Nations Document A/C 3/L 489; *United Nations Yearbook* (1955), pp. 154–6. See also *the Universal Declaration of Human Rights* (1948): I. Brownlie, *Basic Documents in International Law* 2nd edn. (1972), p. 144.

6 Resolution 1803 (XVII) of December 1962. On the interpretation and legal implications see G. Schwarzenberger, *Economic World Order* (1970), p. 42; S. K. Banerjee, 'The Concept of Permanent Sovereignty over Natural Resources: An Analysis', 8 *Indian J.I.L.* (1968), 515–46; J. N. Hyde, 'Permanent Sovereignty over National Wealth and Resources', 50 *A.J.I.L.* (1956), 854.

7 G.A. Res. 3210 (S-VI) of 1 May 1974, reproduced in 13 *I.L.M.* (1974), 715 and 68 *A.J.I.L.* (1974), 799.

8 G.A. Res. 3281 (XXIX) of 12 December 1974, reproduced in 14 *I.L.M.* (1975), 716 and 68 *A.J.I.L.* (1974), 799. For further discussion see *post*, pp. 128–40. In agreement see Oppenheim, *International Law*, vol. 1, 8th edn. (1955); G. H. Hackworth, *Digest of International Law* (1941), vol. 11, 618; J. B. Moore, *Digest of International Law*, vol. 4 (1906), p. 13; B. Sen, *A Diplomat's Handbook of International Law*, vol. 11, 2nd edn. (1970), p. 698; A. A. Fatouros, *Government Guarantees to Foreign Investors* (1962), pp. 141–53; The Treaty Establishing the European Common Market, 1957, Article 48, 298 U.N.T.S., No. 1, 11; The Treaty Establishing the Benelux Economic Union, 1958, Article 2, 381 U.N.T.S., 165, No. 1, 5471; Treaty of Friendship, Commerce and Navigation (F.C.N.) between United States and Japan, 1953, Article 8, U.N.T.S. No. 1, 376; Treaty of F.C.N. between United States and Germany, 1954, Articles 3 and 8, 273 U.N.T.S., No. 1, 3943; the Final Report and Commentaries of the Arab Experts of Supply (unpublished), submitted to the Third Conference of the Arab Experts of Supply, April 1967 (Kuwait); and the Convention on Investment of Arab Capital and its Transfer among the Arab States, 1970, Article 3. The Convention has been signed by the countries which are members of the Council of Arab Economic Unity, which does not include Saudi Arabia.

9 *The Impact of Multinational Corporations on Development and on International Relations*, report by the Group of Eminent Persons studying the role of multinational corporations on development and international relations; U.N. Doc. E/5500/Rev./ST/ESA/16 (1974). The report has been prepared in response to Economic and Social Council Resolution 1721 (IV). On the multinational corporations in black Africa, see Leslie L. Rood, 'Foreign Investment in African Manufacturing', *J.M.A.S.*, 13, 1 (1975), 19–34.

10 I.C.C. Soc. Res. 1913, 57 E.C.O.S.O.C. Suppl. (No. 1A) 31 U.N. Doc. E/5570/Add. 1 (1975).

11 The Commission, at its fourth session, held from 20 to 31 March 1978, began discussion of a working paper prepared by its subsidiary organ, the Centre on Transnational Corporations, containing tentative formulations and common elements on sections of an annotated outline of a code of conduct for transnationals; see *U.N. Chronicle* January to December, 1975, vol. 7, pp. 31–2, 9 April 1978, 59. The idea of formulating a code of conduct to regulate the activities of multinational corporations is gaining momentum not only in the United Nations fora, but also in other organizations, such as O.E.C.D., I.C.C. and E.C.C. For more details, see *post*, pp. 134–9. See also, Sir David Orr, 'The Contribution of Multinational Business to Development', 6 *The Magazine of the Cambridge University Industrial Society* (1980), 9.

12 See the Report of the International Commission on International Development Issues, under the chairmanship of Willy Brandt: *North–South: a Programme for Survival* (1979), published by Pan Books Ltd.

13 Osman Abdalla El Nazir, 'Role of Private Enterprise in the Less Developed Countries', *Sudan Economic and Financial Survey* (Special issue No. 3) (1964), pp. 86–93. Also, the agreed part of the *Report of the United Nations on International Economic Co-operation states:* 'The countries participating in the conference recognize that foreign private capital flows and investments play an important complementary role in the developing economic process.' U.N. Doc. Dist. General, A/31/478/Add.1, 9 August 1977; Annex to Note by the Secretary-General, p. 23. It is noteworthy that the participating countries in the conference were only twenty-seven countries, out of which nineteen were developing countries, which did not include the Sudan and Saudi Arabia.

The industrialized countries, notably the United Kingdom under the Conservatives, have denounced the Brandt Report, arguing against increasing aid to the developing countries, on the plea that such aid is often wasted or misdirected. This is perhaps another factor impelling the developing countries to attract the inflow of private foreign investment which is subject to the severe discipline of the profit and loss account and measurement of return in capital employed: *The Times*, 12 September 1980; David Orr, 6 *The Magazine of the Cambridge University Industrial Society* (1980).

14 Kwame Nkrumah, *Neo-Colonialism: The Last Stage of Imperialism* (1965), p. x. See also the Report of the U.N. Independent Commission on International Development Issues: *North–South*. See also the U.N.C.T.A.D. rounds.

15 Mountjoy, *Industrialization*, p. 86.

16 Some developing countries and especially the non-oil primary-commodity-producing countries have claimed several times greater control over their own resources, and foreign exchange earnings therefrom. This trend has been particularly observed with respect to bauxite, copper and iron-ore. Thus, countries producing bauxite, like Jamaica and Guyana, have been eager in seeking additional payments or ownership, because aluminium prices shot very high in 1974. After eight-fold taxes paid by aluminium companies, Jamaica nationalized 51% of Kariser Aluminium's Jamaican mining assets as

well as the company's entire assets. Similar measures of raising taxes were taken by the Guyana government. Zambia made an arrangement designed to terminate existing managerial consultancy and marketing contracts concluded between the Anglo-American corporations and Zambia Copper Investments for the local Nchanga Consolidated Copper Mines in order to make these mines self-managing: *Development Co-operation, Efforts and Policies*, O.E.C.D., 1975 *Review*, p. 157; see also Tigani E. Tayeb, *Developing Countries and the Tokyo Round*, Development Studies and Research Centre, Faculty of Economic and Social Studies, University of Khartoum (1979).

17 D.A.C., O.E.C.D., 1974 *Review*, p. 145. For an analytical discussion of the new sophisticated forms of legal arrangements by some developing countries with transnational corporations see, 'Transnational Investment Law and National Development', a lecture delivered by Dr Asante in December 1978 at the University of Lagos, Nigeria (unpublished); a copy was given to the writer by the author. On the advantages and disadvantages of joint ventures, see Roy Blough, 'Joint International Business ventures in Less Developed Countries', *Proceedings of the 1960 Institute of Private Investments Abroad* (1960), p. 513, also, generally, W. Friedmann and J. P. Beguin, *Joint International Business Ventures in Developing Countries* (1971), pp. 1–77, 364–419.

18 It has been reported that a massive 'consortium' consisting of British Petroleum, Shell and some French and American companies, has concluded production-sharing agreements with Abu Dhabi, Qatar, Kuwait and Saudi Arabia. Libya also followed suit by concluding similar agreements with some American companies: J. Fawcett, *International Economic Conflicts* (1977), pp. 66–7, see also D.A.C., O.E.C.D., 1974 *Review*, p. 145.

19 For a descriptive account of these alternative methods of investment see Nasrollah S. Fatemi and others, *Multinational Corporations*, 2nd edn., (1976), pp. 241–58.

20 Development Co-operation, O.E.C.D., 1975 *Review*, p. 154.

21 Ibid.

22 Ibid.

23 Ibid.

24 Ibid. The Rahad Agricultural Project of the Sudan is of this type. It combines the funds from the World Bank and Kuwait, the technology and expertise of the British company of MacDonald, and Sudanese manpower, fertile land and water supply.

25 Development Co-operation, O.E.C.D., 1975 *Review*, p. 154.

26 Examples are: O.E.C.D.; the Arab League; Organization of American States (O.A.S.).

27 Such as the International Chamber of Commerce (I.C.C.).

28 575 U.N.T.S., 154. For further discussion, see *post*, pp. 307–16.

29 For instance, the Convention on Investment of the Arab Capital and its Transfer among the Arab States (1971), which has been ratified by the Sudan. For the text, see *S.D.R.S.G.*, No. 1119 dated 15 July 1971, p. 704 (text in Arabic only). Saudi Arabia is not a party to this convention, which is applicable only to the Arab States which are members of the Council of the Arab Economic Unity which comprises Jordan, Sudan, Iraq, Syria, Egypt, Yemen Arab Republic and Kuwait.

30 For instance, the United Nations Development Programme: I.L.O., *Growth, Employment and Equity, a Comprehensive Strategy for the Sudan*, a report of I.L.O./U.N.D.P. Employment Mission, 1975. Saudi Arabia relies on the advice of the World Bank before embarking on large-scale petrochemical and steel industries: James M. Bedore and Louis Turner, *Middle East Industrialization* (1979), p. 23. The U.N.I.D.O. has recently established the Investment Co-operative Programme Office as a department to make feasibility studies on certain industrial investment projects in developing countries. The activity of

this new office also includes convening meetings between potential investors and governments with a view to attracting investors to developing countries and recommending certain investment projects to them. This 'U.N.I.D.O. valuable' service also extends to rendering advice on industrial investments to developing countries. It is interesting to note that at the time of writing the writer was informed by the Head of the U.N.I.D.O. Investment Co-operative Programme Office that they are planning to convene a meeting in Khartoum in November 1980 between the Sudanese Government and foreign investors: interview by the writer with the Head of the Investment Co-operative Programme Office, U.N.I.D.O., Vienna, 26 August 1980. See also U.N.I.D.O., *Industrial Investment Project Proposals*, June 1979.

31 An example of the direct involvement of international organization in financing and sharing in investment projects is the Agricultural Seleit Project (Khartoum), where the I.F.C. has taken a stake in that project jointly with the Sudan Development Corporation, some Sudanese businessmen and a British company. See also *ante*, pp. 000–00.

32 Examples of development banks include, *inter alia*, the Arab Bank for Economic Development in Africa (Khartoum); the Islamic Development Bank (Jeddah); the African Development Bank. On the other hand, the examples of the financing institutions are: the Gulf International Bank (Bahrain); the Arab European International Trading Co. (Kuwait); U.B.A.F. Bank Limited (London) and the Petroleum Investment Corporation (Saudi Arabia).

For an able exposition of the role of international organizations in investment, see Nwogugu, *Legal Problems*, ch. 7.

33 In United Nations' parlance, the Sudan is identified as one of the twenty-five least developed countries in the world. The *per capita* income, as of 1975, was only $130: U.N.I.D.O., *Industrial Development Survey*, U.N. Doc. ID/CONF. 3/3 (ID/134), 1975. For an economic review of the Sudan, see Francis A. Lees and Hugh C. Brooks, *The Economic and Political Development of the Sudan* (1977), ch. 3.

34 Peter K. Bechtold, *Politics in the Sudan. Parliamentary and Military Rule in an Emerging African Nation* (1976), pp. 211–13.

35 Cecil Epvile, *War and Peace in The Sudan 1955–1972* (1974), p. 123. These measures are discussed in chapter 6.

36 *Focus on the Sudan*, a *Progress International Publication* (October 1975), p. 7, published by London International Press Centre.

37 For a detailed discussion on the State as a regulator and entrepreneur, see W. G. Friedmann, *The State and the Law in a Mixed Economy* (1971), chapters 2 and 3.

38 See chapter 11 on economic fundamentals of the Permanent Constitution of the Democratic Republic of the Sudan, 1973, Attorney-General's Chambers, *D.R.S.G.*, issued on 8 May 1973, p. 7.

39 Article 32.

40 Ibid.

41 Ibid.

42 Ibid.

43 These are: the Development and Promotion of Industrial Investment Act 1974, the Encouragement of Investment in Economic Services Act (as amended), 1975; the Agricultural Investment Act 1976 and the Encouragement of Investment Act, 1980. Full discussion of these acts will be made in the following chapters.

44 For instance, the Sudan Development Corporation, which was established on 23 March 1974; the Sudanese Investment Bank, which was formed in July 1976 and the Petroleum

Public Corporation, established in 1975 by the Petroleum Public Corporation Act 1975, *L.S.D.R.S.G.* No. 915, 15 January 1976, p. 259.

45 This policy has been repeated on several occasions, the most recent being the speech of the President to the Union of Sudanese Farmers on the seventh anniversary of the May Revolution, May 1979 in Khartoum; *Economic Survey 1976/1977*, Research Studies of Economic Policy Administration, Ministry of Finance and National Economy, Khartoum, pp. 260–3.

46 As from 1979, some sixteen Arab companies have registered in the Sudan with a combined nominal capital of £S 138 million. The largest group of them is in the field of general investment, mainly in transportation, warehouses and commerce. The second largest group is in agriculture. Other areas where there is considerable Arab investment is in construction and real estate (the Sudanese–Kuwaiti Building and Construction Company). In industry we find the Arab Company for Cement and Gulf International of Kuwait.

It is interesting to note that almost all the companies with Arab capital are in the form of joint ventures with the government, public corporations and/or private companies. One scholar rightly pointed out that this pattern of ownership was due to the fact that Arab investors are rather cautious and want to involve the locals to minimize the risk. He cited the example of the Emirates Conglomerate, which formed a total of six separate joint venture companies with the Sudan Government and three provinces in the country: Dr Ahmed A. Ahmed 'Foreign Investment in the Sudan: A Survey', a paper prepared for the training course on Regulating and Negotiating with Transnational Corporations, run by the United Nations Centre on Transnational Corporations, the Development Studies and Research Centre, and the Government of Sudan, February–March 1980, pp. 3–4.

47 Sudan is called today the 'bread basket' of the Arab world. This is because the Sudan has enormous tracts of potentially good soil. It has 80% of the cultivatable land held by all the Arab League nations and only 10% of this land is now being farmed. An area of 200 million feddans is believed to be arable, but barely 17 million feddans are at present under the plough. At the Food Conference in 1974 in Rome, Sudan was counted as one of three countries to solve the world food crisis in the future: *Focus on the Sudan*, pp. 9, 10; *El Sahafa*, 26 January 1976, issue no. 5037, p. 1; *Sudan Survey* 1975, January Survey, prepared by *African Development*, pp. 9, 11, 12, 13, 15. The Arab planners have worked out that by 1985 Sudan could supply the Arab world with 42% of vegetable oil imports; 20% of sugar imports; 15% of wheat requirements and 58% of requirements for foodstuffs: *The Guardian*, Tuesday, 24 August 1976, p. 3. In fact, Sudan as a Moslem nation and a member of the Arab League is better placed to lay claim to spare petro-dollars than any other Arab or African nation.

The plan of the Arab Fund has been included in the Six-Year Socio-Economic Development Plan 1977/78 to 1982/83, prepared by the National Planning Commission. The plan was approved by the Central Committee of the Sudanese Socialist Union: *The Times*, Sudan, a Special Report, Saturday, 26 February 1977; also ibid. Tuesday 10 January 1978; *New Africa*, Sudan Special Survey, January 1978, pp. 39–78; *The Economist*, Sudan Review, 3 *et seq.*, 18 March 1978; *Financial Times*, 13 July 1978, Special Report; see chapter 5 of The Six-Year Plan for Economic and Social Development 1977/78 to 1982/83, vol. 1, Ministry of National Economy (Khartoum), April 1977. For projected investments, see tables 1 and 2 below. It is interesting to note that the main branches of industries in the Sudan, at present, are cotton ginning, flour milling, sugar refining, brewing, the manufacture of soft drinks, clothing, footwear, cigarettes, soap, furniture, metal products, cement, glass and chemicals: *Quarterly Economic Review of Sudan*, Annual Supplement, (1980), The Economist Intelligence Unit Ltd, p. 13.

48 Ibid., p. 16.

49 Some American companies have responded to the President's invitation. Thus Tenneco entered into a joint venture with the Sudanese Sahara Engineering Co. of Khartoum, to invest in the agricultural sector. The joint venture has embarked upon establishing a farm in the Altad plain along the west bank of the Nile River. About 23,000 acres are put at the disposal of the company. For more details, see Scott Pendleton, 'Altruism in Sudan', *Saudi Business*, 28 September 1979.

50 Between 1973 and 1979 some sixty-five foreign companies were registered in the Sudan. This figure does not include those from the Organization for Arab Petroleum Exporting Countries (O.A.P.E.C.). The largest group among these companies, '19', operates in the field of construction and installation, e.g. buildings, roads, bridges, etc. The second largest group, '16', is in the service area, e.g. technical consultation, communications, airlines and banking. Manufacturing, industry and agriculture are poorly represented among the sixty-five companies.

Regarding the national origin of the the sixty-five companies registered in the Sudan till the middle of 1976, the largest number were American (nineteen companies), and Italian (eleven companies), with French companies ranking third in number and British, fourth. These formed thirty-eight of the sixty-five. The rest were mostly of different European origin, e.g. Belgian and Swiss. See *A Directory to Private and Foreign Direct Investment in the Sudan*, a memorandum prepared by the Prime Minister's office, Khartoum, 1979. See also Dr Ahmed A. Ahmed, 'Foreign Investment', p. 2.

51 *Newsweek Magazine*, 22 December 1975, p. 8; *El Sahafa*, 15 March 1976.

52 For instance, the Sudan Development Corporation.

53 Examples include:

(a) *The Sudanese–Kuwaiti Company for Investment Ltd*, a holding company owning five subsidiaries formed jointly by the Sudan Government, Kuwait and some Kuwaiti businessmen. Remarkably in this case another State is involved in the venture.

(b) *The Kenana Sugar Company Ltd*, established in 1975 with an initial capital of £S 10 million which was later raised to £S 80 million. This was distributed into 40,000,000 shares. The Sudan Government at the beginning, held 50% of the shares. The other subscribers were Kuwait with 6,200,000 shares; the Lonrho Company (English), with 2,200,000 shares; the Gulf International Company, with 900,000 shares; and Nicho, a Japanese company, with 900,000 shares. At the time of writing, it has been resolved by the shareholders to raise the capital from £S 80 million to £S 330 million. This will happen partly through the issuing of any remaining shares to new shareholders, including the Arab Authority for Agricultural Investment and Development (A.A.A.I.D.) and a consortium of Sudanese banks, and partly through the conversion of £S 82 million worth of existing loans into convertible 8% shares. However, under the new capital structure, the main shareholders are, and will continue to be, the governments of Sudan (33.47%), Kuwait (19.25%) and Saudi Arabia (18.96%). The other shareholdings bring in the Arab World in general, through the Arab Investment Company (with 14.22%) and the A.A.A.I.D.: see *The Middle East*, August 1980, no. 70, p. 60. It is needless to imagine the complexity involved in such a multinational institution, which not only comprises the Sudan and foreign investors (multinationals), but also two other States. For a detailed account of the activities of Lonrho, in Africa generally, and the Sudan in particular, see S. Gronje, M. Ling and G. Gronje, *Lonrho, Portrait of a Multinational* (1976).

(c) *The Damazein Agricultural and Animal Production Company*, with a capital of £S 3 million subscribed by investors from Saudi Arabia, a number of Sudanese businessmen, and the People's Council of Blue Nile Province: *Economic Survey*.

54 In the deliberations of the Conference of the British Labour Party on 6 October 1978 it was asserted by Mr Anthony Wedgwood Benn, then Secretary of State for Energy, that a 51% holding of the Government in the British National Oil Corporation is not satisfactory and does not represent effective public control over the activity of the Corporation. He emphasized that the arrangement should be revised so as to increase the share of the British Government in the holding of the Corporation: *The Times*, Friday, 6 October 1978.

55 *New Africa*, Sudan Special, January 1978, pp. 71–3; *The Economist*, 18 March 1978; *Review*, pp. 9–15; Bechtold, *Politics*, p. 272.

56 *The Times*, 13 April 1978; *The Guardian*, 13 April 1978.

57 There were to be five petrochemical complexes, each of which would produce 500,000 tons of ethylene a year. There would also be three export refineries; two one-million-tons-a-year fertilizer plants; one 210,000-tons-a-year aluminium plant, and one 3.5 million-tons-a-year steel plant: *The Guardian*, 22 October 1976, p. 18; Turner and Bedore, *Middle East Industrialization*, pp. 7–8; *Quarterly Economic Review of Saudi Arabia*, 3rd quarter, 1980, the Economic Intelligence Unit Ltd, p. 11.

58 *The Middle East*, June 1980, No. 68, p. 62.

59 *A Guide to Industrial Investment in Saudi Arabia*, 5th edn (1977), published by the Industrial Studies and Development Centre, Kingdom of Saudi Arabia, p. 47.

60 Formed under the Encouragement of Foreign Capital Investment Act 1979, which was passed in order to improve the regulation of foreign investment in the industrial sector. For the text of the Act, see Appendix 2.

61 Bedore and Turner, *Middle East Industrialization*, pp. 9–10.

62 For a survey of foreign companies making joint ventures with Petromin and S.A.B.I.C., see *Financial Times*, Monday, 26 March 1979. In the construction sector it is noteworthy that western construction companies are getting cold feet in Saudi Arabia, and leaving the work to the South Koreans, who have picked up almost all the basic construction contracts that have not gone to local companies: *Quarterly Economic Review*, p. 16.

2. Prerequisites for the admission of investments

1 This is the situation in the case of foreign private investment. In the case of foreign public investment, the problem is not so complicated, because the investment transaction involves only two parties, namely the capital-importing and capital-exporting countries or institutions thereof. As mentioned before, this book deals only with the legal aspects of foreign *private* investment.

2 See The Sudanese Nationality Act, 1957, extract from *S.L.S.D.R.S.G.* No. 910, dated 25 July 1957. Under this act, a person can acquire Sudanese nationality by descent, naturalization, marriage or otherwise, if he satisfies the conditions prescribed by sections 5, 6, 7, 8 and 9 respectively. For a detailed discussion on the acquisition of Sudanese nationality, see 'Development of Nationality Laws in the Sudan', a thesis submitted by the present writer, for part-fulfilment of requirements for the degree of Master of Laws (LL.M.) in the University of Khartoum, Sudan, in May 1975. The details of the procedure for the acquisition of Sudanese nationality are spelled out in The Sudanese Nationality Regulations, 1957, *S.L.S.D.R.S.G.* No. 911, dated 15 August 1957, p. 127. As regards acquisition of Saudi nationality, see the Acquisition of Saudi Nationality Law.

3 *P.C.I.J.* Series B, No. 4, 1923, p. 24, also the *Nottebohm* case, *I.C.J. Reports* (1955), p. 4.

4 C. Parry, *Nationality and Citizenship Laws of the Commonwealth and Ireland* (1957), vol. 1, p. 4; Oppenheim, *International Law*, vol. 1, p. 643; M. S. MacDougal, 'Nationality and Human Rights', 83 *Y.L.J.*, no. 5 (April 1974), 981.

5 For the text, *L.S.D.R.S.G.* no. 983 dated 1 June 1963, p. 77; Article 8.

6 For text, see *Investment Laws of the World*, vol. 4; as regards German treaties with other countries, e.g. Ceylon (Sri Lanka), Zambia, ibid. vol. 6.

7 *L.S.D.R.S.G.* no. 1164 dated 15 August 1974, p. 26. Cf. the Egyptian–Swiss Agreement which contains an identical provision: text, *Investment Laws of the World*, vol. 1, p. 69.

8 575 U.N.T.S., 159; the convention has been ratified by the Sudan by the Convention on the Settlement of Investment Disputes between States and Nationals of Other States (Ratification) Act, 1974, *L.S.D.R.S.G.* no. 1139 dated 15 December 1974, p. 281. For a critical examination of the convention see ch. 10 below. The convention was also ratified by the Kingdom of Saudi Arabia by a Royal Decree.

9 Article 25(2)(a). See C. F. Amerasinghe, 'Jurisdiction *Ratione Personae* Under the Convention on the Settlement of Investment Disputes between States and Nationals of Other States', 47 *B.Y.B.I.L.* (1977), pp. 227–67.

10 Section 1(d); D. P. O'Connell, *International Law*, 2nd edn. (1970), vol. 2, p. 1041.

11 *Investment Laws of the World*, vol. 3. Cf. Articles 2(2) and (3) of the Investment Code of Islamic Republic of Mauritania, no. 71–028 (1971), *Investment Laws of the World*, vol. 3.

12 *P.C.I.J. Reports*, series A, no. 1.

13 This test was applied by the British and American courts to determine the enemy character of companies. For this purpose, it was sufficient that financial interest of the German State yielded potential control over a company's operation. But the question of 'enemy character' is somewhat distinct and irrelevant to this study: see O'Connell, *International Law*, p. 1042; *Daimler Co.* v. *Continental Tyre and Rubber Co.* [1916] A.C. 307; F. A. Mann, 'The Confiscation of Corporations', 11 *I.C.L.Q.* (1962), 471; *idem, Studies in International Law* (1973), pp. 565–8; M. Domke, 'The Control of Corporations', 3 *I.C.L.Q.* (1950), 52.

14 O'Connell, *International Law*, p. 1042; the *I'm Alone* case, *U.N.A.A.R.*, vol. 3, p. 1609 at p. 1617.

15 *I.C.J. Reports* (1952), at p. 102; Davies Harris, 'The Protection of Corporations in International Law in the Light of the Barcelona Case', 18 *I.C.L.Q.* (1969), 275.

16 Ibid.; also Mann, *Studies*, pp. 565–8.

17 *I.C.J. Reports* (1970), p. 3.

18 Ibid. Section 57 of the Sudan Civil Code, 1971, *L.S.D.R.S.G.* No. 1118 dated 15 June 1971 (issued in Arabic only) (repealed), provided: 'A juristic person shall enjoy, within the limits prescribed by the law, all rights, except those that are peculiar to a natural person, and shall have a "deputy" acting for it, and shall also have:

(a) an independent financial existence
(b) such capacity as its memorandum of association may prescribe
(c) an independent nationality
(d) an independent domicile and its domicile shall be the place where its administrative office is situated. A juristic person whose seat of management is situate abroad, whereas it is carrying on business within the Sudan, shall, for the purpose of the laws of the Sudan, be considered as having its seat of management at the place where its local seat of management is situate.'

This is an ambiguous provision. Though it did indicate how the domicile of the juristic person could be ascertained, yet it omitted to do the same in the case of nationality. For criticism of this provision and the whole code, see Zaki Mustafa, 'Opting Out of the Common Law', 17 *J.A.L.* (1973), 133–47. As the Code originated in the civil system it could be presumed that the '*siège sociale*' test would have been intended to determine the nationality of a corporation under the Code.

19 Enacted by Royal Decree no. 38, dated 22 Shawal 1377 A.H. Translated from Arabic into English by Nicola H. Karam.

20 Promulgated by Royal Decree no. M/4 of 2.2.1399 A.H. See Appendix 2.

21 R. B. Lillich, *International Claims: Their Adjudication by National Commissions* (1962), p. 89; also U.S.–Bulgarian Claims Agreement, 1963, 58 *A.J.I.L.* (1964), 686.

22 R. R. Wilson, *U.S. Commercial Treaties and International Law*, (1960), ch. 7; also H. Walker, 'Provisions on Companies', 50 *A.J.I.L.* (1956), 373.

23 Article 1(2); cf. Article 12(a)(ii) of the Netherlands–Indonesia Treaty, 1963, *Teil*, p. 992; Article 1(a) of the Iraqi–Kuwait Treaty, 1964, 5 *I.L.M.* (1965), 1140.

24 For discussion on the relation between treaties and statutes before the Sudanese courts, see *post*, pp. 143–7.

25 For instance, the German–Pakistan Treaty.

26 For text, 11 *I.L.M.* (1972), 126–46. This convention is sometimes referred to as the Andean Foreign Investment Code; cf. the Convention on Investments of the Central African Economic and Customs Union (A.E.C.U.), which came into force on 1 January 1966, 7 *I.L.M.* (1968), 221–32.

27 Article 1. As Saudi Arabia has not made bilateral investment treaties with other countries, the discussion here centres on the Sudan only.

28 The text of the convention was reprinted from *The Courier* no. 31, special issue, March, 1975, European Community–Africa-Caribbean-Pacific. The Sudan is a signatory of the Convention and ratified it by the Lomé Convention (Ratification) Act, 1976, *D.R.S.G.* no. 919, dated 15 January 1976, p. 31. The Convention has been renewed for another term of five years.

29 For text see 9 *J.P.L.* (1960), 116–32.

30 Cf. (a), p. 164.

31 Published in the *Sudan Trade and Investment Guide*, 1960–61, p. 72.

32 Ibid. This same act has been repealed by the Development and Encouragement of Industrial Investment Act, 1974.

33 Section 3(1).

34 *Sudan Trade and Investment Guide.*

35 'Establishment' is defined by the same section as meaning 'every existing industrial establishment or one under construction or proposed to be set up to work in a project, the main purpose of which is the production of a commodity for immediate public consumption or the production of a material whether investment, intermediary or otherwise...' Reference is also made by the same section to the word 'craft' which is defined as 'any industrial work carried out by any person or persons which work basically depends upon various primary or intermediary materials and in which some simple equipment, tools and machinery are used or manual production used for production of final intermediary commodities liable for direct circulation or consumption or any other industrial work decided by the Minister of Industry and Mining'.

36 Section 4 continues.

37 *L.S.D.R.S.G.* no. 1146 dated 15 May 1973 (amended up to 22 November 1975).

38 Section 3; for the text, *L.S.D.R.S.G.* no. 1196 dated 15 July 1976 (Law no. 19, 1976). The majority of municipal investment laws of other developing countries follow the same pattern whereby the definition of the term 'investment' is expressed under the heading of 'capital' or 'asset'. Thus, e.g. the Investment Law of Bolivia contains the following definition: 'investment means capital destined to increase the productive capacity of the country': Law No. 10045, 10 December 1971, section 7, 11 *I.L.M.* (1972), 357.

39 *Manual of Exchange Control Regulations* (revised) 1977, ch. 3, section A, published by the Bank of Sudan.

40 The amount allowed to be transferred abroad by every foreigner who did not bring to the Sudan foreign currency usually does not exceed £S7,000.

41 See section 28 of the *Organization of Dealings in Foreign Currency Regulations*, 1979 (as amended up to January 1980), published by the Bank of Sudan. See also *Manios* v. *Bank of Sudan*, Khartoum P.C.–C.S.–951–1975 (unreported); also M. R. Shuster, *The Public International Law of Money* (1973), p. 31.

42 The writer interviewed the director of the Foreign Exchange Control Department, Bank of Sudan, on 12 January 1976, who confirmed this practice.

43 Sections 10(d), 9 and 8 of the Industrial Investment Act, 1974, the Agricultural Investment Act, 1976, and the Investment in Economic Services Act, 1973, respectively. Cf. Article 9(2) of the Libyan Law on Investment of Foreign Capital, 1968, 7 I.L.M. (1968), 215; also Article 3(2) of the Statute for Investment by Foreign Nationals in Taiwan, *Investment Laws of the World*, vol. 7.

44 Sections 10, 4 and 3 of the Investment in Economic Services Act, the Industrial Investment Act, and the Agricultural Investment Act, respectively.

45 The Law Reform Commission for Revising the Investment Laws, constituted by an Order issued by the Prime Minister in 1977.

46 See Appendix 1.

47 *Investment Laws of the World*, vol. 6; Cf. section 4 of the Foreign and Domestic Private Investment Law of Afghanistan, 1967, ibid. vol. 1.

48 Section 1(a).

49 Also, section 2 of the Implementing Regulations of the Foreign Capital Investment Law, 1979.

50 Ismail S. Nazer, 'Doing Business in Saudi Arabia', in Warren G. Wickersham and Benjamin P. Fishburne (editors), *Current Legal Aspects of Doing Business in the Middle East – Saudi Arabia, Egypt and Iran*, American Bar Association (1977), p. 116, at p. 119.

51 A similar definition of the term 'investment' is produced in Article 1 of the Agreement between the Arab Republic of Egypt and the Democratic Republic of the Sudan on Encouragement and Protection of Investment, 1978 (referred to hereinafter as the Egypt–Sudan Investment Agreement).

52 Cf. the West Germany–Pakistan Treaty, 1959, *Bundesgesetzblatt*, Teil 11 (1961), p. 793; also 457 U.N.T.S. 28.

53 The same definition has been adopted in many investment protection treaties concluded by Switzerland with other countries: e.g. Switzerland–Tunisia Treaty, 1964, 3 *I.L.M.* (1964), 524; Egypt–Switzerland Treaty, 1974, *Investment Laws of the World*, vol. 1.

54 An example of this type of guaranty treaty is the United States–Brazil Treaty, 1965, 6327 *U.S.T.I.A.* Sudan concluded an investment guaranty treaty with the United States in 1959. For the text, see The American–Sudan Guaranty of Private Investments Agreement, 1959, *U.S.T.I.A.*, vol. 10 (part 1), 1959, p. 408. See ch. 7 for a wide definition under the current American investment guarantee programme, see *post*, pp. 164–5.

55 For text and commentary, see 9 *J.P.L.* (1960), 116. For a discussion of the earlier draft, see Miller, 'Protection of Private Foreign Investment by Multilateral Conventions', 53 *A.J.I.L.* (1959), 371. Cf. E. Snyder draft, 11 *J.P.L.* (1963), 201. The O.E.C.D. Draft Conventions of 1965 and 1967 on the Protection of Foreign Property, following the Abs–Shawcross Draft Convention, defines 'property' widely as including 'all property rights and interests whether held directly or indirectly'. In the commentaries, it is correctly stated that the term includes, but is not limited to, 'investment'; for the text of this Draft Convention, see O.E.C.D. publication no. 15637, December 1962, appendix B.

56 G. Schwarzenberger, *Foreign Investments and International Law* (1969), p. 114.

57 Ibid. at p. 17.

58 Ibid.

59 S. Friedman, *Expropriation in International Law* (1953), pp. 145–6; G. White, *Nationalisation of Foreign Property* (1961), p. 48. For a contrary view, see Nwogugu, *Legal Problems*, p. 65.

60 See *ante*, pp. 1–3. See also the Egyptian Investment Laws before 1971, S. Habachy, in Friedmann, *The State and the Rule of Law*, p. 562; for an analysis of the present Egyptian Foreign Investment Law, see H. Salucuse, 'Egypt's New Law on Foreign Investment: The Framework for Economic Openness', *Int.L.L.*, vol. 9, no. 4, p. 647.

Nigeria divided its economy into the private sector and the public sector which monopolizes investment in certain projects relating to public utilities, like generating and distributing electric power and water supply and telecommunication. Investment in mining is assigned to a quasi-governmental Corporation: Act No. 1957–27, 4 June 1957 *Laws of Nigeria* P.A. 103; Act No. 1958–8, 15 April 1958, Official Gazette Extraordinary, vol. 45, no. 34, 24 April 1958, p. 43; also U.N. publ., E/CN, 141 INR/28/Rev. 2, p. 55. A similar policy was adopted in Uganda: Act no. 17, 1964, 3 *I.L.M.* (1964), 1062; also Liberia: Act of 21 March 1961 adopting the Investment Incentive Code, 5 *I.L.M.* (1966), 607. For a general survey and analysis of investment laws in Africa, see Krishna Ahooja, 'Investment Legislation in Africa', 2 *J.W.T.L.* (1968), 495–520. See also in *Re the Palmolive Company*, Mexico, Supreme Court, 26 October [1929], A.D., vol. 5, case no. 161, pp. 261–2; Cf. *Bank voor en Scheepvaat, N.* v. *Slatford and Another* [1953] 1 Q.B. 24, also the Asian–African Consultative Committee (A.A.L.C.C.) Final Report of 3rd Session, Colombo, 1960, p. 113. The Sudan has been admitted to this Committee with effect from 1 October 1958, but was unable to attend this session.

61 Section 4, Industrial Investment Act.

62 Mining in the Sudan is governed by the Mines and Quarries Act, 1972 (Act No. 60) and regulations made thereunder, *L.S.D.R.S.G.* No. 1134, dated 30 August 1972, also published in *Mining and Oil Exploration Laws in the Sudan* (1974), published by the Geological and Mineral Resources Department, Ministry of Power and Mining, p. 38.

63 See the Petroleum Resources Act, 1972 (Act No. 59) and regulations made thereunder, *L.S.D.R.S.G.* No. 1134, dated 30 August 1972, also ibid. pp. 1–37. For allocation of investment by sector, see table 2. The private sector is expected to finance itself for half its total investment out of domestic savings, the other half coming from foreign sources during the Six-Year Plan 1977/1983.

64 Section 6(2).

65 Section 5.

66 Section 51 of the Bank of Sudan (Amendment) Act, 1976, *L.S.D.R.S.G.* no. 919 dated 15 July 1976, p. 20.

67 At the time of writing there were at least seven foreign banks which had started to do

business in the Sudan. These include, *inter alia*: Faisal Islamic Bank; National Bank of Abu Dhabi; Citibank: Chase Manhattan: Bank of Credit and Commerce International and Oman Bank. However, at present there are more than ten foreign banks doing business in the Sudan.

68 Sections 3 and 4.

69 It is noteworthy that Saudi Arabia's average production of natural gas is estimated at over 3.5 billion cubic feet daily, most of which is flared away, since as yet the domestic consumption is rather insignificant: *A Guide to Industrial Investment in Saudi Arabia*, 5th edn (1978), published by the Industrial Studies and Development Centre, Kingdom of Saudi Arabia.

70 Ibid. p. 25.

71 The development of the natural resources such as crude oil, natural gas, and minerals is entrusted to the General Petroleum and Minerals Organization (Petromin) under the Mining and Petroleum Regulations.

72 Article 2 of the Saudi Arabian Foreign Capital Investment Law.

73 For the formation and the function of this Committee, see *post*, p. 355.

74 Article 3 of the Foreign Capital Investment Law. Recently, the Saudi Minister of Industry and Electricity has exercised his discretion under this section, on the recommendations of the Foreign Investment Committee, and determined the following by a ministerial decision as investment projects: productive industrial investments; productive agricultural investments; health developmental projects; services and construction projects.

The same ministerial decision defines each of these investment projects by giving general descriptions and offering examples thereof. Thus, by productive industrial investments, the ministerial decision meant those projects which transform raw materials into manufactured or semi-manufactured goods, or those which transform the semi-manufactured goods into complete manufactured goods or their preparation and packing.

The agricultural investment projects were described by the ministerial decision as including the production of fruits, vegetables, crops, horticultural products, and beans. The agricultural projects also comprised animal husbandry of all kinds, poultry, dairies and fishing of all kinds. On the other hand, the ministerial decision describes the health developmental projects as the building and administration of hospitals and clinics or similar institutions.

As regards service projects, the ministerial decision, similar to the Sudanese Investment in Economic Services Act, only gives examples which include, *inter alia*, banking; hotels and tourism; training; maintenance; workshops; cleaning; protection of the environment from pollution; transport; loading; advertisement and publication; computer services; warehousing; refrigeration stores; central markets; commercial centres; specialized restaurants etc.

The construction projects were intended by the ministerial decision to include the construction of civilian buildings; assembling of prefabricated houses; building of airports, highways, roads, dams and barracks; building of ports; drainage systems; hydro-electric power stations; mechanical construction such as desolation of water stations or factories, etc. For the text of the ministerial decision, see *Al-Riyadh*, No. 4635, Saturday, 20 September 1980, p. 2.

75 *Information Guide, Doing Business in Saudi Arabia*, published by Price Waterhouse & Co. (1979), U.S.A., p. 17. The Saudization of Citibank was completed on 12 July 1980, ahead of the expected schedule: *Quarterly Economic Review of Saudi Arabia*, 3rd Quarter 1980, the Economist Intelligence Unit Ltd. p. 15; see also 2nd Quarter 1980, p. 15.

76 Article 3 of the New Regulations on Agents' Commission, 1978.

77 Work permits are issued in Saudi Arabia in accordance with the Labour and Workers' Regulation, 1969 and the proceedings and rules laid down by the Ministry of Labour. Similarly, foreigners are not allowed in the Sudan to engage in any employment without the permission of the Passports and Immigration Department, which usually does no grant such permission without consultation with the Commissioner of Labour. In practice, he will not consent to the employment of foreigners unless it is proved that there are no qualified Sudanese nationals to be employed. This is a question of high policy and it is normally applicable in cases of technicians and experts. See Sections 17–18 of the Sudanese Passports and Immigration Regulations, 1969, *S.L.S.D.R.S.G.* No. 1091, dated December 1969.

78 See the Sudanese Passports and Immigration Act, 1960, extracts from *L.S.D.R.S.G.* no. 932, dated 15 November 1960.

79 Vattel, *Law of Nations* (1874), translated from French by Joseph Chitty, p. 122; Oppenheim, *International Law*, p. 676; Hackworth, *Digest*, pp. 717–18; Lord McNair, *International Law Opinions* (1956), vol. 11, p. 105; B. Sen, *Diplomat's Handbook*, pp. 296–340; Guy S. Goodwinn–Gill, *International Law and the Movement of Persons between States* (1978), p. 23 *et seq.*

80 For instance, the International Conference on 'Treatment of Foreigners', held in Paris in 1929, League of Nations Doc. C.I.T.E. 62, 1930 11. 5, 419–21; the *Havana Convention on the Status of Aliens*; Sen, *Diplomat's Handbook*, pp. 297–8; A.A.L.C.C., 1960, 3rd session, Final Report.

81 For instance, *Abdou* v. *Attorney-General of Kenya*, Kenya High Court, 24 April 1951, 18 I.L.R., 282; the decision of the Egyptian Conseil d'Etat (Council of State) in case no. 1484/1954, May 1953, *Collection of Decisions of Egyptian Councils of State.*

82 For instance, section 11 of the Industrial Investment Act, 1974; section 8(2) of the Investment in Economic Services Act, 1973; section 17 of the Agricultural Investment Act, 1976.

83 Article (1) of the treaty provides: 'Each contracting party shall in its territory admit investments, in accordance with its legislation, policies and administrative practices, by nationals or companies of the other contracting party and promote such investments as far as possible. It shall treat these investments in a fair and equitable manner'.

84 Letter dated 17 February 1963 of Deputy Permanent Under Secretary, Ministry of Finance and Economics (now Ministry of Finance and Economic Planning), Chairman of Sudanese delegation. This undertaking was confirmed by the German delegation in a similar letter on the same day.

85 Cf. the Agreement between the Democratic Republic of the Sudan and Bulgaria, 1970, *L.S.D.R.S.G.* dated 15 August 1970, p. 439, which contains identical provisions.

86 Section 6.

87 Sections 5, 6 and 21 of the Agricultural Investment Act, 1976.

88 Saud Shawaf's office file no. 55-L 89/79, Riyadh, Saudi Arabia.

89 Ibid.

90 Articles 2 and 4.

91 Under the present Saudi law the Foreign Capital Investment Committee consists of the following persons: the Deputy Minister of Industry and Electricity or his substitute, to act as Chairman; a representative from the Ministry of Planning; a representative from the Ministry of Finance and National Economy; a representative from the Ministry of Agriculture and Water; a representative from the Ministry of Petroleum and Mineral Resources and a representative from the Ministry of Commerce. For more detailed

provisions on the procedure of meetings and organizing the work of the Committee, see Article 4 of the Foreign Capital Investment Law and the regulations passed thereunder.

92 Article 5.

93 The documents include feasibility studies; properly authenticated documents showing the activities and experience of the foreign investor; an authenticated certificate of incorporation etc. All these documents must be accompanied by approved Arabic translation.

94 Information obtained from Saud Shawaf, Attorney-at-Law, also his office file no. 55-L 169/79, Riyadh, Saudi Arabia.

95 Ibid.

96 *Laws of the Sudan*, vol. 4, title XIII: sub-title 5, p. 134. This ordinance was another version of the English Companies Act, 1908. Since 1964 attempts have been made to introduce reform, but nothing was done till 1973 when a Law Reform Commission was formed and work is still going on to re-enact all Sudanese laws. In fact the Committee has finished the Contract, Agency, Sales and other laws which were duly promulgated. The Sudanese Courts used to apply English Common Law in interpreting the Companies Ordinance in cases not provided for. For a detailed account of reception of Common Law in the Sudan, see Zaki Mustafa, *The Common Law in the Sudan*, 1971. But recently, the Government formed another Law Reform Commission with special terms of reference leading to the Islamization of laws in the Sudan.

97 Section 247 of the Companies Ordinance.

98 Section 248(1), ibid.

99 Section 248(2)(a), ibid.

100 Section 248(2)(b), ibid.

101 Section 248(2)(c), ibid.

102 Section 248(2)(d), ibid.

103 Section 248(3), ibid.

104 Section 248(4)(i) and (ii), ibid.

105 Section 248(6), ibid.

106 Section 249, ibid.

107 Section 251; for further details see sections 252–5.

108 This section has been interpreted restrictively by the Attorney-General. It is noteworthy that the Registrar of Companies has been transferred to the Attorney-General's Chambers and is considered an integral part thereof. It is prudent that the Registrar and his aides are lawyers. And any reference to the Minister of Finance and National Economy, under the Company Act, will be deemed to be to the Attorney-General.

109 The Insurers Control (Amendment) Act, 1970, *L.S.D.R.S.G.* no. 1109, dated 15 September 1970, p. 382.

110 See The Public Companies (Grant of Concessions) Act, 1969, *L.S.D.R.S.G.*, 15 November 1969, p. 292.

111 Section 8(a) of the Petroleum Resources Act, 1972.

112 Section 8(b), ibid.

113 For adopting the English Partnership Act, see *Heirs of Khedir Mohammed Khalid* v. *Heirs of Babiker Kannan*, *S.L.R.*, vol. 11 [1932–40], p. 20 (Court of Appeal).

114 For applying English cases, see ibid. where the rule in *Polden* v. *Bostard* [1865] L.R. 1.Q.B., p. 156, was followed.

115 *Laws of the Sudan*, vol. 4, title XIII: sub-title 6, pp. 262–72.

116 Ibid. title XIII: sub-title 1, p. 1.

117 *L.S.D.R.S.G.*, 15 May 1970, p. 230. During the period 1976–77, about 105 companies

have been registered with the Registrar of Companies. On the other hand, about 303 business names, 466 trade marks and 109 partnerships have been registered in the same period. The capital of the companies exceeded £S 55 millions investing in industry, transport, construction works and services: *El Iyam*, Issue no. 9011, dated 17 February 1977, p. 1.

118 Translated and compiled in *Business Laws of Saudi Arabia*, by Nicola H. Karam.

119 Zaki Mustafa, 'Forms of Doing Business in Saudi Arabia', in Wickersham and Fishburne (editors), *Current Legal Aspects*.

120 Nazer, in *Current Legal Aspects*, p. 119.

121 Article 157 of the Companies Regulations.

122 Article 158.

123 Ibid.

124 Article 159.

125 These are: the name, the object and the head office of the company; the names of the partners, their addresses, occupations and nationalities; the names of the members of the board of controllers, if there is a board of controllers; the amount of the capital, and the contributions in cash and in kind. The articles must also include a statement by the partners that all the shares have been allotted and paid up in full. They must also define the method of the distribution of profits and the dates for the commencement and termination of the company, etc.

126 Article 10 of the Companies Regulations. The Notary Public in Saudi Arabia is an official of the Government, part of the judicial system. He is not a private individual with a commission.

127 Article 4 of the Commercial Register Regulations.

128 See the Commercial Agents' Regulation. The practice is that foreign companies doing business in the Kingdom through agents usually establish technical advisory offices to render advice to the agent and the consumer. Several of such consulting and advisory offices have been registered.

129 See Part II of the Law.

130 Article 7.

131 Part III of the Law. This point will be investigated further in ch. 5.

3. Impediments to foreign investment

1 For general descriptions and discussions, see League of Nations, Special Joint Committee on Private Foreign Investment, *Conditions of Private Foreign Investment* (1946).

2 B. Higgins, *Economic Development* (1959), pp. 571–2, 579–82; Diamond, 'Economic Problems of Foreign Trade and Investment in Underdeveloped Countries', 17 *Ohio State Law Journal* (1956), 254–6; R. Nurkse, 'International Investment To-day in the Light of Nineteenth-century Experience', 64 *Econ.J.* (1954), 744, 753–4; Myrdal, *Economic Theory and Underdeveloped Regimes* (1957), p. 110. For a comprehensive account of the economic background of the Sudan, see the United Nations Development Programme, *Country and Inter-Country Programming*, Doc. DP/GC/SUD/R.I, 30 March 1973, pp. 1–70; Ali Mohamed El Hassan (editor), *An Introduction to the Sudan Economy*, (1976), pp. 1–38; also I.L.O., *Growth, Employment and Equity, a Comprehensive Strategy for the Sudan* (1976), pp. 3–199, 241–97.

3 Fatouros, *Government Guarantees*, p. 31; I.L.O., *Comprehensive Strategy*, pp. 191–9, 495–503.

4 See *The Times*, Saturday 26 February 1977, a Special Report; *The Economist*, 24 March

1978; *New Africa*, January 1978; sections 11 and 12 of the Industrial Investment Act; section 5 of the Investment in Economic Services Act; section 4 of the Agricultural Investment Act. See generally, Leslie L. Rood, 'Foreign Investment in African Manufacturing', 13 *J.M.A.S.* (1975), 25–7.

5 Fawcett, *Conflicts*, pp. 29–51; R. E. Hudec, 4 *J.W.T.L.* (1970), 615. For the text of the G.A.T.T., see U.N.T.S., vol. 55, p. 188.

6 For an account on transport, communications and energy in the Sudan, see Lees and Brooks, *Economic and Political Development*, pp. 67, 131–3; *Financial Times*, 13 July 1978, *Sudan, Survey*.

7 Press interview by Al Safa with President Nimeiri, 12 June 1978.

8 *Financial Times*, 13 July 1978.

9 See Ali Ahmed Suliman, *Issues in the Economic Development of the Sudan* (1975), p. 2 *et seq*.

10 Fatouros, *Government Guarantees*, p. 32.

11 Sections 10(5), 7(2) and 18 of the Industrial Investment Act, the Investment in Economic Services Act, and the Agricultural Investment Act, respectively, under section 20(2) of the Encouragement of Investment Act, 1980, no foreign investor will be allowed to borrow money from banks and financial institutions working in the Sudan, save with the consent of the Minister of Finance and National Economy.

12 The Rent Restriction Ordinance 1953, *Laws of the Sudan*, vol. 7, title XX: sub-title 7, p. 95; the Rent Restriction (Amendment) Act, 1972, *L.S.D.R.S.G.* no. 1117, dated 15 March 1971, p. 187; the Rent Restriction (Amendment) Act, 1973, *L.S.D.R.S.G.* no. 1141, dated 15 February 1973, p. 60.

13 The effect of political instability on foreign investment is thoroughly considered by R. O. Ekundare in relation to Nigeria in, 'The Political Economy of Private Investment in Nigeria', 10 *J.M.A.S.* (1972), 37–56.

14 The Approved Enterprises (Concessions) Act (repealed), 1956.

15 Fatouros, *Government Guarantees*, p. 34.

16 *Financial Times*, 13 July 1978.

17 The devaluation was imposed by the I.M.F. in exchange for a standby credit, and effected on 8 June 1978, *Financial Times*, 10 June 1978.

18 Ibid. issue of 13 July 1978.

19 For a general survey of screening procedure and criteria, see U.N. Document A/AC.97/Rev. 1, 27 December 1960, pp. 52–60.

20 Cf. for instance, The International Chambers of Commerce, *Fair Treatment for International Investments: International Code*, Appendix, 19 (I.C.C. Brochure no. 129, 1949).

21 These are: the Investment in Economic Services Act; the Industrial Investment Act and the Agricultural Investment Act.

22 These ministries are: the Ministry of Industry and Mining (now the Ministry of Energy and Mining); the Ministry of Finance, Planning and National Economy; the Ministry of Agriculture and Natural Resources.

23 El Jareeda El Rasmia, 30 September 1974; see Professor Salacuse in *International Lawyer*, vol. 9, no. 4, p. 647; *The Times*, Monday, 9 October 1978, *Egypt, A Special Report*, p. 20.

24 Hyde, 50 *A.J.I.L.* (1956), pp. 216–18; A. H. Roth, *The Minimum Standard of International Law Applied to Aliens* (1949), p. 46; also Nwogugu, *Legal Problems*, pp. 16–17.

25 Most countries impose restrictions on the entry of aliens and foreign capital in a number of sectors, mainly in construction, transportation, ownership and exploitation of land,

public utilities, banking and insurance: U.N. Doc AC/AC. 97/5/Rev., p. 150 *et seq.*: Nwogugu, *Legal Problems*, pp. 14–15. In several developing countries certain sectors are state-controlled and foreign investors are not allowed to enter therein: U.N. Document, 1960, AC/AC/97/5/Rev., p. 161–6.

26 U.N. Doc. AC/AC/97/5/Rev. 1. 27 December 1960, p. 80; the document contains similar rules in other countries, pp. 81–96; see also W. G. Friedmann and R. C. Pugh, *Legal Aspects of Foreign Investment* (1959), pp. 742–54. Mexico followed the same pattern, ibid. pp. 357–8. This practice has been followed in many countries, for example: Greece, Lambadarios, ibid. p. 233; Columbia, Kalmanoff-Salalmananca, ibid. p. 173; Philippines, Manzon, ibid. p. 414; Portugal, Constantine Fernandes, ibid. p. 499; Tunisia, U.N. Publ., E/CN. 14/INR/28/Rev. 2, (1960), p. 65.

27 William J. Gibbons in Friedmann and Pugh, *Legal Aspects*, p. 647. This has been slightly modified by recent legislation.

28 Act No. 35, 11 December 1964, 4 *I.L.M.* (1965), 241; U.N. Publ., E/CN. 14/INR/28/Rev. 2, p. 42.

29 G.A. Res. No. 2158 (XXI), 28 November 1966, adopted on the Report of the Second Committee (A/6518). On national participation in the foreign investment enterprises generally, see Friedmann and Pugh, *Legal Aspects*, p. 747.

30 Article 7 of the Foreign Capital Investment Law.

31 Fatouros, *Government Guarantees*, p. 43.

32 Nwogugu, *Legal Problems*, pp. 11–12.

33 Fatouros, *Government Guarantees*, p. 45; Osam El Deen Mustafa Baseem, *The Legal Regime of Foreign Private Investments in the Developing Countries* (1972), pp. 39–47.

34 Barbara Ward, J. D. Runnalls and Lenore d'Anjou (eds.), *The Widening Gap* (1971), ch. 4, p. 245.

35 *U.N. Investment Laws* (1951), pp. 2–3.

36 Habachy, in Friedmann and Pugh, *Legal Aspects*, p. 562. This has been modified by Article 11 of Law No. 32 of 1977.

37 Decree of August, 1958; cf. Habachy, in Friedmann and Pugh, *Legal Aspects*, pp. 562–72. This provision has been also modified to some extent by Law No. 32 of 1977.

38 Cf. Iran, Nasr in Friedmann and Pugh, *Legal Aspects*, pp. 280–5; Mexico, Hidalgo, ibid. pp. 355–65.

39 *Loc. cit.*, section 6; cf. Section 6 of the Organization and Promotion of Industrial Investment Act, 1967 (repealed).

40 For instance, Article XVI of the Petroleum Production-Sharing Agreement with Chevron, 1975 provides for the employment and training of Sudanese personnel in the operations relating to discovery and exploitation of petroleum in which the company is engaged in the Sudan. See also, I.L.O., *Growth, Employment and Equity*, pp. 192–250.

41 For a survey of labour legislations and industrial relations in the Sudan, see Lees and Brooks, *Economic and Political Development*, pp. 25–7; on termination of service, see Abdel-Rahman E. Ali Taha and Ahmed H. El Jack, *The Regulation of Termination of Employment in the Sudanese Private Sector* (1973).

42 I. Foighel, *Nationalization* (1957), pp. 57–69. For the history of nationalization and expropriation, see White, *Nationalisation*, pp. 1–32.

43 Nationalization Act, 1951; *I.C.J. Pleadings, Anglo-Iranian Oil Co.* Recently the Iranian Revolutionary Government has nationalized all banks and insurance companies in Iran: *The Guardian*, 25 July 1979.

44 Suez Canal Nationalization Decree, 51 *A.J.I.L.* (1957), 673.
45 5 *Neth. Int.L.R.* (1958), 227.
46 Cuban Nationalization Decree, 55 *A.J.I.L.* (1961), 822.
47 Shawcross, *Hague Recueil* (1961), vol. 1, pp. 349–50.
48 Baseem, *Legal Regime*, p. 351; Nwogugu, *Legal Problems*, p. 21.
49 See the Award on the Merits in Disputes between Texaco Overseas Petroleum Company/California Asiatic Oil Company and the Government of Libya Arab Republic, 18 *I.L.M.* (1978), 1. (The Award will be referred to hereinafter as the Libya–Oil Companies Award.)

A voluminous literature has been written on the subjects of 'expropriation' and 'nationalization'. The following are among other references dealing with these subjects: K. Katzarov, *The Theory of Nationalization* (1960); Friedmann, *Expropriation*; Foighel, *Nationalization*; White, *Nationalisation.*

50 See ch. 8, where the appropriate measure of compensation is discussed.
51 White, *Nationalisation*, pp. 27–31.
52 See *post*, pp. 128–40; see also Sir David Orr, 6 *The Magazine of the Cambridge University Industrial Society* (1980), p. 9, at p. 11.
53 The theory that nationalization and expropriation discourage investment finds support in the effect of the British Labour Party resolution passed at the end of its Conference in October 1978 to take over the oil industry in the North Sea operated by private companies. It has been reported that this slackened negotiations over new explorations for oil fields in the area: *The Times*, 5 October 1978, 9 October 1978, respectively.

Nationalization and expropriation will be discussed at length in chapters 5 and 6. Compensation will be discussed in chapter 8.

54 I.M.F. 12th Annual Report on Exchange Restrictions, Washington (1961), p. 27.
55 Ibid. p. 56; cf. Egypt, Law no. 65, 1971, El-Jareeda-el-Rasmia, 30 September 1971, Section 9(2) (repealed); Somalia, Law no. 10, 18 February, 1960, Official Bulletin, Supplement No. 5 to No. 2, 19 February 1960.
56 The text was made available to the writer by Dr Hamza Abdalla Kunna, Legal Counsel, Bank of Sudan. These regulations replaced the Finance (Exchange Control) Regulations, 1966, *L.S.D.R.S.G.* no. 1025 dated 25 August 1966, p. 57. On the historic background of exchange control in the Sudan, see Mahdi El Faki, the Deputy General Manager of the Bank of Sudan, 'The Background of Exchange Control in the Sudan', *The Journal of Banking Studies* (*Sudan*) (1977), vol. 2, January, 7–8; Ali El Hassan Omer, 'Sudan Foreign Exchange Control Policy Impact on its Economic Development', ibid. 19–21.
57 Section 4.
58 Section 11.
59 Sections 12, 13 and 14.
60 Section 10.
61 Section 16.
62 Section 15.
63 Section 2 of the Order Concerning the Carrying of Foreign Currency Notes and other Means of Payment by Travellers Abroad, 1979 (issued by the Minister of Finance and National Economy on 29 October 1979).
64 See Banks Control Law, in Nicola H. Karam, *Business Laws.*
65 See Saudi Arabian Monetary Agency Law, ibid.
66 F. A. Mann, *The Legal Aspects of Money*, 3rd edn., 1971, p. 485; *idem*: 26 *B.Y.B.I.L.* (1949),

p. 259; Nwogugu, *Legal Problems*, p. 18; Hyde, 50 *A.J.I.l.* (1956), 690–2. Fatouros advocated that international customary law has not evolved special rules concerning the right of a State to have exchange control, but he alleged that the general principles applied by civilized nations recognize such a right. Fatouros, *Government Guarantees*, p. 48.

67 *P.C.I.J.* series A, no. 20–1 at p. 44.

68 I.L.R. (1953), p. 242; Lauterpacht in 5 *I.C.L.Q.* (1956), 426–7.

69 Baseem, *Legal Regime*, p. 138.

70 Nwogugu, *Legal Problems*, p. 19; see, generally, Shuster, *Law of Money* (1973), pp. 156–64.

71 U.N.T.S., vol. 55, at p. 194.

72 [1956], 1 All E.R., p. 129; also I.L.R., vol. 22, p. 481.

73 Per Upjohn, J., at p. 142. The principle has been impliedly recognized by the Draft Convention on the Protection of Foreign Property of O.E.C.D., O.E.C.D. publication No. 23081, November 1963. Exchange control is permitted under the provisions of the International Monetary Fund (I.M.F.) Articles of Agreement: Article VI(3), 2 U.N.T.S., 39.

74 *Eisner* v. *United States* (1954), I.L.R., p. 476.

75 Article I (iii); cf. Mann, *Legal Aspects*, pp. 339–40, 378–87; Richard W. Edwards, 'The Currency Exchange Rate Provisions of the Proposed Amended Articles of Agreement of the International Monetary Fund', 70 *A.J.I.L.* (1976), 722–62. Hans Aufricht, *The International Monetary Fund* (1964), ch. 3.

76 Article I (iv).

77 This Article was amended on 30 April 1976. The amended Article gives particular attention to purposes and effects. Obligations are defined in general terms. Emphasis is put on fundamental economic policies and on the underlying economic conditions of the member countries. For a detailed analysis of the amendment, see Edwards, 70 *A.J.I.L.* (1976), 722–62.

78 Article VIII(2) and (3).

79 For instance, Mann, *Legal Aspects*, pp. 533–47; Nwogugu, *Legal Problems*, pp. 20–1.

80 F. E. Koch, *The Double Taxation Conventions*, vol. 1 (1947), p. 3; Ehrenzweig and Koch, *Income Tax Treaties* (1950), p. 41.

81 Sudan adopts both the test of residence and source of income: section 10 of the Law no. 65, 1971. However, under paragraph (b) of this section, the Minister of Finance may exempt any person resident in the Sudan who has income which is taxed at the place of the source. For the text, see *S.L.D.R.S.G.* no. 1123 dated 17 October 1971, p. 840. For an analytical study of taxation laws in the Sudan see Zakria Mohammed Bayiomi, *Daribat el-Dakl-fi-el-Teshria el Sudani* (*Income Tax in the Sudan Legislation*) (1972), pp. 14–75.

Conversely, the Saudi tax system is based on the concept of source and does not seek to tax operations considered to take place outside the Kingdom. Taxation in Saudi Arabia is levied solely by the Central government, under a system of royal decrees, ministerial decisions and governmental circulars. There are no regional or municipal taxes. For more details, see the Income Tax Law, in Nicola H. Karam, *Business Laws*.

82 Oppenheim, *International Law*, p. 680; Sen, *Diplomat's Handbook*, p. 317; Baseem, *Legal Regime*, p. 109; Harold Wurzel, 'Foreign Investment and Extra-territorial Taxation', 38 *Columb.L.R.* (1938), 814–16.

83 Income Tax Act, 1952, section 122, 31 *Halsbury's Statutes* (2nd edn), 390; also section 478 of the Income and Corporation Taxes Act, 1970, *Statute in Force*, 1971, revised edition. For an incidence of double taxation in the United Kingdom, see *Financial Times*, Saturday, 16 October 1976, p. 4; also *Lord Chetwode* v. *Inland Revenue Commissioners* [1977] 1 All.E.R. 638.

84 J. P. Crockett, *The Federal Tax System of the U.S.* (1955); S. S. Surrey, 56 *Columb.L.R.* (1956), 815.
85 Price Waterhouse & Co., *Information Guide*, p. 47.
86 *The Government of India* v. *Taylor* [1955] A.C. 491; cf. *Regazzoni* v. *Sethia* [1958] A.C. 301.
87 Hyde, *International Law*, p. 664; Albrecht, 'The Taxation of Aliens Under International Law', 29 *B.Y.B.I.L.* (1952), p. 145; S. S. Surrey, 'Tax Administration in Underdeveloped Countries", 12 *U. of Miami L. Rev.* (1958), 158.
88 These three branches of the law have already been codified for the first time in the Sudan. The codification is based on common law except in cases where deviation is dictated by the necessity to adapt the law according to Sudanese realities, customs and Sharia law. For the texts, see the Conracts Act, 1974, the Sales Act, 1974, and the Agency Act, 1974, *S.L.S.D.R.S.G.*, dated 25 June 1974, pp. 273, 298, 321, respectively.
89 Thus the Companies Ordinance was enacted in 1925, the Bankruptcy Ordinance in 1929, and the Bills of Exchange Ordinance in 1917, see the *Laws of the Sudan*, vol. 4.
90 Mustafa, 17 *J.A.L.* (1973), 133.
91 See Asante's lecture, 'Transnational Investment Law', p. 25.
92 In Colombia, dividends may be distributed only after 10% of the annual profits have been set aside for the 'legal reserve' until the reserve amounts to at least 50% of the subscribed capital: Friedmann and Pugh, *Legal Aspects*, p. 180.
93 See J. Albert Burgoyne, 'Specific Problems and Unique Aspects of Doing Business in Saudi Arabia', in Wickersham & Fishburne, *Current Legal Aspects of Doing Business in the Middle East*, p. 142.
94 Ibid.
95 Procurement of Government Purchases and Execution of its Projects and Works Law and Implementing Regulations, 1977. For the translated text, see Nicola H. Karam, *Business Laws*.
96 Article 7.
97 Ibid. (d).
98 Unreported case in which the present writer was an advocate.
99 Friedmann and Pugh, *Legal Aspects*, p. 779.
100 See *post*, pp. 128–40; *Proceedings of U.N.C.T.A.D.*, 4th session, 1976.
101 Note by Professor Jeswald W. Salacuse of the Ford Foundation to Dr Zaki Mustafa, Legal Counsel to the President for Legal Reform (Khartoum). The note was delivered to the writer by its author.
102 Cf. the Egyptian Law No. 43.
103 The Commission was formed by the decision of the Prime Minister, no. 177 of 26 July 1977. The Commission was formed of 8 senior officials, of whom one was a lawyer.
104 The Encouragement of National, Arab and Foreign Investment Draft Bill, 1977.
105 These are the Petroleum Resources Act, 1972; the Mines and Quarries Act, 1972; the Investment in Economic Services Act, 1973; the Industrial Investment Act, 1974; the Agricultural Investment Act, 1976.
106 Sections 18 and 19 of the Draft Bill.
107 Section 19.
108 Draft Bill, sections 5, 18 and 21.
109 Explanatory Note of the Draft Bill; also section 21.
110 Section 7.
111 Section 20.
112 See Appendix I. This Act repealed the Investment in Economic Services Act, the Industrial

Investment Act and the Agricultural Investment Act. It left untouched the Petroleum Resources Act and the Mines and Quarries Act.

113 Sections 3 and 5 of the Encouragement of Investment Act, 1980.

114 Section 25.

115 Sections 5, 26, 27 and 29.

116 Section 26.

117 Section 28.

118 See a short review of the Encouragement of Investment Act, 1980 by Alfred Taban in *The Middle East* (June 1980), No. 68, p. 67.

119 Encouragement of Investment Act, section 29.

120 Sections 31 and 33.

121 Sections 8 and 17.

4. Legal incentives

1 For instance U.N. Economic and Social Council, *Taxation in Capital-exporting and Capital-importing Countries of Foreign Private Investment*, Doc. E/2865, para. 18, May 1958. G.A. Res. 824 (IX), 11 December 1954; G.A. Res. 1313 (XIII), 21 December 1960; E.C.O.S.O.C., Res.

2 U.N. Doc. E/3325, para. 172, 26 February 1960.

3 The Investment in Economic Services Act, the Industrial Investment Act, the Agricultural Investment Act respectively.

4 Sections 10(3)(a) and 8(a) of the Industrial Investment Act, 1974 and the Agricultural Investment Act, 1976, respectively; for a detailed examination of the Sudanese taxation and financial system, see Lees and Brooks, *Economic and Political Development*, ch. 6.

5 Section 10(3)(c) of the Industrial Investment Act; Cf. section 8(b) of the Agricultural Investment Act, 1976, which provided that in assessing the business profits tax, only 25% of the prescribed rate will be levied on the first 30% of the increase, 50% on the second and 30% on the third. The remaining 10% was to be fully taxed. See generally, Standford G. Ross, 'Foreign Government Tax Incentives for Investment' in *Proceedings of the Institute on Private Investments Abroad* (1959), the Southwestern Legal Foundation, pp. 292–7.

The Chad Investment Code, 1962, exempts profits earned by a new enterprise during the first five years from taxes. Such an enterprise is entitled to a deduction, for the purpose of tax calculation, of one half of the profits applied to the purchase of heavy equipment; Decree no. 156/PR, U.N. Doc. E/CN/28, 30 October 1963.

6 The Faisal's Islamic Bank Act, 1977, *D.R.S.G.* No. 1218, dated 15 May 1977; Lees and Brooks, *Economic and Political Development*, pp. 120–3.

7 Section 7(1)(b). Cf. Article 16 of the Egyptian Law No. 32, 1977.

8 Section 7(1) of the Investment in the Economic Services Act, 1975. For the definition of economic services see *ante*, p. 25.

Obviously, the attractiveness of tax relief on profits becomes nugatory if no profits are gained within the grace period. To cater for such contingencies, some countries have enlarged the scope of the ordinary tax holiday. The Industrial Development (Income Tax Relief) Decree, 1971 of Nigeria is a striking example. It broadens the tax holiday of 'pioneer industries' by counting as part of the exemption period only those years in which taxable profits were earned. Moreover, as is the case in the Sudan, dividends received from tax-free profits are also immune from Nigerian tax: Law No. 22 of 1971. For a general analysis of this issue in Nigeria, see R. O. Ekundare 'The Political Economy of Private Investment in Nigeria', 10 *J.M.A.S.* 1 (1972), 40–1. The issue of tax exemption has been analysed and evaluated by the F.A.O. of the U.N. in relation to investment in agriculture in developing countries: *Foreign Investment Laws and Agriculture* (1970), a study by Julian Henderson, Legislation Branch, pp. 69–82.

9 Section 7(2), ibid.

10 The Approved Enterprises (Concessions) Act, 1956 (repealed). Under section 10(1) of the Ghana Capital Investments Act, 1963, approved enterprises are entitled to exemption from income tax for a period of five years. This tax holiday may be extended to ten years beginning from the date of production, 2 *I.L.M.* no. 4 (1963). Cf. Ethiopia, Decree No. 5, 16 September 1963 (no longer applicable), 3 *I.L.M.* (1964), 41; Burundi Investment Code, 1976, *Investment Laws of the World*, vol. 1; Egypt Law no. 43 of 1974, as amended by Law no. 32, 1977.

11 See generally Ross in *Proceedings of the Institute on Private Investments Abroad* (1959), p. 332.

12 Sections 8 and 29 of the Encouragement of Investment Act, 1980.

13 In cases of government contracts, there are sometimes 'tax reimbursement' clauses under which the foreign corporation would be responsible for filing accounts and paying the income tax, but the payment is reimbursed by the sponsoring ministry. Obtaining such a clause depends on negotiation: information obtained by the writer orally from the Tax Department, Jeddah, Saudi Arabia.

14 F.A.O., *Foreign Investment Laws.*

15 Section 10(3)(c)(i) of the Industrial Investment Act, 1974; cf. the Indonesian Law no. 1, 1967, concerning investment of foreign capital, article 15(3), whereby allowance for accelerated depreciation of fixed capital is permitted without showing rates or periods; for text, *Investment Laws of the World*, vol. 11. A similar provision was contained in the Afghanistan Foreign and Domestic Private Investment Law, article 4, ibid. vol. 1; Kenya, Act No. 35 11 December 1964, 4 *I.L.M.* no. 2, March, 1965.

16 Section 10(3)(c)(ii) of the Industrial Investment Act; Section 8(2) of the Agricultural Investment Act, 1976. This is resurrected in section 9(3) of the Encouragement of Investment Act, 1980, but with specification that the resulting loss will be considered in the last year of the period of exemption.

17 For different depreciation rates, see Price Waterhouse & Co., *Information Guide*, p. 56.

A detailed system of depreciation is followed in the Philippines where fixed assets may enjoy accelerated depreciation at the option of the taxpayer, and in accordance with the procedure established by the Bureau of Internal Revenue. Fixed assets may be depreciated in two ways: first, to the extent of not more than twice as fast as the normal rate of depreciation, or depreciated at the normal rate of depreciation if the expected life is ten years or less. Secondly, over any number of years between five years and expected life, if the latter is more than ten years, and the depreciation thereon is allowed as a deduction from taxable income. It is obligatory on the taxpayer to notify the Bureau of Internal Revenue at the beginning of the depreciation period which depreciation rate will be used: the Investment Incentives Act, 1967, section 7(B), F.A.O., *Foreign Investment Laws*, p. 84.

18 Section 10 of the Encouragement of Investment Act, 1980. Cf. section 10(3)(d) of the Industrial Investment Act, 1974; section 8 of the Investment in the Economic Services Act, 1975; section 9 of the Agricultural Investment Act, 1976; cf. the Nigerian Act of

Industrial Development (Income Tax Relief) of 1971. Nwogugu, *Legal Problems*, p. 36; the Egyptian Law No. 43; Algerian Law No. 277, 26 July 1963, section 10(3), *El Jareeda El Rasmia*, 2 August 1963; Brazil Law No. 6, 3 *I.L.M.* no. 6, (1964).

19 Section 10(3)(g) of the Industrial Investment Act, 1974.

20 Section 10(5).

21 The legal nature of the development contracts will be dealt with in chapter 9.

22 Petroleum Agreement, Article XII.

23 Article XII.

24 Ball Collins Co.; American Pacific and Texaco Inc. These agreements are not operative at present.

25 Agreement with the Canadian firm Johns Manville, digging for chrysolite asbestos; agreement with the Japanese firms of Marubeni and Mitsubishi, digging for chromite; agreement with the British firm of Robertson Research International for making metallurgical studies for gold near Gebeit.

26 *L.S.D.R.S.G.* no. 1164, dated 15 August 1974, p. 1. The Contract has been signed and ratified by both the Sudan and Saudi Arabia. Cf. The Convention on the Arab Capital and its Transfer Among the Arab States, 1971.

27 *Guide to Industrial Investment*, pp. 111–12; also Price Waterhouse & Co., *Information Guide*, p. 16.

28 Cf. Section 10(3)(f) of the Industrial Investment Act, 1974; section 9 of the Investment in Economic Services Act, 1975; Section 10 of the Agricultural Investment Act, 1976. For instance, the Kenana Sugar Company paid only 10 piastres per feddan under this arrangement. For a general survey of the practice of different developing countries in relation to agricultural investments, see F.A.O.

29 Section 12 of the Encouragement of Investment Act, 1980.

30 Sections 11 and 14–19 of the Industrial Investment and the Agricultural Investment Acts, respectively.

31 *Guide to Industrial Investment*, p. 38.

32 Ibid. pp. 38–9; also Price Waterhouse & Co., *Information Guide*, pp. 17–18.

33 See report on Double Taxation submitted to the Financial Committee of the League of Nations, L. of N. Doc. E.F.S. 73F 19 (1923); report presented by the Committee of Technical Experts on Double Taxation Evasion, L. of N. Doc. P. 1927.11.40.

34 L. of N. Fiscal Committee: London and Mexico Model Tax Conventions: for commentary and text, see L. of N. Doc. C.88. M.88, 1946. 11.A.Geneva, 1 November 1946. For analysis and comments, see Bayiomi, *Daribat-el-Dakl*, pp. 47–57.

35 Resolution 4868 (XVI) of 9 July 1953.

36 I.C.C. Brochure 180, *Avoidance of Double Taxation*, February 1955.

37 Report of Eminent Person, see p. 371, n. 9 to ch. 1. On the advantages and disadvantages of double taxation treaties to developing countries, see Charles Irish, 'International Double Taxation Agreements', 23 *I.C.L.Q.* (1974), 292–316.

38 Nwogugu, *Legal Problems*, p. 48; Baseem, *Legal Regime*, pp. 118–20; Sen, *Diplomat's Handbook*, p. 319; Hyde, *International Law*, pp. 663–4, 671–2; Fatouros, *Government Guarantees*, p. 222.

39 For various double taxation treaties, see the U.N. Doc. E/3492, 18 May 1961. See also Eldon P. King, 'Tax Conventions to which the United States is a Party', in the *Proceedings of the 1960 Institute on Private Investments Abroad* (1960), p. 479 *et seq.* Nearly 200 countries, ranging from large industrial nations to small island States, have negotiated more than 1,100 international tax treaties offering relief from double taxation to foreign investment.

For compilation, see *International Tax Treaties*, series A, Vols. 1–11 and series B, vols. 1–6, Oceana Publications Inc.

40 The agreement was approved by the Ratification Act no. 98; for the text see *S.L.S.D.R.S.G.* No. 1091, dated 31 December 1969, Supplement No. 1; General Legislation; also, the Sudan–Kingdom of Saudi Arabia Reciprocal Exemption from Taxation of the Income of the Designation Airlines Agreement, *L.S.R.S.G.* no. 1098, dated 15 October 1963, p. 203; cf. Article 11 of the Agreement between the United Kingdom and the Republic of Zaire Arising from the Avoidance of Double Taxation on Revenues Arising from the Business of Shipping and Air Transport in International Traffic, 1977, for text, see *Statutory Instruments*, 1977, no. 1298, p. 3685.

41 Article 2 (L).

42 Ibid. (2).

43 For the text, see *Statutory Instruments*, 1977, no. 1719. The convention was concluded with a view to affording relief from double taxation in relation to income, corporation tax or capital gains tax and taxes of a similar character imposed by the Democratic Republic of the Sudan on British companies. The convention is very detailed and comprehensive. The instruments of ratification were exchanged on 7 September 1977. The Sudan ratified the convention by the Ratification Act No. 35, 1977, *L.S.D.R.S.G.* no. 992 dated 15 June 1977, p. 193.

44 The Treaty between Norway and India of 1959, followed the same pattern. Thus under Article XVII (3), income from sources within India under the laws of India is subject to tax in India either directly or by deduction will not be subject to Norwegian tax: 356 U.N.T.S. 257. A similar provision was contained in the Ceylon–Sweden Convention of 1957, whereby income from sources in Ceylon (Sri Lanka) which has been taxed there, is exempted from Swedish tax: 315 U.N.T.S. 86.

45 344 U.N.T.S. 204; cf. the Sudan–Italy Treaty. On the United States tax credit practice in this respect, see Malcolm Johnson, 'Foreign Tax Credit' in *Proceedings of the 1959 Institute on Private Investments Abroad* (1959), pp. 45–103; also Howard M. Liebam, 'A formula for Tax-Sparing Credits in the U.S. Tax Treaties with Developing Countries', 72 *A.J.I.L.* (1978), 296.

46 384 U.N.T.S. p. 3.

47 Article XI(3)(h).

48 Cmnd 1347.

49 Ibid.

50 Article XIV(2)(b)(ii).

51 Nwogugu, *Legal Problems*, p. 52. Article 11 (L) of the United Kingdom–Pakistan Treaty, defined 'Permanent establishment' as: 'A branch, management, factory or other fixed place of business, but does not include an agency unless the agent has, and habitually exercises, a general authority to negotiate and conclude contracts on behalf of such enterprise or has a stock or goods or merchandise from which he regularly fills orders on its behalf.'

52 For instance, Sweden–India Treaty, 1958, Article 3(1), 369 U.N.T.S., p. 211; A. R. Albrecht, 'Taxation of Aliens Under International Law', 29 *B.Y.B.I.L.* (1952), p. 168; Moore Digest (1906), vol. 2, p. 65.

53 Cf. Article XVII(i) of the *U.S.–Pakistan Treaty*, 344 U.N.T.S., p. 204; Albrecht, 'Taxation of Aliens'.

54 Nwogugu, *Legal Problems*, pp. 52–3; for further exposition of the standard of treatment; see *post*, pp. 109–15.

55 For instance, *Guidelines for Industrial Projects*, prepared by the Industrial Unit, Ministry of National Planning (Khartoum).

56 On how a ministerial discretion be exercised, see generally De Smith, *Judicial Review of Administrative Actions* (1973), pp. 252–62.

57 See sections 14, 22, and 11 of the Industrial Investment Act, the Investment in Economic Services Act and the Agricultural Investment Act respectively.

Under section 23 of the Encouragement of Investment Act, 1980, the Minister of Finance and National Economy may cancel any investment licence or concessions acquired under the Act in the following cases:

(a) If the investor has not established the project within the period specified in the licence or any extension thereof.

(b) If the investor has broken any of the terms according to which any privileges, facilities, guarantees or licences have been granted thereby.

(c) If the investor has provided any false information or used unlawful means by which he obtained a benefit under the Act.

(d) If the project, without reasonable cause, stopped.

(e) If the investor so contravenes the law as may threaten the security and safety of the land.

Under sub-section 2 of the same section the investor whose licence or concessions are cancelled must restitute the pecuniary benefit he has obtained as a result of the conferment of any privileges or concessions.

Under sub-section 3 the aggrieved investor may file an application to the Ministerial Committee for revision of the cancellation order and the decision of the Committee is final. See de Smith, *Judicial Review*, pp. 246 *et seq.* Also *post*, pp. 284–9.

Similarly, under Article 10 of the Saudi Foreign Capital Investment Law, 1979, any project licensed under that law, violating therein, shall be warned by the Minister of Industry and Electricity to abide by the investment law. Should the project not comply with the said warning, the Minister may, following a recommendation by the Foreign Investment Committee, withdraw the licence granted to that project or order its final liquidation and closure. Following a recommendation by the said Committee, the Minister may, in lieu of withdrawing the licence, deprive such project of all or part of the privileges provided under the investment law.

However, parties concerned may appeal to the Board of Grievances against the Minister's decision imposing such penalty within thirty days as of the date on which the decision has been officially notified. The verdict of the Board of Grievances shall be final and binding.

58 Cf. Section 7(1)(b); the Approved Enterprise Concessions Act, 1956 (repealed). Ali Mohamed El Hassan, *An Introduction to the Sudan Economy* (1976), p. 87. Note by the writer on the Draft Bill for the Encouragement of Investment, 1980 to the Head Department of Legislation and Legal Affairs, the Presidency of the Republic, Khartoum, dated 20 March 1980.

59 For instance, Nigeria, Burundi, Kenya, Ethiopia; S. M. Nimeiri, 'Tax Incentives for Promotion of Private Industry in the Sudan: Their Impact on Industrial Development and Government Revenue', *Sudan Notes and Records* (1975).

60 Report of the Technical Commission. For simplicity, the Technical Commission for reforming the investment laws will be referred to hereinafter as the Commission.

61 See for instance, the Land Acquisition Ordinance 1930, *Laws of the Sudan*, vol. 7, title

XX: sub-title 3; the Native Disposition of Lands Restriction (no. 1), 1918, ibid., p. 79.

62 See above, p. 389 for the description of the Commission.

63 The Commission's Final Report, p. 7.

64 Statement by the representative of the Bank of Sudan at the Sixth Session of the Commission.

In practice some investors investing in banking, after obtaining their investment licences from the Bank of Sudan, immediately embark on their business, which actually depends on local capital; though they keep the bulk of the foreign capital outside the Sudan. This is a serious snag which enables these investors to siphon off local resources and hence the policy of the investment law would be defeated. Unfortunately, as yet this is not well screened. The investment licences should not be used unless the foreign investor has deposited substantial foreign capital with the Bank of Sudan or any other local commercial bank before starting his business in the Sudan.

65 The Commission's Report, p. 10.

66 I.C.C. Brochure 218, *Taxation Policies in Relation to International Investment* (June 1961), pp. 26–7.

67 Nwogugu, *Legal Problems*, p. 38.

68 Friedmann and Pugh, *Legal Aspects*, p. 741.

69 For further discussion, see *post*, pp. 128–40.

70 Decree-law No. 258 of 30 March 1960, Diario Official No. 2461, 4 April 1960. Cf. the Cameroun Investment Code of 11 June 1960, which confers on high priority enterprises immunity from tax increase for up to twenty-five years: U.N. Doc. E/3492, 18 May 1961, p. 17. The document also contains similar provision on tax exemption in different developing countries.

71 The Draft Bill was intended to supersede the major Sudanese investment laws. As mentioned before, these are: the Investment in Economic Services, the Industrial Investment, the Agricultural Investment Acts. The Petroleum Resources and the Mineral Resources Acts, are not affected, and hence they operate cumulatively with the new law.

72 Section 6(1).

73 Section (2).

74 Section 6(3).

75 Under section 5 the purposes of the Draft Bill are to regulate and encourage foreign, Arab and national investments in private, co-operative and mixed sectors for the contribution by capital and expertise for the realization of the objectives of development of the Sudan in accordance with the priorities and activities to be specified by the Regulations of the Objectives Activities and Priorities of Private Investment. (to be enacted).

76 Section 6(4).

77 It has been revealed in the deliberations of the Commission that about sixty-one firms, purely Sudanese, received tax and customs exemptions in addition to obtaining land below the official sale price in accordance with the Investment in Economic Services Act only during the period 1975–77. Before that, it has been estimated that about £S 60m. of revenue was lost in the period 1961–70 because of exemption from business profits tax and customs duties and because of selling land for erection of new enterprises below market prices. The total amount of private investment in manufacturing and mining industries according to industrial survey in 1969/1970 was £S 43.7m. The amount of current revenue of the Central Government over the same period was about £S 800m. As the

sum of £S 60m. of lost revenue does not include the loss due to reductions in other facilities, it seems that the amount of actual lost revenue over this period makes about 10% of the current revenue: for details and analysis, see Ali Ahmed Suliman, *Issues*, pp. 10–58. Cf. John M. Paxman, 'Argentine Foreign Investment Incentives: Quixotic Nationalism Challenges the Windfall', 12 *Virginia Journal of International Law* (1972), 241–60.

78 The World Bank and the U.N.I.D.O. after examining the incentives furnished by the Sudanese investment laws came to the conclusion that they are extremely exaggerated and may arouse suspicion to foreign investors in view of the near past experience of the Sudanese confiscation and nationalization.

79 Information obtained orally from Mr M. N. El Deen El Tahir, ex-legal adviser to the Council of Ministers, (Khartoum).

80 Part V.

81 Article 89.

82 Articles 90 and 91.

83 Law no. 43 of 1974, as amended by Law no. 32 of 1977.

84 Section 12.

85 See *post*, ch. 9. For a contrary view, see Fatouros, in Friedmann and Pugh, *Legal Aspects*, p. 713.

5. Unilateral guarantees

1 See the United States Department of State *Report on Nationalisation, Expropriation, and Other Takings of United States and Certain Foreign Property* since 1960, reproduced in 11 *I.L.M.* (1972), 84.

2 I.C.C. Brochure 200, *Attracting Foreign Investment* (March, 1959), p. 5.

3 During 1969–71.

4 The original Arabic text of the Article under discussion is very awkward in its drafting and does not contain any Arabic punctuation which tends to distort the meaning, let alone the translated version.

5 *S.L.S.D.R.S.G.* no. 1153, dated 15 September 1975, p. 273.

6 Ibid. no. 1158, dated 14 March 1974, p. 8.

7 Parry, *Nationality*, p. 5.

8 Irving, *Dictionary of Legal Terms* (1969), p. 35.

9 Professor White has observed that during the inter-war period the term nationalization was not widely known, and instead expropriation and confiscation were in common use: White, *Nationalisation*, p. 3.

10 Recently, in the negotiations between Tanzania and Lonrho for fixing the amount of compensation to be paid to Lonrho for its assets, which have been nationalized by Tanzania, the term 'taking' has been used instead of nationalization: *Financial Times*, 16 September 1978. This also finds tenets in political statements in the deliberations of the British Labour Party Conference in relation to the North Sea Oil in October 1978: *The Times*, 5 October 1978.

11 B. A. Wortley, *Expropriation in Public International Law* (1959), pp. 36–7.

12 G. C. Christie, 'What Constitutes A Taking of Property Under International Law', 38 *B.Y.B.I.L.* (1962), pp. 307–38.

13 Ibid. p. 309.

14 Judgment No. 7, *P.C.I.J.*, series A, no. 7.

15 *Norway* v. *U.S.*, 1. U.N.A.A.R., p. 307.

16 Article 10(1) and (2); for the text of the proposed draft, see 55 *A.J.I.L.* (1961), 545–84. The draft was greatly relied on by the American Law Institute: Draft Restatement of the Foreign Law Relations of the United States dealing with State responsibility for economic injury to aliens, *American Law Institute Restatement, The Foreign Law of the U.S.*, ss. 190, 197 (proposed offical Draft, 1962). For comments on the Harvard Draft, see Professors Sohn and Baxter in 55 *A.J.I.L.* (1961), 558–9. For an elaborate definition of the word 'expropriation' for the purpose of insuring foreign investment, see *post*, pp. 166–7.

17 See for instance, *Jabez C. Casto* case, M. M. Whiteman, *Damages in International Law* (1937), vol. 2, p. 860; *German Interests in Polish Upper Silesia* case; the *Norwegians Claims* case; the decisions and panel opinions of the United States Foreign Claims Settlement Commission, cited and reported by Professor Christie, 38 *B.Y.B.I.L.* (1962), 322–4.

18 'The measures Taken by the Indonesian Government Against Netherlands Enterprises', 5 *Neth.Int.L.Rev.* (1958), pp. 227–42; also at p. 235.

19 Ibid. at pp. 227, 242.

20 Ibid. at p. 242.

21 *Expropriation*, p. 3.

22 Ibid. p. 1; also Herz, 'Expropriation of Foreign Property', 35 *A.J.I.L.* (1961), 250–1; Oppenheim, *International Law*, vol. 1, p. 352.

23 *Robert Wilson* case (1841), Moore *Digest of International Arbitrations*, vol. 4, p. 3373; cf. *The Rebecca* (1929), 23 *A.J.I.L.* (1929), 860.

24 Moore, *Digest*, vol. 6, pp. 5036, 5081.

25 Friedmann, *Expropriation*, pp. 1–13; Herz, 'Expropriation', pp. 247–8.

26 White, *Nationalisation*, p. 41.

27 Ibid. p. 43.

28 See ibid. p. 42, f.n. 3.

29 Ibid. pp. 43–5.

30 Nazer, 'Doing Business in Saudi Arabia', p. 117.

31 For further study, see Muhammad Hamidullah, *The Muslim Conduct of State*, 7th revised and enlarged edn., (1977), pp. 120–1: This principle is one of the Command of the Prophet cited by Abu Yusuf, *Kharaj*, p. 71; see also Sarakhsiy, "IV 11«١٧» شرح السير الكبير".

32 M. Khadduri, 'The Islamic System: Its Competition and Co-existence with Western Systems', *Proc. A.S.I.L.* (1959), p. 50.

33 For text in translation see *Investment laws of the World*, vol. 1.

34 Cf. Article 33 of the Afghanistan Constitution, ibid. vol. 1 (now suspended in the wake of the military coup of April, 1978).

35 Order in Council, 1961, Second Schedule, Chapter II, cited and discussed by Nwogugu, *Legal Problems*, p. 60. Cf. Article 18 of the Constitution of Zambia, 1973, *Investment Laws of the World*, vol. 7. The most accurate provision on the guarantee againt illegal nationalization is Article 75 of the Constitution of Kenya, 1969, which sets out exhaustively the exceptions of when private property can be taken or acquired by the State, ibid. vol. 4.

36 *Investment Laws of the World*, vol. 4; for comment, see Nwogugu, *Legal Problems*, pp. 60–1.

37 Settlement of disputes will be discussed in ch. 10.

38 Cf. section 14 of the Organization and Promotion of Industrial Investment Act, 1967 (repealed).

39 Section 20. Cf. Article 8 of the Foreign Investments Protection Act, 1964 of Kenya, 4 *I.L.M.* (1964), 241.

40 *Laws of the Sudan*, vol. 3, title XII: sub-title 1, p. 73.
41 Section 210, ibid.
42 *L.S.D.R.S.G.* no. 1157, dated 30 June 1974, p. 332.
43 Ibid. 1973, no. 9120, dated 15 December 1973, p. 375.
44 Section 9.
45 Cf. the Southern Rhodesia Boycott Act, 1966, *L.S.D.R.S.G.* no. 1027 dated 15 October 1966, p. 146.
46 Section 10.
47 Oppenheim, *International Law*, pp. 679–80; W. E. Beckett, 'The Exercise of Criminal Jurisdiction Over Foreigners', 6 *B.Y.B.I.L.* (1925), pp. 44–60.
48 43 *A.J.I.L.* (1949), 379.
49 *S.L.J.R.* (1971), 35.
50 *S.L.S.D.R.S.G.*, no. 1162, dated 1 July 1974, p. 842.
51 Ibid. no. 1098, dated 15 January 1970, p. 12.
52 Ibid. p. 98.
53 Ibid. p. 105.
54 Ibid. p. 105.
55 *R.S.G.*, October 1964.
56 Ibid. May 1969.
57 Ibid. 1972; also section 7 of the Acquisition Act; section 16 of the Central Bureau Act; the Civil Procedure Act, 1972 (the latter two laws have been repealed).
58 The rather different doctrine of 'act of State' will be discussed in ch. 10.
59 An example, however, was the Italian Embassy Diplomatic Note of 30 December 1971, to the Minister of the Treasury, through the Minister of Foreign Affairs on behalf of Amedco Crescenzi (an Italian national) whose company was confiscated in the Sudan in 1970.
60 These are: the Economic Services Act, 1973; the Industrial Investment Act, 1974; and the Agricultural Investment Act, 1976.
61 Section 16 of the Industrial Investment Act; section 20 of the Agricultural Investment Act.
62 Nwabueze, *Presidentialism*, ch. 9.
63 Section 20 of the Agricultural Investment Act.
64 D. P. O'Connell, *International Law*, vol. 2, 2nd edn. (1970), p. 778.
65 M. Domke, 'Foreign Nationalizations', 55 *A.J.I.L.* (1961), 600.
66 The Banks Nationalization Act, 1970; the Companies Nationalisation Act, 1970: for texts, *S.L.S.D.R.S.G.* No. 1104 dated 12 June 1970, pp. 263, 266.
67 *Tameem-el-Masarif-fe-el-Sudan*, 1970 (*Nationalization of Banks in the Sudan*), prepared by the Information and Publication Committee, Bank of Sudan.
68 Section 3(1); see A. W. Bradley, 'The Nationalisation of Companies in Tanzania', in *Private Enterprise and the Eastern African Company*, pp. 207–28.
69 Cf. the Charter of Economic Rights and Duties of States, 1974 (*post*, pp. 128–40).
70 See also the *Walter Fletcher Smith* case, where the expropriation of alien property for private gain was held to be contrary to international law: 'The expropriation proceedings were not, in good faith, for purpose of public utility... While the proceedings were municipal in form, the properties seized were turned over immediately to the defendant company, ostensibly for public purposes of amusement and private profit, without any reference to public utility.' *U.N.R.I.A.A.*, vol. 2, p. 917.
71 Friedmann, *Expropriation*, p. 142; S. D. Metzger, 'Multilateral Conventions for the Protection of Private Foreign Investment', 9 *J.P.L.* (1960), 133; J. H. Herz, 'Expropriation

of Foreign Property', 35 *A.J.I.L.* (1941), 251–3. Also the decision of the Permanent Court of International Justice in the *Oscar Chinn* case, *P.C.I.J.* series A/B, no. 63, at p. 79. The same view was expressed by the arbitrator in the *Shufeldt* case, 2 *U.N.R.I.A.A.* 1079 at p. 1059. White doubts the application of the limitation of 'public interest' to nationalization as it is vague and not susceptible to legal proof: White, *Nationalisation*, pp. 149–50.

72 F. J. Nicholson, 'The Protection of Foreign Property under Customary International Law', 6 *Boston College Industrial and Commercial Law Review* (1960), 400.

73 *I.C.J.Rep.*, 1970, p. 4.

74 U.N.Doc.A/AC.79/Rev.1, 27 December 1960, p. 149. This act was repealed by the law Concerning Investment of Foreign Capital, 1967. This latter act removed the time-limit during which expropiation was impossible; for the text of the new act, see *Investment Laws of the World*, vol. 2.

75 U.N.Doc.A/AC/97/Rev., 27 December 1960, p. 150.

76 Examples are: Somalia, Brazil and Chile, see p. 386, ns. 26 and 27 to ch. 3 respectively.

77 United States note to Romania, 19 *Department of State Bulletin* (1948), p. 408.

78 Section 7 of the Encouragement of Investment Act, 1980.

79 For the standard of treatment under the investment treaties, see *post*, pp. 109–15.

80 White, *Nationalisation*, pp. 131–44; also the *Oscar Chinn* case, at p. 87.

81 Donke, 55 *A.J.I.L.*, (1961), 602.

82 *Banco Naional de Cuba* v. *Sabbatino* 376 U.S. 398 (1964); also 56 *A.J.I.L.* (1962), 1085, at 1104–5.

83 Wickersham and Fishburne, *Current Legal Aspects*, p. 149.

84 Thus in the *Sura* 'Nissa' ('The Women' IV, v. 29): 'Eat not up your property amongst you in vanities; but trade with it together in mutual good will.' 'Mutual good will' implies that to use someone else's property without his consent is malversation and sin.

85 For further study, see Abdel Salam Dawod El Abdi, *El-Milkia-fe-El-Sharia-El-Islamia*, (*Private Ownership in Islamic Law*) (1975), vol. 2.

86 See Mustafa El Subaa, *Ishtrakiat-El-Islam* (*Socialism of Islam*), 3rd edn. (1960), pp. 101–4; cf. Mohammed Bagir El Sadr, *Igtisaduna* (*Our Economy*), *2nd edn.* (*1968*), *pp. 207–505.*

87 Extracted from a message by Sayed Ahmed Khair, Minister for Foreign Affairs in the Abboud Military Government (1958–64). This message was designated as an opening note to the *Sudan Trade and Industrial Guide, 1960–61*, p. 3.

88 Ibid. p. 7.

89 *Investment Guide*, p. 29.

90 The President's address on the occasion of the seventh Anniversary of the 25 May revolution in the inaugural session of the First Conference of Sudanese Farmers in the Socialist Union, 1976, Khartoum.

91 *Africa Development* (1976).

92 President Nimeiri's Press Conference at the Sudan Embassy, London on 26 March 1973.

93 *Guide to Industrial Investment*, p. 38.

94 U.N. Doc. E/3492, 18 May 1961, p. 89.

95 As there is no restriction on the transfer of money abroad in Saudi Arabia, this section relates only to the Sudan.

96 Section 17, 10(1) and II of the Industrial Investment Act, the Investment in the Economic Services Act and the Agricultural Investment Act, respectively. These provisions have been resurrected in section 20 of the Encouragement of Investment Act, 1980.

97 Sections 18(2) and 12 of the Industrial Investment and the Agricultural Investment Act, respectively.

98 *Adams* case, Moore, *Digest*, vol. 3 (1898), pp. 3066–7; *Muresam Claim*, I.L.R., 1958–11 pp. 294–5; Mann, *Legal Aspects*, p. 229. For practice of States, see E. Borchard, *State Insolvency and Foreign Bondholders* vol. 1, (1953), pp. 127–8.

99 Shuster, *Law of Money*, p. 48.

100 Act of 21 March 1966, 5 *I.L.M.* (1966), 607.

101 Decree No. 51, 16 September 1963, 3 *I.L.M.* (1964), No. 1. It is noteworthy that this decree is no longer operative in the wake of the existing Marxist regime in Ethiopia.

102 13 *I.L.M.* (1974), 1270.

103 Law No. 61–122, 1960, *Investment Laws of the World*, vol. 3.

104 Law No. 43, as amended by Law No. 32, 1977.

105 Section 10.

106 Law No. 10, 18 February, 1960, *Official Bulletin*, Supplement No. 5.

107 *Investment Laws of the World*, vol. 3.

108 Legislative Decree on Encouragement of Investment of Syrians Abroad and Arab Nationals, 30 December 1969, section 4, *Official Gazette*, 1970.

109 Brazilian Law Relating to the Expatriation of Profits Earned by Foreign Investors, 1962 as amended by Law no. 390 of August 29 1964, 3 *I.L.M.* (1964), 236 of Chile, Decree-Law Containing the Foreign Investment Statute, 1974, 13 *I.L.M.* (1974), 1176.

110 *I.M.F., 12th Annual Report.*

111 Nwogugu, *Legal Problems*, p. 61.

112 *Foreign Investment Laws*, 1973; 12 *I.L.M.* (1973), 11489.

113 For the discussion of the theory of vested rights, see pp. 259–60.

114 Nwogugu, *Legal Problems*, pp. 62–3

115 Friedmann, *Law in a Changing Society* (1959), p. 456; also Fatouros in Friedmann and Pugh, *Legal Aspects*, p. 722.

116 *I.C.J. Reports* (1970), p. 4, at 32.

117 *I.C.J. Reports* (1974), pp. 267–72.

118 At p. 267.

119 Sir H. Lauterpacht, *Private Law Sources and Analogies of International Law* (1927), p. 203; B. Cheng, *General Principles of Law* (1953), p. 1411; I. C. MacGibbon, 'Estoppel in International Law', 7 *I.C.L.Q.* (1958), 468–77; D. W. Bowett, 'Estoppel before International Tribunals and its Relation to Acquiescence', 33 *B.Y.B.I.L.* (1957), 176; *The Temple* case, *I.C.J. Rep.* (1962), p. 6, at pp. 29–35. For further discussion on estoppel in relation to development agreements, see *post*, pp. 261–3.

120 Section 32 of the Encouragement of Investment Act, 1980. See chs. 8 and 10.

121 R. R. Wilson, *The International Law Standard in Treaties of the U.S.* (1953), p. 95. On incorporation of international law as part of municipal law in the Commonwealth Countries, see R. R. Wilson, *The International Law Standard and Commonwealth Developments* (1966), pp. 75–88; *idem*, 'International Law in New Constitutions', 58 *A.J.I.L.* (1964), 432–6.

122 Published especially by the Attorney-General's Chambers.

123 Article 218 of the Permanent Constitution of the Sudan. For an analytical discussion on the procedure of amending the constitution in a one-party system in Commonwealth Africa, see Nwabueze, *Presidentialism*, ch. 13.

124 See Article 4 of the Constitution. See generally Nwabueze, *Presidentialism*, p. 396.

6. Investment treaties: bilateral and multilateral

1 It is the first time that the African Organization has taken serious steps towards solving the continent's economic problems. The efficacy of this new strategy, of course, cannot be judged by the words only, but requires strenuous efforts to implement what has been agreed upon. And this needs time.

2 Zouhir A. Kronfol, *Protection of Foreign Investment* (1972), p. 15.

3 Cited by Edwin M. Borchard, *The Diplomatic Protection of Citizens Abroad* (1927), p. 36.

4 For the text, *L.S.D.R.S.G.*, No. 1112 dated 31 December 1970 p. 721. As regards Libya, the agreement no longer exists, as it was renounced in 1977 by the Sudan for political reasons.

5 It should be 'securing'.

6 Treaty with Israel (1951), U.N.T.S., vol. 219, Article XXIII.

7 Treaty between W. Germany and Pakistan, 1961.

8 Agreement between the Federal Republic of Germany and the Republic of Indonesia Concerning the Encouragement and Reciprocal Protection of Investments, 1970: Investment Laws of the World, vol. 3.

9 Treaty between Ceylon (Sri Lanka) and W. Germany, 1966, ibid., vol. 6.

10 The English authentic text of Article 2(2) reads as follows: 'Neither Contracting Party shall in its territory subject nationals or companies of the other Contracting Party, as regards occupations or business matters in connection with investments made by them, to conditions less favourable than it imposes on its own nationals or companies or on nationals or companies of any third State. The same shall apply in respect of the management, use, or enjoyment of such investments.'

11 An identical clause has been recently contained in Article 4 of the Agreement on Exchange Encouragement and Protection of Investments between the Democratic Republic of the Sudan and the Republic of France, 1979.

12 Fatouros, *Government Guarantees*, p. 139.

13 J. L. Brierly, *The Law of Nations*, 6th edn. (1961), p. 220; Oppenheim, *International Law*, vol. 1, p. 350; Roth, *Minimum Standard*, p. 8.

14 Brierly, *Law of Nations*, p. 220.

15 G. Schwarzenberger, 'The Province and Standards of International Economic Law', 2 *I.C.L.Q.* (1948), 402.

16 W. E. Beckett, 'Diplomatic Claims in Respect of Injuries to Companies', 17 *Grotius Society Transactions* (1931), 175, at 179.

17 Nwogugu, *Legal Problems*, p. 123.

18 Cf. Article 2(2) of the Egypt–United Kingdom Agreement on Promotion and Protection of Investments, 1975, which provides that 'investments of all nationals of either party shall at all times be accorded fair and equitable treatment and shall enjoy full protection and security in the territory of the other contracting party'; for the text, 14 *I.L.M.* (1975), 1470; cf. Article 1 of the Treaty between the Swiss Confederation and the Tunisia Republic, 1961, 3 *I.L.M.* (1964), 524; Article 29 of the Treaty between W. Germany and Cameroun, 1962 *Investment Laws of the World, vol. 1.*

19 Section 17.

20 Commands of the Prophet cited by Yusuf, *Kharaj*, p. 71.

21 For instance, Article 2 of the Brazilian Law Relating to the Expatriation of Profits Earned by Foreign Investors, 1964, 3 *I.L.M.* (1964), 662: Article 5 of Chile Decree-Law

Containing the Foreign Investment Statute, 1974, 13 *I.L.M.* (1974), 1176; Article 19 of the *Argentinian Foreign Investment Law*, 1973, 12 *I.L.M.* (1973), 1489, which expressly provides that in no case may foreign investors receive better treatment than Argentinian investors.

22 United States–Korean Treaty, 1956, Article XXII(2), U.N.T.S., vol. 302; also G. Schwarzenberger, 'The Most-Favoured-Nation standard in British State Practice', 22 *B.Y.B.I.L.* (1945), 96–121; Oppenheim, *International Law*, vol. 1, p. 971. For the ablest exposition of the most-favoured-nation standard of treatment see Jacob Viner, *International Economics* (1951), chs. 1 and 5; also I.L.C. 'Most-Favoured-Nation clause', Doc. A/CN4/228 and Add. 1, second report, by Mr Endre Ustor, Special Rapporteur, *Y.B.I.L.C.*, vol. 11 (1970), pp. 201–42, also I.L.C. 13th session 8 May to 28 July 1978, 'First Report on the Most-Favoured-Nation Clause', by N. A. Ushakov, Special Rapporteur, U.N.G.A., Doc. A/CN.4/309/Add.1. Fawcett explained that the most-favoured-nation standard is to be applied when Country A (the promissor) undertakes to accord to Country B (promisee) treatment in the course of trade, transport or establishment of companies or individuals, no worse in any respect than that accorded to Country C (third party) by Country A: *Conflicts*, p. 27. Recently in the negotiations between the Iranian Oil Consortium and Iran for a new long-term relationship, Iran insisted on a 'Most-favoured-nation' clause, which would give her the same benefits as those likely to be achieved by Saudi Arabia in its complete take-over of the Aramco consortium operating there: *Financial Times*, 16 September 1978, p. 2.

23 *Rights of U.S. Nationals in Morocco, I.C.J. Rep.* 1952, p. 176, at p. 192.

24 Article 3(3), (4), (5). Identical clauses were contained in the German treaties with Pakistan and Sri Lanka. The German treaty with Cameroun has blended together the two standards of national and most-favoured-nation treatment in a non-contingent standard of fair and equitable treatment at least equal to that accorded to nationals, or, if more favourable, the same as that granted to nationals of the most-favoured-nation.

25 The most-favoured-nation treatment is also accorded by Article 111 of the Economic Agreement between the State of Kuwait and the Democratic Republic of the Sudan (hereinafter referred to as the Sudan–Kuwait Economic Agreement). The agreement has been ratified by 1970 Act 9; for text see *L.S.D.R.S.G.* no. 1095, dated 15 March 1970, p. 35. According to the League of Arab States, the standard of treatment accorded by one Arab country to another member of the League cannot be the basis of treatment to be claimed under the most-favoured-nation clause in a non-Arab State. Privileges granted by an Arab State to another Arab State may not be applicable to non-Arab parties, since relations among Arab countries are governed by special considerations, see I.L.C., thirteenth session, 8 May to 28 July 1978, *U.N.G.A. Distr.* General, A/CN.4/308/ and 2, p. 2.

26 Cf. the German treaty with Cameroun, n. 24, ch. 6, p. 113. An identical clause is obtained in Article 111 of the Egypt–Sudan Investment Agreement, 1978.

27 G. Schwarzenberger, *International Law*, 3rd edn. (1957), pp. 200–7.

28 The agreement was signed at London on 7 November 1933, for the text, see 142 L.N.T.S. 330.

29 *Y.B.I.L.C.*, Summary Records of the twenty-seventh session, 5 May to 26 July, 1975, p. 263. Fawcett observed that it is a matter of dispute how far the most-favoured-nation standard has evolved into a general principle of law; Fawcett, *Economic Conflicts*, p. 28.

30 Kronfol, *Protection*, p. 16.

31 *U.N.R.I.A.A.*, vol. 4, pp. 61–2.

32 Article 3(1).
33 U.N.T.S. 79, p. 172.
34 Nwogugu, *Legal Problems*, p. 124.
35 See also, White, *Nationalisation*, ch. 6.
36 The Latin-American countries affirm their sovereign right to accord foreign investors national treatment even in treaty arrangements: cf. the Andean Pact, 11 *I.L.M.* (1972), 126.
37 For promises to admit foreign investors in the Sudan, by way of exceptions to the immigration laws, see *ante*, pp. 27–8.
38 Cf. Article 2 of the *Investment Treaty between the Sudan and France.*
39 A similar provision is obtained in Articles IV and 11 of the Economic Agreement between the State of Kuwait and the Democratic Republic of the Sudan, and the Agreement on the Encouragement and Protection of Investment between the Arab Republic of Egypt and the Democratic Republic of the Sudan, respectively.
40 For example, United Kingdom–Iran Treaty (Cmnd 698) 1959, Article 3(4).
41 Example: U.S.–Israel F.C.N. Treaty, 1951 U.N.T.S. 219, p. 252. Also Articles V and VI of the Sudan–Kuwait Economic Agreement and the Egypt–Sudan Investment Agreement, respectively.
42 Article 6(3). A detailed provision on this point is included in Article 6 of the Investment Treaty between the Sudan and France. Section 3 of Article IV of the I.M.F. Articles of Agreement provides that the maximum and minimum rates of exchange transactions between the currencies of members taking place within their territories shall not differ from parity as specified by the same section; for the text, see 2 U.N.T.S. 39. For a comprehensive exposition of the I.M.F. Articles of Agreement, see Aufricht, *The International Monetary Fund* p. 7 *et seq.*, Shuster, *Law of Money*, p. 111 *et seq.* For the meaning of current transactions, see F. A. Mann, *Legal Aspects*, p. 545.
43 Article 6 (3).
44 Article 6.
45 For assessment of compensation, see ch. 8.
46 The authentic text is the Arabic version.
47 Article 111.
48 Article VI(1), U.N.T.S. vol. 25, p. 69.
49 Cf. article V(2) of the Cameroun–U.K. Agreement of 29 July 1963, Cmd 2133.
50 For instance, U.S.–Korea treaty, 1956, Article XI, U.N.T.S. 302.
51 29 *B.Y.B.I.L.* (1952), at p. 180.
52 Herman Walker, 'Modern Treaties of Friendship, Commerce and Navigation', 42 *Minnesota Law Review* (1958), 821.
53 Cheng, *General Principles*, ch. 14.
54 For a convenient text of the Arab League Pact, 1944, see 39 *A.J.I.L.* (1944), 266; for comments see D. W. Bowett, *The Law of International Institutions*, 3rd edn. (1975), pp. 203–6; also M. Khadduri, 'The Arab League as a Regional Arrangement', 40 *A.J.I.L.* (1946), 756. The text of the Agreement for Economic Unity Among the Arab League Countries is reproduced in *L.S.D.R.S.G.* no. 1089, dated 15 November 1969, p. 298.
55 For the text, see *L.S.D.R.S.G.* no. 1119, dated 15 July 1971, p. 704 (text in Arabic only).
56 Article 7.
57 Article 1.
58 Article 9.
59 See, generally, Mann, *Studies*, ch. 17.

60 Cf. The Sudanese Sequestration Act.
61 Article 7.
62 Article 11.
63 U.N.Doc. E/3325, 26 February 1960, p. 71.
64 Clair Wilcox, *A Charter for World Trade* (1949), pp. 231–327. The *Havana Charter* was the outcome of the United Nations Conference on Trade and Employment held at Havana, Cuba, from 21 November 1947 to 24 March 1948. The conference agreed on the text of the Havana Charter for an International Trade Organization which received the signature of fifty-four countries: U.N. Conference on Trade and Employment: Final Act and related Documents, New York (April 1948).
65 Ch. III of the Charter.
66 Article 12(1)(a) and (b).
67 Article 12(1)(c).
68 See Nwogugu, *Legal Problems*, pp. 138–9.
69 Kronfol, *Protection*, p. 31.
70 Richard N. Gardner, 'International Measures for Promotion of Foreign Investment', 9 *J.P.L.* (1960), 182.
71 U.S. Dept. of State Publication No. 3263, November 1948; also G. G. Fenwick, 'The Ninth International Conference of American States', 42 *A.J.I.L.* (1948), 561.
72 Article 25.
73 Nwogugu, *Legal Problems*, p. 141; S. J. Rubin, *Private Foreign Investment* (1956), p. 82.
74 I.C.C. Brochure no. 129, April 1949.
75 Article 3–4.
76 Article 11.
77 Articles 9–10.
78 See E. Snyder: 'Protection of Private Foreign Investment', 10 *I.C.L.Q.* (1961), 480; Fatouros, *Government Guarantees*, pp. 120–61; Friedmann and Pugh, *Legal Aspects*, pp. 204–5.
79 U.N.Doc.E/C.3 2/568, 31 January 1961.
80 For the text, 9 *J.P.L.* (1960), 116; discussed and evaluated by G. Schwarzenberger, 'The Abs/Shawcross Draft Convention on Investments Abroad', ibid. 147 *et seq.*; *idem*, 'The Protection of British Property Abroad', 14 *C.L.P.* (1961), 213; M. Brandon, 'Recent Measures to Improve the International Investment Climate', 9 *J.P.L.* (1959), 125–32.
81 One draft was prepared by the German Society to Advance the Protection of Foreign Investment under the chairmanship of Dr Abs, published in 1957, which was reviewed by Miller in 53 *A.J.I.L.* (1959), 371–8. The other draft was prepared by a group of English and European lawyers and businessmen led by Lord Shawcross; for text and analysis, see Brandon 9 *J.P.L.* (1959), 125–32.
82 Article III.
83 A. Larson, 'Recipients' Rights under an International Investment Code', 9 *J.P.L.* (1960), 172–5.
84 Ibid.
85 O.E.C.D. Publication no. 15637, December 1962, appendix B.
86 For critical analysis of the Draft Convention, see Schwarzenberger, *Foreign Investments*, p. 84.
87 See ch. 8. From an international political point of view, it is hardly possible for the Sudan to support this Draft Convention in view of its voting in favour of the Charter of Economic Right and Duties of States, which will be examined below.

88 O.E.C.D., *Code of Liberalization of Capital Movement* (Paris 1969), pp. 9–19.
89 For text, 55 *A.J.I.L.* (1961), 548.
90 Article 9.
91 Article 10.
92 International Bar Association, Seventh Conference Report (1958), p. 484; the 1958 Conference of the International Parliamentary Union, as reported by Brandon, 'Recent Measures', 127–8.
93 G. W. Haight, 'Activities of International Chambers of Commerce and Other Business Groups', 54 *Am.Soc.Int.Law Proceed.* (1960), pp. 200–3.
94 Successive reports of the Commission's Special Rapporteur Dr Garcia-Ahmador, in 1956-II *Y.B.I.L.C.*, p. 173; 1957-II, ibid., p. 104, and 1958-II, ibid.
95 A. A. Fatouros, 'An International Code to Protect Private Investment – Proposals and Perspectives', 14 *University of Toronto Law Journal* (1961), 77, at 101.
96 Larson, 9 *J.P.L.* (1960), 172.
97 Paul O. Proehl, 'Private Investment Abroad', 9 *J.P.L.* (1960), 362, at 371.
98 Fatouros, 14 *University of Toronto Law Journal*, 100.
99 The Charter was adopted by the General Assembly on 12 December 1974, by a roll-call vote, 120 in favour, six against with ten abstentions (G.A. Resolution 3281 (XXIX)). Among those countries which voted against the Charter were: Belgium, Denmark, Germany (Federal Republic of), Luxembourg, United Kingdom, United States, Countries abstaining were: Austria, Canada, France, Ireland, Israel, Italy, Japan, Netherlands, Norway and Spain. The Charter was originally proposed by the President Luis Echeveria Alavares of Mexico on 19 April 1972, at the Third Session of the United Nations Conference on Trade and Development (U.N.C.T.A.D.) at Santiago, Chile, see *Proceedings of the U.N.C.T.A.D., Third Session, Vol. 1, Report and Annexes* (*United Nation Publication, Sale No.: E.73.11.D.4*) *Annex 1.A.* For a comprehensive account of the origin and negotiations preceding the final adoption of the Charter, see Peter D. Maynard in his doctoral thesis on 'The Charter of Economic Rights and Duties of States – A legal Analysis of the Divisive Issues', submitted to the Johns Hopkins University in conformity with the requirements for the degree of Doctor of Philosophy, Baltimore, Maryland (1976), pp. 1–22; also see Remarks by Ambassador Alfonse Garcia Robles, in *Proceedings of the 69th Annual Meeting of Am.Soc.I.L.* (April 24–26, 1975), pp. 227–31.
100 G.A. Res. 3201 (S-VI) of 1 May 1974, reproduced in 13 *I.L.M.* (1974), 715 and 68 *A.J.I.L.* (1974), 799.
101 Ibid. p. 720.
102 For compensation, see chapter 8 below.
103 'The Charter', p. 41.
104 Brierly, *Law of Nations*, 6th edn., p. 110.
105 For instance, D. H. N. Johnson, 'The Effects of Resolutions of the General Assembly of the United Nations', 32 *B.Y.B.I.L.* (1955–56), p. 106, also F. Blaine Sloan, 'The Binding Force of a Recommendation of the General Assembly of the United Nations', 25 *B.Y.B.I.L.* (1948), pp. 1–33; G. G. Fitzmaurice, 'The Status of Resolutions of the United Nations General Assembly', 25 *B.Y.B.I.L.* (1948), p. 1 *et seq.*; also J. Castaneda, *Legal Effects of United Nations Resolutions* (1969), p. 1 *et seq.*
106 C. N. Brown and J. B. Tepe, 'The Charter of Economic Rights and Duties of States, A Reflection or Rejection of International Law', 9 *Int.L.L.* (1975), 302–3. Professor O'Connell expressed the view that the resolutions of the General Assembly have only moral force and as such they are not legally binding: deliberations of the session on 'State

Participation in Exploitation of Natural Resources', 5th Commonwealth Law Conference, 24–29 July, 1977 (Edinburgh). The writer was present at this conference as an observer.

107 G. W. Haight, 'The New International Economic Order and the Charter of Economic Rights and Duties of States', 9 *Int.L.L.* (1975), 591. See Article 10 of the *United Nations Charter*. In agreement, I.C.C., *Bilateral Treaties for International Investment*, Brochure (1977), p. 11.

108 The International Arbitral Tribunal convened in Geneva, 19 January 1977. Though the Award was *ex parte* the Libyan Government it contains a valuable and substantial discussion, which is very illuminating and worthy to be considered at length. For further discussion of the Award see ch. 9.

109 At pp. 105–6 of the Award.

110 17 U.N. G.A.O.R. 112, U.N. Doc. A/PV.1193, 1962.

111 The Libya–Oil Companies Arbitration Award, p. 109; Maynard 'The Charter', pp. 110–11.

112 For an analytical examination of this Convention, see *post*, pp. 307–16.

113 In agreement Dupuy in the Libya–Oil Companies Arbitration Award, p. 116; Maynard, 'The Charter'.

114 Translated from an article in a French Journal by Dupuy in the Libyan Award, p. 117; also Maynard, 'The Charter', p. 34. In agreement, Ambassador Alfonso Garcia Robles, in *Proceed. of 69th Annual Meeting of Am. Soc. I.L.* (24–26 April 1975) at p. 227. But the rejection of an amendment which would have included an express reference to expropriation and compensation therefore being exercised within the constraints of international law served to emphasize the stress of national law, nationally interpreted.

115 U.N. Doc., A/9946, para. 8, 20.

116 'The Charter', p. 596. In agreement, Dupuy in the Libya–Oil Companies Award, pp. 114–15.

117 Robin C. A. White, 'A New International Economic Order', 24 *I.C.L.Q.* (1975), 544. Castaneda, *Legal Effects*, pp. 35–6 and in U.N. Doc. A/C.2/SR.1638, p. 8.

118 *I.C.J. Reports* (1951), p. 49.

119 Ibid. p. 52.

120 For example, R. A. Falk, 'On the Quasi-Legislative Competence of the General Assembly', 60 *A.J.I.L.* (1966), 782.

121 U.N.C.T.A.D. Doc. TD/B/AC.12/1, para. 18, p. 5.

122 Ibid. para. 19, p. 6.

123 'The Charter', p. 40.

124 U.N. Doc. A/PV.2315, p. 12.

125 Professor Rosalyn Higgins, *Conflict of Interests: International Law in a Divided World* (1965).

126 See the report prepared by the Commission on Permanent Sovereignty over Natural Resources established by G.A. Resolution 1314 (XIII) of 12 December 1958 (U.N. Doc./A/5433 and Add. 1). See also 'The Status of Permanent Sovereignty over Natural Wealth and Resources: Study by the Secretariat' (U.N. Doc.A/AC.97/5/Rev.2). More recently, see the 1973–75 reports of the Secretary-General (U.N. Docs. E/5425 and Corr. 1 and Add.1, E/5549, A/9716 and E/C/7/53).

127 See Hyde, 50 *A.J.I.L.* (1956), 854.

128 61 *A.J.I.L.* (1967), 869.

129 'A New International Economic Order', 545.

130 Resolution 1803 used to be widely regarded as enunciating accepted customary international law in the area of nationalization and compensation. It is in this resolution that

the interests of the developed countries, as sources of private investment, were variously accommodated.

131 For a comprehensive study on the *Calvo* clause, see K. Lipstein, 'The place of Calvo Clause in International Law', 22 *B.Y.B.I.L.* (1945), p. 130; M. M. Whitemann, *International Law* (1967), vol. 8, pp. 916–33.

132 'The Charter', p. 153.

133 General Assembly Resolutions 3201 (S-VI) and 3202 (S-VI). For survey of the work of the United Nations on a Code of Conduct for regulating the activities of transnational corporations, see Coonvod, 'The United Nations Code of Conduct for Transnational Corporations', 18 *Harv.Int.L.J.* (1977), 273; also 'The United Nations and the Regulations of Transnational Corporations', an unpublished paper by S. A. Tiewl, Legal Adviser in the Attorney-General's Chamber, Ghana. The paper was released privately to the writer.

134 *70th Annual Meeting of Am. Soc. Int. Law* (April 22–24 1976), pp. 16–34. It is noteworthy that the U.N. parlance has gradually shifted from the term 'multinational corporations' to 'multinational enterprises' to 'transnational enterprises'. It seems that the change is motivated by the desire to encompass many business institutions in a single terminology. In this book the terms are used interchangeably. For distinguishing these terms, see Fawcett, *Conflicts*, pp. 24–25.

135 See U.N. Doc. 5655; E/C 10/6, 17 March 1975, Programme of Issues to Transnational Corporations: report by the UN Commission on Transnational Corporations to E.C.O.S.O.C. For antecedents and analytical comments on the Report, see Seymour J. Rubin, "Reflections Concerning the United Nations Commission on Transnational Corporations", 70 *A.J.I.L.* (1976), 73.

136 For instance, U.N.C.T.A.D. Intergovernmental Group on the Transfer of Technology: U.N. Doc. TD/B/C. 6114 (1976); see, generally, Jeffries, 'Regulation of Transfer of Technology, An Evaluation of the U.N.C.T.A.D. Code of Conduct', *Harv. Int. L.J.* (1977), 309; O.E.C.D., 'Guidelines for Multinational Enterprises', *Declaration on International Investment and Multinational Enterprises* (1976), reproduced in 15 *I.L.M.* (1976), 297. For an extensive survey of other organizations, see Joel David and Lisa Chiles, 'The United States and the Issues of the Binding or Voluntary Nature of International Codes of Conduct Regulating Restrictive Business Practices', 72 *A.J.I.L.* (1978), 247 *et seq.*; the Andean Foreign Investment Code, 1970; see also U.N. Doc. E/C 10/9, at 18 (1976); International Chamber of Commerce, *Guidelines for International Investment* (1972).

137 Memorandum prepared by Professor K. Vasdev, Faculty of Law, University of Khartoum for the training course on Regulating and Negotiating with Transnational Corporations, organized jointly the U.N. Centre on Transnational Corporations, Government of the Sudan and the Development and Research Centre, Khartoum, February–March 1980; also, 'The Negative Aspects of the Sudanese Investment Laws', a paper submitted by the writer for the same U.N. training course.

138 See U.N. Conference on An International Code of Conduct on the Transfer of Technology, U.N. Doc. TD/Code TOT/20, 5 December 1979; also generally, see Norbert Horn (ed.), *Legal Problems of Codes of Conduct for Multinational Enterprises* (1980). For different codes of conduct by other organizations, see *Multinational Corporations Law* (1979), compiled and edited by Kenneth R. Simmonds, published by Oceana Publications, Inc. for the Workshop on International Law and the Multinational Corporation sponsored by New York University School of Law and the British Institute of International and Comparative Law, London, 18–19 August 1980. The writer was a delegate to this workshop.

139 For a general survey of national legislation and regulations of developing countries on control of transnational corporations, see *National Legislation and Regulation Relating to Transnational Corporations*, a document prepared by the U.N. centre on Transnational Corporations for the Training Course on Regulating and Negotiating with Transnational Corporations Khartoum, Sudan, February to March 1980.

140 Vagts, 'The Multinational Enterprises, A New Challenge for Transnational Law', 83 *Harv.L.R.* (1970), 639; U.N.Doc.TD/B/600, at para. 7 (1976).

141 See D. L. Guertin, *Proceedings of the 69th Annual Meeting of the Am. Soc. I.L.* (1975), pp. 236–7.

142 David and Chiles, 'International Codes of Conduct', 256–7. For a contrary view, see Seymour J. Rubin, 'The Multinational Enterprise at Bay', 68 *A.J.I.L.* (1974), 476–7.

143 *Proceedings of the 69th Annual Meeting of the Am. Soc. I.L.* at p. 31.

144 *Formulation of a Code of Conduct: Elaboration of the Chairman's Annotated outline on the Basis of Discussion in Intergovernmental Working Group of a Code of Conduct*, a note by the Secretariat, Commission on Transnational Corporations, Fourth Session, March, 1978, provided to the writer by Dr Asante, the Chief Legal Adviser, Centre on Transnational Corporations, U.N., New York. By May 1980, the Group had drafted more than 40% of the Code's provisions, agreeing on about half of them: Sortirios G. Mousouris, 'Formulating the Code of Conduct on Transnational Corporations: Process, Problems, Prospects', a paper submitted for the Workshop on International Law and the Multinational Corporation, 18–19 August 1980, London.

145 See U.N. Doc. 5655; E/C 10/6, Annex 1, where it has been reported that the Group of 77 (the developing countries) asserted that the following guidelines should be contained in a binding code, namely: that the transnational enterprises should be subject to the laws of the receiving (host) country and the exclusive jurisdiction of its courts; that they should abstain from all interference; that they should supply all pertinent information; should conduct their operations so as to result in net receipt of financial resources for the host nation; should contribute to development; should refrain from restrictive commercial practices; and should respect the socio-cultural identity of the host nation. Conversely, Annex 11 disclosed that the developed countries have persistingly claimed that the codes of conduct and transfer of technology should only be guidelines and 'instruments of moral persuasion', and hence should not create legal rights or obligations for States or enterprises. Concerning the content of the code, they set out in their list 'of areas of concern' that the code should include such matters as whether the host country's legislation discriminates either for or against transnational corporations, on the basis of foreign membership, and the extent to which such treatment might affect the contribution of these corporations to development objectives. Adding spice to this they enlisted an item on prompt, adequate and effective compensation in the event of nationalization. The developed countries also included arbitration, presence or absence of a stable investment climate, the extent to which domestic laws might help or hinder in labour relations and a call for consideration of the extent to which the transnational corporations' take host nations' interest into account in establishing capital and dividend repatriation polices.

It is noteworthy that in the 1950s and late 1960s, direct foreign investment came from transnational corporations of the developed countries. Recently, some developing countries have established their own multinationals. Thus, Argentina, Peru, Brazil, the Philippines, Singapore, Hong Kong, India, South Korea, and Taiwan, to mention a few, who have already embarked on industrial and infrastructural investments by their multinationals in other developing countries. The Korean construction companies are executing heavy infrastructural investments in the Arab countries, especially Saudi Arabia. They will install flour mills in the Sudan in the Geziva Province and one Korean company has built a first-class hotel in Khartoum: see Bodour O. Abu Affan, 'The Impact of Direct Private Foreign Investment on the Future Development of the Sudan Economy', Economic and Social Research Council, National Council for Research, Bulletin No. 8, Khartoum (January 1980), pp. 20–3.

146 Interview with Dr Asante; the Working paper.

147 Ibid.

148 'United Nations and International Regulation of Transnational Corporations', a lecture delivered by Dr Asante to the Cambridge University International Club, on 22 November 1978 (unpublished).

149 See section 23 of the Sudanese Encouragement of Investment Act, 1980.

150 See n. 139 to this chapter (page 408); also Mousouris, 'Formulating the Code of Conduct'.

151 See ibid. for further detail see the Working Paper.

152 This was expressly stated by Ambassador Scalf of the United States when commenting on the Reservation by the United States on the Charter; for the statement, see 13 *I.L.M.* (1974), 746, also Charles N. Brown, *Proceed. of 69th Annual Meeting of the Am. Soc. I.L.* (April 24–26, 1975), p. 232.

153 Maynard, 'The Charter', p. 26.

154 *Bilateral Treaties*, I.C.C. booklet, p. 10.

155 For instance, the Sudan–Kuwait Investment Protection Treaty; the Sudan–Egypt Investment Treaty.

156 I.C.C. Booklet, *Bilateral Treaties*.

157 Joseph L. Kunz, 'The Meaning and the Range of the Norm *Pacta Sunt Servanda*, 39 *A.J.I.L.* (1945), 180–97; Harvard Research 1935, Part III, 29 *A.J.I.L.* (1935), 775–86; Lord McNair, *The Law of Treaties* (1961), ch. 30.

158 The *Mavrommatis Palestine Concessions* (Merits) case, *P.C.I.J.* series A, no. 5, p. 6; *Forests in Central Rhodopia* (Greece v. Bulgaria), *U.N.R.I.A.A.*, vol. 3, p. 1405.

159 Fatouros, *Government Guarantees*, p. 222.

160 Judgment No. 13, *P.C.I.J.* series A, no. 17, p. 13.

161 Judgment No. 7 (The Merits) *P.C.I.J.* series A, no. 5.

162 Ibid. p. 24.

163 Examples are the cases of the *Anglo-Iranian Oil Co.*, *I.C.J. Pleadings and Documents*, 1952, pp. 74–9; and the nationalization of the *Suez Canal*: Nwogugu, *Legal Problems*, pp. 162–3. In these two cases the parties disagreed on whether or not the legal instruments in dispute had created treaty obligations under international law.

164 For instance, Nwogugu, *Legal Problems*, p. 165.

165 Fatouros, *Government Guarantees*, p. 227.

166 Oppenheim, *International Law*, vol. 1, pp. 35–77; *Walker* v. *Baird* [1892] A.C., p. 491. More recently, Lord Denning, in *Trendtex Trading Corporation Ltd.* v. *Central Bank of Nigeria* [1977] I All E.R., p. 881, advocated that the doctrine of incorporating international law as part of English law should prevail. He rejected the doctrine of transformation, which maintains that international law is not to be considered as part of English law except in so far as it has been already adopted and made part of English law by the decisions of the courts or by Act of Parliament, pp. 888–90. For the American view, see Louis Henkin, *Foreign Affairs and the Constitution* (1975), pp. 156–9, 162–222, 410. For a general survey of the practice of different Commonwealth countries, see Wilson, *Commonwealth Development*, pp. 25–91. For a contrary view under the West German

constitution, see Hans G. Rupp, 'International Law as Part of the Law of the Land: Some Aspects of the Operation of Article 25 of the Basic Law of the Federal Republic of Germany', 11 *Tex. Int. L.J.* (1976), 541–7.

167 Oppenheim, *International Law*, p. 36; O'Connell relying on the Judgment of Lord Atkin in the *Att-Gen. for Canada* v. *Att-Gen. for Ontario* [1937] A.C. 326, advocated that unless the treaty proceeds to authorize the Executive to alter municipal law by regulations, it is of no other significance: O'Connell, *International Law*, vol. 1, p. 62. For a survey of the practice in different legal systems, see ibid. pp. 62–88.

168 Supreme Court-Major Court, 104–74.

169 Kh-P-C-1972 (unreported).

170 Fatouros, *Government Guarantees*, p. 231.

171 For example, India: see D. D. Basu, *Commentary on the Constitution of India* (1962), vol. 11, p. 55; Burma: Article 213 of *the Constitution*, O'Connell, *International Law*, p. 66; Mexico: *Re Conde*, *I.L.R.* (1950), case no. 6; Brazil: *Federal Government* v. *Comporhia de Radio Int. de Brazil*, *I.L.R.* (1953), case No. 1; Argentina: *Montero* v. *Farnendez*, *A. D.* (1938–40), case no. 188.

172 Oppenheim, *International Law*, pp. 45–6; Hyde, *International Law*, vol. 2, pp. 1464–5; Hackworth, *Digest*, vol. 5, pp. 186–95; recently, F. A. Mann, 'The Consequences of an International Wrong in International and National Law', 48 *B.Y.B.I.L.* (1978), p. 1, at pp. 22–8.

173 A.D. (1923–24), at pp. 320–2.

174 Article 102.

175 Article 106.

176 *L.S.D.R.S.G.*, no. 1162, 15 June 1974, p. 139.

177 Hackworth, *Digest*, vol. 5, p. 185; F. A. Mann, 48 *B.Y.B.I.L.* (1978), at pp. 25–7, Henkin, *Foreign Affairs*, p. 185.

178 *Ibn Sad*, 2/1; Hamidullah, *Muslim Conduct of State*, pp. 1290–4.

179 Fatouros, *Government Guarantees*, p. 231.

180 *P.C.I.J.*, series A, no. 1, pp. 29–30.

181 Ibid. at pp. 29–30.

182 Case of the *Greco-Bulgarian 'Communities'*, Advisory Opinion of 13 July 1930, ibid. series B, no. 17 p. 32; *cf. Case of Free Zones of Upper Savoy*, ibid. series A, no. 24, p. 12: 'it is certain that France cannot rely on her own legislation to limit the scope of her international obligations'; also *idem.*, Advisory Opinion, 4 February 1932, series A/B, no. 44, p. 24: 'a state cannot adduce as against another State its own constitution with a view of evading obligations incumbent upon it under international law or treaties in force', Treatment of Polish Nationals and other Persons of Polish Origin of Speech in the Danzig Territory.

183 For example, The Advisory Opinion Concerning Reparation for Injuries Suffered in the Service of the U.N., I.C.J. Rep. (1949), p. 180.

184 *The Norwegian Shipowners claims*, *U.N.R.I.A.A.*, vol. 1, p. 331; *The Tinoco Case*, ibid. vol. 3, pp. 393–4.

185 The defendant States too generally agreed with the view that conformity to municipal law does not exclude international responsibility. For example, in the Memorandum submitted to the League of Nations regarding the dispute between the Swiss Confederation and other States concerning reparation of damage suffered by Swiss citizens as a result of events during the war, the Swiss Federal Council expressly confirmed that municipal law cannot relieve a State from the necessity of fulfilling its international obligations: *League of Nations, Official Journal*, 15th year, no. 11 (November 1934), 1486, reproduced in the

Y.B.I.L.C. (1971), vol. 11, p. 229; for similar statements by different states, see ibid. pp. 222–30.

186 H. W. Briggs, *The Law of Nations*, 2nd ed. (1952), pp. 62–3; Wright, 'The Legal Nature of Treaties', 10 *A.J.I.L.* (1916), 722; Mann, 48 *B.Y.B.I.L.* (1978) at p. 25.

187 U.N. Publication, Sales No. E 70 v. 6, pp. 53–4, 13th Meeting, paras. 30–40; for the text of the Vienna Convention on the Law of Treaties, see Brownlie, *Basic Documents*, p. 233. See also, Article 5 of the Draft Code prepared by the Japanese Association of International Law in 1926, *Y.B.I.L.C.* (1969), vol. 11, p. 141, document A/CN.2/217 and Add. I, annex 11; Article 2 of the Draft prepared by the Harvard Law School; see the *Third Report on State Responsibility* by the International Law Commission, by Mr Roberto Ago, Special Rapporteur, *Y.B.I.L.C.* (1971), pp. 193–232.

188 Obviously, this view, may be restrictive of the developing countries' sovereign right to pass laws necessary for the exploitation of their natural resources.

189 *Bilateral Treaties*, I.C.C. Booklet, 1977.

190 The developing countries which adopted the Charter of Economic Rights and Duties of States.

7. Investment insurance programmes

1 Fawcett, *Conflicts*, p. 66; Mann, 48 *B.Y.B.I.L.* (1978), p. 15.

2 Theodor Meron, *Investment Insurance in International Law* (1976), p. 37.

3 Ibid.

4 Ibid., p. 1.

5 *I.C.J. Rep.* (1970), at p. 32.

6 Meron, *Investment Insurance*, p. 2. Also the *Nottebohm* case, *I.C.J. Rep.* (1955), p. 5.

7 For the British Foreign Compensation Commission, see R. B. Lillich, *International Claims: Postwar British Practice* (1967), pp. 59, 122–3; for French practice, see Meron, *Investment Insurance*, pp. 7–8; also B. H. Weston, *International Claims: Postwar French Practice* (1971), pp. 87–8.

8 See Whiteman, *Damages*, vol. 2, at p. 1296.

9 Meron, *Investment Insurance*, p. 19.

10 Ibid.

11 O'Connell, *International Law*, vol. 2, p. 1137.

12 For instance, *The Caldera* (1859), Whiteman, *Damages*, at p. 1320. Also Borchard, *Diplomatic Protection*, p. 647.

13 Meron, *Investment Insurance*, pp. 12–13.

14 Ibid.

15 For instance, McNair, *International Law Opinions*, vol. 2, p. 290.

16 Cases cited by O'Connell, *International Law*, p. 1136.

17 Meron, *Investment Insurance*.

18 Ibid. pp. 2–3.

19 Ibid. p. 3.

20 Ibid. See *I.C.J. Rep.* (1970), at p. 49. The issue was raised in the pleadings of the parties in the case of the *El Al* case (Israel v. Bulgaria), but the International Court of Justice did not rule on the merits of the case but on procedural grounds. For the arguments of the parties, see *I.C.J.Rep.*, Pleadings (1959), pp. 438–45, 562–4, respectively.

21 Meron, *Investment Insurance*, p. 18.

22 Ibid.

23 See ch. 10.

24 Meron, *Investment Insurance*, p. 20.

25 See, generally, M. M. Whiteman, *Digest of International Law* (1967), p. 1233 *et seq.*

26 See Keeton, *Basic Text on Insurance Law* (1971), pp. 88, 91 *et seq.*; also Meron, *Investment Insurance*, p. 17.

27 On protecting a State from double claims, see *Reparation for Injuries Suffered in the Service of the United Nations, I.C.J. Rep.* (1949), at p. 188.

28 Keeton, *Insurance Law*, p. 160.

29 O'Connell, *International Law*, vol. 2, p. 1137.

30 Meron, *Investment Insurance*, p. 11.

31 For further discussion on nationality of claims, see *post*, pp. 294–6.

32 At present, thirteen industrialized countries provide some form of government-sponsored political risks insurance for direct private investments in developing countries. These include Japan, Australia and Canada, and most of the West European countries and United States. See 'A Comparison of OPIC to the Other Nations' Investment Insurance', Staff of Sub-Committee on Multinational Corporations, Multinational Corporations and U.S. Foreign Policy, Hearing before the Sub-Committee on Multinational Corporations of the Senate Committee of Foreign Relations, 93rd Congress, 1st Session, *Comm. Print.* pt. 3, at 63 (1973), reproduced in Meron, *Investment Insurance*, Annex 111 (2), p. 291. See also Baseem, *Legal Regime*, pp. 303–67.

33 Baseem, *Legal Regime*, pp. 292–3.

34 Ibid., pp. 303–4.

35 Meron, *Investment Insurance*, p. 293.

36 Baseem, *Legal Regime*, p. 293.

37 Fatouros, *Government Guarantees*, p. 117; Baseem, *Legal Regime*, p. 294; also *Multilateral Investment Insurance*, A Staff Report of the International Bank for Reconstruction and Development (March, 1962).

38 This public corporation was established on 30 December 1969 by Public Law 91-175, Foreign Assistance Act, 1969, *83 Stat.* 805.

39 Nwogugu, *Legal Problems*, p. 66; Fatouros, *Government Guarantees*, pp. 117–19.

40 *65 Stat.* 384 (1951).

41 *67 Stat.* 158 (1953).

42 The terms 'guaranty' and 'insurance' are used throughout this chapter interchangeably.

43 'Less developed countries' is taken to refer to 'developing countries'.

44 Meron, *Investment Insurance*, p. 49.

45 Section 221(d), *75 Stat.* 424 (1961); also Baseem, *Legal Regime*, p. 307.

46 For an analytical survey of the application of the programme under the reign of A.I.D., see ibid., pp. 306–38.

47 *Public Law 91-175*, see Annex V (1), Meron, *Investment Insurance*, p. 303.

48 Ibid. p. 50.

49 *Public Law 91-175*, section 231.

50 Ibid.

51 Statement by Bradford Mills, President of O.P.I.C., Hearings Before the Sub-Committee on Foreign Economic Policy of the House Committee on Foreign Affairs, 93rd Congress, 1st session (*Comm. Print* 1973), p. 262, reported in Meron, *Investment Insurance*, p. 51.

52 Ibid.

53 Ibid. p. 52.

54 Meron, *Investment Insurance*, p. 53.

55 Section 231(1) of Public Law 93-390, ibid. Annex V(1), p. 303.

56 Section 231(a) of Public Law 93-390.

57 See O.P.I.C.: *Investment Insurance Handbook*, produced in Meron, *Investment Insurance*, Annex V(5), p. 573; O.P.I.C., *Regulations or Policy Guidelines*, ibid. Annex V(6), pp. 587–607.

58 Insurance contacts under O.P.I.C.'s programme can categorically be identified as follows:

1. Insurance Contract 234 KGT 12-70 used for equity and some debt transactions.
2. Insurance Contract 234 LGT 5-73 has been developed for insurance of debt only and is used primarily for insurance of large loans.
3. Insurance Contract 234 GGT 5-73 has been developed for insurance of the guaranty of debt.
4. Insurance Contract 424 PGT 6-75 (Rev. 9-75) covers construction projects only.
5. Insurance Contract 001 PGT 6-75 used for the political risks of inconvertibility and expropriation.

The text of these contracts is provided in annexes by Meron, *Investment Insurance*, Annex V(4), pp. 337–525.

59 Section 230.

60 O.P.I.C., *Investment Insurance Handbook* 7 (1975); also O.P.I.C., *Regulations on Eligibility of Investor* (1970).

61 Meron, *Investment Insurance*, p. 55.

62 Ibid.

63 234 KGT 12.70.

64 Meron, *Investment Insurance*, p. 56.

65 S. D. Metzger, 'Nationality of Corporate Investment under Investment Guaranty Schemes – The Relevance of Barcelona Traction', 65 *A.J.I.L.* (1971), at 532.

66 Meron, *Investment Insurance*, p. 57.

67 Ibid. The enjoyment of non-United-States nationals of the programme is a clear violation of the nationality of claims rule if subrogation is to fully operate, unless the company is incorporated in the United States, for in this case the rule in the *Barcelona Traction* case applies.

68 Reported in Meron, *Investment Insurance*, p. 59. See generally, D. N. Smith and L. J. Wells, 'Mineral Agreements in Developing Countries: Structures and Substance', 69 *A.J.I.L.* (1975), 560.

69 Public Law 93-390.

70 *Insurance Handbook*, 15–16.

71 *O.P.I.C. Incentive Handbook*, 6.

72 *O.P.I.C. Application for Political Risk Investment Insurance* (O.P.I.C. Form 52), reported in Meron, *Investment Insurance*, p. 63.

73 Ibid.

74 Ibid. p. 64.

75 Ibid. See table explaining by statistics cases where the O.P.I.C. rejected applications for insurance for certain reasons, ibid. pp. 64–5.

76 Meron, *Investment Insurance*, p. 66.

77 Ibid.

78 The specific obligations of O.P.I.C. and of the investor with respect to the inconvertibility risk (coverage A) are governed by Articles 13–17 of the Insurance Contract 234 KGT 12-70.

79 O.P.I.C. *Incentive Handbook* 14.

80 This means the effective rate of exchange recognized and used on the relevant date by the Central Bank of the host country in selling U.S. dollars for its currency: *Contract of Insurance*, 234 KGT 12-70, Articles 1–30, 14–15.

81 Meron, *Investment Insurance*, p. 67; also Baseem, *Legal Regime*, p. 292.

82 Reported in Meron, *Investment Insurance*, pp. 105–6.

83 In determining claims arising from insurance contracts, O.P.I.C. applies Internal Action and Claims Determination Memoranda which contain important source of law bearing upon the construction and application of O.P.I.C. insurance contracts, reported in Meron, *Investment Insurance*, p. 105.

84 234 KGT 12-70, Article 1.13.

85 Ibid.

86 Ibid. Article 1.13(1).

87 Ibid. Article 1.13(2).

88 Ibid. Article 1.13(3).

89 See, generally, in the *Matter of the Arbitration between International Telephone and Telegraph Corporation of America* (*I.T.T.A*) *and O.P.I.C., Arbitration*, 13 *I.L.M.* (1974), 1307. For a succinct description of the risk of expropriation, see the statement of Seymour Rubin, then General Counsel of A.I.D. (the predecessor of O.P.I.C.), 'The Investment Guaranty Programme of the United States', 77 *Proceed. of the Am. Soc. Int. Law* (1962), at p. 78.

90 9 *I.L.M.* (1970), 889.

91 Ibid. p. 896; cf. the *Aramco* Award, discussed in ch. 9.

92 For instance, *I.T.T.A.–O.P.I.C. Arbitration; In the Matter of the Arbitration between Anaconda Company and Chile Copper Company and O.P.I.C.* (1975), reported in Meron, *Investment Insurance*, p. 73.

93 O.P.I.C. *Incentive Handbook* 14.

94 *Insurance Contract 234 KGT 12-70*, Article 2.13.

95 Ibid.

96 Article 1.05 of the *Insurance Contract*.

97 O.P.I.C. *Incentive Handbook*.

98 *Insurance Contract 234 KGT 12-70*, Article 22.01.

99 *Insurance Contract 234 KGT 12-70*, Articles 24–25.

100 The fees charged up to 1976 are given in an Annex reported in Meron, *Investment Insurance*, p. 607.

101 Ibid. p. 76.

102 See section 237 (a) or Public Law 93-390.

103 Also section 237(b) of Public Law 93-390. For a list of countries considered by O.P.I.C. eligible for investment insurance, see O.P.I.C. *Annual Report*, Fiscal 1974, at p. 4, reported in Meron, *Investment Insurance*, pp. 79–82.

104 Ibid. p. 77.

105 342 U.N.T.S. 13, No. 1: 4896. Article 2.

106 Walsh Construction Co. The disputes arose from a construction contract which was financed from an American loan granted to the Sudan under the Foreign Assistance Act, 1961. Due to the severance of diplomatic relations in the wake of the Middle East War in 1967, the Company suspended the work under the Contract. The Sudan Government expropriated the equipment and machinery left behind by the Company. The Company succeeded in its claim against the American insurance agency, and was paid the amount of insurance which it had bought, in $222,352.

107 The American companies affected by the Sudanese nationalization measures are: Sterling

Drug Company; American Life Insurance Company; United States banking interests: National City Bank's 40% interest in National and Grindlays, and Bank of America's 3% interest in Barclays Bank; Hartford Fire Insurance Company; National Cash Register: 6 *I.L.M.* (1972), 106. Compensation due to these companies and banks had been settled by mutual agreements under the Nationalization Laws of 1970. See ch. 8.

108 Meron, *Investment Insurance*, p. 77.

109 *68 Stat.* 199 (repealed).

110 Article 1.

111 Article 2.

112 Article 3(a), (c) cf. Article 5 of the Agreement between the United States and the Arab Republic of Egypt, 1963, *U.S.T.I.A.S.* No. 5383; also 479 U.N.T.S. 207. The agreement entered into force on 29 June 1963.

113 Article 3(b).

114 Article 3(h).

115 Article 3(c).

116 Meron, *Investment Insurance*, pp. 81–2. For a list of countries with which the United States concluded Guaranty Agreements till 1975, see ibid. pp. 83–7; also, M. V. N. Whiteman, *Government-Sharing in Foreign Investment* (1965), pp. 88–9 (up to 1964).

117 The code was agreed upon by Bolivia, Chile, Colombia, Ecuador and Peru. Cf. Article 3 of the Mexican Foreign Investment Code, 1973, text in 12 *I.L.M.* (1973), p. 643. Both instruments deal with the *Calvo* clause.

118 A recent example of the modern American investment guaranty agreements is the agreement with Barbados, signed in Bridgetown on 11 March 1968; for the text, see 6463, Treaties and other International Acts Series (T.I.A.S.).

119 Text in U.S.T.I.A., vol. 26, part 1 (1975), p. 459. The agreement was signed at Washington on 27 February, and entered into force on 26 April of the same year.

120 Fatouros, *Government Guarantees*, pp. 117–18; Baseem, *Legal Regime*, p. 296.

121 'Europe's Business Tasks: How U.S. Can Help', U.S. News and World Report, 16 Dec. 1952, p. 71, reported in Whiteman, *Government-Sharing*, p. 104.

122 Ibid. pp. 103–4.

123 Ibid.

124 Meron, *Investment Insurance*, p. 111.

125 Senate Report no. 93-676, reported by Meron.

126 A summary of the German programme is contained in the Staff Report of the I.B.R.D.: A Multilateral Investment Insurance, Annex. A.3, pp. 28–9 (referred to hereinafter as the World Bank Report).

127 Article 18, par. 1, for the text, see *Bundesgesetzblatt*, part II, p. 793. Also, Baseem, *Legal Regime*, p. 339; William Conant Brewer, 'The Proposal for Investment Guarantees by an International Agency', 58 *A.J.I.L.* (1964), 67.

128 Fatouros, *Government Guarantees*, p. 112; Nwogugu, *Legal Problems*, p. 67.

129 The World Bank Report, p. 28.

130 The Sudan–German Investment Protection Treaty, 1963, Article 5.

131 Article 11.

132 Article 2; see ch. 10.

133 Article 3.

134 Article 6.

135 Ibid.

136 The World Bank Report, p. 28.

137 Article 14(2).
138 The World Bank Report, p. 28; Fatouros, *Government Guarantees*, p. 112.
139 World Bank Report, p. 28.
140 Ibid.
141 Fatouros, *Government Guarantees*, p. 112; Baseem, *Legal Regime*, pp. 344–5.
142 Baseem, *Legal Regime*, p. 348.
143 Fatouros, *Government Guarantees*, pp. 112–13.
144 Ibid. p. 114; also the World Bank Report, p. 28.
145 The World Bank Report, p. 28; Baseem, *Legal Regime*, pp. 350–2.
146 The World Bank Report, p. 28.
147 The book value is usually indicated in an audited balance sheet.
148 The World Bank Report, p. 28.
149 Ibid. Baseem, *Legal Regime*, p. 351.
150 The World Bank Report, p. 29.
151 Ibid.
152 Ibid.
153 Ibid.; Baseem, *Legal Regime*, p. 350.
154 Ibid.
155 These paragraphs of Article 3 have already been discussed before (see pp. 115–17). The Swiss counterpart anticipates a very simple procedure for subrogation. Article 7 of the Sudan–Swiss Investment Agreement, provides that: 'in case one Contracting Party has granted any financial security against non-commercail risks in respect of an investment by a national or a company in the territory of the other Contracting Party, the latter recognizes the subrogation by assignment of the grantor to the rights of the investor as to damages, if payment has been made under that security, to the extent of that payment and within the rights of the investor.' For details on the Swiss investment guaranty programme, see the World Bank Report.
156 Cf. the investment insurance programme of Japan, which does not require the conclusion of a bilateral agreement. For detailed survey, see the World Bank Report, p. 27. For this reason we do not want to discuss the Japanese programme, though there are some Japanese investments in the Sudan at present.
157 Earl Snyder, 'Foreign Investment Protection: A Reasoned Approach', 61 *Michigan L.R.* (1963), 1097.
158 Ibid.
159 Fatoruos, *Government Guarantees*, p. 114; Baseem, *Legal Regime*, pp. 365–6; R. Y. Don, *Protection of Foreign Investment Under International Law* (1979), pp. 492–4.
160 For a general survey of the various proposals on a multilateral investment insurance programme, see the World Bank Report, Annex 2.
161 For an informative account of the corporation, see Baseem, *Legal Regime*, pp. 407–35 (in Arabic); Dr Hisham Saddiq, *El nizam Al-Arabi Le-deman El-Ithtithar Dhid-El-Makhatir Gir El-Tigaria* (*The Arab Regime for Guarantee of Investment against Non-commercial Risks*) (1977); Don, *Protection*, pp. 494–5.
162 Ibrahim F. I. Shihata, 'Arab Investment Guarantee Corporation: A Regional Investment Insurance Project', 6 *J.W.T.L.* (1972), 185.
163 Shihata, 6 *J.W.T.L.* (1972), 187.
164 Shihata, 6 *J.W.T.L.* (1972), 187–8; Baseem, *Legal Regime*, pp. 407–8.
165 Ibid.

166 Kuwaiti Fund for Arab Economic Development: *Towards a Convention for the Guarantee of Arab Investments* (1967).
167 Baseem, *Legal Regime*, p. 408.
168 The Council works as an specialized agency of the Arab League.
169 The Sudan ratified the Convention by the Arab Investment Guarantee Corporation (Ratification) Act, 1971, *L.S.D.R.S.G.* no. 1118 dated 15 June 1971, p. 669. Saudi Arabia refused at the beginning to join the corporation, but subsequently has decided to be a party thereto, as of 1977.
170 Articles 1 and 7.
171 Article 3.
172 Article 7(1).
173 On the international personality of an international organization, see Bowett, *International Institutions*, ch. 11.
174 Article 8(1).
175 Article 8(2).
176 Article 8(6). On apportionment of expenses in international organizations generally, see Bowett, *International Institutions*, p. 369 *et seq.*
177 Article 8(7).
178 On this, see the World Bank Report.
179 Article 10(6).
180 Article 9.
181 Ibid.
182 Shihata, 6 *J.W.T.L.* (1972), 191.
183 Article 10(5).
184 Article 18(1)(a).
185 Article 18(1)(b).
186 Article 18(1)(c).
187 Article 18(2)(a).
188 Article 18(2)(b).
189 Article 18(2)(c).
190 Shihata, *J.W.T.L.* (1972), 193–4. See also Osam El deen Mustafa Baseem, 'Namazig El Dhaman El-Mutabagga-fe-El Moussassa Al-Arbia-le-dhaman El-Ithitthar (Models of Guaranty Contracts Applied by the Arab Investment Guarantee Corporation)', *Journal of Law of Sharia* (Kuwait 1980), 121–72.
191 Baseem, *Legal Regime*, pp. 416–17.
192 All through, the Convention uses the term 'country' instead of the legal term 'State' in order to allow for participation of Arab Emirates and Sheikhdoms which are not fully sovereign States.
193 Article 17(1).
194 Article 17(3).
195 Article 15.
196 Ibid. (4).
197 Article 15(3).
198 Baseem, *Legal Regime*, p. 419.
199 A partial exception may be found in Pontzen's proposal that private as well as public 'loans' may be eligible for investment insurance: The World Bank Report, pp. 30–7.
200 Article 16.

201 Shihata, 6 *J.W.T.L.* (1972), 197.
202 Article 20(4).
203 Article 20(1).
204 Article 20(3).
205 Ibid. and Article 20(2).
206 Article 19(1), (2).
207 Ibid.
208 Shihata, 6 *J.W.T.L.* (1972), 197.
209 Cf. the American National Programme.
210 Article 21(1).
211 Under Articles 25–26.
212 Article 25(3). On immunities of international organizations generally, see Bowett, *International Institutions*, pp. 311–22.
213 Article 21(3).
214 Article 6.
215 Meron, *Investment Insurance*, p. 31.
216 Thus the Sudanese insurance companies explicitly decline to issue any insurance policy againt war, revolutions, commotion, civil strife and similar risks. An example of this attitude is demonstrated by Clause 5 of *Fire Insurance Policy and Marine Insurance*, the Blue Nile Insurance Company Ltd, Khartoum. Neither policy covers loss through hostilities, war-like mutiny, riot, civil commotion, look-out, insurrection, rebellion, revolution, etc.
217 See, in general, Martin, 'Multilateral Investment Insurance: The O.E.C.D. Proposal", 8 *Harv. Int.L.J.* (1967), 280.
218 For an analytical account of the 1968 World Bank Proposal, see Baseem, *Legal Regime*, pp. 368–407.
219 For the text, see Meron, *Investment Insurance*, Annex 11(3), p. 259.
220 Article 1(a).
221 Ibid. (a) (iv).
222 Ibid.
223 This will be examined in detail in ch. 10.
224 Meron, *Investment Insurance*, p. 34.
225 Ibid.
226 Ibid. at pp. 35–6. It is worth mentioning that the General Assembly of the United Nations adopted Resolution 32/177 on 19 December 1977 requesting the Secretary-General to prepare a report on the feasibility and desirability of establishing a multilateral insurance and reinsurance agency. This reflects a positive gesture to securing consensus on the issue of investment insurance which might result in a favourable and stable investment climate. For the text of the resolution, see *U.N. Chronicle*, January 1978, p. 134.
227 Meron, *Investment Insurance*, p. 36.
228 O.P.I.C., Hearing Before the Sub-Committee on Foreign Economic Policy of the House of Committee of Foreign Affairs, 93rd Cong. reported in Meron, *Investment Insurance*. On the advantages and disadvantages of a Multilateral Insurance Programme, see the Report of the World Bank.
229 Thus, the European Commission proposed in 1972 the setting-up of a European Community guarantee scheme for private investment in third countries, Meron, *Investment Insurance*, p. 37. In the conference of Islamic countries for drafting an investment treaty between the member countries, 27–30 March 1980, there was a proposal for setting

up an insurance scheme attached to the Islamic Development Bank at Jeddah. The writer participated in this conference.

230 For a general account, see Meron, *Investment Insurance*, ch. 7; for the text of the Act, see Cmnd No. 4656, at p. 5 (1971). For a detailed examination of the British scheme for insuring overseas investment against non-commercial risks, see Clive M. Schmitthoff, *The Export Trade* (1980), 7th edn., ch. 22.

231 Turriff Construction (Sudan) Ltd, For further discusion of the case, see chs. 9 and 10.

232 Interview by the writer with J. R. Blair, Chairman of the Panel of Investment Insurance Contracts of the Confederation of British Industry (C.B.I.), on 5 May 1978, at the Shell Centre, London.

8. Assessment of compensation

1 Ignaz Seidl-Hohenveldern, 'Communist Theories on Confiscation and Expropriation', 7 *A.J.C.L.* (1958), 541–71. See, R. B. Lillich and B. H. Weston, *International Claims: Their Settlement by Lump Sum Agreements* (1975), chs. 4 and 5.

2 The *Chorzow Factory* case, *P.C.I.J.*, series A, no. 17 (1928), p. 47; Mann, 48 *B.Y.B.I.L.* (1978), 2.

3 Fatouros, *Government Guarantees*, p. 308.

4 *P.C.I.J.*, series A, no. 13, p. 29.

5 Mann, 48 *B.Y.B.I.L.* (1978); J. Brownlie, *Principles of Public International Law*, 2nd edn. (1973), p. 448, who regards *restitutio in integrum* as exceptional.

6 For a contrary view, see H. W. Baade, who asserted the exclusivity of claims of damages: 'Indonesian Nationalization Measures Before Foreign Courts – A Reply', 54 *A.J.I.L.* (1960), 801.

7 Fatouros, *Governmental Guarantees*, p. 310, D. W. Bowett, 'Libyan Nationalisation of American Oil Companies' Assets', 37 *Camb.L.J.*, part 1 (1978), 5, at 7.

8 In English municipal law the expression '*restitutio in integrum*' is also used to indicate the measure of damages to which the victim is entitled: see e.g. H. McGregor, *The Law of Damages*, 13th edn. (1972), section 10. It would seem that the expression was used in the same sense by Lauterpacht, *Private Law Sources*, p. 147. For further discussion, see *post*, pp. 271–6.

9 In agreement F. A. Mann who states: 'Accordingly, he who asks for a declaration as to his rights does not ask either for *restitutio in integrum* (reparation) or specific performance. The three remedies are entirely distinct.', 48 *B.Y.B.I.L.* (1978), at 64. Furthermore, in the words of Mosley and Whiteley, *Law Dictionary*, ed. by John B. Saunders, 8th edn. (1970), 'a suit for specific performance is one which a person with whom another has made a contract prays that the latter may be deemed specifically to perform it. The specific performance has in general been decreed in equity, where contract is not a positive contract of a personal nature "as to sing at a theatre", nor one for the nonperformance of which damages would be a sufficient compensation "as to pay a liquidated sum of money",' p. 345.

10 Rapalje and Lawrence, *Law Dictionary*, vol. 11, p. 117.

11 W. W. Buckland, *A Text-Book of Roman Law from Augustus to Justinian*, 3rd. edn. (1963), pp. 719–20.

12 Ibid. p. 720. For instances where the remedy of *restitutio in integrum* was applied in Roman law, see ibid. pp. 721–4. According to Rapalje and Lawrence's *Law Dictionary*, *restitutio*

in integrum was applied in Roman law where a person who, according to strict law, had lost a right, was restored to his original position by a judgment of a court acting on equitable grounds: vol. 11, pp. 1117–18.

13 *P.C.I.J.*, series A, no. 13, p. 47.

14 Kronfol, Protection, p. 101.

15 See the Introductory Note to the Arbitration Award by Robert B. von Mehren, 17 *I.L.M.* (1978), 1. It has been reported that Libya and the American companies reached a settlement, whereby Libya agreed to provide the companies over fifteen months with $152 million of crude oil and the companies agreed to terminate the arbitration proceedings: *The New York Times*, 26 September 1977.

16 See p. 436, n. 75 to ch. 10.

17 *I.C.J. Rep.* (1970), at p. 24.

18 Frank G. Dawson and Burns H. Weston, 'Prompt, Adequate and Effective: A Universal Standard of Compensation', 30 *Fordham L. Rev.* (1962), 727.

19 Quoted by Lord McNair, 'The Seizure of Property and Enterprises in Indonesia', 6 *Neth. I.L. Rev.* (1959), 250.

20 For instance, the Abs–Shawcross Draft Convention on Investment Abroad, 1959.

21 Kronfol, *Protection*, p. 110.

22 For instance, Article 545 of the French Civil Code, White, *Nationalisation*, p. 12.

23 *U.N.R.I.A.A.*, vol. 11, p. 909.

24 Ibid. vol. 1, p. 309.

25 Article 2(2).

26 Article 6.

27 U.N. International Law Commission, Fourth Report on International Responsibility by Gracia Amador, Special Rapporteur, *Responsibility of the State for Injuries Caused in its Territory to the person or property of Aliens – Measures Affecting Acquired Rights*, Doc. A/CN 4/119, 2 *Y.B.I.L.C.*, (1959), p. 22.

28 Kronfol, *Protection*, p. 111.

29 I. Foighel, *Nationalization: A Study in the Protection of Alien Property in International Law* (1957), p. 127.

30 Ibid. pp. 128–9.

31 Ibid. p. 121.

32 Fatouros, *Government Guarantees*, p. 326.

33 Oppenheim, *International Law*, vol. 1, p. 352 Lillich and Weston, *International Claims*, ch. 5.

34 K. Katzarov, *The Theory of Nationalization* (1964), p. 349.

35 F. S. Dunn, 'International Law and Private Property Rights', 28 *Columb.L.R.* (1928), 166.

36 Arthur K. Khun, 'Nationalization of Foreign-Owned Property and its Impact on International Law', 45 *A.J.I.L.* (1951), 709.

37 Ibid. 711–12.

38 Francesco Francioni, 'Compensation for Nationalization of Foreign Property: the Borderland between Law and Equity', 24 *I.C.L.Q.* (1975), 272–83.

39 Ibid. 285. In agreement, Dr Asante, Taylor Lecture.

40 Francioni, 24 *I.C.L.Q.* (1975), 278.

41 The idea of previous excess income as a justifiable cause for paying a correspondingly diminished compensation was recently articulated in Latin-American practice, especially by Chile at the time of the Allende Government: text, 10 *I.L.M.* (November, 1971), 1235 *et seq.* For comment, see F. O. Vicuna, 'Some International Law Problems Posed by the

Nationalization of the Copper Industry by Chile', 67 *A.J.I.L.* (1973), 711; *idem.* 'The International Regulation of Valuation Standards and Processes: A Re-examination of Third World Perspectives', in R. B. Lillich (ed.), *The Valuation of Nationalized Property in International Law*, vol. 3 (1975), p. 134.

42 U.N.G.A., Official Records, 17th session, supplement (1962), No. 17 (Al 52*7), pp. 15–16. See ch. 6.

43 24 *I.C.L.Q.* (1975), 545.

44 See U.N. Doc. A/C.2/SR 835, p. 5 and U.N. Doc. A/C/2./L, 668.

45 See Lipstein, 22 *B.Y.B.I.L. (1945), p. 130.*

46 For the text of the amendment, see 14 *I.L.M.* (1975), 262–3. The amendment was proposed by Austria, Belgium, Canada, Denmark, France, Federal Republic of West Germany, Ireland, Italy, Japan, Luxembourg, Netherlands, United Kingdom and United States.

47 White, 24 *I.C.L.Q.* (1975), at 547.

48 Article 3, 4 and 6.

49 Article 6.

50 *P.C.I.J.*, series A, no. 1, p. 32.

51 White, *Nationalisation*, p. 16.

52 Ibid. p. 215.

53 Ibid. p. 205. Cf. the *Libya–Oil Companies Settlement*, where compensation is being paid in crude oil.

54 Kronfol, *Protection*, pp. 101–2. Generally the developing countries have rejected the market value method, and used book value instead. For the practice of African countries, see Nwabueze, *Presidentialism*, ch. 12.

55 Fatouros, *Government Guarantees*, p. 317.

56 The market-value method was utilized by the Foreign Claims Commission of the United States in determining the value of the nationalized property at the time of taking. Fair market value derives from book value less speculative items such as goodwill Lillich, (ed. and contributor), *Valuation*, vol. 1, pp. 96–100.

57 Ibid. p. 16, by Dale R. Weigel and Burns H. Weston.

58 Ibid. p. 17.

59 Fatouros, *Government Guarantees*, p. 317.

60 Ibid. p. 321; also Eagleton, 'Measure of Damages in International Law', 39 *Y.L.J.* (1938), 66–75. For general survey of the cases, see Whiteman, *Damages*, vol. 3, pp. 1765–876.

61 *P.C.I.J.*, series A/B, no. 63, Judgment of 12 December 1934, at p. 88.

62 Kronfol, *Protection*, p. 106.

63 Ibid.

64 Ibid. For various cases, see Borchard, *Diplomatic Protection*, ss. 172, 173.

65 See Dale R. Weigel and Burns H. Weston, in Lillich (ed.), *Valuation*, vol. 1, pp. 19–20.

66 Ibid. p. 20.

67 Fatouros, *Government Guarantees*, p. 324.

68 Ibid. pp. 318–19; also Kronfol, *Protection*, p. 102. As regards the application of tax declaration method to real property valuation, see Roger P. Smith in Lillich (ed.), *Valuation*, pp. 152–4.

69 Kronfol, *Protection*, p. 102; also, *Re London Country Council & London Street Tramways Co.* [1894], 2 Q.B., 189, 219; Roger P. Smith, 'Real Property Valuation for Foreign-Wealth Deprivations', in Lillich (ed.), *Valuation*, pp. 156–8.

70 Kronfol, *Protection*, p. 103.

71 Lillich, *International Claims*, p. 116; also Roger P. Smith, in Lillich (ed.), *Valuation*, 154.
72 Ibid.
73 Lillich, *International Claims*, p. 117.
74 *I.C.J.Rep.*, 1970, At p. 40. See also Gillian White, 'Problems of Valuation in the Barcelona Traction Case', in Lillich (ed.), *Valuation*, ch. 2, pp. 43–63.
75 *S.L.S.D.R.S.G.* no. 1104, dated 12 June 1970, p. 263.
76 Ibid. p. 266.
77 *L.S.D.R.S.G.* no. 919 dated 15 July 1970, p. 25.
78 For the British practice, see for example *Melbourne Tramway & Omnibus Co.* v. *Tramway Bd.* [1919] A.C. 667; also Roger P. Smith in Lillich (ed.), *Valuation*, vol. 1.
79 For the Canadian practice in allowing depreciation see e.g. *The Queen* v. *Sisters of Charity* (1952) Can. Exh. 113, 126.
80 For instance, *Lindheime* v. *Illinois Bell Tel. Co.*, 292 *U.S.* 151, 167 (1934).
81 Section 4 and 3 of the Banks Nationalization Act, and the Companies Nationalization Act, respectively.
82 The Advisory Committee was constituted of a senior legal counsel from the Attorney-General's Chambers, a senior representative from the Auditor-General, and was presided over by an Under-Secretary, Minister of Finance and National Economy, assigned to the Affairs of Nationalized Companies, who was also a certified accountant.
83 Section 4(3) of the Banks Nationalization Act; section 3(2) of the Companies Nationalization Act.
84 For instance, petition of Sudan Tunnel Cement Co. which was a majority shareholder in Sudan Portland Cement Co. Ltd (nationalized).
85 Ibid. This was put in the words: 'a substantial profit-earning capacity and reasonable expectation of maintaining such capacity'.
86 This material was taken from confidential files of the Ministry of Finance and National Economy which could not be specifically mentioned here.
87 Memorandum of the Advisory Committee, 'Claims of Nationalised Companies', dated 1 December 1971.
88 Like patent medicines or stationery; see Sir James Henry in Lillich (ed.), *Valuation*, vol. 1, p. 86.
89 *Bailey* v. *Isle of Thanet Light Railways Co.* [1900] 1Q.B.722, 724; R. P. Smith, 'Real Property Valuation for Foreign-wealth Deprivations', in Lillich (ed.), *Valuation*, vol. 1, chap. 7, p. 161.
90 R. B. Lillich, 'The Valuation of Nationalized Property by the Foreign Claims Settlement Commission', in *Valuation*, p. 96.
91 Sir James Henry, in ibid. p. 86.
92 Fatouros, *Government Guarantees*, p. 316.
93 Ibid.
94 Ibid. This modality of securing the instalments of compensation by promissory notes had been a dominant feature of the practice of States since the Eastern European countries compensation agreements with western countries and private enterprises. See White, *Nationalisation*, pp. 185–92.
95 See, for instance, the Barclays Bank Agreement, and the Mitchell Cotts Agreement.
96 Tunnel Cement Ltd. (a British Company) and Dr Schmidheiny (Switzerland) were the principal shareholders of the Sudan Portland Cement Company Ltd, a company incorporated under the Sudan Law which was nationalized on 4 June 1970 in accordance with the Companies Nationalization Act, 1970.
97 Information obtained from confidential files.

98 The Companies Nationalization (Amendment) Act, 1973 Law no. 36, section 4(1), the Democratic Republic of the Sudan Gazette no. 1154, dated 15 October 1973.

99 The Companies Nationalization (Amendment) Act, 1975 L.S.D.R.S.G. No. 1196 dated 15 March 1976, p. 25. For the deliberations of the People's Assembly on the proposed amendment, see *The People's Assembly Deliberations*, Second Session, 7 January 1976 (Khartoum), pp. 16–24.

100 Section 3(1) of the Banks Nationalization (Amendment) Act, 1975, the *D.R.S.G.* no. 1196 dated 15 March 1976.

101 *Government Guarantees*, p. 325.

102 E.g. submission on behalf of Mitchell Cotts.

103 *L.S.D.R.S.G.*, no. 1116 dated 15 April 1971, p. 123.

104 The Technical Committee for Revising the Confiscation Measures.

105 Republican order no. 111, dated 10 August 1972. The text of the order was obtained by the writer during his work in the Committee as a legal adviser, among five other lawyers. The writer was also a member of the main subsidiary Committee for sorting out and studying the merits of all claims before being considered by the Technical Committee, which was presided over by a judge from the Court of Appeal. The other nine members were mainly the Under-Secretaries and Deputy Under-Secretaries of all the Ministries and departments related to investment as well as security officers.

106 These were legal officers from the Attorney-General's Chambers and judges from the Judiciary. There had been also some economists and accountants from the Auditor-General's Chambers.

107 Cf. Sidney Freidberg and Bert B. Lockwood, 'The Measure of Damages in Claims Against Cuba', in Lillich (ed.), *Valuation*, vol. 1, ch. 6. Also White, *Nationalisation of Foreign Property*, pp. 186–7.

108 For instance, Mexico paid compensation to the United States for the nationalized American property over a period of nine years; France is being paid compensation for its nationalized property by Poland over a period of fifteen years; Sweden by Poland over seventeen years, see Stanley D. Metzger, 'Property in International Law', 50 *Virginia Law Review* (1964), 603; Kronfol, *Protection*, pp. 110–12; White, *Nationalisation*, pp. 193–243.

109 For instance, the Compensation Agreement between United Kingdom and Poland of 1958, U.N.T.S., vol. 87, p. 3. Cf. David A. Gantz, 'The Marcona Settlement: New Forms of Negotiation and Compensation For Nationalized Property,' 71 *A.J.I.L.* (1977), 474, where the settlement was reached by negotiation and not through a formal mixed commission.

110 Reproduced in 26 *A.J.I.L.* (1932), 272, at 279.

111 On the legal effect of compensation agreements, see Lillich and Weston, *International Claims*, chs. 4 and 5; White, *Nationalisation*, pp. 183–243.

112 The Investment in Economic Services Act; the Industrial Investment Act and the Agricultural Investment Act.

113 Sections 10(d), 16(b)(i), (ii) and 20(b)(2) of the Investment in Economic Services Act, the Industrial Investment Act, and the Agricultural Investment Act, respectively.

114 Section 16(h)(iii) of the Industrial Investment Act and Section 20(b)(2) of the Agricultural Investment Act.

115 Article 222 of the Permanent Constitution of the Sudan, 1973.

116 White, *Nationalisation*, pp. 205–6.

117 *Libya–Oil Companies Settlement*.

118 The *Marcona Settlement*.

9. Economic development agreements

1 Rainer Geiger, 'The Unilateral Change of Economic Development Agreements', 23 *I.C.L.Q.* (1974), 73.

2 A narrative from the award is extracted by Dr L. Erades in 17 *Neth.Int.L.R.* (1970), 200–2.

3 Geiger, 23 *I.C.L.Q.* (1974), 73.

4 *Legal Problems*, pp. 166–7.

5 D. P. O'Connell, *State Succession in Municipal Law International Law* (1967), vol. 1, p. 304; T. T. F. Huang, 'Some International and Legal Aspects of the Suez Canal Question', 51 *A.J.I.L.* (1957), 289–96, where the legal structure of a concession is considered.

6 At p. 29. of the Award which is *ex parte* the Libyan Arab Republic.

7 Hyde, 50 *A.J.I.L.* (1956), at 862; McNair, 'The General Principles of Law Recognized by Civilized Nations', 33 *B.Y.B.I.L.* (1957), p. 1; G. W. Ray, 'Some Reasons for the Binding Force of Development Contracts between States and Foreign Nationals', 16 *Bus. Lawyer* (1960–61), 942.

8 33 *B.Y.B.I.L.* (1957), p. 1.

9 *Legal Problems*, pp. 180–6.

10 The term 'concession' is used in the Sudanese investment laws only in the sense of an exemption from taxes, customs duties and similar dues; see ch. 3 of the Investment in Economic Services Act and the Industrial Investment Act.

11 For instance, *Contract between the Republic of the Sudan and Turriff construction (Sudan) Ltd* 1962; see also the Award in 17 *Netherlands International Law Review; Contract between the Republic of the Sudan and Brown International (Sudan)*, 1962; also *Sudan Government* v. *Brown International Inc.* Ac-Rev-368-1967 (unreported). These two contracts and the decisions thereunder will be discussed later in this chapter. Cf. the contract between the *Delagoa Bay Railway Co.* and *Portugal*; see the award in Moore, *Digest*, vol. 6, p. 647.

12 For instance, the Petroleum Production-Sharing Agreement between the Democratic Republic of the Sudan and Chevron Company (Sudan) 1975; the Petroleum Production-Sharing Agreement between the Democratic Republic of the Sudan and Texaco Company (Sudan). Another two identical agreements have been concluded with the two American companies of Ball Collins (Sudan) and American Pacific (Sudan) 1975. The agreements have been concluded pursuant to the Petroleum Resources Act, 1972, and the Petroleum Resources Regulations, 1973. The latter agreements are not operative.

13 E.g. Agreement between the Democratic Republic of the Sudan, Mitsubishi Corporation (Japan) and Japan Metals and Chemicals Co. Ltd. (Japanese Group), 1976, for digging for chromite resources; Agreement among Gulf International Group, Johns-Manville Corporation and the Democratic Republic of the Sudan, 1976, for exploration and development of asbestos resources in the Sudan; the Exploration and Development Agreement between the Democratic Republic of the Sudan and Chevron Exploration Corporation of Sudan, 1979. Apart from the latter agreement, these agreements are joint ventures. Unlike the petroleum agreements, they are concluded pursuant to the Mines and Quarries Act, 1972 and the Mines and Quarries Regulations, 1973. Cf. Contract of Lena Goldfields Ltd with the Government of the U.S.S.R., arbitral award: 36 *Cornell L.Q.* (1950), 31.

14 The Sugar Agreement between the Democratic Republic of the Sudan and Lonrho Ltd. (English Co.), 1972 (joint venture); see Kalmanof, 'Manufacturing in Developing Countries, 10 *J.Transn. L.* (1971), 303.

15 Sugar Sales Agreement between Kenana Sugar Co. Ltd. and the Democratic Republic of the Sudan, 1972.

16 Rahad Irrigation Project, Supply Contracts between the Democratic Republic of the Sudan and Sir Malcolm MacDonald & Partners, Cambridge, 1976; Contract between the Saudi Ministry of Agriculture and Water (Riyadh Additional Water Supply), and Sir Malcolm MacDonald Partners, Cambridge.

17 For instance, guarantee to Vickers Vandergreeten S.A. Co. (Belgium) by the Bank of the Sudan for the loan of 35,638,000 Belgian francs to the Blue Nile Brewery (Khartoum), 1975; guarantee to Bomar (Polish Company) by the Bank of Sudan to the Loan to the Ministry of Local Government, 1973; guarantee by the Bank of Sudan to Angra Yugoslav Co. to the Loan to the Nile Cement Co.

18 For instance, guarantee by the State Bank of Sudan for Foreign Trade to the Agricultural Bank (State Bank) for the supply of 1,000 tractors and spare parts by Massey-Ferguson Ltd.

19 Guarantee provided by the Sudanese Ministry of Finance to Massey-Ferguson Ltd for the credit facilities to the Sudanese Agricultural Bank.

20 Bechtet's Programme Management Services Agreement with the Royal Commission for Jubail and Yanbu, 1976, Saudi Arabia.

21 O'Connell, *State Succession*, p. 107; K. S. Charlston, 'International Role of Concession Agreements', 52 *N.Y.U.L.R.* (1957), 618, at 636–40; *idem*, 'Concession Agreements and Nationalization', 62 *A.J.I.L.* (1958), 260–1. Some writers consider the instruments of approval 'licences' issued by virtue of investment laws as economic development agreements: see Fatouros, *Government Guarantees*, p. 234; Kronfol, *Protection*, p. 68. As has been established before, it is very difficult to accept such an idea. These instruments of approval lack the essential elements of contract, as they are unilateral in character, though they may have some similarities in their content with contracts under discussion. However, for present purposes they will be assimilated to contracts.

22 33 *B.Y.B.I.L.* (1957), p. 3.

23 This result has been radically modified where investment agreements specifically state that the ownership of the natural resources rests in the investee State itself. This point has been investigated at length by Dr Asante in his Lagos Lecture by examining the development agreements concluded by some African countries with transnational corporations: 'Transnational Investment Law and National Development', pp. 5–12. Dr Asante concludes his investigation by observing that: 'some developing countries have attempted to restructure their relations with transnational corporations by replacing the traditional concession regime with new and reputedly more sophisticated forms of legal arrangements, such as joint ventures, service contracts, production-sharing agreements and technical assistance agreements'. The basic assumption of this development is that these new forms provide a more effective institutional framework for realizing national development goals such as ownership, control and high financial return. Dr Asante goes on to explore the validity of this observation with respect to every type of the above-mentioned new arrangements: at pp. 21–55 of his unpublished lecture.

24 See ch. 4.

25 In agreement, see Fatouros, *Government Guarantees*, p. 208.

26 This will be discussed in ch. 10.

27 Kronfol, *Protection*, p. 68.

28 *I.C.J. Rep.*, 1952, p. 112.

29 53 *Am. Soc. Int. Law Proceed.* (1959), p. 267.
30 Alfred von Verdross in 'The Status of Foreign Private Interests Stemming from Economic Development Agreements with Arbitration Clauses', *Selected Readings on Protection by Law of Private Foreign Investments*, The Southwestern Legal Foundation (1964), p. 121.
31 At p. 43 of the Award. The same view is shared by Mann, *Studies*, p. 223; also Professor R. Y. Jennings, 'State Contracts in International Law', 37 *B.Y.B.I. L.* (1961), p. 156, at pp. 175–81.
32 *Government Guarantees*, p. 208.
33 Henry Cattan, *The Law of Oil Concessions in the Middle East and North Africa* (1967), p. 30.
34 Ibid.
35 I.L.R., vol. 27 (1958), 117.
36 Ibid.
37 See George W. Ray, 'Law Governing Contracts between States and Foreign Nationals', in 2 *Proceedings of the 1960 Institute on Private Investments Abroad* (1960), pp. 12–13.
38 Ibid.
39 Cecil J. Olmstead, 'Economic Development Loan Agreements, Part II: Agreements Between States and Aliens; Choice of Law and Remedy', 49 *Calif. L. Rev.* (1961), at 507.
40 Ibid. Cf. Restatement, Foreign Relations law of the United States 102 (Tent. Draft No. 3, 1959).
41 Olmstead, 49 *Calif. L. Rev.* (1961), p. 507.
42 Financial Circulars of Concluding Government Contracts, Ministry of Finance and National Economy (Khartoum).
43 Section 7 of the Mines and Quarries Act, 1972.
44 Section 25 of the Petroleum Resources (Amendment) Act, 1975.
45 See generally, Colin Turpin, *Government Contracts* (1972), chs. 1, 2. and 3.
46 For instance, *Smith* case (*United States* v. *Mexico*), Moore, *International Arbitration*, vol. 4, p. 3456; also Bernadou (*United States* v. *Brazil*, 1851), ibid. vol. 5.
47 See the *Shufeldt Arbitration* (*United States* v. *Guatemala*, 1930), *U.N.R.I.A.A.*, vol. 2, p. 1081.
48 Ibid.
49 *Trumbull case* (*Chile* v. *United States*), Moore, *International Arbitration*, vol. 4, p. 3569.
50 'Repudiation of Ultra Vires State Contracts and the International Responsibility of States', 6 *I.C.L.Q.* (1957), 279.
51 Ibid. 289.
52 Olmstead, 49 *Calif. L. Rev.* (1961), 507–8.
53 Restatement, Foreign Relations Law of the United States, 103(2). See Legal Status of Eastern Greenland, *P.C.I.J.*, Series A/B, No. 53 (1933).
54 See P. M. North (ed.), *Cheshire's Private International Law*, 9th edn. (1974), ch. 8.
55 Cattan, *Law of Oil Concessions*, p. 33.
56 George W. Ray, 2 *Institute on Private Investments Abroad* (1960), pp. 20–33; J. Anderson and N. J. Coulson, 'The Moslem Ruler and Contractual Obligations', 33 *N.Y.U.L.R.* (1958), pp. 917–33; also P. Nicholas Kourides, 'The Influence of Islamic Law on Contemporary Middle Eastern Legal Systems: The Formation and Binding Force of Contracts', 9 *Columb. J. Trans. L.* (1970), no. 2, pp. 384–435.
57 *S.L.S.D.R.S.G.* no. 1162, dated 25 June 1974, p. 275.
58 Sections 1 (2) and 2.

59 Kenneth S. Charlston, 'International Role of Concession Agreements', 52 *N.Y.U.L.R.* (1957), at 630.
60 A. Von Verdross, 'Quasi-International Agreements', 27 *Year Book of World Affairs* (1964), p. 230.
61 E.g. Kronfol, *Protection*, p. 72. Fatouros, *Government Guarantees*, p. 286.
62 McNair, 33 *B.Y.B.I.L.* (1957), p. 7.
63 F. A. Mann, 'The Proper Law of Contracts Concluded by International Persons', 35 *Y.B.I.L.* (1959), p. 34, at p. 49.
64 See the Libya–Oil Companies Arbitration Award, p. 35.
65 Mustafa Ahmed El Zarga *Al-Madkhal-el-Fighe-Al-AAM* (1964) (*Introduction to General Islamic Jurisprudence*).
66 Professor R. Y. Jennings, 'Rules Governing Contracts Between States and Foreign Nationals', in *Selected Readings*, p. 127.
67 *P.C.I.J.*, series A, no. 20/21, p. 41.
68 Ibid. p. 42.
69 Libya–Oil Companies Award, p. 35. Cf. *Rex* v. *International Trustees* (1937) A.C. 500, where the House of Lords applied the doctrine of the free choice of law and rejected the contention of the United Kingdom that English Law should apply. It was held that the governing law was the law of the United States.
70 *Sudan Arbitration* (Turriff case).
71 Clause 13. Cf. *The Ghana–Valco Agreement of 1961*: Nwogugu, *Legal Problems*, p. 248. Also *Sudan Government* v. *Brown International* Inc.
72 A similar provision is contained in the Loan Agreement between the Sudanese Ministry of Planning and the National Bank Voor Middellang (Dutch Bank), where the law of the Netherlands is applicable.
73 Geiger, 23 *I.C.L.Q.* (1974), 76–7.
74 Jennings, 37 *B.Y.B.I.L.* (1961), p. 156.
75 Geiger, 23 *I.C.L.Q.* (1974), 76. The legal effect of the 'stabilization clause' has been examined at length by René-Jean Dupuy, sole Arbitrator in the Libya–Oil Companies Award with respect to the doctrine of sovereignty, p. 57, *et seq.*
76 J. C. Hurewitz, *Diplomacy in the Near and Middle East, 1935–1956*, vol. 2 (1956), p. 349, at p. 374.
77 Cf. the Agreements: N.I.O.C.–Agip, N.I.O.C.–Pan American, Kuwait–Shell; Cattan, *Law of Oil Concessions*, p. 59; Geiger, 23 *I.C.L.Q.* (1974), 76; E. H. Wall, 'The Iranian–Italian Oil Agreement of 1957', 7 *I.C.L.Q.* (1958), 736.
78 Nwogugu, *Legal Problems*, p. 248. For a contrary view, see S. Asante, 'Stability of Contractual Relations in the Transnational Investment Process', 28 *I.C.L.Q.* (1979), 401.
79 I.L.R. (1956), p. 633.
80 Ibid. p. 637.
81 Hurewitz, *Diplomacy*, p. 377. Similar provisions were included in the National Iranian Oil Company's Agreement with Assienda Generale Italiana Petroli (Agip) (1957), the Kuwait–Arabian Oil Company Concession (1958), the Kuwait–Shell Concession (1961) and the UAR–Pan American Concession (1963 and 1964), Cattan, *Law of Oil Concessions*, p. 59.
82 Emphasis added. See Petroleum Working Contract between Indonesia and P.T. Stanvoc, Indonesia, and notes on Contracts of P.T. Shell Indonesia, P.T. Caltex Pacific Indonesia and California Asiatic Oil Company and Overseas Petroleum Company, 3 *I.L.M.* (1964), 248 *et seq.*

83 Mann, 35 *B.Y.B.I.L.* (1959), 34, at 43; *idem*, *Studies*, p. 223.

84 'The Theoretical Approach Towards the Law Governing Contracts between States and Private Persons', *Rev. Belge D.I.* (1975), p. 562.

85 P. 44.

86 At p. 46 of the Libyan Award. For a critical comment on the Libyan Award see, D. W. Bowett, 'Libyan Nationalisation of American Oil Companies Assets', 37 *Camb. L.J.* (April, 1978), 5–8.

87 See Professor Jennings in 37 *B.Y.B.I.L.* (1961), p. 181.

88 'Rules Governing Contracts Between States and Foreign Nationals', *International and Comparative Law Centre*, the Southwestern Legal Foundation (1965), pp. 127–8. *Pacta sunt servanda* and 'acquired rights' will be discussed later in this chapter.

89 See C. W. Jenks, *The Common Law of Mankind* (1958), p. 3; Cheng, *General Principles*, *passim*; Schlesinger, 'Research on the General Principles of Law Recognized by Civilized Nations', 51 *A.J.I.L.* (1957), 734.

90 See the judgment of the Permanent Court of International Justice in the *Lotus* Case, (1927) *P.C.I.J.*, series A, no. 10 at p. 16.

91 At p. 51 of the *Award*; other international contracts referred to the general principles of law: the contract between Iran and AGIP, 1954 (Art. 40); contract between Kuwait and Kuwait Shell Petroleum Company, 1961 (Art. 35); the contract between the United Arab Republic and Pan American U.A.R. Oil Company, 1936 (Art. 42).

92 The awards delivered in *Lena Goldfields* v. *Sovereign U.S.S.R.*, A.D. (1929–30), Case No. 1; Nussbaum: 36 *Cornell L.Q.* (1950–51), 31–53; *Petroleum Development Ltd.* v. *Sovereign of Abu Dhabi in* 1951, 1 *I.C.L.Q.* (1952), 249; International *Marine Oil Company* v. *Sovereign of Quatar*, I.L.R. (1953), p. 541, and *Sapphire International Petroleum Ltd.* v. *N.I.O.C.*, 13 *I.C.L.Q.* (1964), 1013. In all these cases the Arbitrators noted a reference to the general principles of law in reaching their conclusions as to the internationalization of the contract.

93 McNair, 33 *B.Y.B.I.L.* (1975), p. 19.

94 Cattan, *Law of Oil Concessions*, p. 62. Fatouros, *Government Guarantees*, pp. 289–301. On transnational law generally, see P. C. Jessup, *Transnational Law*, (1956). In the opinion of Fatouros, transnational law is that body of law applicable to relations between international organizations or State and individuals. 'Contractual relation between States and aliens would also seem to fall within this general category' (at p. 284). The writer went on to say: 'transnational law is founded on the general principles of law common to civilized nations' (at p. 289).

95 Mann, in 35 *B.Y.B.I.L.*, at p. 44.

96 Ibid. Fatouros, *Government Guarantees*, pp. 285–95.

97 Wolfgang Friedmann, *The Changing Structure of International Law* (1964), p. 194.

98 1 *I.C.L.Q.* (1952), 247.

99 Ibid. 250–1.

100 Friedmann, *Changing Structure*, p. 193; Kronfol, *Protection*, p. 78.

101 I.L.R. (1953), 534. Cf. *Aramco* v. *Saudi Arabia*.

102 Fatouros, *Government Guarantees*, pp. 293–4; the Libya–Oil Companies Award, pp. 53–4.

103 Ibid. pp. 53–4.

104 At p. 172.

105 The Libya–Oil Companies Award, p. 54. Cf. clause XXIII of the Petroleum Production-Sharing Agreement between the Sudan and Chevron; clause 38 of the *Rahad Contract*, the Sudan–Lonrho Sugar Agreement, 1972. Charlston suggests, on the other hand, that

an obligation to have recourse to negotiations and arbitrations for the settlement of any dispute is imposed on the parties of State contracts by the 'living law' of their contract. Charlston, 52 *N.W.U.L.Rev.* (1957), 618, 640; also *idem*, 52 *A.J.I.L.* (1958), 260, 265.

106 M. Bourguin, 'Arbitration and Economic Development Agreements', 15 *Bus. Lawyer* (1960), 860; Fatouros, *Government Guarantees*, pp. 275–6; S. M. Schwebel, *Am. Soc. Int. Law Proceed.* (1959), p. 266.

107 The Libya–Oil Companies Award, p. 55.

108 Clause 17 of the Petroleum Production-Sharing Agreement between the Democratic Republic of the Sudan and Chevron.

109 35 I.L.R. (1967), at pp. 175–6.

110 C. F. Amerasinghe, *State Responsibility for Injuries to Aliens* (1967), p. 96; Kronfol, *Protection*, p. 76. Brownlie, *Public International Law*, who advocates the application the rules of private international law to contracts between aliens and government, pp. 537–4.

111 Southwestern Legal Foundation, at p. 127.

112 The Libya–Oil Companies Award, p. 58.

113 *I.C.J. Rep.* (1949), at p. 178.

114 The Libya–Oil Companies Award; also Professor Garcia Amador, 2 *Y.B.I.L.C.*, U.N. Doc. A/CN.4/119 (1959), at p. 32.

115 For the distinction between the claim of the individual and the claim of his State, see the *Mavrommatis Concessions* case, *P.C.I.J.*, series A., no. 5.

116 Jennings, in 37 *B.Y.B.I.L.* (1961), p. 164.

117 Ibid.

118 Cattan, *Law of Oil Concessions*, p. 82; Ḳronfol, *Protection*, pp. 79–80.

119 Cattan, *Law of Oil Concessions*, p. 82.

120 Friedmann, *Changing Structure* (1964), at p. 196.

121 Cattan, *Law of Oil Concessions*, p. 84.

122 McNair, *International law Opinions*, vol. 2, p. 201; Fatouros, *Government Guarantees*, p. 243; Cf. Schwebel, 53 *Am. Soc. Int. Law Proc.* (1959), 266–8.

123 Fatouros, *Government Guarantees*, p. 247.

124 Ibid. p. 261 *et seq.*

125 For the discussion of these arguments, see ibid.

126 For instance, Hendrix: 'A Sovereign Nation's Legal Ability to Make and Abide by a Petroleum Concession Contract', a paper delivered to the Arab Oil Conference held in Cairo in April 1959, cited and criticized by Ray, in *Proceedings of the 1960 Institute on Private Investments Abroad*, pp. 501–2, who identified the adherents to this view as 'the Absolutists'. See also L. T. Kissan and E. K. Leach, 'Sovereign Expropriation of Property and Abrogation of Concession Contracts', 28 *Fordham L.R.* (1959–60), 177, at 199.

127 Nwogugu, *Legal Problems*, p. 174; Kronfol, *Protection*, p. 83; the Libya–Oil Companies Award, and the authorities cited therein, pp. 75–118.

128 Nwogugu, *Legal Problems*, pp. 173–4; Kissan and Leach, 28 *Ford.L.Rev.* (1959–60), 177–214; Schwebel, *Am.Soc.Int.Law Proceed.*, p. 268; *the Libya–Oil Companies Award.*

129 27 I.L.R., 1963, at 168. The same rule was followed in the Sapphire Award.

130 For instance, Ray, *Institute of Private Investments Abroad*; Nwogugu, *Legal Problems*, p. 175; Kronfol, *Protection*, p. 83.

131 At pp. 101–18 of the Award; Bowett, 37 *Camb. L.J.* (1978), 6–7.

132 For cases, see *Radio Corporation of America* v. *China*, 30 *A.J.I.L.* (1936), 535; *Czechoslovakia* v. *R.C.A.*, ibid. 523; Anglo-Iranian Dispute (United Kingdom Memorial), *I.C.J. Pleadings*, p. 90. See, generally, Don, *Protection*, pp. 242–52.

133 294 *U.S.* 330.
134 For instance, *Robertson* v. *Minister of Pensions* [1948] 2 All E.R., 767 at p. 770.
135 See, *Sudan Government* v. *Brown International Inc.*
136 2 *U.N.R.I.A.A.*, 1080; 24 *A.J.I.L.* (1930), 799.
137 *U.S. Foreign Relations*, 1902, p. 857. The same result obtained in the *Rudolff* case, 9 *U.N.R.I.A.A.*, p. 244.
138 F. M. Auburn Aukand, 'The 1973 Conference on the Law of the Sea in the Light of Current Trends in State Seabed Practice', 50 *C.B.R.* (1972) at 102–3.
139 Sanctioned by Royal Decree M/27 of 1 October 1968 reported by Aukand, ibid.
140 Brownlie, *Basic Documents*, pp. 107–11. For the *Ratification* Act of the Convention, see *S.L.S.D.R.S.G.* no. 991, dated 15 June 1978, p. 218.
141 *I.C.J.Pleadings*, 1968; *I.C.J.Rep.* (1969) (Judgment), pp. 4–56.
142 The Sudan–Saudi Arabia Kingdom Agreement Concerning the Mutual Exploitation of Natural Resources in the Red Sea Bed in the Common Area Between Them (Ratification) Order, 1974 (Presidential Order No. 215), for text, *L.S.D.R.S.G.* no. 1162, dated 15 June 1974, p. 131.
143 An authoritative support for 'vested right' as a principle of international law is found in O'Connell, *International Law*, vol. 1, p. 10; McNair, 33 *B.Y.B.I.L.* (1957); Wortley, *Expropriation*, pp. 125–8. The ablest exposition of the principle of 'acquired' rights was given by Professor Pierre A. Lalive, 'The Doctrine of Acquired Rights', in *Rights and Duties of Private Investors Abroad* (1965), Southwestern Legal Foundation, pp. 145–200.
144 R. Y. Jennings, in *Rights and Duties*, Southwestern Legal Foundation, pp. 221–37.
145 Ibid.; Nwogugu, *Legal Problems*, p. 178.
146 *Certain German Interests* (Merits); *Chorzow Factory* case, cases reviewed by McNair, 33 *B.Y.B.I.L.* (1957), pp. 221–37.
147 I.L.R., at p. 205; cf. the abrogation of the exploration licences of Sudanese Minerals Co. Ltd.
148 H. Wehberg, 'Pacta Sunt Servanda', 53 *A.J.I.L.* (1959), 775–86.
149 Hans Kelson, *Principles of International Law* (1967), p. 447.
150 See the authorities cited by Wehberg, 53 *A.J.I.L.* (1959); Cheng, *General Principles*, p. 113; Kunz, 39 *A.J.I.L.* (1945), 180; Oppenheim, *International Law*, vol. 1, pp. 880–1; McNair, *The Law of Treaties*, ch. 30.
151 Nwogugu, *Legal Problems*, p. 186; Kronfol, *Protection*, p. 90.
152 *Permanent Court of International Justice, Pleadings, Oral Statements and Documents*, series C, no. 78, p. 32.
153 53 *A.J.I.L.* (1959), at 786. For a contrary view of the applicability of the principle of *pacta sunt servanda* to State contracts, see Fatouros, *Government Guarantees*, pp. 265–71.
154 Jennings in *Rights and Duties*, Southwestern Legal Foundation, pp. 131–2.
155 30 *A.J.I.L.* (1936), 523.
156 Ibid. at 531. In the Libya–Oil Companies Award the Arbitrator found that both Libyan Law (Acts 147 and 148 of the *Civil Code*) and international law embodied the principle of *pacta sunt servanda*, so the binding force of the concessions was beyond doubt.
157 Fatouros, *Government Guarantees*, pp. 253–61; Nwogugu, *Legal Problems*, pp. 179–80; Kronfol, *Protection*, pp. 87–8. See also *ante*, pp. 104–6, where the principle has been argued to be applicable to unilateral measures.
158 Cheng, *General Principles*, p. 236; see also Bowett; 33 *B.Y.B.I.L.* (1957), p. 176, at p. 177.
159 Lauterpacht, *Private Law Sources*, pp. 203–4; *idem*, *The Development of International Law by International Court* (1958), pp. 168–72; Friedmann, *Legal Theory*, pp. 505–6; *The Temple* case, *I.C.J.Rep.* (1962), pp. 39–41.

160 2 *U.N.R.I.A.A.*, p. 1081, at p. 1094.
161 The Sudan Arbitration; see also *The Financial Times*, 29 April 1970.
162 At first it was thought wise to have the housing project carried out partly by one contractor and partly by another. Even the earmarking of the area was not agreed upon and after that issue was determined it was considered necessary to appoint consulting engineers, a process which took a long time. Futhermore, the preparation and issuing of tender documents added to the delay before concluding the contract with Turriff. For a detailed narrative of the facts, see 17 *Neth. Int. L.R.* (1970), 200–2.
163 For an elaborate study of this principle, see H. C. Gutteridge and R. J. A. David: 'The Doctrine of Unjust Enrichment', 5 *Camb. L.J.* (1933–35), 204, Wortley, *Expropriation*, pp. 95–102.
164 *Landreau Claim* (*United States* v. *Peru*), 1 *U.N.R.I.A.A.*, 347.
165 Nwogugu, *Legal Problems*, p. 180.
166 Ibid.; Gutteridge and David, 5 *Camb. L.J.* (1933–35), 204–23.
167 Friedmann, *Changing Structure*, p. 206; also D. P. O'Connell, 'Unjust Enrichment', 5 *A.J.C.L.*, (1959), 2.
168 A.D. (1929–30), case no. 1; Nussbaum: 36 *Cornell L.Q.* (1950–51), 31–53.
169 A.D. (1929–30), at p. 51.
170 Fatouros, *Government Guarantees*, 296; Kronfol, *Protection*, p. 88; Nwogugu, *Legal Problems*, p. 183.
171 Sir H. Lauterpacht, *The Function of Law in International Community* (1958), ch. 14; Cheng, *General Principles*, p. 122 *et seq.* Garcia Amador: *Y.B.I.L.C.* (1959–11), pp. 7–8.
172 Schwarzenberger: 'Abuse of Rights in International Law', 42 *Grotius Society Transactions* (1957), p. 147; J. M. Jones, 'The Nottebohm case', 5 *I.C.L.Q.* (1956), 230, at 236–43.
173 Nwogugu, *Legal Problems*, p. 183; also Lauterpacht, *Development of International Law*, at p. 162.
174 Gutteridge & David, 5 *Camb. L.J.* (1933–35), at 44.
175 Wortley, *Expropriation*, p. 102.
176 E.g. *German Interests in Polish Upper Silesia*, *P.C.I.J.*, series A, no. 7, 1926, at p. 30; *The Free Zones of Upper Savoy and Gex*, *P.C.I.J.*, series A, no. 24, p. 12.
177 See *The Walter Fletcher Smith* case, (*U.S.* v. *Cuba*, 1929), 2 *U.N.R.I.A.A.*, p. 913; Harvard Draft Convention on the International Responsibility of States for Injuries to Aliens, 55 *A.J.I.L.* (1961), 548.
178 David C. Baldus, 'State Competence to Terminate Concession Agreements with Aliens', 53 *Kentucky L.J.* (1964), p. 59. The most articulate exposition of the policy view which combines moral motivations with pragmatic considerations is given by Charlston, 'Concession Agreements and Nationalization', 52 *A.J.I.L.* (1958), 260–77, 279.
179 *Am. Soc. Int. Law Proceed.* (1959).
180 Quoted by Kronfol, *Protection*, p. 97.
181 4 *U.N.R.I.A.A.* 691 at 698–700; cf. the *Turriff* case.
182 Cf. the *Hughes* Case (*U.S.* v. *Mexico* 1930), 4 *U.N.R.I.A.A.* 617; F. A. Mann, 'State Contracts and State Responsibility'. 54 *A.J.I.L.* (1960), at 574–75; Fatouros, *Government Guarantees*, p. 237.
183 Nwogugu, *Legal Problems*, p. 187.
184 Kronfol, *Protection*, p. 92; Foighel, *Nationalization*, p. 74; Charlston, 52 *A.J.I.L.* (1958).
185 Fatouros, *Government Guarantees*, p. 247.
186 Wortley, *Expropriation*, p. 110.
187 Jennings, in Southwestern Legal Foundation, *Rights and Duties*, p. 132.
188 Nwogugu, *Legal Problems*, p. 188; Meron, 6 *I.C.L.Q.* (1957), 288.

189 *Free Zones of Upper Savoy case*, pp. 156–8; *Nationality Decrees in Tunis and Morocco* (1923), *P.C.I.J.* series B, no. 4, p. 29; Advisory Opinion on International Status of S.W. Africa, *I.C.J.Rep.* 1950, pp. 132–3.

190 Oppenheim, *International Law*, pp. 941–2; section 73 of the Sudanese Contracts Act, 1974.

191 52 *A.J.I.L.* (1958), p. 265.

192 *Am. Soc. Int. Law Proc.* (1959), p. 273. For the practice of African countries in re-negotiating their investment agreements with transnational corporations, see Dr Asante's Lagos lecture, *Transnational Investment Law*, pp. 59–76.

193 A typical example of such *force majeure* clauses is mentioned in other petroleum and mining agreements between the Sudan and the Chevron Co.

194 Mann, 54 *A.J.I.L.* (1960), 102; Schwarzenberger, 5 *C.L.P.* (1952), 572, at 582; Jennings, 37 *B.Y.B.I.L.* (1961), p. 170 *et seq.*

195 *A.J.I.L.* (1961), 548 *et seq.*

196 Jennings: 37 *B.Y.B.I.L.* (1961), at pp. 161–81; Hyde, *International Law*, vol. 2, p. 991; Nwogugu, *Legal Problems*. Cf. United Nations International Law Commission in its 1959 report, *U.N.Y.B.I.L.C.* (1959), vol. 2 (A/CN.4 SER.A/1959/ADD.1), pp. 31–2.

197 *Cheek's Claim* (*U.S.* v. *Siam*), Whiteman, *Damages*, vol. 3, p. 1651; *Delagoa Bay Coy.* case, ibid. p. 1698.

198 Also White, *Nationalisation*, pp. 45–50.

199 Jennings, *Selected Readings*, Southwestern Legal Foundation, pp. 136–7.

200 At pp. 139–40 of the Libya–Oil Companies Award. The order of *restitutio in integrum* in this Award has been criticized by Bowett as impractical. In his words: 'One may also wonder at the practicability of specific performance as the primary remedy in such cases, or even at the wisdom of postponing the assessment of damages in lieu of further proceedings' 37 *Camb. L.J.*, 8.

201 48 *B.Y.B.I.L.* (1978), at p. 63.

202 In agreement, S. M. Schwebel, 'Speculations on Specific Performance of a Contract between a State and a Foreign National', *Rights and Duties*, Southwestern Legal Foundation, p. 201.

203 Nwogugu, *Legal Problems*, p. 191; *Cheeks' Claim.*

204 Whiteman, *Damages*, p. 1692; also *Antoine Fabianni Claim* (*France* v. *Venezuela*), ibid. pp. 1785–6; *Delagoa Bay Co. Case*, ibid. p. 1698; article 34 of the Harvard Draft Convention on the Responsibility of States 1961 provides: 'Damages for the violation, annulment, or modification of a contract or concession . . . shall include compensation for losses caused and gains denied as a result of such wrongful act or omission or compensation which will restore the claimant to the same position in which the injured alien was immediately preceding such act or omission', 55 *A.J.I.L.* (1961), 548.

205 *Rudolf* case, 9 *U.N.R.I.A.A.*, p. 244; *Shufeldt* Claim, p. 1079.

206 Nwogugu, *Legal Problems*, p. 192.

207 Report on the Arbitration Between the Government of the Republic of the Sudan and Turriff Construction (Sudan) Ltd., dated March 1968, addressed to Herbert Smith & Co., the solicitors of the Sudan Embassy. Cf. the table of calculation of damages due in the Shufeldt case at pp. 100–1.

208 C. J. Olmstead, 32 *N.Y.U.L.Rev.* (1957), 1122, at 1133–4.

209 Moore, *International Arbitration*, vol. 4, p. 3248.

210 *Shufeldt Claim* at p. 1099.

211 See Cheng, *General Principles*, p. 243 *et seq.*; Nwogugu, *Legal Problems*, p. 194.

212 P. 1099. Cf. the English Cases of *Hadley* v. *Baxendale* [1894] 9 Ex. 341, at pp. 354–5; *Victoria Laundry* v. *Newman* [1949] 2 K.B. at pp. 539–40.
213 *Chorzow Factory (Indemnity)* Case, p. 53.
214 Whiteman, *Damages*, vol. 3, pp. 1871–2; Cf. *Michel* Claim (1953) I.L.R., p. 628.
215 Ibid.
216 Nwogugu, *Legal Problems*, p. 195.
217 I.L.R. (1956), 299. Cf. *May* Claim.
218 *U.N.R.I.A.A.*, vol. 1, p. 309.
219 S. I. B. Asante, 'Restructuring Transnational Mineral Agreements', 73 *A.J.I.L.* (1979), 335 *et seq.*

10. Settlement of investment disputes

1 For an elaborate discussion of the maxim, see Cheng, *General Principles*, p. 290.
2 Nwogugu, *Legal Problems*, p. 230.
3 *U.N.R.I.A.A.*, vol. 2, p. 1098.
4 Kronfol, *Protection*, pp. 123–4.
5 Nwogugu, *Legal Problems*, p. 233. On recent developments on sovereign immunity in the British Courts, see Lord Denning in *Trendtex Trading Corporation Ltd.* v. *Central Bank of Nigeria* [1977], 2 W.L.R. 356; 16 *I.L.M.* (1977), 471. In this case Lord Denning adopted a restrictive view on sovereign immunity. See also Rosalyn Higgins, 'Recent Developments in the Law of Sovereign Immunity in the United Kingdom', 71 *A.J.I.L.* (1977), 427; also the State Immunity Act, 1978, published by Her Majesty's Stationery Office, London. On the United States practice see the Foreign Sovereign Immunity Act, 1976 which has taken effect as from 19 January 1977, 15 *I.L.M.* (1976), 1388; also Eleanor C. McDowell, 'Sovereign Immunity', 71 *A.J.I.L.* (1977), 338–43.
6 Article III deals with the right of the President to declare a state of emergency in case of imminent danger threatening the independence or integrity of the country and the safety of its territory or its economy.
7 *S.L.S.D.R.S.G.* no. 1162 dated 2 July 1974, p. 661.
8 Section 323.
9 Section 324(1).
10 Ibid. (2).
11 Sections 325 and 327.
12 See for details sections, 326, 328, 329, 330, 331, 332, 333, 334 and 335.
13 Section 309(1).
14 Section 309(2).
15 Section 309(3).
16 Section 310(1).
17 Section 312. Before the enactment of this section, the rule was that the appeal from an administrative decision was available only in cases provided for by law, or where the administrative authority was exceeded or abused. Thus, in *Re Tiweisha and Wadaa Boundaries Disputes*: *Adam Bishara and Others* v. *District Commissioner, El Fasher*, the Province Court of Darfour held that in the absence of statutory provision, an appeal does not lie to a Civil Court from the decision of a District Commissioner pertaining to a boundary dispute between two omodias (districts), [1964] *S.L.J.R.*, 156.
18 Section 313.

19 Introduced by the Statutory Instrument, 1977, 1955 (L. 30) Supreme Court of Adjudication, *Rules of the Supreme Court* (Amendment No. 1977), *Statutory Instruments Reports*, 1977.

20 Section 14 of the Industrial Investment Act.

21 [1969] 2 W.L.R. 163. For a critical evaluation of the case, see H. W. R. Wade, 'Constitutional and Administrative Aspects of the Anisminic Case', 85 *L.Q.R.* (1969), 198–212; also, D. M. Gordon, 'Judicial Review in Administrative Law: The Ever-Open Door', 27 *Camb. L.J.* (1969), 161–6.

22 *L.S.D.R.S.G.* No. 1107 dated 15 July 1970, p. 252.

23 *L.S.D.R.S.G.* No. 1148 dated 7 June 1973, p. 109.

24 Extract from *S.L.S.D.R.S.G.* No. 910 dated 25 July 1957 (1957 Act no. 22).

25 See Article 188 of the Permanent Constitution of the Sudan, 1973, sections 16, 29 and 57 of the Judiciary Act, 1973. See generally, B. O. Nwabueze, *Judicialism in Commonwealth Africa* (1974), ch. 3.

26 On the independence of the Judiciary generally see E. C. S. Wade & G. Phillips, *Constitutional Law*, 9th edn., 1977, ch. 19.

27 [1970] A.C. 179.

28 Ibid. p. 212.

29 Ibid. See also Lord Denning, M.R., in *Butts Gas & Oil Co.* v. *Hammer* [1975] 2 W.L.R. 425. According to the Supreme Court order 18/8/2 'Act of State': 'The exact limits of the so-called doctrine of "act of State" whether it be of a foreign government or of Her Majesty's Government, are and still remain a matter of controversy into which it is most undesirable to embark on the hearing of an interlocutory appeal, and although there are certain classes of acts by or on behalf of foreign governments or Her Majesty's Government which the courts of England will not allow to be questioned before them there is in English law no established or defined doctrine, similar to the 'act of State' doctrine developed in the U.S.A., which requires the court to strike out a pleading or particulars on the proceedings between private litigants....' *The Supreme Court Practice* (1976), vols. 1 and 2, *First Supplement*. Similarly, by Order 18/12/4 it is provided that: 'The circumstances in which the defence of "act of State" is available are very ill-defined, and it is still in the process of being worked out in the cases but it is for the courts to determine in any particular case as it comes up whether, as a matter of policy (the policy of the law), the defence of "act of State" should be available.' ibid.

30 Ibid. pp. 212–13. For the application by the American courts of the 'act of State' doctrine, see K. R. Simmonds, 'The Sabbatino Case and the Act of State Doctrine' 14 *I.C.L.Q.* (1965), 452–90.

31 [1970] A.C., 179 at 213.

32 For the practice of the English courts in reviewing the administrative decisions even in cases of prerogatives, see *Laker Airways Ltd.* v. *Department of Trade* [1977], 2 All E.R. 182.

33 Article 59 of the Constitution provides: 'The State is subject to the Rule of Law and the Supremacy of the Rule of Law shall be the basis of Government.'

34 *Misr Printing Press* v. *Kamil Mohamed Kamil and Mahir Habib Gutta* [1959] *S.L.J.R.*, p. 3; *Amin Abdel Maseeh & Sons* v. *Manoli Chadzoghlou & Sons* (1962), ibid. p. 251.

35 L. of N., *Official Journal*, vol. XIV (1933), pp. 198–204.

36 For text, see *L.S.D.R.S.G.* No. 1245, dated 15 July 1978, p. 18.

37 For the text, see U.N.T.S. 575, 159. For a detailed exposition, see *post*, pp. 307–16.

38 The Grievances Board Regulations, 1976.

39 Cited by Kronfol, *Protection*, p. 124.

40 *United States Supreme Court Reports* 168 [1897], p. 250.

41 56 *A.J.I.L.* (1962), 1105.

42 *United States Supreme Court Reports* 376 [1964], p. 1105.

43 *78 Stat. 1013* (1964).

44 Kronfol, *Protection*, p. 125. For later developments to the *Hickenlooper Amendment* see *First National City Bank of New York* v. *Banco National de Cuba*, 66 *A.J.I.L.* (1972), 856; Robert Delson, 'The Act of State Doctrine – Judicial Deference or Abstention', ibid. pp. 82–93; S. D. Metzger editorial comment, 'The State Department's Role in the Judicial Administration of the Act of State Doctrine', ibid., pp. 94–101; *D. Angelo* v. *Petroleos Mexicanos*, 68 *A.J.I.L.* (1974), 740–1; *Alfred Dunhill of London Inc.* v. *Republic of Cuba*, 96 *S.ct.* 1854 (full text in 15 *I.L.M.* (1976), 485). In this latter case, the United States Supreme Court refused to apply the doctrine of 'act of State' to commercial transactions. The court positively stated: 'the concept of an act of State should not be extended *to include the repudiation of a purely commercial obligation owed by a foreign sovereign or by one of its commercial instrumentalities.* Italics added. See also, Robert MacCrate, *Proceed. Am. Soc. I.L.* (1973), p. 73.

45 M. Zander, 'The Act of State Doctrine', 53 *A.J.I.L.* (1959), 635. For a contrary view, see Robert K. Goldman, *Proceed. Am. Soc. I.L.* (1973), 78.

46 *The Mavrommatis* case, *Permanent Court of International Justice*, series A, no. 2, p. 12.

47 *P.C.I.J.* series A/B, no. 76.

48 Oppenheim, *International Law*, vol. 1, 8th edn. (1955), pp. 347–8; Nwogugu, *Legal Problems*, p. 101.

49 See *ante*, p. 15; also the case of *Nationality Decrees in Tunis and Morocco*, Advisory opinion of the *P.C.I.J.* series B, no. 4.

50 The place of nationality in international law was discussed at the Hague Conference of 1930. Article 1 of the Hague Convention on Certain Questions Relating to the Conflict of Nationality Laws stated that the right of each State to determine by municipal law who are its nationals can only be recognized by other States 'in so far as it is consistent with international conventions, international custom, and the principle of law generally recognized with regard to nationality'. See Hudson, *International Legislation*, vol. 5, p. 359. The Sudan and Saudi Arabia have not ratified the Convention.

51 *Baron Frederic de Born* v. *Yugoslavia State*, A.D. [1925–26] Case No. 205; *Barthez de Montfort* v. *Treuhander Hauptverwaltung*, ibid. Case No. 206; The *Nottebohm* Case, *I.C.J. Rep.*, 1955, p. 4; see 'The Development of Nationality Laws in the Sudan', a thesis submitted by the writer for the part fulfilment of the requirements of LL.M. Degree in the University of Khartoum in May 1975. For a critical examination of the *Nottebohm* case, see Nwogugu, *Legal Problems*, pp. 103–5.

52 Nwogugu, *Legal Problems*, p. 108.

53 *A.J.I.L.*, Special Supplement (1928), 205, para. 6.

54 *I.C.J. Rep.*, 1970 at p. 32. For criticism see F. A. Mann, 'The Proctection of Shareholders' Interests in the Light of the Barcelona Traction case', 67 *A.J.I.L.* (1973), 259–74. The U.S.'s practice seems not to follow the rule in *Barcelona Traction* Case on diplomatic protection, particularly in claims under the investment insurance programme, see *ante*, pp. 162–3.

55 *I.C.J. Rep.* (1970), at pp. 35–6.

56 Ibid. at p. 48. Cf. A. Bagge, 'Intervention on the Ground of Damage Caused to Nationals, with Particular Reference to Exhaustion of Local Remedies and the Rights of Shareholders', 34 *B.Y.B.I.L.* (1958), p. 162.

57 Jones, 'Claims on Behalf of Nationals who are shareholders in Foreign Companies', 26 *B.Y.B.I.L.* (1949), p. 225; Bagge, 34 *B.Y.B.I.L.* (1958), pp. 169–75; Nwogugu, *Legal Problems*, p. 112. The first case in which the principle of protecting shareholders was dealt with was the *Ruden*'s case, Moore, *International Arbitrations*, vol. 2 (1898), p. 1653.

58 Nwogugu, *Legal Problems*, p. 113.

59 This is true of some foreign companies nationalized by the Sudan in 1970 which had been voluntarily incorporated under the Sudanese Companies Ordinance, 1925, e.g. Contomathalios Companies.

60 Nwogugu, *Legal Problems*, p. 113; see in general, Whiteman, *Digest*, vol. 8, p. 1233 *et seq.*; Bochard, *Diplomatic Protection*, p. 29.

For the practice of the United States, see J. Gillis Wetter, 'Diplomatic Assistance to Private Investment', 29 *University of Chicago Law Review* (1962), 275.

61 Ibid.; also *Delagoa Railway* case, Moore, *Digest of International Law*, vol. 6 (1906), p. 647; Nwogugu, *Legal Problems*, pp. 113–16. On the British practice, in the concrete case, the majority of shareholders were British subjects – see the Note of 20 April 1938, of the Government of the United Kingdom to the Mexican Government (Cmd 5758–1938, p. 7 *et seq.*).

62 For instance, the Kenana Sugar Company; also the Plastic Sacks Company, the mining industry and the various agricultural projects under construction and implementation by transnational companies owned by businessmen of multiple nationalities; see Lees and Brooks, *Economic and Political Development*, p. 123. In agreement, Schwarzenberger, *Foreign Investments*, pp. 27, 112, and 189.

63 Oppenheim, *International Law*, p. 361; C. Eagleton, *The Responsibility of States in International Law* (1928), pp. 95–124; Bagge, 34 *B.Y.B.I.L.* (1958), at p. 165 *et seq.*

64 *P.C.I.J.* series A/B, no. 77, p. 64.

65 Ibid. p. 79. Cf. The *Interhandel* case, *I.C.J. Rep.* (1959), p. 6.

66 Oppenheim, *International Law*, vol. 2, p. 362.

67 Ibid.

68 Ibid. See the award of Osten Unden in the case of *Some Forests in Central Rhodopia* (*Greece* v. *Bulgaria*), 28 *A.J.I.L.* (1934), at 789.

69 Nwogugu, *Legal Problems*, p. 107.

70 Oppenheim, *International Law*, vol. 2, p. 874.

71 I. C. MacGibbon, 'Some Observations on the Part of Protest in International Law', 30 *B.Y.B.I.L.* (1953), p. 293.

72 See for State practice, Hackworth, *Digest*, vol. 5 (1943), p. 588; Nwogugu, *Legal Problems*, pp. 117–18.

73 Examples are the British protests against Mexico's expropriation of the Eagle Oil Company in 1938: Hackworth, *Digest*, vol. 3, p. 661; the United States protest against Guatemalan expropriation of the property of the United Fruit Company, and the Cuban expropriatory laws: *Department of State Bulletin* 29 (1953), pp. 357–60, 42 (1960), p. 158, respectively.

74 Kronfol, *Protection*, pp. 127–8.

75 Ibid. p. 128.

76 Text in Brownlie, *Basic Documents*, p. 2, at p. 12.

77 Oppenheim, *International Law*, vol. 2, p. 10; Nwogugu, *Legal Problems*, p. 230.

78 I.B.R.D. 13th Annual Report 1957–58, p. 6; Sir H. Lauterpacht, *The Suez Canal Settlement* (1960), p. 3; 54 *A.J.I.L.* (1960), 498. For the present World Bank procedure for the settlement of investment disputes by the International Centre for the Settlement of

Investment Disputes (I.C.S.I.D.), see H. D. Darwin, 'Mediation and Good Offices', in *International Disputes: The Legal Aspects* (1972), pp. 77–92, Report of a Study Group of the David Davies Memorial Institute of International Studies (cited hereinafter as the David Davies Institute on Settlement Procedures). For an inside account of the negotiations which preceded the agreement, see Jacques-Georges Picot (translated from French by W. G. Rogers) *The Real Suez Crisis* (1978), pp. 139–77.

79 I.B.R.D. 14th Annual Report, 1958–59, p. 7; A. Broches, 'Arbitration between Governments and Foreign Private Firms', *Am.Soc.Int.Law Proceed.* (1961), p. 72.

80 It is an open question whether western foreign investors would be prepared to utilize the good offices of the Arab League and the Organization of African Unity in preference to the U.N. or other organization of similar prestigious status.

81 Nwogugu, *Legal Problems*, p. 231.

82 For the text of the Statute of the Court, see Brownlie, *Basic Documents*, p. 267.

83 *P.C.I.J.* series A, nos. 20/1 (1929).

84 Article 36 of the Statute of International Court of Justice.

85 For instance, the *Anglo-Iranian* case; the *Barcelona Traction* case.

86 For the texts of the Sudan and U.S.A. declarations see *Yearbook of the International Court of Justice* (1977–78), pp. 73 and 77 respectively. For a critical evaluation of the Sudan's declaration, see Faisal Abdel Rahman Ali Taha, 'A Plea for the Withdrawal of the "Automatic Reservation" from the Sudan's Declaration Under the Optional Clause', *S.L.J.R.* (1970), 345–53.

87 Separate Opinion in the *Norwegian Loans* case, *I.C.J. Rep.* (1957), at p. 34.

88 Taha, *S.L.J.R.* (1970), p. 350 *et seq.*

89 C. H. M. Waldock, 'The Plea of Domestic Jurisdiction before International Legal Tribunals', 31 *B.Y.B.I.L.* (1954), p. 96, at p. 133.

90 *Idem*, 'Decline of the Optional Clause', 32 *B.Y.B.I.L.* (1955–56), p. 244 at p. 272.

91 *I.C.J. Rep.* (1959), at p. 23; R. Y. Jennings, 'Recent Cases on "Automatic Reservations" to the Optional Clause', 7 *I.C.L.Q.* (1958), 117 at pp. 118–19.

92 See *Yearbook of the International Court of Justice* (1977–78), pp. 32, 48–78.

93 See L. Gross, 'Participation of Individuals in Advisory Proceedings Before the International Court of Justice: Equality between the Parties', 52 *A.J.I.L.* (1958), 16.

94 Quoted in Nwogugu, *Legal Problems*, p. 237; see also Baseem, *Legal Regime*, pp. 176–9.

95 P. J. Allott, 'The International Court of Justice', in the David Davies Institute *Studies on Settlement Procedures*, pp. 128–57.

96 Nwogugu, *Legal Problems*, pp. 240–1, See, generally, C. M. Schmitthoff, (Editor–Compiler), *International Commercial Arbitrations*, Loose-leaf Service, Oceana Publications Inc. (1974).

97 See generally, Hazel Fox, 'Arbitration', in the David Davies Institute's *Studies on Settlement Procedures*, pp. 101–27; Baseem, *Legal Regime*, p. 117; G. White, *The Use of Experts by International Tribunals* (1965), chs. 1 and 7.

98 Kronfol, *Protection*, p. 138.

99 Cf. the *Turriff* case, where the sovereign immunity of the Republic of the Sudan was not raised at all throughout the proceedings before it withdrew and the *ex parte* award was rendered.

100 Quoted by Cattan, *Law of Oil Concessions*, p. 143.

101 Article 33 of the *Statute of the International Court of Justice*; Bowett, *International Institutions*, pp. 247–8.

102 For instance, the *Sudan Government* v. *Brown International Inc.*; the *Turriff* case.

103 For instance, the American Arbitration Association; the London Court of Arbitration; the Netherlands Arbitration Institute; the Inter-American Commerce Arbitration Commission etc. For a detailed survey, see Kronfol, *Protection*, p. 139; also William T. Ketcham, 'Arbitration Between a State and a Foreign Private Party', *International and Comparative Law Centre*, Southwestern Legal Foundation (1965), p. 402, *et seq.*

104 International Chamber of Commerce, International Arbitration of the I.C.C. (Paris, August, 1966), p. 1.

105 Ibid. Gerald Aksen, remarking on the I.C.C. arbitration/conciliation, appraised conciliation as follows: 'When confronted with a dispute arising from a contract containing an I.C.C. arbitration/conciliation clause, the practitioner often overlooks the possibilities offered by conciliation as a preliminary attempt at resolution of the dispute. Two main advantages of conciliation as conditions precedent to arbitration are noteworthy. First, conciliation may produce a settlement without the need of arbitration. Such a result would be considerably less expensive and would tend to preserve the friendly atmosphere between the parties. Second, and most important to the practising attorney, is the fact that where conciliation has failed to produce a friendly settlement, if properly used, it can bring out important elements of the dispute prior to arbitration much like pretrial discovery in an adjudicatory proceeding', *Am. Soc. Int. Law Proceed.* (1975), pp. 164–5.

106 International Chamber of Commerce, International Arbitration, p. 6.

107 Kronfol, *Protection*, p. 140.

108 Ibid.

109 Ibid. p. 141.

110 The Nigerian Government, for instance, has concluded an investment contract containing an I.C.C. arbitration clause with a Canadian oil company: K. H. Bockstiegel, 'Arbitration of Disputes between States and Private Enterprises in the I.C.C.', 59 *A.J.I.L.* (1965), 581. The I.C.C. rules are to be found in a similar contract between the Pakistan Government and a French company, ibid. Syria's pipelines construction agreement with a consortium of British companies of 1965 has also envisaged the settlement of any dispute in accordance with the Rules of Conciliation and Arbitration of the I.C.C.: Cattan, *Law of Oil Concessions*, p. 167.

111 Kronfol, *Protection*, p. 141; Baseem, *Legal Regime*, p. 185.

112 J. B. Scott, *The Hague Conventions of 1899 and 1907*, 2nd edn. (1915), p. 57. The Sudan has ratified the revised convention by the Convention for the Pacific Settlement of International Disputes (Ratification) Act, 1966 (Act No. 40, 1966), *L.S.D.R.S.G.* No. 1027 dated 15 October 1966, p. 185. Till now Saudi Arabia has neither acceded to nor ratified this convention. Hazel Fox, 'Arbitration', p. 103; see N. Bar-Yaacov, *The Handling of International Disputes by Means of Inquiry* (1974), chs. 1 and 4.

113 Nwogugu, *Legal Problems*, p. 243; Kronfol, *Protection*, p. 129; Baseem, *Legal Regime*, p. 180.

114 9 *Neth. Int. L.R.* (1962), July p. 339; 57 *A.J.I.L.* (1963), 500; Ketcham, p. 407.

115 17 *Neth. I.L. Rev.* (1970), 200.

116 Article 47 authorizes the International Bureau of the Court to put that organization at the disposal of the contracting governments for an especial arbitral jurisdiction. The article is not limited expressly to arbitration between States nor to use of the Permanent Court panel.

117 *U.N.Y.B.I.L.C.* (1958), vol. 2 (A/CN.4/SER. a/1958/ADD.1) (New York, 1958), p. 83.

118 Clause 4(1) of the Submission.

119 Clause 4(7).

120 For the text, U.N.T.S. 575, 159; Centre Document I.C.S.I.D./2: 4 *I.L.M.* (1965), 524. The Sudan ratified the Convention by the International Centre for Settlement of Investment Disputes between States and Nationals of Other States (Ratification) Act, 1972, *L.S.D.R.S.G.* no. 1139, dated 15 December 1972, p. 281. Also, Saudi Arabia ratified the convention by a Royal Decree quite recently. As of September 1979 the number of Signatory States increased from 77 to 80, while the number of Contracting States (i.e. States which both signed and ratified the convention) rose from 71 to 75: see I.C.S.I.D. *Thirteenth Report* 1978/1979, Annex 1, pp. 8–9.

121 International Centre for Settlement of Investment Disputes (I.C.S.I.D.), Convention on the Settlement of Investment Disputes between States and Nationals of Other States (Washington, D.C., 1965), pp. 1–26 (hereinafter referred to as Report of the Executive Directors). For the negotiating history of the Convention, see Baseem, *Legal Regime*, pp. 198–201; Convention on the Settlement of Investment Disputes between States and Nationals of Other States: Analysis of Documents Concerning the Origin and the Formulation of the Convention (1970), (hereinafter referred to as History); Schwarzenberger, *Foreign Investments*, pp. 135–8; J. F. McMahon and Michael Akehurst, 'Settlement of Disputes in Special Fields', in David Davies Institute's *Studies on Settlement Procedures*, pp. 257–62.

122 Article 2.

123 Article 18.

124 Report of the Executive Directors, p. 4.

125 Report of Executive Directors, para, 9, p. 4; Amerasinghe, 47 *B.Y.B.I.L.* (1974–75), p. 227.

126 Articles 4 and 6; Schwarzenberger, *Foreign Investments*, p. 140. For the list of members of the Administrative Council and Officials of the Centre as at 30 June 1979, see *The Thirteenth Annual Report* of I.C.S.I.D., p. 10.

127 Article 5.

128 Article 67.

129 Article 10(1).

130 Article 10(2); see Baseem, *Legal Regime*, pp. 203–4; Report of Executive Directors, para. 20.

131 Articles 12 and 13. For the list of the Members of the Panel of Conciliators and Arbitrators of the Centre as at 30 June 1979, see the *Thirteenth Annual Report*, pp. 11–21.

132 Article 14(2); also Baseem, *Legal Regime*, p. 205; Schwarzenberger, *Foreign Investments*, p. 141.

133 Amerasinghe, 47 *B.Y.B.I.L.* (1974–75), 250.

134 I.C.S.I.D., History, p. 9.

135 Ibid.; Schwarzenberger, *Foreign Investments*, p. 142.

136 Article 25(4). Kronfol, *Protection*, p. 147; Baseem, *Legal Regime*, p. 210.

137 Amerasinghe, 47 *B.Y.B.I.L.* (1974–75), p. 229.

138 Ibid. p. 233.

139 Meron, *Investment Insurance*, pp. 24–5; also Amerasinghe, 47 *B.Y.B.I.L.* (1974–75), pp. 242–8.

140 For the criteria followed in determining the nationality of a juridical person, see *ante*, pp. 16–19.

141 Amerasinghe, 47 *B.Y.B.I.L.* (1974–75), p. 249.

142 Meron, *Investment Insurance*, p. 26.
143 Ibid. p. 28.
144 I.C.S.I.D., Report of Executive Directors, p. 8.
145 Article 26.
146 Article 27.
147 Articles 28–35. On the definition and the advantages of conciliation commissions, see Bar-Yaacov, *Handling of International Disputes*, pp. 225–46.
148 Article 29.
149 Article 30.
150 Articles 48 and 53.
151 Articles 13–15. See Baseem, *Legal Regime*, pp. 213–15.
152 Article 38. Thus in *Guadalupe Gas Products Corporation* v. *The Federal Military Government of Nigeria* (Case ARB/78/1) the chairman, pursuant to article 38 of the convention, appointed the third arbitrator and the President of the tribunal, because the parties did not reach agreement on the appointment: *Thirteenth Annual Report*, p. 6.
153 Articles 38 and 40.
154 I.C.S.I.D., Report of the Executive Directors, p. 15; Baseem, *Legal Regime*, pp. 221–3.
155 Article 42(2); Baseem, *Legal regime*, p. 222.
156 Article 42(3).
157 Article 53.
158 Article 50.
159 Article 51.
160 Article 52.
161 I.C.S.I.D., Report of the Executive Directors, p. 14.
162 Article 53.
163 Article 64.
164 Article 27.
165 Kronfol, *Protection*, pp. 149–50.
166 Interview with R J. Blair, Shell Centre, London, see *ante*, p. 419, n. 232 to ch. 7); Fawcett, *Conflicts*, pp. 69–70.
167 Interview with R. J. Blair, Shell Centre, London, see n. 232, ch. 7, p. 419; Fawcett, *Conflicts*, 1977, pp. 69–70.
168 *Thirteenth Annual Report*, 1978/1979, Annex 6.
169 Ibid. at pp. 5–6.
170 *Twelfth Annual Report* 1977/1978, p. 5.
171 Ibid.
172 See generally, Sir H. L. Lauterpacht, 'Restrictive Interpretation and the Principle of Effectiveness in the Interpretation of Treaties', 26 *B.Y.B.I.L.* (1949), p. 48, at pp. 65 *et seq.*; the *Free Zones* case, *P.C.I.J.* series A, no. 22 (1929), at p. 13; Articles 31–33 of the Vienna Convention on the Law of Treaties.
173 *Thirteenth Annual Report*, p. 3.
174 Amerasinghe, 47 *B.Y.B.I.L.* (1974–75), p. 267.
175 Ibid. Annex 4.
176 The Convention was concluded on 10 June 1974. It has been ratified by the Sudan by Act No. 34, 1978; for text see *L.S.D.R.S.G.* No. 1243, dated 15 July 1978, p. 18.
177 Arab State members of the Council of Arab Economic Unity and signatories of the Convention are: Jordan, Sudan, Syria, Iraq, Kuwait, and the Arab Republic of Yemen. Saudi Arabia has not signed the Convention.

178 Article 4.
179 Article 3.
180 Articles 4, 5, 6 and 7.
181 Article 6.
182 Articles 10 and 14.
183 Article 36.
184 Articles 11–19.
185 Article 25.
186 Article 22.
187 Article 23.
188 Article 25.
189 Article 19.
190 Article 39.
191 Article 11(1) of the Sudan–German Investment Treaty; Article 10 of the Sudan–Swiss Investment Agreement; Article 11(1) of the German–Pakistan Investment Treaty. The same approach is followed in F.C.N. of the United States, Kronfol, *Protection*, p. 136.
192 For instance, Article 11(2) and (3) of the Sudan–German Treaty; the Sudan–Swiss Agreement, Article 10.
193 *L.S.D.R.S.G.* No. 1095, dated 15 March 1970, p. 35.
194 Article VII, ibid.
195 See the Sudan–United States Investment Guaranty Agreement, see p. 414, n. 106 to ch. 7.
196 Article XXIII. Cf. The Rahad Project Supply Contracts; the Sugar Sales Agreement (Joint Venture) between the Sudan and Lonrho Co., *ante*, p. 425.
197 *Laws of the Sudan*, vol. 9.
198 Kronfol, *Protection*, p. 126; Stephen M. Schwebel and J. Gillis Wetter, 'Arbitration and the Exhaustion of Local Remedies', 60 *A.J.I.L.* (1960), 484, at 499; also Olmstead, 49 *Calif. L. Rev.* (1961), 504, at 511.
199 *International Court of Justice, Pleadings, Oral Arguments and Documents*, 1952, p. 267.
200 See *ante*, pp. 124–5. For summary and discussion of the relevant provisions of these proposed codes and conventions, see Kronfol, *Protection*, pp. 134–5.
201 For history of the Commission see, G.A. Res. 2205 (XXI) of 17 December 1966 which established the Commission, U.N.G.A. Doc. A/CN.9/1 14 November 1967 – 'Note by the Secretariat'. The United Nations Commission on International Trade Law adopted these U.N.C.I.T.R.A.L. Arbitration Rules at its ninth session (12 April to 7 May 1976). At that session the Commission decided to invite the General Assembly of the United Nations at its 31st session in 1976 to recommend the use of the Rules in the settlement of disputes arising in the context of international commercial relations, particularly by reference to the U.N.C.I.T.R.A.L. Arbitration in commercial contracts.
202 Article 6.
203 Article 2.
204 Article 3.
205 Article 4.
206 Articles 14, 24, 25 and 29.
207 Article 16.
208 Articles 18–23.
209 Articles 31–41.
210 The model Arbitration Clause reads as follows: 'Any dispute, controversy or claim arising

out of or relating to this contract, or the breach, termination or invalidity thereof, shall be settled by arbitration in accordance with the U.N.C.I.T.R.A.L. Arbitration Rules as at present in force.

Note – Parties may wish to consider adding:

(a) The appointing authority shall be...(name of institution or person);

(b) The number of arbitrators shall be...(one or three);

(c) The place of arbitration shall be...(town or country);

(d) The language(s) to be used in the arbitral proceedings shall be...'

211 Kronfol, *Protection*, p. 132; C. Wildred Jenks, *The Prospects of International Adjudication* (1964), pp. 692–5; Bowett, *International Institutions*, pp. 246–7.

212 For the possibility of securing compliance with international decisions or awards by recourse to the General Assembly, other organizations of specialized agencies of the United Nations, regional organizations, co-operation of other States or municipal legal proceedings, see Jenks, *Common Law of Mankind*, pp. 695–715; in agreement, O. Schachter, 'Enforcement of International Judicial and Arbitral Decisions', 54 *A.J.I.L.* (1960), 1.

213 [1923] 1. ch. 385. The decision was confirmed by the House of Lords: [1924] A.C. 797.

214 *Rossignol* v. *State of Czechoslovakia*, A.D. (1949), Case No. 40 (France); *Federated People's Republic of Yugoslavia* v. *Kafr El-Zayat Cotton Co. Ltd.*, I.L.R. (1951), case no. 54 (Egypt); *Weilamann* v. *Chase Manhattan Bank*, 54 *A.J.I.L.* (1960), 410 (U.S.); Drachsler: 54 *A.J.I.L.* (1960), 790.

215 For instance, *U.A.R.* v. *Dame X*, 55 *A.J.I.L.* (1961), 167; *Scocobelge* v. *Greek State*, 47 *A.J.I.L.* (1953), 508; and the excellent discussion by W. L. Griffin, 'Execution Against the Sovereign's Property: The Current Scene', *Am.Soc.Int.Law Proceed.* (1961), 107–13.

216 For the text of the Convention, see 11 *I.L.M.* (1972), 470; see generally, Georges R. Delaume, 'Three Perspectives on Sovereign Immunity', 71 *A.J.I.L.* (1977), 399; also the British State Immunity Act, 1978.

217 Monroe Leigh, 'Enforcement of Judgments and Awards', *International and Comparative Law Centre*, the Southwestern Legal Foundation (Dallas, 1965), p. 439, at pp. 465–6.

218 Kronfol, *Protection*, p. 132.

219 For the text, see 8 *I.C.L.Q.* (1959), 228; also U.N.T.S., Vol. 330, p. 38.

220 Ibid.

221 These are: absence of a valid arbitration agreement; lack of a fair opportunity to be heard; the award is in excess of the submission; improper arbitral procedure; or lack of finality of the award in the rendering State (Articles IV and V).

222 Article V(2).

223 Sanders, 'New York Convention on the Recognition and Enforcement of Foreign Arbitral Awards', 6 *Neth. Int. L.R.* (1959), 43; P. Contini, 'International Commercial Arbitration. The United Nations Convention on the Recognition and Enforcement of Foreign Arbitral Awards', 8 *A.J.C.L.* (1959), 283, at 294.

224 Nwogugu, *Legal Problems*, p. 254.

225 O'Connell, *International Law*, 2nd edn., vol. 1, (1970), pp. 80–106; *Reparations for Injuries Suffered in the Services of the U.N.*, case, *I.C.J. Rep.* (1949), p. 174.

226 In agreement, Kronfol, *Protection*, p. 133.

227 Article III.

228 Article 4 of the Convention.

11. Unilateral sanctions by home States

1 As regards the International Court of Justice, see *ante*, pp. 300–3.

2 Nwogugu, *Legal Problems*, p. 260.

3 E.g. the freezing of Egyptian assets in Britain when Egypt nationalized the Suez Canal Company, *New York Times*, 2 March 1957, p. 1, col. 5. See, for a similar American practice, Christenson, 55 *A.J.I.L.* (1961), at 620.

4 *The Guardian*, Tuesday, 14 October 1980.

5 For a discussion of global settlements, see Wortley, *Expropriation*, p. 146; White, *Nationalisation*, pp. 206–26; Schwarzenberger, *Foreign Investments*, ch. 4.

6 E.g. the U.S.–Polish Agreement, 1960; 55 *A.J.I.L.* (1961), 540. Cf. U.K.–U.A.R. Agreement of 1959 concerning financial and commercial relations and British property in Egypt – Cmd 639.

7 Customary international law limitations on reprisals are contained in the *Nauilaa* case, 1928, A.D. (1927–28) case no. 360: (i) there must be a violation of a rule of international law by the State against which the reprisals are directed; (ii) they must be preceded by a request for redress of the alleged wrong; (iii) the measure adopted must not be excessive or out of proportion with the injury suffered. For confirmation see D. W. Bowett, 'Economic Coercion and Reprisals by States', *Virginia Journal of International Law* (1972), at pp. 9–10.

8 This article controls the use of force or threat of force for settling disputes between States.

9 Hyde, *International Law*, vol. 2, p. 1662.

10 See generally, Bowett, 13 *Virginia Journal of International Law* (1972), 1–13.

11 Nwogugu, *Legal Problems*, pp. 167–8.

12 Ibid.

13 Ibid. For the boycott of Japanese goods by China, see C. L. Bouve, 'The National Boycott as an International Delinquency', 28 *A.J.I.L.* (1934), 19. See generally the proceedings of the American Society of International Law on 'International Boycotts and Embargoes', 71 *Am.Soc.Int.L.Proc.* (1977), 170–94; *idem.*, 'Policy Conflicts in Foreign Trade and Investments: the Anti-boycott Regulations', 72 *Am.Soc.Int.L.Proc.* (1978), 80–97; Ibrahim F. I. Shihata, 'Destination Embargo of Arab Oil: Its Legality Under International Law', 68 *A.J.I.L.* (1974), 591–627. See also a wide variety of articles on international coercion assembled in *Economic Coercion and the New International Economic Order* (R. Lillich, ed., 1976) and in a symposium in 12 *Texas Int.L.J.* (1977).

14 H. Lauterpacht, 'Boycott in International Law', 14 *B.Y.B.I.L.* (1933), p. 128.

15 *Legal Problems*, p. 271.

16 Ibid. p. 272.

17 Borchard, *Diplomatic Protection*, p. 448 *et seq.*; Oppenheim, *International Law*, p. 309.

18 P. C. Jessup, *Modern Law of Nations* (1948), p. 169; Wright, 'The Goa Incident', 56 *A.J.I.L.* (1962), 617, at 621; Baty, *Canons of International Law* (1930), pp. 102–5.

19 D. W. Bowett, *Self-Defence in International Law* (1958), p. 101.

20 Ibid. pp. 102–3.

21 Ibid. pp. 102–3.

22 The Porter Convention 1907; Scott, the Hague Conventions and Declarations of 1899 and 1907, 2nd ed., (1915), p. 89; Kellog–Briand Pact, 1928, L.N.T.S. 94, p. 57; Cmd 3410. Also, in agreement is the General Assembly's Declaration on Principles of International Law Concerning Friendly Relations and Co-operation among States of 24 October 1970. This declaration was adopted by acclamation and contained the following phrase: 'States

have a duty to refrain from acts of reprisal involving the use of force.' G.A. Res. 2625, 25 U.N. GAOR Supp. 28, at p. 112, U.N. Doc. A/8082 (1970). Cf. Bowett, 'Reprisals Involving Recourse to Armed Conflict', 66 *A.J.I.L.* (1972), 1, at 2–10; *idem* 13 *Virginia Journal of International Law* (1972), 7–8.

23 In agreement, Nwogugu, *Legal Problems*, p. 278; Jenks, *International Adjudication*, pp. 690–2.

24 The former practice of Britain to exercise the right of self-defence to protect the property of its nationals abroad can best be illustrated by the intervention in Egypt on the nationalization of the Suez Canal Company in 1956, of which Britain was a majority shareholder. The United States has adopted the policy of non-intervention militarily in such cases: Wetter, 29 *Univ. of Chicago Law Review* (1962), p. 275, at p. 325. For practice of Italy, Germany and additional examples of the British practice, see ibid. pp. 298–9.

25 There may be cases where the public property involved may be vital for the existence of the State and failure of the respondent State to make amends or submit to impartial settlement will justify the use of force in self-defence. Thus, if the Sudan deviated the course of the Nile and Egypt had to receive no water as a result, there would be good reason for Egypt to justify its action of armed intervention in the Sudan on the basis of self-defence, because the action of the Sudan would threaten the very existence of Egypt, which would perish. But it is inconceivable to justify the same action if the Sudan nationalized without compensation the assets of an Egyptian company owned by Egyptian citizens in the Sudan.

26 Bowett, *Self-Defence*, p. 105.

27 Foreign Assistance Act, 1962; also Wetter, 29 *Univ. of Chicago Law Review*, 300–3; William D. Rogers, 'Of Missionaries, Fanatics and Lawyers: Some Thoughts on Investment Disputes in the Americas', 72 *A.J.I.L.* (1978), 1, at 14–16.

28 American aid was also suspended when Ceylon (Sri Lanka) nationalized the oil properties of two American companies and payment of compensation was delayed: Nwogugu, *Legal Problems*, p. 279. In 1979 the U.S. also suspended its economic aid to Ethiopia, as the latter refused to pay compensation to the American firms for their investments which were nationalized by the military leftist junta.

29 See section 621(e)(2) of the Foreign Assistance Act 1961 as amended; section 21 of the Inter-American Development Bank Act; section 12 of the International Development Association Act, applicable to the World Bank; section 18 of the Asian Development Act and section 502(b)(4) of the Trade Act of 1974. Seen Gantz, 73 *Am.Soc.I.L.Proc.* (1979), 250–1.

30 This has been applied to block a major World Bank project of $40 million: *The Guardian*, Tuesday, October 14 1980.

31 Gantz, 73 *Am.Soc.I.L.Proc.* (1979), 251.

32 Nwogugu, *Legal Problems*, p. 279. In agreement, Bowett, 13 *Virginia Journal of International Law* (1972), 8–11.

33 Fawcett, *Conflicts*, pp. 79–82.

34 Expropriation and nationalization are considered as political measures, though the situation may be different if the loss suffered by a foreign investor is caused by riots or physical violence. See Gantz, 73 *Am. Soc. I.L. Proc.* (1979), 253–5.

35 Interview by the writer with R. J. Blair who was referring to certain figures and statistics which the writer could not look at. See p. 419, n. 232 to ch. 7.

Appendix 2

1 Promulgated by Royal Decree No. M/4, 1979, Kingdom of Saudi Arabia.

Addendum

1 About 400 investment licences were issued under the Encouragement of Investment Act, 1980 in various economic sectors.

2 The conference was organized under the auspices of the Minister of Finance and Economic Planning in Khartoum in November, 1982.

3 February, 1983.

4 See the report of Sudan Taxation Commission, 1983, Ministry of Finance and Economic Planning.

5 For a contrary view see Prof. Mohamed Hashim Awad, 'Pipeline to Prosperity', *Sudanow*, vol. 8, no. 4 (April 1983), p. 19.

6 See Kamal Hassain, *Law and Policy in Petroleum Development* (1979).

7 The award is reproduced in vol. 21, no. 5. *I.L.M.* (1983), 976.

8 See *ante*, pp. 232–79.

9 See Libya-Oil Companies Award, 17 *I.L.M.* (1978), p. 1.

10 End of para. 33 of the Award, p. 1006.

11 See p. 1026 of the Award.

12 P. 1036 of the Award.

13 The North Sea Continental Shelf Cases, *I.C.J. Rep.* (1969), p. 3.

SELECT BIBLIOGRAPHY

Books

Aufricht, H. *The International Monetary Fund*. London, 1964.

Bar-Yaacov, N. *The Handling of International Disputes by Means of Inquiry*. Oxford University Press, 1974.

Baseem, O. E. M. *El Nizam-el-Ganouni-l-el-Isthitthmarat-el-Ajanabia-el-Khasa-f-el-Dowal-el-Namia* (*The Legal Regime of Foreign Private Investments in the Developing Countries*). Cairo, 1972.

Basu, D. D. *Commentary on the Constitution of India*, vol. 2, 4th edn. Calcutta, 1962.

Bayiomi, Z. M. *Daribat-el-Dakl-fi-el-Teshria El Sudani* (*Income Tax in the Sudan Legislation*). Alexandria, 1972.

Double Taxation. Alexandria, 1972.

Bechtold, P. K. *Politics in the Sudan. Parliamentary and Military Rule in an Emerging African Nation*. New York, 1976.

Bedore, J. M. and Turner, L. *Middle East Industrialization*. New York, 1979.

Borchard, E. M. *The Diplomatic Protection of Citizens Abroad*. New York, 1927.

State Insolvency and Foreign Bondholders, vol. 1. New Haven, 1951.

Bowett, D. W. *Self-Defence in International Law*. Manchester, 1958.

The Law of International Institutions, 3rd edn. London, 1975.

Brierly, J. L. *Law of Nations*, 6th edn. Oxford University Press, 1963.

Brownlie, I. *Basic Documents in International Law*, 2nd edn. Oxford University Press, 1972.

Principles of Public International Law, 2nd edn. Oxford, 1973.

Buckland, W. W. *A Text-book of Roman Law from Augustus to Justinian*, 3rd edn. Cambridge University Press, 1963.

Castaneda, J. *Legal Effects of United Nations Resolutions* (translated by Alba Amonia). New York and London, 1969.

Cattan, H. *The Law of Oil Concessions in the Middle East and North Africa*. New York, 1967.

Cheng, B. *General Principles of Law as Applied by International Courts and Tribunals*. London, 1953.

Crockett, J. P. *The Federal Tax System of the U.S.* New York, 1955.

The David Davies Memorial Institute of International Studies, *International Disputes: The Legal Aspects*. London, 1972.

Don, R. Y. *Protection of Foreign Investment Under International Law*, Modern Management Foundation, People's Republic of China, 1979.

Dunning, J. H. (ed. and cont.) *International Investment*. Harmondsworth, 1972.

El Abdi, A. S. D. *El-Milkia-fe-El-Sharia-El-Islamia* (*Private Ownership in Islamic Law*). 1975.

Eagleton, C. *The Responsibility of States in International Law*. New York, 1928.

El Hassan, A. M. *An Introduction to the Sudan Economy*. Khartoum, 1976.

El Sadr, M. B. *Igtisaduna (Our Economy)*, 2nd edn. Beirut, 1968.

El Sheikh, F. A. 'Development of Nationality Law in the Sudan', a thesis submitted for part fulfilment of the degree of Master of Laws in the University of Khartoum, May 1975.

El Subaa, M. *Ishtrakiat-El-Islam (Socialism of Islam)*, 3rd edn. Syria, 1960.

El Tayeb, T. *Developing Countries and the Tokyo Round*. Research and Development Studies, Khartoum, 1979.

Fatouros, A. A. *Government Guarantees to Foreign Investors*. New York, 1962.

Fawcett, J. *International Economic Conflicts: Prevention and Resolution*. London, 1977.

Foighel, I. *Nationalization: A Study in the Protection of Alien Property in International Law*. London and Copenhagen, 1957.

Ford, A. W. *The Anglo-Iranian Oil Dispute of 1951–1952*. Berkeley and Los Angeles, 1954.

Friedman, S. *Expropriation in International Law*. London, 1953.

Friedmann, W. G. *Law in a Changing Society*. London, 1959.

The Changing Structure of International Law. New York, 1964.

The State and the Law in a Mixed Economy. London, 1971.

Friedmann, W. G. and Beguin, J. P. *Joint International Business Ventures in Developing Countries*. New York, 1971.

Friedmann, W. G. and Pugh, R. C. *Legal Aspects of Foreign Investment*. London, 1959.

Gronje, S., Ling, M. and Gronje, G. *Lonrho: Portrait of a Multinational*. Harmondsworth, 1976.

Hackworth, G. H. *Digest of International Law*, 7 vols. Washington, 1940–43.

Hamidullah, M. *The Muslim Conduct of State*, 7th revised and enlarged edn. Lahore, 1977.

Henderson, J. (ed.). *Foreign Investment Laws and Agriculture* (F.A.O.). London, 1970.

Henkin, L. *Foreign Affairs and the Constitution*. New York, 1975.

Horn, N. (ed.). *Legal Problems of Codes of Conduct for Multinational Enterprises*. Khuwer, 1980.

Hurewitz, J. C. *Diplomacy in the Near and Middle East; A Documentary Record, 1935–1956*, 2 vols. New York, 1956.

Hyde, C. H. *International Law Chiefly as Interpreted and Applied by the United States*, 3 vols., 2nd edn. Boston, 1947.

Institute on Private Investments Abroad, *Proceedings for 1959* (ed. R. A. Wilson), The Southwestern Legal Foundation, Dallas. New York, 1959.

Jenks, C. W. *The Prospects of International Adjudication*. London, 1964.

Jessup, P. C. *A Modern Law of Nations – An Introduction*. New York, 1948.

Transnational Law. New Haven, 1956.

Katzarov, K. *The Theory of Nationalization*. The Hague, 1964.

Koch, F. E. *The Double Taxation Conventions*, vol. 1, Taxation of Income. London, 1947.

Kronfol, Z. *Protection of Foreign Investment*. Leiden, 1972.

Lauterpacht, Sir H. *Private Law Sources and Analogies of International Law*. London, 1927.

The Development of International Law by International Court. London, 1958.

Lawrence and Rapalje, S. *Law Dictionary*, vol. 1. Jersey City, N.J.

Lees, F. A. and Brooks, H. C. *The Economic and Political Development of the Sudan*. London, 1977.

Lillich, R. B. *International Claims: Postwar British Practice*, Syracuse University Press, 1967.

(ed. and cont.). *The Valuation of Nationalized Property in International Law*, 3 vols. Charlottesville, 1972 (third volume, 1975).

(ed.). *Economic Coercion and the New International Law Order*. Virginia, 1976.

Lillich, R. B. and Weston, B. H. *International Claims: Their Settlement by Lump Sum Agreements*. Charlottesville, 1975.

McNair, Lord. *International Law Opinions*, 3 vols. Cambridge, 1956.
The Law of Treaties. Oxford, 1961.
McGregor, H. *The Law of Damages*, 13th edn. London, 1972.
Mann, F. A. *The Legal Aspects of Money*, 3rd edn. Oxford, 1971.
Studies in International Law. Oxford, 1973.
Maynard, P. D. 'The Charter of Economic Rights and Duties of States – A Legal Analysis of the Divisive Issues', a doctoral thesis submitted in the University of Johns Hopkins, Baltimore, Maryland, 1976.
Meron, T. *Investment Insurance in International Law*. New York, 1976.
Moore, J. B. *A Digest of International Law*, 8 vols. Washington, 1898–1906.
Mustafa, Z. *The Common Law in the Sudan*. Oxford, 1971.
Nwabueze, B. O. *Presidentialism in Commonwealth Africa*. London, 1974.
Judicialism in Commonwealth Africa. London, 1974.
Nwogugu, E. I. *The Legal Problems of Foreign Investment in Developing Countries*. Manchester, 1965.
O'Connell, D. P. *State Succession in Municipal Law and International Law*, vol. 1. Cambridge University Press, 1967.
International Law, 2 vols., 2nd edn. London, 1970.
Oppenheim, L. *International Law*, vol. 1, 8th edn., (ed. Sir H. Lauterpacht). London, 1955.
International Law, vol. 2, 7th edn., (ed. Sir H. Lauterpacht). London, 1952.
Parry, C. *Nationality and Citizenship Laws of the Commonwealth and Ireland*, vol. 1. London, 1957.
Peaslee, A. J. *Constitutions of Nations*, 3 vols., 2nd edn. The Hague, 1956.
Roth, A. H. *The Minimum Standard of International Law Applied to Aliens*. Leiden, 1949.
Saddig, H. *El-Nizam Al-Arabi-le-deman-el-Istthithmar-dhid-el-Makhatir Gir-el-Tigarig*, (*The Arab Regime for Guarantee of Investment against Non-Commercial Risks*). Alexandria, 1977.
Saunders, J. B. (ed.). *Mosely and Whitely's Law Dictionary*, 8th edn. London, 1970.
Schmitthoff, C. M. *The Export Trade*, 7th edn. London, 1980.
Shuster, M. R. *The Public International Law of Money*. Oxford, 1973.
Schwarzenberger, G. *International Law*, 3rd edn. London, 1957.
Foreign Investments and International Law. London, 1969.
Scott, J. B. *The Hague Conventions of 1899 and 1907*, 2nd edn. New York, 1915.
Sen, B. *A Diplomat's Handbook of International Law and Practice*. The Hague, 1965.
Shuster, M. R. *The Public International Law of Money*. Oxford, 1973.
Simmonds, K. R. (ed.). *Multinational Corporations Law, the UN and Transnational Law*. London, 1979.
Smith, S. A. De. *Judicial Review of Administrative Actions*, 3rd edn. London, 1973.
Thomas, B. V. A. (ed.). *Private Enterprise and the East African Company*. Tanzania Publishing House, 1974.
Turpin, C. *Government Contracts*. Harmondsworth, 1972.
Viner, J. *International Economics*. London, 1951.
Wade, E. C. S. and Phillips, G. *Constitutional Law*, 9th edn. London, 1977.
White, G. *Nationalisation of Foreign Property*. London, 1961.
White, G. M. *The Use of Experts by International Tribunals*. Syracuse University Press, 1965.
Whiteman, M. M. *Damages in International Law*, 3 vols. U.S. Government Printing Office, Washington, D.C., 1937.
Digest of International Law, 8 vols., U.S. Government Printing Office. Washington, D.C., 1967.

Whiteman, M. N. *The U.S. Investment Guaranty Program and Private Foreign Investment.* Princeton University Press, 1959.
Wickersham, W. G. and Fishburne, B. P. (eds.). *Current Legal Aspects of Doing Business in the Middle East.* American Bar Association, 1977.
Wilcox, C. *A Charter for World Trade.* New York, 1949.
Wilson, R. R. *The International Law Standard in Treaties of the U.S.* Cambridge, Mass., 1953.
United States Commercial Treaties and International Law. New Orleans, 1960.
(ed.). *The International Law Standard and Commonwealth Developments.* Durham, 1966.
Wortley, B. A. *Expropriation in Public International Law.* Cambridge University Press, 1959.

Articles

Ahooja, K. 'Investment Legislation in Africa', 2 *J.W.T.L.* (1968), 495.
Albrecht, A. R. 'The Taxation of Aliens Under International Law', 29 *B.Y.B.I.L.* (1952), p. 145.
Amerasinghe, C. F. 'Jurisdiction *Ratione Personae* Under the Convention on the Settlement of Investment Disputes between States and Nationals of Other States', 47 *B.Y.B.I.L.* (1977), p. 227.
Anderson, J. N. D. and Coulson, N. J. 'The Moslem Ruler and Contractual Obligation', 33 *N.Y.U.L.R.* (1958), 917.
Baade, H. W. 'Indonesian Nationalization Measures Before Foreign Courts – A Reply', 54 *A.J.I.L.* (1960), 801.
Bagge, A. 'Intervention on the Ground of Damage Caused to Nationals, with Particular Reference to Exhaustion of Local Remedies and the Rights of Shareholders', 34 *B.Y.B.I.L.* (1958), p. 162.
Beckett, W. E. 'The Exercise of Criminal Jurisdiction Over Foreigners', 6 *B.Y.B.I.L.* (1925), p. 44.
'Diplomatic Claims in Respect of Injuries to Companies', 17 *Grotius Society Transactions* (1931), 175.
Blough, R. 'Joint International Business Ventures in Less Developed Countries', *Proceedings of the 1960 Institute of Private Investments Abroad*, Southwestern Legal Foundation, Dallas, p. 513.
Bourguin, M. 'Arbitration and Economic Development Agreements', 15 *Bus. Lawyer* (1959–60), 860.
Bouve, C. L. 'The National Boycott as an International Delinquency', 28 *A.J.I.L.* (1934), 19.
Bowett, D. W. 'Estoppel before International Tribunals and its Relation to Acquiescence', 33 *B.Y.B.I.L.* (1957), p. 176.
'Economic Coercion and Reprisals by States', 13 *Virginia Journal of International Law* (1972), 1.
'Reprisals Involving Recourse to Armed Conflict', 66 *A.J.I.L.* (1972), 111, 176.
Brandon, M. 'Recent Measures to Improve the International Investment Climate', 9 *J.P.L.* (1959), 125.
Brewer, W. C. 'The Proposal for Investment Guarantees by an International Agency', 58 *A.J.I.L.* (1964), 67.
Broches, A. 'Arbitration between Governments and Foreign Private Firms', *Am. Soc. Int. Law Proceed.* (1961), p. 72.

Brown, C. N. and Tepe, J. B. 'The Charter of Economic Rights and Duties of States. A Reflection or Rejection of International Law', 9 *Int.L.L.* (1975), 295.

Charlston, K. S. 'International Role of Concession Agreements', 52 *N.Y.U.L.R.* (1957), 618.

'Concession Agreements and Nationalization', 52 *A.J.I.L.* (1958), 260.

Christie, G. C. 'What Constitutes a Taking of Property Under International Law', 38 *B.Y.B.I.L.* (1962), p. 307.

Dawson, F. G. and Weston, B. H. 'Prompt, Adequate and Effective: A Universal Standard of Compensation', 30 *Ford.L.Rev.* (1962), 727.

Delson, R. 'The Act of State Doctrine – Judicial Deference or Abstention', 66 *A.J.I.L.* (1972), 82.

Doman, N. R. 'Postwar Nationalization of Foreign Property in Europe', 20 *Columb. L.R.* (1948), 1128.

Domke, M. 'The Control of Corporations', 3 *I.C.L.Q.* (1950), 52.

'Foreign Nationalizations', 55 *A.J.I.L.* (1961), 585.

Ekundare, R. O. 'The Political Economy of Private Investment in Nigeria', 10 *J.M.A.S.* (1972), 31.

El Faki, M. E. 'The Background of Exchange Control in the Sudan', 2 *The Journal of Banking Studies* (January 1977), 7.

Falk, R. A. 'On the Quasi-Legislative Competence of the General Assembly', 60 *A.J.I.L.* (1966), 782.

Fatouros, A. A. 'An International Code to Promote Private Investment: Proposals and Perspectives', 14 *University of Toronto Law Journal* (1961), 77.

'Obstacles to Private Foreign Investment in Underdeveloped Countries', 2 *Current and Social Problems* (1961), 194.

Fenwick, G. G. 'The Ninth International Conference of American States', 42 *A.J.I.L.* (1948), 553.

Fitzmaurice, G. G. 'The Status of Resolutions of General Assembly', 25 *B.Y.B.I.L.* (1948), p. 1.

Francioni, F. 'Compensation for Nationalisation of Foreign Property: The Borderland between Law and Equity', 24 *I.C.L.Q.* (1975), 255.

Friedmann, W. 'The Principle of Unjust Enrichment in English Law', 16 *C.B.R.* (1938), 243.

Gantz, D. A. 'The Marcona Settlement: New Forms of Negotiation and Compensation for Nationalized Property', 71 *A.J.I.L.* (1977), 474.

Gardner, R. N. 'International Measures for Promotion of Foreign Investment', 9 *J.P.L.* (1960), 182.

Geiger, R. 'The Unilateral Change of Economic Development Agreements', 23 *I.C.L.Q.* (1974), 73.

Gillis, J. G. 'Diplomatic Assistance to Private Investment', 29 *University of Chicago Law Review* (1906), 647.

Gordon, D. M. 'Judicial Review in Administrative Law: The Ever-Open Door', 27 *Camb. L.J.* (1969), 161.

Griffin, W. L. 'Execution Against the Sovereign's Property: The Current Scene', *Am.Soc.Int.Law Proceed.* (1961), 105.

Gutteridge, H. C. and David, R. J. A. 'The Doctrine of Unjust Enrichment', 5 *Camb.L.J.* (1933–35), 204.

Haight, G. W. 'Activities of International Chambers of Commerce and Other Business Groups', 54 *Am.Soc.Int.Law Proceed.* (1960), 200.

'The New International Economic Order and the Charter of Economic Rights and Duties of States', 9 *Int.L.J.* (1975), 591.

Harris, D. 'The Protection of Corporations in International Law in the Light of the Barcelona Case', 18 *I.C.L.Q.* (1969), p. 275.

Herz, J. H. 'Expropriation of Foreign Property', 35 *A.J.I.L.* (1941), 243.

Higgins, R. 'Recent Developments in the Law of Sovereign Immunity in the United Kingdom', 71 *A.J.I.L.* (1977), 423.

Hyde, J. N. 'Permanent Sovereignty Over Natural Wealth and Resources', 50 *A.J.I.L.* (1956), 854.

Irish, C. R. 'International Double Taxation Agreements and Income Taxation at Source', 23 *I.C.L.Q.* (1974), 292.

Jennings, R. Y. 'Recent Cases on "Automatic Reservations" to the Optional Clause', 7 *I.C.L.Q.* (1958), 249.

'State Contracts in International Law', 37 *B.Y.B.I.L.* (1961), p. 156.

'Rules Governing Contracts Between States and Foreign Nationals', *Rights and Duties of Investors Abroad*, International and Comparative Law Centre, Southwestern Legal Foundation, Texas, 1965.

Johnson, D. H. N. 'The Effects of Resolutions of the General Assembly of the United Nations', 32 *B.Y.B.I.L.* (1955–56), p. 97.

Jones, J. M. 'Claims on Behalf of Nationals Who are Shareholders in Foreign Companies', 26 *B.Y.B.I.L.* (1949), p. 225.

'The Nottebohm Case', 5 *I.L.C.Q.* (1956), 230.

Khadduri, M. 'The Arab League as a Regional Arrangement', 40 *A.J.I.L.* (1946), 756.

'The Islamic System: Its Competition and Co-existence with Western Systems', *Am. Soc. of Int. Law Proceed.* (1959), p. 50.

Khun, A. K. 'Nationalization of Foreign-owned Property and Its Impact on International Law', 45 *A.J.I.L.* (1951), 709.

Kissan, L. T. and Leach, E. K. 'Sovereign Expropriation of Property and Abrogation of Concession Contracts', 28 *Ford. L. Rev.* (1959–60), 177.

Kunz, L. J. 'The Meaning and the Range of the Norm of Pacta Sunt Servanda', 39 *A.J.I.L.* (1945), 180.

Lalive, P. A. 'The Doctrine of Acquired Rights', *Rights and Duties of Private Investors Abroad* (1965), Southwestern Legal Foundation, p. 14.

Larson, A. 'Recipients' Rights under an International Investment Code', 9 *J.P.L.* (1960), 172.

Lauterpacht, H. 'Boycott in International Relations', 14 *B.Y.B.I.L.* (1933), p. 125.

'Restrictive Interpretation and the Principle of Effectiveness in the Interpretation of Treaties', 26 *B.Y.B.I.L.* (1949), p. 48.

Leigh, M. 'Enforcement of Judgments and Awards', *Rights and Duties of Investors Abroad,* International and Comparative Law Centre, Southwestern Legal Foundation (1965), p. 465.

Lipstein, K., 'The Place of Calvo Clause in International Law', 22 *B.Y.B.I.L.* (1945), p. 130.

MacGibbon, I. C. 'Some Observations on the Part of Protest In International Law', 30 *B.Y.B.I.L.* (1953), p. 293.

'Estoppel in International Law', 7 *I.C.L.Q.* (1958), 468.

McNair, Lord. 'The General Principles of Law Recognized by Civilized Nations', 33 *B.Y.B.I.L.* (1957), p. 1.

'The Seizure of Property and Enterprises in Indonesia', 6 *Neth.Int.L.Rev.* (1959), 250.

Mann, F. A. 'The Law Governing State Contracts', 21 *B.Y.B.I.L.* (1944), p. 11.

'The Proper Law of Contracts Concluded by International Persons', 35 *B.Y.B.I.L.* (1959), p. 34.

'State Contract and State Responsibility', 54 *A.J.I.L.* (1960), 572.

'The Confiscation of Corporations, Corporate Rights and Corporate Assets and Conflict of Laws', 11 *I.C.L.Q.* (1962), 471.

'The Protection of Shareholders' Interests in the Light of the Barcelona Traction Case', 67 *A.J.I.L.* (1973), 259.

'The Consequences of an International Wrong in International and National Law', 48 *B.Y.B.I.L.* (1978), p. 1.

Meron, T. 'Repudiation of Ultra Vires State Contracts and the International Responsibility of States', 6 *I.C.L.Q.* (1957), 273.

Metzger, S. D. 'Multilateral Conventions for the Protection of Private Foreign Investment', 9 *J.P.L.* (1960), 133.

'Nationality of Corporate Investment under Investment Guaranty Schemes – The Relevance of the Barcelona Traction', 65 *A.J.I.L.* (1971), 532.

'The State Department's Role in the Judicial Administration of the Act of State Doctrine', 66 *A.J.I.L.* (1972), 94.

Miller, A. S. 'Protection of Private Foreign Investment by Multilateral Conventions', 53 *A.J.I.L.* (1959), 371.

Mustafa, Z. 'Opting Out of the Common Law: Recent Development in the Legal System of the Sudan', 17 *J.A.L.* (1973), 133.

Nimeiri, S. M. 'Tax Incentives for Promotion of Private Industry in the Sudan: Their Impact on Industrial Development and Government Revenue', *Sudan Notes and Records* (1975).

Nussbaum, A. 'The Arbitration between the Lena Goldfields Ltd. and the Soviet Government', 36 *Cornell Law Quarterly* (1950–51), 31.

O'Connell, D. P. 'Unjust Enrichment', 5 *A.J.C.L.* (1956), 1.

Olmstead, C. J. 'Economic Development Loan Agreements, Part II: Agreements between States and Aliens; Choice of Law and Remedy', 49 *Calif.L.Rev.* (1961), 504.

Omer, A. H. 'Sudan Foreign Exchange Control Policy Impact on its Economic Development', *Journal of Banking Studies* (January 1977), 19.

Orr, D., Sir. 'The Contribution of Multinational Business to Development', 6 *The Magazine of the Cambridge University Industrial Society* (1980), 9.

Paxman, J. M. 'Argentine Foreign Investment Incentives: Quixotic Nationalism Challenges the Windfall', 12 *Virginia Journal of International Law* (1972), 240.

Proehl, P. O. 'Private Investment Abroad', 9 *J.P.L.* (1960), 362.

Ray, G. W. 'Law Governing Contracts between States and Foreign Nationals', *Proceedings of the 1960 Institute on Private Investments Abroad*, p. 5.

Reisman, W. M. 'The Enforcement of International Judgments', 63 *A.J.I.L.* (1969), 1.

Rood, L. L. 'Foreign Investment in African Manufacturing', *J.M.A.S.* (1975), 19.

Rubin, S. J. 'Reflections Concerning the United Nations Commission on Transnational Corporations', 70 *A.J.I.L.* (1976), 73.

Rupp, H. G. 'International Law as Part of the Law of the Land: Some Aspects of the Operation of Article 25 of the Basic Law of the Federal Republic of Germany', 11 *Texas International Law Journal* (1976), 541.

Simmonds, K. R. 'The Sabbatino Case and the Act of State Doctrine', 14 *I.C.L.Q.* (1965), 452.

Sanders, P. 'New York Convention on the Recognition and Enforcement of Foreign Arbitral Awards', 6 *Neth.Int.L.R.* (1959), 43.

Schwarzenberger, G. 'The Most-Favoured-Nation Standard in British State Practice', 22 *B.Y.B.I.L.* (1945), p. 96.

'The Province and Standards of International Economic Law', 2 *I.C.L.Q.* (1948), 402.

'The Protection of British Property Abroad', 5 *C.L.P.* (1952), 295.

'The Abs/Shawcross Draft Convention on Investments Abroad', 9 *J.P.L.* (1960), 147.

Schwebel, S. M. 'International Protection Arrangements', *Am.Soc.Int.Law Proceed.* (1959), p. 266.

Seidl-Hohenveldern, I. 'Communist Theories on Confiscation and Expropriation: Critical Comments', 7 *A.J.C.L.* (1958), 541.

Shihata, I. F. I. 'Arab Investment Guarantee Corporation: A Regional Investment Insurance Project', 6 *J.W.T.L.* (1972), 185.

'Destination Embargo of Arab Oil: Its Legality under International Law', 68 *A.J.I.L.* (1974), 591.

Smith, D. N., and Wells, L. T. 'Mineral Agreements in Developing Countries: Structures and Substance', 69 *A.J.I.L.* (1975), 560.

Surrey, S. S. 'Current Issues in the Taxation of Corporate Foreign Investment', 56 *Columb.L.R.* (1956), 815.

Taha, F. A. R. A. 'A Plea for the Withdrawal of the "Automatic Reservation" from the Sudan's Declaration under the Optional Clause', *S.L.J.R.* (1970), 345.

Verdross, A. von. 'Quasi-International Agreements', 27 *Yearbook of World Affairs* (1964), 230.

'The Status of Foreign Private Interests Stemming from Economic Development Agreements with Arbitration Clauses', *Selected Readings on Protection by Law of Private Foreign Investments*, Southwestern Legal Foundation (1964), p. 121.

Vicuna, F. O. 'Some International Law Problems Posed by the Nationalization of the Copper Industry by Chile', 67 *A.J.I.L.* (1973), 711.

Wade, H. W. R. 'Constitutional and Administrative Aspects of the Anisminic Case', 85 *L.Q.R.* (1969), 198.

Waldock, C. H. M. 'The Plea of Domestic Jurisdiction before International Legal Tribunals', 31 *B.Y.B.I.L.* (1954), p. 96.

'Decline of the Optional Clause', 32 *B.Y.B.I.L.* (1955–56), p. 244.

Wehberg, H. 'Pacta Sunt Servanda', 53 *A.J.I.L.* (1959), 775.

Wetter, J. G. 'Diplomatic Assistance to Private Investment', 29 *University of Chicago Law Review* (1961–62), 275.

White, R. C. A. 'A New International Economic Order', 24 *I.C.L.Q.* (1975), 542.

Wilson, R. R. 'International Law in New Constitutions', 58 *A.J.I.L.* (1964), 432.

Woolsey, L. H. 'Expropriation of Oil Properties by Mexico', 32 *A.J.I.L.* (1938), 519.

Wright, Q. 'The Goa Incident', 56 *A.J.I.L.* (1962), 617.

Wurzel, H. 'Foreign Investment and Extra-territorial Taxation', 38 *Columb.L.R.* (1938), p. 809.

Magazines and Newspapers

Africa no. 61, September 1976.

Al-Riyadh, no. 4635 Saturday, 20 September 1980, p. 2.

The Economist, 5 June 1976; 18 March 1978.

El-Iyam, 17 Feburary 1977.

El Sahafa, 6 January 1976.

The Financial Times, 10 October 1976; 29 April 1978; 26 May 1978; 13 July 1978; 16 September 1978.

The Guardian, 13 April 1978.

The Middle East International, January 1978; June 1980; August 1980.

The Middle East, June 1980, no. 68, p. 62.
New Africa, January 1978.
Newsweek Magazine, 22 December 1974.
New York Times, 12 March 1957.
Quarterly Economic Review, *Sudan*, no. 1, 1976.
Sudan Survey, prepared by Africa Development, 1976.
The Times, 30 April 1976; 16 February 1977; 10 January 1978; 5 October 1978.

Published Documents

1. League of Nations and United Nations

1923 'Report on Double Taxation', the Financial Committee: L. of N. Doc. E. F.S.73F.19 (1923–27).

1928 'Report of the League of Nations Commission of Experts on the Nationality of Commercial Corporations and their Diplomatic Protection', 22 *A.J.I.L.* (1928), 205, para. 6.

1929 'International Conference on the Treatment of Foreigners', Geneva, 5 November 1929 – Preparatory Documents: Draft Convention prepared by the Economic Committee of the League of Nations as a basis of discussion at the International Conference: L. of N. Doc. C.I.T.E.L.c.36.M. 21.1929 11.

1946 'Model Tax Conventions': L. of N. Doc. C.88 M.88 November 1946, prepared by the Fiscal Committee, London and Mexico.

1952 U.N. Doc. A/C 3/L 489 G.A. Res. 626 (VII) of 21 December 1952 on the Exploitation of Natural Resources, *U.N.Y.B.I.L.C.* 1952.

1955 U.N. Doc. A/C 3/L 489, 17 November 1955: 'Draft International Covenants on Human Rights: report of working party on Article 1', *U.N.Y.B.I.L.C.* 1955, p. 158.

1956 U.N.I.L.C. Doc. A/CN.4/96, 20 January 1956: 'State Responsibility: report by F. V. Garcia Amador', Special Rapporteur, *U.N.Y.B.I.L.C.*, 1956, vol. 11, p. 137.

1957 U.N.I.L.C. Doc. A/CN.4/106, February 1957, 'State Responsibility: second report by F. V. Garcia Amador', *Y.B.I.L.C.* (1957), vol. 11, p. 104.

1958 U.N.I.L.C. Doc. A/3859, 28 April 1958: 'Model Rules on Arbitral Procedure: report of the I.L.C. covering the work of its tenth session', *Y.B.I.L.C.* (1958), vol. 11, p. 83.

1959 U.N.I.L.C. Doc. A/CN.4/119, 26 February 1949: 'State Responsibility: Fourth report by Garcia F. V. Amador, Special Rapporteur', *Y.B.I.L.C.* (1959), vol. 11, p. 2.

1960 U.N. Doc. Soc. A/AC.97/5/Rev. 1, 27 December 1960: 'The Status of Permanent Sovereignty over Natural Wealth and Resources Revised Study by the Secretariat'.

1960 U.N. Doc. E/3369, 13 May 1960: 'Economic Development of Underdeveloped Countries. International flow of Private Capital, 1958–9: Report by the Sectretary-General'.

1961 U.N. Doc. 1/AC 97/L.11, 20 May 1961: 'Report of U.N. Commission On Permanent Sovereignty over Natural resources.'

1961 U.N. Doc. E/3492, 18 May 1961: 'The Promotion of the International flow of Private Capital: report by the Secretary-General'.

1962 U.N.G.A., Resolution 1803 (XVII), 14 December 1962: 'Permanent Sovereignty over Natural Resources', General Assembly, *Official Records*: Seventeenth Session, Supplement No. 17 (A/5217), New York, 1963.

1963 U.N. E/CN. 14/INR/28, 30 October 1973: 'Investment Laws and regulations in Africa'.
1964 U.N.C.T.A.D. Proceedings, 3rd Session, vol. 1, *Final Act and Report*, Doc. Sales No. 64 11.B.11., 1964.
1967 U.N. Doc. A/CN.9/1, 14 November 1967, 'Note by the Secretary-General: UNCITRAL'.
1969 U.N. Doc. I.C.J.: 'Declaration of the Sudan and U.S.A. accepting the compulsory jurisdiction of the I.C.J. (Connally Amendment)', *Yearbook of I.C.J.* (1969–70), p. 75.
1970 U.N.I.L.C. Doc. A/CN.4/228 and Add. 1, 9 March and 18 May 1970: 'Most-favoured-Nation Clause: Second report by Mr Endre Ustor, Special Rapporteur', *U.N.Y.B.I.L.C.*, 1970, vol. 11, p. 199.
1970 U.N. Doc. A/8082 4 October 1970: Declaration on Principles of International Law Concerning Friendly Relations and Co-operation among States.
1971 U.N.I.L.C. Doc. A/CN.4/246 and Add. 1–3, 5 May, 7 April and 18 May 1971: 'Third Report on State Responsibility, by Mr Roberts Ago, Special Rapporteur', *U.N.Y.B.I.L.C.* (1971), vol. 11, p. 199.
1973 U.N. Doc. DP/GC/SUD/R.1., 30 March, 1972: 'U.N. Development Programme: Country and Inter-Country Programming, Sudan, U.N.D.P. Assistance requested by the Government of the Sudan for the period of 1972–1974'.
1973 U.N. Doc. ST/ECA/190, *Multinational Corporations in World Development*.
1974 G.A. Res. 3210 (S-VI), 1 May 1974. The Declaration on the Establishment of a New International Economic Order, U.N.G.A. Sixth Special Session, 13 *I.L.M.* (1974), p. 715.
1974 U.N.G.A. Resolution 3202 (S-VI) 16 May 1974: Programme of Action on the Establishment of a New International Economic Order, Sixth Special Session, 13 *I.L.M.* (1974), 720.
1974 U.N.G.A. Res. 3281 (XXIX) 12 December 1974: The Charter of Economic Rights and Duties of States, U.N. Monthly Chronicle, vol. 12, No. 1, (Jan. 1975), p. 108; 14 *I.L.M.* (1975), p. 251.
1974 U.N. Doc. E/5500/Rev./ST/ESA16 'The Impact of Multinational Corporations on Development and International Relations: report by the Group of Eminent Persons'.
1975 U.N. Doc. E/5570/Add. 1, E.C.O.S.O.C. Res. 1913, 57 ESCOR, Supp. (No. 1A) 31, establishing the United Nations Commission on Transnational Corporations.
1975 U.N. Doc. E/5655; E/C 10/6, 17 March, 1975: 'Programme of Work on the Full Range of Issues relating to Translational Corporations to E.C.O.S.O.C.'.
1975 U.N.G.A. Res. 3362 (S-VII), *Official Proceedings*: Special Session, 1–16 September, 1975, Suppl. No. 1 (C/A/10301), p. 3.
1975 UN ILO/U.N.D.P., *Growth, Employment and Equity, a Comprehensive Strategy for the Sudan*: Report of ILO Employment Mission, 1975.
1975 U.N. Doc 5655; E/C 10/6, 17 March 1975: 'Programme of Issues to Transnational Corporations: report of UN Commission on Transnational Corporations to E.C.O.S.O.C'.
1975 U.N. Doc. ID/CONF. 3/3 (ID/134), U.N.I.D.O., Industrial Development Survey, Special Issue for the Second Conference at Lima, Peru, 12–26 December 1975.
1976 The *U.N.C.I.T.R.A.L. Arbitration Rules*, Report of the UN Commission on International Trade Law, ninth session, 12 April–7 May 1976, *General Assembly Official Records*, Thirty-first Session, Suppl. No. 17 (A/31/17), 1976.
1976 U.N.C.T.A.D., U.N. Doc. TD/B/C.6114 (1976), Intergovernmental Group on the Transfer of Technology.

1976 U.N.I.L.C. Doc. A/31/10, 3 May–23 July 1976: 'Report on State Responsibility' on the Work of its 28th Session, *U.N.Y.B.I.L.C.* (1976) vol. 11, p. 69; the same document, ch. 11: 'The Most-Favoured-Nation clause', p. 4.

1977 U.N.I.L.C. Doc. A/CN.4/302 and Add. 1–3, 14 July 1977: 'State Responsibility', *U.N.Y.B.I.L.C.* (1977), vol. 1, p. 240.

1977 U.N.G.A. Res. 32/174, 19 December 1977. 'Progress Made in the Establishment of the New International Economic Order', *U.N. Chronicle* (Jan. 1978), p. 56.

1977 U.N. Doc. Dist. General, A/31/478/Add.1, 9 August 1977: 'Report on International Economic Cooperation: Annex to Note by the Secretary-General'.

1978 U.N.I.L.C. Doc. A/CN 4/309/Add. 1: 'Report on the Most-Favoured-Nation Clause: report by Special Rapporteur', U.N.I.L.C. 13th Session, 8 May–28 July 1978.

1979 Industrial Investment Project Proposals, U.N.I.D.O., Investment Co-operative Programme Office, June 1979.

1979 The Report of the UN Independent Commission on International Development Issues, *North–South: A Programme for Survival*, 20 December 1979.

2. I.C.C. Documents

1949 I.C.C. Brochure No. 129: *International Code of Fair Treatment for Foreign Investment.*

1955 I.C.C. Brochure No. 180: *Avoidance of Double Taxation*, February 1955.

1959 I.C.C. Brochure No. 197: *Taxation and Developing Nations.* March 1959.

1961 I.C.C. Brochure No. 218: *Taxation Policies in Relation to International Investment.* June 1961.

1966 I.C.C. *International Arbitration of I.C.C.* August 1966.

1972 I.C.C. 'Guidelines for International Investment', *The National Charter*, 1972.

1980 I.C.C. Booklet, *Bilateral Treaties for International Investment*, 1980.

3. *Other Published Documents*

1938 British Protest against Mexican expropriation of Eagle Oil Company, 1938, Cmd 5758–1938.

1951 Harvard Draft Convention on the Responsibility of States for Injuries to Aliens, 55 *A.J.I.L.* (1951), 545.

1954 4 I.M.F. Staff Papers 113 (1954).

1957 I.B.R.D. 13th Annual Report.

1958 I.B.R.D. 14th Annual Report.

1958 International Bar Association, 7th Conference Report.

1960 A.A.L.C.C., Final Report, Colombo.

1960 *Sudan Trade and Investment Guide*, 1960–61, published by the Diplomatic press and Publishing Co. in co-operation with the Government of Republic of the Sudan.

1961 I.M.F. Annual Report on Exchange Restrictions, Washington (1961).

1962 Multilateral Investment Insurance, A Staff Report of I.B.R.D., March 1962.

1962 Draft Restatement on Foreign Law Relations of U.S., *American Law Institutes.*

1962 Permanent Court of Arbitration Bureau Rules for arbitration proceedings between States and Public International Bodies and Individuals, 9 *Neth.Int.L.R.* (1962), 339; 57 *A.J.I.L.* (1963), 500.

1963 O.E.C.D. Draft Convention on Protection of Foreign Property, O.E.C.D. Publ. No. 15637, 1963, Appendix B.

1965 Report of the Executive Directors of the World Bank, I.C.S.I.D., Convention on Settlement of Investment Disputes between States and Nationals of Other States (Washington D.C., 1965).

1967 I.B.R.D. Draft Articles of the International Investment Insurance Agency (111A).

1969 *Investment Opportunities in Nigeria*, published by Ministry of Information, Lagos.

1969 O.E.C.D. Code of Liberalization of Capital Movements (Paris).

1970 *Tameem-el-Masarif-fe-el-Sudan* (*Nationalisation of Banks in the Sudan*), prepared by the Information and Publication Committee, Bank of Sudan, University of Khartoum Press.

1971 Documents Concerning Nationalization of Copper Companies in Chile, 10 *I.L.M.* (1971), 1235.

1972 Report on Nationalization, Expropriation and Other Takings of the United States and Certain Foreign Property since 1960, 11 *I.L.M.* (1972), 84.

1974 Proposed Amendment of the Charter of Economic Rights and Duties of States, 1974, 14 *I.L.M.* (1975).

1975 *Focus on the Sudan*: A Progress International Publication, October 1975, published by London International Press Centre.

1975 O.E.C.D., D.A.C., Efforts and Policies, 1975 Review.

1975 *Sixth Annual Report of Bank of Sudan*, Government Press, Khartoum.

1976 *Quarterly Economic Review*, Sudan.

1977 *The Six-Year Plan for Social and Economic Development*, Ministry of Planning, Khartoum, Government Press, July 1977.

1978 *A Guide to Industrial Investment in Saudi Arabia*, Industrial Studies and Development Centre, Saudi Arabia, 5th edn., 1978.

1978 *Thirteenth Annual Report* of the International Centre for Settlement of Investment Disputes, 1978/1979.

1979 Information Guide: *Doing Business in Saudi Arabia*, Price Waterhouse & Co., New York, 1979.

Unpublished Documents

(1) Official Documents

(*a*) *Sudan and Saudi Arabia*

The material which forms the basis of this book is mainly derived from unpublished official and private documents. The official documents are kept in official files. In the Sudan the files consulted are obtained from the Council of Ministers, the Attorney-General's Chambers, Ministry of Finance and National Economy, Bank of Sudan, Department of Geology in the Ministry of Energy and Mining, the Sudan Embassy (London) and other governmental departments. The documents contained in these files are not grouped in specific classes, but scattered in several sub-departmental files which contain, *inter alia*, advice rendered by the legal officers or deliberations and reports of Special Committees.

As regards Saudi Arabia, the unpublished documents were basically obtained from the Royal Commission for Jubail and Yanbu, the Ministries of Agriculture, Petroleum and Mining and Industry and Electricity.

(*b*) *Foreign Documents*

Among the official unpublished sources used in this study are the following:

(i) *The Report of the Kuwaiti Fund for Arab Economic Development Towards a Convention for Guarantee of Arab Investment* (1967) (text in Arabic).

(ii) *The Final Report on Recommendations of the Arab Experts of Supply*, submitted to the 3rd Conference of the Arab Experts of Supply (1967) (Kuwait) (text in Arabic).

(iii) *Formulation of a Code of Conduct: Elaboration of the Chairman's Annotated Outline of the Basis of Discussion in the Intergovernmental Working Group on a Code of Conduct*, Commission on Transnational Corporations, 4th Session, 20–31 March 1978, provided by Dr Samuel B. Asante, Deputy Attorney-General of Ghana and Chief Legal Adviser, United Nations Centre on Transnational Corporations (1977–79), Visiting Fellow, Clare Hall, Cambridge University (1978–79).

(2) Private Unpublished Sources

These comprise documents, notes, lectures and researches made by private institutions or individuals by way of contribution in conferences or otherwise. The following documents and manuscripts were utilized:

(*a*) *Fire Insurance Policy*, the Blue Nile Insurance Company (Khartoum).

(*b*) Advocate Attabani file no. 3–2, vol. 11 (Khartoum).

(*c*) 'Protection of Patents in the Arab Countries', a paper submitted by the writer in collaboration with Sayed Osman El Tahami, Senior Legal Counsel, Attorney-General's Chambers (Khartoum) to the 4th Symposium of Arab Lawyers, 2–10 March 1972 (Khartoum).

(*d*) 'Transnational Investment Law and National Development', a lecture delivered by Dr S. K. B. Asante at the University of Lagos, Nigeria, December 1978, in contribution to Taylor Lectures, 1978.

(*e*) 'United Nations Efforts at International Regulation of Transnational Corporations', a lecture delivered by Dr Asante to the International Club, at Jesus College, Cambridge, on 22 November 1978.

(*f*) 'The United Nations and the Regulation of Transnational Corporations', July 1978, by S. A. Tiewl, Legal Counsel, Attorney-General's Chambers, Ghana.

(*g*) Saud Shawaf Office's file No. 55-L 89/79, Riyadh, Saudi Arabia.

INDEX